GLENN'S

BOBCAT

TUNE-UP AND REPAIR GUIDE

by Harold T. Glenn

HENRY REGNERY COMPANY • CHICAGO

Library of Congress Cataloging in Publication Data

Glenn, Harold T
Glenn Bobcat tune-up and repair guide.

1. Bobcat automobile. I. Title. II. Title: Bobcat tune-up and repair guide.
TL 215.B58G53 1975 629.28'7'22 75-23465
ISBN 0-8092-8167-8

Printed in the United States of America
Library of Congress Catalog Card Number 75-23465
International Standard Book Number 0-8092-8167-8

Books by HAROLD T. GLENN

Youth at the Wheel
Safe Living
Automechanics
Glenn's Auto Troubleshooting Guide
Exploring Power Mechanics
Automobile Engine Rebuilding and Maintenance
Automobile Power Accessories
Glenn's Auto Repair Manual
Automotive Smog Congrol Manual
Glenn's Emission-Control Systems
Glenn's Foreign Car Repair Manual
Glenn's Triumph Repair and Tune-Up Guide
Glenn's Alta Romeo Repair and Tune-Up Guide
Glenn's Austin, Austin-Healey Repair and Tune-Up Guide
Glenn's Sunbeam-Hillman Repair and Tune-Up Guide
Glenn's MG, Morris and Magnette Repair and Tune-Up Guide
Glenn's Volkswagen Repair and Tune-Up Guide
Glenn's Volkswagen Repair and Tune-Up Guide (Spanish Edition)
Glenn's Mercedes-Benz Repair and Tune-Up Guide
Glenn's Foreign Carburetors and Electrical Systems Guide
Glenn's Renault Repair and Tune-Up Guide
Glenn's Jaguar Repair and Tune-Up Guide
Glenn's Volvo Repair and Tune-Up Guide
Glenn's Peugeot Repair and Tune-Up Guide
Glenn's Fiat Repair and Tune-Up Guide
Glenn's Toyota Tune-Up and Repair Guide
Glenn's Tune-Up and Repair Manual for American and Imported Car Emission-Control Systems
Glenn's Chrysler Outboard Motor Repair and Tune-Up Guide for 1 & 2 Cylinder Engines
Glenn's Chrysler Outboard Motor Repair and Tune-Up Guide for 3 & 4 Cylinder Engines
Glenn's Evinrude Outboard Motor Repair and Tune-Up Guide for 1 & 2 Cylinder Engines
Glenn's Evinrude Outboard Motor Repair and Tune-Up Guide for 3 & 4 Cylinder Engines
Glenn's Johnson Outboard Motor Repair and Tune-Up Guide for 1 & 2 Cylinder Engines
Glenn's Johnson Outboard Motor Repair and Tune-Up Guide for 3 & 4 Cylinder Engines
Glenn's McCulloch Outboard Motor Repair and Tune-Up Guide
Glenn's Mercury Outboard Motor Repair and Tune-Up Guide
Glenn's Sears Outboard Motor Repair and Tune-Up Guide
Glenn's Honda One-Cylinder Repair and Tune-Up Guide
Glenn's Honda Two-Cylinder Repair and Tune-Up Guide
Glenn's Suzuki One-Cylinder Tune-Up and Repair Guide
Glenn's Yamaha Enduro Tune-Up and Repair Guide
Glenn's Triumph Two-Cylinder Motorcycle Tune-Up and Repair Guide
Glenn's Chevrolet Tune-Up and Repair Guide
Glenn's Chevrolet Camaro Tune-Up and Repair Guide
Glenn's Ford/Lincoln/Mercury Tune-Up and Repair Guide
Glenn's Chrysler/Plymouth/Dodge Tune-Up and Repair Guide
Glenn's Pontiac Tune-Up and Repair Guide
Glenn's Pontiac Firebird Tune-Up and Repair Guide
Glenn's Oldsmobile Tune-Up and Repair Guide
Glenn's Buick Tune-Up and Repair Guide
Glenn's Complete Bicycle Manual
Glenn's Opel Tune-Up and Repair Guide
Glenn's Datsun 510/610/710 Tune-Up and Repair Guide
Glenn's Pinto Tune-Up and Repair Guide
Glenn's Mustang II Tune-Up and Repair Guide
Glenn's Capri and Capri II Tune-Up and Repair Guide
Glenn's Bobcat Tune-Up and Repair Guide
Glenn's OMC Inboard/Outboard Tune-Up and Repair Guide
Glenn's Volkswagen Tune-Up and Repair Guide
Glenn's Kawasaki-3 Tune-Up and Repair Guide
Glenn's Honda-4 (750) Tune-Up and Repair Guide
Glenn's Mazda Tune-Up and Repair Guide
Glenn's Basic Repair Guide
Glenn's Hornet Tune-Up and Repair Guide
Glenn's Flat Rate Manual

foreword

This is a comprehensive tune-up and repair guide for Ford automobiles. It is a reference book for professional mechanics and also a completely usable manual for car owners who want to make their own repairs, those who are interested in keeping their autos running smoothly and economically, and performance-minded drivers who want to obtain as much power and fuel economy as possible from their engines.

The four "roadmaps" in the first chapter ("Troubleshooting") are especially important in helping to pinpoint the trouble before beginning repairs. This feature also helps to save time while repairs are in process, because it shows the mechanic what to look for as the unit is being disassembled. Many simple procedures are demonstrated that require no elaborate equipment for testing and that can be made by any interested car owner. The book includes servicing the engine, running gear, driveline, brakes, and fuel and electrical systems. Comprehensive specification tables are provided.

Among the many special features of this guide is the use of step-by step illustrated instructions. Another is the use of "exploded illustrations" of major mechanical and electrical units. There are many photographs of worn parts so that the reader will recognize such wear when he sees it. These pictures take the place of years of experience.

The author wishes to express his appreciation to the Ford Motor Company for its gracious assistance in furnishing material for this guide, and specifically to the following: Russell M. Hart, Larry A. Weis, George E. Trainor, Steve E. Madeline, Owen W. Bombard, E. S. Gorman, and Jim Milum. Appreciation must also be expressed to the following firms, which generously loaned the author illustrations: AC Spark Plug Division; Ammco Tools, Inc.; Champion Spark Plug Company; Federal-Mogul Service; McQuay-Norris Manufacturing Company; Offenhauser Sales Corporation; Perfect Circle Division, Dana Corporation; Sun Electric Corporation; Toledo Steel Products Company.

Special thanks are due to my wife, Anna Glenn, for her gracious and devoted assistance in helping to proofread the manuscript and galley proofs and to Mark Tsunawaki for his contribution to the artwork of this book.

HAROLD T. GLENN

table of contents

1 troubleshooting

Troubleshooting must be a well thought-out procedure. To be successful with it, you must start by accurately determining the problem; then you must use a logical approach to arrive at the proper solution. Obviously, if the instructions are to be of maximum benefit as a guide, they must be fully understood and followed exactly.

ROADMAPS

When an engine does not start, the trouble must be localized to one of four general areas: cranking, ignition, fuel, and compression. Each of these areas must be systematically inspected until the trouble is located in one of them, and then detailed tests of that system must be made to isolate the part causing the starting problem.

To assist you, four roadmaps have been developed so that the testing program can be visualized in its entirety and the logical approach determined. ROADMAP ONE concerns EMERGENCY TROUBLESHOOTING, and it represents some quick and simple tests that can be made on the cranking, ignition, and fuel systems and the compression to determine which one requires further investigation. ROADMAP TWO deals with a detailed inspection of the various units which make up the cranking system. ROADMAP THREE details the various tests that are used for isolating ignition system troubles, while ROADMAP FOUR covers the tests that are used to pinpoint fuel system problems.

ROADMAP ONE—EMERGENCY TROUBLESHOOTING

In using this EMERGENCY TROUBLESHOOTING ROADMAP, proceed sequentially through each of the tests until a defect is uncovered. Then skip to the detailed testing procedure and roadmap for that system. For example, if, when using the EMERGENCY TROUBLESHOOTING ROADMAP, the first two systems, cranking and ignition, test OK, but the third test shows that there is trouble in the fuel system, then skip ROADMAPS TWO and THREE and proceed to the detailed tests under ROADMAP FOUR —FUEL SYSTEM TESTS.

①**CRANKING SYSTEM TEST:** Turn the ignition switch to the START position, and the starter should crank the engine at a normal rate of speed. If it does, it is an indication that the battery, cables, starting relay, and starter are in good condition and you should proceed with the testing program by going on to Test ② on the EMERGENCY TROUBLESHOOTING ROADMAP.

If the starter cranks the the engine slowly or doesn't crank it at all, the trouble is in the cranking system, and you should proceed to ROADMAP TWO—CRANKING SYSTEM TESTS for the detailed testing procedure that will help you uncover the starter trouble.

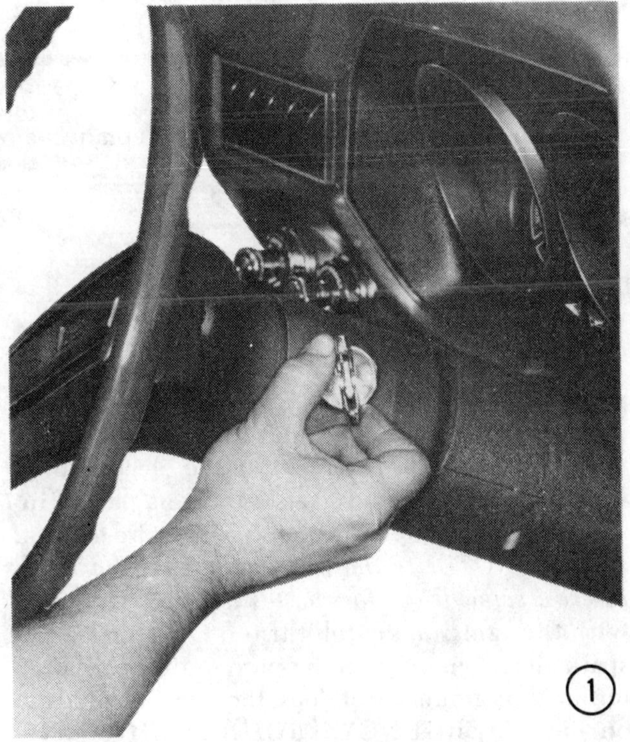

①

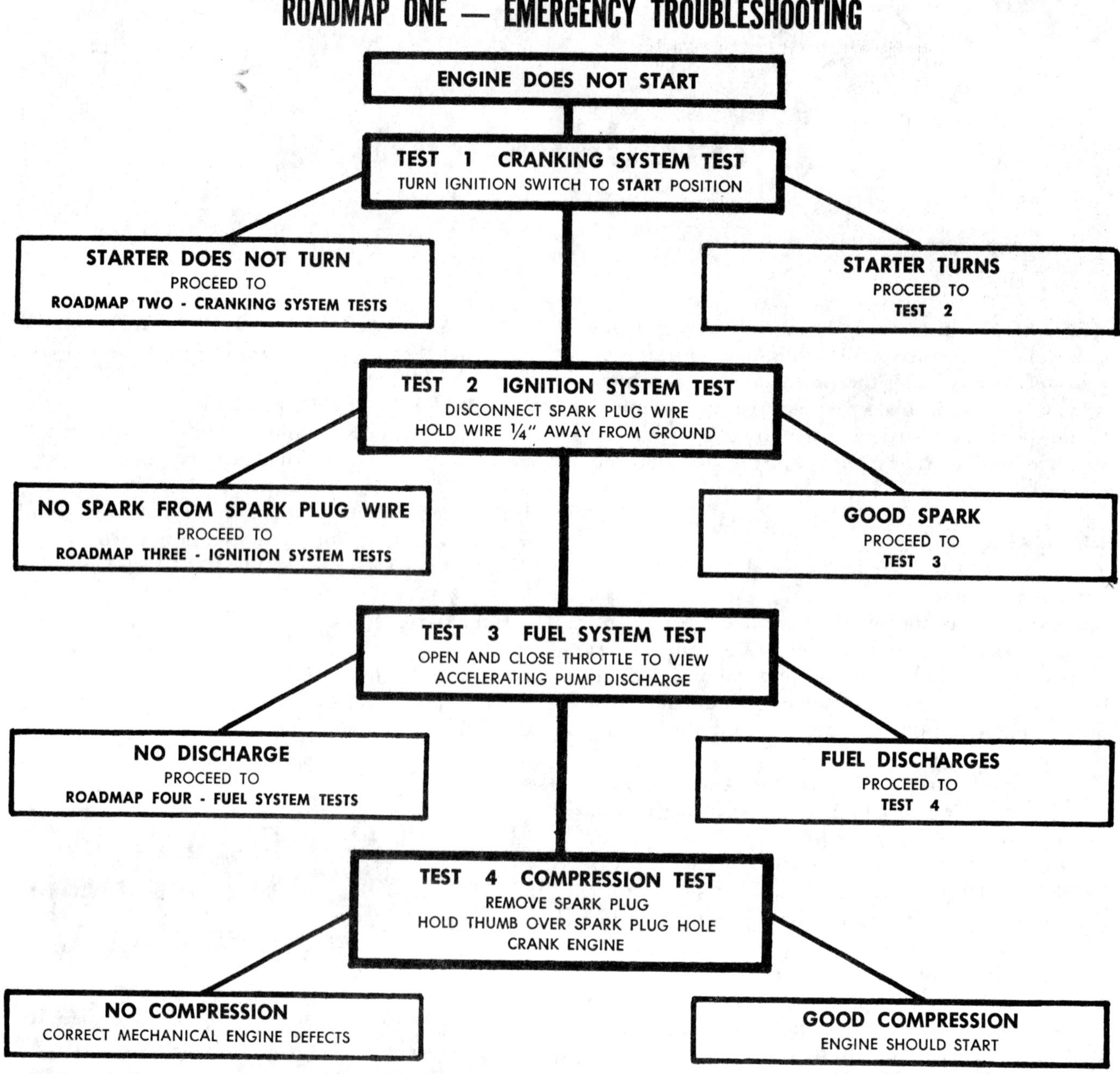

② **IGNITION SYSTEM TEST:** Disconnect a spark plug wire and hold it about 1/4" from a spark plug terminal or ground. **CAUTION: Because of the very high voltages generated by the electronic ignition system, it is advisable to use a pair of insulated pliers to hold the high-tension wire to avoid a shock.** *NOTE: If the boot cannot be slid back, insert a screwdriver for the test.* Crank the engine with the ignition switch turned ON, and a good spark should jump from the wire to the spark plug terminal or ground. If it does, then go on to Test ③ on the EMERGENCY TROUBLESHOOTING ROADMAP.

If there is no spark or the spark is very weak, the trouble is in the ignition system, and you should proceed to ROADMAP THREE—IGNITION SYSTEM TESTS for the detailed testing procedure that will help you to uncover the ignition system trouble.

③ **FUEL SYSTEM TEST:** This test is to determine whether or not there is fuel in the carburetor. Remove the air cleaner, and then look down into the throat of the carburetor. Open and close the throttle several times to see if fuel is squirted out of the pump jets as shown in the accompanying illustration. *NOTE: The*

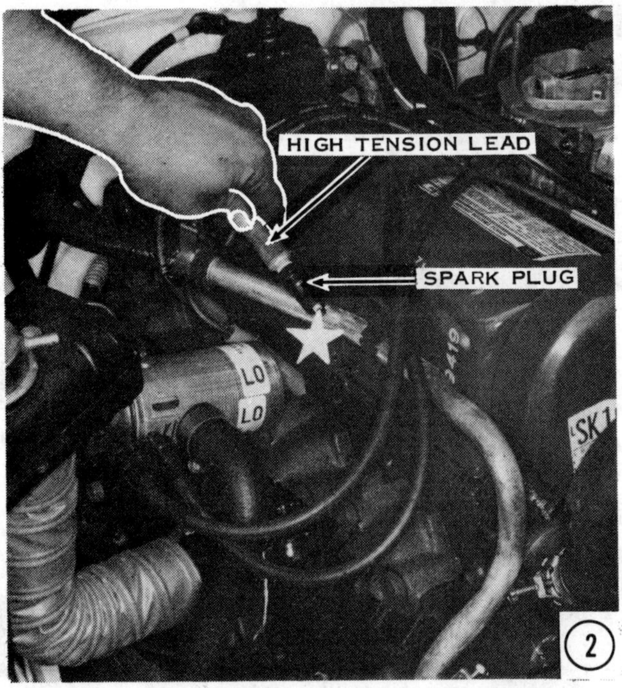

top of the carburetor has been removed in this illustration for photographic purposes.

If fuel is discharged, it is an indication that there is fuel in the carburetor bowl and that the fuel system must be functioning properly; therefore, go on to Test ④ on the EMERGENCY TROUBLESHOOTING ROADMAP.

If no fuel is discharged from the pump jets, then the trouble is in the fuel system, and you should proceed to the detailed tests on ROADMAP FOUR—FUEL SYSTEM TESTS to isolate the trouble.

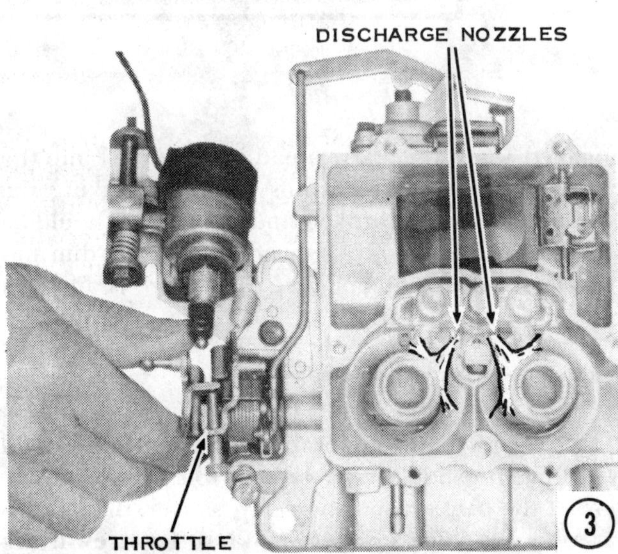

④ **COMPRESSION TEST:** Remove a spark plug and hold your thumb over the spark plug hole. Have someone crank the engine. You should be able to feel pressure pulses as the piston comes up on each of the firing strokes. It is not necessary in this rough test to determine the exact pressure, as you only have to know whether or not there is compression. Strong pressure pulses indicate that the mechanical parts of the engine are sound.

ROADMAP TWO—CRANKING SYSTEM TESTS

This roadmap provides a sequential series of tests that can be made to isolate trouble in a cranking system that does not function properly. Obviously, an engine cannot be started properly if it cannot be turned fast enough to draw in a full charge of fuel, compress it properly, and have enough voltage reserve left for igniting the mixture. The cranking system includes the starter and drive, battery, starting relay, ignition switch, and the necessary wiring and cables to complete the various circuits. Vehicles with an automatic transmission have, in addition, a neutral-safety switch which prevents operation of the starter in all transmission selector positions except NEUTRAL or PARK.

Every cranking system problem falls into one of three situations: the starter does not turn at all, it spins rapidly but does not crank the engine, or it cranks the engine very slowly.

ROADMAP TWO — CRANKING SYSTEM TESTS

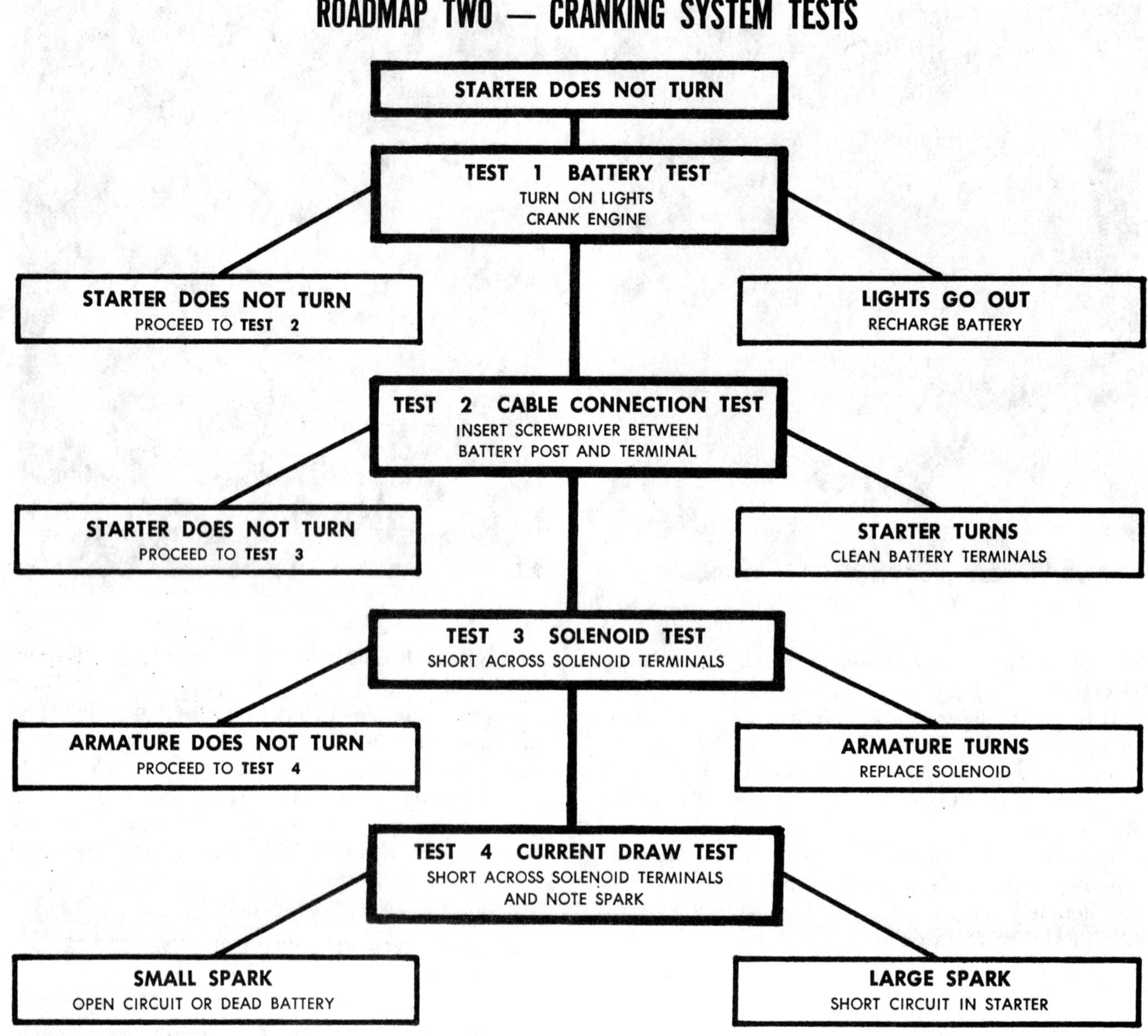

BATTERY TEST

①Turn on the headlights, and then crank the engine by turning the ignition switch to the START position. On a car with a normal electrical system, the lights will dim somewhat and the starter will crank the engine at a normal rate of speed. On a vehicle with a defect, there are several possible results, depending upon the amount of charge left in the battery or the condition of the cables. If the lights go out completely, or dim considerably, the battery is dead and must be recharged. If the starting relay clicks like a machine gun, the battery charge is too low to keep the relay engaged when the starter load is connected into the circuit. If the starter spins without cranking the engine, the drive is broken and the starter should be removed for repairs. If the headlights do not dim and the starter does not operate, then there is an open circuit. Go on to Test ②.

CABLE CONNECTION TEST

②If the starter is inoperative and the headlights do not dim, you should troubleshoot for a poor connection at the battery, starting relay, starter, or neutral-safety switch. The first test is to insert a screwdriver

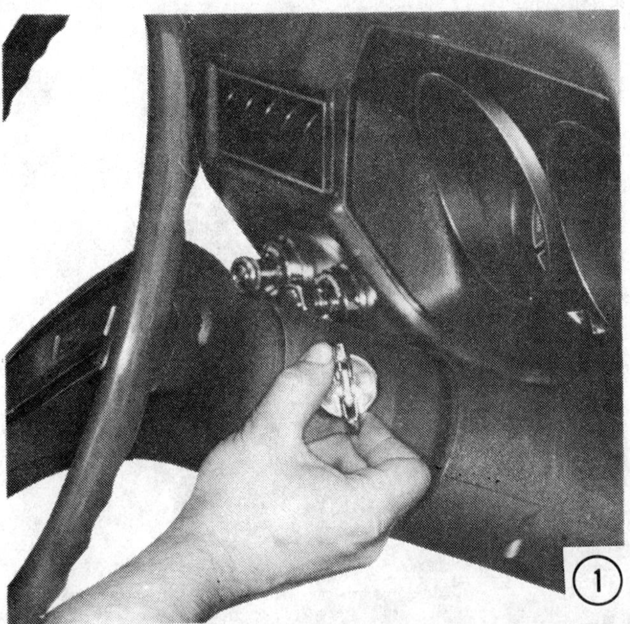

blade tip between a battery post and cable while trying to crank the engine. If the starter now turns, the battery cable connection is corroded and must be disassembled, cleaned, and reassembled. Make this screwdriver test between each of the two battery terminals. *NOTE: This is a very common cause of trouble because of the corrosive nature of battery electrolyte.* If the starter still does not turn with the screwdriver blade tip between the battery post and cable, try moving the transmission selector lever from NEUTRAL to PARK to see if the neutral-safety switch is out of adjustment or has a poor connection. Sometimes jiggling the selector lever will restore a connection temporarily so that the engine can be started. If the starter still does not turn, go on to Test ③.

SOLENOID TEST

③The solenoid (sometimes called a starting relay) should be checked next by holding a pair of pliers so that the handles short across the two large cable terminals. **CAUTION: Make sure that the uninsulated pliers handles do not touch any other metallic part of the car, or sparks will fly.** You can use a heavy jumper cable or screwdriver in place of the pliers to short across the terminals. **CAUTION: Don't use thin wire, as it will get very hot under the heavy load and will burn your hands.** If the starter armature now turns, the trouble is in the relay, which should be checked to see if the circuit from the ignition switch to the starting relay is complete. Check out this circuit by holding a piece of wire from the heavy terminal (battery) on the starting relay to the small terminal, which is the energizing circuit wire from the ignition

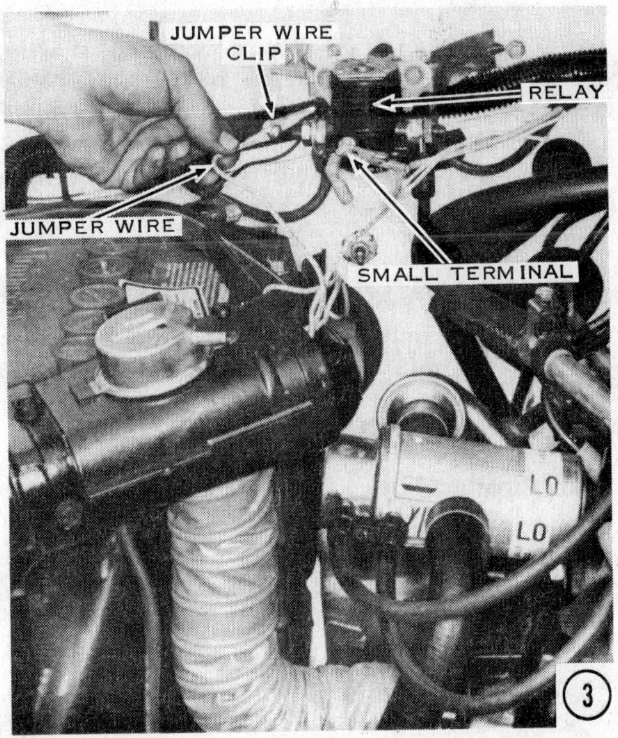

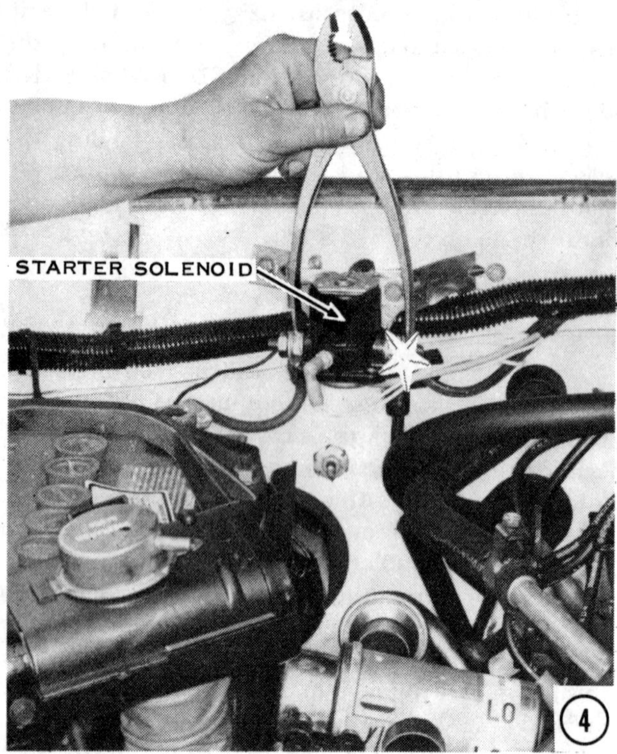

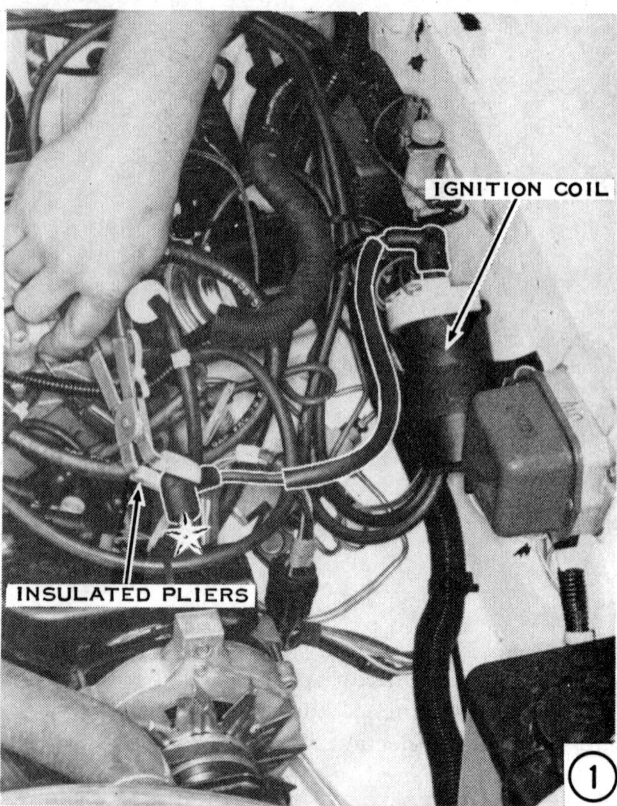

switch. If the relay now operates, the trouble is in the circuit to the ignition switch. **CAUTION: The ignition switch must be turned to the START position in order to energize this circuit.** If the starter still does not turn, go on to Test ④.

CURRENT DRAW TEST

④On some engines, it must be noted, shorting across the two large terminals of the starter relay (solenoid) will cause the starter armature to turn, but it may not crank the engine because the relay is not energized to pull the drive into engagement with the flywheel ring gear. In such a case, this test is still valuable in determining the current draw of the starter. With a normal starter, the size of the spark across the plier handles should be rather small. If you do get a large spark, it indicates that there is a short in the starter, which must be removed for service.

ROADMAP THREE – IGNITION SYSTEM TESTS

This roadmap describes two basic tests to determine whether or not the trouble is in the electronic ignition system. If the system is defective, you will need an ohmmeter and a voltmeter to make the detailed tests described in Chapter 10.

ROADMAP THREE — IGNITION SYSTEM TESTS

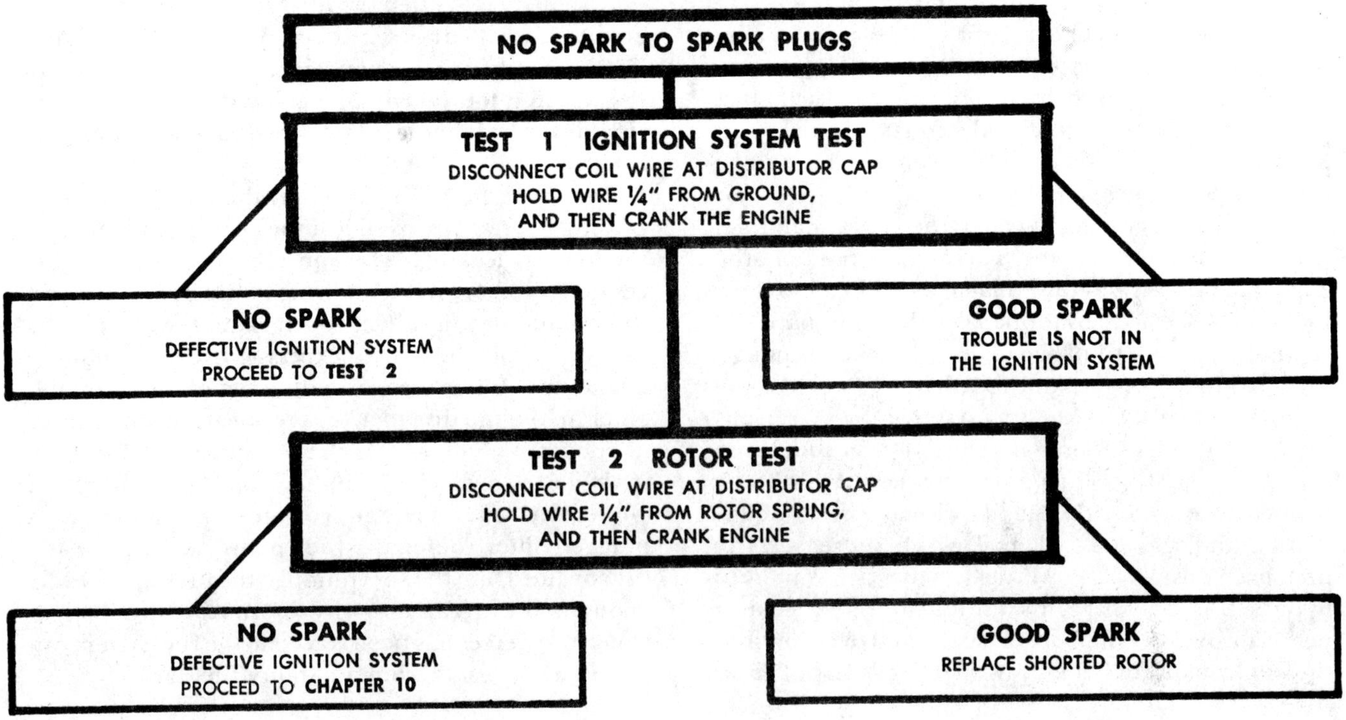

NO SPARK TO SPARK PLUGS

TEST 1 IGNITION SYSTEM TEST
DISCONNECT COIL WIRE AT DISTRIBUTOR CAP
HOLD WIRE 1/4" FROM GROUND,
AND THEN CRANK THE ENGINE

NO SPARK
DEFECTIVE IGNITION SYSTEM
PROCEED TO **TEST 2**

GOOD SPARK
TROUBLE IS NOT IN
THE IGNITION SYSTEM

TEST 2 ROTOR TEST
DISCONNECT COIL WIRE AT DISTRIBUTOR CAP
HOLD WIRE 1/4" FROM ROTOR SPRING,
AND THEN CRANK ENGINE

NO SPARK
DEFECTIVE IGNITION SYSTEM
PROCEED TO **CHAPTER 10**

GOOD SPARK
REPLACE SHORTED ROTOR

Engine Cranks But Does Not Start

① Disconnect the high-tension coil wire from the center of the distributor cap and hold it about 1/4" from a good ground. *NOTE: If the rubber boot cannot be pushed back enough, insert a paper clip or a screwdriver.* **CAUTION: Because of the high voltages involved, use a pair of insulated pliers to avoid getting a shock.** Have a helper turn the ignition switch to the START position to crank the engine. If there is a good spark here, you can have trouble in the secondary circuit, a shorted rotor, or a cracked distributor cap. To make the rotor test, proceed to Test 2.

Rotor Test

② Hold the high-tension coil wire about 1/4" from the rotor spring, and then crank the engine. If a spark jumps to the rotor, then it is shorted to ground and must be replaced. If no spark jumps to the rotor, then check the distributor cap for a crack, which can short the voltage to ground. If the cap is not defective, then you have trouble in other than the secondary circuit, and this must be checked by a series of voltage and resistance tests to determine the exact cause as discussed in Chapter 10.

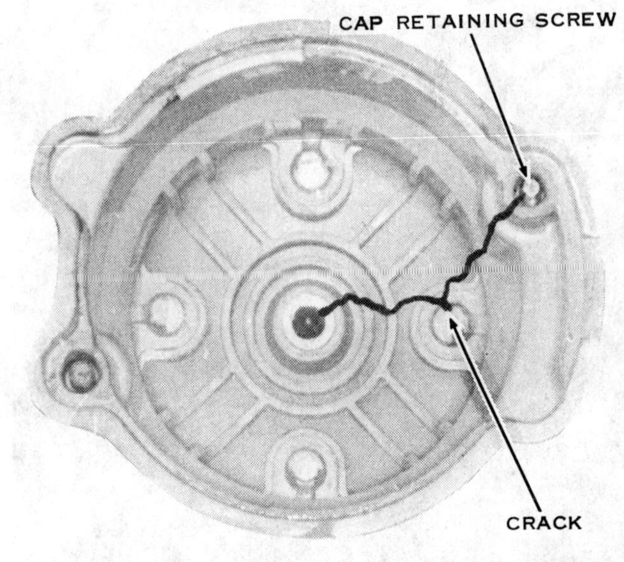

A cracked distributor cap or rotor can keep the engine from starting.

ROADMAP FOUR—FUEL SYSTEM TESTS

This roadmap details a series of tests to localize trouble in the fuel system. It is seldom that starting trouble can be caused by the carburetor itself. It is possible for an automatic choke to stick in the open position and cause starting trouble, but this can be overcome to some extent by pumping the accelerator pedal to discharge some fuel into the intake manifold. If the automatic choke sticks in the shut position, the engine will flood, and this will make it difficult to start. Depressing the accelerator pedal to the floorboard will cause the unloader linkage to open the choke enough for starting the engine in this case.

On the other hand, the fuel system can be a serious source of trouble when hard starting is encountered with a hot engine. When a hot engine is shut off, the temperature within the fuel bowl may rise to 150° - 200°F., and the fuel will boil which increases the pressure considerably. All carburetors are vented to bypass this pressure, but some of the fuel may percolate over the high-speed nozzle and overflow into the intake manifold. This raw fuel needs lots of air to vaporize and dilute it for a combustible mixture. The only remedy is to open the throttle wide and crank the engine until it draws in enough air to start. **CAUTION: Under no circumstances should you pump the accelerator pedal, or you will be adding fuel through the accelerating jets to compound the trouble.**

A plugged fuel filter can keep your carburetor from receiving fuel, and this can cause hard starting. Always change the fuel filter every 15,000-20,000 miles.

Too much fuel can also enter the intake manifold, causing hot starting trouble if the needle valve and seat assembly is leaking. After an engine is shut off, the residual pressure in the fuel line forces excess fuel past the leaking needle valve, which raises the level in the fuel bowl and causes the excess to overflow into the intake manifold. Excessive amounts of fuel can also enter an engine due to a "heavy" float, which reduces its buoyancy. The result is an excessively high fuel level in the float bowl, which causes a continuous overflow. Generally, fuel system troubles are caused by a plugged filter, defective fuel pump, or leak in the suction line from the fuel pump to the fuel tank. Oddly enough, the great majority of starting troubles in which the defect has been traced to the fuel system can be found to result from an empty fuel tank.

FUEL PUMP TEST

①Connect a jumper wire from the primary (distributor) side of the ignition coil to ground to keep the

ROADMAP FOUR — FUEL SYSTEM TESTS

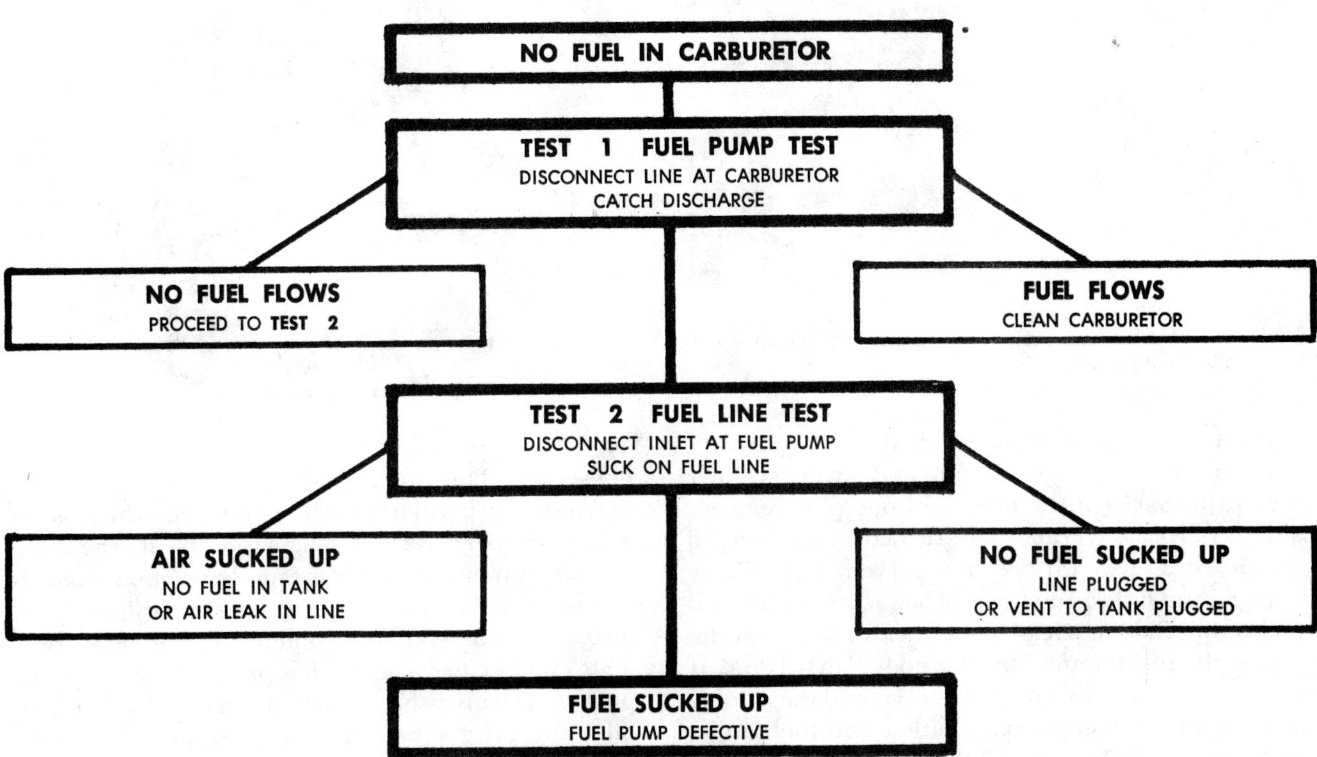

engine from starting. It is also possible to pull the high-tension wire out of the distributor cap and ground it. **CAUTION: Because gasoline will be flowing in the engine compartment during this test, it is very important to guard against fire by securely grounding the high-tension wire so that it cannot spark.** Disconnect the fuel line to the carburetor, position a container so that the discharged fuel can be caught, and then crank the engine. A good-size stream of fuel should pulse out of the line if the fuel pump is functioning properly. Catch at least 10-15 pulses to check the possibility that the size of the stream might decrese, which would indicate a restricted line or defective valve in the gas tank cap on vehicles with evaporative emission-control systems.

In case the fuel line is plugged, it is possible for the fuel stream to stop entirely. If adequate fuel flows to the carburetor, and the engine still does not start, there is the possibility that a strainer in the carburetor inlet or fuel tank is plugged, or that the fuel inlet needle valve and seat are gummed together, which would not allows fuel to pass. Or it can be automatic choke trouble, as discussed before.

If no fuel flows, a defective fuel pump can be the cause or the line from the fuel tank to the fuel pump can be plugged or leaking air. In this case, no fuel will flow. Check out these possibilities by proceeding to Test ②.

FUEL LINE TEST

② The fuel line can be tested by sucking on it.

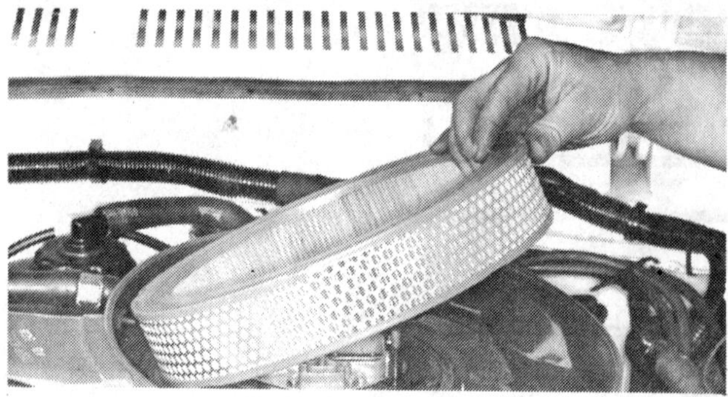

A plugged air filter can cause poor engine performance and increased gas consumption.

Because of the inaccessibility of the line, it is necessary to disconnect it at the fuel pump and attach a rubber tube to it. Suck on the tube, and one of three conditions will occur: (1) air will be sucked up, (2) fuel will be sucked up, or (3) the fuel or vent line will be plugged and little or no fuel will be sucked up. If air is sucked up, there is a leak in the suction line from the tank to the fuel pump or there is no fuel in the tank. If fuel is sucked up, then the line is clear and the trouble must be in the fuel pump. If little or no fuel can be sucked up, then the suction line is plugged, the strainer in the fuel tank is clogged, or the vent to the fuel tank is not open. Without an open vent to the fuel tank, suction builds up and keeps the fuel from flowing to the fuel pump.

SPARK PLUGS

①By way of confirmation, carefully examine the spark plugs you removed from the engine. Line them up in the order of removal so that you can "read" the firing end of the spark plugs and thereby ascertain what has been going on in each cylinder of the engine.

②This is the way a normal spark plug should look after use. The deposits should be dry and powdery. The hard deposits inside the shell indicate that the engine is starting to use some oil, but the condition is not serious. The most important evidence, however, is the light gray color of the porcelain, which is an indication that this spark plug has been running at the correct temperature. This means that the spark plug is one with the correct heat range and that the air-fuel mixture is correct. The combustion temperature is high enough to raise the temperature of the spark plug porcelain so that it burns off the small amount of oil that is normally present in the combustion chamber during the firing period.

③This black, sooty condition on both the shell and porcelain is caused by an excessively rich air-fuel mixture, both at low and high speeds. The rich mixture lowers the combustion temperature so that the spark plug does not run hot enough to burn off the deposits.

1

2

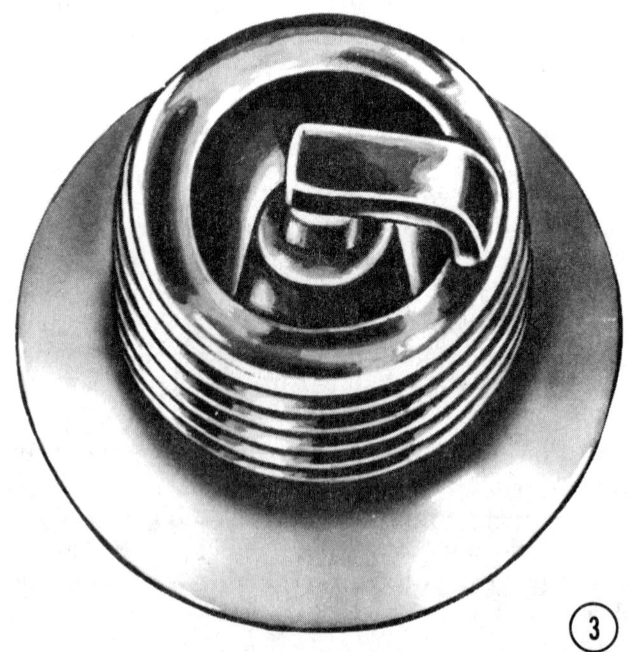

3

④If the deposits are formed only on the shell, it is an indication that the low-speed air-fuel mixture is too rich. With a normal mixture at high speeds, the combustion chamber temperature is high enough to burn off the deposits on the insulator.

⑤This dark insulator, with very few deposits, indicates that the spark plug is running too cool. This condition can be caused by low compression or by using a spark plug of an incorrect heat range. If the condition is isolated to one cylinder, low compression can be suspected. If all of the spark plugs look like this, they are probably of a heat range that is too cold.

⑥Heavy carbon-like deposits are an indication of excessive oil consumption. This can result from worn piston rings, worn valve guides, or from a valve seal that is either worn or incorrectly installed.

⑦This wet, fouled spark plug is not firing. Any combustion would have dried off the deposits until the spark plug looked like the one in the preceding picture. This fouled condition of the spark plug can be caused by the wet oily deposits on the insulator shorting the high-tension spark to ground inside the shell. Or the condition can be caused by ignition trouble, in which case no high-tension pulse is delivered to the plug to fire it.

(8) Overheating and pre-ignition are indicated by a dead white or gray insulator, which is generally blistered. The electrode gap wear rate will be considerably more than normal and, in the case of pre-ignition, will actually cause the electrodes to melt as the ones in this spark plug did. Overadvanced ignition timing, detonation from using a fuel of too low octane rating, an excessively lean air-fuel mixture, or cooling system troubles can cause overheating.

(9) Excessive electrode wear results in a wide gap and, more important, the carbonized electrode surfaces form a high-resistance gap path for the spark to jump across. This condition will cause the engine to misfire under acceleration. If all of the spark plugs are in this condition, it can cause an increase in fuel consumption and a restricted top speed, especially so if the rest of the ignition system is not operating at maximum efficiency. The remedy, of course, is to replace the

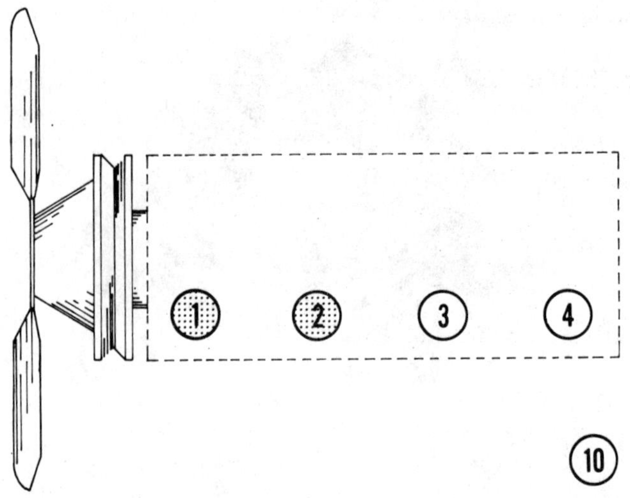

spark plugs. However, it is possible to use this spark plug if the electrodes are filed to remove the resistance surfaces and then regapped to the correct specifications.

(10) If you find two adjacent spark plugs fouled, check for a blown cylinder head gasket or for incorrect

The spark plug insulator must be cleaned periodically of all foreign matter because this becomes a leakage path for the high-tension voltage to cross over.

connections of the high-tension wires to these plugs.

EMISSION-CONTROL SYSTEMS

There are three kinds of emissions that must be controlled on a modern engine: crankcase, exhaust, and evaporative. The troubleshooting of these systems will be covered in Chapter 4, along with the theory of operation.

FUEL AND IGNITION SYSTEM PROBLEMS

Rough Engine Idle

A rough idle can be caused by any of numerous conditions and maladjustments of the engine. This problem is best approached by first doing a complete engine tune-up to take care of such possible ignition conditions as spark plugs burned, fouled, or improperly gapped, or the ignition timing set too far advanced or retarded.

Other engine conditions which can cause a rough idle are intake manifold air leaks, uneven compression, sticking valves, and troubles in the fuel system which can affect the idle mixture. These troubles include a high fuel level, a heavy float, a leaking needle valve and seat, a leaking power valve diaphragm, a

When the dirty insulator gets wet, flashover occurs, and the cylinder misfires. This condition causes hard starting in wet weather.

Engine misfire is generally caused by ignition system defects. Worn-out spark plugs with corroded electrodes and an excessively wide gap can cause the engine to misfire on acceleration.

To check out the PCV system, clamp the hose shut, and the engine speed should drop about 60 rpm. CAUTION: If the hose is old, it is better to pull if off the valve and cover the end with your finger. Clamping off an old hose will often loosen particles from the brittle inside walls, which may then plug the valve.

restricted air filter element, an automatic choke malfunction, and poor idle mixture and/or speed adjustments.

With the advent of exhaust, evaporative, and crankcase emission control systems, the modern engine induction system has been designed with a calibrated amount of air leaking into the intake manifold. This is necessary to vent the crankcase of unburned vapors. Also, some of the late-model engines are passing intake manifold vacuum through calibrated bleeds to operate diaphragms for controlling valves in the power brakes, hand brake releasing mechanisms, heater and air conditioning door systems, and vacuum motors for regulating the temperature of the incoming air in the thermostatically controlled air cleaner. If an excessively large amount of air is bleeding into the intake manifold through a leak in one of the air hoses, by an improper vacuum connection, or by an incorrectly installed part with an improper air bleed, the result will be a rough engine idle. The only way to isolate troubles of this type is to pinch off one at a time the hoses leading to the intake manifold and to note the effect on a vacuum gauge and tachometer. In the case of a vent, such as the one to the PCV valve in the manifold, pinching it off should cause a drop in engine speed of about 60 rpm. If there is no drop then the PCV valve is plugged, and the calibrated air bleed is shut. If the drop is excessive, the PCV valve has an incorrectly calibrated air bleed.

Check for a vacuum leak in each of the other vacuum systems by pinching off each hose in turn and noting the effect of so doing on the vacuum gauge and the tachometer.

On engines with an Exhaust-Gas Recirculation (EGR) system, a valve that is stuck open can cause a very rough idle. See Chapter 4 for testing this system.

Inconsistent Engine Idle Speed

The most common cause of an inconsistent idle speed is sticking or binding in the throttle linkage and/or the automatic transmission throttle control and kickdown linkages. It is also possible for the carburetor throttle shaft to be either sticking or loose on the throttle lever, or to have a loose throttle plate which can shift in the body and cause this trouble.

If the carburetor is equipped with a dashpot, check the operation of the plunger for sticking or binding. Clean the end of the plunger and the plunger seat on the throttle lever. A dirty and gummy plunger and seat can cause a sticking condition.

Excessive Fuel Consumption

This condition can be the result of poor driving habits, a faulty condition of the vehicle, or inefficient engine operation. Quite often, it is a combination of all three. If the fuel consumption has been normal for some time, and then suddenly increases, defects other than the driver are indicated.

Preliminary checking should include an inspection for correct tire inflation, dragging brakes, or a fuel leak. Check for a fuel leak both with the engine running and not running. Fuel leaks show up more readily between the fuel pump and carburetor when the fuel pump is operating. On the other hand, a leak between the fuel pump and tank will not be evident when the fuel pump is operating. This is due to the vacuum that is created on the suction side of the system, which will keep the fuel from leaking.

Ignition performance can have a decided effect on gasoline mileage. Some of the factors which can adversely affect mileage are fouled or burned spark plugs, ignition system defects, and late ignition timing.

If the other factors check out or have been corrected and the fuel consumption is still excessive, then the carburetor must be overhauled. Check the power valve and the needle valve and seat for leaking. Care must be taken when making the adjustments which affect fuel consumption, such as those to the float level, automatic choke, vacuum-kick, and power valve. When checking the operation of the automatic choke, make sure that the heat tube is open and that the vacuum system works properly. Be sure to clean the filter element of the air cleaner.

Acceleration Stumble

A stumble on acceleration is generally caused by insufficient delivery of fuel during a stroke of the

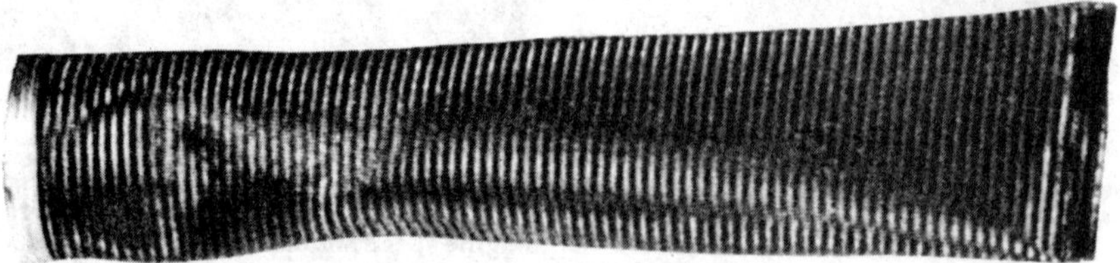

If you get water in the gas tank through condensation or through the gas station hose, the filter at the end of the pickup tube in your gas tank will swell and restrict the flow of fuel, resulting in the carburetor running out of fuel during high-speed driving.

One way to check the air-fuel mixture is to speed up the engine and restrict the flow of air through the carburetor. This can be done by closing the choke valve partially or restricting the opening with the palm of your hand. If the mixture is too lean, restricting the air will cause the engine to speed up. If the mixture is too rich, restricting the air will cause the engine to slow down.

Improperly adjusted ignition timing has a decided effect on the performance of the engine, emissions, and gasoline mileage. Use a timing light to adjust the ignition timing to specifications.

A cracked fuel pump diaphragm (arrow) causes a leak of fuel into the engine crankcase, and this lowers the gas mileage considerably. You can smell the gasoline in the oil on the dipstick. It is necessary to replace the fuel pump, because they cannot be repaired on late-models.

carburetor accelerator pump. This deficiency could be the result of too short a pump stroke or leaking accelerator pump check valves. The remedy is to remove the carburetor, clean it thoroughly (paying particular attention to the parts of the acceleration system), and then reassemble it. Be sure to make the bench adjustments, paying special attention to those which are concerned with the parts of the accelerating circuit.

It is quite possible that other systems can cause a stumble on acceleration. If the manifold heat control valve is stuck in the open position, it can cause a stumble when the engine is warming up. Trouble in the ignition system secondary circuit will also cause a stumble, but this condition may better be referred to as a miss on acceleration.

Engine Surge

A surging engine is one which runs as if the load on the car were being intermittently increased and decreased. This is best detected while maintaining a constant car speed. Surging can take place at any car speed. However, surging generally is detected in the mid-speed range and may not be in evidence at other speeds.

In general, surging is caused by a lean fuel condition, resulting from dirt or a restriction in the fuel system. A defective fuel pump or any condition that does not permit a normal flow of fuel mixture into the intake manifold can cause surging. Another cause, though quite remote, is a distributor vacuum-advance system that may be hunting or constantly changing the spark timing.

Poor High-Speed Performance

This problem can be caused by either the fuel system or the ignition system. A fuel system that does not supply adequate fuel for high-speed operation usually causes the engine to cut out entirely as car speed is increased. As the car slows down, a speed will be reached where operation will again be normal.

An ignition problem is usually evidenced by the engine misfiring during acceleration, but it is possible for a malfunctioning ignition system, without sufficient reserve, to pass out at higher engine speeds. Generally, the feeling is one of rough engine operation rather than of a complete cutting out.

Other conditions which should be checked for poor high-speed performance are preignition and over-advanced ignition timing. Fuel system troubles include the following: a restricted air cleaner, restricted exhaust system, defective fuel pump, clogged fuel filter in the line, and partially clogged vent in the gas tank.

Poor Low-Speed Performance

If the engine performance is sluggish at low speeds only and high-speed operation is normal, the fuel supply system must be operating satisfactorily. The spark plugs, distributor, compression, and exhaust system must also be normal.

If the trouble occurs only at low speeds, it can be in the low-speed or range circuits of the carburetor, in an incorrect low-speed calibration of the distributor, or in a failure to set the ignition timing to specifications. Also, check the vacuum advance diaphragm of the distributor for a leak and passage in the carburetor to be sure it is open. An automatic transmission with a defective one-way clutch will aslo cause a loss of performance at low speeds.

Engine Stalling

When an engine starts normally but fails to keep running, the trouble is probably in the fuel system. If the temperature is below freezing, water in the fuel line or carburetor may have frozen, thereby restricting the flow of fuel. Stalling when cold can be caused by the fast-idle speed being too low, the choke plate sticking, an incorrect setting of the choke cover, or the choke plate pull-down adjustment being incorrect.

If a hot engine stalls and cannot be restarted, the trouble can be caused by vapor lock. Such an engine cannot usually be restarted until the vaporized fuel has condensed back into a liquid. If the hot engine stalling condition is general, the trouble can be caused by the idle speed being too low, the idle mixture being incorrectly adjusted, or the choke plate sticking partially closed.

Under certain weather conditions, an engine will run normally, both when it is cold and when it is hot, but will stall at idle or near-idle speeds during the engine warm-up period. This condition can be caused by carburetor icing, and it is most likely to occur when winter-grade gasoline (more volatile than summer grade) is used and when the atmospheric temperature ranges from 30° to 60°F. at relative humidities above 65%.

When carburetor icing occurs, moisture is drawn from the air passing through the carburetor. It condenses and forms ice on the throttle plates and the surrounding throttle body. When the throttle is almost completely closed for idling, this ice tends to bridge the gap between the throttle plate and body, thereby cutting off the air supply and causing the engine to stall. Opening the throttle for restarting breaks the ice bridge but does not eliminate the possibility of further stalling until the engine and carburetor are warmed up.

In some instances, an engine will run normally in all phases of its operation but will stall just as the car is brought to a stop. This condition usually is confined to cars equipped with an automatic transmission. Most cars so equipped have an anti-stall dashpot attached to the carburetor to control the closing rate of the throttle plates. A dashpot that is out of adjustment or one that is defective generally causes this type of engine stalling. However, if the stalling is accompanied by engine roughness, a contributing cause could be a high

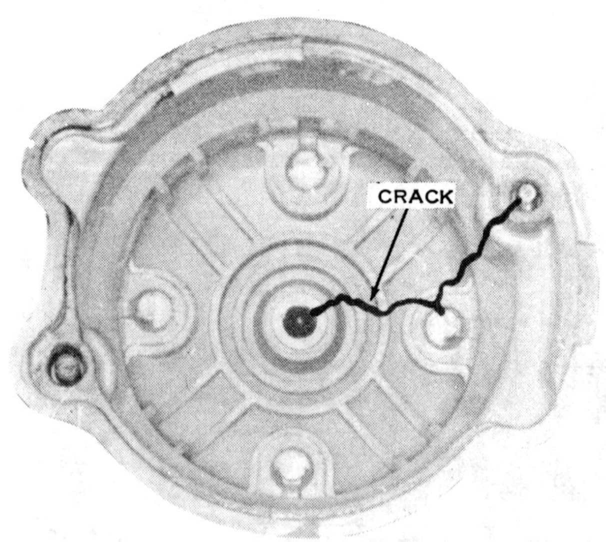

A cracked distributor cap can cause the engine to misfire or stop entirely if the crack runs from the center connector to any grounded point.

carburetor fuel level due to a leaking needle valve and seat or to a heavy float, or a combination of dashpot adjustment and high fuel level.

Engine Starts Hard

When an engine is hard to start when cold but starts easily when hot, the trouble is usually caused by defects in the ignition system or by a lean supply of fuel through the carburetor. A choke coil that is set too lean, sticking choke plate, and binding choke linkage are the most common causes of this particular lean condition. If this cold-starting problem exists only when the temperature is below freezing, the most likely cause is water in the carburetor which freezes and restricts the flow of fuel.

Hard starting of a hot engine generally is caused by an oversupply of fuel through the carburetor, which results in engine flooding. The more common causes of flooding are a choke coil that is set too rich, sticking choke plate, and binding choke linkage. Flooding also can be caused by a dirty, worn, or leaking float valve needle and seat or by a sticking float. Another cause of flooding is percolation, whereby the fuel in the carburetor bowl boils over into the intake manifold. This condition, when it exists, is most likely to occur shortly after a hot engine is shut off. High fuel pump pressure occasionally contributes to flooding.

Engine Misfire

In most instances, this condition is caused by spark plug troubles; the plugs can be fouled, have broken insulators, be improperly gapped, or offer high resistance at the electrodes, or the wrong type may have been installed. The condition can also be caused by other defects in the ignition system secondary circuit—in the ignition coil, rotor, distributor cap, or high-tension wiring

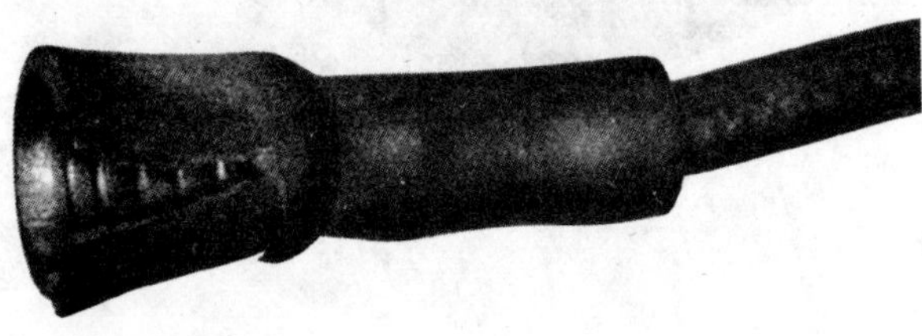

Hardened and cracked spark plug boots allow moisture to seep onto the spark plug insulator, and this can cause hard starting and flashover.

TROUBLESHOOTING MECHANICAL ENGINE CONDITIONS

Good compression is the key to engine performance. An engine with worn piston rings, burned valves, or a blown gasket cannot be made to perform satisfactorily until the mechanical defects are repaired. Generally, a compression gauge is used to determine the cranking pressure within each cylinder. However, today's big displacement engines generally have considerable valve overlap, and the resulting compression reading may be much lower than the manufacturer's specifications of around 150-170 psi. It is entirely possible to obtain a reading as low as 120 psi on a modern engine which is in good mechanical condition. Such an engine is said to "exhale" at cranking speed, even though everything is perfectly normal at operating speeds.

To make a compression test, remove the spark plugs and lay them out in the order of removal. This is extremely important so that you can "read" the firing end of each spark plug. After the spark plugs are removed, insert the rubber adapter of a compression

For an engine to idle smoothly, it must have compression that does not vary over 15 psi for any cylinder. The actual reading is not as important as the amount of variance between cylinders.

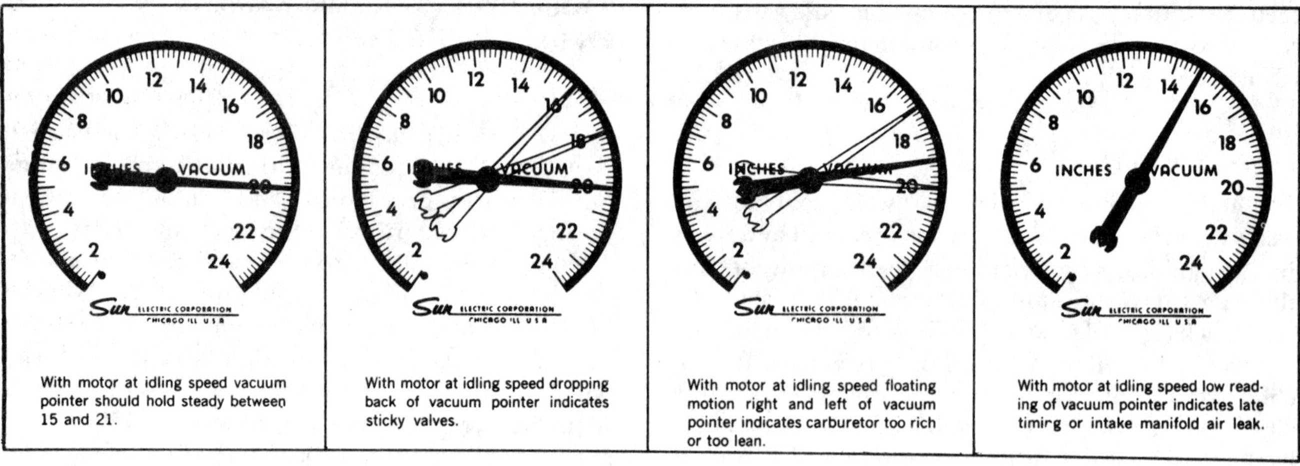

With motor at idling speed vacuum pointer should hold steady between 15 and 21.

With motor at idling speed dropping back of vacuum pointer indicates sticky valves.

With motor at idling speed floating motion right and left of vacuum pointer indicates carburetor too rich or too lean.

With motor at idling speed low reading of vacuum pointer indicates late timing or intake manifold air leak.

A vacuum gauge is a handy diagnostic tool for isolating troubles in an internal-combustion engine. The interpretations are shown under each of the gauge readings.

gauge into one cylinder and have a helper crank the engine. **CAUTION: Ground the primary terminal of the coil to prevent damage to it. CAUTION: The throttle valve and choke must be in the wide-open position in order to obtain maximum readings.** Crank the engine through several revolutions to obtain the highest reading on the compression gauge, or record an equal number of pulses for each cyliner.

The significance in a compression test is the variation in pressure readings between cylinders. As long as this variation is within 20-30 psi, the engine is normal. If a greater variation exists, then the low-reading cylinder should be checked by making a cylinder leak test to determine where the trouble lies. You can do this by introducing compressed air into the combustion chamber through the spark plug hole with the piston at TDC, firing position. If an exhaust valve is defective, you will be able to hear air escaping through the tailpipe. If an intake valve is burned, air will escape through the intake manifold, and it can be heard through the top of the carburetor.

VACUUM GAUGE

A vacuum gauge is a relatively inexpensive piece of test equipment that can be very handy in isolating trouble in an internal-combustion engine. As with a compression gauge, a numerical reading cannot be counted on. Instead, relative readings and typical actions of the needle provide clues to some types of troubles.

Normal idle vacuum in the intake manifold ranges from 15 to 22" Hg. On later-model engines, lower and less steady intake manifold vacuum readings are becoming increasingly common because of the greater use of high-lift cams and the increase in the amounts of valve overlap. Also, altitude affects a vacuum gauge reading. In mountainous areas, a vacuum gauge will read about one inch lower for each 1,000' of elevation above sea level. It is also possible for a change in barometric pressure to affect a vacuum gauge reading, which emphasizes the fact that it is much more important to watch the needle action than its actual reading. With experience, you will come to recognize easily such conditions as sticking valves, a tight valve lash adjustment, or a restriction in the exhaust system.

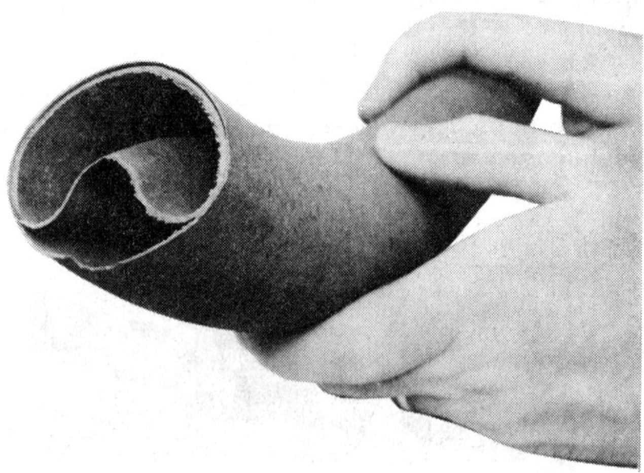

This is part of an exhaust pipe that collapsed. This kind of defect can be checked with a vacuum gauge by accelerating the engine and allowing it to return to idle. A restricted exhaust will cause a momentary stop in the return of the needle when the throttle is closed quickly.

ENGINE NOISES

Noises are generally referred to as knock, slaps, clicks, and squeaks; they are caused by loose bearings, pistons, gears, and other moving parts of the engine. In general, the most common types of noises are either synchronized to engine speed or to one-half engine speed. Those that are timed to engine speed are sounds that have to do with the crankshaft, rods, pistons, and pins. The sounds that are emitted at one-half crankshaft speed concern valve-train noises. Whether or not the sound occurs at engine speed or one-half engine speed can usually be determined by operating the engine at a slow idle and noting whether the noise is synchronized with flashes of a timing light.

A main bearing knock is usually a dull thud that is noticeable under load. Trying to move the car under power with the brakes applied will bring out this noise. Pull the spark plug wires from the plugs, one at a time. If the noise disappears when a plug wire is removed, then it is probably coming from that cylinder. This category would include rod bearings, piston pins, and piston slap. If a rod bearing is loose, the noise will be loudest on deceleration. Piston pin noise and piston slap are, in general, louder when a cold engine is first started. **CAUTION: Don't pull off a spark plug wire on a vehicle with a catalytic converter, or you will destroy it.**

A stethoscope is handy for determining the source of an engine noise. You can also use a screwdriver with the handle against your ear to determine the noise source.

The use of a stethoscope or other listening device will often aid in locating the source of an unusual sound. However, a great deal of care and judgment must be used, because noise travels through other metallic parts as well as parts not involved in the problem.

Carbon build-up in the combustion chamber can cause interference with a piston. Fuel pumps can knock, belts can be noisy, distributors can emit clicking noises, and generators can contribute to unusual sounds. Flywheels, clutches, transmissions, water pumps, and loose manifolds can also cause noise problems.

EXCESSIVE OIL CONSUMPTION

High oil consumption complaints are often the result of oil leaks rather than actual consumption by the engine. Therefore, before assuming that an engine is burning oil, examine the exterior for evidence of oil leaks.

In analyzing a mechanical engine leak problem, consideration must be given to the fact that oil can enter the combustion chambers in only three ways: (1) past the piston rings, (2) through the valve guides, and (3) through the intake manifold. Evidence of excessive oil consumption usually is in the form of carbon deposits in the exhaust outlet pipe and oil-fouled spark plugs. The following items are generally responsible for internal oil consumption problems: (1) a clogged positive crankcase ventilation system, (2) piston rings not sealing, (3) excessive valve stem-to-guide clearance, (4) ineffective valve stem seals, or (5) a cracked intake manifold (the type that serves as a valve chamber cover).

A quick check to determine if the PCV (Positive Crankcase Ventilation) system is working can be made by removing the oil filler cap and placing the palm of your hand over the oil filler tube opening for 30 seconds with the engine idling. If there is suction when removing your hand, the system is working. If there is pressure against your hand, the system is inoperative and must be repaired.

OVERHEATING

Without The Loss Of Coolant

Overheating can be caused by the front of the radiator being obstructed by leaves, bugs, and/or dirt. Restricted hoses in the cooling system can affect the flow of coolant, and this is also true if the pump drive belt is loose. Any restriction in the exhaust system, too, will cause overheating. This can be a bent exhaust pipe or an exhaust control valve that is stuck in the closed position.

Circulation can also be impaired by a loose or broken pump hub or impeller, or the thermostat can be defective. The thermostat can be checked by removing it from the engine and testing it in a pail of heated water.

When the thermostat is removed for checking, inspect the casting for a foundry flash inside the manifold. This can be done by a visual inspection or by probing through the thermostat opening with a piece of welding rod or heavy wire. If there is a flash, it will restrict the flow of coolant through the manifold, causing the coolant to boil after the engine is stopped. This condition can also cause the engine to overheat after long driving periods.

If the car is equipped with a fluid-coupling type of fan drive, check the operation of the unit as follows: (1) Run the engine at approximately 1,000 rpm until normal operating temperature is reached. This process can be speeded up by blocking off the front of the radiator with cardboard. (2) Stop the engine and, using a cloth to protect your hand, immediately check the effort required to turn the fan. If considerable effort is required, the coupling is operating satisfactorily. If very little effort is required to turn the fan, it is an indication that the coupling is not operating properly and that it should be serviced or replaced.

Retarded ignition timing and a lean air-fuel mixture will also cause overheating.

The pressure rating of the radiator filler cap can be checked with a pump and gauge arrangement as shown.

With Loss Of Coolant

When it becomes necessary to add coolant to the system at regular intervals, the cause of the trouble should be investigated. Visually inspect the radiator, pump, engine, and hoses for leaks. Check the pressure rating and operation of the radiator filler cap.

If the loss of coolant is due to an internal leak caused by a crack in the combustion chamber, the coolant will be rusty and the engine will overheat. If this is the case, evidence of the crack can be determined by looking for bubbles in the coolant as the engine is accelerated. Do this by draining the coolant to the top of the block and then removing the top hose. Add coolant until the level is even with the top of the thermostat housing. Start the engine and accelerate it quickly. Check the coolant surface for evidence of bubbles.

If you suspect a crack in the combustion chamber, you can introduce air pressure into each cylinder while checking the coolant at the thermostat housing for bubbles. To do this, install an air hose adapter (an old spark plug shell to which a tire valve has been brazed)

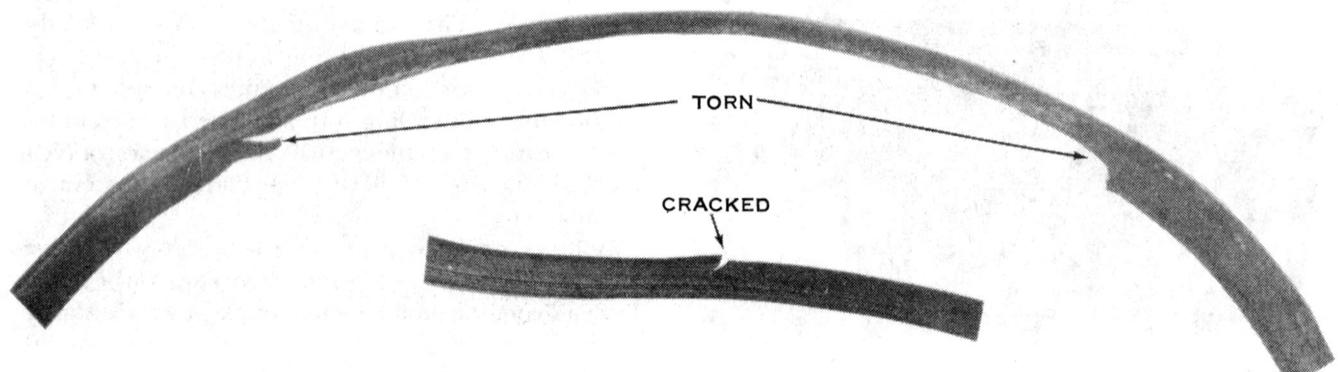

A broken or cracked fan belt or power steering pump drive belt will often cause a noise that is clearly audible from the driver's seat. Always replace belts with defects before they actually break.

A crack in the head or block can be checked by introducing compressed air into each cylinder with the piston at TDC firing position and checking for bubbles in the coolant at the thermostat housing, as discussed in the text.

in No. 1 spark plug hole. Start the test by rotating the crankshaft until No. 1 cylinder is at TDC, firing position. Introduce air at full line pressure. Check each cylinder in turn by rotating the crankshaft until the piston is at TDC, firing position for the next cylinder in the firing order. Transfer the air hose adapter to that cylinder, and then repeat the test.

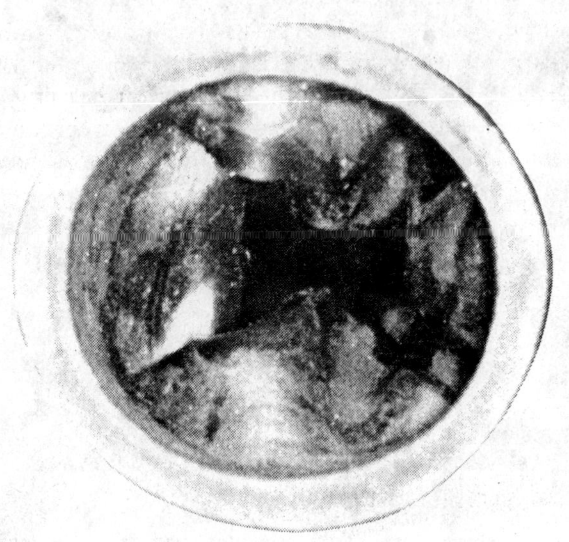

A clogged radiator hose is an indication that the rest of the cooling system is plugged in a similar fashion. The remedy is to reverse-flush the system and replace the hoses. It may be necessary to remove the radiator for cleaning by a speciality shop.

ELECTRICAL SYSTEM

BATTERY AND CHARGING SYSTEM

The charging system consists of an alternator, a regulator, a battery, a charge indicator gauge, and the necessary wiring to connect the components. Many late-model alternators have the regulator built into one end cap.

Battery problems are not always due to charging sytstem defects. Excessive use of lights and accessories while the engine is either off or running at low speed, voltage losses, corroded battery cables and connectors, low water level in the battery, or prolonged disuse of the battery which would permit a self-discharging condition are all possible reasons which should be considered when a battery is run down or low in charge.

Charging system troubles such as low alternator output or no alternator output (indicated by the in-

An induction-type ammeter can be used to measure the charging system output by holding the meter over the main wire to the battery with the engine running at a fast-idle speed.

dicator gauge showing discharge while the engine is running) require testing of both the alternator and the alternator regulator. Alternator regulator problems usually do not make themselves known except by their direct effect on the alternator output and, of course, eventually by creating a battery problem. Proper adjustment of the regulating units contained in the regulator assembly is very important.

Test the alternator output at the battery with a voltmeter connected across the terminals. Start the engine, and the voltmeter reading should advance from the battery voltage of 12 to the regulated voltage of approximately 14. If it doesn't increase above the battery voltage (12 volts), then the alternator or regulator is defective.

Isolating The Trouble

To isolate trouble between the alternator and regulator, hold a screwdriver blade against the back plate of the alternator. Turn on the ignition switch (engine not running), and you should have magnetism, indicating that the regulator is exciting the field circuit.

If there is no magnetic attraction, then the regulator is defective. If there is a magnetic field, and the system does not charge, then the alternator is defective.

Noise Alternator

When investigating the complaint of alternator noise, first try to localize and pinpoint the noise area to make sure that the alternator is at fault rather than the drive belt or water pump or another part of the engine. Start the engine and listen for the area and the type of noise. Use a stethoscope or similar sound-detection instrument to localize the noise. An alternator bearing, pump bearing, or belt noise is usually a squealing sound.

An alternator with a shorted diode will normally whine (magnetic noise) and will be most noticeable at idle speeds. Perform an alternator output test; if the output is approximately 10 amperes less than specifications, a shorted diode is indicated. To eliminate the belt as the cause of noise, apply a light amount of belt dressing. If the alternator belt is at fault, adjust the betl to specifications or replace it, if necessary. If the belt is satisfactory and the noise is believed to be in the alternator or pump, remove the alternator belt. Start the engine and listen for the noise as a double check to be sure the noise is not caused by another component. If the noise is traced to the alternator, remove it and inspect the bearings for wear, scoring, or an out-of-round condition.

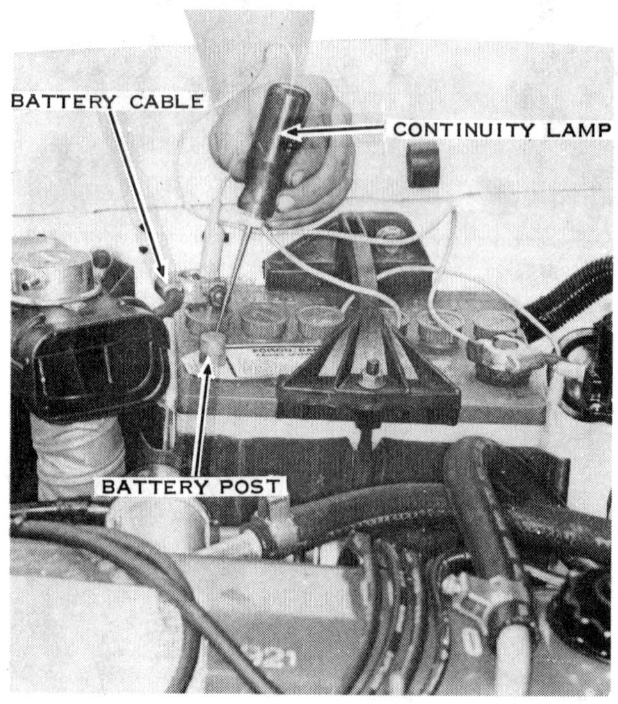

To check for a short circuit, connect a test lamp between the disconnected battery cable and the battery post. If the test lamp lights, then there is a short circuit.

A simple check to see if the regulator contacts are in good condition is to hold a screwdriver against the end of the alternator with the ignition key in the running position but with the engine stopped. If the regulator contact points are good, the field will be energized and the screwdriver will be attracted by the resulting magnetic field. CAUTION: Don't make contact at the positive diode heat sink which is at battery voltage, or sparks will fly.

TURN SIGNALS

The turn signal system includes a fuse, flasher unit, switch, front and rear signal lights, instrument panel indicator lights, ignition switch (accessory terminal is used as the power source), and the necessary wiring to connect the components.

As a visual aid in troubleshooting turn signal problems, connect an ammeter in series with the battery. Any indication of an excessive current draw can then be readily observed. **CAUTION: The ignition switch must be either in the ACC or ON position for the turn signal lights to operate.**

One Signal Light Fails To Operate

This type of trouble is most often the result of a burned-out bulb. If one bulb is burned out, the remaining bulb(s) will remain on but will not flash. Also, the respective right or left instrument panel indicator light will remain on. Switch failure, shorted or open wiring, loose connectors, or corroded bulb socket assemblies are other causes of inoperative signal lights.

All Signal Lights Fail To Operate

This trouble is most often the result of a blown fuse or a defective flasher unit. However, a turn signal switch failure or shorted or open wiring could also be contributing causes. As the fuse or turn signal power supply is fed from the accessory terminal of the ignition switch, check that other accessories, such as the radio, are operative. If other accessories are not operative, it is possible that the ignition switch may be defective.

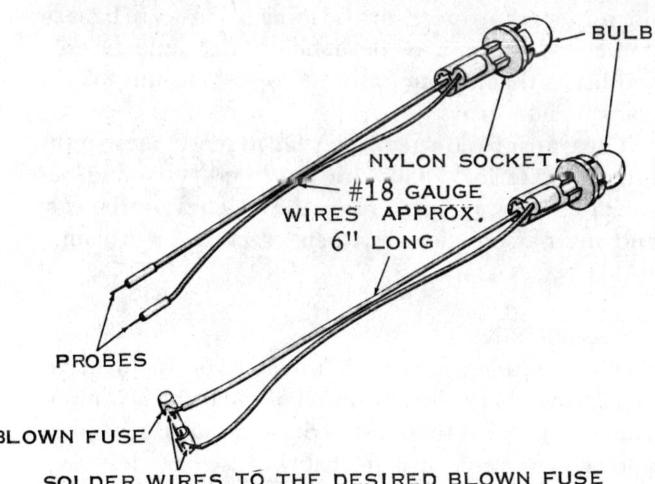

A testing probe can be made with an old socket and a bulb. This device can be used to check terminals for current without blowing out the fuse. If a similar probe is soldered to a blown fuse(lower), the fuse can be inserted into the fuse receptacle of a circuit for testing so that fuses are not blown out at each test.

A 12-volt test light can be substituted for a voltmeter. A voltage or test light indication should be obtained only at the connectors which lead to the lights in question. If there is voltage or a test light indication at connectors other than those for which the turn signal switch is positioned, then the turn signal switch or wiring has a short circuit. If there is no voltage at the connections, then an open circuit through the switch is indicated. In either case, the switch or wiring assembly must be removed for repair or replacement.

CONSTANT-VOLTAGE SYSTEM

The CV (Constant Voltage) system consists of the fuel level indicator gauge, fuel tank sending unit, temperature indicator gauge, temperature sending unit, and the oil pressure indicator gauge and sending unit except on cars equipped with an oil pressure indicator light.

If all gauge indicators read maximum, the condition is caused by sticking points or an open heater winding in the CV regulator. If all gauge indicators remain on the low end of the scale, an open CV regulator or an open circuit on the input side of the regulator is the probable cause. If one or two gauge indicators register incorrectly, a defective indicator or sending unit is the

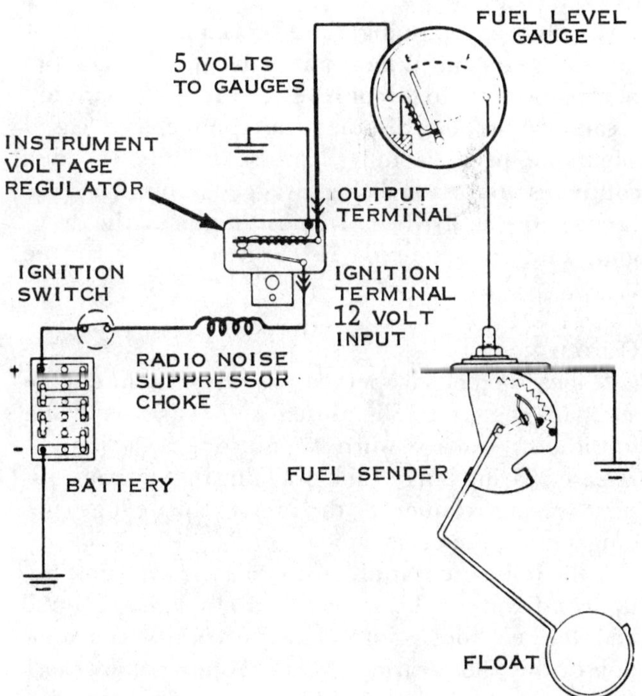

A constant voltage regulator is designed to furnish 5 volts for energizing the gauges. The battery voltage cannot be used for the gauge system because it varies with the state of battery charge and the charging rate of the alternator.

most probable cause. Substitute a new fuel tank sending unit to check out a suspected gauge. Disconnect the wire from the suspected sending unit and connect it to the test unit. **CAUTION: Be sure that the test unit is grounded properly to the metal of the car.**

If the gauge indicator operation is erratic, loose wiring connectors or a defective sending unit is the most probable cause. If all gauge indicators read higher than conditions warrant, the probable cause is a poor ground at the CV regulator. Clean and tighten the CV regulator ground connections, and then retest the system. If the gauge indicators still read higher than operating conditions indicate, replace the CV regulator.

TROUBLESHOOTING THE DRIVELINE

Clutch Chatters

Rapid gripping or slipping of the clutch assembly while the unit is being engaged will cause a clutch to chatter. Some of the conditions resulting in clutch chatter are release bearing binding, worn linkage, clutch pedal and assist spring being out of adjustment, loose engine mounts, and a warped or sticking clutch disc.

Clutch Drags

Clutch drag (spinning) causes clashing of the transmission gears and is most noticeable in shifting from neutral position to low or reverse gear. The condition is caused by a clutch disc that is not completely released when the pedal is fully depressed. Thus, the disc continues to rotate, being dragged around by the rotation of the flywheel. In most instances, the dragging condition is caused by excessive clutch pedal free travel.

Clutch Noisy

If the clutch pedal operation is noisy with the engine stopped, the trouble is caused by linkage requiring lubrication, linkage worn or improperly adjusted, release bearing burred and dragging on the transmission bearing retainer, or the pressure plate lugs rubbing against the cover.

If the noise occurs only when the engine is running, the condition can be caused by a misaligned engine and flywheel housing or by looseness or a worn condition of the pilot bearing. *NOTE: A faulty or dry clutch pilot bearing is characterized by a high-pitched noise when the clutch pedal is depressed with the engine idling.*

If the noise occurs only when the clutch pedal is partially depressed, the trouble is a defective release bearing. The pedal action brings the release bearing into contact with the clutch release fingers when the pedal is partially depressed, causing the bearing to spin.

Clutch Slips

Clutch disc slippage will be encountered if the friction surface of the clutch plate fails to hold the disc against the friction face of the flywheel. If severe clutch slippage exists, a greater than normal engine speed will be noticed in high gear when the accelerator is depressed to full throttle. If the slippage is slight but continuous, it may go unnoticed until excessive temperature caused by friction results in failure of the disc and/or friction surfaces.

In most cases, slippage is caused by insufficient clutch pedal free-travel. Normal clutch disc facing wear causes a gradual reduction in free-travel and when a point of no free-travel is reached, clutch slippage will begin.

STANDARD-GEARED TRANSMISSION

The problems related to a geared transmission are the transmission jumping out of gear, excessive noise, hard shifting efforts, clashing of gears when the transmission is shifted, and lubricant leakage.

Transmission Jumps Out Of Gear

The gears will not slip out of low or reverse gear on cars that are equipped with a properly installed and adjusted exterior interlock linkage. This linkage has been designed to make certain the transmission low and reverse shift lever is locked in place after the clutch pedal has been fully released. If the linkage is not adjusted properly or the linkage parts are bent or damaged, there may be a binding or interference condition that will not allow proper meshing of the transmission gears.

The transmission gears may fail to stay in mesh if the internal interlock balls are damaged, the interlock spring is weak or broken, or the notches on the cam and shaft assemblies are worn, cracked, or broken.

Transmission Noisy

To determine the cause of the noise problem, drive the car and check the operation of the transmission in each gear ratio. If the noise is present only during one specific gear ratio, it is probably caused by defective gears pertaining to that respective gear ratio. If the transmission is noisy in each gear ratio, the noise could be caused by improper lubrication, damaged bearings, flywheel housing misalignment, loose transmission mount bolts, or a damaged mainshaft or cluster gears.

Check the synchronizers for damaged parts or improper operation. Make sure that the synchronizer parts are properly assembled. The insert springs should properly secure the inserts into the insert area of the hub. The sleeve and blocking rings should be free of nicks and burrs. The splines of the hub and shaft have to be free of burrs and nicks that could restrict the hub from moving on the shaft. The cam-and-shaft assembly of the gear-shift housing should be checked for restricted travel.

Check all the transmission and flywheel housing bolts for the proper torque. Start with the flywheel housing. **CAUTION: Make sure that the flywheel housing is properly positioned against the engine.** Check the torque on the engine rear mounting bolts and crossmember-to-body bolts. Loose mounting bolts allow misalignment of the transmission in relationship to the torque transfer from the engine to the transmission main drive gear. Misalignment between the flywheel housing and the engine will cause the same type of problem as loose mounting bolts.

Check the lubricant for proper level. If necessary, drain some of the old lubricant and make sure that it isn't contaminated with metal chips or dirt. The wrong type of lubricant can be a factor in causing noise.

Hard Shifting

Excessive shifting efforts are usually caused by an improperly adjusted clutch or transmission manual linkage. If the transmission has the exterior interlock type linkage, make sure that the cam or wedge parts are not binding and that the interlock is adjusted properly. The last items to be checked should be the internal shift linkage and synchronizers. If the problem exists only during cold weather, a pint of automatic transmission fluid can be added to the lubricant. Also, make sure that the transmission contains the specified lubricant.

If the linkage is not adjusted properly or bent, there will be a binding or interference condition when shifting from one gear to another. To check this out, disconnect the linkage at the end of the steering column and move the selector lever to check for any binding condition. Next, disconnect the linkage rods at the transmission shift levers, and then try the levers for freedom of movement.

If there are no linkage problems, then the transmission will have to be disassembled in order to check the synchronizers for proper operation. Check the splines on the sleeve and hub for nicks or burrs. Make sure that the synchronizer ring is not damaged and that the inserts are properly assembled and retained in the hub by the insert springs.

AUTOMATIC TRANSMISSION

The routine for diagnosing troubles in an automatic transmission requires that you follow certain procedures. Before any repairs or adjustments are made, certain checks must be made, and then the vehicle must be taken for a road test. For example, the transmission fluid level and the manual throttle linkage adjustment must be checked before any road test in undertaken.

See Chapter 6 for detailed tests and service procedures for automatic transmissions.

REAR AXLE

The most common axle or driveline complaint is noise. Excessive rear axle or driveline noise can indicate a malfunction. However, it must be noted that axle gears inherently make some noise and an absolutely quiet unit is seldom found. When evaluating the rear axle, make sure that the noise is not caused by the road surface, by a grounding exhaust system, by the engine, tires, transmission, or wheel bearings, or by some other external component of the car.

Road Test

Before a road test of the car is performed, make sure that there is sufficient lubricant of the specified type in the rear axle housing. Drive the car far enough to warm the lubricant to normal operating temperature before testing. A car should be tested for axle noise by being operated in high gear under the following four driving conditions:

1. DRIVE: Higher than normal road load power where the speed gradually increases on level road acceleration.

2. CRUISE: Constant speed operation at normal road speeds.

3. FLOAT: Using only enough throttle to keep the car from driving the engine. In float, the car will slow down with very little load on the rear axle gears.

4. COAST: Throttle closed—engine is braking the car. Load is on the coast side of the gear set.

When a rear axle is noisy, the following tests are to be performed to pinpoint the problem and eliminate the possibility that the noise is of external origin.

Road Noise

Road surfaces, such as those of brick or rough-surfaced concrete, can cause a noise condition which may be mistaken for tire or rear axle noise. Driving on a smooth asphalt surface will quickly show whether the road surface is the cause of the noise. A road noise usually has the same pitch on DRIVE or COAST.

Tire Noise

Tire noise can easily be mistaken for rear axle noise, even though the noisy tires may be located on the front wheels. Sounds and vibrations are caused by unevenly worn tire surfaces or ply separations. Also, some designs of non-skid treads on low-pressure tires, snow tires, and other assorted types cause vibrations. *NOTE: Temporarily inflate all tires to approximately 40 pounds pressure for test purposes only.* This will alter any noise caused by tires but will not affect noise caused by the rear axle. Excessive rear axle noise usually diminishes or ceases during COAST at speeds under 30 miles per hour. However, tire noise continues, but with a lower tone as car speed is reduced. Rear axle noise usually changes when comparing DRIVE and COAST. However, tire noise remains about the same.

Front Wheel Bearing Noise

Loose or rough front wheel bearing noises can be confused with rear axle noise. However, front wheel bearing noise does not change when comparing DRIVE and COAST. Drive the car through a series of left and right turns, which will put a load on the wheel bearings and emphasize a noisy condition, if it exists. A light application of the brake while holding the car speed steady will often cause wheel bearing noise to diminish. This action takes some weight off the bearings. If front wheel bearing noise is suspected, you can easily check it by jacking up the front wheels and spinning them while feeling and listening for roughness. Also, shake the wheels to determine if the bearings are loose.

Body Noises

The car body and/or one of the attached components can have a wind noise condition that sounds like a noisy rear axle. Items such as the grille, radio antenna, and hood can cause the condition which must be isolated. In some cases, loose body hold-down bolts or brackets can be a source of noise.

Rear Axle Noise

Sometimes a noise which seems to originate in the rear axle is actually caused by the engine, exhaust, transmission, or power steering. To determine which unit is actually causing the noise, observe the approximate car speeds and conditions under which the noise is most pronounced, and then stop the car in a quiet place to avoid interfering noises. With the transmission in neutral, run the engine slowly up and down through engine speeds corresponding to the car speed at which the noise was most pronounced. If a similar noise is produced with the car standing still, it is caused by components other than the rear axle or driveline assemblies.

If a careful road test of the car shows that the noise is not caused by the road surface or by components previously described, it is reasonable to assume that the noise is caused by the rear axle or driveline units. The rear axle should be tested on a smooth level road to avoid road noise. **CAUTION: It is not advisable to test the rear axle assembly for noise by running it with the rear wheels jacked up because the load distribution is different.**

Noises in the rear axle assembly can be caused by faulty rear wheel bearings; loss of pinion pre-load; faulty differential or pinion shaft bearings; worn differential side gears and pinions; or by a mismatched, improperly adjusted, or scored ring-and-pinion gear set. It is sometimes impossible to determine from a test exactly which internal repairs are required to correct a noisy axle unit. The needed repairs can best be determined by a careful inspection of wear on the individual parts when the unit is disassembled.

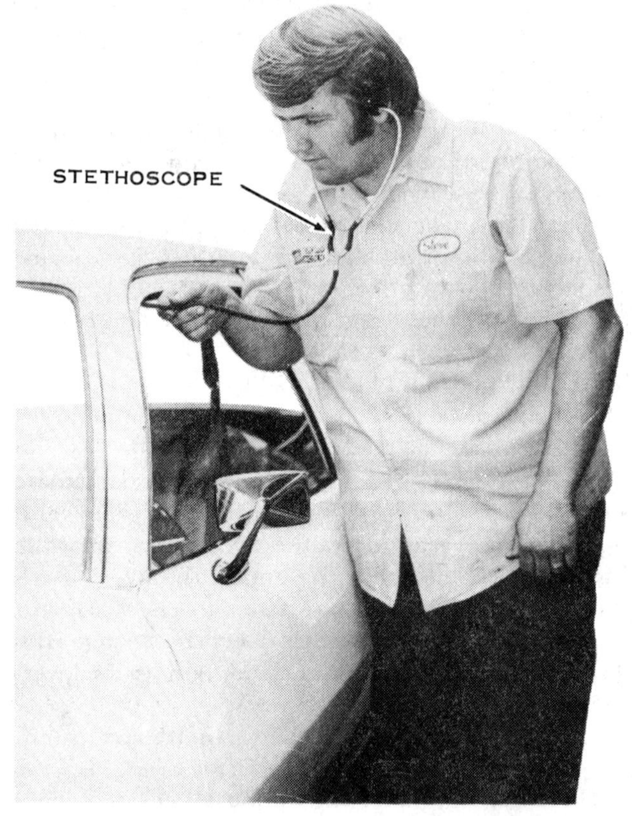

Wind noises can be traced by using a stethoscope with the indicating end removed. Close all windows and air vents and turn the ventilating fan to HIGH SPEED. Move the hose along the edges of all openings to trace wind noises caused by leaking seals. Some mechanics paint suspected areas with a soapy water solution and check for bubbles.

Rear Wheel Bearing Noise

A rough rear wheel bearing produces a heavy grinding or "growling" noise in DRIVE and CRUISE, which will continue when the transmission is positioned in neutral with the car coasting. A brinelled rear wheel bearing causes a knock or click approximately every two revolutions of the rear wheel, since the bearing rollers do not travel at the same speed as the rear axle shaft and wheel. To accentuate the noise of a suspected bearing, drive the car in a series of right and left turns to put a load on the bearings. Sometimes the bearings can be tested with the rear wheels jacked up. Spin the rear wheels by hand while listening at the hubs for evidence of rough or brinelled wheel bearings.

Differential Side Gears And Pinion Noise

Differential side gears and pinions seldom cause noise since their movement is relatively small on straight-ahead driving. Noise produced by these gears will be most pronounced on turns. As a rule, the noise heard will be a "chuckling" sound, similar to the sound given by two steel balls when rattled together. The noise can be attributed to excessively worn or loosely fitted differential side gears.

Pinion Bearing Noise

Rough or brinelled pinion bearings produce a continuous "whine" that starts at a relatively low speed. The noise is most pronounced on FLOAT between 20 and 35 mph. In most instances, pinion bearing noise can be pinpointed by raising the rear axle on a hoist and running it with the transmission in high gear. If the pinion bearing is bad, the noise will be obvious.

Ring And Pinion Gear Noise

Noise produced by the ring-and-pinion gear set generally shows up as DRIVE, COAST, or FLOAT noise. As the gears become worn or out of adjustment, a heavy "humming" sound will be noticed. The noise in DRIVE, COAST, and FLOAT will be very rough or irregular if the differential pinion shaft bearings are rough, worn, or loose, and will vary in tone with speed. As a rule, DRIVE noise is caused by a heavy heel contact, and a COAST noise is caused by heavy toe contact. Heavy face contact is usually the trouble when the rear axle is noisy in FLOAT or CRUISE.

Backlash

Excessive backlash ("clunk noise") can be caused by worn axle shaft splines; loose axle shaft flange nuts; worn, broken, or loose universal joint flange or slip yoke mountings; excessive play between the drive pinion and ring gear; excessive backlash in the differential gears; bearings worn or out of adjustment; or the engine idle speed is too high.

Vibration

Excessive noise or vibration can be caused by a lack of lubrication in the driveshaft U-joint bearings, worn bearings, a bind between the universal joint and the rear axle companion flange (universal joint not seated properly), a sprung or damaged driveshaft, or a missing driveshaft balance weight. **CAUTION: Undercoating carelessly applied to the driveshaft can destroy the balance and cause vibration.**

Vibration or shudder, which is noticeable either on fast acceleration in DRIVE or when in COAST, can be caused by the rear axle housing being loose on the rear springs or by an excessive driveline angle.

TROUBLESHOOTING THE RUNNING GEAR

When troubleshooting a front suspension problem, it is important to follow a pattern before and during a road test that will isolate the area or item that is causing the trouble. This is because several of the problems attributable to front suspension components are also common to steering gear and linkage, rear suspension, and wheel or tire problems. For example, wrong or uneven tire pressures can cause steering problems. Also, a misaligned rear suspension, a binding steering linkage, or an improperly aligned front suspension component has a similar effect on the steering ability of a car.

QUICK CHECKS

Check the attitude of the car for an unbalanced load condition or sagging springs. Jounce the front and rear of the vehicle to check for noisy, weak, loose, or damaged springs, and shock absorbers. After it has settled, check the front and rear of the car for obviously improper front or rear spring riding heights.

If the vehicle looks uneven, measure the riding heights at the same places on each side. Although sagging may be apparent at one or more wheels, the action of all four shock absorbers and springs must be checked. One or more binding shock absorbers or springs can hold other corners of the car abnormally high or low, causing uneven weight distribution, with resulting abnormal tire wear.

Check the air pressure in each tire and the tires for uniformity in size. Also, observe the tread wear pattern for signs of misalignment. Rotate the front and rear wheels to make sure that they turn freely without brake or bearing bind. Check the front wheel bearings for noise, looseness, wear, or improper adjustment. Spin the wheels again to check the tires for run-out, ply separation, or an unbalanced condition.

Inspect the steering column, steering gear, linkage, and stabilizer for loose mountings, wear, or damaged parts. Check the engine and transmission mounts for looseness or damage. Inspect the front and rear springs, shock absorbers, and suspension components for loose mountings, excessive wear, cracks, or damaged parts.

ROAD TEST

Perform a short road test over a smooth and level surface, rough surfaces, and a roadway with a series of small dips. On a level road, check the car for steering bind, side-to-side wander, looseness in the steering gear, shimmy, wheel tramp, pulling to one side, noisy conditions, excessive front-end vibration, and steering wheel vibration.

Drive the car over a surface that has roughness or dips and check for wander, rough ride, noisy conditions, excessive vibration at the steering wheel, weak or bottoming springs, and defective shock absorbers. Perform a series of quick stops in both forward and reverse gears and check for excessive dipping action, bounce, or bottoming, any of which is attributable to weak or damaged springs or shock absorbers. Perform a series of slow turns to the right and left and check the steering mechanism for excessive play, hard steering, and poor steering recovery. Check for excessive body sway, which can be attributed to weak springs, a weak shock absorber, or a loose stabilizer.

From a given point in a wide roadway, turn the steering wheel fully to the left. Then drive the car in a complete circle and observe the diameter of the turn. Perform a similar turn to the right. If the diameter is not the same on both turns, the steering mechanism is out of adjustment or the steering linkage or suspension arms are bent, worn, or damaged.

If misalignment or dog tracking of the front and rear suspension is suspected, drive the car straight ahead on a section of pavement, part of which is wet, and then stop about ten feet beyond the wet area. If alignment is correct, the rear tire imprints will overlap the front equally. If misalignment exists, it can be attributed to an improperly or loosely mounted rear axle or to damaged rear suspension components.

If the vehicle pulls to one side, the condition can be caused by faulty front-end alignment, defective wheel bearings, steering gear defects, or chasis misalignment. Specific defects which can cause the car to pull to one side are the steering gear off the center position, brakes out of adjustment, contaminated brake linings, drums out of round, damaged or worn interior brake components, restricted hydraulic line to one cylinder, or worn wheel bearings.

Abnormal tire tread wear indicates a front-end alignment problem. To check this out, drive the car on a fairly level road in a straight-ahead direction, and then momentarily release the steering wheel to observe if the car pulls to one side. Make a few normal stops to determine how much the steering or front-end alignment problem is related to the amount of direction that the car pulls when the brakes are applied.

VEHICLE LEADS TO ONE SIDE

Rear suspension misalignment is usually the cause of the vehicle leading to one side, and generally the trouble is the result either of bent parts or of a rear spring not being centered in a locating hole. To determine whether this condition exists, measure the distance between a locating hole at the rear of the spring mounting bracket common to both side rails and the forward edge of the axle. The dimension must be the same on both sides of the vehicle. Other causes of the vehicle leading to one side are front-end misalignment, uneven tire pressure, non-uniformity of tire sizes, a dragging brake, improperly adjusted wheel bearing, the steering gear out of adjustment, or binding of the steering linkage.

VIBRATION OR SHIMMY

This common complaint is generally due to an unbalanced condition of the front wheels. Low-speed vibration results from a static unbalanced condition, while high-speed problems are always caused by dynamic imbalance. Shimmy results from a combina-

Uneven tire wear can cause road noise that can be mistaken for rear axle noise. Uneven tire wear should always be investigated.

tion of an unbalanced condition and worn front-end parts. To check for an unbalanced condition during a road test, hold the steering wheel lightly and note the amount of vibration during various speeds.

Before balancing a tire, all foreign matter must be removed from the tread and bead. Check the wheels and tires for lateral and radial run-out, the total of which must not exceed 0.080", with a tolerance of 0.060" even more desirable. **CAUTION: Adding balance weights cannot counteract for wheel and tire run-out.** *NOTE: If excessive weight is required to balance a front tire, replace it.with a new one or the spare.*

Other conditions which could cause vibration are damaged springs, inoperative shock absorbers, loose engine supports, worn universal joints, or a driveshaft that is loosely mounted or out of balance.

POWER STEERING

Power steering gear troubles generally include the following conditions: excess or loss of steering effort, partial steering assist or assist in only one direction, poor returnability, or leaks. Because the internal parts of the power gear assembly are always under high hydraulic pressure, lubrication and wear problems do not occur. However, because of the high pressures, seal problems and leaks are quite general.

Preliminary checks must include the drive belt condition and tension. Check the fluid level in the reservoir and add fluid if necessary. Start the engine and turn the steering wheel back and forth. Shut off the engine and recheck the fluid level. If the level is low, add fluid, but do not overfill.

A pressure check should be made on the pump, with and without the rest of the system, in order to isolate the trouble . This can be done by installing and closing a shut-off valve between the pump and the power steering gear unit. If the pressure builds up to specifications with the shut-off valve closed, then the pump is OK, and the pressure loss must be in the power steering gear assembly. If the pump does not build up to the specified pressure, then the pump is defective. *NOTE: The pitman arm must be disconnected from the sector shaft in order to perform steering gear checks and/or adjustments.*

Some of the conditions that could cause a loss of power assist are drive belt loose, worn, broken, or slipping; fluid level low or air in the system; fluid leaking or damage to the lines; pump pressure too low; and control valve and/or power steering gear assembly defective.

If there is a partial assist or an assist in only one direction, the condition causing this trouble could be the control valve out of adjustment; fluid level too low; air in system; drive belt loose, worn, or slipping; pump pressure too low; control valve defective; or power steering gear assembly defective.

Excessive steering effort and/or poor returnability can be caused by front-end misalignment, tire pressures too low, tires oversize, steering gear fluid low, steering gear out of adjustment, or steering linkage binding or bent.

IRREGULAR TIRE WEAR

Loose, worn, or bent front suspension parts and/or steering linkage can cause irregular tire wear.

Underinflation Wear

Tires are designed so that, under a given load and with the proper air pressure, the tire will make a full pattern across the entire width of the tread, thereby distributing the wear evenly over the entire surface. When a tire is run underinflated, the side walls and the shoulders of the tread carry the load, while, due to the low internal air pressure, the center section folds in, or compresses. With the shoulders thus taking most of the driving and braking loads, they wear much faster than the center section.

Overinflation Wear

When a tire is overinflated, the outside or shoulder sections of the tread are lifted away from the road surface. The center section of the tread then receives most of the driving and braking loads, and this causes it to wear much faster than the shoulder sections.

Scuffing Wear

When the front wheels have an excessive amount of either toe-in or toe-out, the tires are actually dragged sideways when they travel straight down the road and a cross-wear or scraping action takes place, rapidly wearing away the tread. This scuffing action will produce a feather-edge on the ribs of the tread. In many instances, this can be detected by rubbing your hand across the face of the tire. If the feather-edges are on the inside of the tire ribs, too much toe-in is indicated. If the feather-edges are on the outside of the ribs, it indicates that the tires are being run with a toe-out condition.

Camber Wear

Excessive wheel camber causes the tire to run at a slight angle to the road surface, resulting in more wear on one side of the tread than on the other. With too much positive camber, the outside of the tread will show the most wear. Too much negative camber will show a similar wear pattern on the inside of the tread.

Cornering Wear

Cornering wear can be identified by a rough, diagonal wear pattern across the face of the tread. This pattern is the result of the driver making high-speed turns, resulting in an abrasive action caused by tire slippage.

Cup- And- Flat Spot Wear

Cups and flat spots generally are the result of road tramp, caused by wheels and tires being out of balance. Wheel misalignment, along with the unbalanced condition, can cause unusually severe tire cupping. Cupped or spotty tread wear on a front tire cannot be corrected by wheel alignment or balancing. A cupped tire, if transferred to a rear wheel, will true itself up to a certain degree by absorbing the driving and braking loads.

SERVICE BRAKES

The function of the hydraulic system is to deliver equal pressure to each of the four wheel cylinders. This pressure must cause each of the wheel cylinder pistons to move outward to apply the brake shoe linings against the braking surface of each brake drum with equal force. It is also important to remember the effect of the tire treads; each tire must be capable of creating equal friction at the road surface. Another fact to remember is that power brakes do not stop a vehicle better than manual brakes; they only reduce the amount of effort needed to depress the brake pedal.

Some typical problems with service brakes are grabbing, dragging, fading, and noise. Problems associated with brake pedal action are low pedal, soft or spongy pedal, and hard pedal action.

Grabbing Brakes

When one wheel brake grabs, the condition is caused by too much braking friction between the brake linings and brake drum of one wheel or unequal friction between the tread of one tire and the road surface. When all the brakes grab, the problem is at all four wheel brake assemblies.

If all four brakes grab, check the master cylinder piston for partially restricted movement. Check the push rod length adjustment if the car has power brakes. Also, check the internal parts of the power brake that could cause the problem; it could result from a sticking poppet valve, leaking reaction diaphragm, restricted diaphragm passage, or sticking actuating valve assembly.

Remove the brake drums and check the brake linings for defects or the wrong type of material. Wheel cylinder leakage and consequent lining contamination caused by improper overhaul or defective parts can also create a grabbing condition. Make sure that all of the internal brake parts are properly lubricated at the friction areas.

Dragging Brakes

If the brakes are dragging at one wheel only, the trouble can be one wheel brake out of adjustment, a restriction in the hydraulic line, a front wheel bearing

	RAPID WEAR AT SHOULDERS	RAPID WEAR AT CENTER	CRACKED TREADS	WEAR ON ONE SIDE	FEATHERED EDGE	BALD SPOTS
CONDITION						
CAUSE	UNDER INFLATION	OVER INFLATION	UNDER-INFLATION OR EXCESSIVE SPEED	EXCESSIVE CAMBER	INCORRECT TOE	WHEEL UNBALANCED
CORRECTION	ADJUST PRESSURE TO SPECIFICATIONS WHEN TIRES ARE COOL			ADJUST CAMBER TO SPECIFICATIONS	ADJUST FOR TOE-IN 1/8 INCH	DYNAMIC OR STATIC BALANCE WHEELS

Uneven and excessive tire wear, causes, and corrections. The conditions are discussed in the text.

damaged or out of adjustment, weak return springs, or improper assembly of the brake shoes, causing their return to be restricted or the friction areas to be rusted or corroded. *NOTE: Rotate the defective wheel to determine just how much drag exists at the wheel, and then release the bleeder screw to determine if excessive hydraulic pressure is causing the shoes to be held against the drum.*

If a rear wheel brake is dragging, the trouble could be as described in the material just covered. In addition, check the parking brake adjustment and the operating linkage. If the brakes are dragging on all four wheels, the trouble could result from any of the following: restricted pedal return, a push rod of too great length, a defective residual check valve, a plugged compensator port, or a stuck piston or swollen rubber parts in the master cylinder.

If the vehicle is equipped with a power brake unit, see that all parts are free and allow the unit to return to the fully released position. Some of the following can cause trouble: a leak at the diaphragm assembly, sticking or unseated atmospheric check valve, sticking valve plunger, broken piston return spring, or a faulty check valve.

Fading Brakes

Fading is generally due to an overheated drum expanding away from the brake linings after many hard stops. Fading is nonexistent with disc brakes, because the expansion of the rotor is against the friction pads. Any condition which causes overheating of the brake system can contribute to fading: riding the brake pedal, repeated panic stops, incorrect brake linings, glazed brake linings, thin brake drums, and weak brake shoe return springs.

Noisy Brakes

Brake noises take several forms, one of the most annoying of which is squeal. This condition is caused by vibration due to loose parts or to misalignment of the brake shoes, which prevents the proper shoe contact with the drum.

When checking out noises, rotate each wheel. Noise related to defective or loose wheel bearings or incorrectly assembled and rubbing internal brake parts should be evident. Rotate the wheel again and have someone depress the brake pedal lightly so that the noise level can be determined with the linings contacting the drums or rotors. Check the drum surfaces for evidence of threads cut during a drum-turning process; cut threads could cause the linings to shift to the side and then snap back during a brake application.

Chatter

The problem of brake chatter is caused by the brake lining's failure to maintain constant pressure on the braking surface of the drum. Make a road test: apply and release the brakes while checking for any clicking or other unusual noises that are audible at the four wheels. A noise indicates loose internal parts or parts that may not have been assembled correctly. Check to see if one particular wheel is causing the problem.

Brake chatter can be caused by loose backing plate retaining bolts; loose brake linings; oil, grease, or hydraulic fluid on the brake linings, causing unequal friction when the linings contact the drum; bent or distorted brake shoes; loose retaining springs; or distorted or out-of-round brake drums.

Low Pedal Action

With a low pedal, the brakes may be capable of stopping the car under normal conditions, but there may not be enough reserve left in case of emergency. Also, the depressed pedal height does not position the leverage at its most advantageous point.

A low pedal is generally caused by excessive brake shoe travel in relation to the distance that the brake pedal has to be depressed. Check for the following troubles: air in the hydraulic lines, low fluid level, or improper adjustment of the brake shoes.

If the car has self-adjusting brakes, first try a few firm reverse stops to see if the brakes will adjust themselves. If they won't, try adjusting the brakes by hand. You can determine which wheel is giving the trouble by the amount of adjustment required. If the trouble is a loose adjustment at one wheel, check the self-adjuster mechanism to see if the cable and springs are properly installed and if the adjusting lever and wheel are free from burrs.

A low fluid level in the master cylinder indicates possible fluid leakage. Add fluid and then check the complete system for improper assembly or defective parts. If the trouble is in the master cylinder, remove and disassemble it. Check the valve, valve seat, springs, cups, pistons, and cylinder bore for excessive wear or damage.

If the pedal action remains soft or spongy, check the complete brake system for leakage. Start at the master cylinder, and then check the brake lines and connections to each wheel. Check the backing plate and the wheel area for evidence of wheel cylinder leakage. A fluid leak can cause inconsistency in building up pressure in the brake lines.

Soft Or Spongy Pedal Action

Soft pedal action is generally due to air in the

hydraulic lines. If the brake shoes are out of adjustment or if the shoes are bent or out of alignment, the entire face of the lining may not make full contact with the brake drum. Use of an improper lining, one that is too soft, can also cause this type of trouble.

Hard Pedal Action

Hard brake pedal action can be caused by any mechanical restriction in either the brake pedal linkage or the brake shoe assembly parts. Or it can be caused by a restriction in the hydraulic system.

Remove the brake drums and examine the brake shoes for restrictions in travel. **CAUTION: Don't move the shoes out too far or you will pop out the wheel cylinder cups.** Make sure that the return and hold-down springs are properly installed. Lubricate all friction points. Tighten the backing plate bolts, as a loose backing plate will allow the shoes to be out of position in relationship to the braking surface of the drum. Brake linings that have hard or glazed surfaces will cause hard pedal action, because the cushioning effect between the face of the lining and the braking surface of the drum has been lost.

Check the hydraulic system for a restriction which could cause difficulty in moving the hydraulic fluid. Check the vent in the master cylinder cover and the compensating port for restrictions.

DISC BRAKES

The caliper-type disc brake saddles a rotating disc, often called a rotor. Frictional pads compress against the sides of the rotor. It is important to note the following advantages of a disc brake system: (1) Heat radiation is very efficient, making brake application very effective without fading. (2) Due to heat expansion, the rotor does expand radially, but the thickness does not alter, thus the pedal stroke does not change. (3) Pad replacement and system maintenance are relatively easy as compared with drum-type brakes. (4) Brake effectiveness-recovery from water occurs quickly due to dispersion by centrifugal force. (5) Disc brakes are self-adjusting. As the pads wear, the piston is returned by the stretch of the piston seal within the cylinder.

TROUBLESHOOTING THE DISC BRAKE SYSTEM

Warning Lamp

The brake warning lamp and the parking brake lamp utilize the same bulb, which can be tested by depressing the brake pedal with the ignition switch turned ON. If it doesn't light, replace the bulb or check for an open circuit.

After checking the warning lamp, test the switch assembly by raising the car and loosening one of the wheel cylinder bleeder screws. Slowly depress the brake pedal with the ignition switch turned ON. The pressure differential should activate the switch and light the warning lamp. If the lamp does not light, replace the safety switch. To recenter the safety switch piston, tighten the bleeder screw, and then apply light brake pedal pressure. The piston will center itself automatically.

Proportioning Valve

A proportioning valve (brake pressure control valve) is connected into the rear brake hydraulic line, where it controls the rear brake line pressure on a fast, hard brake application to minimize rear wheel lockup.

A rough test can be made by making a hard brake application at about 40 mph. If the rear wheels lock up (skid), the trouble can be a defective proportioning valve.

Caliper Assembly

Check the caliper seals and piston boots for evidence of leaks or damage. If any brake fluid leakage is evident, it is necessary to disassemble the caliper and install a new seal kit. Replace the brake pads when the lining is worn to 1/16" thickness.

DISC BRAKE TROUBLESHOOTING CHART

Symptoms & Causes

1. **Insufficient braking action**
   - 1a. Fluid leaking
   - 1b. Pad wear excessive
   - 1c. Pad contact surfaces wet with water or oil
   - 1d. Rotor worn
   - 1e. Proportioning valve defective
2. **Noisy brakes**
   - 2a. Deposits on pad surfaces
   - 2b. Improper pad seating
   - 2c. Front wheel bearing adjustment loose
   - 2d. Lining material glazed
   - 2e. Backing plate bolts loose
3. **Car pulls to one side**
   - 3a. Pads wet with water or oil deposits
   - 3b. Tire inflation incorrect
   - 3c. Front end misaligned
   - 3d. Backing plate bolts loose
   - 3e. Wheel bearings loose
4. **Excessive pedal travel**
   - 4a. Air in hydraulic system
   - 4b. Excessive play at master cylinder push rod
   - 4c. Fluid leaking
5. **Rear wheel lockup**
   - 5a. Defective proportioning valve

2 | tuning for performance

Engine tune-up is a very important service procedure that affects the efficiency of your engine and also determines the gasoline mileage obtained. It is very important to perform the service work in the sequence detailed in this section. Use the specification tables in the appendix for making all adjustments.

TUNING FOR PERFORMANCE

Remove the spark plug wires by grasping, twisting, and then pulling on the molded cap only. **CAUTION:**

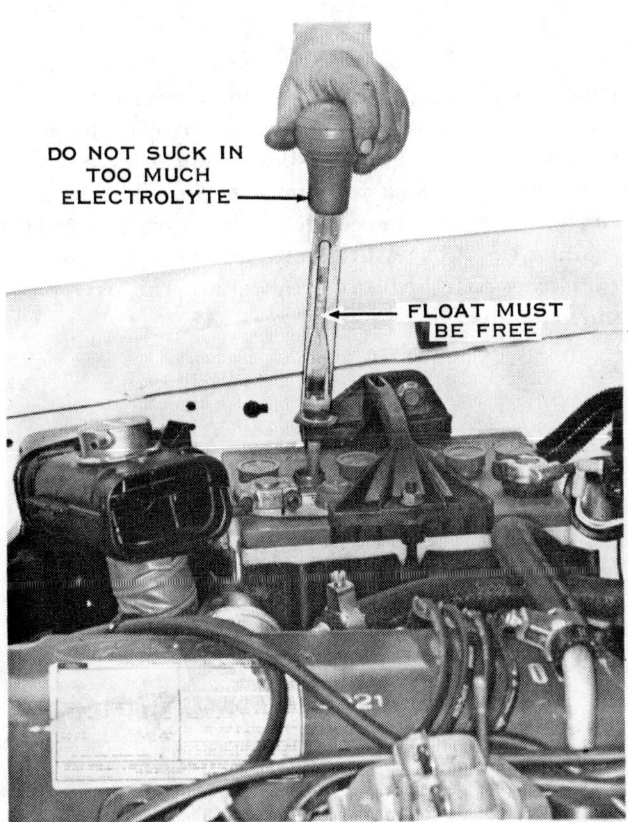

One of the first tune-up checks is to see that the battery is fully charged. Do this by using a hydrometer. A reading of 1,300 indicates a fully charged battery, while one of 1,150 means that the battery is discharged. Such a battery will make starting the engine difficult.

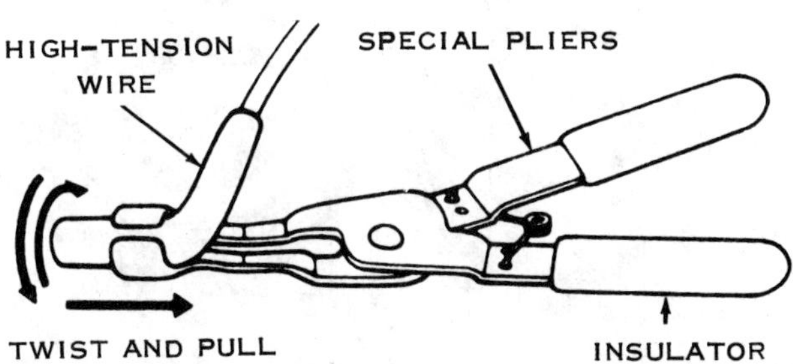

Use a special pair of insulated pliers to pull off the fragile high-tension wire boots.

Don't pull on the wire, or the connection inside of the cap may become separated or the boot may be damaged. Remove the spark plugs. **CAUTION: Don't tilt the spark plug socket, or you will crack the spark plug insulator.** Check the spark plugs against the illustrations to determine the operating conditions of

To check the belt tension, position a tension gauge as shown. The tension is correct when the indicator marks are lined up with the gauge body.

Spark plug identification guide. (1) Black, dry fluffy deposits, (2) wet deposits, (3) build-up closing the gap. (4) yellow or tan deposits, (5) light tan or gray deposits, (6) eroded electrodes, (7) melted or spotty deposits, (8) white or very light gray insulator, with bluish-burnt electrodes.

the engine. Clean and gap the spark plugs, and then place them on the bench for later installation. Test the compression by cranking the engine with a gauge inserted in each spark plug hole in turn. The actual reading is not as important as is a variation between cylinders which, if over 20 psi, indicates ring or valve trouble. Insert a teaspoonful of oil on top of the piston of a cylinder that reads abnormally low, and then crank the engine a few times to distribute the oil. Recheck the compression to see if the oil changed the reading. If the pressure increases, then the compression loss is past the piston rings; if not, the loss is past a burned valve.

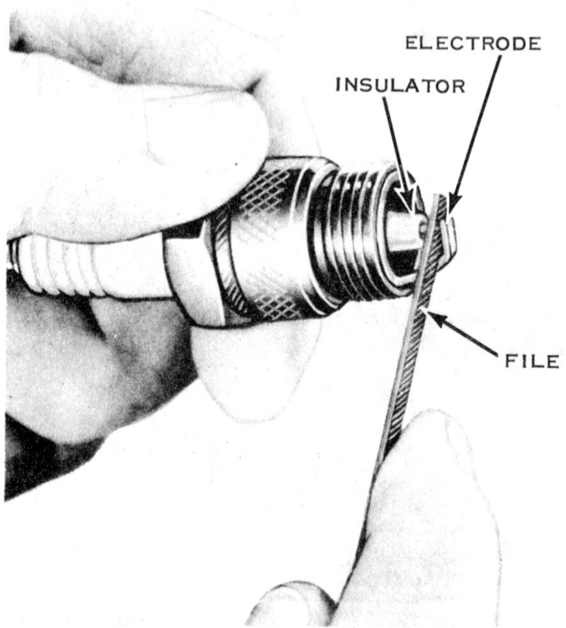

One of the most important service procedures is filing the spark plug electrodes. These elements corrode and form a high-resistance path for the spark to jump across, resulting in engine misfire on acceleration.

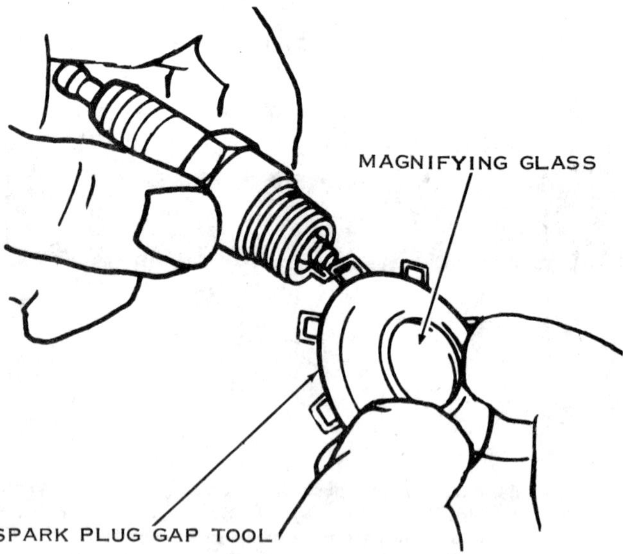

Always measure the spark plug gap with a round gauge. A flat gauge will give an erroneous reading.

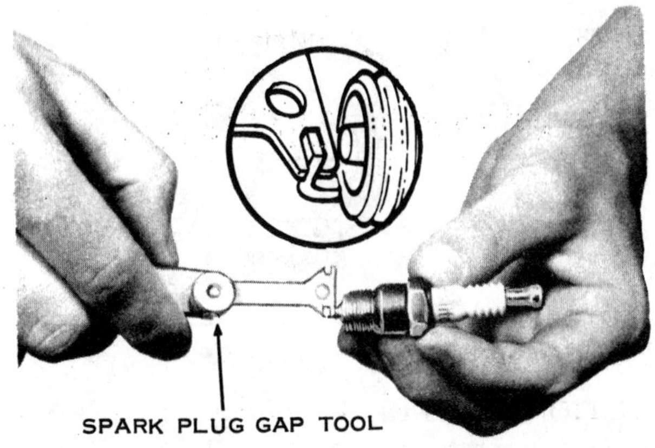

Bend the side electrode to adjust the gap, never the center one, or you will crack the insulator.

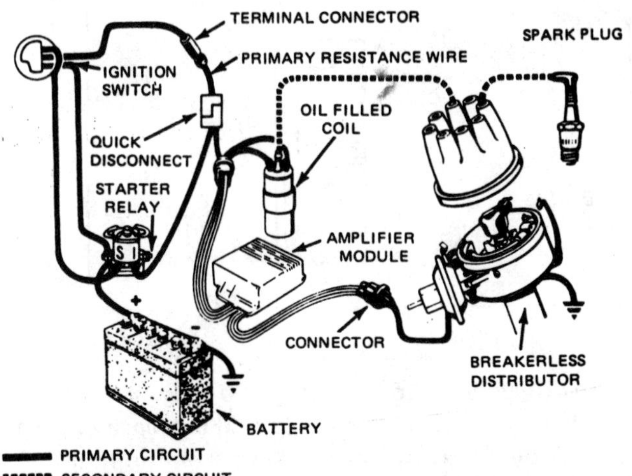

Schematic diagram for the electronic ignition system.

MECHANICAL SERVICES

Tighten the cylinder head and the intake manifold bolts to the correct torque. Be sure to tighten the bolts in the sequence detailed by the illustrations in the chapter on Engine Service. **CAUTION: Uneven tightening can result in distortion.** Replace the cleaned and gapped spark plugs, tightening them to 15-20 ft-lbs of torque.

Clean the air filter and reinstall it. Start the engine and allow it to warm to operating temperature.

IGNITION SYSTEM

The only adjustments that can be made to the breakerless ignition system are the timing and the centrifugal advance and vacuum advance adjustments. The air gap between the armature and magnetic pickup coil in the distributor is not adjustable, nor are there any adjustments for the amplifier module. Defective components are replaced. Any attempt to connect components outside the vehicle can result in component failure.

IGNITION TIMING

Disconnect the vacuum hoses at the distributor and plug the ends. Connect a tachometer and adjust engine speed to the specifications on the tuning decal. Connect a power timing light to No. 1 spark plug. **CAUTION: Never puncture the wire or boot as this could start a high-voltage leak. Use an adapter.**

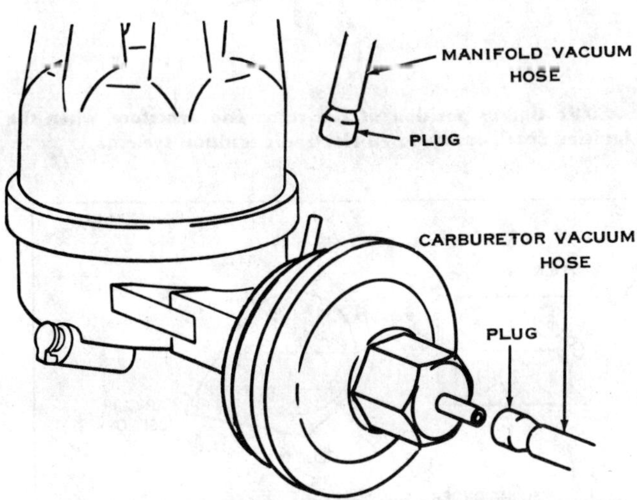

Before setting the ignition timing, it is essential that both vacuum hoses are disconnected and the ends plugged.

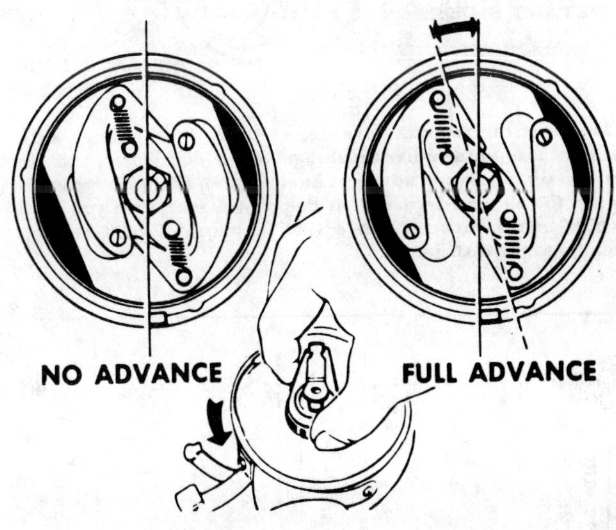

Check the automatic advance weights for freedom of action by twisting the rotor, which must feel springy in one direction and solid in the other. If the rotor does not turn, or if it turns sluggishly, the ignition timing will not advance with engine speed; power and gas mileage will suffer.

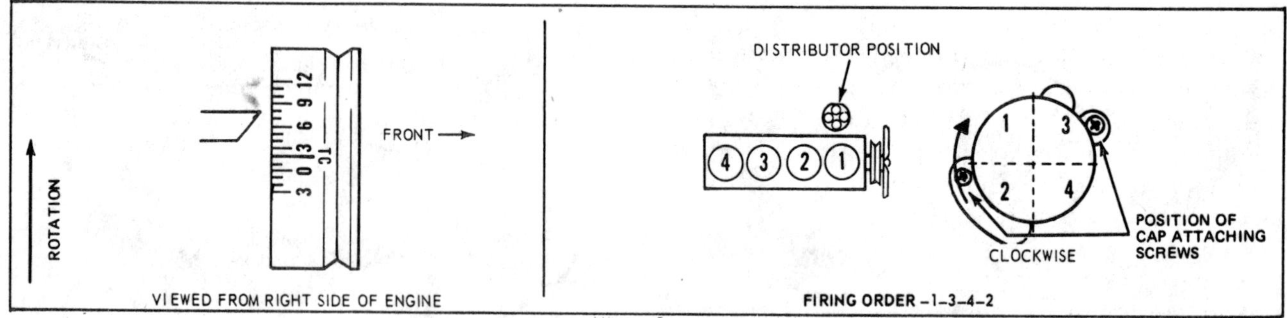

Ignition timing marks for the 2,300cc engine.

Start the engine and idle it at 600 rpm or less to be sure that no centrifugal advance is taking place. Adjust the ignition timing by rotating the distributor housing. Tighten the hold-down bolt.

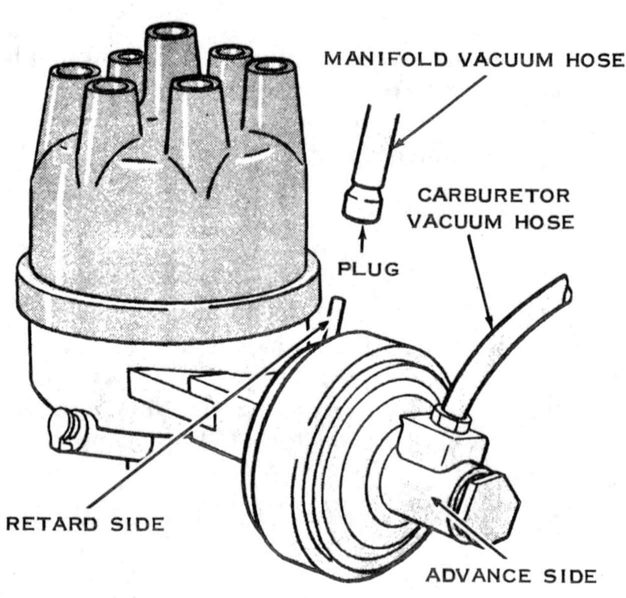

To check the vacuum advance, connect the advance-side vacuum hose to the outer diaphragm of the distributor, and the ignition timing should advance. Engine speed should increase to reflect the added advance. If it doesn't advance, then you have trouble in the vacuum unit or in the control system feeding vacuum to the distributor.

IGNITION ADVANCE

All engines have centrifugal and vacuum advance units to vary ignition timing according to engine speed and load. In addition, some engines have a dual-diaphragm unit on the distributor which has an added function of retarding ignition timing at idle speed for emission control. During a tune-up, it is essential to check the operation of these units. This can be done accurately if you have a timing light with a timing gauge and an advance control knob. If not, you can make the following rough checks to be sure that each of the systems is functioning.

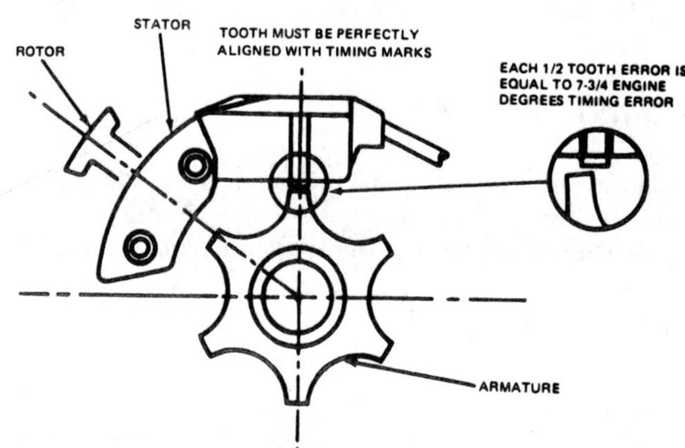

Static timing position of the rotor and armature when the ignition spark occurs in an electronic ignition system.

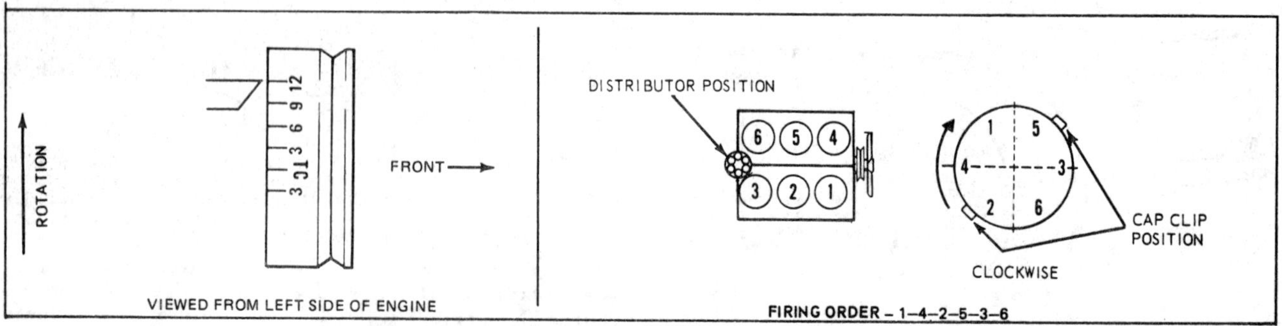

Ignition timing marks for the 2,600/2,800cc engines.

Checking The Mechanical Advance

With the ignition timing properly adjusted and the timing light connected to No. 1 spark plug wire, increase engine speed to about 2,000 rpm. The ignition timing must advance at least 10°. If it doesn't, you must remove the distributor to check the advance mechanism under the breaker plate.

Checking The Vacuum Advance

With the engine running at about 2,000 rpm (engage the fast-idle cam), connect the vacuum hose to the advance side of the distributor control unit (outer on a dual-diaphragm unit), and the ignition timing should advance at least 10° more than with the mechanical advance. **CAUTION: On an engine with a vacuum-delay valve, you must keep the throttle steady until vacuum passes through the valve, which may take as long as 30 seconds. Varying the throttle will change the vacuum in the line, which will lead to an erroneous interpretation.**

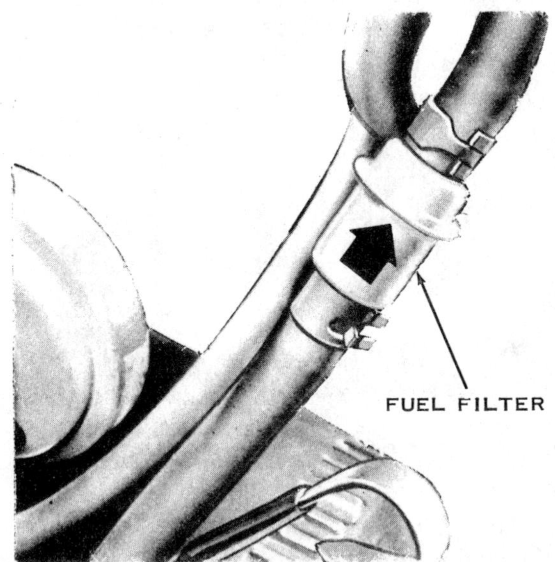

Position of the in-line fuel filter element for the 2,000/2,300cc engines. Make sure that the arrow points in the direction of fuel flow.

To remove the air filter, take out the two wing nuts, and disconnect the vacuum hoses. CAUTION: Always replace the gasket between the carburetor and air cleaner to keep unfiltered air from entering the engine.

The air filter element can be lifted out for replacement.

CHECKING THE VACUUM RETARD

With the engine idling, connect the vacuum hose to the retard (inner) side of the distributor control unit, and the ignition timing should retard at least 5° if this diaphragm is operating properly. Engine idle speed should slow down slightly to reflect the added retard.

CARBURETOR ADJUSTMENTS

The ignition adjustments must have been accurately made and underhood temperatures must be stabilized before making any carburetor adjustments.

Make sure that the choke valve is fully open and that the hot-idle compensator is seated. Turn the headlights to HIGH BEAM and the air conditioner to OFF. **CAUTION: The air cleaner must be in position when making all adjustments.** If it is not possible to make an adjustment with the air cleaner in place, remove it and note the change in engine mixture or speed. Compensate for this change so that the idle mixture and speed will return to specifications when the air cleaner is installed.

On vehicles with a manual-shift transmission, the idle setting must be made with the shift lever in NEUTRAL; with an automatic transmission the selector lever must be in DRIVE.

If the engine has a Ported-Vacuum Switching (PVS) valve, always remove the vacuum hose from the distributor and plug it while making the idle adjustments. This is to insure that the valve has not switched the distributor over to full intake manifold vacuum due to an excessively high coolant temperature.

Adjust the curb-idle speed to the specifications on the tuning decal. On engines with a throttle-stop solenoid, make the adjustment with the solenoid plunger screw or by turning the adjusting nut at the bottom of the solenoid. Disconnect the solenoid lead wire at the connector, and then adjust the throttle-stop screw to obtain 500 rpm, which is designed to prevent after running. Connect the solenoid wire at the connector and open the throttle slightly by hand; the solenoid plunger should extend as long as the ignition switch is ON.

Turn the mixture adjusting screw inward to obtain the smoothest idle possible (within the range of the idle limiter cap); turn each screw in an equal amount. If a

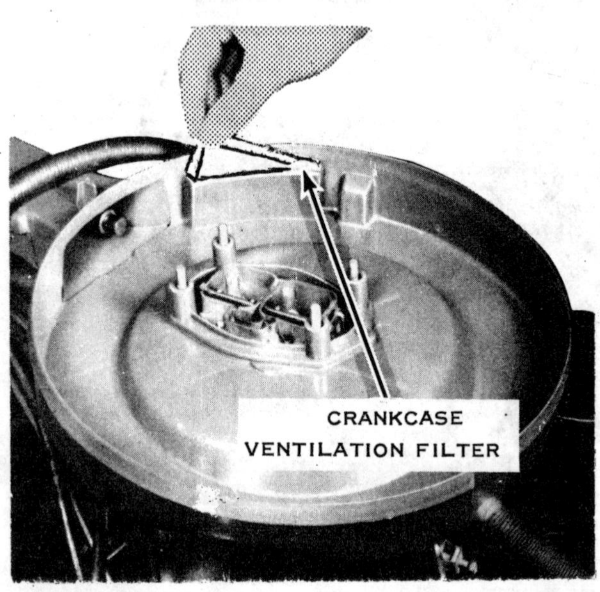

Always replace the crankcase ventilation filter element during each tune-up.

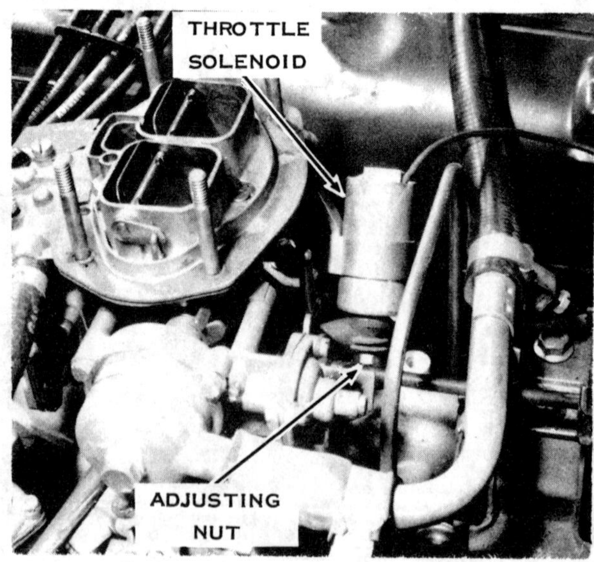

The curb-idle speed adjustment on the 2,000/2,300cc and V-6 engine carburetor is made by turning the hex nut at the base of the solenoid with it energized and the stem extended.

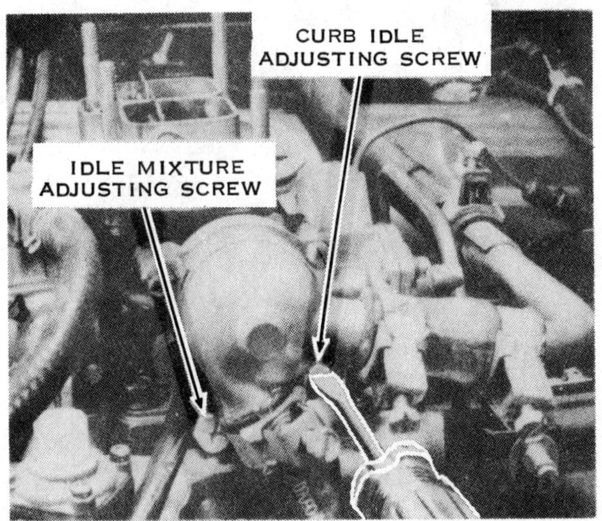

Making the carburetor adjustments on the 2,000/2,300cc and V-6 engine.

satisfactory idle adjustment cannot be obtained after tuning the engine properly, check for a vacuum leak. If the poor idle condition is due to a lean condition that is not caused by mechanical or ignition troubles and cannot be remedied because of the idle limiter, it is possible to make an idle mixture adjustment provided an exhaust gas analyzer is used to verify the results.

Lean-Drop Method

Where a CO meter is not available, the mixture can be adjusted by the lean-drop method, which is quite accurate. To make the adjustment, break off the tabs on the mixture caps using needle-nosed pliers. Adjust the idle speed screw to 50 rpm **above** specifications and the mixture screw to obtain the maximum engine speed or the highest vacuum gauge reading.

Now turn the idle mixture screw in (lean) until engine speed decreases 50 rpm to the specification on the tuning decal. With two adjusting screws, turn each in equally. **CAUTION: Don't change the idle speed screw to make this adjustment.** Note that you are slowing engine speed 50 rpm by **leaning** the air-fuel mixture, and this will result in as lean a mixture as possible, and the CO reading will generally be within specifications.

Artificial Enrichment

On some late-model engines, the emission-control decal has specifications for artificial enrichment, and the rpm gain is due to the addition of the artificial enrichment substance (a pure hydrocarbon fuel). The specified rpm gain with this method is the same as the rpm loss used when making the adjustment with the lean-drop method discussed above.

The rpm gain with artificial enrichment would be equivalent to the curb-idle speed increase above specifications for using the "lean-drop" method discussed above.

Ford **VEHICLE EMISSION CONTROL INFORMATION**

ENGINE FAMILY 2.3 CATALYST EGR/AIR (1CEF)
ENGINE DISPLACEMENT CID 140 CID
SPARK PLUG AGRF-52 GAP .032-.036
DISTRIBUTOR—BREAKERLESS

CHOKE HOUSING NOTCH SETTING		MAN/TRANS 1 LEAN AUTO/TRANS 1 LEAN		
TRANSMISSION		AUTO NEUTRAL	AUTO DRIVE	MANUAL NEUTRAL
IGNITION TIMING		10° BTDC		6° BTDC
TIMING RPM		550		550
CURB IDLE RPM	A/C		750	900
	NO A/C		750	900
IDLE MIXTURE—ARTIFICIAL ENRICHMENT				
RPM GAIN			20-60	20-60
RPM RESET			40	40

THIS VEHICLE REQUIRES MAINTENANCE SCHEDULE "B"

MAKE ALL ADJUSTMENTS WITH ENGINE AT NORMAL OPERATING TEMPERATURES, A/C AND HEADLIGHTS OFF

CURB IDLE—ADJUST WITH THROTTLE SOLENOID POSITIONER ENERGIZED, THERMACTOR AIR ON, ALL VACUUM HOSES CONNECTED AND AIR CLEANER IN POSITION. WHENEVER CURB IDLE IS RESET, CHECK AND ADJUST THE DECEL VALVE ACCORDING TO THE SERVICE MANUAL

IDLE MIXTURE—PRESET AT THE FACTORY. DO NOT REMOVE THE LIMITER CAP(S). CONSULT THE SERVICE MANUAL FOR DESCRIPTION OF ARTIFICIAL ENRICHMENT METHOD OF IDLE MIXTURE ADJUSTMENT TO BE USED ONLY DURING TUNE-UPS AND MAJOR CARBURETOR REPAIRS: IDLE MIXTURE MUST BE MEASURED WITH THERMACTOR AIR OFF

INITIAL TIMING—ADJUST WITH HOSES DISCONNECTED AND PLUGGED AT THE DISTRIBUTOR

REFERENCE TO A/C, THROTTLE SOLENOID, THERMACTOR AIR AND DECEL VALVE APPLICABLE ONLY IF THE ENGINE IS SO EQUIPPED. CONSULT SERVICE PUBLICATIONS FOR FURTHER INSTRUCTIONS ON TIMING AND IDLE SET

THIS VEHICLE CONFORMS TO U.S.E.P.A. REGULATIONS APPLICABLE TO 1975 MODEL YEAR NEW MOTOR VEHICLES.
THIS VEHICLE ALSO CONFORMS TO THE STATE OF CALIFORNIA CERTIFICATION STANDARDS APPLICABLE TO 1975 MODEL YEAR NEW MOTOR VEHICLES.

FORD MOTOR COMPANY D52E-9C485-DA

Vehicle emission control decal.

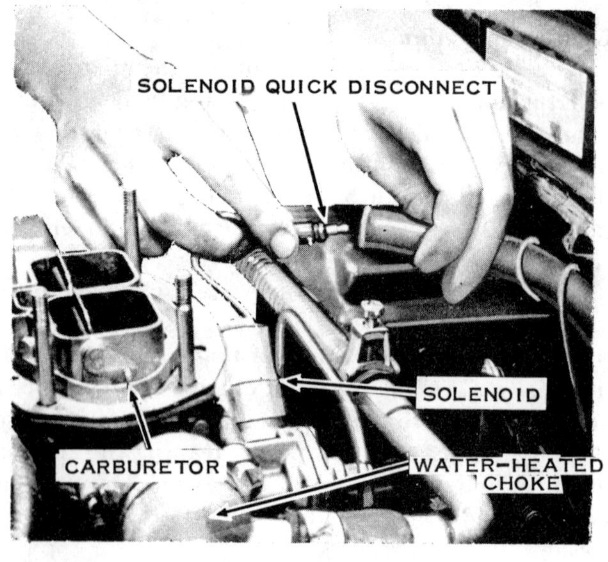

The solenoid quick-disconnect connection on the 2,000/2,300cc or V-6 engine carburetor must be broken to make the slow-idle speed adjustment, which is to prevent dieseling.

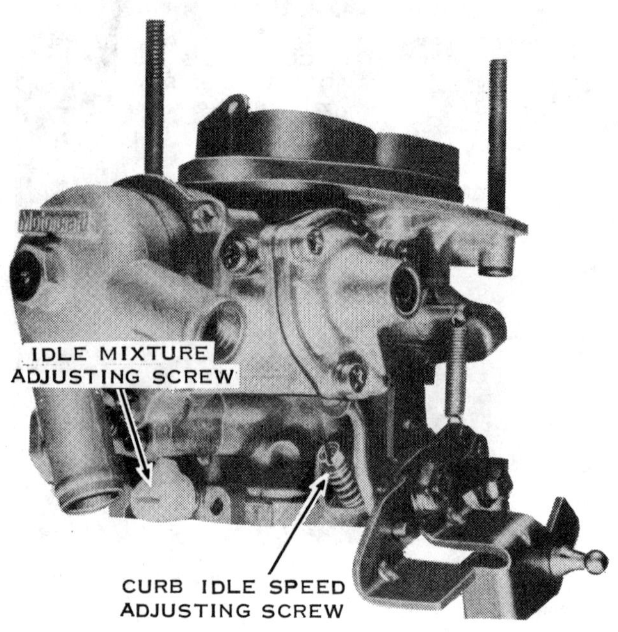

Idle mixture and curb-idle speed (throttle-stop screw) adjustments with the 2,000/2,300cc and V-6 engine carburetor.

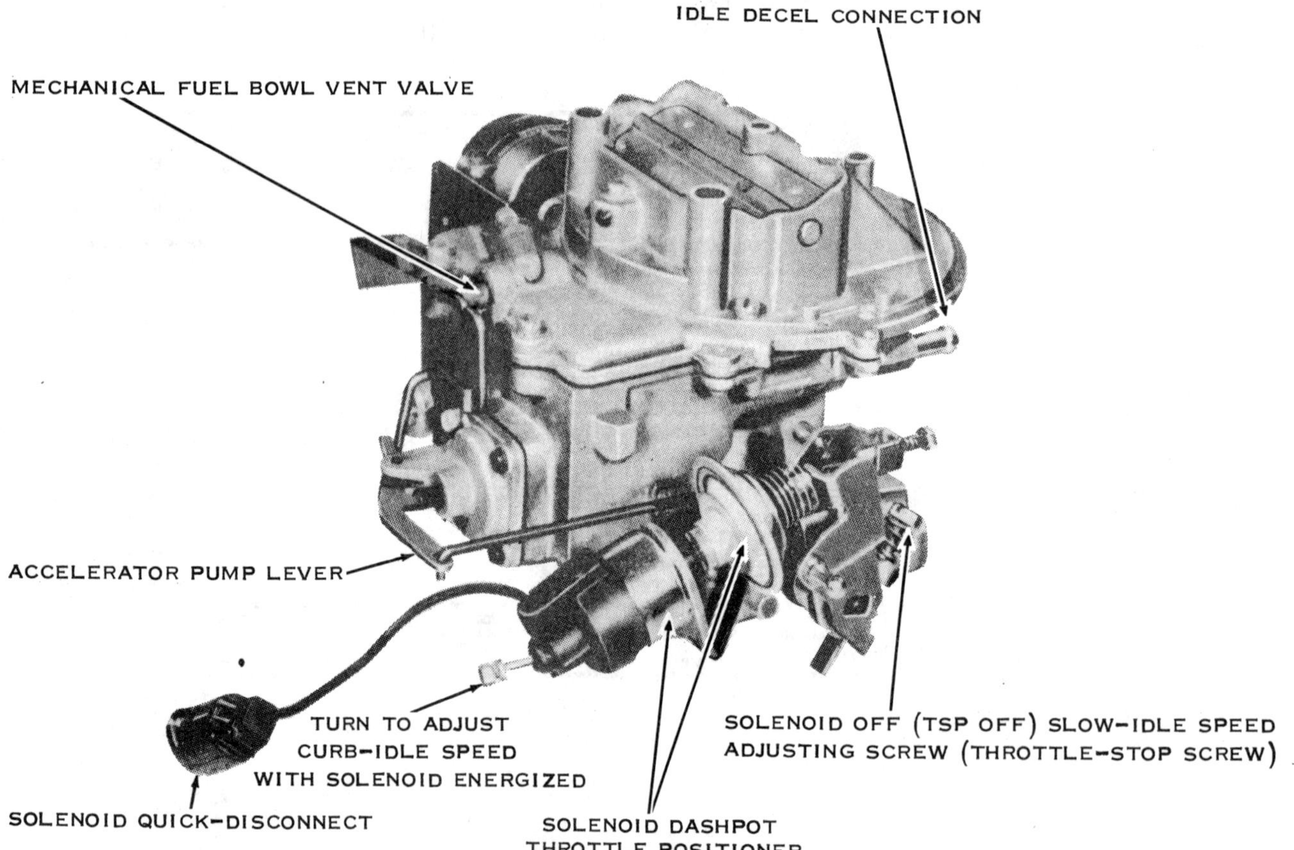

Idle mixture and curb-idle speed speed adjusting screws on the 2150 - 2V carburetor used on the V-6 engine since 1975. The adjustments are made in the same manner as for the earlier model carburetors.

3 | PREVENTIVE MAINTENANCE

Preventive maintenance is a term used to indicate those commonly performed jobs that are necessary to prevent major breakdowns if performed periodically. Many of these operations are covered in greater detail in other sections of this book, but they are grouped here as a guide to help the mechanically inclined owner keep his car in tip-top shape.

The time or mileage intervals are intended as a general guide for establishing regular maintenance and lubrication periods for your car. Sustained heavy duty or high-speed operation, or a great deal of short stop-and-go driving can necessitate more frequent servicing.

ENGINE

LUBRICATION

Crankcase oil should be selected to give the best performance under the climatic and driving conditions in the territory in which the vehicle is driven. During warm or hot weather, an oil which will provide adequate lubrication under high-operating temperatures, is required. During the colder months of the year, an oil which will permit easy starting at the lowest atmospheric temperature likely to be encountered should be used.

When the crankcase is drained and refilled, the oil should be selected on the basis of the lowest temperature anticipated for the period during which the oil is to be used. Unless the crankcase oil is selected on the basis of viscosity or fluidity of the anticipated temperature, difficulty in starting will be experienced at each sudden drop in temperature.

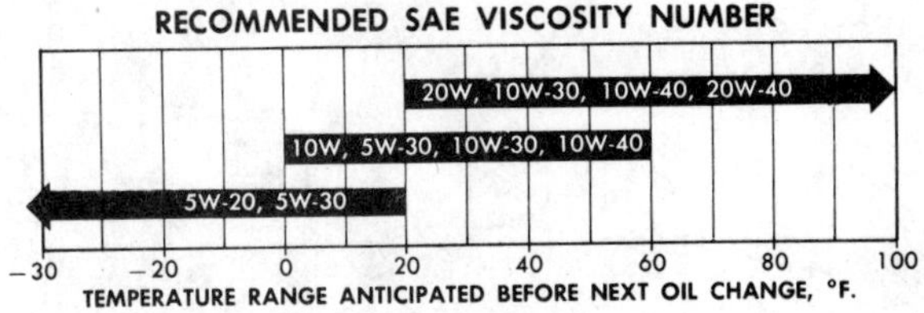

Recommended oil viscosity numbers.

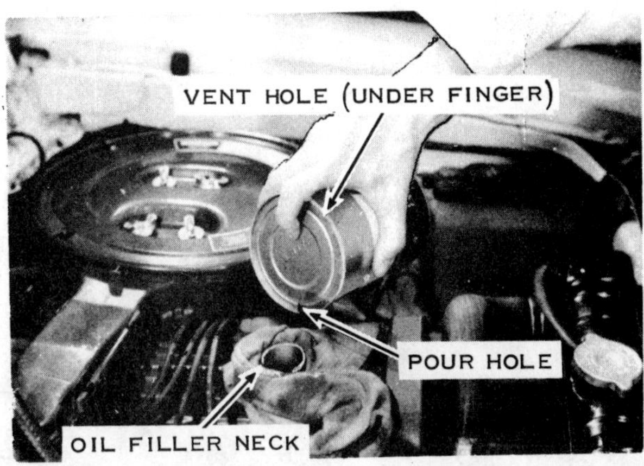

Cover the oil filler neck with a rag to catch the overflow. If you don't have a pouring spout, punch two holes in the cover of the can. Hold the can over the oil filler neck with your finger over the vent hole to control the flow of oil.

CHANGING THE ENGINE OIL AND OIL FILTER

DRAINING

With the car raised, remove the oil pan drain plug,

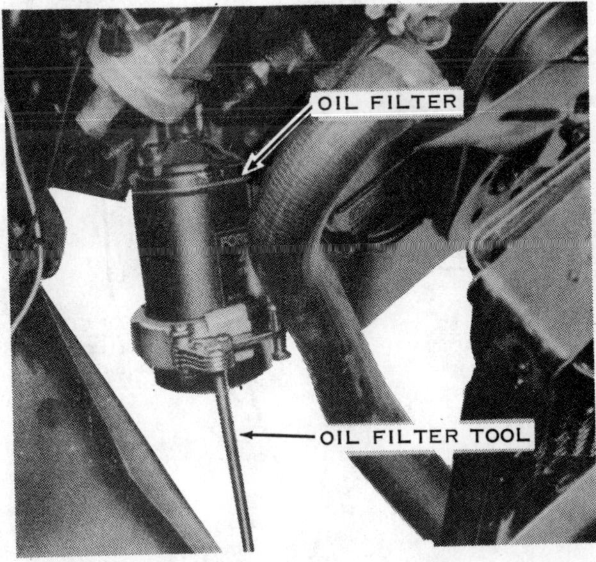

A special tool is available to uncrews the oil filter. Position a drain pan under the engine to catch the drippings.

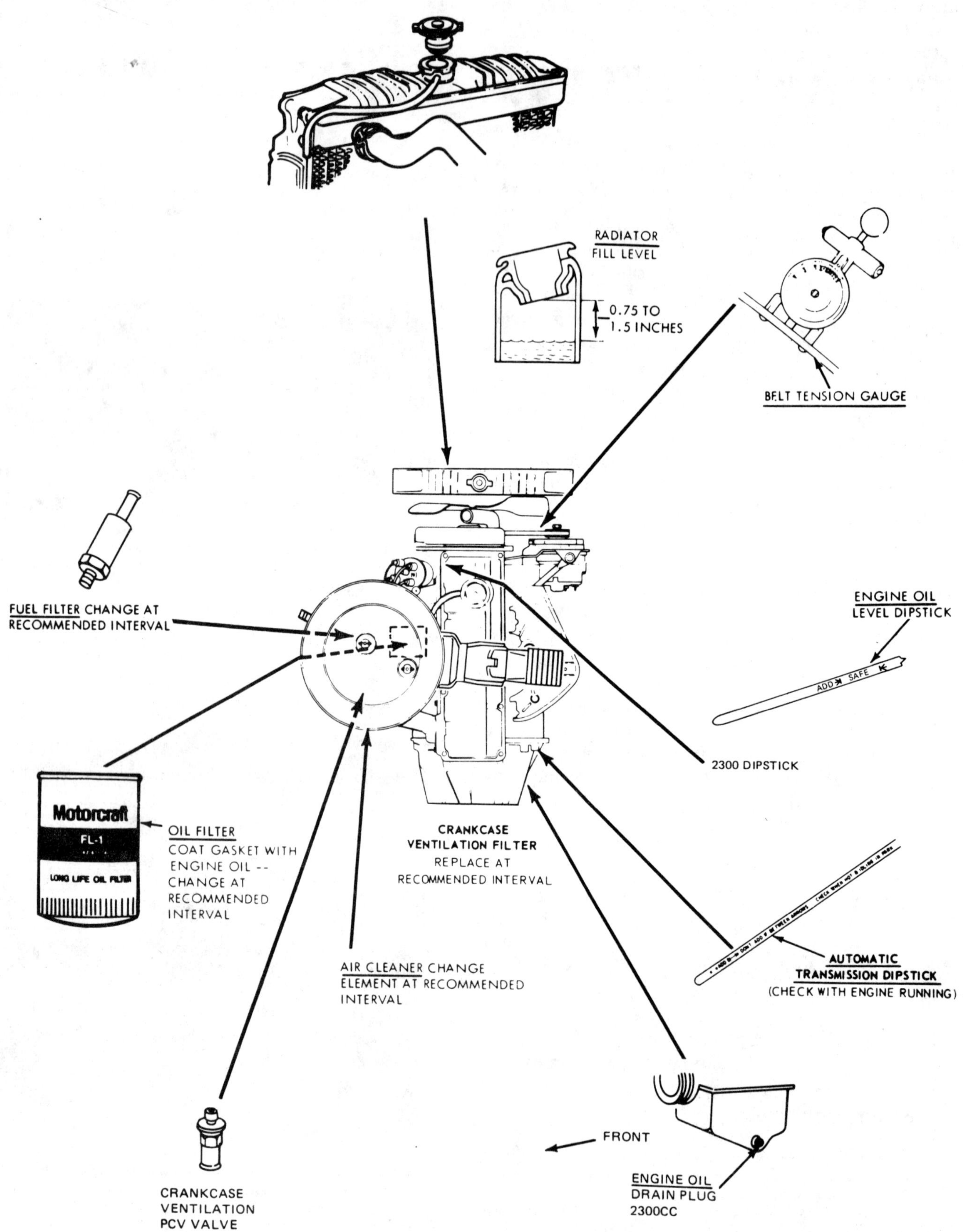

Four-cylinder engine lubrication and service points.

allowing the engine oil to drain into a container. *NOTE: The engine should be warm.*

Place a drip pan under the oil filter. Turn the filter counterclockwise, and then remove it from the engine.

REPLACING THE OIL FILTER

Clean the gasket surface at the cylinder block. Coat the gasket on the filter with a light film of oil. Thread the filter onto the adapter until the gasket contacts the sealing surface; then, advance it an additional 1/2 turn. **CAUTION: Do not overtighten the filter.** Remove the drip pan.

Replace the oil pan drain plug gasket if cracked or mutilated. Install the oil pan drain plug and torque it to 15 to 20 ft-lbs. Lower the car.

Fill the crankcase to the required level with the proper type and grade of lubricant. Start the engine and operate it at a fast idle. Check for oil leakage.

DRIVE BELTS

INSPECTING

Replace any belt that is broken, cracked, glazed, worn or stretched so that it cannot be sufficiently tightened. On a vehicle with matched belts, check both belts. **CAUTION: Use only the specified type of belt.**

To install a new oil filter, coat the gasket surface with engine oil and thread the filter onto the adapter until it contacts the gasket surface, and then tighten it an additional half turn.

Any belt that has operated for a minimum of 10 minutes is considered a used belt and must be adjusted accordingly.

When installing new belt(s), first adjust the belt to the new belt specification. Proper tension minimizes noise and prolongs belt service life. It is recommended that a belt tension gauge be used to check and adjust the belt tension.

ADJUSTING THE ALTERNATOR DRIVE BELT TENSION

Install the belt tension tool on the drive belt. Check the tension following the instructions furnished with the tool. If an adjustment is necessary, loosen the alternator mounting bolts and the alternator adjusting arm bolt. Move the alternator toward or away from the engine until the correct tension is obtained. **CAUTION: Apply pressure on the alternator front housing only.**

Remove the gauge. Tighten the alternator adjusting arm bolt first, and then the mounting bolts. Install the tension gauge and recheck the belt tension.

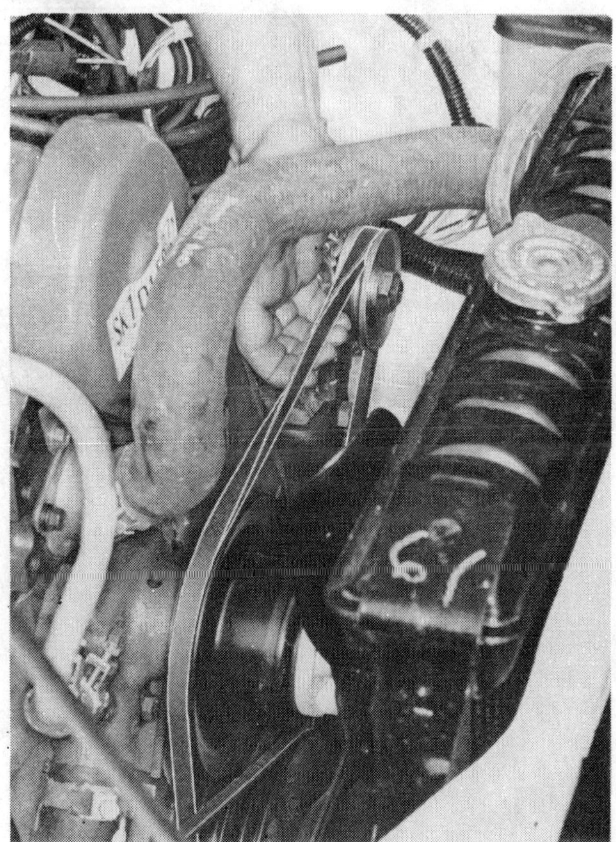

The condition of the drive belt should be checked every year, and the belt replaced every two years, or 24,000 miles. This is very important in today's engines with emission-control systems, where the underhood heat is much greater than ever before. Replace any belt with a crack or tear.

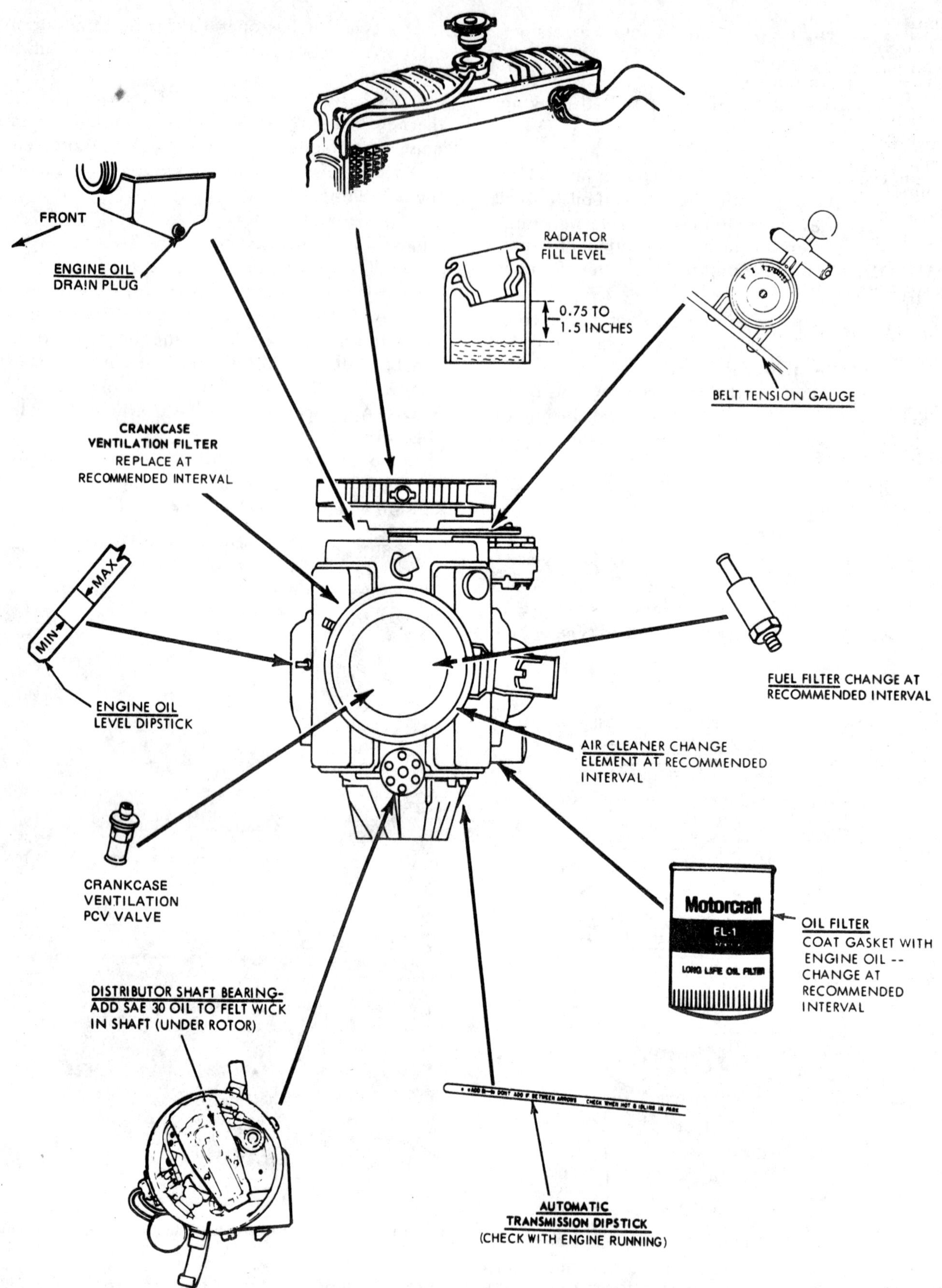

V-6 engine lubrication and service points.

Adjusting The Power Steering Drive Belt

Loosen the adjusting and mounting bolts on the front face of the pump cover plate (hub side) and the one nut at the rear. Attach a 9/16-inch open-end wrench on the projecting 1/2-inch boss and pry upward to correct tension on 4-cyl. engines.

To adjust the belt on an 8-cyl. engine, loosen the mounting bolt in the adjusting slot and the nut directly above the adjusting slot. Place a suitable pry bar between the cast boss on the pump cover plate; pry upward to correct tension. **CAUTION: Do not pry against the reservoir as it can be deformed and cause a leak.**

Recheck the belt tension. When the tension has been correctly adjusted, tighten the bolts to specifications.

Adjusting The Air Conditioning Compressor Belt

With A Rotary Compressor

Loosen the three belt tensioning adjusting screws; one at the compressor rear and two at the compressor front mounting brackets. Install the belt tension gauge on the compressor clutch drive belt. Insert a flex handle, having a 1/2-inch drive, into the belt tensioning pry bar slot, and then move the compressor toward or away from the engine to obtain the specified belt tension.

To check the belt tension, position a tension gauge as shown. The tension is correct when the indicator marks are lined up with the gauge body.

Tighten the three adjusting screws and recheck the belt tension.

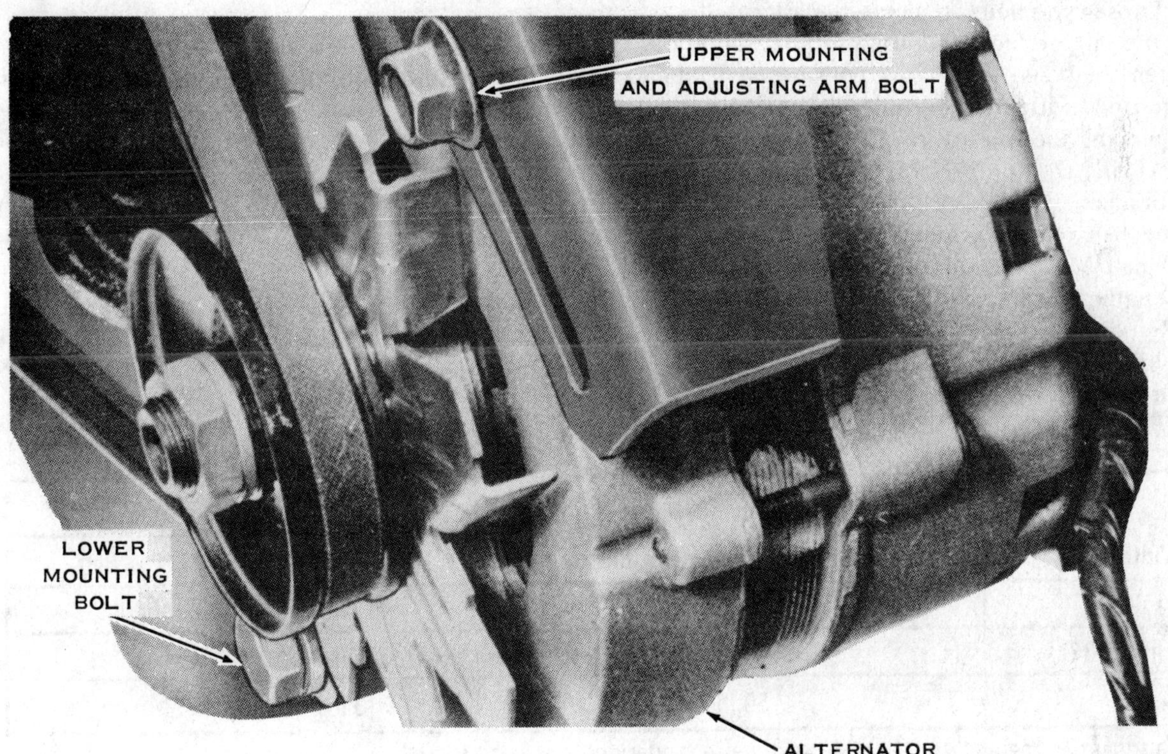

Typical alternator mounting and adjusting bolts.

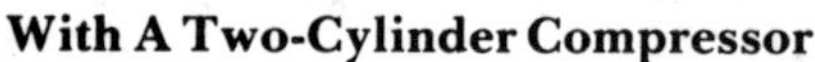

The drive belt should be adjusted so that there is about ½" free play when depressed in the center of the longest span.

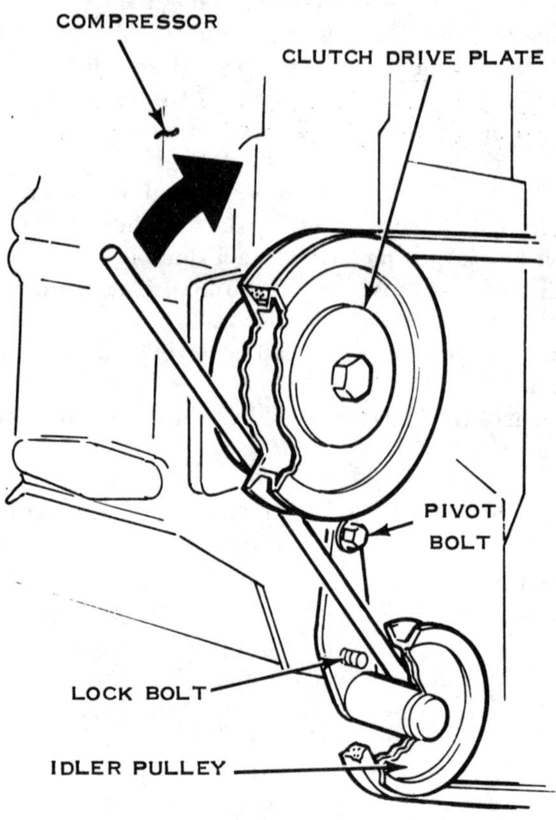

To adjust the air conditioner drive belt, it is necessary to insert a pry bar between the two pulleys, as shown. To increase belt tension, push upward on the pry handle.

With A Two-Cylinder Compressor

Adjust the belt by repositioning the idler pulley, if so equipped. Loosen the bolts attaching the idler pulley bracket to the engine block, reposition the assembly and retighten the bolts.

If not equipped with an idler pulley, adjust the belt tension by moving the compressor. To do this, loosen the bolts securing the compressor to the compressor mounting bracket.

Install the belt tension gauge on the compressor clutch drive belt. Move the compressor toward or away from the engine until the specified belt tension is obtained. Remove the gauge. Tighten the compressor-to-support bracket bolts. Install the tension gauge and recheck the belt tension.

Adjusting The Air Pump Drive Belt

Install the belt tension gauge on the drive belt and check the tension. Adjust as necessary by loosening the air pump mounting and adjusting arm bolts. Move the air pump toward or away from the engine until the correct tension is obtained. Use a suitable bar and pry against the pump rear cover to hold belt tension while tightening the mounting bolts. **CAUTION: Do not pry against the pump housing or you will destroy it.**

Remove the gauge. Tighten the air pump adjusting arm and mounting bolts. Install the tension gauge and recheck the belt tension.

Belt Width	Minimum Tension (for use at maintenance interval only) (Hot Engine)	Installation Tension	
		Used Belt ①	New Belt
1/4"	30 lbs.	60 lbs.	80 lbs.
3/8" and 15/32"	50 lbs.	110 lbs.	140 lbs.
1/2"	50 lbs.	110 lbs.	140 lbs.

① Any belt that has operated for ten minutes or more is considered a used belt.

Drive belt tension specifications.

COOLING SYSTEM

CHECKING THE COOLANT LEVEL

CAUTION: Avoid injury when checking a hot radiator. Muffle the radiator cap in a thick cloth and turn it slowly counterclockwise until the pressure escapes. After the pressure has completely dissipated, finish removing the cap.

Fill a vertical-flow type radiator only to the COLD FILL mark. **CAUTION: Check the level cold, the engine must not be running.**

If equipped with a constant-full (coolant recovery) system, check the level in the radiator COLD, and then add coolant as necessary to the radiator and to the overflow tank (plastic bottle).

Use the recommended mixture of permanent anti-freeze and water to maintain adequate protection against the temperatures to be encountered in the area of operation. To provide sufficient protection against corrosion and boiling, this level should be at least 0 degrees F.

To avoid chemical damage to the cooling system, do not mix different brands of anti-freeze. Use only those permanent anti-freeze brands which meet manufacturer's specifications.

CHECKING THE ANTI-FREEZE PROTECTION

Be sure the engine is at operating temperature. Check the anti-freeze in the cooling system by using a permanent anti-freeze test hydrometer. Standard protection is to -20 degrees F. (-35 degrees F. for Canadian and Alaskan vehicles) with a solution of water and permanent anti-freeze meeting your car's specifications.

CAUTION: Use extreme care when removing the cap from a hot radiator. Avoid rapid escape of pressurized fluid that can cause injury.

INSPECTING THE HOSES

Inspect the cooling system hoses for evidence of cracking, checking or weathering. Replace all cracked hoses. Check for leaking or porous hoses and tighten or replace. Make sure all supporting brackets for the hoses are in place and that the hoses are properly installed in the brackets.

Inspect the radiator core and tanks for seepage or leaks. Check all fittings to see that they are tight and in good condition. Examine the hoses at the fittings for cuts or weakness.

REPLACING THE COOLANT

To drain the radiator, open the drain cock located at the bottom of the radiator and remove the cylinder block drain plug(s). The 4-cylinder engines have one plug in the side of the engine block; the V-8 and V-6 engines have a drain plug on each side of the cylinder block.

To fill the cooling system, close the drain cock. Install the block drain plug(s). Disconnect the heater outlet hose at the water pump to release trapped air in the system. When the coolant begins to escape, connect the heater outlet hose.

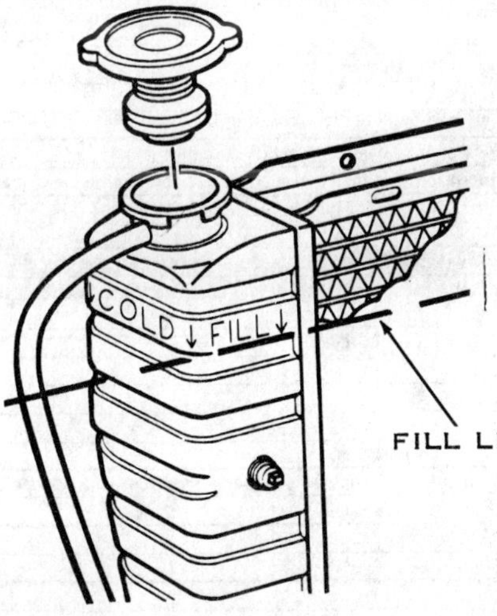

Fill a cross-flow type radiator only to the COLD FILL line. Fill a vertical-flow type radiator to one inch below the lower flange of the radiator filler neck.

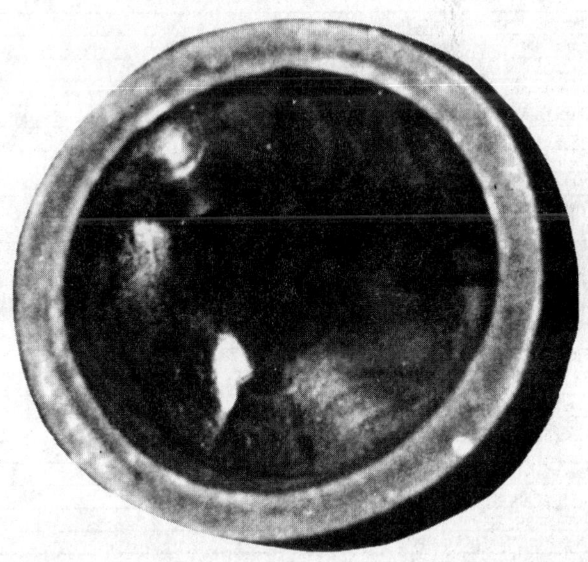

A rusted radiator hose is an indication that the rest of the cooling system is in a similar condition. Overheating and engine damage can result.

NON-EMISSION SYSTEMS SCHEDULED MAINTENANCE

Vehicles Designated Schedule "A" or "B" on Glovebox and Engine Emission Control Information Decal.	SERVICE INTERVAL – Time in months or mileage in thousands, whichever occurs first.									
MAINTENANCE OPERATION	**5**	**10**	**15**	**20**	**25**	**30**	**35**	**40**	**45**	**50**
Inspect Exhaust System Heat Shields (3)			AB			AB			AB	AB
Check Automatic Transmission Fluid Level	AB		AB			AB			AB	
Check Manual Transmission Fluid Level	AB		AB			AB			AB	
Check Rear Axle Fluid Level	AB		AB			AB			AB	
Check Brake Master Cylinder Fluid Level	AB		AB			AB			AB	
Inspect Clutch Linkage (2)	AB		AB			AB			AB	
Inspect Steering Linkage for Abnormal looseness or damaged seals			AB			AB			AB	
Adjust Automatic Transmission Bands (at 5,000, 15,000, 30,000 and 45,000 miles for severe service) (1)			AB							
Inspect Brake Lining, Lines, Hoses and front wheel bearing lube (2)					AB					AB
Lubricate Front Suspension and Steering Linkage						AB				
Drain and Refill Automatic Transmission Fluid – Continuous Service Only						AB				

Vehicles Designated Schedule "C" on Glovebox and Engine Emission Control information Decal.	SERVICE INTERVAL – Time in months or mileage in thousands, whichever occurs first.							
MAINTENANCE OPERATION	**6**	**12**	**18**	**24**	**30**	**36**	**42**	**48**
Check automatic transmission fluid level – add fluid if required	C		C		C		C	
Check brake master cylinder fluid level – add fluid if required	C	C	C	C	C	C	C	C
Check steering linkage for abnormal looseness or damaged seals		C		C		C		C
Lubricate front suspension, ball joints						C		
Check rear axle fluid level – add fluid if required	C		C		C		C	
Adjust automatic transmission bands (at 6,000, 18,000, 30,000, 42,000 for severe service) (1)		C						
Inspect brake lining, lines, hoses and front wheel bearing lube (2)				C				C
Check manual transmission fluid level – add fluid if required	C		C		C		C	
Check clutch linkage and adjust clutch pedal free play – adjust if required	C	C	C	C	C	C	C	C
Inspect exhaust system shields (3) (5)		C		C		C		C

NOTES: (1) Severe Service Operation – When vehicle is operated under any of the following conditions, observe severe service recommendations:
- Extended period of idling or low speed operation such as police, taxi or door-to-door delivery.
- Operation when outside temperature remains below +10°F. for 60 days or more and most trips are less than 10 miles.
- Operation in severe dust conditions.

(2) Adjust, repair or replace as required.

(3) Remove accumulated debris or replace shield as required. Inspect for loose weld attachments, damage or deterioration.

(4) Inspect at 5,000 mile intervals whenever the vehicle has been operated under the following conditions: a. On gravel roads b. Off-road use c. Severe road load conditions

(5) Inspect at 6,000 mile intervals whenever the vehicle has been operated under the following conditions: a. On gravel roads b. Off-road use c. Severe road load conditions

Lubrication maintenance schedule. "Inspect" denotes a visual inspection, while "check" means an operational check to uncover defects and make repairs.

Items should be checked periodically and service performed when required. These services are not covered by the Warranty, you will be charged for the labor, parts and lubricants used.

MAINTENANCE OPERATION	WHEN PERFORMED
Inspect wheels and tires for damage and tighten lug nuts.	Periodically or if wheels are noisy.
Balance and rotate wheels and tires.	Tires show uneven wear pattern or vibrate.
Replace tires.	When tread wear indicator appears.
Front suspension check.	Abnormal tire wear.
Check front wheel alignment and steering linkage.	Abnormal tire wear if normal realignment is not required.
Check tire air pressure.	At least monthly.
Check power steering reservoir.	Each time engine oil is checked or when fueling car.
Inspect steering mechanism.	Hard steering, excessive free play, or unusual noise.
Check parking brake operation.	Excessive foot pedal travel required or will not hold car.
Check air conditioning system.	At beginning of warm weather season.
Check headlight alignment.	Light beam appears improperly aimed.
Inspect exterior lights and replace bulbs as required.	When performing regular car services (fueling, cleaning, etc.)
Check operation of turn signals, high beam indicator, and hazard flashers.	When performing regular car services (fueling, cleaning, etc.)
Check operation of engine warning lights.	Each time engine is started.
Check accelerator pedal operation.	If uneven pressure is observed or pedal does not function smoothly.
Inspect brake system components.	When brake light glows with engine running; if brakes are noisy or brake pedal travel is excessive.
Check and lubricate hood latches and auxiliary catch, hood, door, and trunk lid hinges and checks, and all lock cylinders.	When performing regular car service or when noisy or hard to operate.
Replace windshield wiper blade elements.	Blades do not properly clean windshield after wiper blades and glass have been properly cleaned.
Check windshield washers aim and reservoir level.	When insufficient solution is sprayed on windshield or improper cleaning is observed after function.
Clean body drain holes.	Improper water drainage from body is suspected.
Check locking of seatback latches.	Periodically (with doors closed.)
Check seat belt buckles, release mechanisms, and retractor locking.	Regularly.
Inspect seat belt webbing for cuts or broken fibers.	Regularly (replace if cut or broken).
Check horn operation.	Periodically or when malfunction is suspected.
Check for fluid leaks on pavement (water dripping from A/C after use is normal).	After car has been parked a while or when possible to observe underbody when vehicle is raised.
Lubricate transmission controls, kickdown linkage, and clutch linkage.	When moving parts and connections are sluggish in action.
Check engine coolant level and add as required.	When engine overheats, or once a month.
Check heater and radiator hoses.	Regularly (replace if cut or broken).
Check engine oil level and add as required.	When fueling vehicle.
Check battery water and add as required.	Every three months; more often in hot weather.
Lubricate door weatherstrips.	When squeaky or noisy during window operation or visual inspection shows need.
Test anti-theft alarm system operation.	Periodically or when malfunction is suspected.
Lubricate clutch (except cable) and transmission shift linkage.	When moving parts and connections are void of lube or sluggish in action.

Non-scheduled maintanance, which should be checked periodically and serviced when needed.

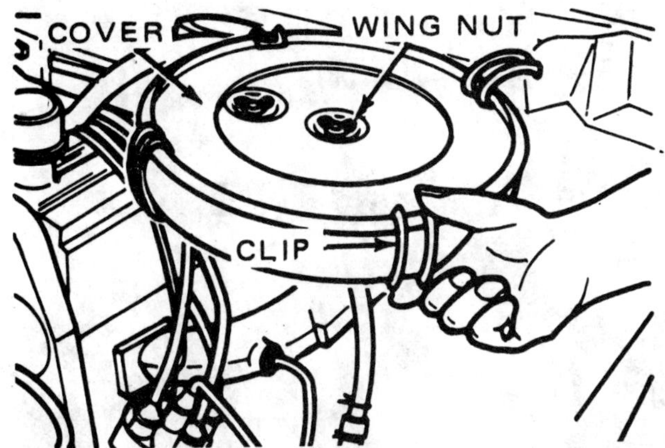

To gain access to the air filter, remove the wing nuts at the top, and then snap off the retaining clips.

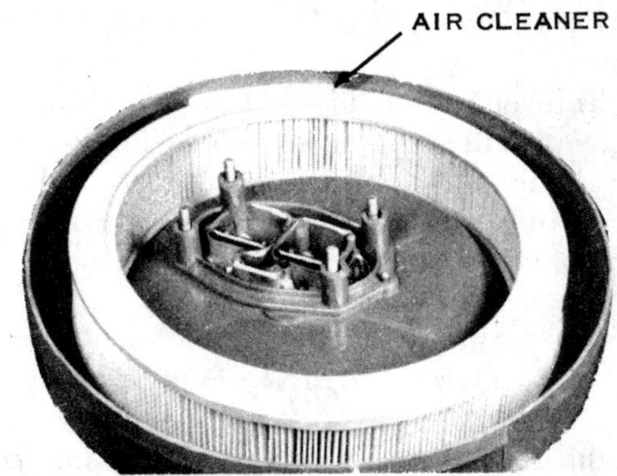

The filter element can be lifted out after removing the cover. CAUTION: If the filter has the word TOP molded into it, make sure that that side faces up.

To avoid overheating in very hot weather, use mixtures with not more than 50 percent anti-freeze, except in areas where anti-freeze protection below 35 degrees F is required. In this case, refer to the coolant mixture chart on the permanent anti-freeze container.

After the initial fill, the coolant level may drop approximately one quart after the engine has been operated about 20 minutes at 2000 rpm. This is due to the displacement of entrapped air. Refill to the proper level.

FUEL SYSTEM

CHECKING THE THROTTLE LINKAGE

Depress the accelerator pedal all the way to the floor and check to see that the throttle is fully open. Release the accelerator pedal and be sure the throttle lever and pedal return to their original positions. Check all pivot points for binding. Check the throttle return springs for broken or damaged springs. Check the accelerator cable for kinks or other restrictions. Replace all broken or damaged parts. Lubricate the moving parts with engine oil.

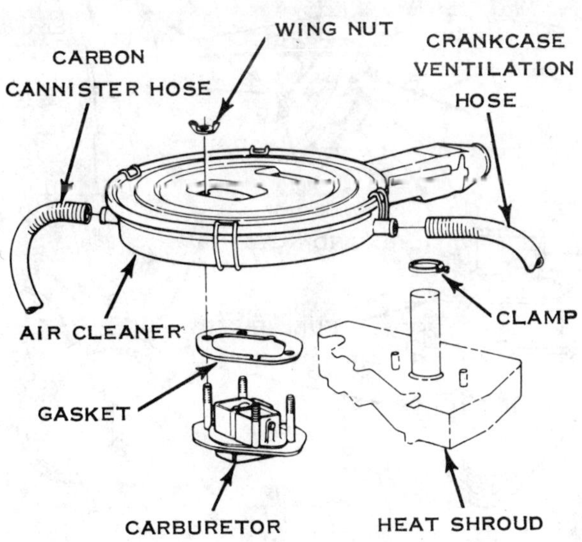

Always replace the gasket under the air cleaner assembly whenever it is removed. Failure to have a good seal at this point will allow unfiltered air to enter the engine.

CHECKING THE CHOKE LINKAGE

Examine the choke external linkage for free operation. If the linkage appears to be sticking or is dirty, clean it using a brush and common mineral-spirits type cleaning fluid. Operate the choke plate manually to make sure that it moves freely. Lubricate the choke plate shaft at each end and the choke operating linkage with engine oil if necessary.

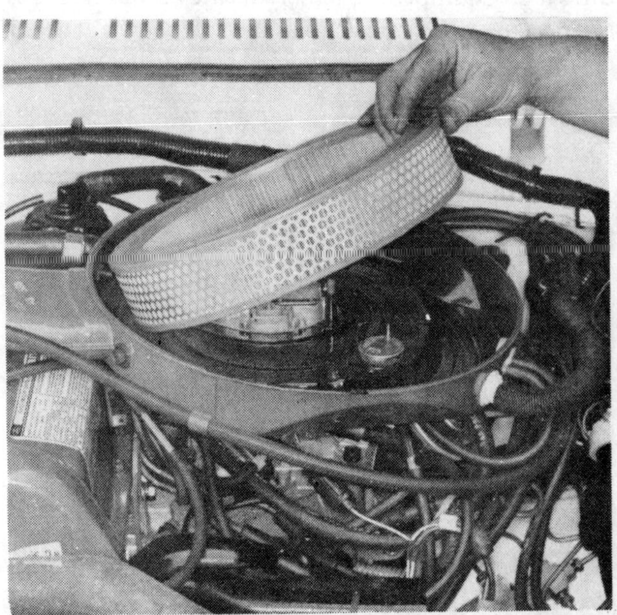

The air filter element can be replaced after taking off the top cover. It should be replaced periodically to minimize any restriction in the flow of air into the engine, which would cause the gas mileage to drop.

CHECKING THE THROTTLE-STOP SOLENOID

With the throttle solenoid connected and the engine running, open the throttle by hand. The solenoid plunger should follow the throttle lever until the plunger is fully extended. Disconnect the solenoid lead. The plunger should retract. If the solenoid does not operate properly, replace it.

INSPECTING THE FUEL LINES FOR LEAKAGE

With the engine off examine the fuel line connections for wetness, washed, or stained areas that indicate a fuel leak. Start the engine and observe all the connections for fuel seepage. Tighten or replace fuel lines as necessary.

CHECKING THE HEATED-AIR SYSTEM (VACUUM MOTOR TYPE,

Look into the snorkel to see if the heat door is wide open with the engine not running. Start the engine, and the door should move quickly to the heat-on position and remain there until the engine starts to heat. Then the door should move gradually to the heat-off position and should be wide open when the engine is fully heated.

REPLACING THE AIR CLEANER FILTER

Remove the wing nuts holding the air cleaner (and duct if so equipped) assembly to the carburetor. Disconnect the crankcase ventilation system hose at the air cleaner.

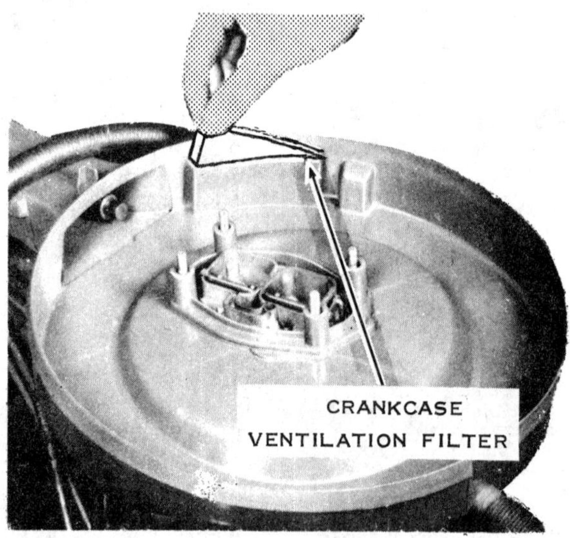

Replacing the crankcase ventilation filter.

The fuel filter should be changed periodically to minimize the possibility of small dirt particles entering the carburetor and causing the float needle valve to remain partially open, thus raising the float level and lowering the gas mileage.

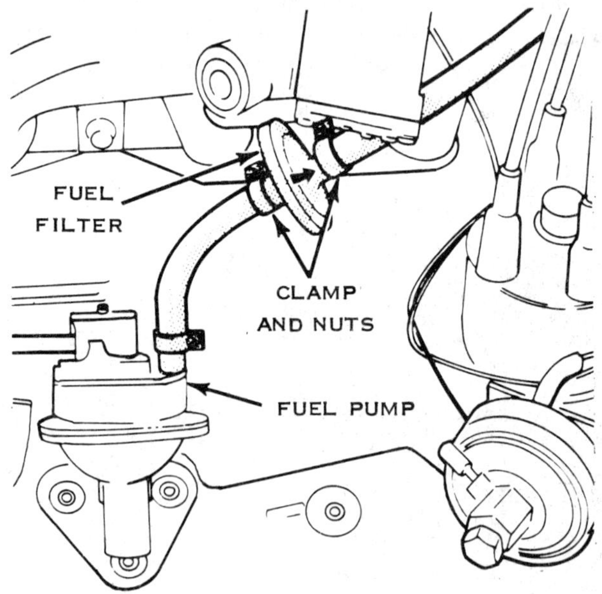

Some in-line filter elements are secured by means of clamps. Note the arrow to designate the direction of fuel flow. In some cases, the filter is screwed into the carburetor fuel bowl.

Remove the air cleaner and duct assembly from the carburetor. **CAUTION: To prevent dirt from entering the carburetor, the filter element must never be removed when the air cleaner body is mounted on the carburetor.**

Remove the air cleaner cover and filter element. Discard the air cleaner mounting gasket.

INSTALLING

Install a new air cleaner mounting gasket on the carburetor. **CAUTION: An air leak here will allow unfiltered air to enter the engine and cause excessive abrasive wear.** Install the air cleaner body on the carburetor, or position the air cleaner and air intake duct-and-valve assembly on the carburetor (and shroud tube if so equipped) so that the word FRONT faces the front of the car.

Place the new air cleaner filter element in the air cleaner body. **CAUTION: Make sure the filter is properly seated. If the word TOP is indicated on the filter element, make sure the word TOP faces up.** Install the cover and tighten the wing bolt. Connect the crankcase vent hose to the air cleaner.

REPLACING THE FUEL FILTER

The fuel filter used on all engines is of one-piece construction and cannot be cleaned. Replace the filter if it becomes clogged or restricted. Otherwise, replace it at the interval specified in the maintenance schedule.

To replace the filter, remove the air cleaner. Loosen the retaining clamp(s) securing the fuel inlet hose to the fuel filter. Unscrew the fuel filter from the carburetor. Disconnect the fuel filter from the hose and discard the retaining clamp.

Install a new clamp on the inlet hose and connect the hose to the new filter. Screw the filter into the carburetor inlet port.

Position the fuel line hose clamp(s) and crimp the clamp(s) securely. Start the engine and check for fuel leaks.

IGNITION SYSTEM

CHECKING THE DISTRIBUTOR

Remove the distributor cap and inspect for cracks. Also check the inside of the cap for carbon build-up. Remove the rotor and check for cracks or a bent or corroded contact arm.

Squirt a few drops of SAE 10W engine oil into the distributor oil cup, if so equipped.

REPLACING SPARK PLUGS

Remove the wire from each spark plug by grasping, twisting, and then pulling the moulded cap of the wire. **CAUTION: Do not pull on the wire because the**

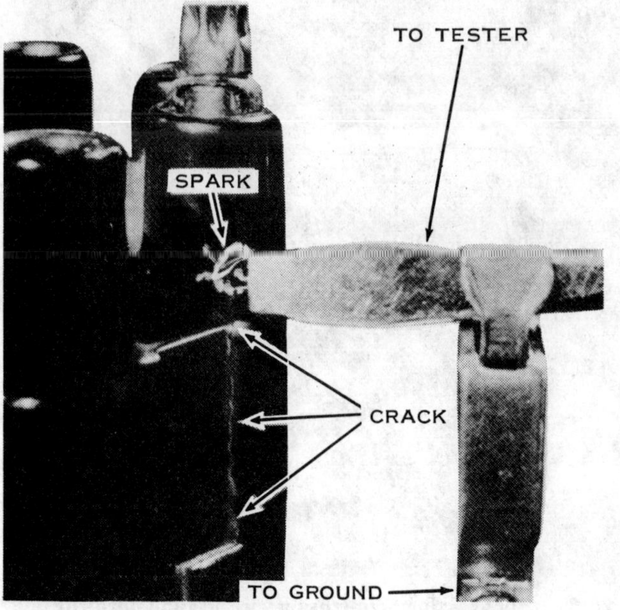

A cracked distributor cap can be checked by using a screwdriver and jumper wire that is grounded at one end. Move the tip of the screwdriver around the cap and along the high-tension wires with the engine running to determine cracks and leaks.

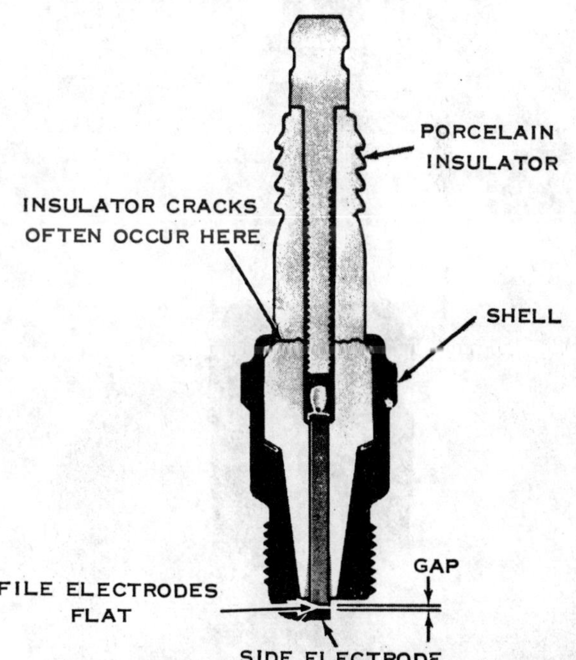

Details of the spark plug. You must file the electrodes to remove the corrosion that causes resistance, which leads to misfiring. Always bend the side electrode to adjust the gap; bending the center electrode will crack the porcelain. Insulator cracks in the area shown are always caused by tilting the socket when removing the spark plug.

After loosening the spark plug a few threads, it is good practice to blow away all dirt to keep it from entering the combustion chamber.

connection inside the cap may become separated or the weather seal may be damaged.

Clean the area around each spark plug port with compressed air; then remove the spark plugs.

Set the spark plug gap by bending the ground electrode. **CAUTION: Never bend the center electrode or you will crack the insulator.**

Dirty insulators cause flash-over and misfiring, especially in damp weather.

Install the spark plugs and torque each to 15 to 20 ft-lbs. Connect the spark plug wires. Check the wire position in the support brackets. Press the wires firmly into the proper bracket slots. Push the all-weather seals firmly into position.

CHECKING THE SECONDARY WIRES

A breakdown or energy loss in the secondary circuit can be caused by: fouled or improperly adjusted spark plugs; defective high-tension wiring; or high-tension leakage across the coil, distributor cap, or rotor resulting from an accumulation of dirt.

To check the spark intensity at the spark plugs, thereby isolating an ignition problem to a particular cylinder, proceed to check the spark intensity of one wire at a time.

When removing the wires from spark plugs, grasp and twist the molded cap back and forth on the plug insulator to free the cap. Use a tool to pull the cap from the insulator. **CAUTION: Do not pull directly on the wire, or it may become separated from the connector inside the cap to cause a loss of energy to that spark plug, which will result in a misfire.**

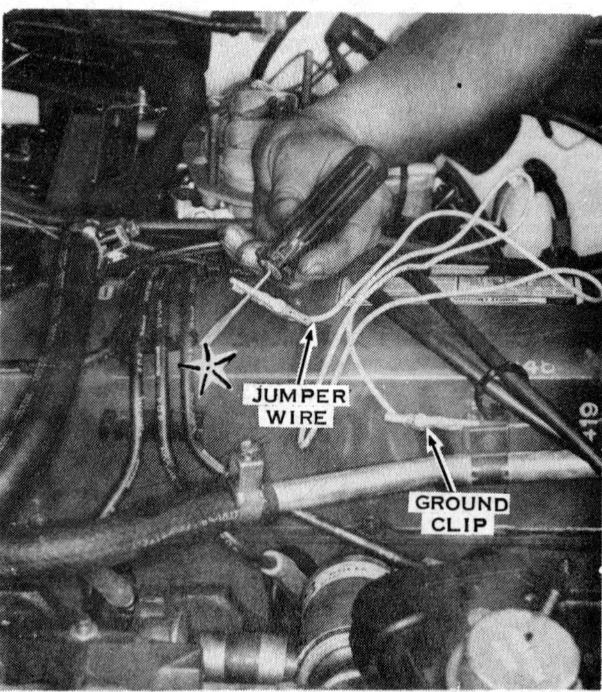

To check for a leaking high-tension wire, use a jumper with one end grounded. Disconnect the high-tension cable to the spark plug to increase the voltage in the cable and make the test more effective. If you draw a spark, you have a crack in the cable. In any case, replace the cables every two years to minimize hard-starting problems.

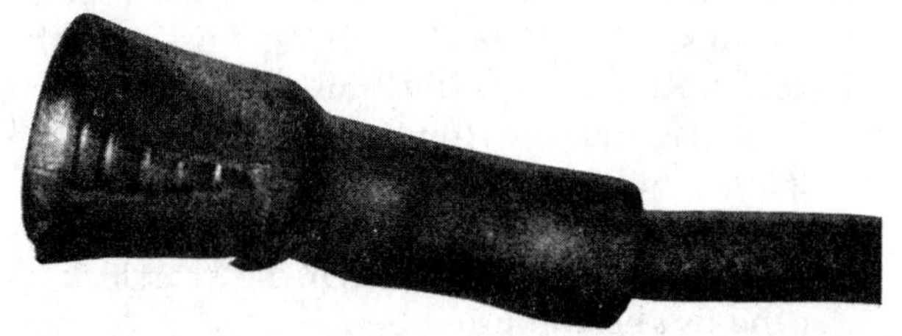

Spark plug wires that are old, dry out and crack, allowing moisture to leak through and this causes misfiring.

Install an adapter in the terminal of the wire to be checked. Hold the adapter approximately 3/16-inch from the exhaust manifold and crank the engine, using an auxiliary starter switch. The spark should jump the gap regularly. If the spark intensity of each wire is satisfactory, the coil, rotor, distributor cap, and the secondary wires are probably satisfactory.

If the spark is good at only some wires, check the resistance of the faulty leads with an ohmmeter, or replace the wire.

If the spark is equal at all wires, but weak or intermittent, check the coil, distributor cap, and the coil-to-distributor high-tension wire. The wire should be clean and bright on the conducting ends and on the coil tower and distributor sockets. The wire must fit snugly and be securely bottomed in the sockets.

BATTERY

CHECKING THE STATE OF CHARGE

With the battery temperature at 80 degrees F, the battery should have a specific gravity reading of not less than 1.230. **WARNING: Hydrogen and oxygen gases are produced during normal battery operation. This combustible mixture can explode if flames or sparks are brought near the vent openings of the battery. The sulphuric acid in the battery electrolyte can cause a serious burn if spilled on the skin or spattered in the eyes. It should be flushed away with large quantities of clear water.**

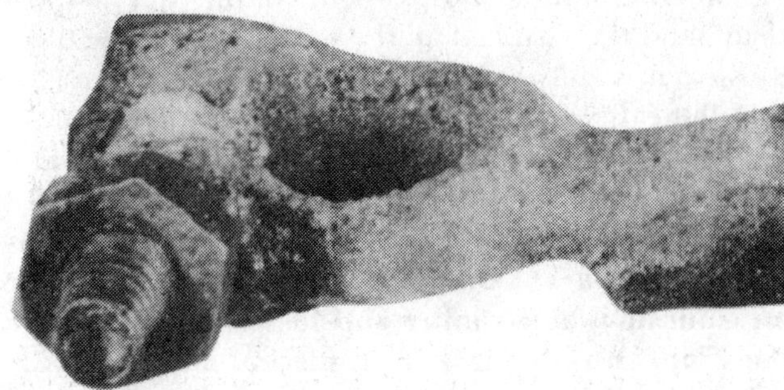

Corroded battery terminal which can cause all kinds of electrical trouble: hard starting, burned out alternator, and short lightbulb life.

Keep the fluid in each battery cell up to the level of the ring in the bottom of the filler well. Generally, tap water can be added unless it has a high mineral content or has been stored in a metal container. If the tap water is unsuitable for these reasons, distilled water should be used.

CHECKING THE BATTERY CABLES

Check the battery cable connections for clean terminals and tightness. Cables must be tight in the terminals and the terminals tight to the posts. A light coating of non-metallic grease can be applied to the terminals and posts to retard corrosion and oxidation.

CLUTCH AND MANUAL TRANSMISSION

LUBRICATING THE CLUTCH AND SHIFT LINKAGE

Clean and lubricate the shift linkage, trunnions, and external shift mechanism (floor shift) with lubricant meeting Ford Chassis and Ball Joint Lube specifications. If excessive shifting efforts are encountered, apply one or two drops of engine oil at the transmission shift arm pivot points.

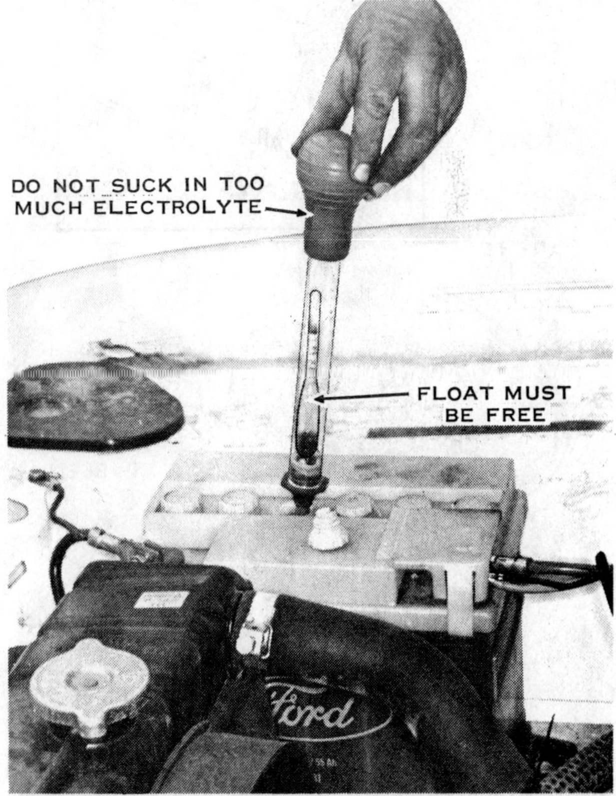

A hydrometer is needed to test the electrolyte of a storage battery. Keep the tube vertical and draw in only enough fluid to lift the float.

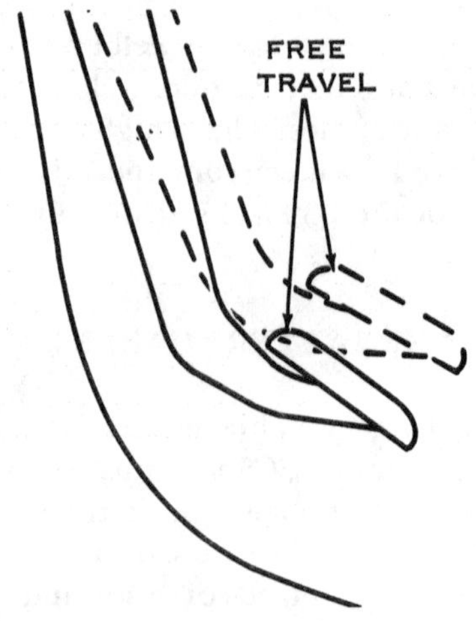

The clutch pedal free travel must be ½" with the engine running at about 3,000 rpm.

ADJUSTING THE CLUTCH PEDAL FREE PLAY

From under the car, loosen the cable locknuts and the adjusting nut at the flywheel housing boss. Pull the cable toward the front of the car until free movement of the release lever is eliminated.

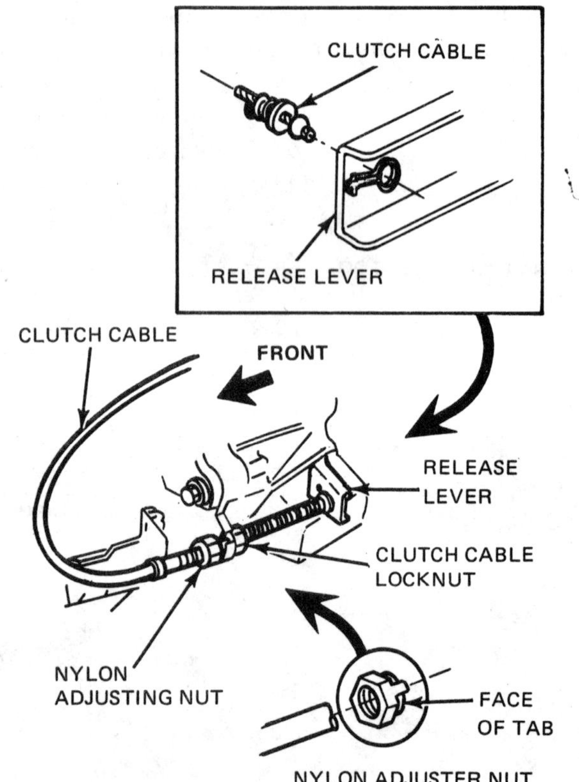

To make the clutch pedal free travel adjustment, loosen the clutch cable locknut, pull the cable to the front of the car until the tabs on the nylon adjuster nut are clear, and then rotate the nut to obtain ¼" clearance.

Holding the cable in this position, place a 1/4 inch spacer against the flywheel housing boss (on the engine side). Run the adjusting nut against the spacer fingertight. Tighten the front locknut against the adjusting nut, being careful not to disturb the adjustment. Torque the locknut to 40-60 ft-lbs.

Remove the spacer and tighten the rear locknut against the flywheel housing boss.

CHECKING THE TRANSMISSION FLUID LEVEL

Clean all dirt and grease from the area around the filler plug, and then remove the plug from the side of the case. If lubricant does not flow from the hole, fill the case with the specified lubricant until it is level with the bottom of the filler hole with the car in a level position. Install the filler plug.

AUTOMATIC TRANSMISSION

LUBRICATING THE LINKAGE

Lubricate all pivot points in the kickdown linkage with lubricant meeting Ford Chassis and Ball Joint Lube specifications.

CHECKING THE FLUID LEVEL

The automatic transmission is designed to operate with the oil level between the ADD and FULL marks on the dipstick at an operating temperature of 150 degrees F to 170 degrees F, and should be checked under these conditions. The operating temperature can be obtained by driving 15 to 20 miles of city type driving with the outside temperature above 50°F.

With the transmission in PARK, engine at curb idle rpm, foot brakes applied, and the vehicle on a level surface, move the transmission selector lever through each range, allowing time in each range to engage transmission units. Return to the PARK position and apply the parking brake.

Clean all dirt from the transmission fluid dipstick cap, and then pull the dipstick out of the tube. Wipe it clean, and then push it all the way back into the tube. Be sure it is fully seated.

Pull the dipstick out of the tube again and check the fluid level, which should be between the ADD and FULL marks. If additional fluid is required, add enough through the filler tube to bring the level between the marks. **CAUTION: Do not overfill the transmission, as foaming and loss of fluid through the vent can result in a transmission malfunction.**

Install the dipstick, making sure it is fully seated in the tube.

Throttle	Range	Shift	OPS–RPM	1	2
Minimum (10" - 15" Vacuum)	D	1-2	590-760	12-16	11-15
	D	2-3	820-1100	17-23	16-22
	D	3-2	680-800	14-17	13-16
	D	2-1	340-450	7-9	6-9
To Detent (Torque Demand)	1	2-1	1060-1570	21-32	20-31
	D	1-2	760-1070	16-22	15-21
	D	2-3	1480-2050	30-42	29-40
	D	3-2	1760 Max.	36 Max.	35 Max.
Through Detent (W.O.T.)	D	1-2	1790-2100	37-43	35-41
	D	2-3	3150-3490	64-72	62-69
	D	3-2	3200 Max.	66 Max.	63 Max.
	D	3-1	1180 Max.	24 Max.	23 Max.

Axle Ratio	Tire Size	Use Column No.
Pinto 3.40:1	BR70 x 13	1
	B78 x 13	1
	BR78 x 13	1
3.55:1	BR70 x 13	2
	B78 x 13	2
	BR78 x 13	2
	CR70 x 13	2

Shift speeds for the four-cylinder engine.

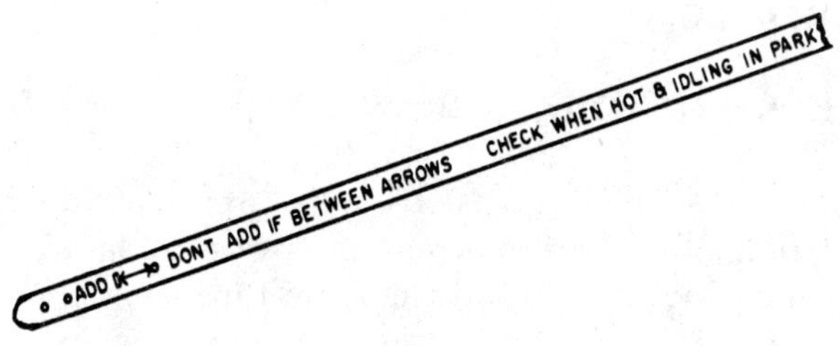

The automatic transmission fluid level dipstick shows a pair of arrows to indicate the two levels which are acceptable. CAUTION: Don't overfill.

CHECKING THE TRANSMISSION INITIAL ENGAGEMENT

Initial engagement checks are made to determine if band and clutch engagements are smooth.

Run the engine until its normal operating temperature is reached. With the engine at the correct idle speed, shift the selector lever from N to 2, D1, and R. Observe the initial band and clutch engagements. Band and clutch engagements should be smooth in all positions. Rough initial engagements in D are caused by high engine idle speed or high control pressure.

Throttle	Range	Shift	OPS–RPM	1	2	3	4	5	6	7	8
Closed (Above 17" Vacuum)	D	1-2	370-440	8-10	8-10	8-10	8-10	7-9	7-9	7-8	7-8
	D	2-3	400-960	9-22	9-22	9-22	9-21	8-19	8-19	8-19	8-19
	D	3-1	370-440	8-10	8-10	8-10	8-10	7-9	7-9	7-8	7-8
	1	2-1	1470-1800	34-42	34-41	33-41	33-41	30-37	30-36	29-36	29-36
To Detent (Torque Demand)	D	1-2	840-1500	19-35	19-34	19-34	19-34	17-31	17-30	17-30	16-30
	D	2-3	1470-2220	34-52	34-51	33-51	33-50	30-46	30-45	29-45	29-44
	D	3-2	1380 Max.	32 Max.	32 Max.	31 Max.	31 Max.	28 Max.	28 Max.	28 Max.	27 Max.
	D	3-1 2-1	440 Max.	10 Max.	10 Max.	10 Max.	10 Max.	9 Max.	9 Max.	8 Max.	8 Max.
Through Detent (W.O.T.)	D	1-2	1720-2210	40-52	38-51	39-50	39-50	35-45	35-45	35-45	34-44
	D	2-3	3082-3800	72-89	71-88	71-87	70-86	64-79	63-77	62-77	62-76
	D	3-2	3270 Max.	76 Max.	75 Max.	75 Max.	74 Max.	67 Max.	67 Max.	66 Max.	66 Max.
	D	3-1 2-1	1950 Max.	45 Max.	45 Max.	44 Max.	44 Max.	40 Max.	39 Max.	39 Max.	39 Max.

Axle Ratio	Tire Size	Use Column No.
3.00:1	DR70-13	1
	CR70-13, B78-13	2
	175-13	3
	BR70-13, BR78-13	4
3.40:1	DR70-13	5
	CR70-13, B78-13	6
	175-13	7
	BR70-13, BR78-13	8

Shift speeds for the V-6 engine.

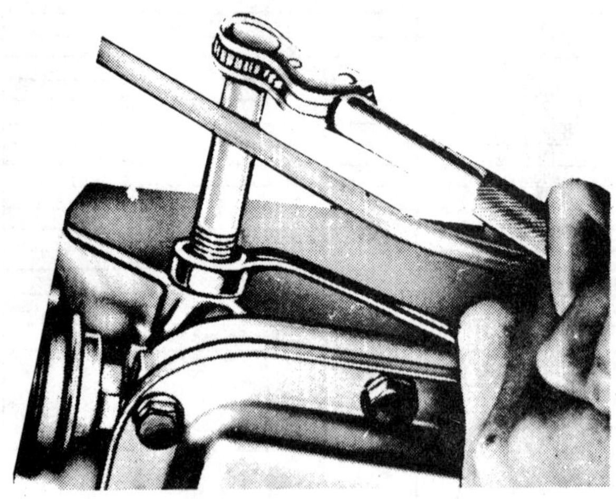

Adjusting the low-reverse band.

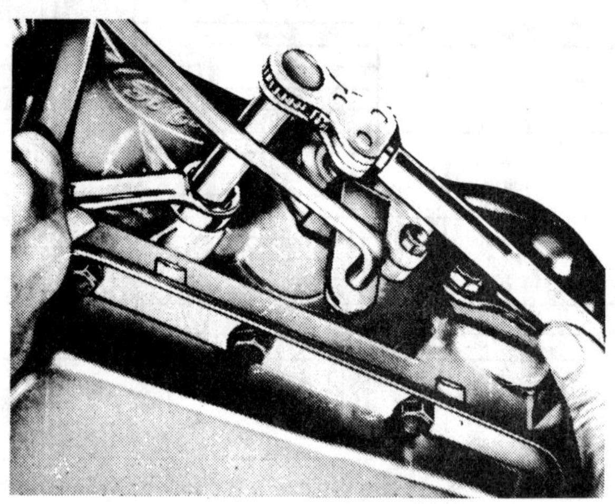

Adjusting the intermediate band.

CHECKING THE SHIFT POINTS

Check the light throttle upshifts in D. The transmission should start in first gear, shift to second, and shift to third within the shift points specified.

With the transmission in third gear, depress the accelerator pedal through the detent (to the floor). The transmission should shift from third to second, or third to first, depending on vehicle speed.

Check the closed-throttle downshift from third to first by coasting down from about 30 mph in third gear. The shift should occur within the limits specified.

CHECKING THE NEUTRAL-START SWITCH

Start the engine with the transmission selector lever in PARK and again in NEUTRAL. The engine should start in these gears only. Adjust the switch, if necessary.

ADJUSTING THE NEUTRAL-START SWITCH

With the manual lever properly adjusted, loosen the two switch attaching bolts. With the transmission manual lever in NEUTRAL, rotate the switch, and then insert the gauge pin (No. 43 drill shank end) into the gauge pin holes of the switch. **CAUTION: The gauge pin has to be inserted to a full 31/64 inch into the three holes of the switch.**

Tighten the two switch attaching bolts to 55 to 75 in-lbs. of torque. Remove the gauge pin from the switch.

Check the operation of the switch. The engine should start only with the transmission selector lever in NEUTRAL and PARK.

REAR AXLE

CHECKING THE LUBRICANT LEVEL

Clean all dirt and grease from the area around the filler plug, and then remove the plug at the location shown on the Lubrication Charts in this manual.

When checking the lubricant level, the axle must be in a normal curb position. If checked on a frame

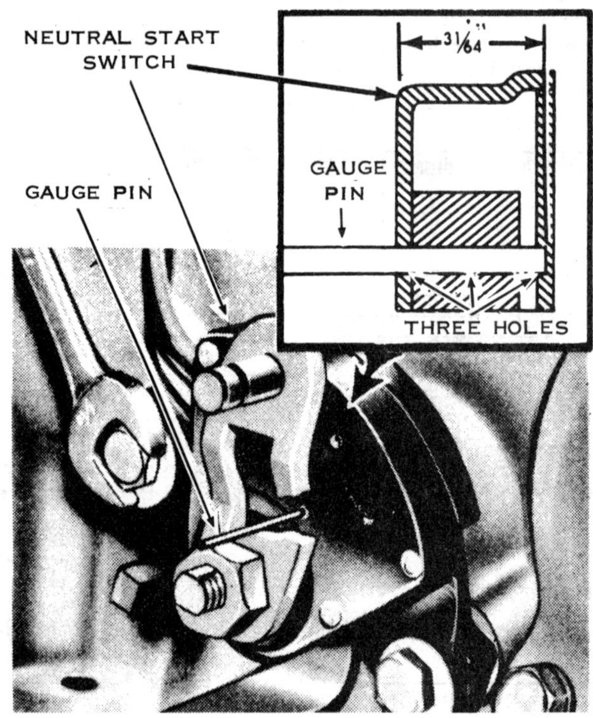

Neutral start switch adjustment. The gauge pin should be a No. 43 drill shank, as discussed in the text.

contact hoist, use safety stands to hold the axle in a normal curb position. Add the specified lubricant until it is level with the bottom of the filler hole. Replace the filler plug.

STEERING MECHANISM

INSPECTING THE STEERING LINKAGE

Check for looseness at the tie-rod ends. Looseness can affect the toe readings and adjustment.

Check the front suspension ball joints and mountings for looseness. Check the brake caliper attaching bolts. Torque all loose nuts and bolts to specifications. Be sure all cotter pins are correctly installed.

Check the steering gear mountings and all steering linkage connections for looseness. Torque all loose mountings to specifications.

CHECKING THE STEERING COLUMN LOCK

Place the transmission selector lever in PARK position on vehicles equipped with an automatic transmission; place it in REVERSE if equipped with a manual transmission.

Turn the key to the LOCK position. Some models are equipped with a lock button on the left side of the steering column, which must be depressed first. Turn the steering wheel left or right slightly until it snaps into the lock detent.

Check to see if the steering wheel is locked in both directions. *NOTE: The selector lever will remain locked only in the PARK position on the column-shift vehicles.* The key can be removed from the ignition lock in the LOCK position only. With the key in the ignition lock, open the driver's door to check the operation of the key removal warning buzzer.

CHECKING THE STEERING CONTROL

Road-test the vehicle and check it for harshness, noise, wander, or free play. Check the steering wheel return for stiffness or inconsistency in either direction.

If the steering is exceptionally stiff, put the vehicle on a hoist and disconnect the pitman arm. Check the steering effort with a scale on the rim of the steering wheel. The effort required to rotate the steering wheel should not exceed specifications. Adjust as required.

INSPECTING THE BALL JOINTS FOR WEAR

UPPER BALL JOINT

Raise the vehicle and place floor jacks beneath the lower arms.

Ask an assistant to grasp the lower edge of the tire and move the wheel in and out. Observe the upper end of the spindle and the upper arm.

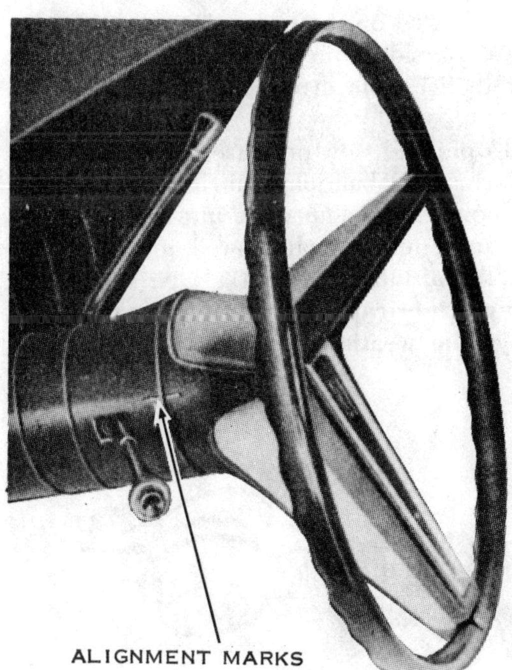

Straight-ahead alignment marks are located on the steering wheel rim and column tube.

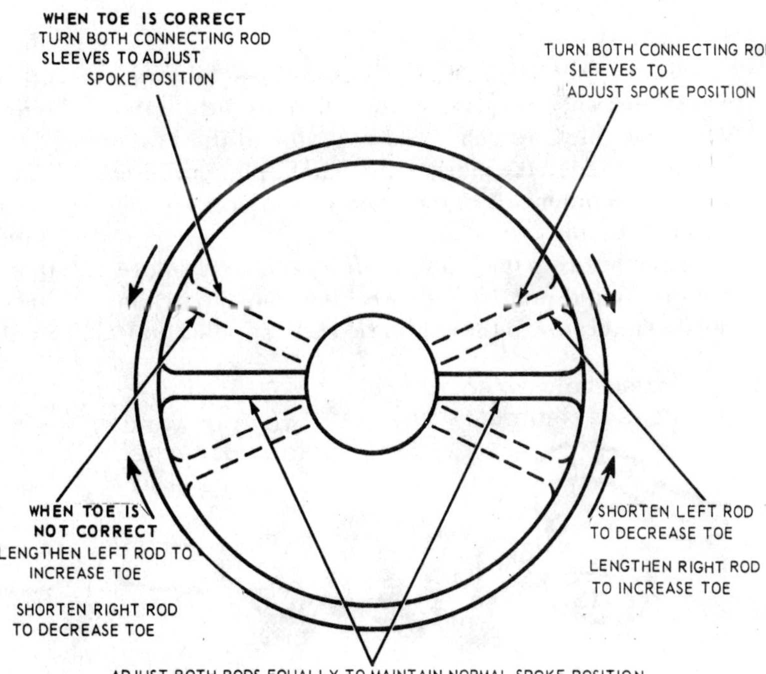

Toe-in adjustments to keep the steering wheel aligned.

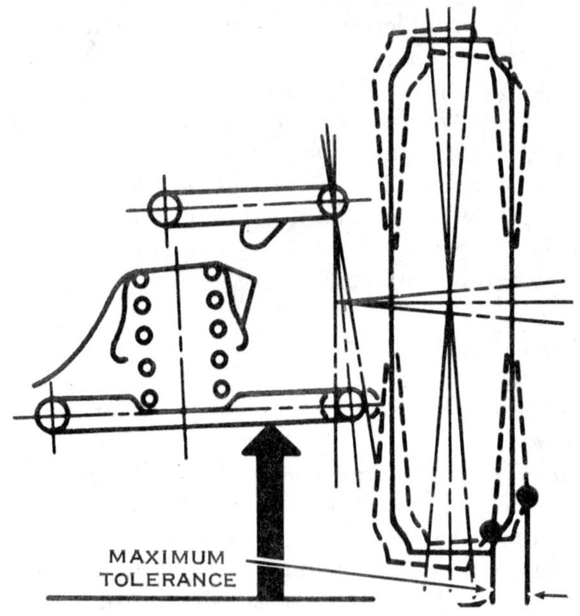

Measuring the lower ball joint radial play.

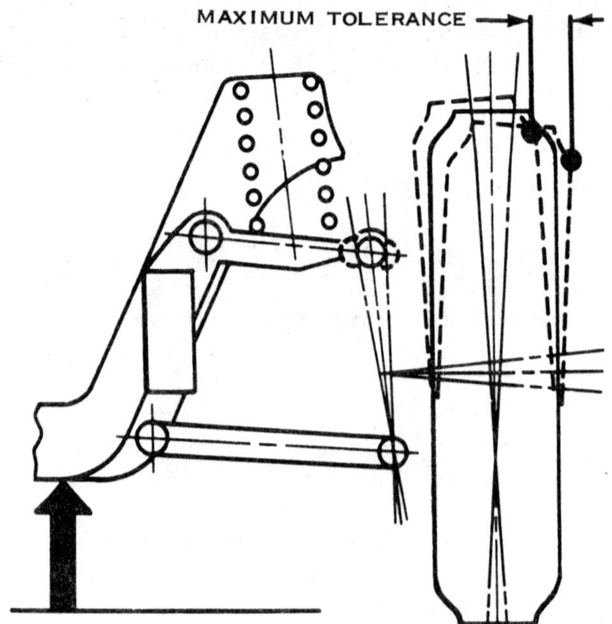

Measuring the upper ball joint radial play.

Any movement between the upper end of the spindle and the upper arm indicates ball joint wear and loss of preload. If any such movement is observed, replace the upper suspension arm. **CAUTION: During the check, the lower ball joint will be unloaded and may move. Disregard all such movement. Also, do not mistake loose wheel bearings for a worn ball joint.**

Lower Ball Joint

Raise the vehicle and place jacks under the lower arms. This will unload the lower ball joints. Adjust the wheel bearings. Attach a dial indicator to the lower arm and position the indicator so that the plunger rests against the inner side of the wheel rim adjacent to the lower ball joint.

Grasp the tire at the top and bottom and slowly move the tire in and out. Note the reading (radial play) on the dial indicator. If the reading exceeds specifications replace the lower suspension arm. **CAUTION: During the check, the upper ball joint will be unloaded and may move. Disregard all such movement. Also, do not mistake loose wheel bearings for a worn ball joint.**

LUBRICATING THE BALL JOINTS

The plugs are located on the top of the upper ball joint and on the underside of the lower ball joint. Wipe all accumulated dirt from around the lubrication plugs.

Use a hand-operated, low-pressure grease gun, loaded with chassis and ball-joint lubricant which meets specifications. Force lubricant into the joint until the boot can be felt or seen to swell, indicating that the boot is full of lubricant. **CAUTION: Do not overlubricate until lubricant escapes from the boot, as this destroys the weathertight seal.** Install the

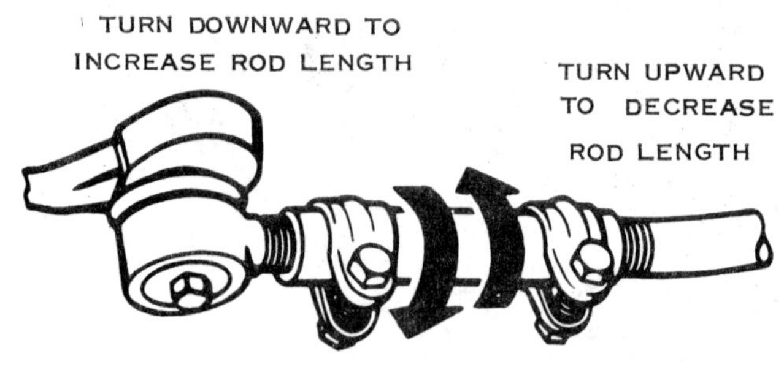

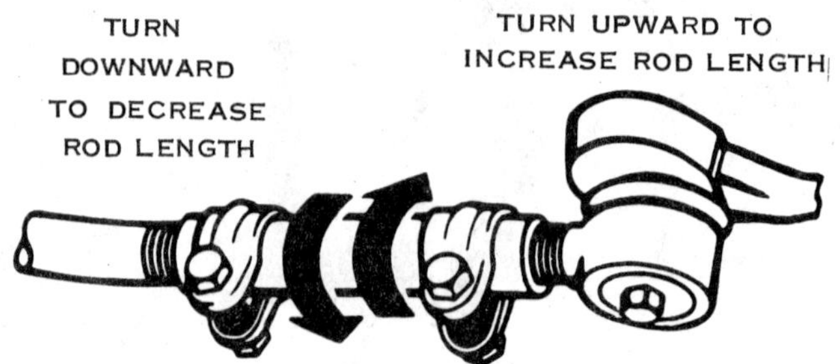

Details for making the spindle connecting rod adjustment.

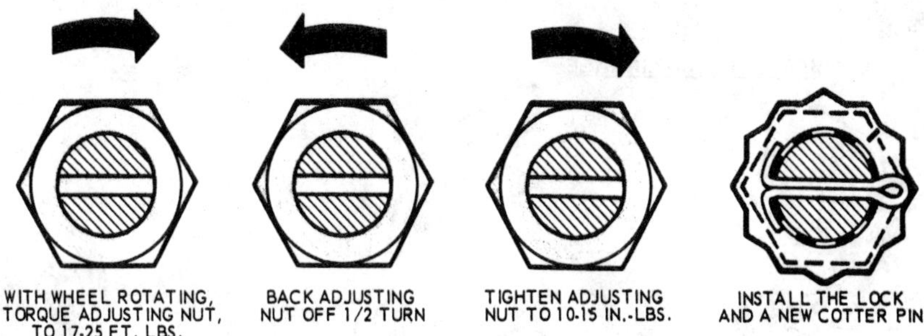

Making the front wheel bearing adjustment.

plugs. *NOTE: If the vehicle has been parked in a temperature below 20 degrees F, park it in a heated garage for 30 minutes, or until the joints will accept lubricant.*

INSPECTING THE FRONT WHEEL LINKAGE

Check for specified air pressures in all four tires. Raise the front of the vehicle off the floor. Shake each front wheel, grasping the upper and lower surfaces of the tire. Check the front suspension ball joints and mountings for looseness, wear, or damage.

Check the brake backing plate mountings. Torque all loose nuts and bolts to specification. Replace all worn parts.

Check the steering gear mountings and all steering linkage connections for looseness. Torque all mountings to specifications. If any of the linkage is worn or bent, replace the parts.

Check the front wheel bearings. If any in-and-out free play is noticed, adjust the bearings to specifications. Replace worn or damaged bearings. Spin each front wheel to check for balance.

Check the action of the shock absorbers. If the shock absorbers are not in good condition, the vehicle may not settle in a normal, level position, and front wheel alignment will be affected.

LUBRICATING THE STEERING LINKAGE

Wipe all accumulated dirt from around the lubrication plugs, and then remove the plugs. Use a rubber-tipped, hand-operated grease gun at low pressure, loaded with lubricant which meets specifications; to force lubricant into the joint until the joint boot can be felt or seen to swell, indicating that the boot is full of lubricant. **CAUTION: Do not overlubricate, until lubricant escapes from the boot, as this destroys the weathertight seal. Install the plug.** *NOTE: If the vehicle has been parked in a temperature below 20 degrees F, park it in a heated garage for 10 minutes, until the joints will accept lubricant.*

LUBRICATING THE STEERING ARM STOPS

Clean and lubricate all friction points. Steering arm stops are located on the inside of the steering arm and the upturned end of the front suspension strut, where it is attached to the lower control arm.

CHECKING THE POWER STEERING PUMP FLUID LEVEL

Run the engine until the fluid is at normal operating

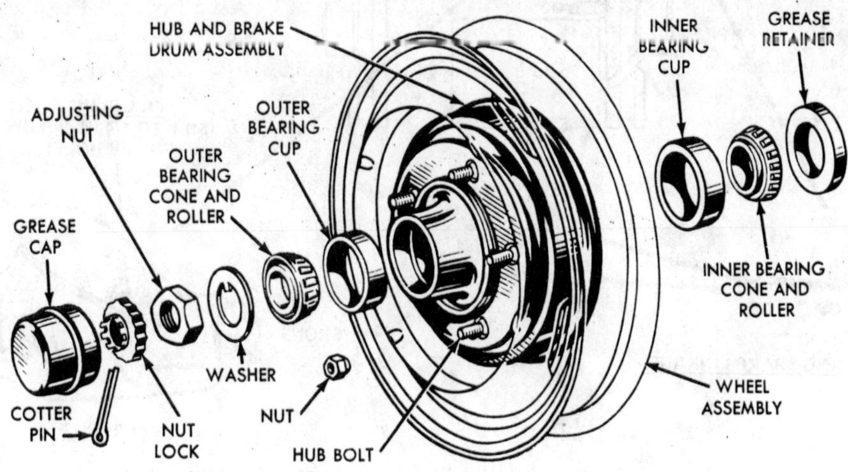

Details of the front wheel and bearing assembly.

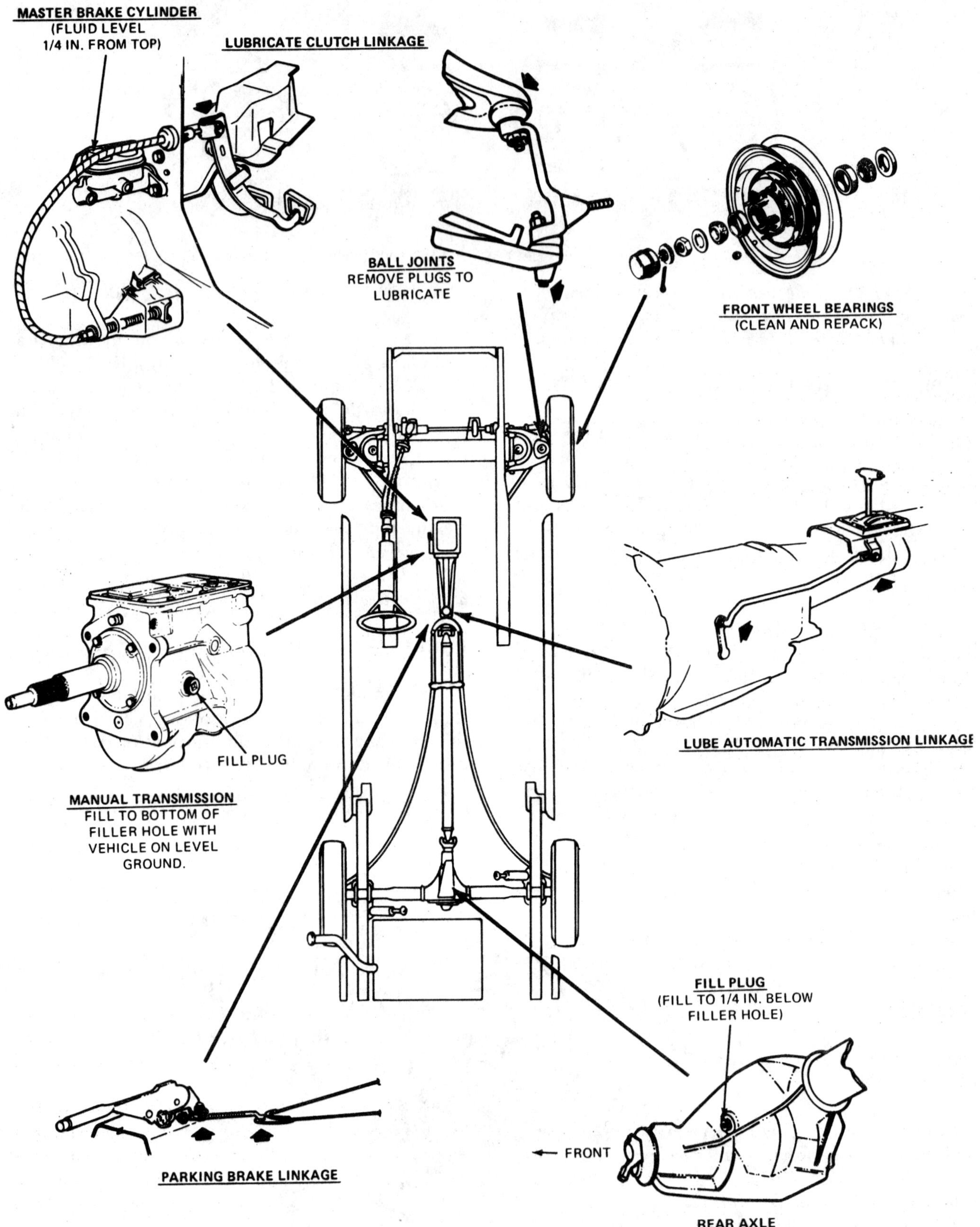

Chassis lubrication points.

Packing a bearing cone with grease.

temperature. Then turn the steering wheel all the way to the left and right several times. Shut off the engine.

Check the fluid level in the power steering reservoir. The level must show on the cross-hatching between the bottom of the dipstick and the full mark. **CAUTION: Do not overfill.** Remove excess fluid with a suction device.

ADJUSTING THE POWER STEERING PUMP DRIVE BELT TENSION

Loosen the adjusting and mounting bolts incorporated on the front face of the pump cover plate (hub side) and the one nut at the rear. Attach a 9/16-inch open-end wrench on the projecting 1/2-inch boss, and then pry upward to correct tension. To adjust the belt on 8 cyl. engines, loosen the mounting bolt in the adjusting slot and the nut directly above the adjusting slot. Place a suitable pry bar between the cast boss on the pump mounting bracket and the cast boss on the pump cover plate, and then pry upward to correct tension. **CAUTION: Do not pry against the reservoir because it can be deformed and cause a leak.**

Recheck the belt tension. When the tension has been correctly adjusted, tighten the bolts to specifications.

BRAKES

INSPECTING THE MASTER CYLINDER FLUID LEVEL

Push the master cylinder cap retainer to one side, and then remove the cover and cover gasket cap from the master cylinder. The gasket which seals the master cylinder should come off with the cap.

Fill the reservoir full or 1/4 inch from the top. Install the cover, making sure that the gasket is properly seated in the cap.

INSPECTING FLEXIBLE BRAKE HOSES

A flexible brake hose should be replaced if it shows signs of softening, cracking, or other damage.

When installing a new front brake hose, position the hose to avoid contact with other chassis parts. Place a new copper gasket over the hose fitting, and then thread the hose assembly into the front wheel cylinder. Engage the opposite end of the hose to the bracket on the frame. Install the horseshoe-type retaining clip, and then connect the tube to the hose with the tube fitting nut.

A rear brake hose should be installed so that it does not touch the muffler outlet pipe or shock absorber. Thread the hose into the rear brake tube connector. Engage the front end of the hose to the bracket on the frame. Install the horseshoe-type retaining clip, and then connect the tube to the hose with the tube fitting nut.

Bleed the hydraulic system to remove all trapped air. **CAUTION: Always check the fluid level in the master cylinder before performing the bleeding procedures.** If the fluid level is not within 1/4 inch of the top of the master cylinder reservoirs, add Ford Brake Fluid—Extra Heavy Duty—Part Number C6AZ—19542-A (ESA-M6C25-A) or equivalent for all brake applications. *NOTE: The extra heavy duty brake fluid is colored blue for identification purposes.*

CHECKING THE OPERATION OF THE BRAKING SYSTEM

Depress the foot brake pedal for good pedal height before road testing. Check and correct, if required, the following conditions: pull in either direction, harshness or noise, excessive pedal effort, spongy feel, and operation of the brake warning light. **CAUTION: Avoid sudden hard stops—make slow, gradual stops.**

INSPECTING THE DISC BRAKE UNITS FOR WEAR

Raise the vehicle until the wheel and tire clear the floor. Remove the wheel cover or hubcap from the wheel. Remove the wheel and tire from the hub and rotor.

Inspect the brake shoes and linings for wear. If a lining is worn to within 1/32 inch of the rivet heads or if there is more than 0.125" taper from end to end, or if the lining shows evidence of brake fluid contamination, replace all shoe-and-lining assemblies on both front wheels.

Check the rotor for scoring. If the rotor is excessively scored, refinish it or replace the rotor. Visually check the caliper. If the caliper housing is leaking, it should be replaced. If a seal is leaking, the caliper must be disassembled and new seals installed. If a piston is seized in the bore, a new caliper housing is required.

Check the brake hoses for signs of cracking, leaks or abrasion. Replace them if necessary. Install the wheel and hub assembly.

CHECKING THE OPERATION OF THE PARKING BRAKE MECHANISM

Check the operation of the parking brake and indicator light. When the parking brake is fully released, the cable should have no slack, and the rear brakes should not drag when the wheels are turned. Adjust as required with the vehicle on a hoist. If equipped with an indicator light, be sure it glows when the parking brake is engaged.

ADJUSTING THE PARKING BRAKES

Make sure the parking brake is fully released. Place transmission in NEUTRAL, and then raise vehicle.

Tighten the adjusting nut on the equalizer rod at the control assembly to cause rear wheel brake drag. Then, loosen the adjusting nut until the rear brakes are fully released. Torque the jam nut to 7 to 10 ft-lbs. **CAUTION: There should be no brake drag.**

Lower the vehicle and check the operation of the parking brake.

WHEELS AND TIRES

INSPECTING THE WHEEL COVERS

Inspect the wheel covers or hub caps for dents or looseness.

To install a wheel cover, center the tire valve stem in the wheel cover hole, and then position the cover on the wheel, with the valve stem side of the cover tight against the wheel. Use a rubber mallet to tap the cover into place, beginning on the outer perimeter opposite the valve stem. **CAUTION: Avoid damage to the wheel cover.** Be sure the cover is fully seated against the wheel all around the perimeter of the cover.

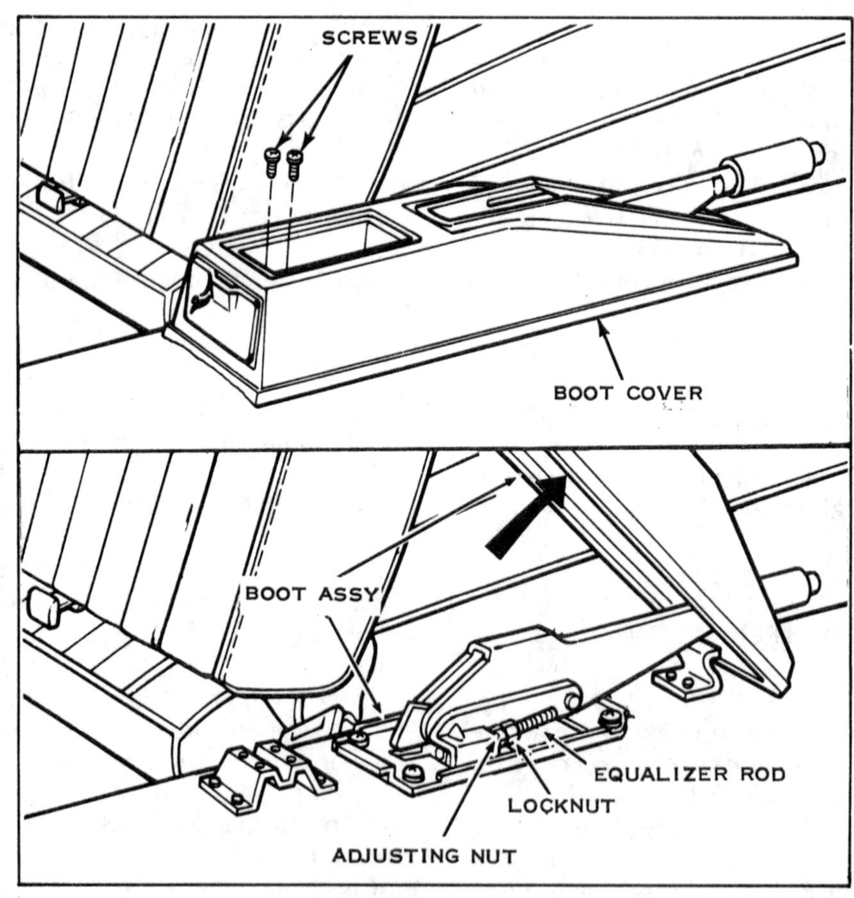

Parking brake adjustment.

INSPECTING THE WHEELS

Wheel hub nuts should be inspected and tightened to specifications. Loose wheel hub nuts can cause shimmy and vibration. Elongated stud holes in the wheels can also result from loose hub nuts.

Keep the wheels and hubs clean. Stones wedged between the wheel and drum and lumps of mud or grease can unbalance a wheel and tire.

Check for damage that would affect the runout of the wheel. Wobble or shimmy caused by a damaged wheel will eventually damage the wheel bearings. Inspect the wheel rims for dents that could permit air to leak from the tires.

CHECKING THE TIRES AND AIR PRESSURE

Inspect the tire treads and remove all stones, nails, glass, or other objects that may be wedged in the tread. Check for holes or cuts that can permit air leakage from the tire. Make necessary repairs. Inspect the tire side walls for cuts and damage. If internal damage is suspected, remove the tire from the wheel for further inspection and repair or replacement.

Check the tire valve for air leaks, and replace the valve, if necessary. Replace all missing valve caps. The tires should be checked frequently to be sure that air pressures agree with those specified for the tires and vehicle model, including the spare.

Inspect the tires for uneven wear that might indicate the need for front-end alignment or tire rotation.

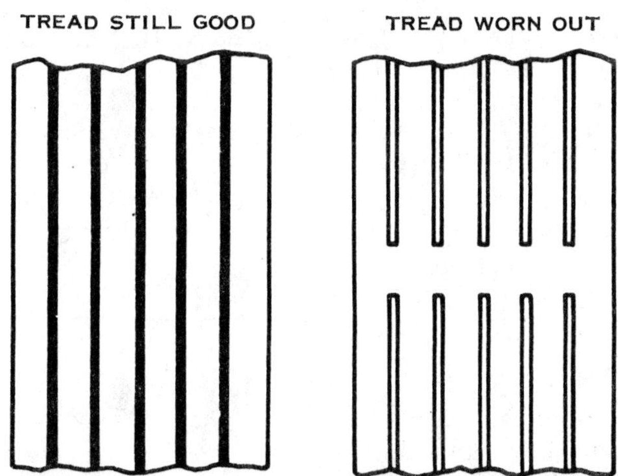

Modern tires have a built-in wear indicator, which shows a band across the tire (right) when the tread is worn to a dangerous condition.

ROTATING THE TIRES

Bias and bias-belted tires should be cross-switched as shown. If the vehicle is equipped with radial ply tires, they can be rotated from front to rear as shown in an accompanying illustration. *NOTE: Cross-switching is not recommended for radial ply tires.* **CAUTION: If the car is equipped with the optional Space Saver Tire, do not include it during rotation of the other four tires. CAUTION: Tires should not be rotated until the cause of unusual or uneven wear is located and corrected.**

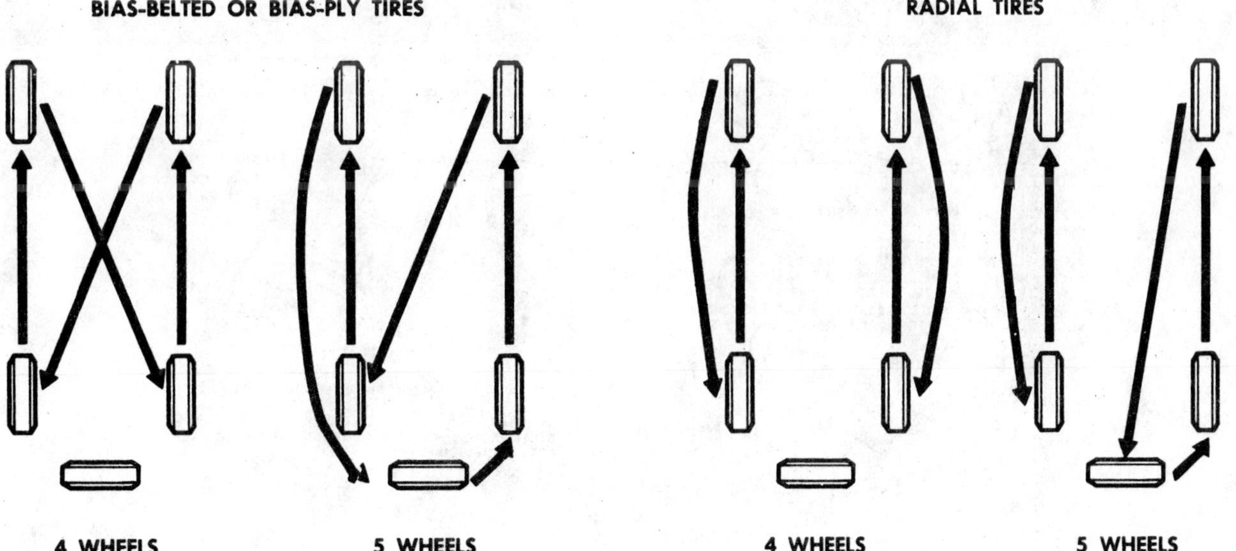

Tire rotation diagram to equalize tread wear. Note the different rotation for radial tires.

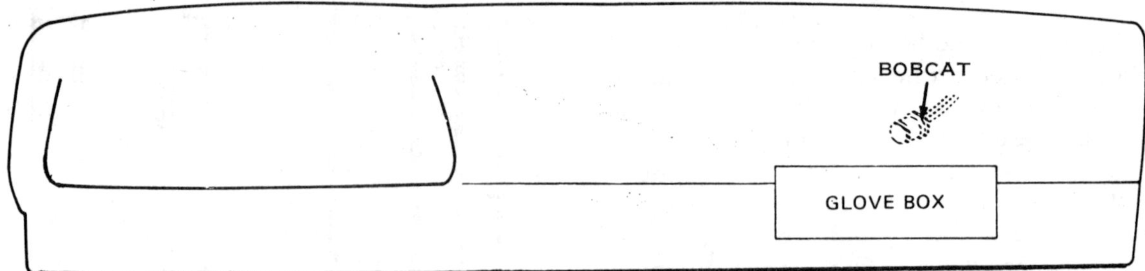

Turn signal and hazzard flasher locations.

BODY

INSPECTING THE BODY DRAIN HOLES

Make sure that the drain holes in the doors, rocker panels, and quarter panels are free from obstruction. A small screwdriver can be used to open plugged or partially plugged drain holes, but it must not be used on rubber dust valves. Visually check the dust valves for proper sealing and draining operation.

LUBRICATING BODY FRICTION POINTS

To eliminate binding conditions on pivot and friction points, spray lubricant on the luggage compartment hinge pivots, fuel filler door hinges, and station wagon and runabout tailgate or rear door support hinges.

Lubricate the lock cylinders, including the ignition lock, by applying lubricant sparingly in the key slot and working the key in the lock.

Spray polyethylene grease on hood and door hinges and hinge checks, and on the auxiliary hood catch.

Work all pivot points several times to be certain the lubricant has been worked in thoroughly.

LIGHTING AND ACCESSORIES

CHECKING THE LIGHTS

Check for proper operation of switches and the brightness of lights, including operation of the oil pressure and alternator warning lights.

Check the detent action and return of the turn signal lever by making full left and right turns during the road test. Check the operation of the hazard warning flasher system.

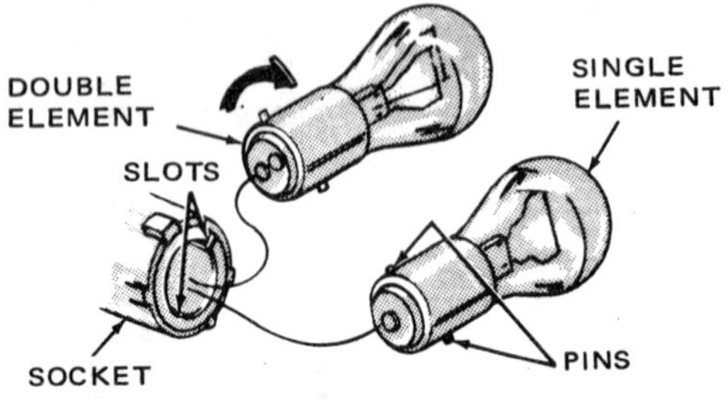

DEPRESS BULB IN SOCKET AND ROTATE COUNTERCLOCKWISE. THEN, PULL BULB FROM SOCKET.

TO INSTALL, INSPECT PINS ON BULB BASE. IF THEY ARE NOT SAME DISTANCE FROM BOTTOM OF BASE, THEY MUST BE INSERTED INTO THE CORRECT SLOT. DETERMINE WHICH SLOT IN SOCKET PINS SHOULD BE INSERTED INTO AND PUSH BULB BASE INTO SOCKET. THEN, ROTATE CLOCKWISE TO ENGAGE PINS. IF BULB WILL NOT ROTATE, PINS ARE IN WRONG SLOTS.

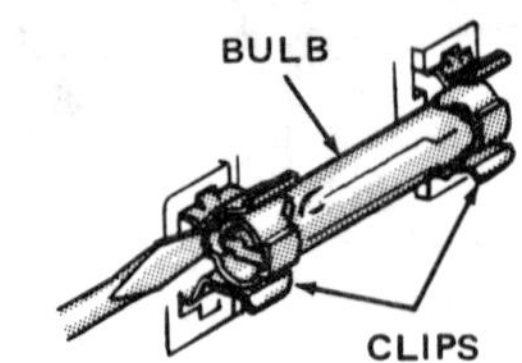

INSERT A SCREWDRIVER UNDER END OF BULB AND PRY BULB OUT OF CLIPS.

TO INSTALL, POSITION BULB TO CLIPS AND PRESS INTO PLACE.

PULL BULB STRAIGHT OUT OF SOCKET TO REMOVE.

TO INSTALL, POSITION BULB TO SOCKET AND PUSH STRAIGHT IN UNTIL SEATED.

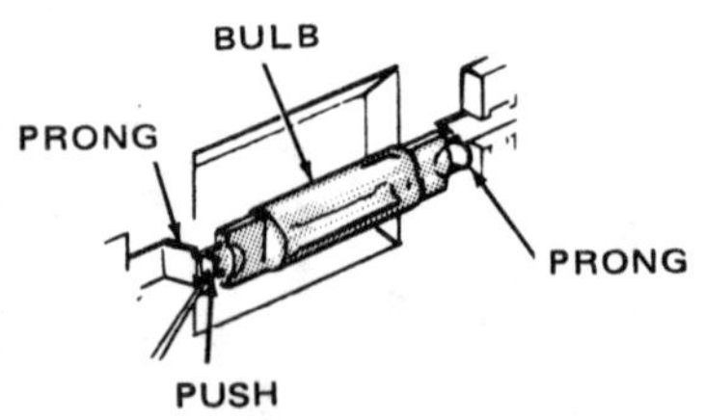

TO REMOVE, PUSH PRONG TOWARD BULB AND LIFT BULB FROM PRONG.

TO INSTALL, ENGAGE ONE END OF BULB OVER ONE PRONG. THEN, PUSH OTHER PRONG TOWARD BULB AND ENGAGE BULB END OVER PRONG. **DO NOT FORCE BULB END OVER PRONG.**

Replacing an interior light bulb.

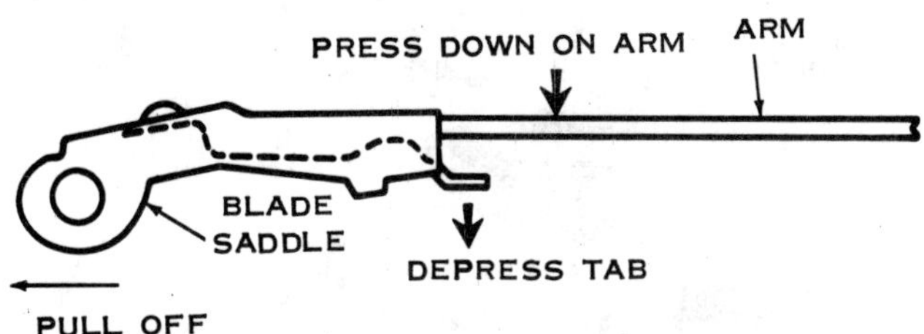

Trico bayonet-type blade removal.

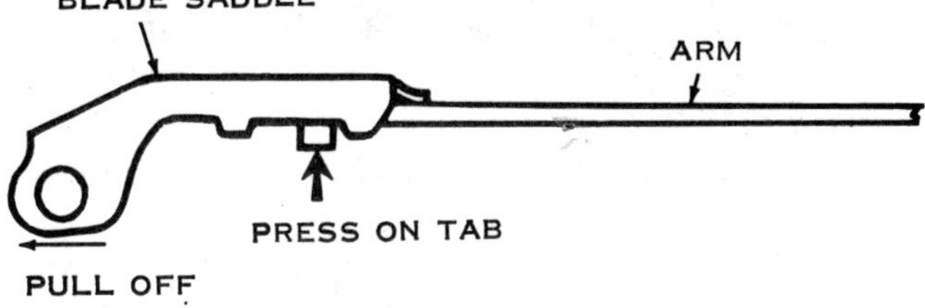

Anco bayonet-type blade removal.

CHECKING THE HORNS

Check the rim-blow and pad-blow horns to be sure the horn(s) blow at all rim or pad contact positions.

CHECKING THE WINDSHIELD WASHER AND WIPERS

Check for proper operation, including wiper sweep and park. Adjust if required. Check washer operation and adjust as required.

Fill with water and solvent meeting specifications. Use as directed on the container. Check the screen-type filter on the pick-up tube. Clean as necessary.

REPLACING WINDSHIELD WIPER BLADES

Wiper blade replacement intervals will vary with the amount of use, type of weather, chemical reaction from road tars or salts, and the age of the blades. Be sure that the windshield glass surface is not contaminated with oil, tree sap, or other substance which cannot be easily rubbed off.

Generally, if the wiper pattern across the glass is uneven and streaks over clean glass, the blades should be replaced.

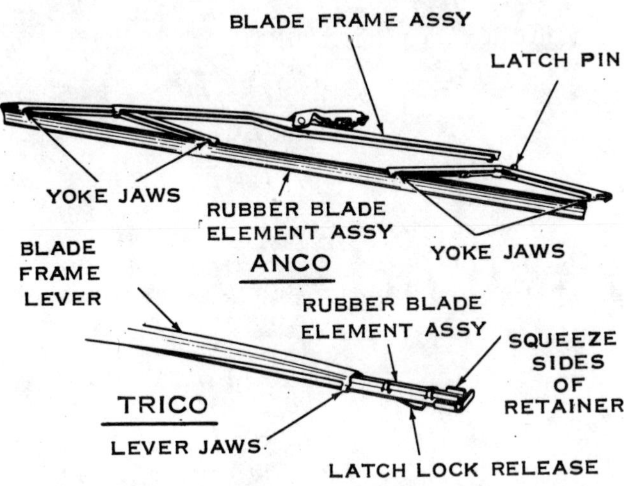

Replacing the windshield wiper blade.

Saddle-Pin Type Blade

To remove a pin type (Trico) blade, insert an appropriate tool into the spring release opening of the blade saddle, depress the spring clip, and pull the blade from the arm.

To install, push the blade saddle onto the pin so that the spring clip engages the pin.

Bayonet-Type Blade

To remove a Trico blade, press down on the arm to unlatch the top stud. Depress the tab on the saddle, and then pull the blade from the arm.

To remove an Anco blade, press inward on the tab, and then pull the blade from the arm.

To install a new blade, slip the blade connector over the end of the wiper arm so that the locking stud snaps into place.

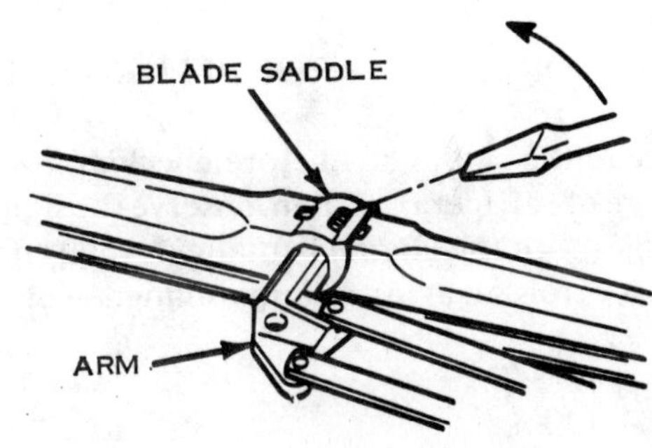

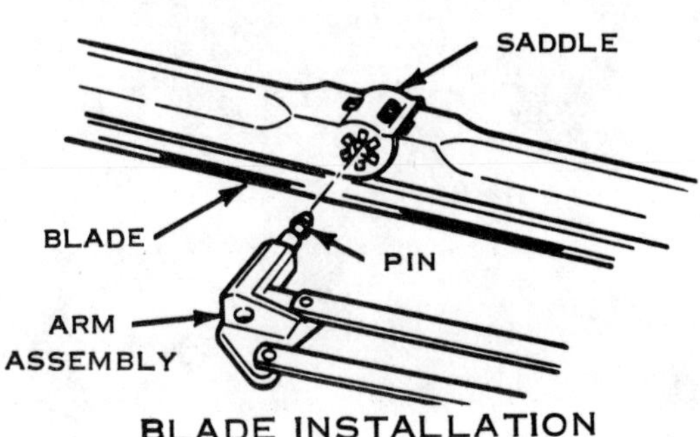

Trico or Anco pin-type wiper blade removal. The left side procedure is shown, which is similar for the right side.

REPLACING A RUBBER BLADE ELEMENT

Trico

To remove, squeeze the latch lock release, and then pull the blade element out of the lever jaws.

To install, insert the new element through each of the lever jaws. Be sure the element is engaged in all lever jaws.

Anco

To remove, depress the latch pin, and then slide the element out of the yoke jaws.

To install, slide the element through the yoke jaws, and then insert the blade frame assembly into the slots of the yoke jaws. **CAUTION: If the arm or blade assembly is bent or distorted, replace the complete blade assembly.**

CHECKING THE HEATER AND AIR CONDITIONER

Check for the following items: leaks, sufficient heat (approximately 140 degrees F at 32 degrees outside temperature and 50 percent relative humidity), blower operation, temperature control operation, operation of open air ducts and vents, operation of air conditioner controls and air conditioning temperatures (approximately 68 degrees F at 100 degrees outside temperature and 50 percent relative humidity). Adjust as necessary.

CHECKING THE AIR CONDITIONER SIGHT GLASS

Clean the sight glass before checking for a proper charge of refrigerant. Then, observe the sight glass for bubbles with the engine running at 1500 rpm and the A/C controls set at maximum cooling. A continuous or

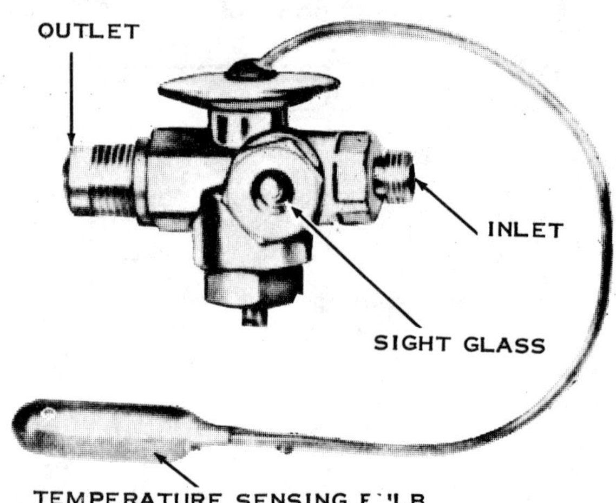

Air conditioner sight glass.

large amount of bubbles in the sight glass indicates an undercharge of refrigerant.

If an undercharge is found, check the system for leaks. Repair any leaks, evacuate the system with a vacuum pump, and charge the system with the proper amount of Refrigerant 12.

No bubbles in the sight glass indicates either too much refrigerant or a complete loss of regrigerant. While observing the sight glass, cycle the magnetic clutch off and on, with the engine running at 1500 rpm. If refrigerant is in the system, bubbles will appear while the clutch is engaged and disappear when the clutch is disengaged.

If no bubbles appear during the on and off cycle of the magnetic clutch, there is no refrigerant in the system, and it will be necessary to test for leaks and repair as required. Then, recharge the system. *NOTE: Under conditions of extremely high temperatures, occasional foam or bubbles may appear in the sight glass.*

4 | emission-control systems

Three kinds of emission-control systems are used on these cars: crankcase, exhaust, and evaporative.

Crankcase-emission control is by means of a Positive Crankcase Ventilation (PCV) valve, with a secondary (overload) hose leading to the air cleaner.

Exhaust emission-control is by means of the Ford IMCO (IMproved COmbustion) system. This varies with engines, but it means that the carburetor air-fuel mixture has been optimized, a heated-air system added, and the ignition advance curve modified to meet increasingly stricter emission standards.

Some engines (depending on transmission and optional equipment) have other control systems: Decel Valve, Thermactor, Transmission-Regulated Spark (TRS), and Spark-Delay System (SDS).

All models since 1974 utilize an electric-assist choke to minimize emissions during engine start up.

Exhaust-Gas Recirculation (EGR) is used to reduce NOx emissions.

Catalytic converters are used on all of the larger 1975 engines (and the 2,300cc engine for California), and it is being used on all 1976 models. The larger engines with a catalytic converter use an exhaust heat-control valve to assist in rapid engine warmup during cold weather.

Evaporation-emission control is by means of a charcoal canister to store the vapors until the engine is running at which time they are purged through the air cleaner to be burned in the combustion chambers of the engine.

CRANKCASE VENTILATION SYSTEM

Ventilation of the crankcase is effected by the vacuum created in the intake manifold when the engine is running and varies with the changes in vacuum. A portion of the fresh air entering the air cleaner bypasses the carburetor to be drawn into the intake manifold via a primary vent hose, cylinder head cover, crankcase, oil separator, ventilation control valve, and secondary vent hose.

TESTING THE SYSTEM

WITH THE ENGINE IDLING

Remove the PCV valve from its mounting. If the valve is functioning properly and not plugged, a hissing air noise will be heard as the air passes through the valve, and a strong vacuum should be felt when a finger is placed over the valve inlet. While your finger is over the valve inlet, check for vacuum leaks in the hose line and at all connections.

Re-install the PCV valve; then, remove the crankcase air inlet hose at the air cleaner connection. Loosely hold a small piece of stiff paper (such as a 3" x 5" memo card or parts tag card) over the opening at the

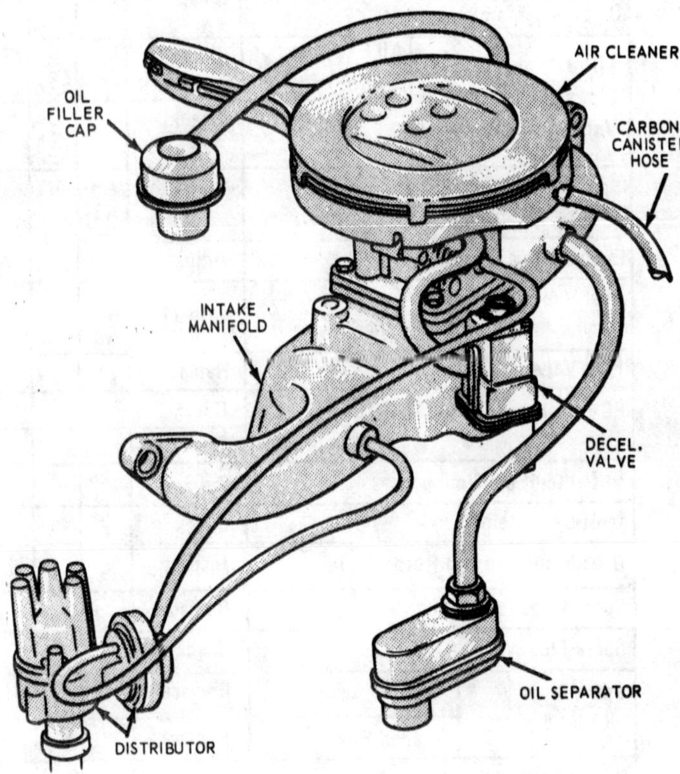

Crankcase ventilation system for the early 2,300cc engine.

EMISSIONS SYSTEMS REQUIRED MAINTENANCE SERVICES – PASSENGER CARS		SERVICE	SERVICE INTERVAL (NUMBER OF MONTHS OR THOUSANDS OF MILES, WHICHEVER COMES FIRST)																
			5	6	10	12	15	18	20	24	25	30	35	36	40	42	45	48	50
Engine Oil (1) (2)		Change	AB	C	AB	C	AB	C	AB	C	AB	AB C	AB	C	AB	C	AB	C	AB
Oil Filter (1) (2)		Replace	AB	C			AB	C			AB	C	AB			C	AB		
Intake Manifold Bolts/Nuts (16)		Torque		C (14)			B	C	A			C (14)				C (14)			
Exhaust Control Valve (3)		Lubricate		C		C	B	C	A	C		B		C	A	C	B	C	
		Check										C							
Fuel System Filter		Replace		C			B		A										
Carburetor Air Cleaner Element (4)		Check				C	B							C			B		
		Replace							A	C		B			A			C	
Emissions Filter in Air Cleaner (4)		Replace							A	C		B			A			C	
Idle Fuel Mixture	All Except 4 Cyl.	Adjust		C			B		A	C		B			A		B		
	4 Cyl.	Adjust		C		C	B		A	C		B		C	A		B	C	
Fast Idle Speed	All Except 4 Cyl.	Adjust	AB	C			B		A	C		B			A		B		
	4 Cyl.	Adjust	AB	C		C	B		A	C		B		C	A		B	C	
Curb Idle Speed		Adjust	AB				B		A			B			A		B		
Curb Idle Speed and TSP Off Speed	All Except 4 Cyl.	Adjust		C						C									
	4 Cyl.	Adjust		C		C				C				C				C	
Throttle Solenoid Off Speed		Adjust	AB																
Air Cleaner Temp Control and Delay Valve (5)		Check				C	B		A	C		B		C	A		B	C	
Throttle and Choke Linkage and Delay Valve or Air Valve	All Except 4 Cyl.	Check		C (5)			B		A	C (5)		B			A		B		
	4 Cyl.	Check		C (5)		C (5)	B		A	C (5)		B		C (5)	A		B		
Fuel Deceleration Valve (5)		Check	AB (14)	C		C	B (14)		A (14)	C		B (14)		C	A (14)		B (14)	C	
Engine Valve Clearance (2800)		Adjust				C	B		A	C		B		C	A		B	C	
Fuel Vapor Emissions (Fuel Filler Cap, Hoses, Lines)		Inspect							A	C		B			A			C	
PCV Valve		Replace							A	C		B			A			C	
PCV System, Hoses, Tubes (5)		Check				C	B		A					C	A		B		
		Clean							A	C		B			A			C	
Initial Ignition Timing		Adjust					B	C	A			B		C	A		B		
Ignition System (6)		Check					B		A			B			A		B		
Distributor Cap and Rotor (7)		Inspect					B	C	A			B		C	A		B		
Spark Plugs (1)		Replace					B		A			B			A		B		
Spark Plug Wires (9)		Check					B		A			B			A		B		
Spark Plugs (1) (8)	Low/No Lead Fuel	Replace						C						C					
	Leaded Fuel	Replace				C				C				C				C	
Crankcase Breather Cap – if so equipped (15)		Check				C				C				C				C	

EMISSIONS SYSTEMS REQUIRED MAINTENANCE SERVICES – PASSENGER CARS		SERVICE	SERVICE INTERVAL (NUMBER OF MONTHS OR THOUSANDS OF MILES, WHICHEVER COMES FIRST)																
			5	6	10	12	15	18	20	24	25	30	35	36	40	42	45	48	50
Spark Plug Wires	Low/No Lead Fuel	Inspect						C						C					
	Leaded Fuel	Inspect				C				C				C				C	
Spark Control System and Delay Valve ⑤		Check				C	B		A	C		B		C	A		B	C	
Thermactor System ⑤		Check					B		A	C		B			A		B	C	
Evaporative Emissions Canister ⑤ ⑩	All Except 4 Cyl.	Inspect							A	C		B			A			C	
	4 Cyl.	Inspect				C			A	C		B		C	A			C	
EGR System and Delay Valve ⑤ ⑪		Check				C				C				C				C	
Drive Belt Tension		Check		C			B		A										
Drive Belt Condition		Inspect				C				C		B		C	A		B	C	
Belt-Driven Accessories (4 Cyl.) ⑫		Check				C	B		A	C		B		C	A		B	C	
Coolant Condition and Protection ⑬		Check				C	B		A	C							B	C	
Coolant		Replace											B	C	A				
Cooling System Hoses and Clamps		Check								C			AB					C	

① For A and B rated cars – When operating your vehicle under severe service conditions, change engine oil every 2½ months or 2,500 miles change engine oil filter the first oil change and every 5 months or 5,000 miles thereafter. Check, clean and regap spark plugs every 5,000 miles.

Ford C rated cars – If you are operating your car under severe service conditions, change the oil every 2 months or 3000 miles and the oil filter every 4 months or 6000 miles. Under severe service conditions, clean and regap spark plugs every 4 months or 6000 miles, whichever comes first.

Severe service conditions include:

- extended periods of idling or low-speed operation such as police, taxi, or door-to-door delivery.
- driving short distances (less than 10 miles) while outside temperature remains below 10°F for 60 days or more.
- excessive dust conditions.

② For C rated cars – Normal oil change is at every 6000 miles or 4 months, whichever occurs first. Normal oil filter change is at first 6000 miles or 4 months and at alternate oil changes thereafter.

③ Lubricate and free up at each oil change (C rated cars only)

④ Replace more often if operated in severe dust conditions

⑤ Adjust, repair or replace as required

⑥ A rated cars – check with scope (recheck after any maintenance or repair)

⑦ Clean or replace as indicated by scope check

⑧ If not replaced at 12,000 or 18,000 mile intervals, replace complete set at time of plug malfunction

⑨ Repair or replace wires as indicated by scope check and verified by continuity check

⑩ Replace canister if contaminated by water, oil, etc.

⑪ Clean exhaust passages in EGR valve, carburetor spacer, and intake manifold

⑫ Check and torque to specifications

⑬ If coolant is dirty or rusty in appearance, the system should be drained, cleaned and refilled with the prescribed solution of cooling system fluid and water. Use only a permanent type coolant that meets Ford Specification ESE-M97B18-C.

⑭ Four-cylinder and V-6 only

⑮ More often if operated in severe dust conditions

⑯ "C" schedule refers to all engine displacements

Required emission systems maintenance services. Three maintenance schedules are specified, identified by the letters A, B, and C, which applies to the vehicle identified by a decal on the glove compartment door. This code also appears on the Vehicle emission Control Information Decal, which is located on the engine valve cover.

end of the inlet hose. The paper should be sucked against the hose opening with a noticeable force **after sufficient time has lapsed for the crankcase pressure to lower** (usually about a minute or more).

With The Engine Stopped

Remove the PCV valve from its mounting and shake it. A metallic clicking noise should be heard, indicating the valve is free.

If the ventilation system passes these tests, the system is functioning and no further service is required. If it fails, either of the tests, replace the PCV valve hoses and tubes. Then, check and clean and repeat the test with the engine idling. If the system still does not pass the test, clean the ventilation system.

CLEANING THE SYSTEM

Remove the PCV system components: filler cap, PCV valve, hoses, tubes, fittings, etc. from the engine. Soak the rubber ventilation hose(s) in a low volatility petroleum base solvent.

Clean the rubber ventilation hose(s) by passing a suitable cleaning brush through them. Thoroughly wash the rubber hoses in a low volatility petroleum base solvent and dry with compressed air. Thoroughly

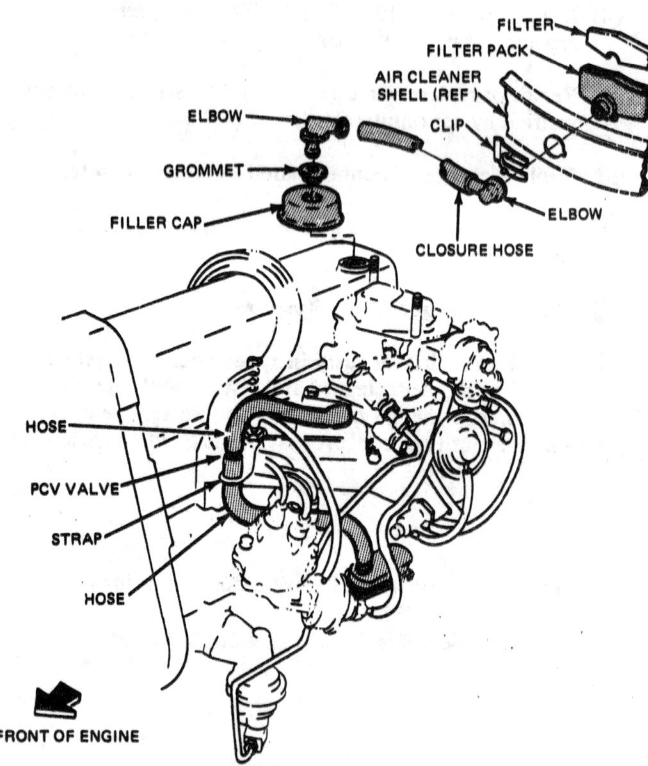

Crankcase ventilation system for the 2,300cc engine.

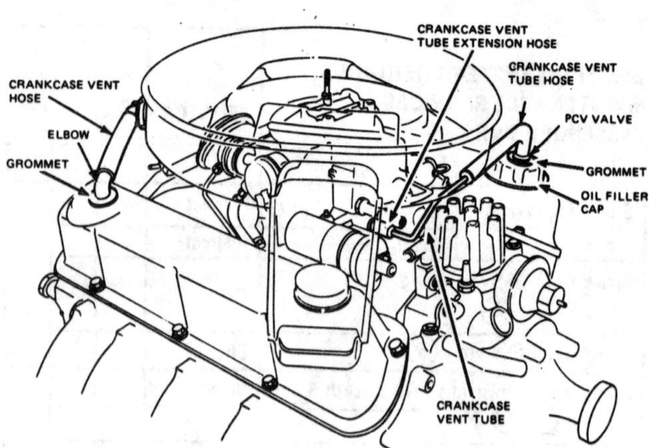

Crankcase ventilation system for the V-6 and V-8 engines.

wash the crankcase breather cap (if so equipped) in a low volatility petroleum base solvent and shake dry. **CAUTION: Do not dry with compressed air, as damage to the filtering media can result.**

Thoroughly clean all tubes, fittings, and connections to assure an unobstructed flow of emission gases.

Install a new PCV valve and re-install the hoses, tubes, fittings, etc. to their proper location. Replace any system component that shows signs of damage, wear, or deterioration. Replace any hose or tube that cannot be cleaned satisfactorily.

CRANKCASE VENTILATION FILTER

Removing

Disconnect the oil filler cap-to-air cleaner hose at the air cleaner. Remove the top of the air cleaner. Remove the crankcase ventilation filter retainer and take out the filter.

Installing

Position the new crankcase ventilation filter in the air cleaner body, and then install the retainer.

Connect the oil filler cap to the air cleaner. Install the top of the air cleaner.

HEATED-AIR SYSTEM

A sheet metal stove is attached to the exhaust manifold where underhood air is heated as it passes over the hot manifold. The heated air is conducted from the stove to the air cleaner through a flexible duct.

The use of a heated-air system does not materially affect the inducted air temperature during warm weather, but it does raise the intake air temperature in cold weather. A decreased spread in the temperature range permits the use of leaner air-fuel mixtures with satisfactory driveability.

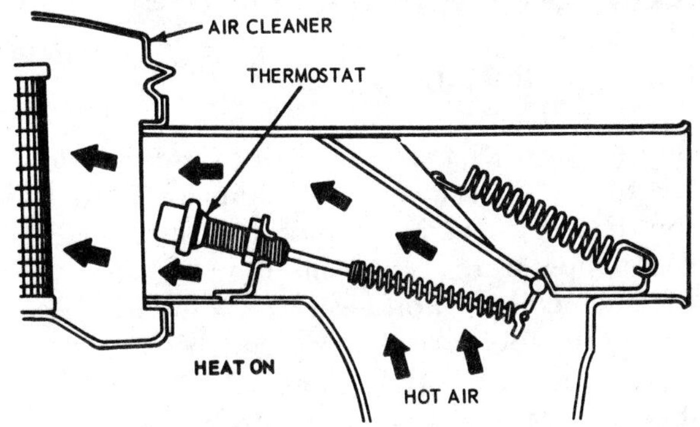

The capsule-type thermostat is used on four-cylinder engines. This drawing shows the unit in the heat-on position during engine warm-up. This unit can be adjusted by turning the thermostat body in the mounting bracket.

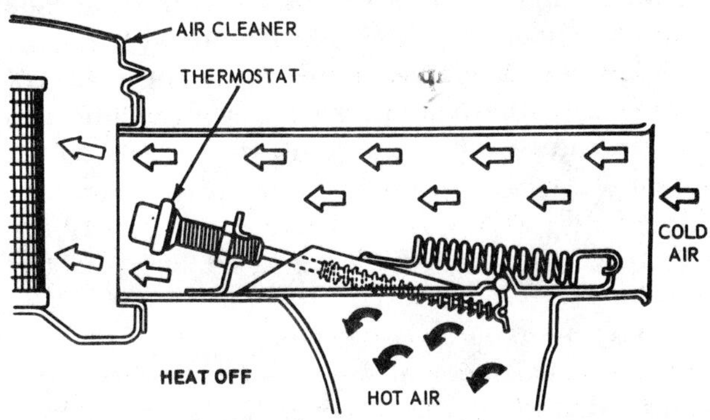

As the engine warms to operating temperature, the heated-air door moves to the heat-off position and only underhood air is admitted to the inducation system.

There are two types of control systems used on Ford engines: capsule and vacuum motor.

Capsule Type

The capsule-type thermostat is sensitive to changes in temperature. Where the incoming air is below about 100°F., the heated-air door is closed to underhood air and open to exhaust manifold-warmed air. As the temperature of the incoming air rises, the heated-air door opens gradually to admit outside underhood air, eventually blending the incoming air to about 105°F.

Vacuum -Motor Type

A vacuum motor is connected to intake manifold vacuum with a bi-metal thermostatic control unit in series with the vacuum source. Vacuum holds the heated-air door in.a position to close off all underhood air until the incoming air reaches about 105°F., at which time the bi-metal thermostat closes off the vacuum to the vacuum motor, and the heated-air door moves to the heat-off position.

At speeds above 70 mph, decreasing intake manifold vacuum and an increasing differential pressure

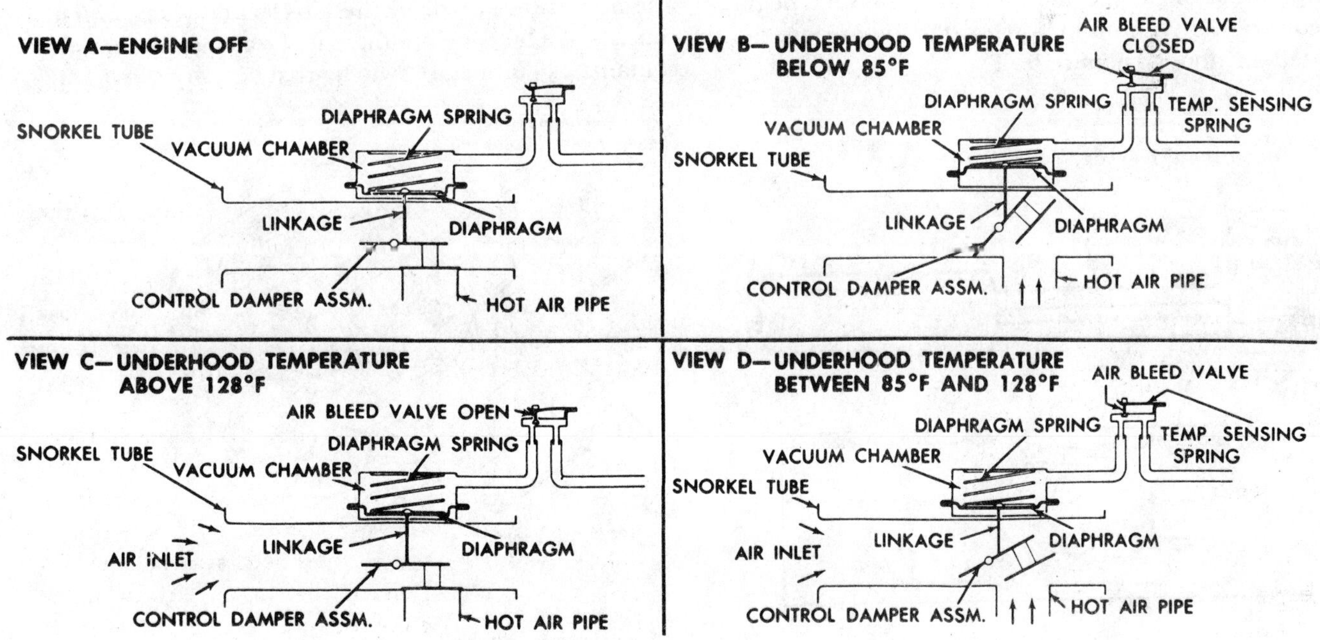

Operation of the vacuum-motor type air cleaner used on the larger engines. A quick check is to see that the heated-air door (control damper assembly) is in the heat-off position (horizontal) before starting the engine, and then shuts as soon as the engine starts.

across the temperature-controlled door cause the door to open gradually until an intake manifold vacuum of about 5.5" Hg is reached; at this time the heat-control door will be in the heat-off position, and the inducted air temperature will be the same as underhood air temperatures.

SERVICE PROCEDURES

Capsule Type

Remove the duct-and-valve assembly from the engine and immerse it in water so that the thermostat capsule is covered. Raise the water temperature to 100°F and allow it to soak at least 5 minutes to stabilize the temperature. The valve must remain in the heat-on position.

Increase the water temperature to 135°F, and the valve plate must move to the heat-off position. If the valve does not function properly, check for interference between the plate and duct, which might cause it to bind. Realign the plate if interference is evident. If the valve does not meet the specifications and binding is not present, replace the duct and valve assembly.

Vacuum -Motor Type

Check to see that the cold-air door is open before the engine is started, and that it closes immediately after starting as vacuum is built up. Then the door should open again gradually as the engine warms to operating temperature. A thermometer can be used to check the temperature of the thermostat, and this should begin to control the vacuum motor for starting to close the heated-air door at about 105°F.

AIR CLEANER-MOUNTED SWITCHES

COLD WEATHER MODULATOR

The cold weather modulator switch used on some models since 1975 is a vacuum modulator located in the air cleaner. During engine operation in cold ambient temperatures, it prevents the air cleaner duct door from opening to non-heated intake air to assist in vaporizing the fuel more quickly. When available air from the "fresh air" intake is above 55°F., the cold weather modulator does not operate.

Normally, the duct air door will be closed to outside air any time vacuum from the bi-metal sensor is applied. This occurs when the outside temperature is low enough to require heated air for carburetor intake. When the vacuum is cut off, the door will open. This occurs when the temperature rises high enough to operate the bi-metal sensor. It also happens during acceleration in cold weather conditions. When this situation is encountered, the cold weather modulator, inserted in the vacuum line between the bi-metal sensor and the vacuum duct motor, will close the vacuum to the motor and hold the duct door open to heated air.

AIR CLEANER TEMPERATURE SWITCH

Engines with Cold Temperature Actuated Vacuum systems (CTAV), and those with Thermactor systems containing catalytic converters, also are equipped with a temperature switch in the air cleaner. This switch consists of a housing mounted in the air cleaner, which contains a bi-metal switch that is operated by

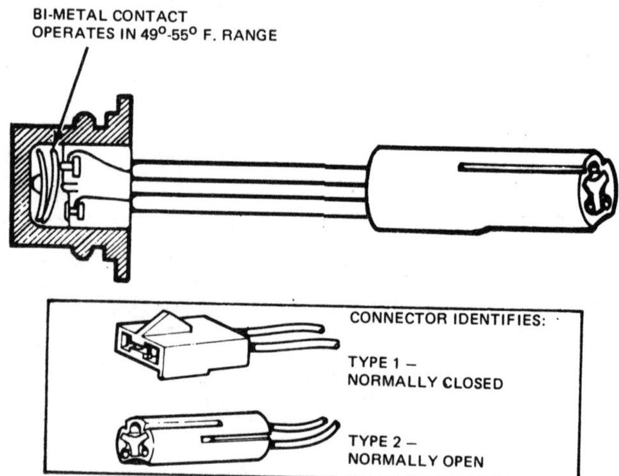

Air cleaner temperature switch located in the 1975 air cleaner of some engines. Its operation is discussed in the text.

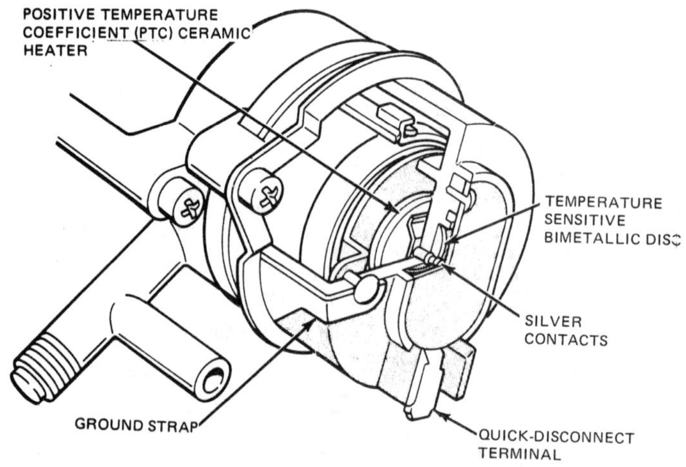

Electric-assist chokes are used on all late-model engines to minimize warm-up time in order for the engine to pass emission tests. This is the temperature-sensitive type used on all carburetors, except the 5,200-2V.

temperature changes. They are of two types, each identified by the connector to the wiring harness: Type 1 has contacts that are normally closed; Type 2 has contacts that are normally open.

ELECTRIC-ASSIST CHOKE

Late-model passenger car engines use an electrically-assisted choke thermostatic spring heater as an aid to fast choke release and better emission characteristics during engine warm-up. The heaters are of two types: temperature sensitive (all except 5200 2V) and constant operating (5200 2V). Both types operate from current supplied from the center tap of the alternator when the engine is running.

The temperature-sensitive electric choke assist

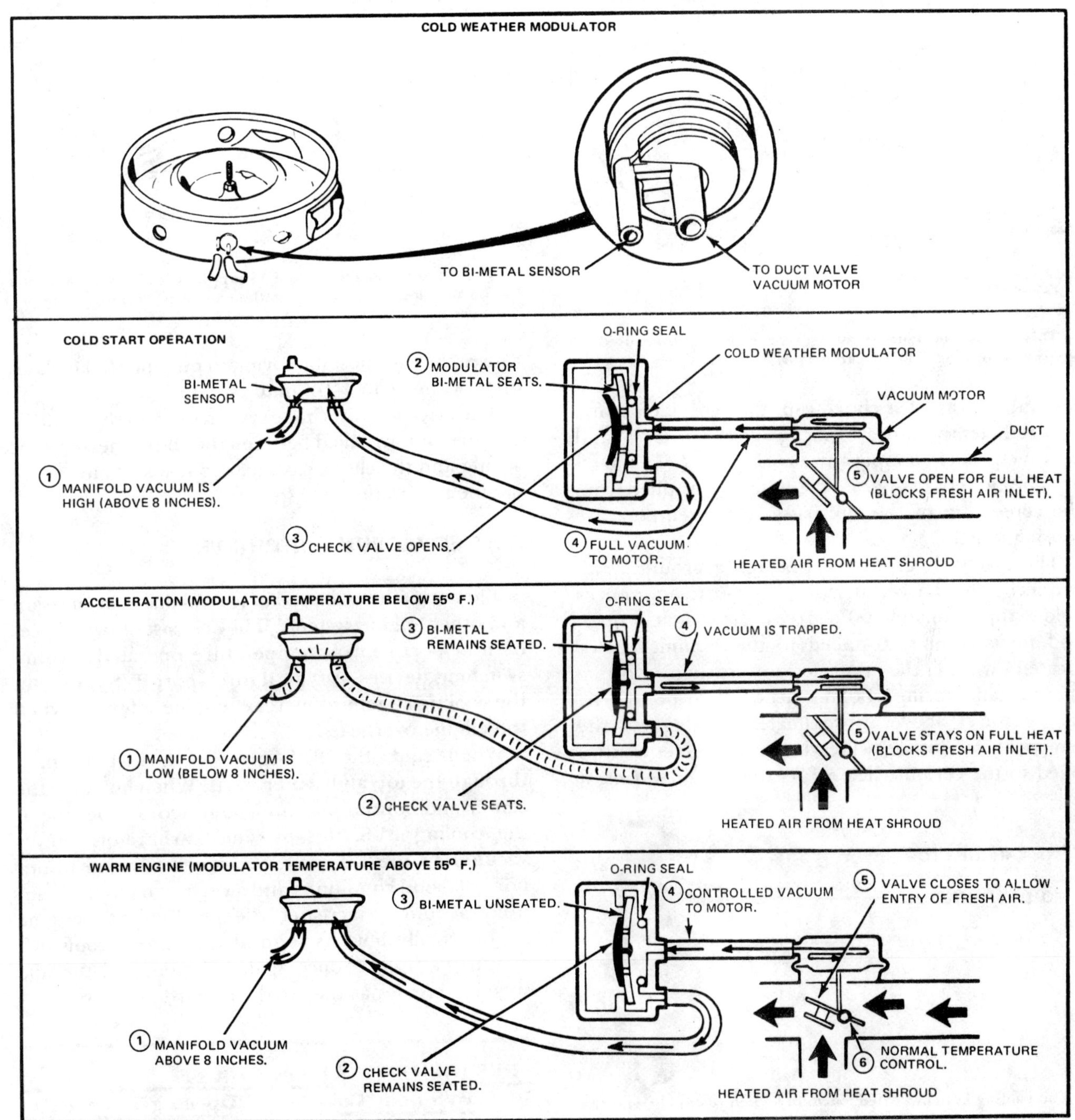

A cold weather modulator switch is used on some 1975 models to keep the heated-air system from opening to underhood air at ambient temperatures below 55° F. to assist in warming the catalytic converter quickly.

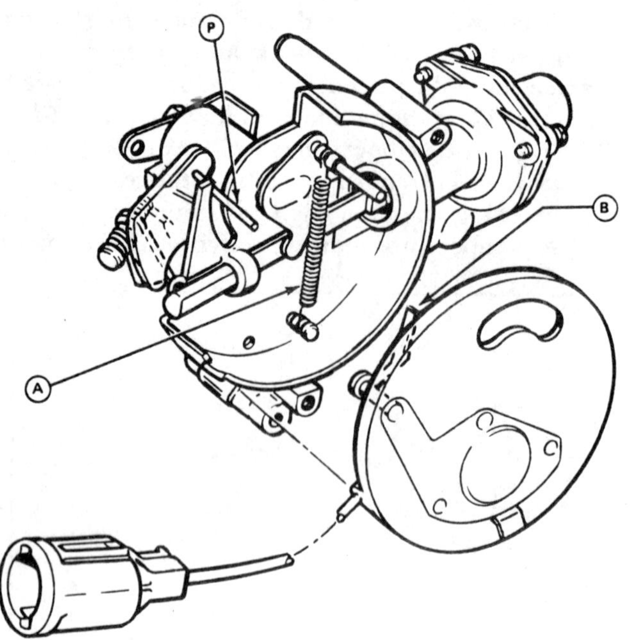

This is the constant-operating type electric choke used on engines with the 5,200-2V carburetor.

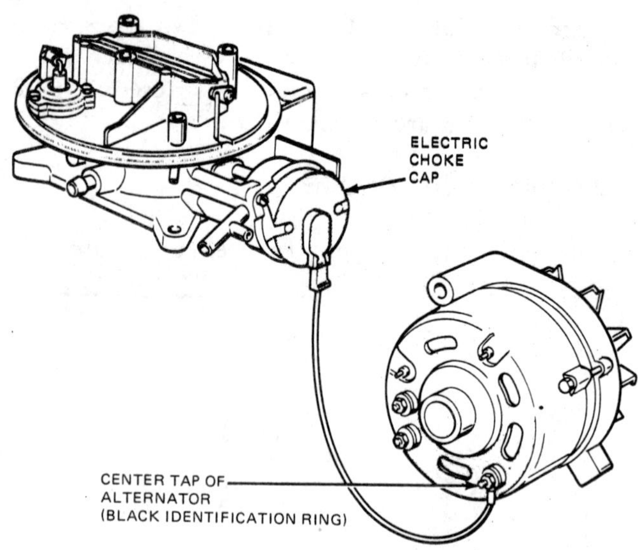

Current to the electric choke is supplied from a special center tap on the alternator as long as the engine is running.

system consists of a choke cap, thermostatic spring, bi-metal temperature sensing disc (switch), and ceramic positive temperature coefficient (PTC) heater. The current to operate the system is supplied from the center tap of the alternator to the temperature sensing switch.

The system is grounded through a ground strap connected to the carburetor body. At temperatures below approximately 60 degrees, the switch is open and no current is supplied to the ceramic heater located within the thermostatic spring. Normal thermostatic spring choking action then occurs. At temperatures above approximately 60 degrees, the temperature sensing switch closes, and current is supplied to the ceramic heater. As the heater warms, it causes the thermostatic spring to pull the choke plates open within 1 to 1-1/2 minutes.

The electric assist choke system used on the 5200-2V carburetor is installed between the choke thermostatic spring and the choke casting, and heats whenever the engine is running.

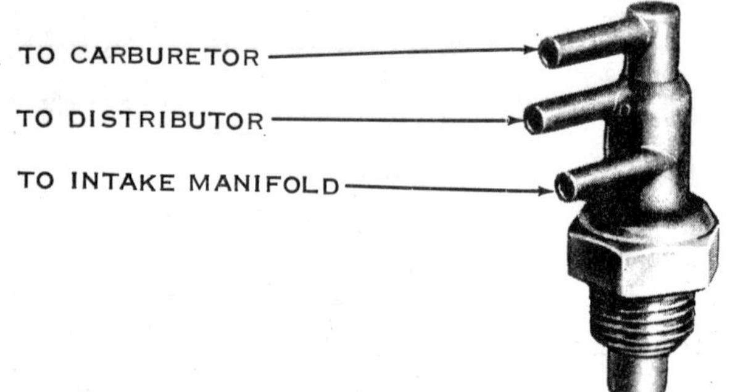

The cooling system Ported Vacuum Switch (PVS) changes the distributor actuator vacuum source from a ported one (just above the throttle blade while the engine is idling) to a direct intake manifold vacuum tap. This same type of switch (with a different temperature rating) is used to control the application of vacuum to other emission-control devices.

PORTED VACUUM SWITCH (PVS)

These switches are used in several places in emission and other engine systems. They consist of two- three- or four-port coolant temperature operated vacuum switching devices. A typical three-port PVS is used in the cooling system to increase engine idle rpm when the engine overheats.

When cold, the PVS provides a vacuum path through the top and center ports. When hot, only the center and bottom port are connected. In the case of the cooling PVS, this provides carburetor venturi vacuum to the distributor vacuum advance under normal (cool) conditions and switches to engine manifold vacuum for increased idle speed when the engine is abnormally hot. As soon as the engine cools off, venturi vacuum is once again selected, and the idle speed decreases as the spark is retarded again.

PVS IDENTIFICATION CHART

PVS Body Color	Opening Temp. (°F.)
Black	92 — 98
Blue	125 — 131
Purple	157 — 163

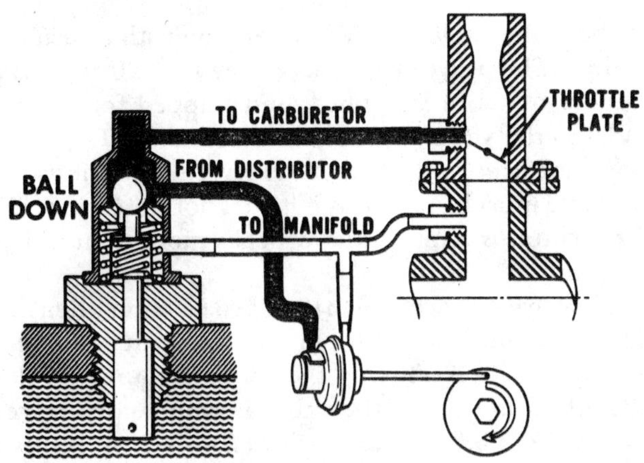

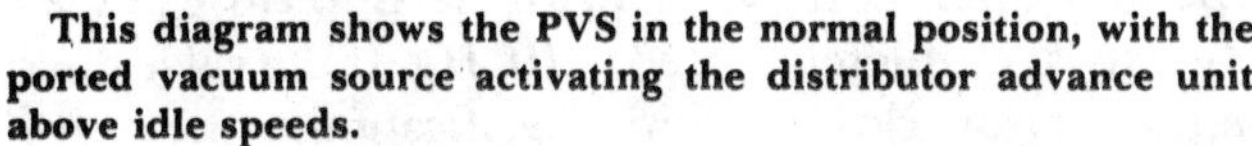
This diagram shows the PVS in the normal position, with the ported vacuum source activating the distributor advance unit above idle speeds.

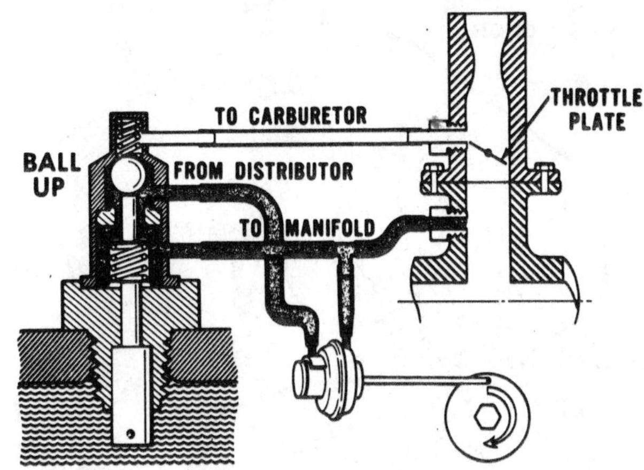

When the engine overheats and the temperature reaches 230° F. while the engine is idling, the vacuum-switching valve opens the intake manifold vacuum line to the distributor actuator to advance ignition timing and, thereby, increase engine speed for better coolant circulation.

ELECTRIC PORTED VACUUM SWITCH

The electric PVS for 1975-76 is used in some Thermactor-equipped engines that have catalytic converters in the exhaust system. It is a combined vacuum switching device and electric signalling device that is used in two versions: normally open electric contacts, and normally closed electric contacts.

HEAT CONTROL VALVE (HCV)—V-6 & V-8, 1975-76

If fuel condenses on the cold surfaces of the fuel induction system, this fuel/air ratios fluctuate. These variations can cause uneven acceleration and increased emission levels. The exhaust heat control valve is designed to provide quick induction system warm-up and better cold engine fuel/air ratio control for protection of the catalytic converter.

Since 1975, all passenger car V-6 and V-8 engines have a vacuum-operated heat control valve mounted between the exhaust pipe and the exhaust manifold. Its function is to preheat the fuel-air mixture by directing a portion of the exhaust gas upward through passages in the intake manifold during engine warm-up.

On cold starts, manifold vacuum is directed to the heat control valve (HCV) through the top two ports in the HCV PVS (ported vacuum switch), closing the HCV valve against the spring in the vacuum motor. When the engine coolant reaches a certain temperature, the PVS seals off the vacuum supply, venting the HCV vacuum motor to the atmosphere and allowing the spring to open the HCV butterfly valve. A separate PVS is used for each of three systems.

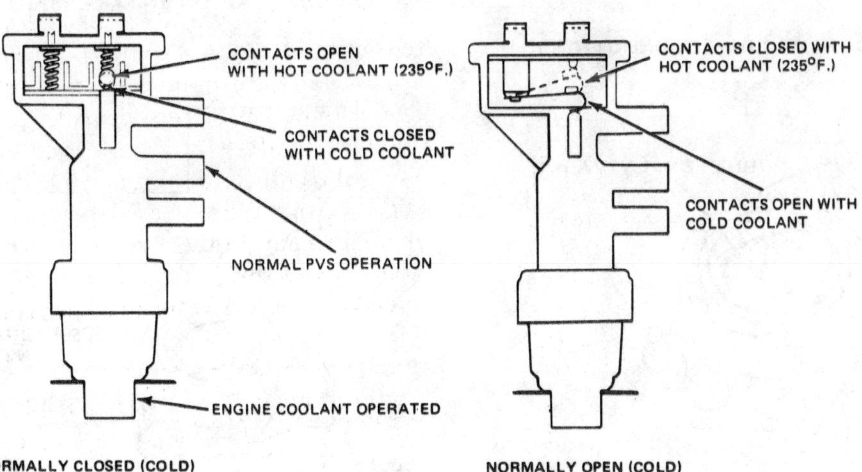

An electric-type PVS is used on some Thermactor-equipped engines. It is a combined unit that switches the vacuum source and is also an electric triggering device for other emission-control units.

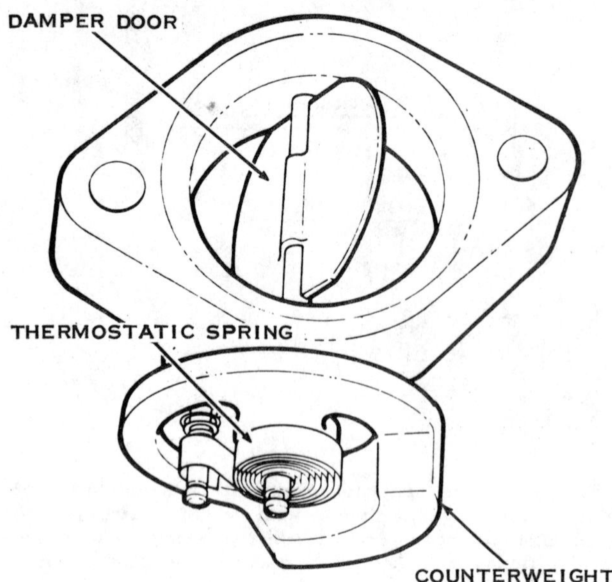

The exhaust manifold of larger engines used this type of thermostatically controlled damper to shut off the exhaust gas flow and force it through the cross-over under the carburetor for vaporizing the incoming air-fuel mixture quickly during engine warm-up. As the exhaust manifold heated, the thermostatic spring relaxed, and the damper door opened.

SERVICE PROCEDURES

Inspect the exhaust heat control valve for abnormal conditions. Inspect the vacuum hoses, connections, and manifold vacuum port for blocks, leakages, and/or proper connections. Substitute a tee for the vacuum valve. Remove the vacuum line from the heat control valve and connect a vacuum gauge. With the engine idling at normal operating temperature, the gauge should register less then 3 inches Hg. If not, replace the PVS valve.

Check the valve assembly operation with a vacuum source. The valve must close when 15-20 inch Hg vacuum or more is applied (and trapped for 60 seconds) to the valve vacuum actuator motor. The valve must not leak more than 2″ Hg vacuum. The valve assembly must be replaced if it does not close when 15″ Hg vacuum is applied and/or leaks more than 2″ Hg vacuum.

The valve must return to the open position when the valve vacuum actuator motor is vented to the atmosphere by removing the vacuum source. If the valve does not open, the valve assembly must be replaced. *NOTE: The valve is closed if the shaft lever comes within 0.065″ (feeler gauge) of the stop.* Check the valve assembly operation to see that it starts to close at 3-6″ Hg and is completely closed at 10″ Hg. If the valve does not open or close within specifications, the valve assembly must be replaced. Reinstall the engine vacuum line on the valve assembly.

Lubricate the valve with C0AZ-19 A501-A or C4AZ-19A501-A graphite lube or equivalent.

FUEL DECELERATION VALVE

Two kinds of fuel deceleration valves have been used, one through 1974 and a new model since then on some models. Deceleration valves provide enriched mixture on engine deceleration with closed throttle. When closed throttle occurs, the valve provides momentary fuel/air flow bypassing the carburetor. The deceleration valve is used with two carburetors the Motorcraft 5200-2V used on the 2.3L engine and the 2150-2V used on the 2.8L V-6.

The deceleration valve has two ports and a threaded base that attaches to the intake manifold of the engine.

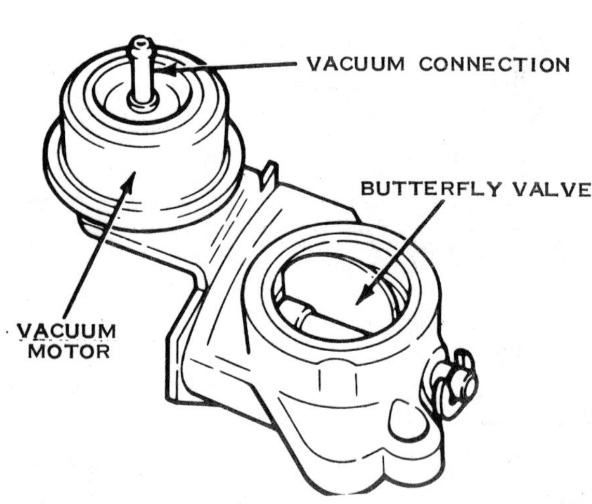

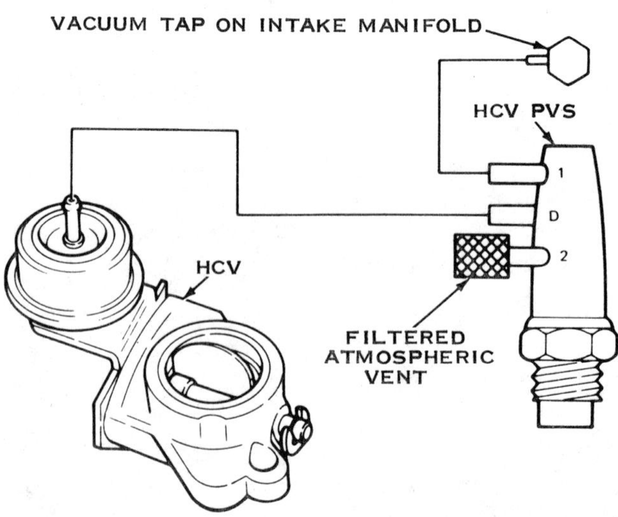

Since 1975, the heat-control valve is vacuum actuated (left) and the vacuum is temperature controlled by a special PVS as shown in the schematic hose diagram at the right.

The operation of the valve is controlled by application of vacuum to the smaller of the two side ports. When the vacuum is applied to the control port, the valve opens and pulls a fuel/air mixture from the carburetor deceleration system into the intake manifold.

On the conventional system, control vacuum is applied directly from the engine intake manifold. In this way, the decel valve will open any time the manifold vacuum reaches the specified limit and close when vacuum falls below this figure.

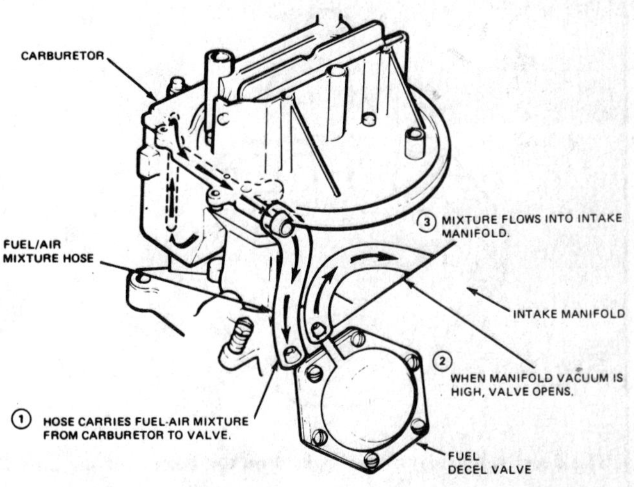

Operation of the conventional fuel deceleration system.

Speed Modulated Fuel Decel System

On some vehicles with the 2.8L V-6 engine, the fuel deceleration system is tied into vehicle speed. In this way, the system is prevented from operating when the vehicle is in a deceleration mode below 11 mph, and allowed to operate when the vehicle is in a deceleration mode above 11 mph. The interlock is designed to prevent the deceleration system from acting upon speeds below 11 mph.

TESTING

Excessively high engine idle speeds can be caused by a "hanging" valve or a mis-adjustment. Check as follows: Attach a tachometer to the engine. Operate the engine for twenty minutes at 1,200 rpm to stabilize engine temperature.

Disconnect the rubber hose between the decel valve and carburetor at the decel valve end and cap the nipple on the valve. **CAUTION: Make sure the ignition timing, idle speed, and carburetor mixtures are set to specifications.**

Increase engine speed to 3,000 rpm and hold for approximately 5 seconds; then release the throttle. If engine speed does not return to normal, check for throttle linkage hang-ups and correct, if necessary, before continuing.

Remove the cap from the decel valve nipple. "Tee" a vacuum gauge into the hose between the decel valve and carburetor. Verify that a 3/16 inch vacuum hose is connected between the small nipple on the valve to a manifold vacuum source (2300cc engines only).

Increase engine speed to 3,000 rpm and hold for approximately 5 seconds. Release the throttle and measure the time required for the vacuum reading to drop to zero. This should take from 2 to 5 seconds.

On 2300cc engines, if the valve is not within specifications, it must be replaced and the test repeated. On 2000cc and 2800cc engines, if the valve is not within specifications, adjust as required to meet specifications (2 to 5 seconds).

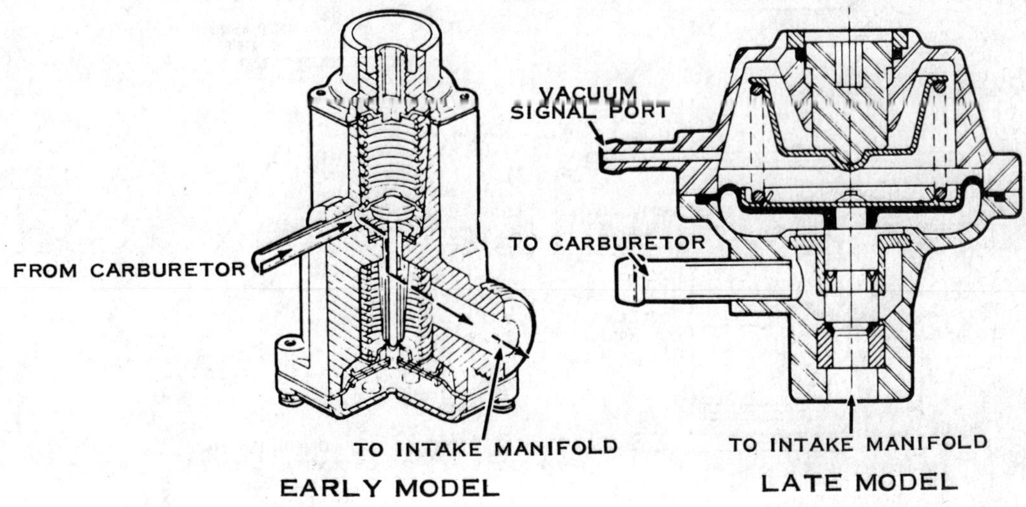

Two kinds of decel valves have been used.

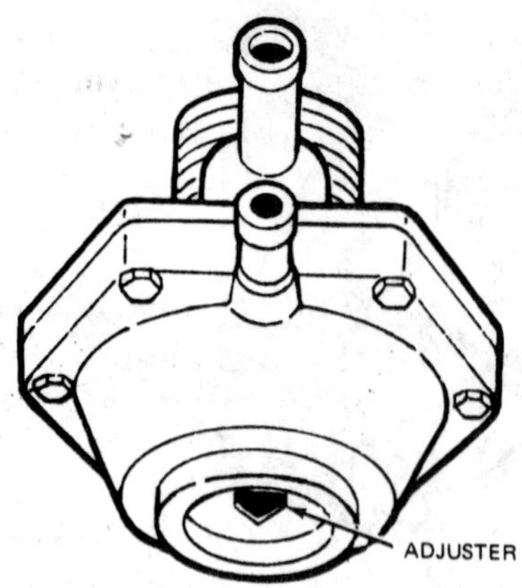

The decel valve adjuster is located on the bottom of the unit.

ADJUSTING

Turning the adjusting screw inward reduces the time the valve is open; outward increases the open time. If the valve cannot be adjusted within the limits of the adjusting screw, replace the valve. **CAUTION: If the valve closes below specifications, emission levels will be high. If the valve stays open longer than 5 seconds, excessive engine speed will be experienced.**

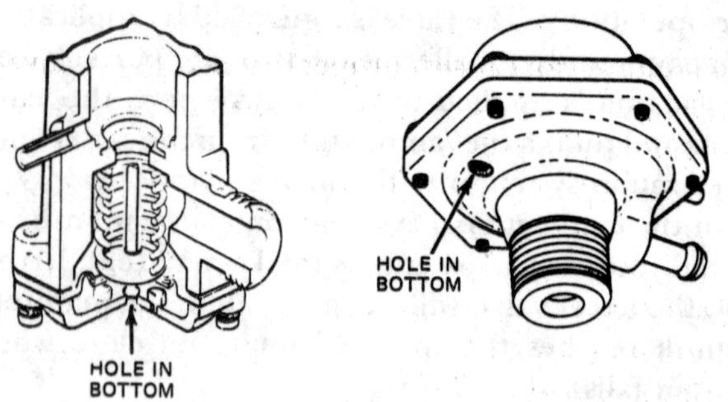

You can check the decel valve diaphragm for a leak by holding your finger over the hole in the bottom. If this changes the idle condition, then the diaphragm is leaking air and the unit must be replaced.

The deceleration valve should be checked and adjusted, if necessary, any time the engine idle speed or fuel mixture has been adjusted. This will assure that factory specifications are met for this system.

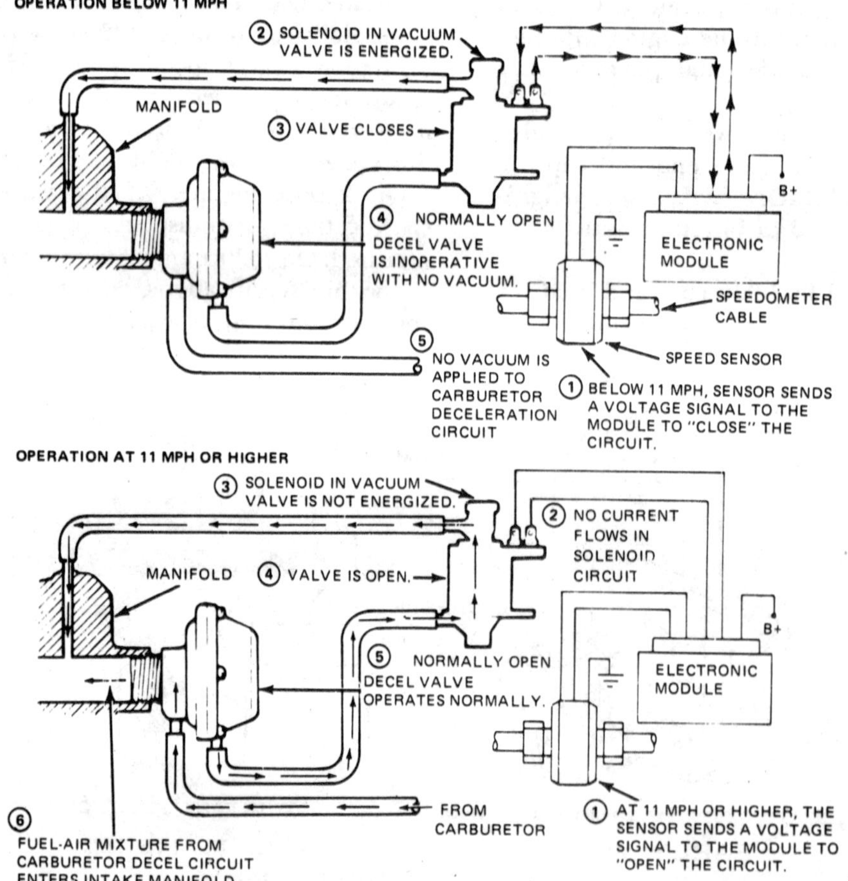

Operation of the speed-modulated deceleration system used on some 1975 engines.

Excessive advance in initial timing and/or an overly rich mixture can cause a properly functioning valve to "hang" open. Obviously, any adjustment that affects manifold vacuum also affects the decel valve opening and closing points. The higher the vacuum, the sooner the valve opens and the later it closes. When checking the decel valve, idle vacuum should not exceed 18.5 inches Hg for engines with dual-diaphragm distributors, or 19.5 inches Hg with a single diaphragm distributor.

ROUGH IDLE

Rough idle or an excessively lean air-fuel mixture can be caused by a ruptured or leaking decel valve diaphragm. Check as follows: (a) To check for a vacuum leak, place a finger over the small hole in the bottom of the decel valve. (b) Improvement of the idle quality and/or significant change in idle speed indicates the diaphragm is leaking and should be replaced.

THERMACTOR SYSTEM

A Thermactor air injection system is installed on many vehicles and on all 1975-76 models. The Thermactor System reduces the carbon monoxide and hydrocarbon content of combustion by-product gases by injecting fresh air into the hot exhaust gas stream as it leaves the combustion chamber. A pump supplies air under pressure to the exhaust port near the exhaust valve, by either an external air manifold, or through internal drilled passages in the cylinder head or exhaust manifold. The oxygen in the fresh air plus the heat of the exhaust gases, causes further oxidation (burning), which converts the exhaust gases into carbon dioxide and water.

The major components of a typical Thermactor system include: (a) Air supply pump—belt driven from the crankshaft pulley or from the alternator. (b) Air bypass valve. (c) Vacuum differential valve (VDV) with catalytic converter(s) only. (d) Air supply system-external or internal. (e) Cylinder heads with air passages to exhaust ports. (f) Air supply check valves. (g) Vacuum reservoir—on some models. (h) Air supply pump muffler.

Air Supply Pump

The belt-driven air pump takes air in through an impeller-type centrifugal air filter fan, thus eliminating the need for a separate air filter. Dust and dirt particles cannot enter the pump because these heavier-than-air contaminants are thrown from the air intake by centrifugal force.

Since 1975, the air supply pump does not have a pressure relief valve, this function being now controlled by the air bypass valve. The pump also incorporates larger ports for reduced outlet air temperature.

Air Bypass Valve

Two air bypass valves are used for 1975, one type for non-catalytic systems and an all new one for catalytic converter equipped systems.

The bypass valve used with non-catalytic systems is

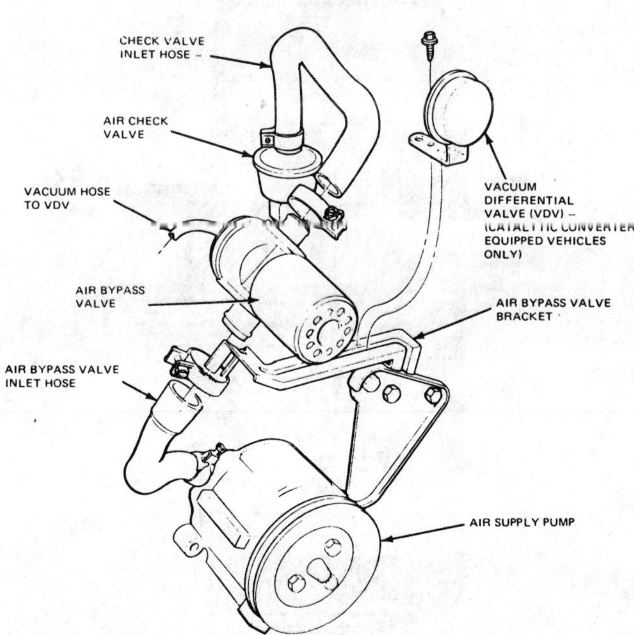

Typical Thermactor system component layout for a vehicle with a catalytic converter.

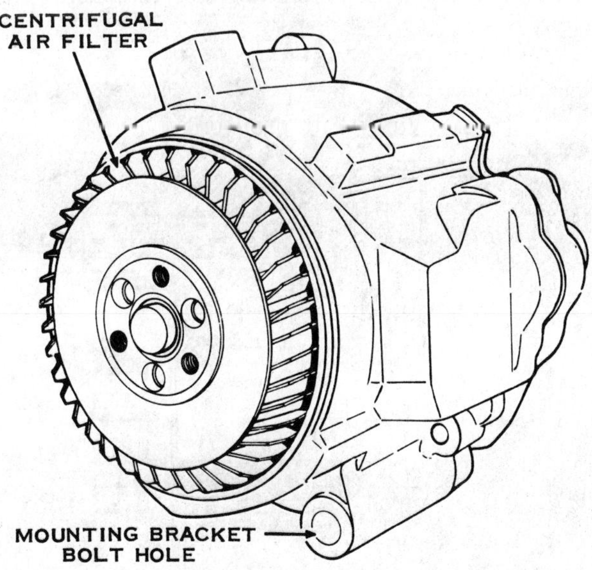

Details of the Thermactor air supply pump.

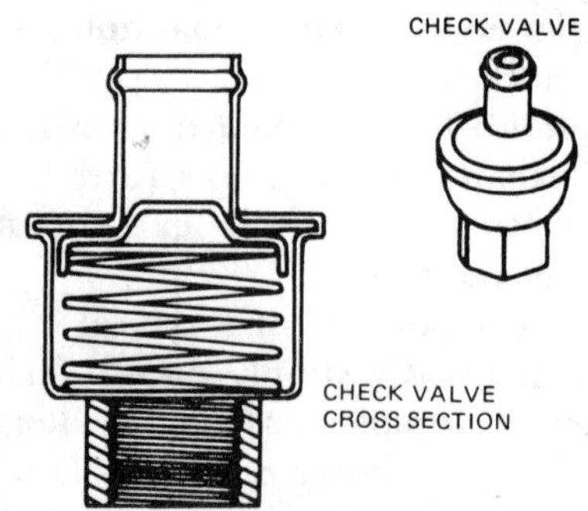

Section through the exhaust check valve used with a Thermactor system to prevent back flow of exhaust gases to the air pump, which would destroy it.

the same as used for all earlier Thermactor systems and operates as follows: During normal operation, vacuum is equalized on both sides of the diaphragm. The diaphragm return spring holds the valve closed, allowing Thermactor pump air to flow to the exhaust ports.

During the deceleration, the sudden rise of intake manifold vacuum under the diaphragm overcomes return spring pressure and pulls the valve downward. Thermactor air is then diverted to the atmosphere momentarily, because vacuum is quickly equalized again on both sides of the diaphragm through a small orifice in the diaphragm.

The bypass valve used with catalytic systems is new since 1975, and its operation differs from the other valve as follows: During normal operation, engine intake manifold vacuum, applied through the VDV holds the valve upward, allowing Thermactor air to flow to the cylinder head(s) and blocking the vent port. When engine intake manifold rises or drops sharply (such as during acceleration or deceleration, or system blockage or failure), the VDV operates and momentarily cuts off the vacuum to the bypass valve. The spring pulls the stem down, seating the valve to cut off pump air to the exhaust manifold and opening the dump valve at the lower end of the bypass valve to momentarily divert the pump air to the atmosphere. In the case of excess pump volume or a down-stream restriction, the excess pressure will unseat the valve in the lower portion of the bypass valve and allow a partial flow of pump air to the atmosphere. At the same time, the valve in the upper part of the bypass is still unseated, allowing a partial flow of pump air to the exhaust manifold to meet system requirements.

Vacuum Differential Valve (VDV)—Catalyst Systems

The vacuum differential valve (VDV) controls the operation of the new bypass valve used with catalytic-converter equipped systems.

The VDV is inserted in the vacuum control line to the bypass valve and serves to cut off the vacuum and de-energize the bypass valve. The differential valve consists of a diaphragm connected to a dump valve that controls the vacuum to the bypass valve. During normal operation, vacuum is equalized on both sides of the diaphragm and the spring holds the dump valve

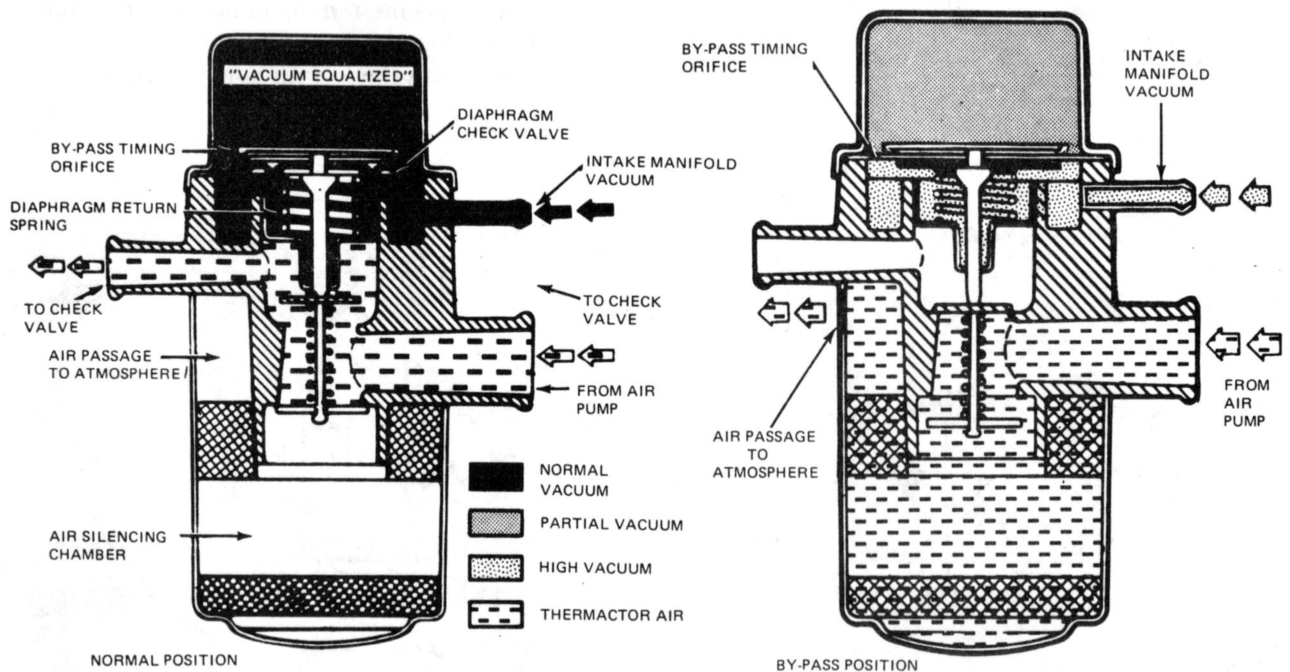

Operation of the by-pass valve used on a Thermactor system without a catalytic converter.

3 DIAPHRAGM RETURN SPRING HOLDS DIAPHRAGM UPWARD, CLOSING DUMP VALVE
2 VACUUM EQUALIZED ON BOTH SIDES OF DIAPHRAGM, THROUGH BYPASS TIMING ORIFICE
BYPASS TIMING ORIFICE
1 NORMAL VACUUM FROM SOLENOID VACUUM VALVE
4 VACUUM TO BYPASS VALVE
VACUUM VALVE DUMP
NORMAL OPERATION
CUT-OFF OPERATION
5 VACUUM FROM SOLENOID VACUUM VALVE IS RESTRICTED DURING DUMP CYCLE BY SMALL ORIFICE.
2 VACUUM DIFFERENTIAL IS CREATED BECAUSE VACUUM CANNOT QUICKLY EQUALIZE THROUGH TIMING HOLE.
1 HIGHER THAN NORMAL VACUUM FROM SOLENOID VACUUM VALVE DURING ENGINE DECELERATION.
4 VACUUM IN BYPASS VALVE LINE IS EQUALIZED TO ATMOSPHERE THROUGH FILTER, CAUSING BYPASS VALVE TO DUMP THERMACTOR AIR.
3 DIFFERENTIAL CAUSES DIAPHRAGM TO MOVE DOWNWARD, MOMENTARILY OPENING DUMP VALVE.

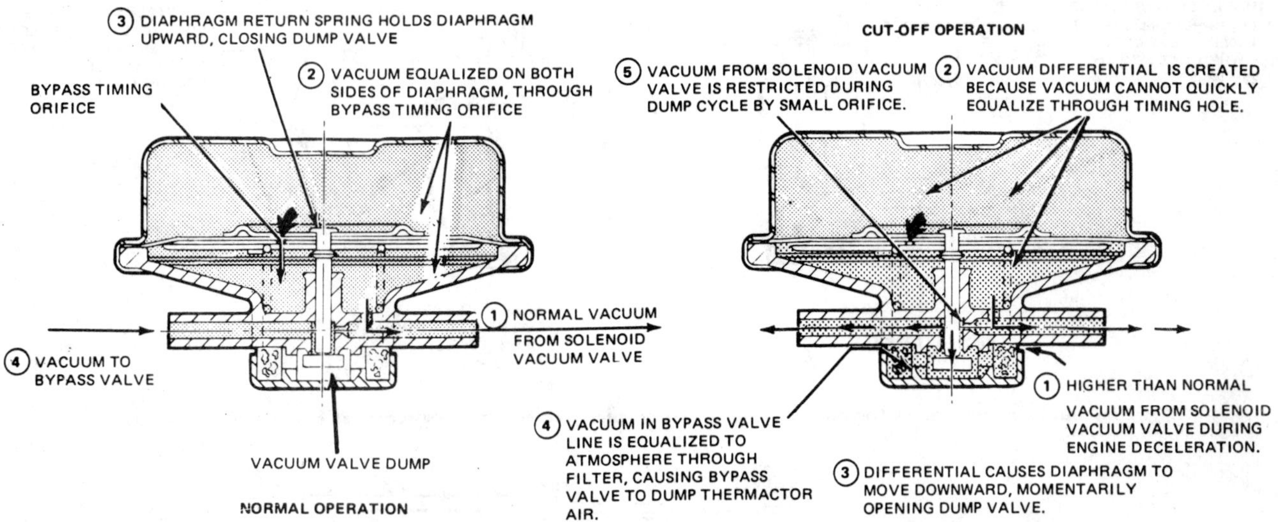

Operation of the vacuum-differential valve used on a 1975 Thermactor system with a catalytic converter. See the text for details.

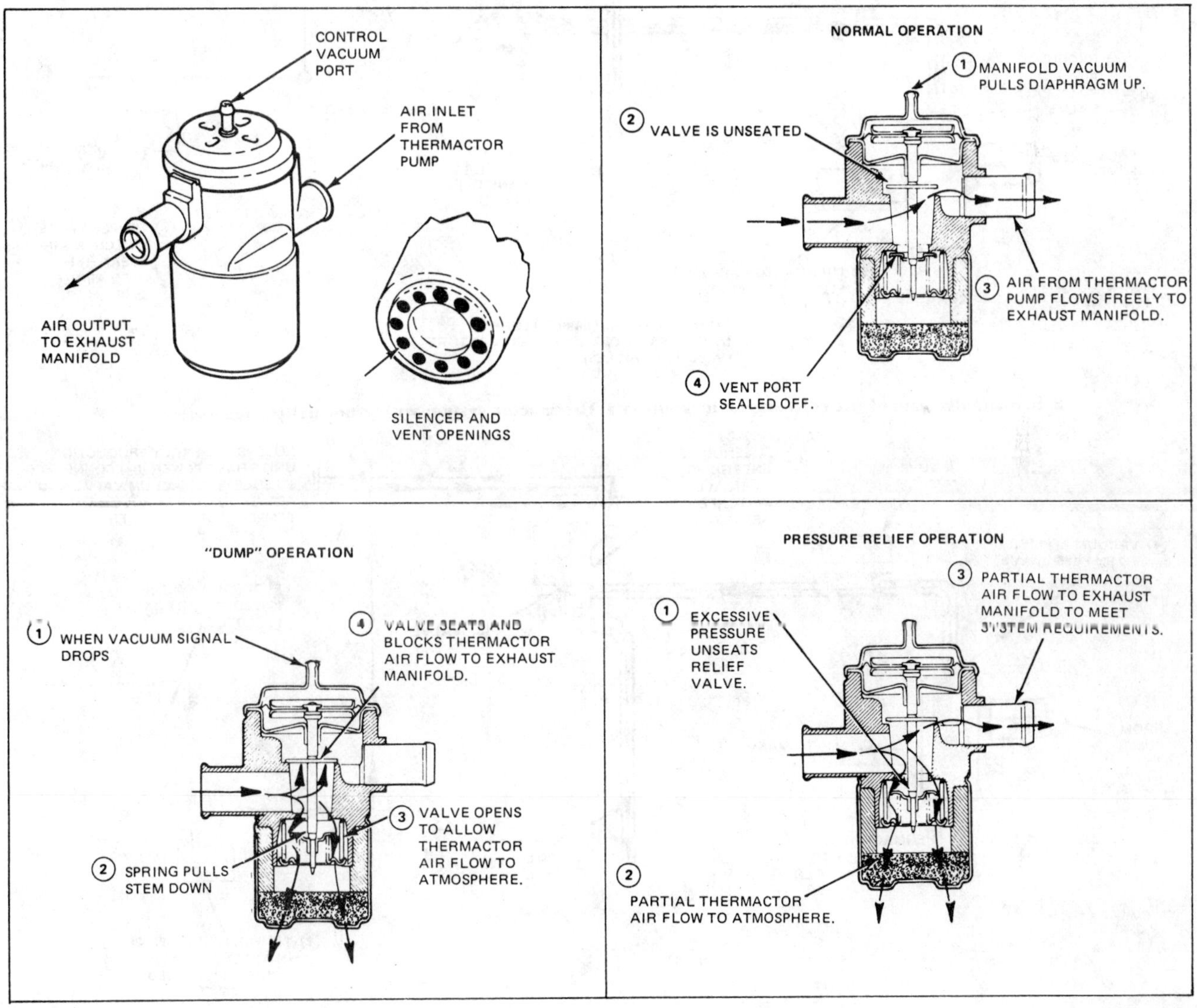

CONTROL VACUUM PORT
AIR INLET FROM THERMACTOR PUMP
AIR OUTPUT TO EXHAUST MANIFOLD
SILENCER AND VENT OPENINGS
NORMAL OPERATION
1 MANIFOLD VACUUM PULLS DIAPHRAGM UP.
2 VALVE IS UNSEATED
3 AIR FROM THERMACTOR PUMP FLOWS FREELY TO EXHAUST MANIFOLD.
4 VENT PORT SEALED OFF.
"DUMP" OPERATION
1 WHEN VACUUM SIGNAL DROPS
4 VALVE SEATS AND BLOCKS THERMACTOR AIR FLOW TO EXHAUST MANIFOLD.
3 VALVE OPENS TO ALLOW THERMACTOR AIR FLOW TO ATMOSPHERE.
2 SPRING PULLS STEM DOWN
PRESSURE RELIEF OPERATION
3 PARTIAL THERMACTOR AIR FLOW TO EXHAUST MANIFOLD TO MEET SYSTEM REQUIREMENTS.
1 EXCESSIVE PRESSURE UNSEATS RELIEF VALVE.
2 PARTIAL THERMACTOR AIR FLOW TO ATMOSPHERE.

Operation of the by-pass valve used on a Thermactor system with a catalytic converter.

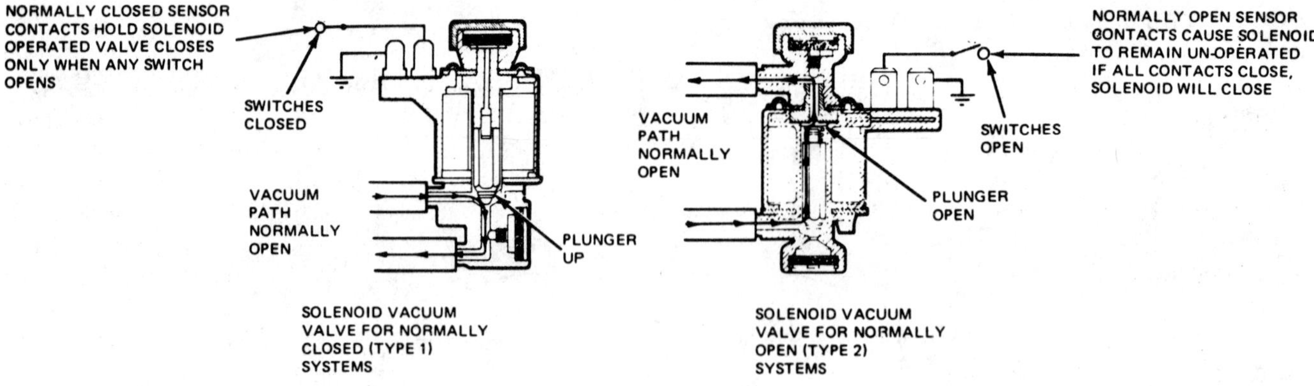

Solenoid vacuum valves for normally open and normally closed type switches, as discussed in the text.

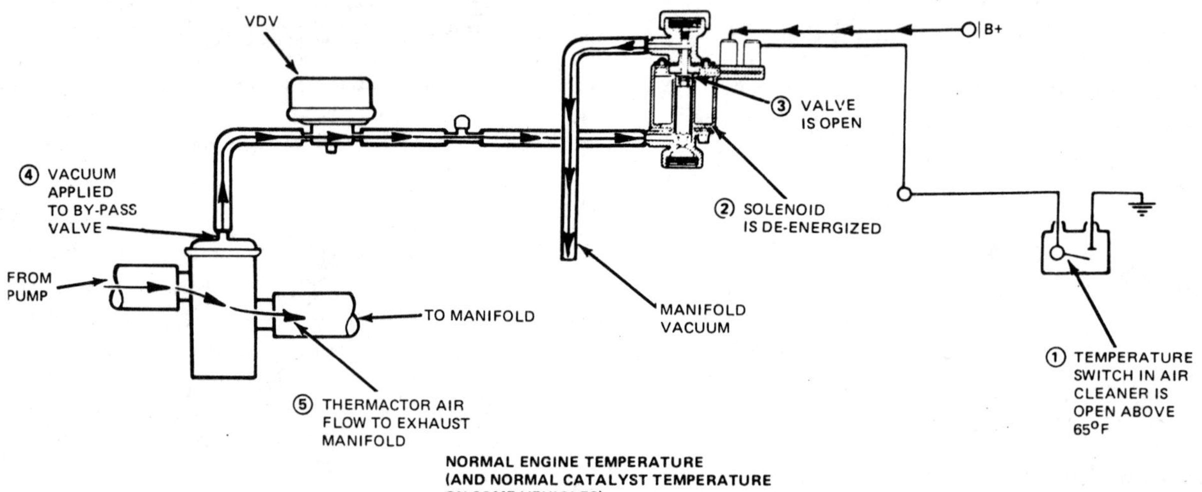

Schematic diagram of the cold-engine lockout on a Thermactor system with a normally open switch.

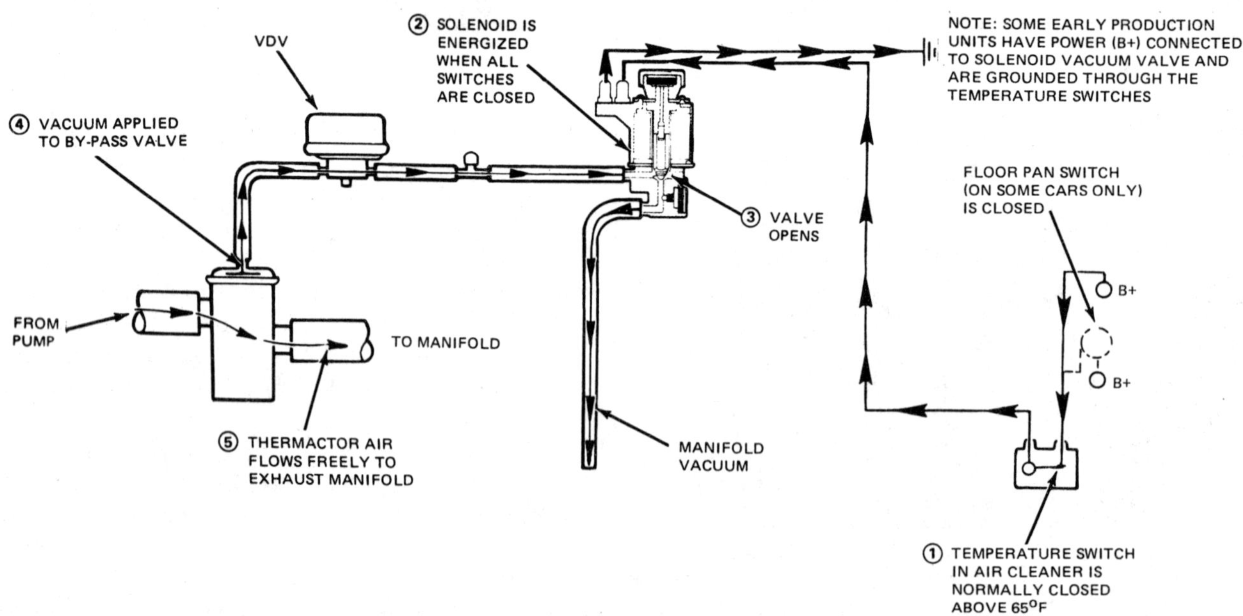

Schematic diagram of the cold-engine lockout on a Thermactor system with a normally closed switch.

closed. When sudden higher than normal vacuum is encountered, such as under deceleration conditions, vacuum is higher on the dump valve side of the diaphragm and the diaphragm operates the dump valve. As the dump valve operates, the vacuum signal to the bypass valve is diverted through the built-in filter system to atmosphere. When the vacuum bleeding through the bypass timing orifice in the VDV has equalized on both sides of the diaphragm, the diaphragm return spring once again closes the dump valve and applies vacuum to the bypass valve, which again applies pump air to the exhaust ports.

Exhaust Check Valve

The exhaust gas check valve allows Thermactor air to enter the exhaust port drillings, but prevents the reverse flow of exhaust gases in the event of improper operation of system components. The valve is located between the bypass valve and the exhaust port drillings, either mounted on the external air manifold or directly on the engine.

COLD ENGINE LOCKOUT—THERMACTOR SYSTEM WITH A CATALYTIC CONVERTER

Overtemperature protection for systems equipped with catalytic converters is provided by an electrically operated vacuum solenoid installed in the vacuum circuit to the bypass valve.

Two different systems are used: a system of normally closed switches where current is supplied to the solenoid except during engine cold conditions and a system of normally open switches where current is supplied to the solenoid only during engine cold conditions.

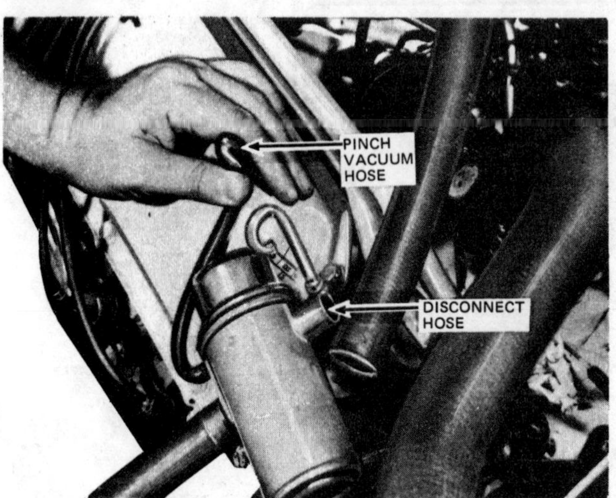

To test the operation of the by-pass valve, pinch off the vacuum signal hose with the outlet hose disconnected. As you release the signal hose, air must exhaust from the by-pass valve port for a few seconds.

Normally Closed (Type I) Switches

When the engine air intake system is at normal operating temperature, with all components functioning normally, an electrical path is provided from the battery through the solenoid vacuum valve windings, through the closed contacts of the air cleaner temperature sensor, through the closed contacts of the floor pan temperature sensor (on some vehicles), to ground. This provides a vacuum path from the vacuum source through the activated solenoid vacuum valve, through the vacuum differential valve (VDV), to the bypass valve, allowing Thermactor air to flow in the system.

If any of the normally closed switches operates, due to low intake air temperature or an overheated floor pan (some vehicles), the solenoid vacuum valve will release, breaking the vacuum path and causing the bypass valve to dump Thermactor air to the atmosphere.

Normally Open (Type II) Switches

With all components functioning normally, the solenoid vacuum valve is inactivated. This provides a vacuum path through the non-operated solenoid vacuum valve, through the vacuum differential valve (VDV), to the bypass valve, allowing Thermactor air to flow in the system. When the engine air intake system is cold, the air cleaner temperature sensor operates, closing the solenoid winding circuit through to ground.

If the solenoid vacuum valve operates, it breaks the vacuum path to the VDV and bypass valve, causing Thermactor air to be diverted to the atmosphere instead of being injected into the exhaust system ports.

TRANSMISSION-REGULATED SPARK (TRS)

In the TRS system, used on some vehicles, the vacuum spark advance is controlled by the transmission so that retarded vacuum spark timing is retained until the transmission shifts into high gear. With an automatic transmission, high gear is sensed by a pressure-sensitive switch in the hydraulic circuit. Manual transmissions employ a switch on the shift linkage. The switch opens in high gear. A three-way, solenoid-control valve is energized in first and second gears to vent the distributor vacuum-advance unit to atmosphere, at the same time plugging the carburetor vacuum port. When the solenoid is de-energized in third (or high) gear, it plugs the vent and reconnects the vacuum port to the distributor spark-advance unit. Thus, high-gear deceleration (and acceleration to 30 mph) is always with a retarded spark.

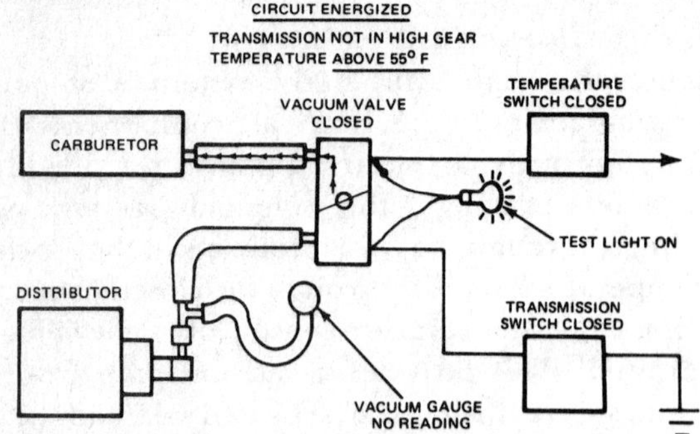

Use a test lamp across the solenoid vacuum valve of the TRS system to determine when it is energized.

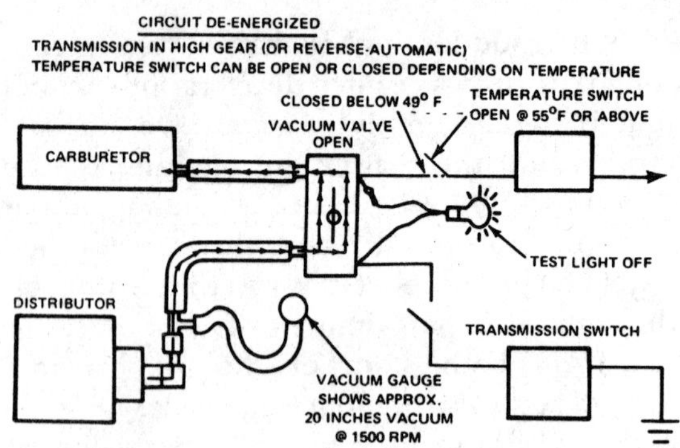

This is the result of the test lamp check across the solenoid vacuum valve when the circuit is de-energized.

FUNCTIONAL TCS SYSTEM CHECKS

A failure in the TCS system could result in either of two troubles: (1) continuous vacuum advance in first and second gears, which would prevent the vehicle from passing the federal emissions standards, or (2) no vacuum advance in third gear, which would result in loss of power and lower gas mileage.

The following checks should be made as part of each engine tune-up: Secure theparking brake and block one wheel in front and back. Hook up a tachometer and timing light. Start the engine and move the transmission selector lever into DRIVE. Increase engine speed to approximately 1,000 rpm by positioning the fast-idle cam. Check the timing mark and there must be no vacuum advance. Shift into REVERSE and there should be full vacuum advance.

With a standard transmission, depress the clutch and shift into HIGH gear, where there should be full vacuum advance.

EXHAUST GAS RECIRCULATION (EGR)

The Exhaust-Gas Recirculation (EGR) system is designed to introduce small amounts of exhaust gas into the combustion cycle to lower the peak flame temperature, and thus reduce nitrous oxides (NOx). Early systems were controlled by ported vacuum from the carburetor so that they became effective above idle speeds. As the yearly statutory limits were reduced, more sophisticated systems for controlling the amount of EGR have been introduced in later model vehicles.

TYPES OF VALVES

There are two types of EGR valves, the poppet type and the modulating type.

Poppet Type

The poppet type consists of spring-loaded

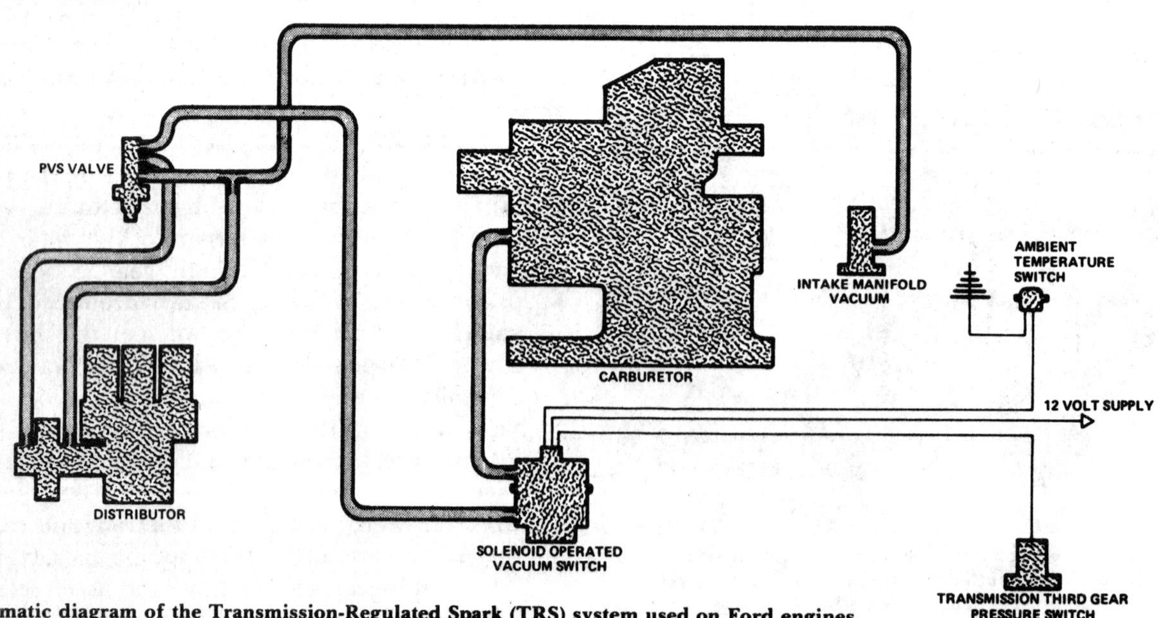

Schematic diagram of the Transmission-Regulated Spark (TRS) system used on Ford engines.

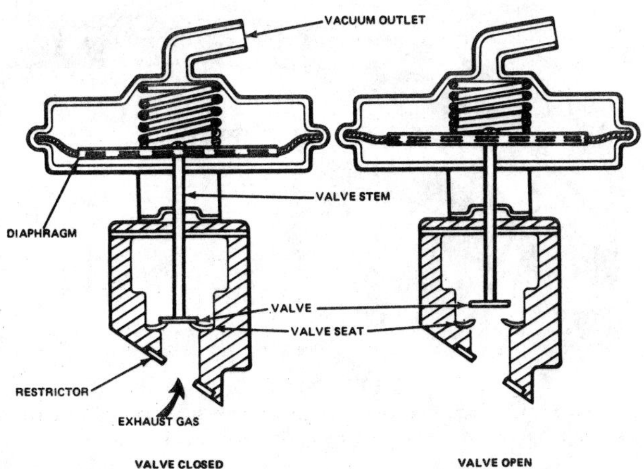

Sectioned view through the poppet-type EGR valve used on many Ford engines.

diaphragm and valve operating in an enclosed valve body. At approximately 3" Hg of vacuum, the valve begins to open. The valve stem is pulled forward, unseating the valve and allowing exhaust gas to flow into the valve chamber. Venturi vacuum then pulls the gas from the chamber into the air-fuel flow and then into the combustion chambers. Once the valve is unseated, the only means of limiting exhaust gas flow is the size of the flow restrictor placed in the inlet port of the valve body. The size of the restrictor will vary according to engine application.

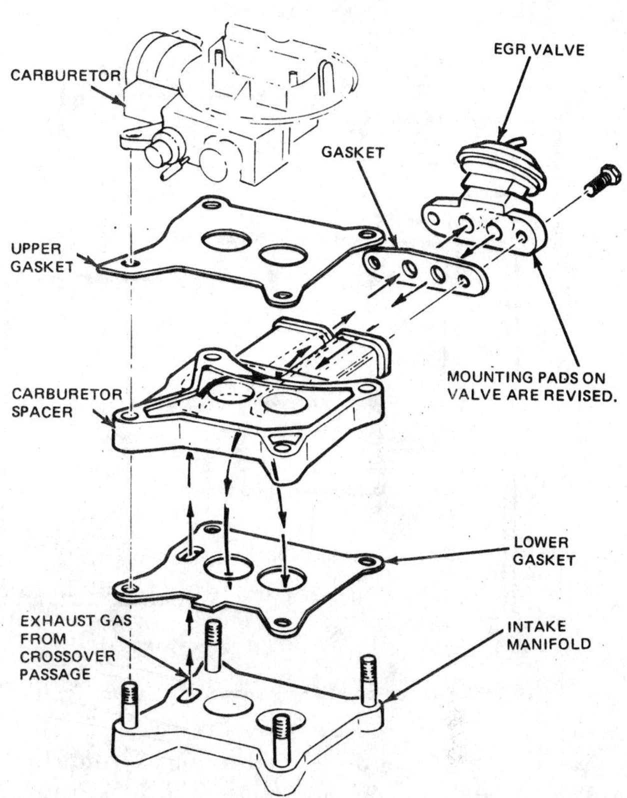

Exhaust-Gas Recirculation system and related parts.

Modulating Type

On the modulating type valve, an additional disc has been added to the valve stem below the main valve. The modulating valve operates exactly like the poppet valve when vacuum is between approximately 3" Hg

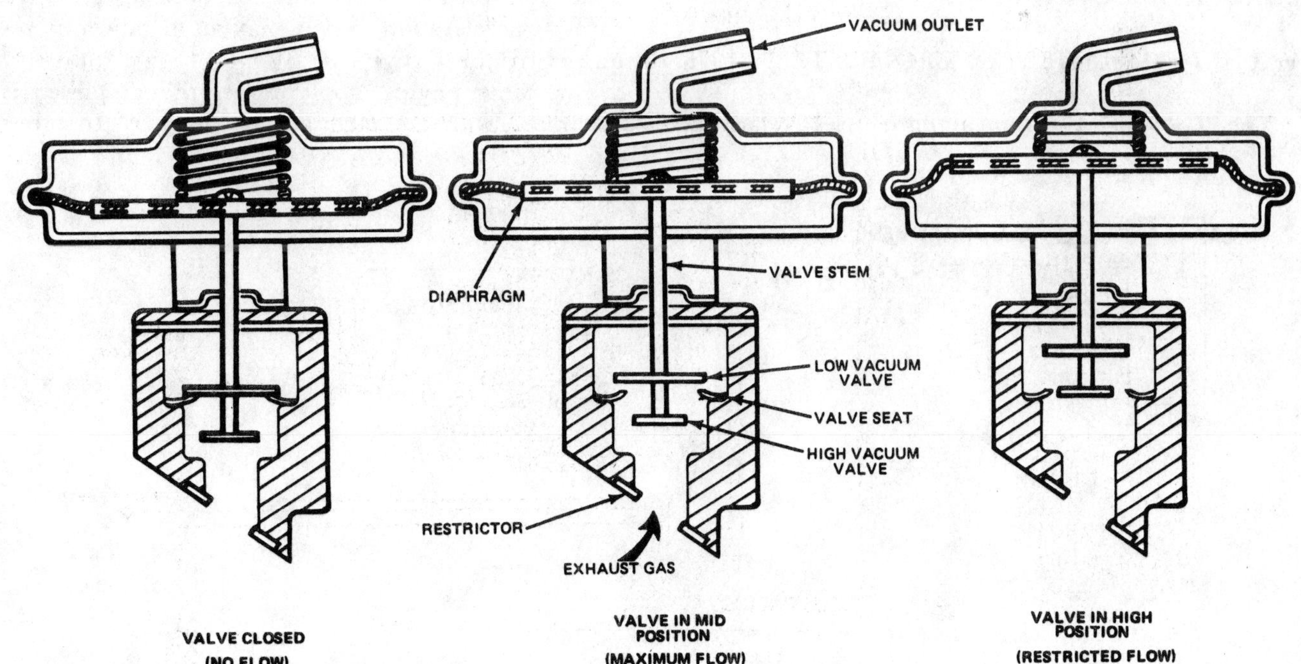

Sectioned view through the modulating-type EGR valve used on some Ford engines.

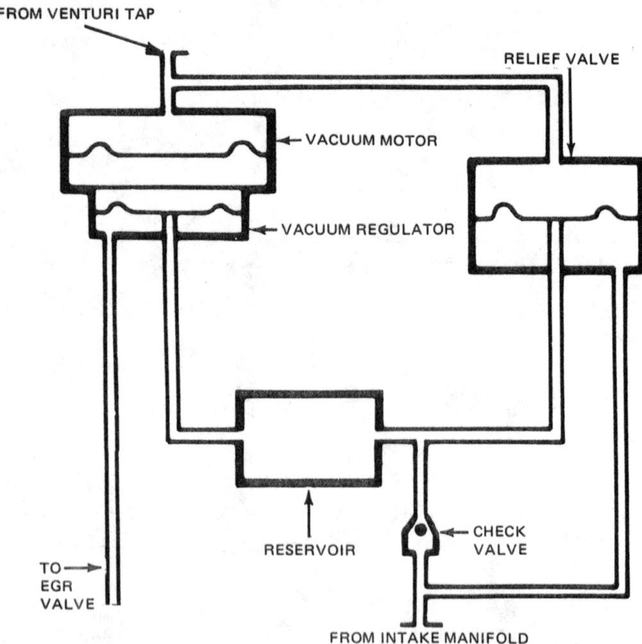

Typical vacuum amplifier schematic diagram.

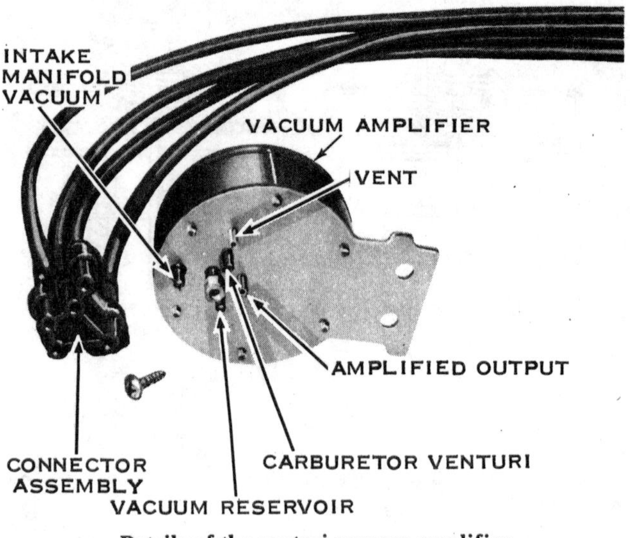

Details of the venturi vacuum amplifier.

and 10.5" Hg. When the vacuum reaches approximately 10.5", the lower disc (high vacuum flow restrictor) approaches the shoulders of the valve seat and restricts the flow of exhaust gas. The purpose of modulating gas flow is to improve driveability on certain models.

The EGR valve and vacuum control valve cannot be repaired and must be replaced if damaged.

EGR CONTROL SYSTEMS

VACUUM AMPLIFIER CONTROL SYSTEM—1975-76

The EGR venturi vacuum amplifier uses a relatively weak venturi vacuum signal in the throat of the carburetor to shape a strong intake manifold vacuum signal to operate the EGR valve. This makes it possible to achieve an accurate, repeatable, and almost exact proportion between venturi air flow and EGR flow. Thus, it assists in controlling oxides of nitrogen emissions with minimal sacrifice in vehicle driveability.

The amplifier features a vacuum reservoir and check valve to maintain adequate vacuum supply, regardless of variations in engine manifold vacuum.

A relief valve is used to "dump" or cancel the output EGR signal whenever the venturi vacuum signal is equal to, or greater than, the intake manifold vacuum. This allows the EGR valve to close at or near wide-open throttle acceleration, when maximum power is required from the engine.

For some engine applications, the amplifier is calibrated with a 2-inch Hg output bias. In other

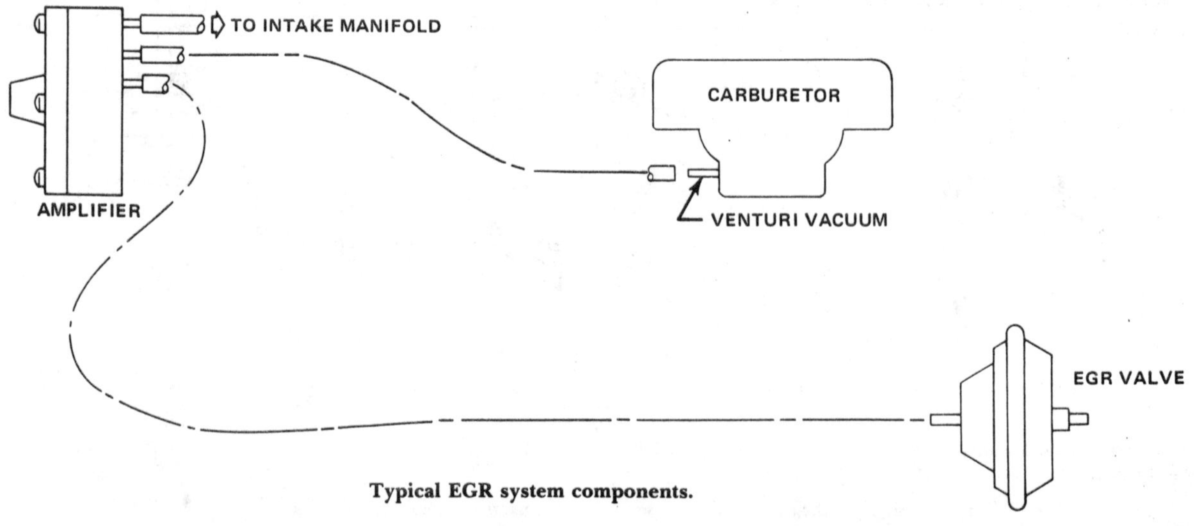

Typical EGR system components.

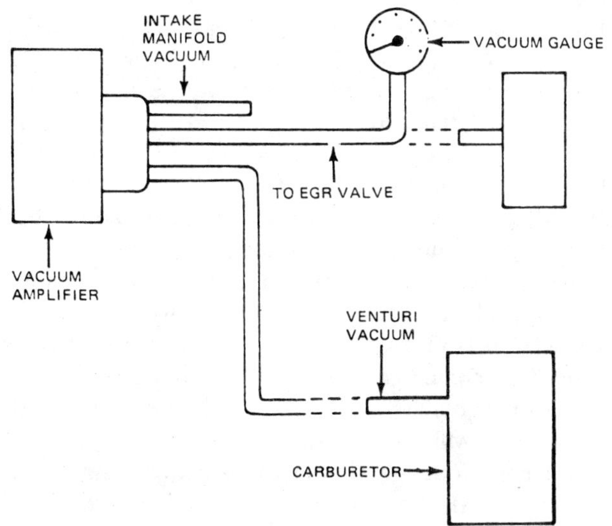

Hook-up for checking the vacuum amplifier bias.

words, when the venturi vacuum signal is at zero, the output signal already reads 2 inches Hg. This feature permits a rapid system response in overcoming the EGR valve spring closing force.

The vacuum amplifier control system has been almost entirely replaced in 1976 by either ported vacuum control or a back-pressure transducer valve.

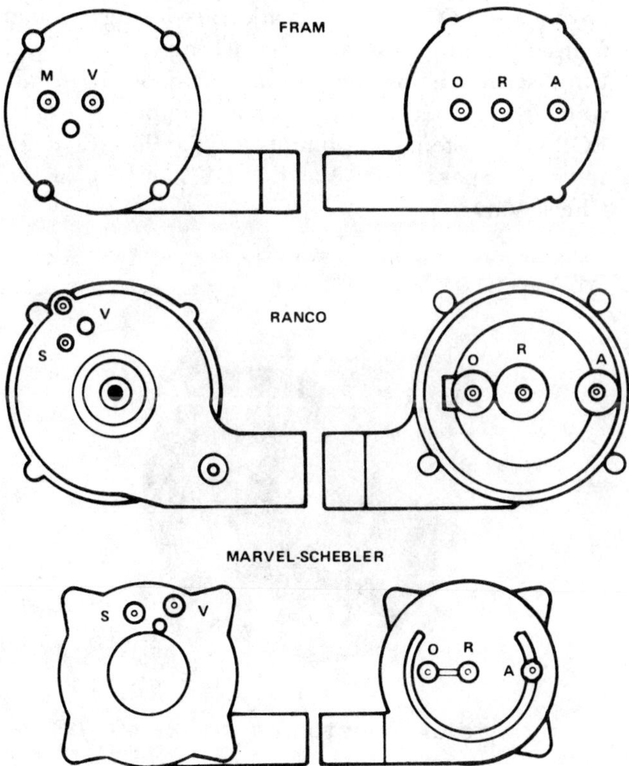

Venturi vacuum amplifiers of the dual-connection type. (O) Output to EGR valve, (R) from reservoir, (S) vacuum source, spark or EGR port, (V) venturi vacuum, (A) atmospheric vent.

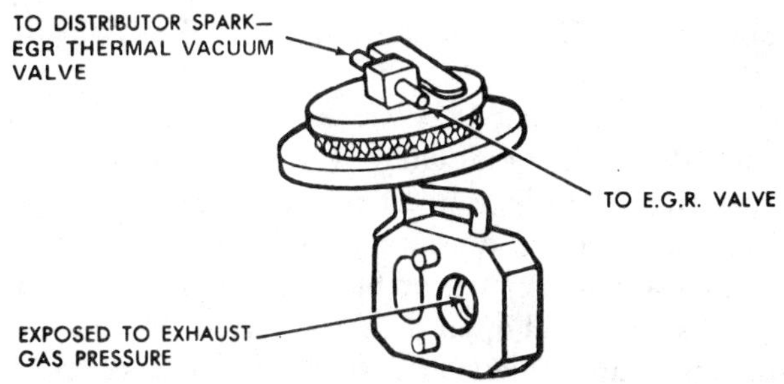

Exhaust back-pressure transducer used for modulating the EGR valve

BACK-PRESSURE TRANSDUCER VALVE

To achieve improvements in engine performance and fuel economy, a control valve (transducer) is incorporated into the system to vary the EGR in proportion to exhaust back pressure.

The control valve works as follows: At idle and very light engine loads, the EGR source vacuum will vary from minimal to manifold vacuum, but the exhaust pressure is not sufficient to overcome the transducer spring force and the vacuum source is bled off through a transducer bleed port thereby leaving the EGR valve closed. At very heavy engine loads (e.g. WOT), the exhaust pressures are high enough to close the EGR vacuum bleed port in the transducer, but manifold and EGR source vacuum will be insufficient

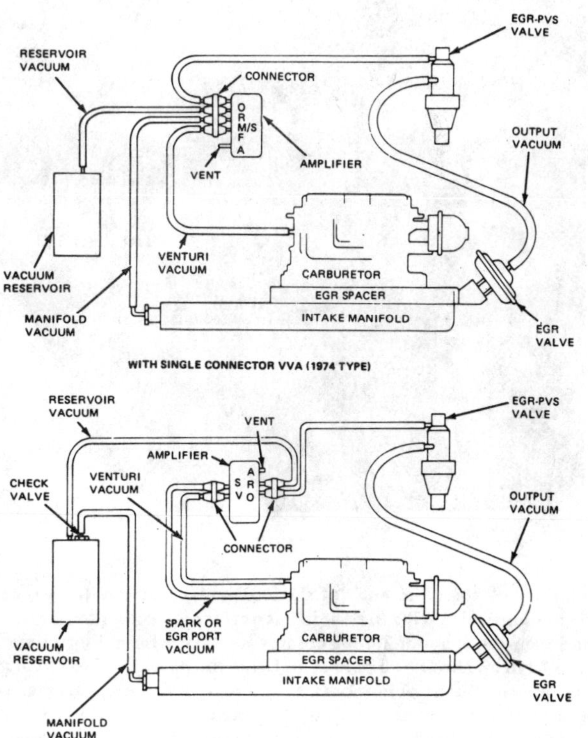

Typical EGR system components.

to open the EGR valve, therefore the EGR will be virtually inoperative.

The operational mode between the idle and WOT is when EGR flow is modulated by the transducer. The exhaust pressure will be great enough to overcome the spring force on the diaphragm and start closing or close the transducer vacuum bleed port. The resulting output vacuum will open the EGR valve. As the EGR valve opens and flow starts, there will be a drop of exhaust pressure to the transducer due to intake manifold vacuum being imposed on the pressure probe cavity. The transducer and EGR valve will tend to seek a balanced condition, providing optimum EGR for this set of exhaust and source vacuum conditions. Any increase or decrease in load will cause the transducer and EGR valve to re-stabalize at a greater or less EGR flow.

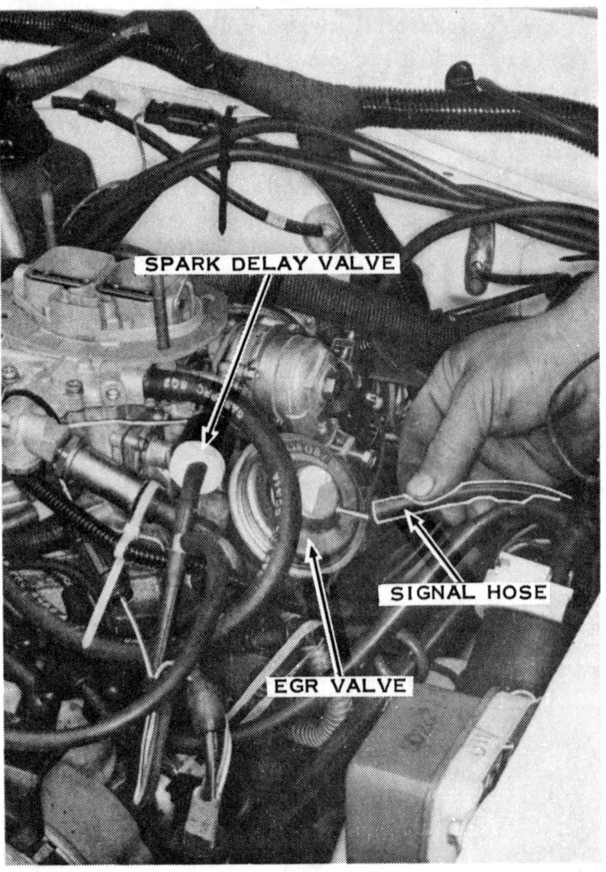

To check the efficiency of the EGR valve, remove the vacuum signal hose and, with the engine at normal operating temperature and running at about 2,000 rpm, reconnect the hose. Engine speed should drop about 200 rpm to indicate the passage of exhaust gas into the combustion chambers. If engine speed doesn't drop as you add EGR, then either you don't have a vacuum signal in the hose, which can be checked by holding your finger over the opening, or the valve is defective. If you don't have vacuum with a warm engine, then the EGR control system is not operating.

TESTING THE EGR SYSTEM

Run the engine until operating temperature is reached so that any thermostatic control units are functioning properly. Operate the engine at about 1,500 rpm, and then open the throttle sharply for a moment. The stem of the EGR valve should move back and forth to indicate that it and its control system is functioning properly. You can see the valve stem move or you can feel under the diaphragm with your finger to check it. **CAUTION: The valve can get rather hot from the exhaust gases so use caution in handling it.**

Another quick test is to disconnect the vacuum hose to the EGR valve. With the engine running at about 1,500 rpm (engage the fast-idle cam), connect and disconnect the hose at the valve. When the hose is connected, engine speed should drop 200-300 rpm to reflect the entrance of exhaust gas and it should speed up when you disconnect the hose. If it doesn't function properly, check the end of the hose to see that you do have vacuum present. If not, then the control system is defective.

EGR/CSC SYSTEM—SINCE 1974

The EGR/CSC (Exhaust-Gas Recirculating/Coolant Spark Control) system regulates both distributor spark advance and EGR valve operation according to coolant temperature by sequentially switching vacuum signals for ease in starting the engine and good driveability when it is cold. It is not used on all engines. The major EGR/CSC system components are: (a) 95°F EGR-PVS valve, (b) Spark Delay Valve, (SDV), and (c) Vacuum Check Valve.

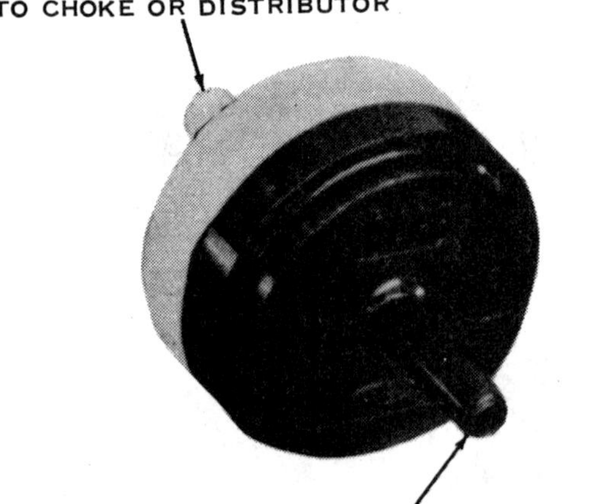

The Spark-Delay Valve (SDV) is used to delay the application of vacuum to the distributor vacuum advance unit on some engines to minimize the formation of NOx. CAUTION: The valve must always be installed with the black side to the vacuum source.

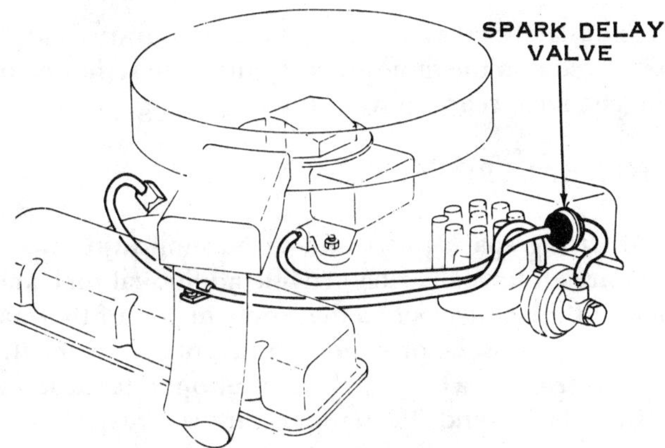

Typical Spark-Delay Valve installation.

To check the efficiency of the spark-delay valve, tee in a vacuum gauge between the valve and the distributor vacuum-advance unit. Vacuum should build up slowly, depending on the color of the valve, as long as you maintain an even throttle opening. If the vacuum doesn't build up, then the valve is plugged and must be replaced.

When engine coolant temperature is below 82°F, the EGR-PVS valve admits carburetor EGR port vacuum (occuring at about 2,500 rpm) directly to the distributor advance diaphragm, through the one-way check valve. At the same time, the EGR-PVS valve shuts off carburetor EGR vacuum to the EGR valve and transmission diaphragm.

When engine coolant temperature is 95°F and above, the EGR-PVS valve is actuated and directs carburetor EGR vacuum to the EGR valve and transmission instead of the distributor. At temperatures between 82°F and 95°F, the EGR-PVS valve may be open, closed, or in mid position.

The SDV valve delays carburetor spark vacuum to the distributor advance diaphragm by restricting the vacuum signal through the SDV valve for a predetermined time. During normal acceleration, little or no vacuum is admitted to the distributor advance diaphragm until acceleration is completed, because of (1) the time delay of the SDV valve and (2) the rerouting of EGR port vacuum, if the engine coolant temperature is 95°F or higher. The check valve blocks

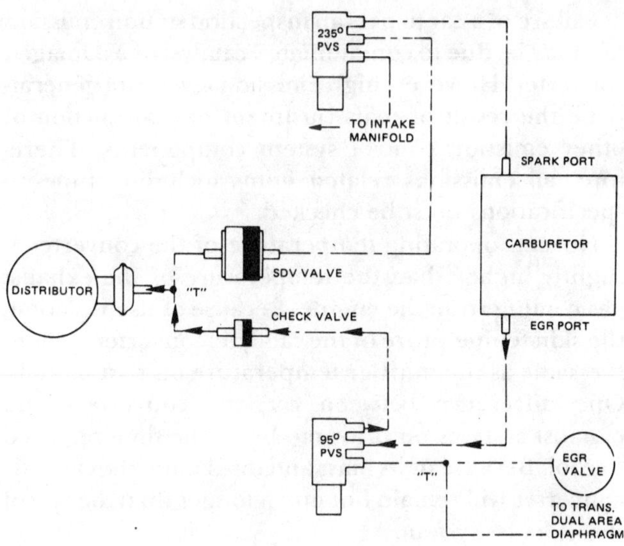

Operation of the EGR/CSC system below 82° F. Note that vacuum reaches the distributor through the 95° PVS and check valve while the engine is cold, by-passing the SDV circuit.

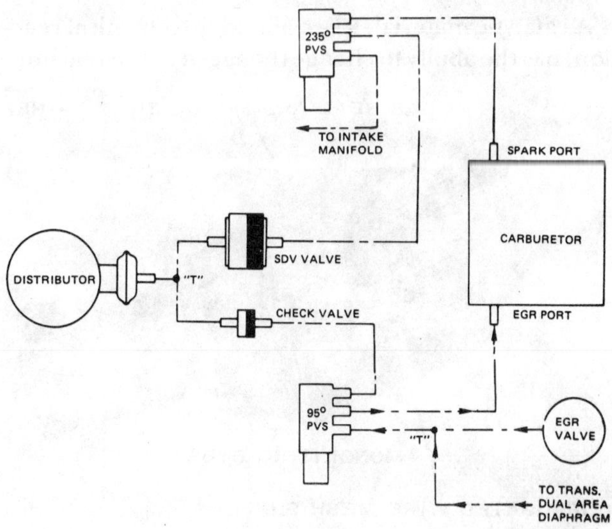

Operation of the EGR/CSC system above 95° F. The 95° PVS shuts off the vacuum source through the check valve, and the SDV delays vacuum to the distributor actuator to minimize the formation of NOx.

TYPE VALVE	I.D.#	TIME IN SECONDS MINIMUM	MAXIMUM
BLACK & GRAY	1	1	4
BLACK & BROWN	2	2	5
BLACK & WHITE	5	4	12
BLACK & YELLOW	10	5,8	14
BLACK & BLUE	15	7	16
BLACK & GREEN	20	9	20
BLACK & ORANGE	30	13	24
BLACK & RED	40	15	28

Spark-Delay Valves and the time in seconds that they delay the application of vacuum to the distributor actuator.

off any vacuum signal from the SDV to the EGR-PVS so that carburetor spark vacuum will not be dissipated when the EGR-PVS is actuated above 95°F.

The 235°F PVS is not part of the EGR/CSC system, but is connected to the distributor vacuum advance to prevent engine overheating while idling (as on previous models). At idle speed, no vacuum is generated at either the carburetor spark port or EGR port, and engine timing is fully retarded. When engine coolant temperature reaches 235°F, however, the valve is actuated to admit intake manifold vacuum to the distributor advance diaphragm. This advances engine timing and speeds up the engine. The increase in coolant flow and fan speed lowers engine temperature.

CATALYTIC CONVERTERS—SINCE 1975

A catalytic converter system provides for one or more containers filled with chemical compounds through which the exhaust gases are passed as they move out of the engine. The catalyst is composed of noble metals, platinum and palladium, both rare and expensive.

A catalytic material, when added to a chemical reaction, has the ability to change the speed of the reaction.

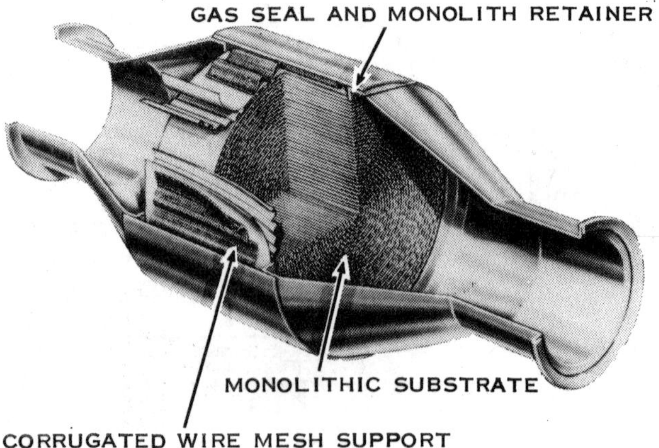

The catalytic converter changes HC and CO emissions into carbon dioxide and water via contact with noble metal catalysts. The platinum is deposited on the surfaces of the honeycomb-like substrate.

While a catalyst may undergo some temporary change, it is present in the same quantity and state at the end of the chemical reaction as at the beginning.

THERMAL PROTECTION

Misfiring spark plugs and carburetor adjustments that are abnormally rich provide additional fuel, and heat, to the converter so that some means of thermal protection must be provided to prevent destroying the unit. Normally, a catalytic converter operates at about 1400-1500°F., and this temperature will rise to about 2000°F. if two spark plugs are shorted out at 30 mph. Total ignition failure at 30 mph will cause the temperature to rise to about 2800°F. With the melting point of the catalyst about 2000°F., it is quite evident that some form of thermal protection is needed. A thermal sensor is used to control the output of the Thermactor pump during warmup, and this controls the oxidation process and, therefore, the operating temperature.

CATALYTIC CONVERTER INFORMATION

A converter may gradually lose effectiveness during its life, but this change will not cause engine performance problems.

Leaded gas should not be used, but in an emergency, a small amount of leaded gas may be used. The pellets will recover most of their effectiveness with the return to unleaded gas. Each time leaded gas is used the pellets lose more of their effectiveness until they are contaminated beyond recovery.

Failure of a car to pass an inspection station emission test may be due to contaminated catalyst or a damaged converter. However, high emission levels will generally be the result of maladjustment or malfunction of other emission control system components. Therefore, all emissions related items including tune-up specifications must be checked.

Normal operating temperature of the converter is slightly higher than the temperature of the exhaust gas coming from the engine. Because of its insulation, the skin temperature of the catalytic converter is about the same as the muffler temperature on past models. One difference between catalytic converters and exhaust systems on prior models is the time required to cool. Because of its mass and insulation, the catalytic converter will remain hot much longer than the rest of the exhaust system.

Moderate oil consumption (for example 500 mile-qt.) will not harm the catalyst. The continuous use of supplemental fuel additives is not recommended. However, if a supplemental fuel additive is to be used for a specific operational reason, first ascertain that the additive manufacturer warrants the product and states that it may be used in vehicles equipped with catalytic converters without harming the catalyst.

Use of a starting fluid will not harm the catalyst.

Some burning of transmission fluid in the engine may be related to a transmission vacuum modulator leak. The burning of this fluid will not harm the catalyst as long as the fluid does not foul the spark plugs.

In an emergency, use of a few gallons of leaded fuel will not seriously impair the catalyst. Continued use of leaded fuel will greatly decrease the effectiveness of the catalyst, but it will not plug the catalytic converter or in any way restrict the exhaust system. Leaded fuel will not damage the engine or the rest of the exhaust system, but its continued use would require more frequent spark plug replacement and other maintenance. *NOTE: There are severe legal penalties for service stations fueling catalyst equipped cars with leaded fuel.*

Occasionally a catalytic converter may produce small amounts of hydrogen sulfide gas which, when detected by the human nose, smells like rotten eggs. It may be produced by a momentary rich air/fuel mixture and a hot converter. There is less tendency to produce this gas as the catalyst ages. The sulfur from which hydrogen sulfide can be produced comes from the gasoline. Some gasolines contain more sulfur than others.

Damage to the catalytic converter, reduced effectiveness of the catalyst or other adverse affect upon emission control may result from the installation on or in the engine of non-original equipment parts. Accordingly, obtain assurance from the manufacturer of these parts that they may be used on vehicles equipped with catalytic converters.

Misadjustments or alterations to the carburetor may cause objectionable odors and increase catalytic converter temperatures. In addition, operation of the vehicle with ignition malfunctions may result in increased catalytic converter temperatures. Continued operation of the vehicle with increased catalytic converter temperatures may result in catalytic converter failures.

Catalytic converter damage due to heat is not the fault of the catalytic converter. If the catalytic converter is bulged or distorted from excessive temperatures, the engine probably has an ignition or carburetor problem which should be corrected before replacing the catalytic converter. Also, when this occurs, the remainder of the exhaust system must be inspected for bulges or distortion from excessive temperature.

PRECAUTIONS

Avoid prolonged idling (after a cold start) on the high step of the fast-idle cam (5 minutes maximum).

When driving a car on or off a hoist, be sure the hoist is all the way down, all hoist cover doors are closed and "flip up" pads are down to avoid damaging under-car components, including the converter. If contact is made, recheck all under-body components for damage and clearance.

When performing collision work or other service to the car: (1) A minimum floor pan-to-exhaust system clearance of ⅝ of an inch must be maintained. (2) Floor covering and insulation pads that are removed must all be reinstalled. (3) If any components located in the vicinity of the exhaust system are moved during service, be sure they are placed back in their original position. Examples of the components are wiring harnesses and fuel and brake lines.

EVAPORATION EMISSION CONTROL SYSTEM

Much of the smog problem can be traced to mixing of nitrous oxides from the exhausts of internal combustion engines and hydrocarbons which evaporate from fuel tanks and carburetors. Evaporative losses have been estimated to be 10%-15% of the total hydrocarbons discharged into the atmosphere. The regulations for limiting evaporative losses are 2 grams per vehicle per test.

Vapors are formed in the gas tank when the vehicle is allowed to stand in the sun. Vapors from the carburetor are caused by engine heat, and this is intensified when a hot engine is shut off, often causing

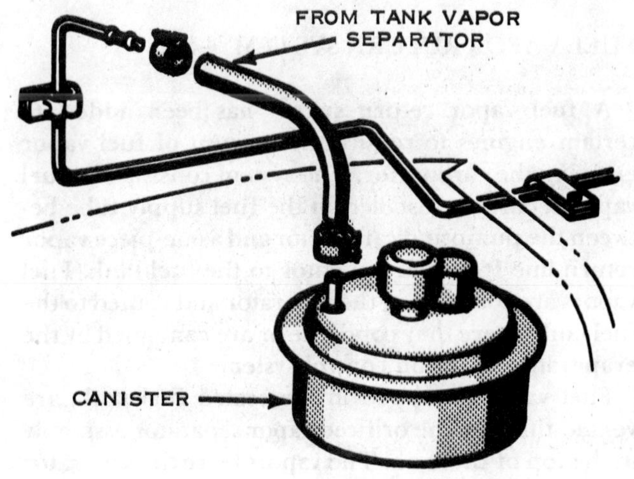

The activated charcoal canister adsorbs the hydrocarbon vapors from the gas tank and carburetor fuel bowl.

the gasoline in the carburetor float chamber to boil. In the past, these vapors have been allowed to flow into the atmosphere through vents designed to relieve the pressure. To reduce these emissions, it has been necessary to eliminate the external vents from the gas tank and the carburetor.

ACTIVATED-CARBON CANISTER

This system is known as an adsorbtion-regeneration system. In it a canister of activated carbon traps the vapors and stores them. Later, fresh air is passed over the carbon, stripping it of the trapped vapors. These vapors are then fed into the engine for burning in the combustion chamber. This burning takes place at times when engine operation would not be adversely affected by the enriched mixture.

To say that the vapors are adsorbed means that they form a layer on the surface of the carbon. This is different from absorption. When a substance is absorbed it soaks into another substance, beyond the surface. To regenerate means to restore or renew. When the vapors are stripped away from the carbon, the canister is ready to adsorb more vapor. This is the regeneration phase.

PRESSURE AND VACUUM RELIEF SYSTEM

The fill cap is a sealed cap with a built in pressure-vacuum relief valve. Fuel system vacuum relief is provided after 1/4 psi and pressure relief beyond 3/4 to 1-1/4 psi. Under normal operating conditions, the fill cap operates as a check valve, allowing air to enter the tank as gasoline is used while preventing vapors from escaping the tank through the cap.

FUEL VAPOR RETURN SYSTEM

A fuel vapor return system has been added to certain engines to reduce the amount of fuel vapor entering the carburetor. The system consists of a fuel vapor separator installed in the fuel supply tube between the pump and carburetor and a one-piece vapor return line from the separator to the fuel tank. Fuel vapors are collected in the separator and routed to the fuel tank where they condense or are contained by the evaporative emission control system.

Fuel vapors, trapped in the sealed fuel tank, are vented through the orificed vapor separator assembly in the top of the tank. The vapors leave the separator assembly through a single vapor line and continue to the carbon canister in the engine compartment for storage until such time as they are purged to the engine by means of a tube connected to the air cleaner.

Vapor generated in the fuel supply line by high engine compartment temperatures is continuously vented back to the fuel tank. This action prevents engine surging from unwanted fuel enrichment and assists in hydrocarbon emission control.

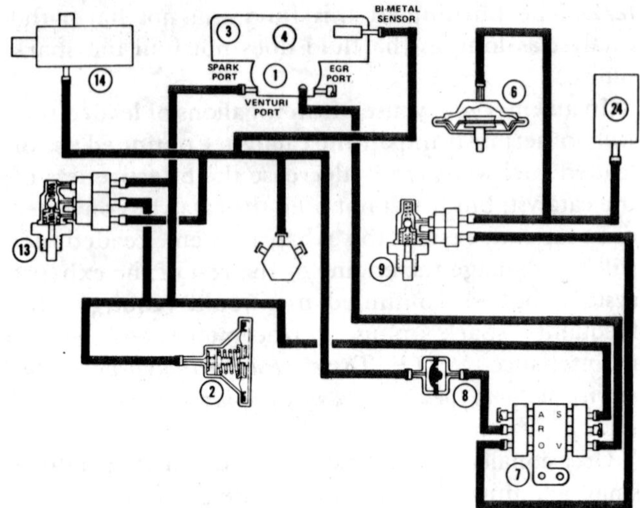

1975 emission-control system vacuum hose schematic diagram for the 2,300cc engine with air conditioning and an automatic transmission for sale in 49 states. Not all of these controls are used on all engines, depending on equipment.

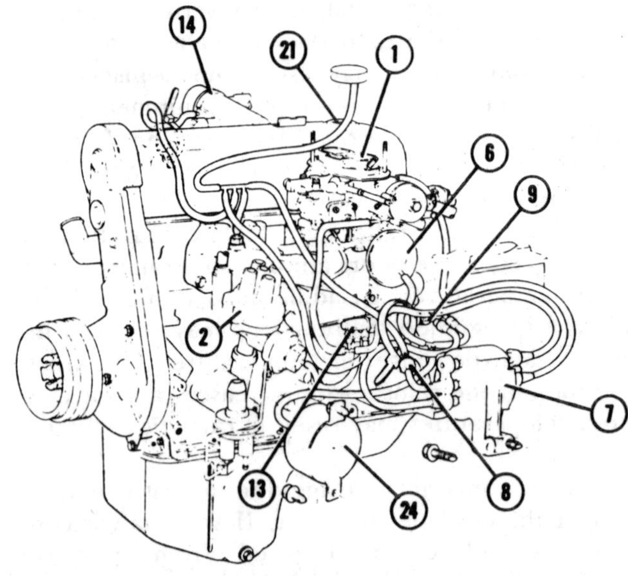

Placement of emission-control devices for the 1975-76 2,300cc engine with air conditioning and an automatic transmission for sale in 49 states. (1) carburetor venturi port, (2) distributor with a vacuum-advance unit, (7) venturi vacuum amplifier (not used in 1976), (8) vacuum-check valve, (9) EGR/PVS valve, (13) cooling system PVS valve, (14) Thermactor air bypass valve, (21) PCV valve, (24) vacuum reservoir.

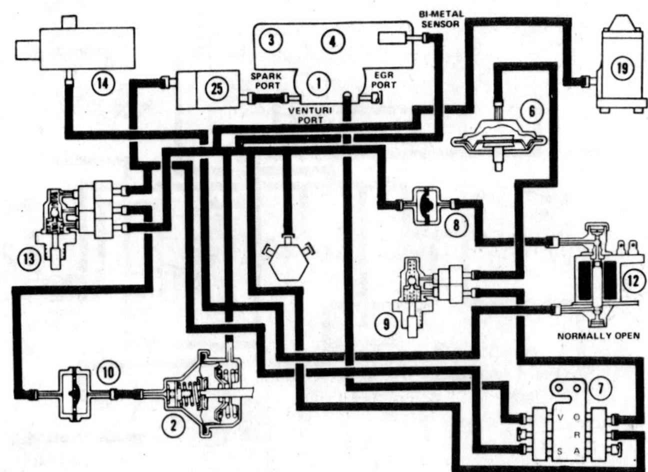

1975 emission-control system vacuum hose schematic diagram for the 2,300cc engine with air conditioning and a manual transmission for sale in California. Not all of these controls are used on all engines, depending on equipment. See the legend of the engine parts placement diagram for the names of the parts.

REPLACING THE CHARCOAL CANISTER

Disconnect the canister purge hose from the air cleaner fitting. Loosen the canister bracket retaining bolt. Lift the canister and hose assembly out of the vehicle. Install a new canister and hose assembly.

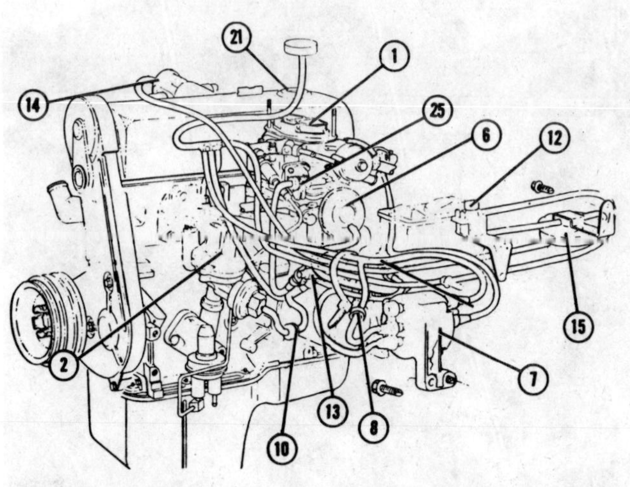

Placement of emission-control devices for the 1975-76 2,300cc engine with air conditioning and a manual transmission, for sale in California. (1) Carburetor, (2) distributor, (6) EGR valve, (7) venturi vacuum amplifier (not used in 1976), (8) vacuum check valve, (10) vacuum-delay valve, (12) vacuum solenoid, (13) cooling system PVS, (14) Thermactor air by-pass valve, (15) Thermactor differential vacuum-control valve, (21) PCV valve, (25) fuel separator.

Placement of emission-control devices for the 1975-76 2,300 engine with air conditioning and a manual transmission for sale in California. (1) Carburetor, (2) distributor, (6) EGR valve, (7) venturi vacuum amplifier (not used in 1976), (8) vacuum check valve, (9) EGR/PVS, (1) (10) vacuum-delay valve, (12) vacuum solenoid, (13) cooling system PVS, (14) Thermactor air bypass valve, (19) fuel decel valve, (21) PCV valve, (25) fuel separator.

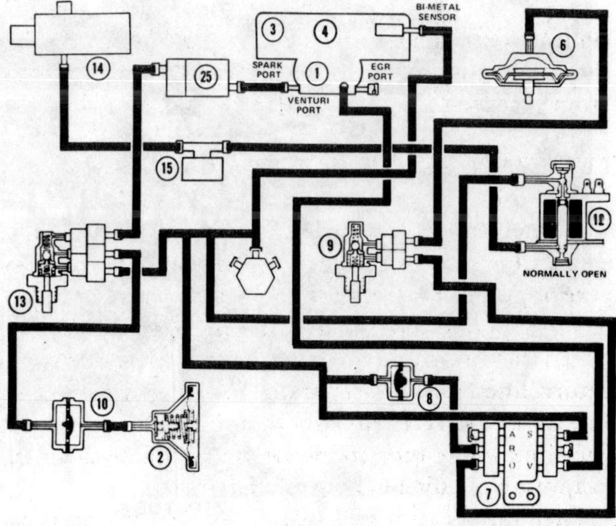

1975 emission-control system vacuum hose schematic diagram for the 2,300cc engine with air conditioning and a manual transmission, for sale in California. Not all of these controls are used on all engines, depending on equipment. See the legend of the engine parts placement diagram for the names of the parts.

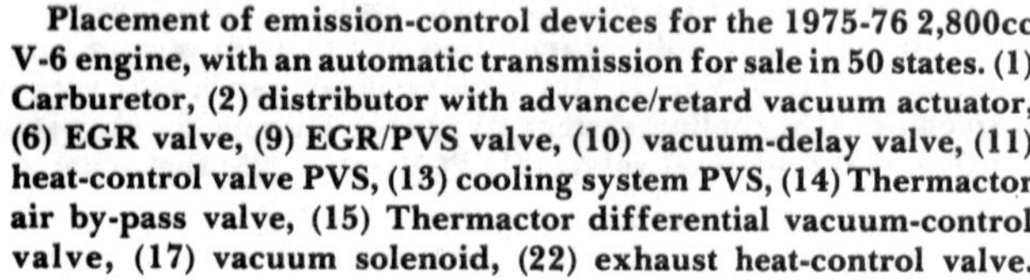

Placement of emission-control devices for the 1975-76 2,800cc V-6 engine, with an automatic transmission for sale in 50 states. (1) Carburetor, (2) distributor with advance/retard vacuum actuator, (6) EGR valve, (9) EGR/PVS valve, (10) vacuum-delay valve, (11) heat-control valve PVS, (13) cooling system PVS, (14) Thermactor air by-pass valve, (15) Thermactor differential vacuum-control valve, (17) vacuum solenoid, (22) exhaust heat-control valve.

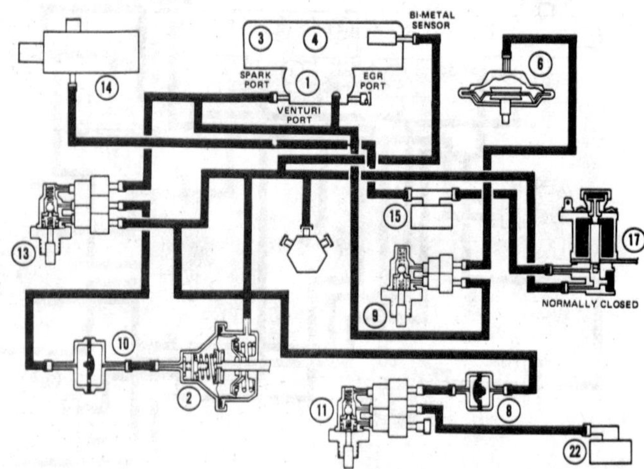

1975 emission-control system vacuum hose schematic diagram for the 2,800cc V-6 engine with an automatic transmission for sale in 50 states. Not all of these controls are used on all engines, depending on equipment. See the legend of the engine parts placement diagram for the names of the parts.

Engine compartment of the 1976 model.

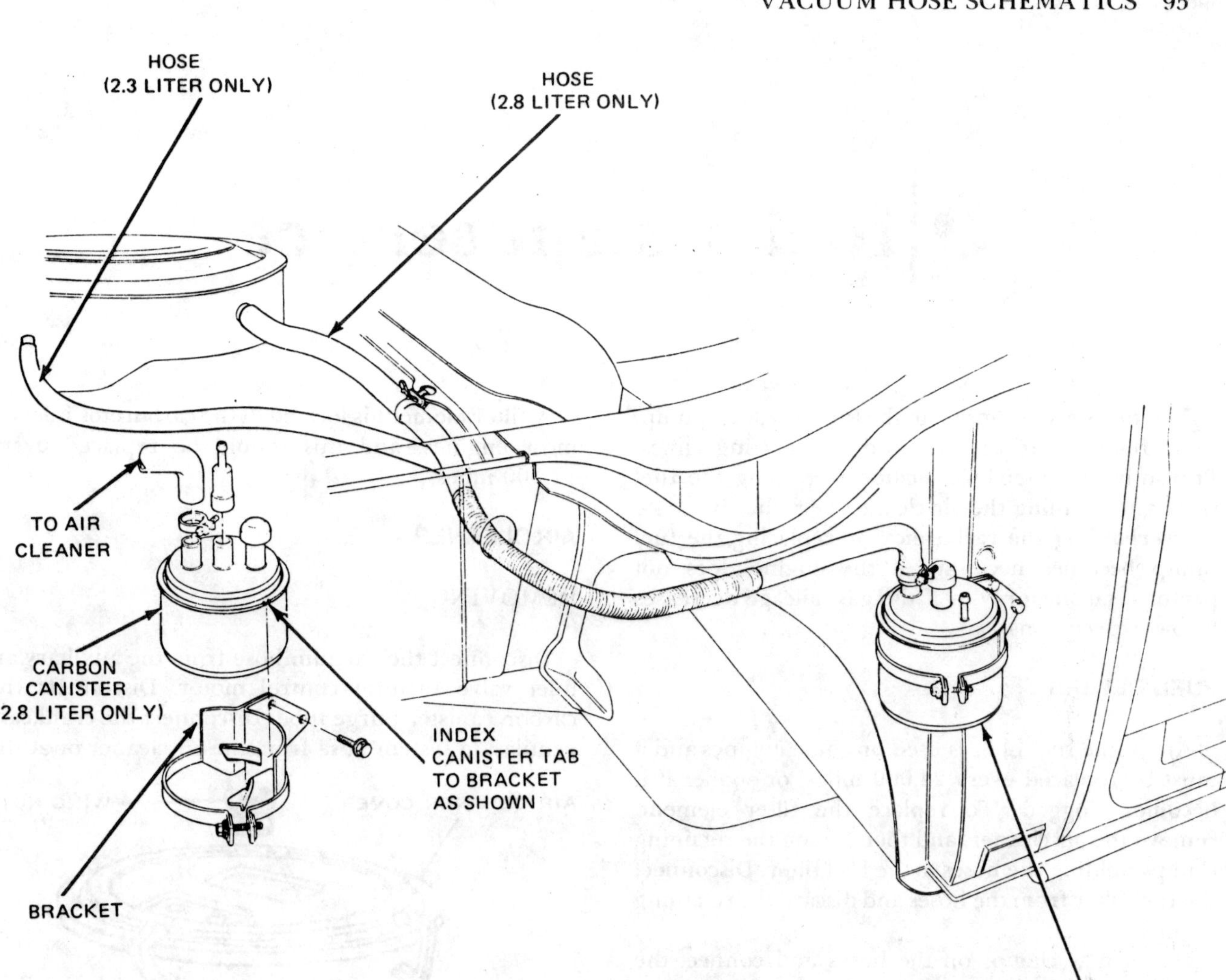

The charcoal canisters for the 2,300cc and 2,800cc engines are positioned as shown. Inspect the canister every 24,000 miles and replace if contaminated by water, oil, etc.

5 | fuel system service

The fuel system consists of the fuel tank, fuel pump, fuel filters, carburetor, and connecting lines. Preventive maintenance includes replacing the fuel filter and cleaning the air cleaner periodically.

Overhauling the carburetor or replacing the fuel pump becomes necessary if the engine does not perform satisfactorily or if the gas mileage decreases below expectations.

FUEL FILTERS

An in-line fuel filter is used on some engines and it must be replaced every 24,000 miles, or sooner if it becomes clogged. To replace the filter element, remove the air cleaner, and then loosen the retaining clamps holding the hoses to the fuel filter. Disconnect the fuel filter from the hoses and discard the retaining clamps.

Install new clamps on the hoses and connect the hoses to the new filter. **CAUTION: Make sure the arrow points in the direction of fuel flow to the carburetor.** Tighten the filter. Position the fuel line hose clamps and crimp them securely. Start the engine and check for fuel leaks.

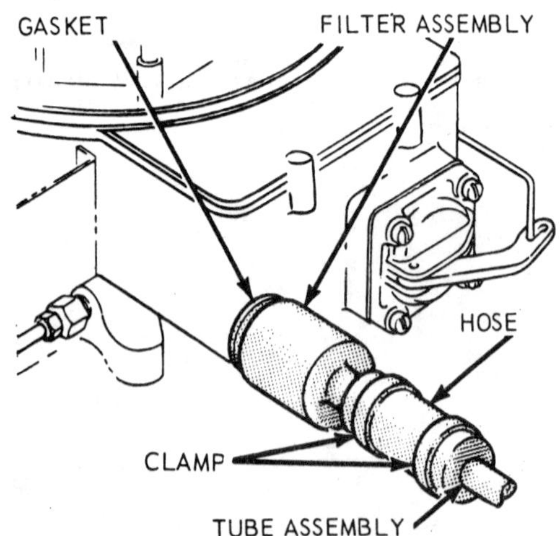

The fuel filter is located in the fuel line at the base of the carburetor; it should be replaced every 12,000 miles.

A filter element is located in the carburetor inlet on most engines, and this should be replaced every 12,000 miles.

AIR CLEANER

REMOVING

Disconnect the vacuum hose from the auxiliary air inlet valve vacuum control motor. Disconnect the carbon canister purge tube. Disconnect the crankcase ventilation system hose from the air cleaner or at the

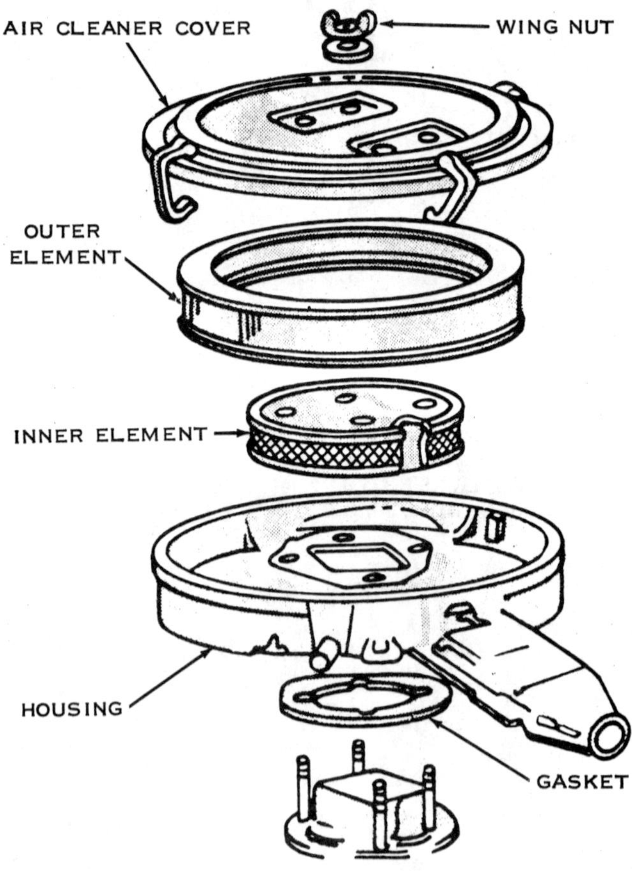

Air cleaner assembly used on the 2,000/2,300cc engines.

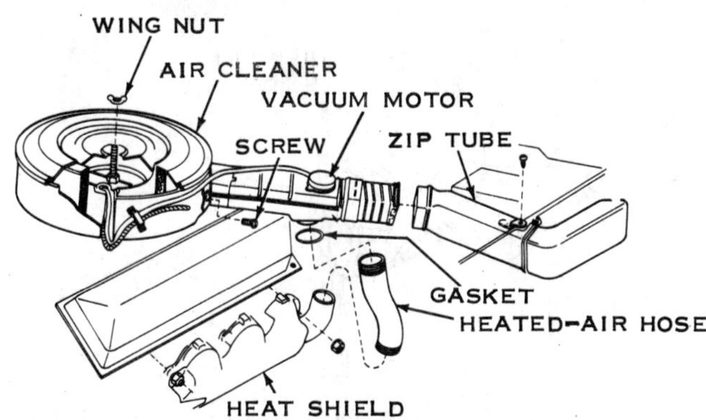

Air cleaner assembly used on late-model engines. Note the vacuum motor to operate the heat door and the Zip tube to allow cool air to enter the carburetor.

valve cover. Loosen the clamp that secures the exhaust shroud tube to the air intake duct.

Remove the wing nuts retaining the air cleaner to the carburetor. Remove the air cleaner and the air intake-duct-and-valve assembly from the carburetor as a unit. Remove the air cleaner cover and filter elements from the air cleaner body. Inspect the air cleaner-to-carburetor mounting gasket.

INSTALLING

Install a new air cleaner-to-carburetor mounting gasket. Position the air cleaner inner element. Position the air cleaner and air intake duct-and- valve assembly on the carburetor and shroud tube. Secure the clamp attaching the shroud to the air duct.

Install a new filter element in the air cleaner body. **CAUTION: If the word TOP is indicated on the filter element, make sure it faces upward. Make sure the filter element is properly seated.**

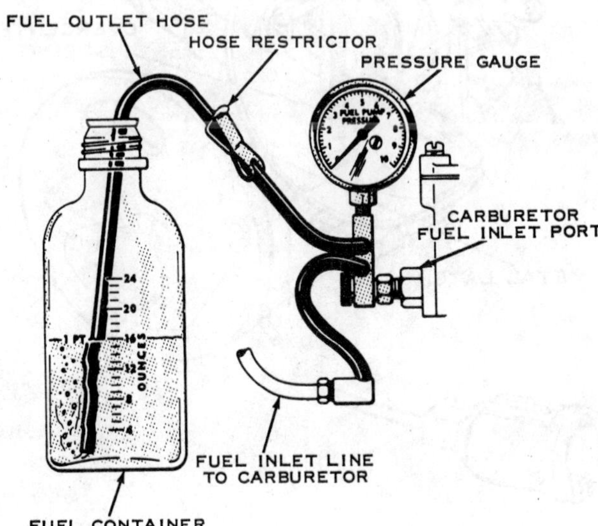

Method of hooking up a gauge and container to test fuel pump pressure and volume.

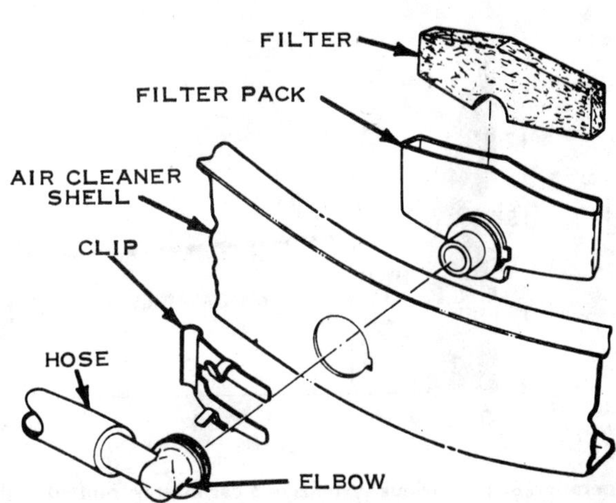

The crankcase ventilation filter should be replaced each time that you service the main air filter element.

Install the air cleaner cover and retaining wing nuts. Connect the crankcase ventilation system hose to the air cleaner body or at the valve cover. Connect the vacuum hose to the vacuum-control motor. Connect the carbon canister purge tube.

FUEL PUMP

Incorrect fuel pump pressure and inadequate volume are the two most likely fuel pump troubles. Low pressure will cause a low fuel level in the float bowl, a lean mixture, and fuel starvation at high speeds; excessive pressure will cause a high fuel level in the float bowl, a rich mixture, and flooding. Low volume will cause fuel starvation at high speeds. Service instructions, therefore, consist of testing the fuel pump to check it out as a source of trouble.

It is possible for the diaphragm of the fuel pump to crack after long service, and this will cause a fuel leak through the diaphragm and into the crankcase. If the gas mileage has decreased suddenly, check the oil dipstick for the tell-tale odor of gasoline, which indicates such a leak.

Modern fuel pumps are sealed units which cannot be taken apart for repairs. Replace the pump if it is defective.

TESTING THE PUMP

Pressure Test

Remove the air cleaner and disconnect the fuel line at the carburetor. **CAUTION: Don't spill gasoline on the hot engine, or it can catch on fire.** Connect a pressure gauge, restrictor, container, and flexible hose between the fuel filter and the carburetor. With the

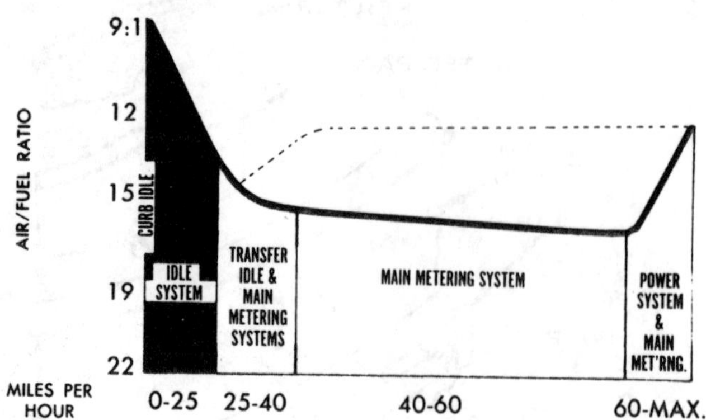

Operation of the various systems of a carburetor, plotted against road speed.

engine idling, vent the outlet hose into the container by opening the hose restrictor momentarily. Close the hose restrictor and allow the pressure to stabilize, which should be 3.5-5.5 psi.

Volume Test

If the fuel pump pressure is within specifications, test the volume by opening the hose restrictor with the engine idling and allowing fuel to discharge into the graduated container. A pint of fuel should be collected in about 40 seconds.

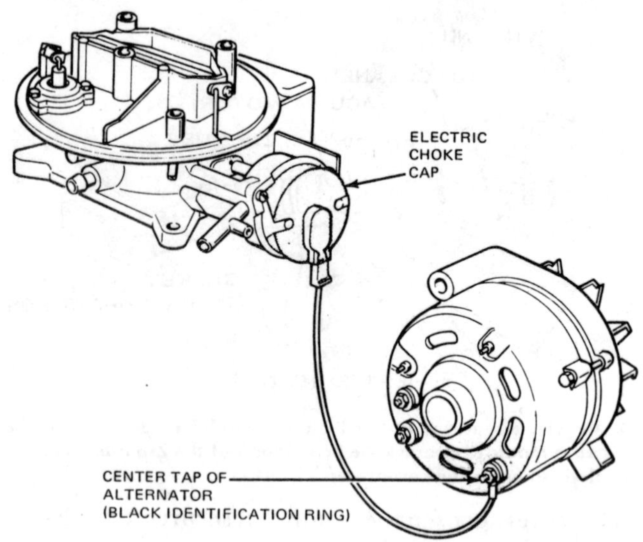

The electric choke receives current from the center tap of the alternator as long as the engine is running.

CARBURETORS

The Bobcat uses a Model 5200-2V carburetor on the 2,300cc four-cylinder engine since 1975.

The 2,800cc V-6 engine is equipped with a Model 2150-2V carburetor for the 1975-76 models.

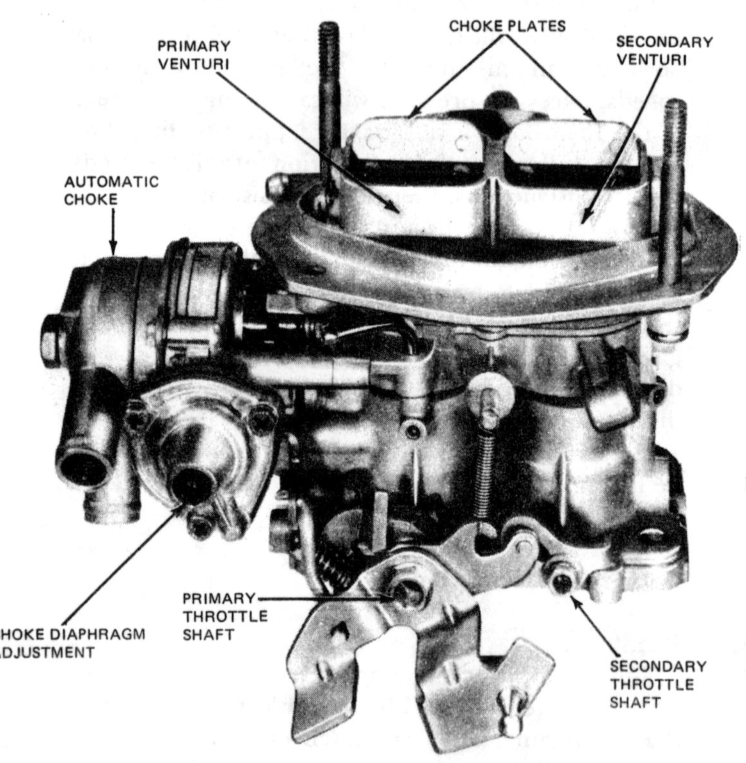

Details of the Motorcraft Model 5200 carburetor.

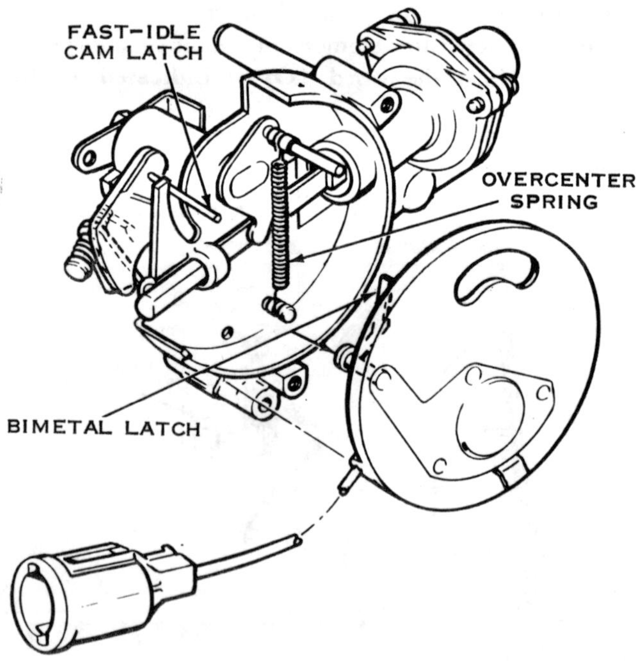

The new model choke is equipped with a fast-idle cam latch and an overcenter spring to assist in closing the choke plate for initial starting of a cold engine.

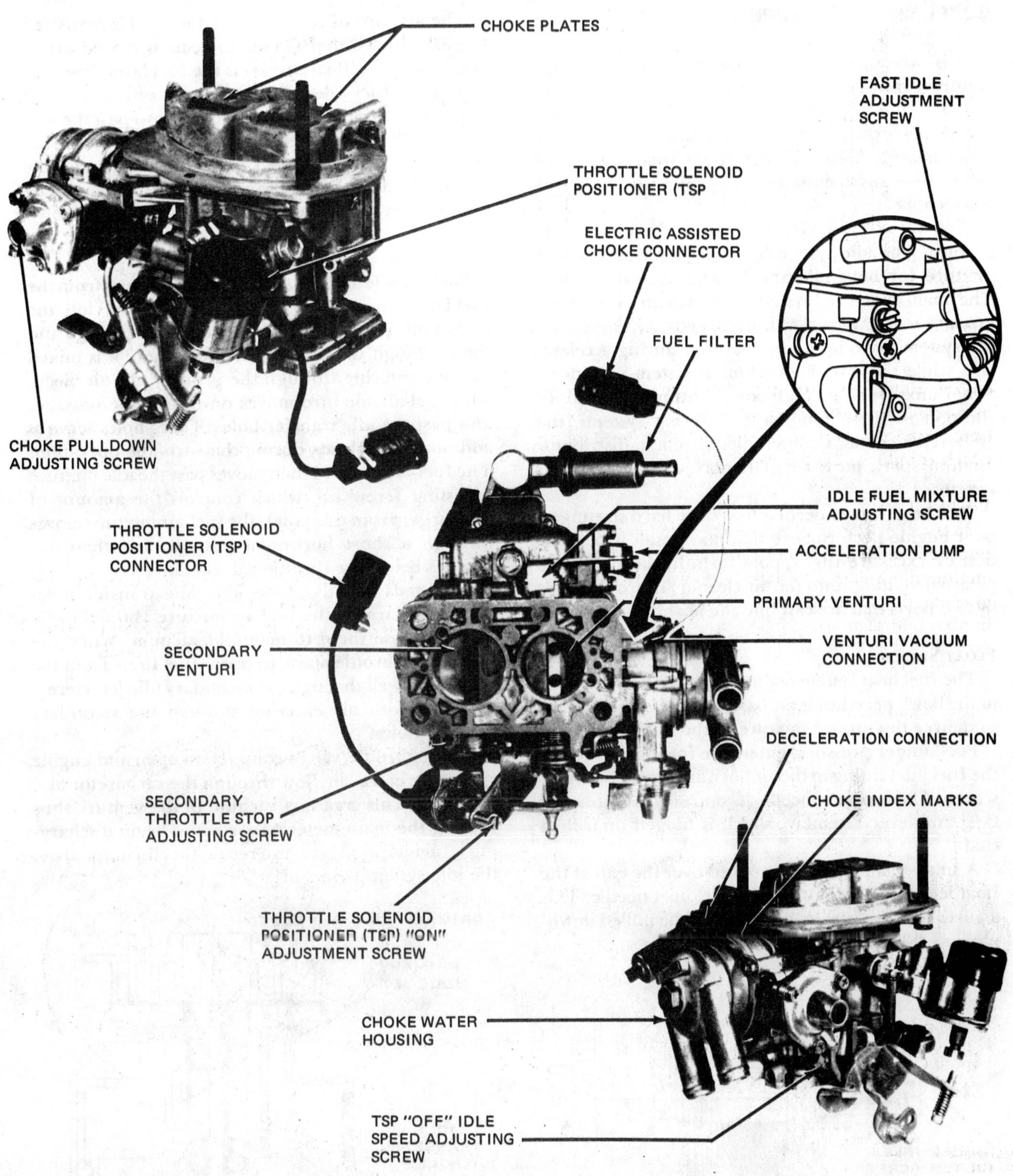

Details of the Motorcraft 5200-2V carburetor used on the Bobcat 2,300cc engine.

MODEL 5200-2V CARBURETOR

This two-stage carburetor has a small primary stage (venturi) for better low-speed performance and economy and a larger secondary stage for better high-speed performance. The automatic choke uses a water-heated bi-metal thermostat housing. Since 1974, these carburetors are equipped with an electric-assist choke.

The carburetor uses four basic fuel metering systems. The idle systems provides a proper fuel-air mixture for both idle and low-speed performance. The main metering system provides an economical mixture for all normal cruising speeds, The accelerating system provides additional fuel during acceleration while the power enrichment system provides a richer mixture when high power output is needed. In addition to these four basic metering systems, the carburetor contains a fuel inlet system, a distributor vacuum spark port, an EGR port, and a bowl-vent system.

This bowl vent is needed to reduce hard starting or poor engine performance that may result if percolation or excessive fuel vapors form in the fuel bowl. Internal venting (into the air cleaner) is provided for by two ports that are cast into the air-horn assembly.

Float System

The fuel inlet system maintains a specified fuel level in the bowl, permitting the basic fuel metering systems to deliver the proper mixture to the engine.

Fuel, under pressure, enters the fuel bowl through the fuel inlet fitting in the air horn and through a filter screen. The fuel inlet needle is controlled by nitrophyl float-and-lever assembly, which is hinged on a float shaft.

A small retaining clip is hooked over the end of the float lever tang and also to the fuel inlet needle. This assures that the fuel inlet needle will be pulled downward as the float drops.

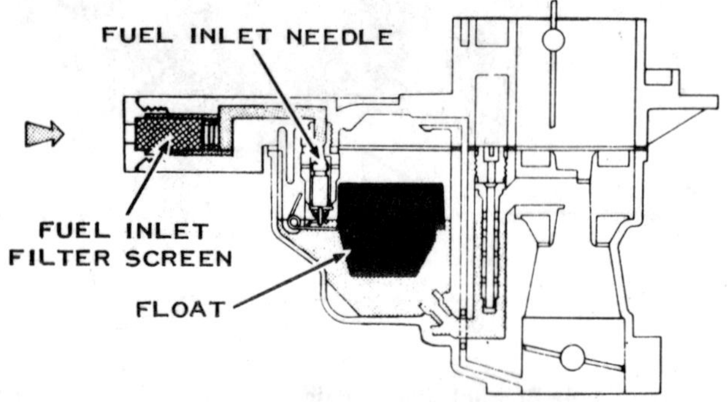

Fuel inlet and float systems of the 5200 carburetor.

The amount of fuel entering the bowl is regulated by the distance the fuel inlet needle is moved off its seat. When the float drops (as the fuel level drops), it causes the fuel inlet needle to move off its seat and permits additional fuel to enter the bowl past the fuel inlet needle. As the fuel reaches the specified level, the fuel inlet needle is raised to a position where only enough fuel is admitted to replace that being used by engine-operating conditions.

Idle System

Fuel for idle and low speed operation flows from the fuel bowl, through the primary main jet, and into the main well. Fuel then flows up through a passage and then through the primary idle jet, where it is mixed with air entering through the primary idle air bleed. This fuel-air mixture moves down the idle passages and past the idle transfer holes. These holes serve as additional air bleeds during the curb-idle operation: The fuel-air mixture then moves past the idle mixture adjusting screw tip, which controls the amount of discharge. From this point, the fuel-air mixture moves through a short horizontal passage, and then discharges below the throttle valves.

At speeds slightly above idle, idle transfer holes begin discharging the fuel-air mixture as the throttle valves expose them to manifold vacuum. When the secondary throttle starts to open, fuel flows from the secondary well through the secondary idle jet. Here it is mixed with air entering through the secondary transfer holes.

As the throttle valves continue to open and engine speed increases, air flow through the carburetor also increases. This creates a vacuum in the venturi, thus causing the main metering system to begin discharging a fuel-air mixture. As a result, the discharge from the idle system tapers off.

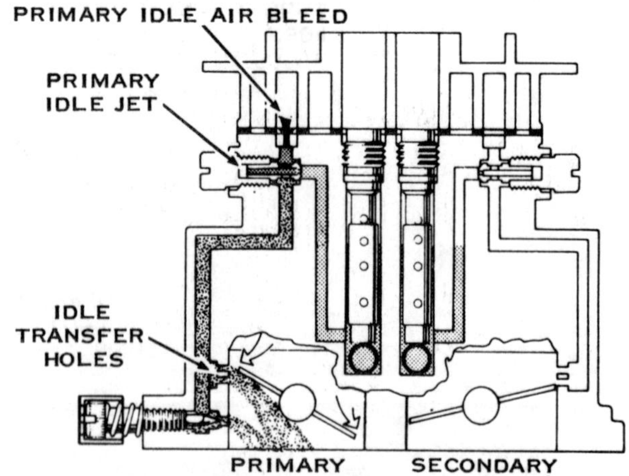

The idle transfer stage comes into operation as the engine is run just above idle speed.

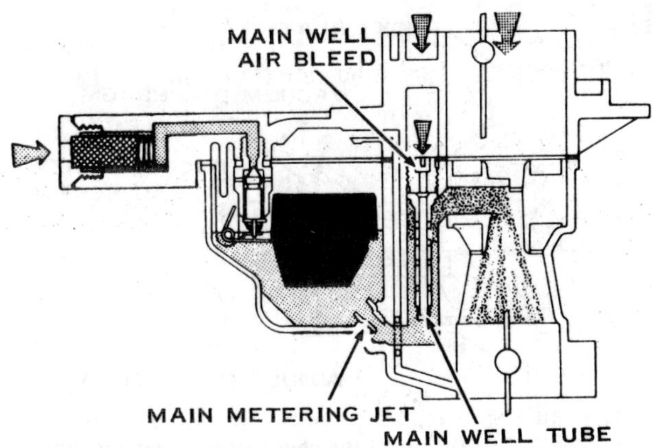

The main metering system takes over from the second idle stage and continues to top speed.

Main Metering System

As engine speed increases, air velocity through the booster venturi causes a vacuum (low-pressure area) in the venturi. Fuel then begins to flow through the main metering system due to the high pressure in the fuel bowl and a low pressure at the main discharge nozzle. Fuel flows from the fuel bowl, through the main jets, and into the main wells.

Fuel then moves up the main well tubes, where it is mixed with air. Air, supplied through the high-speed air bleeds, mixes with the fuel through small holes in the sides of the main well tubes. These air bleeds meter an increasing amount of air, whenever venturi vacuum increases, to maintain the proper fuel-air ratio. This mixture of fuel and air atomizes more readily than raw fuel. As the fuel-air mixture moves from the main well tube to the discharge port, it is discharged into the booster venturi.

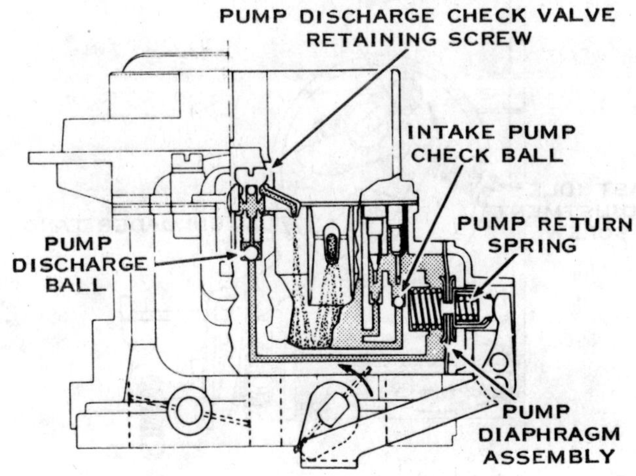

Schematic diagram of the acceleration system of the 5200 carburetor.

Accelerating System

When the throttle valves are opened quickly, the air flow through the carburetor responds almost immediately. However, since fuel is heavier than air, there's a brief time-lag before fuel flow can gain enough speed to maintain the proper fuel-air ratio. During this lag, the accelerating system supplies the required fuel, until the proper fuel-air ratio can be maintained by the other metering systems.

When the throttle valves are closed, the diaphragm return spring pushes the diaphragm against its cover. Fuel is drawn through the inlet, past the inlet ball check valve, and into the pump chamber. A discharge check ball prevents air from being drawn into the pump chamber.

The moment the throttle valves are opened, the diaphragm rod is pushed inward, forcing fuel from the pump chamber into the discharge passages. The inlet ball check valve seals the inlet hole during pump operation, thus preventing fuel from returning to the fuel bowl. Fuel under pressure unseats the discharge check ball and is forced through the pump discharge valve assembly, where it sprays into the primary venturi through the pump discharge nozzle.

Excess fuel and pump chamber vapors are discharged back into the fuel bowl through a restriction.

Primary Power Enrichment System

During heavy load conditions or high speed operation, the fuel-air ratio must be increased for higher engine output. The power-enrichment system supplies the extra fuel during this period and is controlled by intake manifold vacuum.

Manifold vacuum is applied to the power-valve diaphragm from an opening in the base of the carburetor body, where it is connected to passages in the main body and air horn to the power-valve

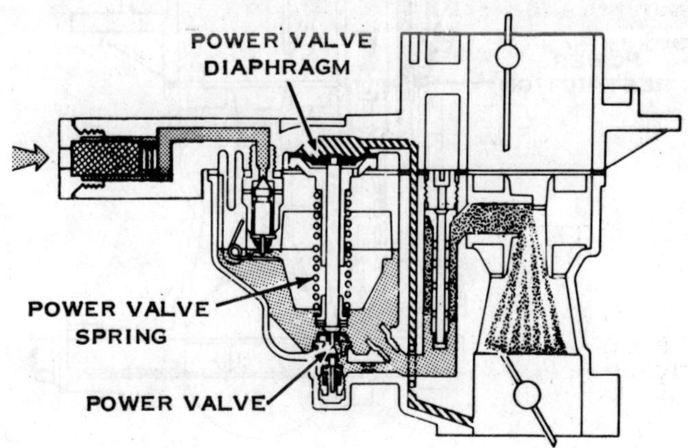

Diagram of the operation of the power-enrichment system of the secondary stage of the 5200 carburetor.

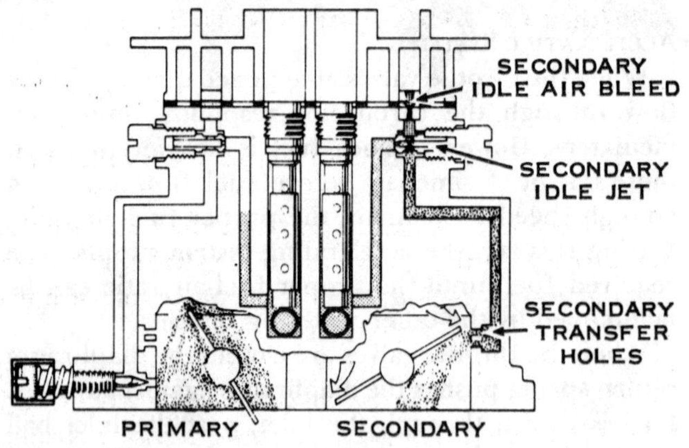

The secondary progression (2nd stage) comes into operation when the primary throttle plates reach 45° opening.

diaphragm. During idle and normal driving conditions, manifold vacuum is high enough to overcome the power-valve spring tension, thus holding the valve closed. When higher engine output is needed, the increased load on the engine results in decreased manifold vacuum. The power-valve diaphragm spring opens the valve when manifold vacuum drops below a predetermined value. Fuel flows from the fuel bowl through the power valve and into passages leading to the main wells. At the main wells, this fuel is added to the fuel in the main metering system to enrich the mixture.

As engine load requirements decrease, manifold vacuum increases and overcomes the tension of the power valve spring, closing the power valve.

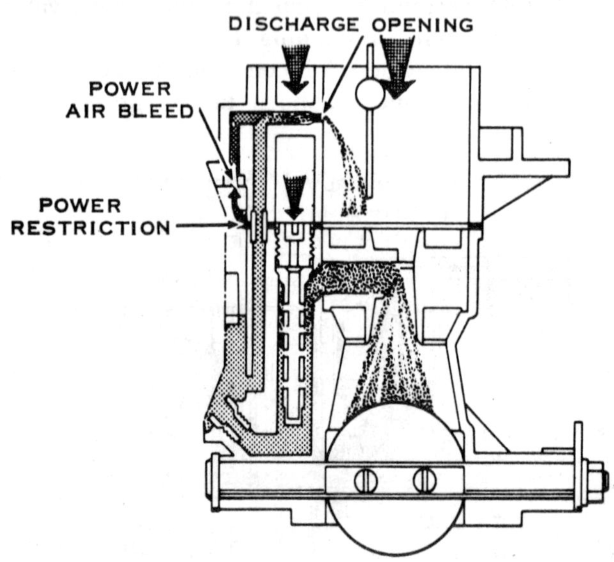

Diagram of the operation of the power-enrichment system of the secondary stage of the Holley carburetor.

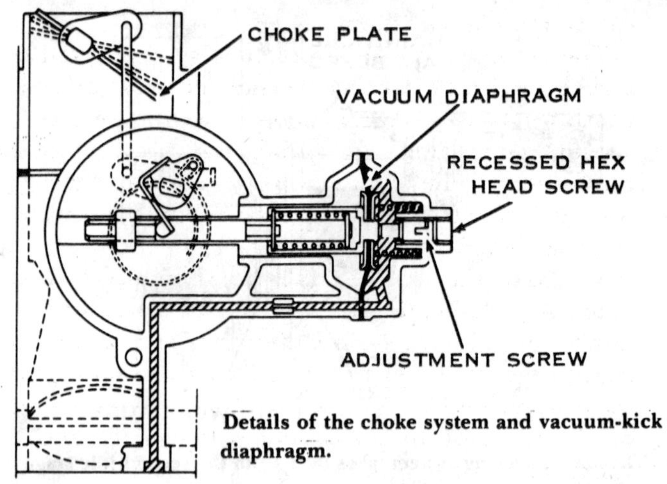

Details of the choke system and vacuum-kick diaphragm.

Secondary Progression

When the primary throttle plates reach approximately 45° opening, the secondary throttle plates start to open. Fuel-air mixture then starts to flow from the secondary transfer holes as they are exposed to manifold vacuum. Further opening of the throttle plates starts operation of the secondary main metering system, which is similar to the primary system.

Secondary Power Enrichment System

The secondary system is also provided with an air-velocity operated power system for full-power operation. As the secondary throttle valve approaches the wide-open position, air velocity through the secondary venturi creates a low pressure at the discharge opening. Fuel flows from the bowl through a restricted vertical channel. As this occurs, air enters through a calibrated air bleed and mixes with the fuel, discharging this mixture through the discharge opening.

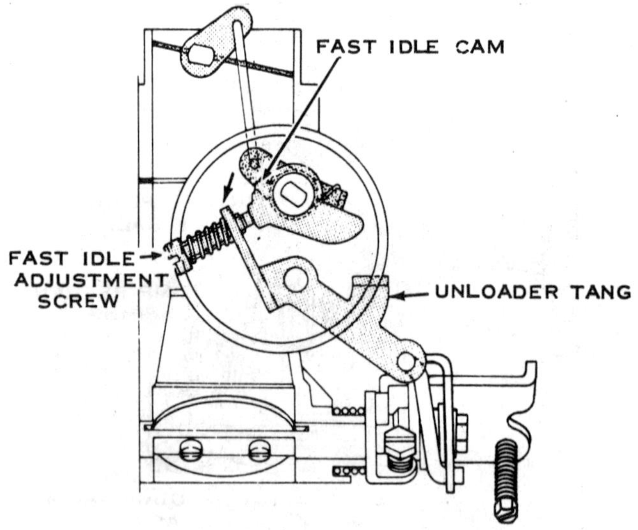

Fast-idle and choke unloader linkage.

AUTOMATIC CHOKE SYSTEM

The automatic choke assembly is mounted on the carburetor body. It has a bimetal thermostatic coil, which winds up when cold and unwinds when hot. A vacuum diaphragm and spring controls the initial operation of the choke. Engine coolant flowing through a choke water cover heats the bimetal coil and controls the final choke opening.

To start the engine, the accelerator pedal is depressed, closing the choke valves. This permits fuel to flow through the main metering system as well as the idle system. When the engine starts, air flows past the off-set choke valves, and manifold vacuum, acting on the choke vacuum diaphragm, opens the choke valves to a predetermined position. As the engine coolant warms up, it circulates through the choke housing, heating the bimetallic choke coil. The coil unwinds, permitting full opening of the choke valves. If the cold engine is suddenly accelerated, the resulting drop in manifold vacuum on the vacuum diaphragm, allows the choke valves to close momentarily.

The fast-idle cam, actuated by the choke rod, controls idle speed during engine warm up. When the choke valves are fully open, the fast-idle cam rotates free of the fast-idle screw. An unloader tang on the throttle lever partially opens the choke valves when the accelerator is fully depressed. This permits unloading or breathing of a flooded engine.

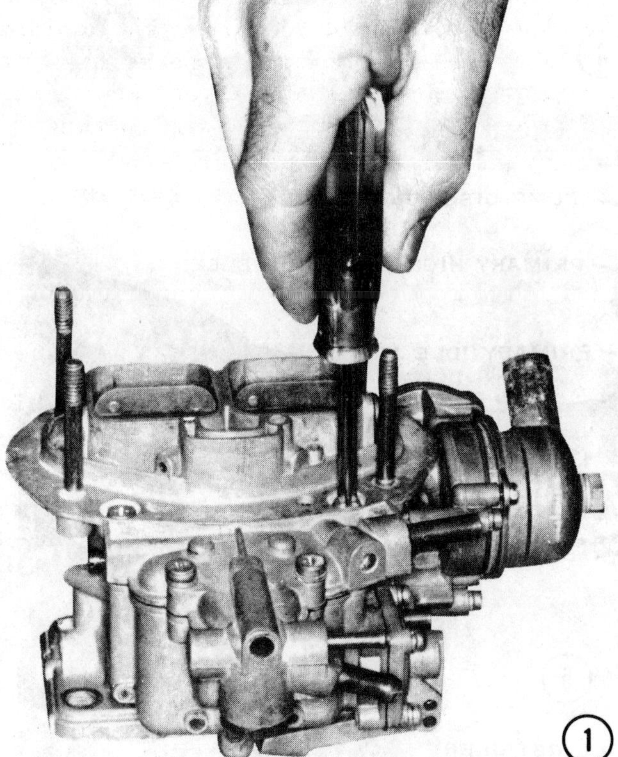

①

OVERHAULING A 5200 CARBURETOR

DISASSEMBLING

①Remove the five Phillip's head screws that hold the air horn to the main body of the carburetor.

②Raise the air horn slightly, and then remove the retainer clip at the lower end of the choke rod. Push out the end of the rod, and then remove the air horn assembly. Discard the gasket.

③To take off the choke thermostatic housing coolant cover, remove the three retaining screws, and then lift off the cover, gasket, and thermostat housing. Take off the thermostat housing gasket. Remove the three choke housing-to-main body retaining screws, using the Phillip's screwdriver, as shown, and then rotate the choke housing toward the bottom of the main casting in order to disengage the fast-idle rod from the fast-idle lever. To remove the choke vacuum-break diaphragm from the choke housing, take out the three cover screws, and then lift out the cover, spring, and diaphragm. **CAUTION: Always replace any diaphragm that is exposed to air.** Generally, it is not necessary to disassemble the fast-idle or choke linkage, unless the parts are damaged.

④ Take out the four accelerator pump cover retaining screws, and then lift off the pump diaphragm and the return spring, which is under the diaphragm. Discard the diaphragm.

⑤Remove the primary idle jet retainer and jet, as shown, and then take out the secondary jet retainer and jet from the other side of the carburetor. **CAU-**

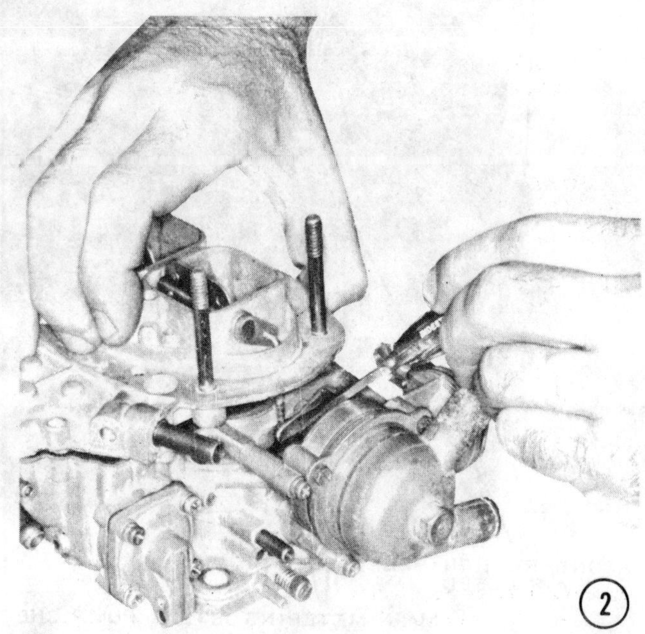

②

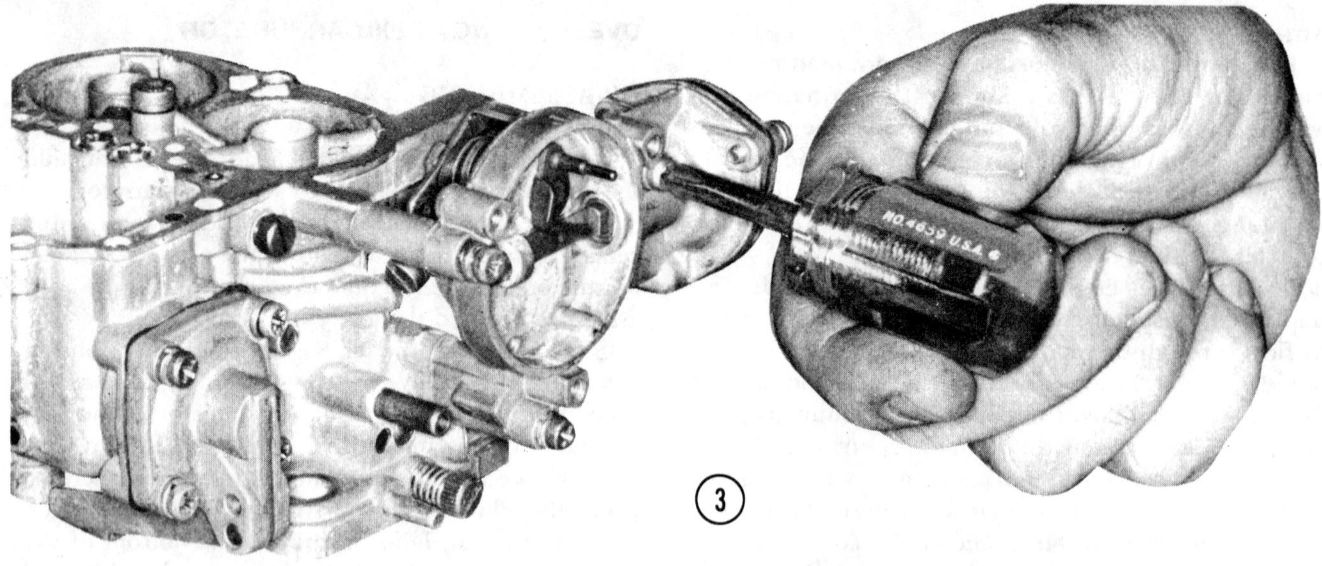

TION: Make a note of the jet sizes for each side of the carburetor, because each jet is stamped differently for the primary and secondary sides. Remove the accelerator intake check ball retainer, and then turn the casting over to catch the intake check ball in the palm of your hand. *NOTE: In some models, the intake check ball is held in place by a plug, which is not removable.* Remove the primary and secondary high-speed air bleeds and the main well tubes under them. **CAU-**

4

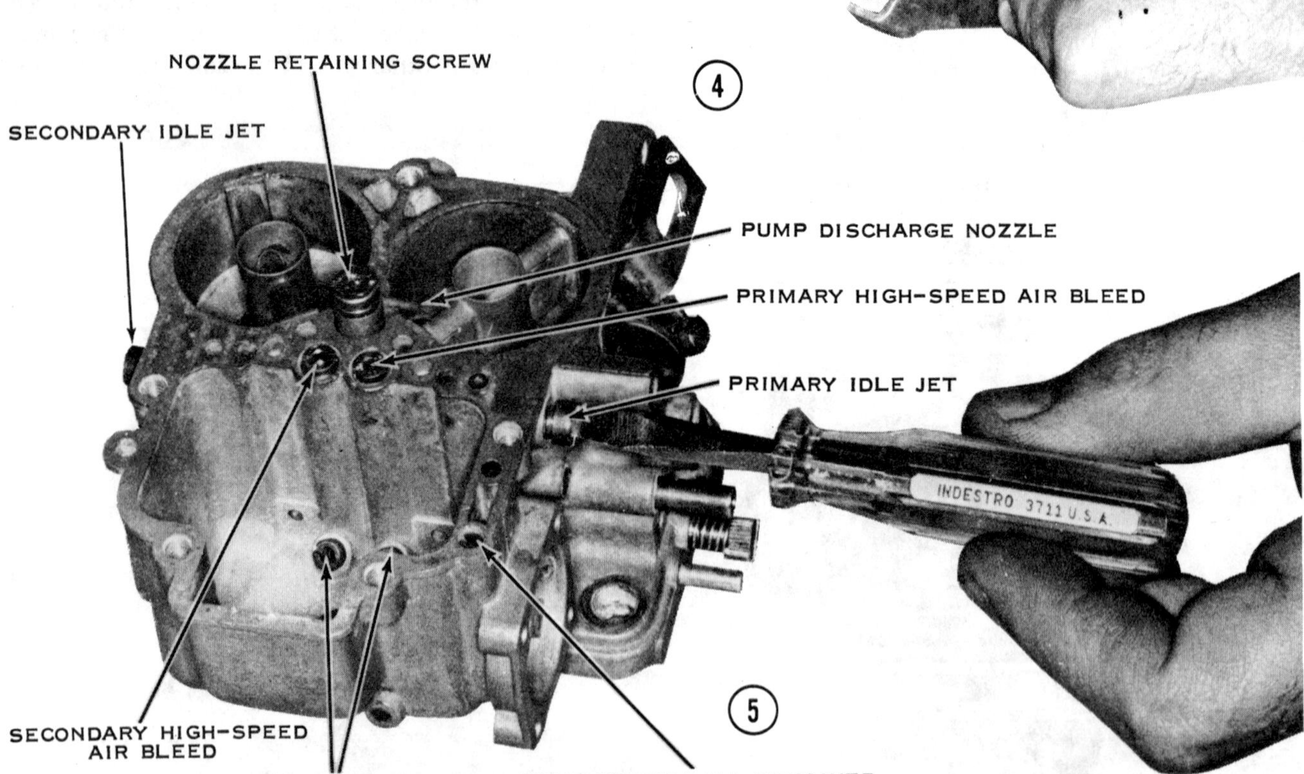

TION: Make a note of the air bleed and main well tube sizes for the primary and secondary sides for replacement purposes. Remove the accelerator pump discharge nozzle-retaining screw, and then take off the pump discharge nozzle. Note that there are two gaskets, one on each side of the nozzle. Turn the casting over and catch the accelerator pump outlet ball check in the palm of your hand. **CAUTION, On some models, there are two such balls, one being a weight to keep the ball check seated, and this is done for emission control.** *NOTE: The pump discharge nozzle retaining screw on some models has a lead plug, which should be pried out to make sure that the small nylon anti-siphon ball check valve is free.* **CAUTION: Don't soak this retaining screw assembly in carburetor cleaner unless you remove the nylon ball check first.** *NOTE: Some models have a solid screw and some a hollow screw to hold the pump discharge nozzle in place.* Remove the two main metering jets and record the sizes.

⑥ Take out the power valve assembly, using special tool J-10185 to avoid damaging the valve. A flat-bladed screwdriver can be modified for this job by grinding a 1/8" notch in the center of the blade. Discard the gasket under the power valve. Check the power valve for seating by alternately applying oral suction and pressure. The valve must not leak;

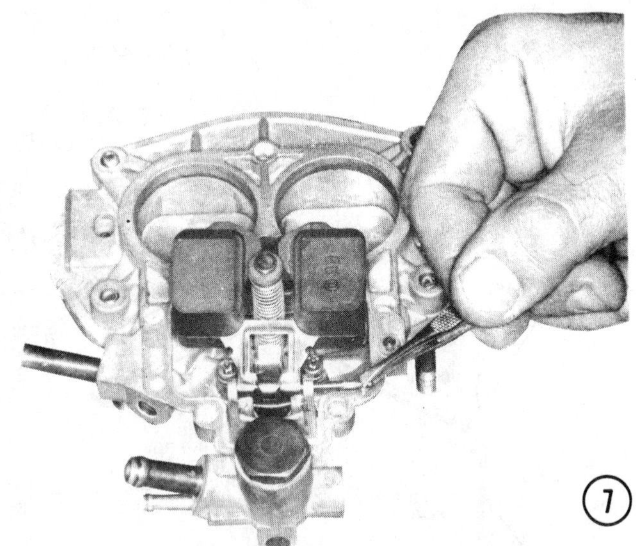

otherwise, gas mileage will suffer. Take out the idle mixture adjusting screw and spring. *NOTE: There is only one adjusting screw on the primary side of the carburetor.*

⑦ To disassemble the air horn, pull out the float hinge pin, and then take off the float assembly. Remove the fuel inlet needle.

⑧ Take out the three screws holding the power valve diaphragm assembly, and then remove the valve. Unscrew the needle valve seat. Discard the gasket under it.

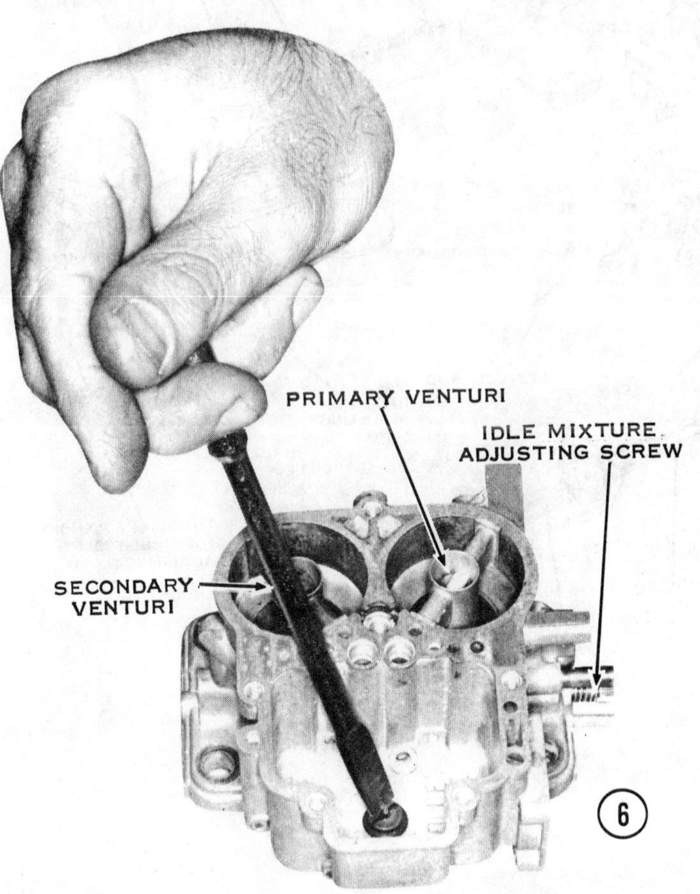

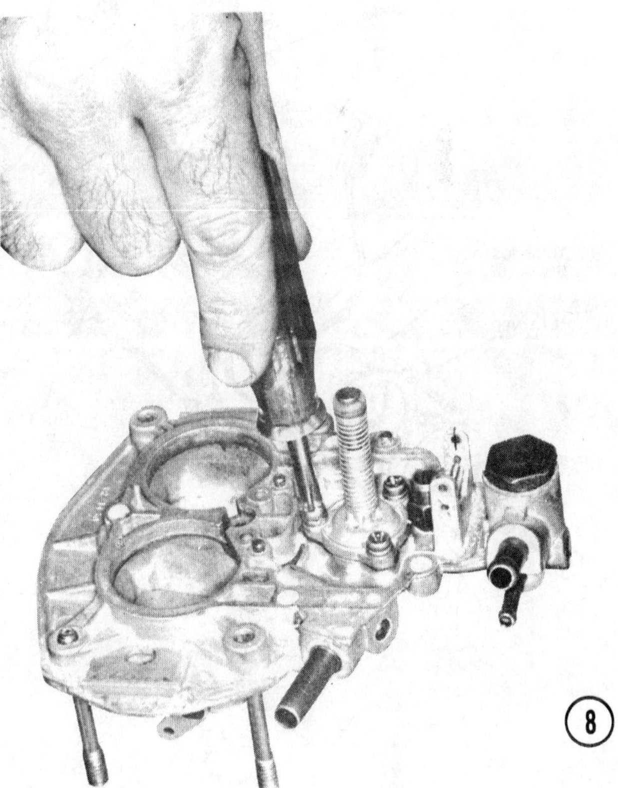

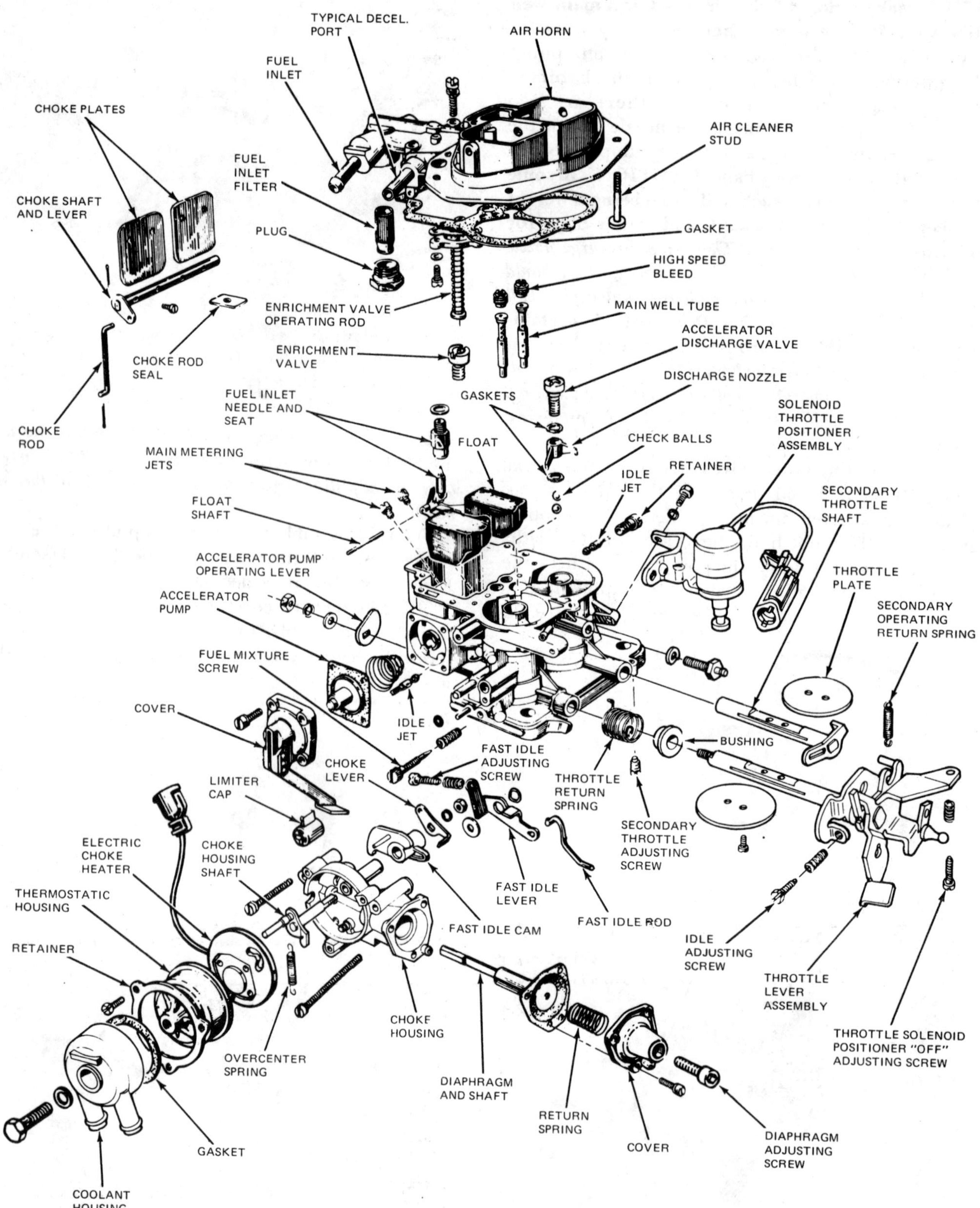

Exploded view of the Motorcraft Model 5200 carburetor.

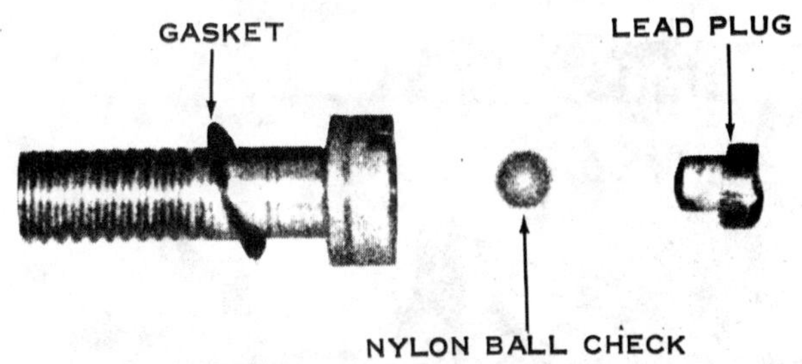

This nylon ball check in the pump discharge nozzle retaining screw operates as an anti-siphon valve. It is necessary to pry out the lead plug to get the ball check out.

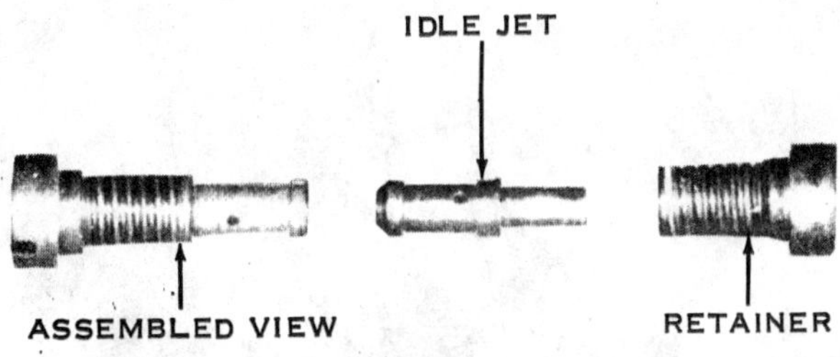

The idle jet can be separated from its retainer by pulling it out. The left view shows an assembled jet.

CLEANING AND INSPECTING

Wash all parts, except diaphragms and parts with rubber, in a commercial carburetor cleaning solvent. Lacquer thinner or denatured alcohol can also be used. Rinse parts in hot water to remove all traces of the cleaning solvent and dry them with compressed air. Direct compressed air through all passageways and jets to make sure that they are clean. **CAUTION: Don't use a wire or drill to clean jets or calibrated openings, or you may enlarge the holes.**

Check the choke and throttle shafts for excessive wear. Inspect the choke plate and throttle valve plate to be sure that they are not nicked. Replace the entire carburetor if the throttle shaft is worn excessively. During manufacture, the location of the idle transfer and spark advance control ports to the throttle valve is carefully established, and it would be very unlikely that the original relationships of the ports to the valve could be obtained if a new shaft were installed.

Replace the float assembly if the arm needle contact surface is worn. Replace the float shaft if it is grooved.

Always inspect the casting impressions in the gasket to see how the two parts are mating. A weak impression can be traced to a warped casting, which can then be dressed flat on emery cloth.

Always replace the needle valve and seat, because it is the most wearing part of the carburetor and is vital in maintaining the fuel level at the designed height.

If the pump discharge nozzle retaining screw has a lead plug in the top with a nylon ball below it, either remove the lead plug to clean the assembly, or blow clean fluid through it to be sure that it seats in one direction and passes the fluid in the other. *NOTE: You can use an aerosol can with penetrant to force fluid through the check valve to be sure that it is free.*

On models where the intake ball check is held in the bowl casting by a non-removable plug, direct the penetrant through the intake port in the bowl side of the casting to be sure that the ball check is free. And then direct the spray in the port from the accelerator pump diaphragm casting side to be sure that the fluid does not pass through the check valve and back into the float bowl. If it does, then you will get a flat spot on acceleration.

Check the choke vacuum diaphragm for an internal leak by depressing the diaphragm stem, and then placing your finger over the vacuum fitting to seal the opening. Release the diaphragm stem. If the stem moves out more than 1/16" in ten seconds, the leakage is excessive and the unit must be replaced.

Always replace all gaskets and parts with diaphragms because of the danger of leaks. It is a good policy to purchase a factory repair kit, which contains all of the parts that wear most and a complete set of gaskets and seals. These factory kits always contain complete specifications, which are important for rebuilding the carburetor properly.

This kind of damage to the idle mixture adjusting needle is done by screwing it into place too hard. The end of the needle strikes the edge of the throttle plate and bends up in this fashion, making it impossible to obtain an accurate adjustment.

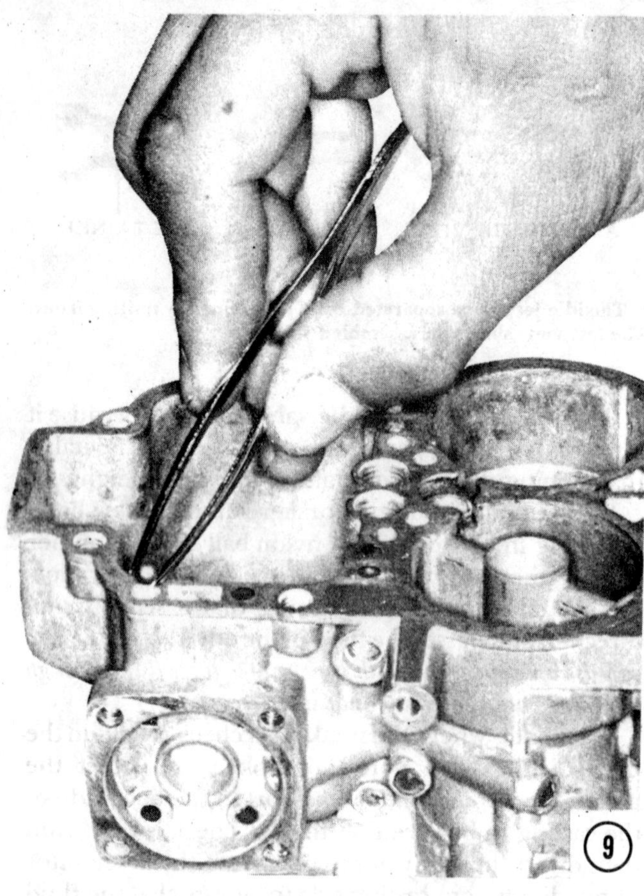

9

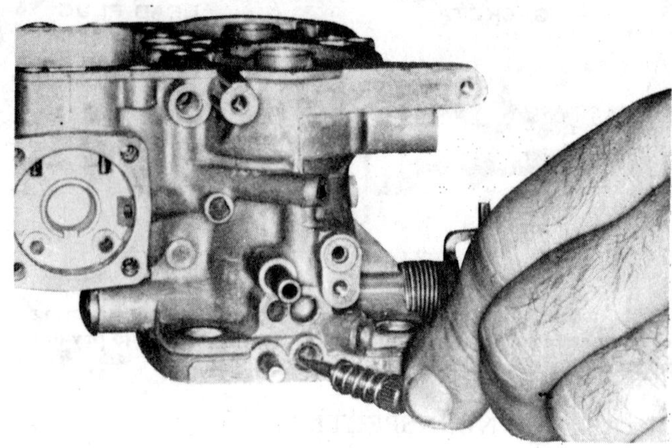

11

ASSEMBLING

⑨Install the accelerator pump inlet ball check. **CAUTION: If the ball check is a non-removable type, make sure that it is free, as discussed in the Cleaning and Inspecting section.**

⑩Install the accelerator inlet ball check retainer. Tighten it securely. No gasket is needed.

⑪Install the idle mixture adjusting screw and spring. Seat the needle gently, and then back it out four turns for a preliminary adjustment. **CAUTION: Don't seat the adjusting screw too hard, or you will damage the tip, making an adjustment difficult.**

⑫Install the venturis into the barrels. **CAUTION: The smaller venturi goes into the primary side. CAUTION: Make sure that the passageway in the venturi is facing the opening in the rear of the carburetor bore, as shown.**

10

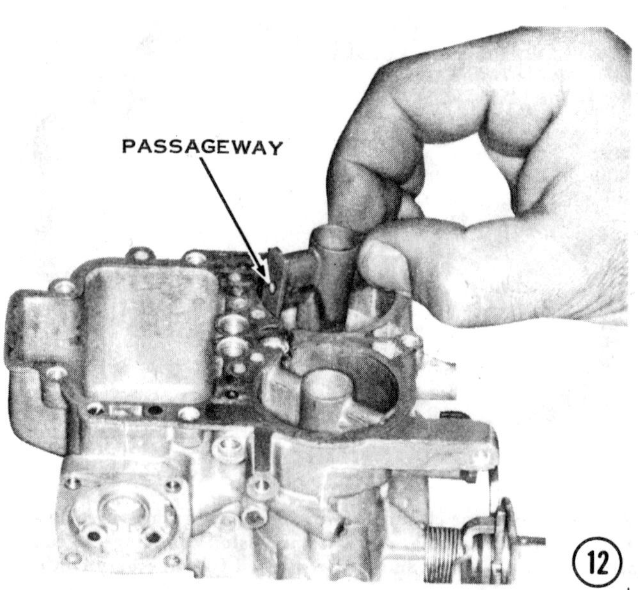

12

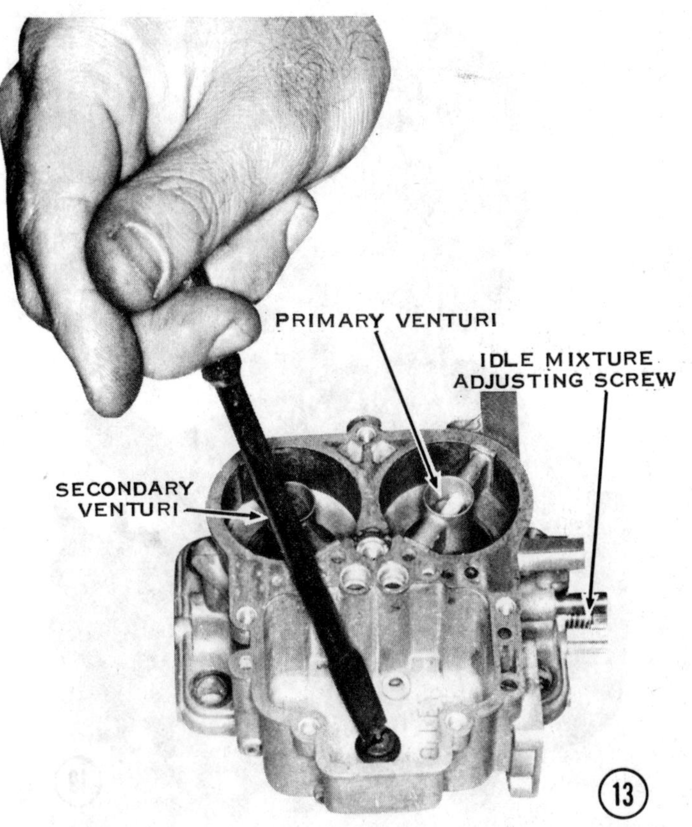

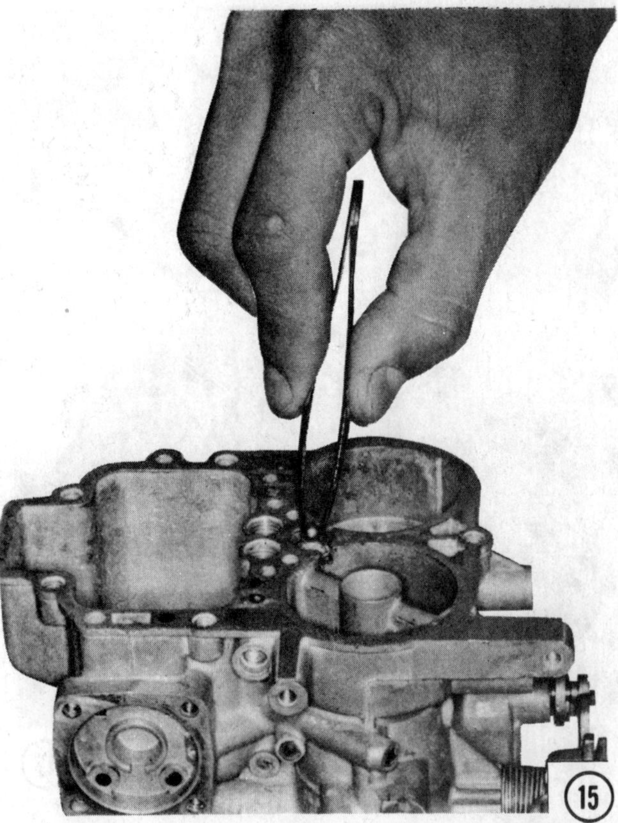

⑬ Install the power valve, using a new gasket under it. **CAUTION: Use the special tool to keep from damaging the valve. If this valve leaks, gas mileage will suffer.**

⑭ Install the two main metering jets. No gaskets are needed. **CAUTION: Check the sizes to make sure you are installing them in the correct sides of the carburetor. If in doubt, consult the specifications.**

⑮ Drop the ball check into the accelerating pump outlet passageway. **CAUTION: Some carburetor models have two such balls, the top one being a weight for emission control.**

⑯ Install the accelerator nozzle assembly. Note the gasket under it.

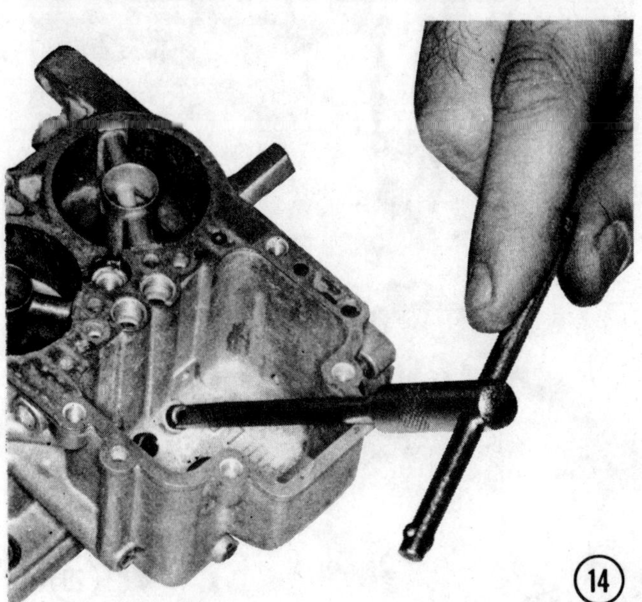

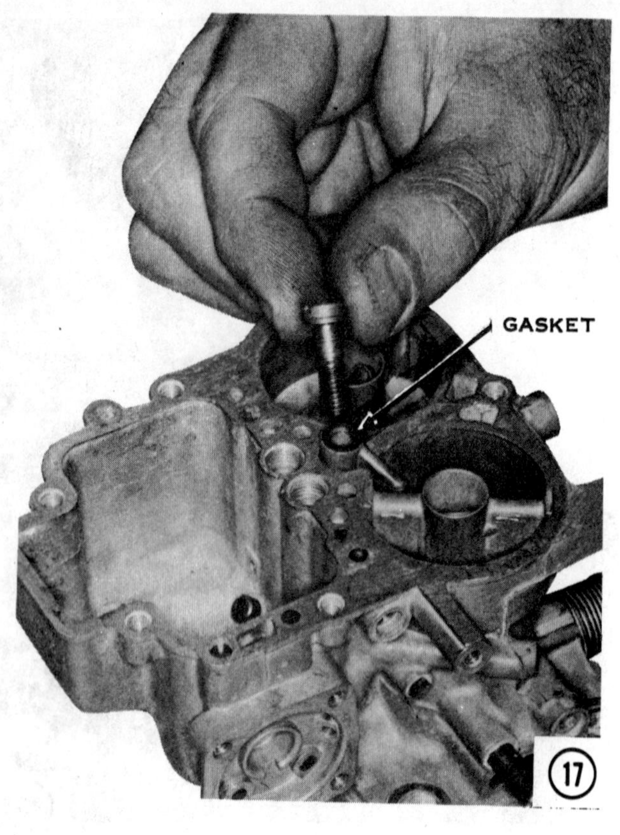
GASKET
17

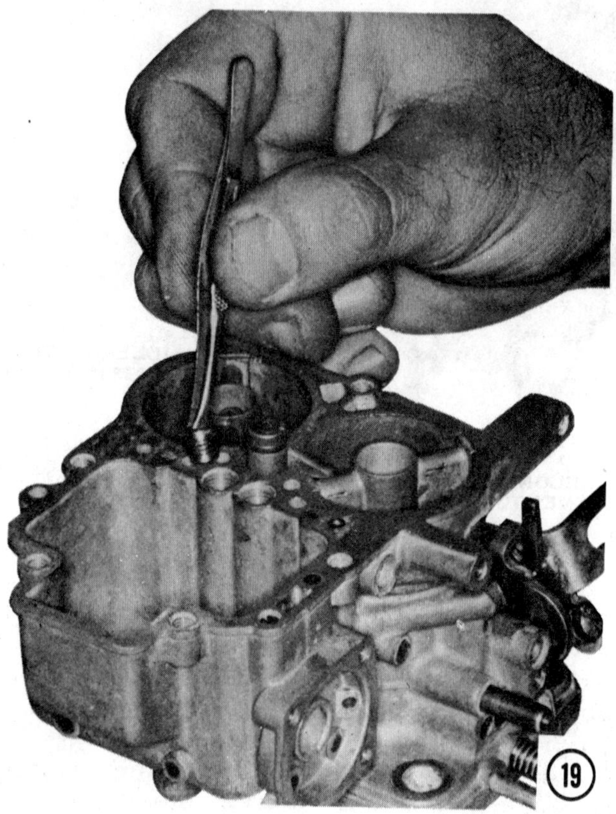
19

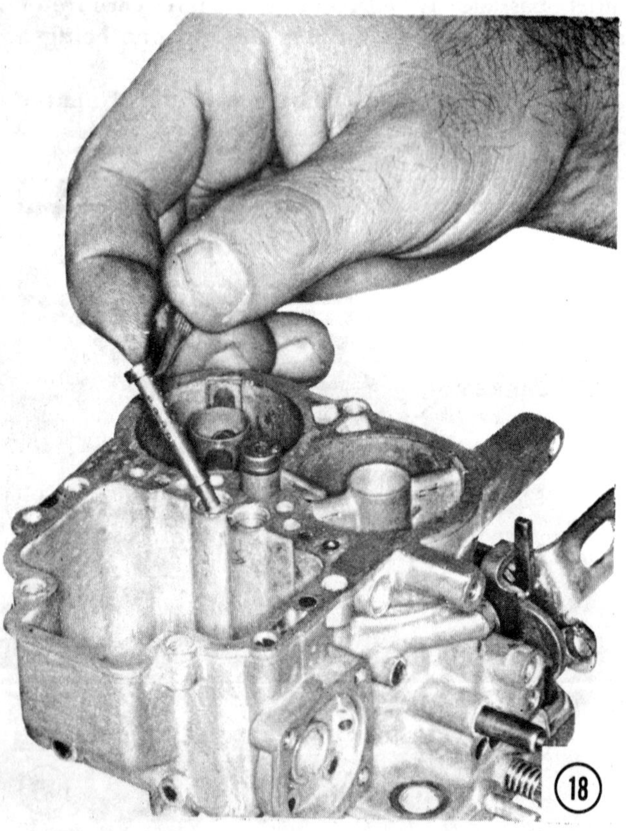
18

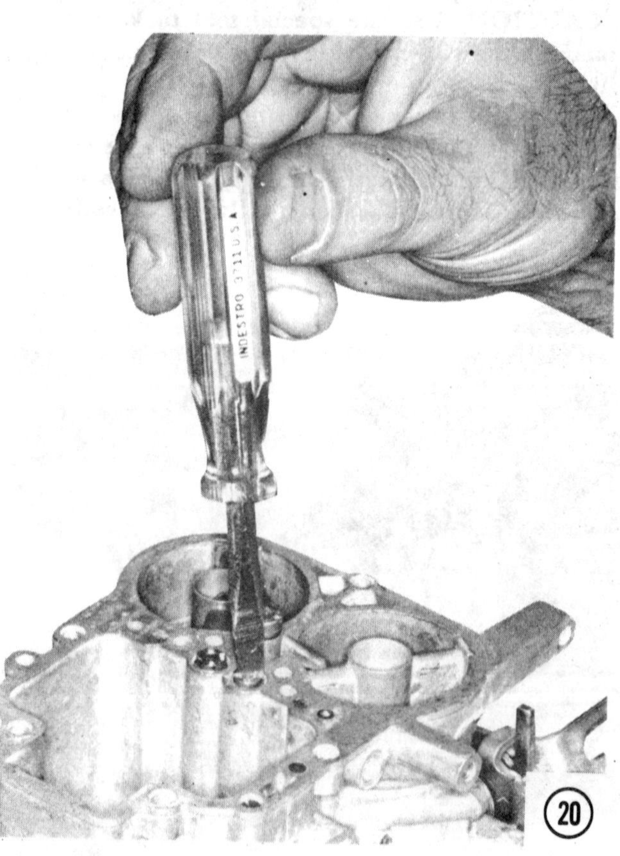
INDESTRO
20

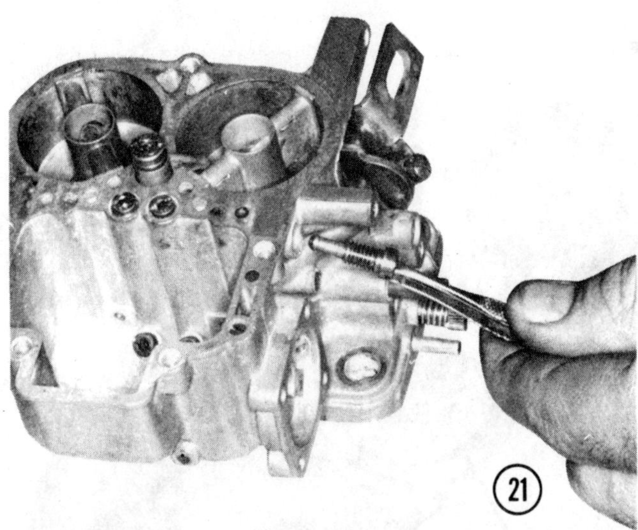
21

(17) Assemble the nylon anti-siphon ball check in the retaining screw if one is used, and then install the screw, tightening it securely. Note the gasket above the accelerator pump nozzle. Make sure that a new lead plug is inserted into the hole in the retaining screw to keep the nylon ball from dropping out.

(18) Slide the main well tube into the secondary side of the carburetor. **CAUTION: Make sure that you are installing the correct one.** No gasket is needed.

(19) Install and tighten the secondary side. **CAUTION: Make sure you are installing the right one for the secondary side.**

(20) Install the primary side main well tube and then the primary high-speed air bleed. Tighten the air bleed securely.

(21) Assemble the primary side idle jet into its holder, and then install the assembly into the primary side of the carburetor as shown. Repeat for the secondary side.

(22) Install the accelerating pump diaphragm return spring, and then position a new diaphragm over it, with the large end of the button facing out, as shown.

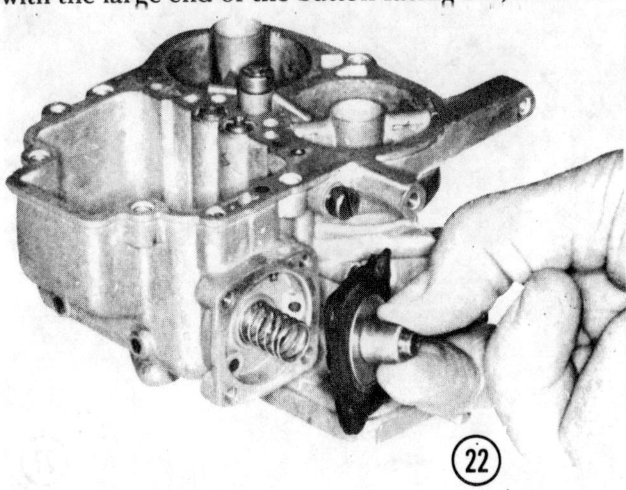
22

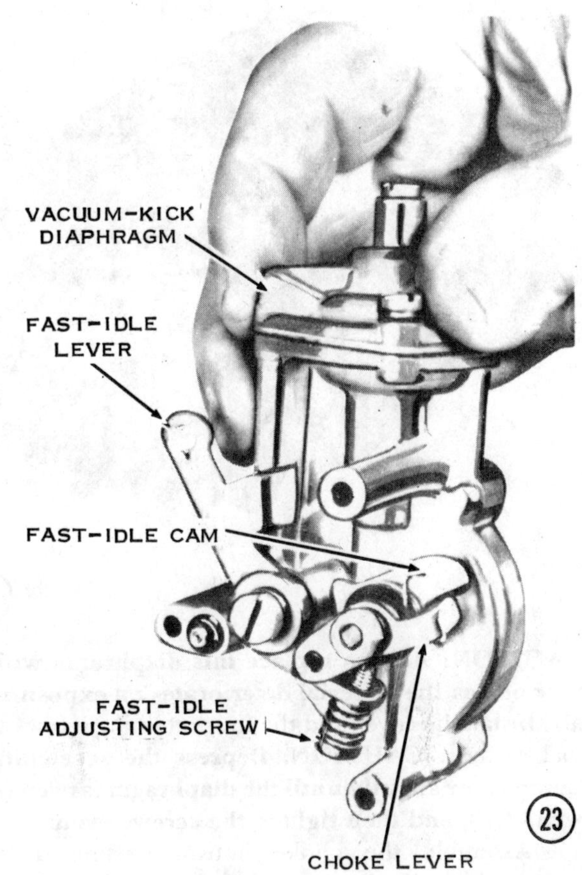

23

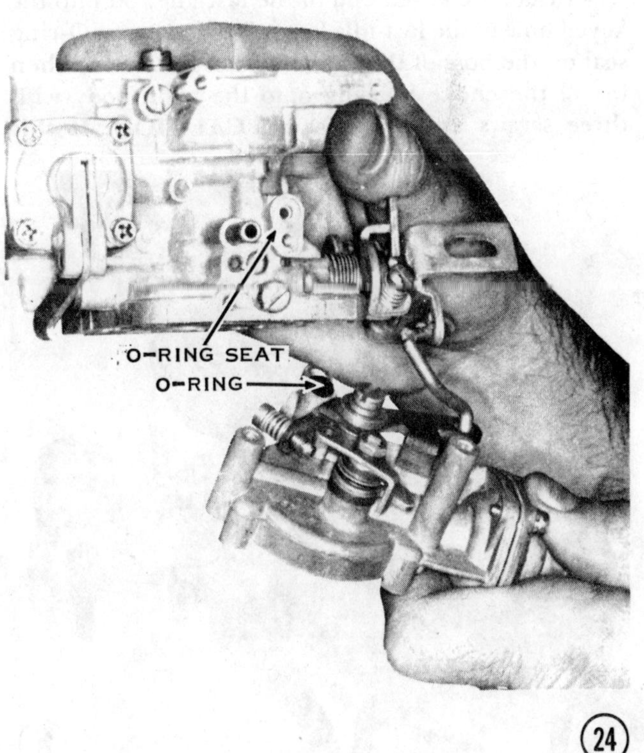

24

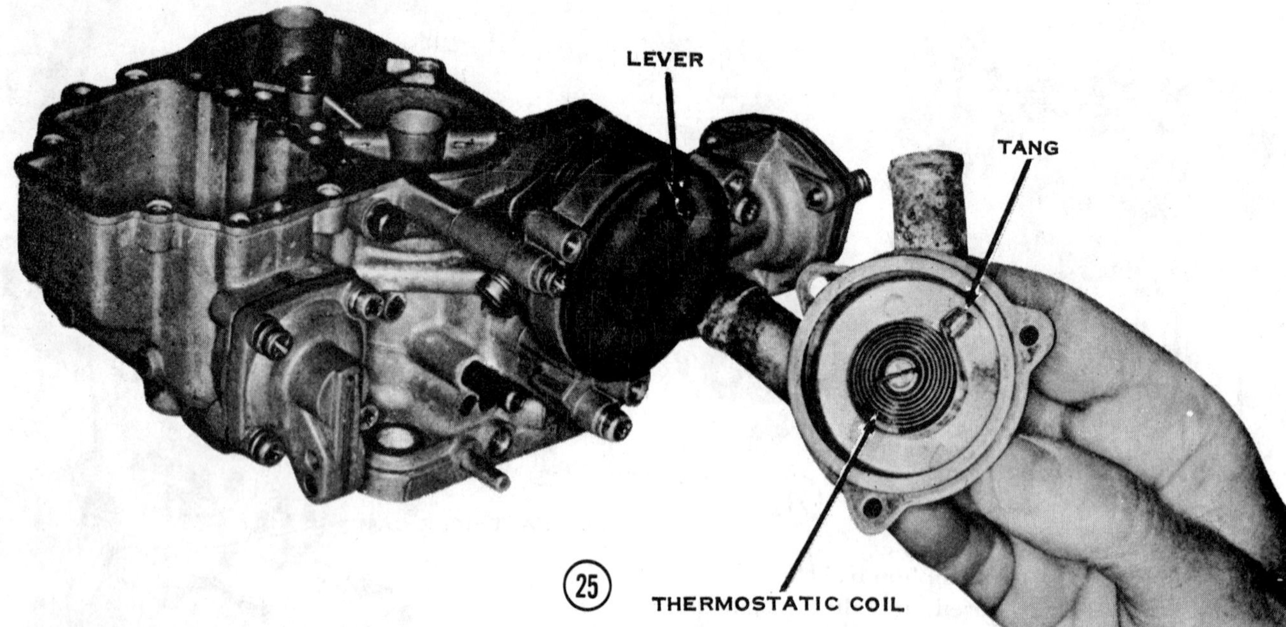

25

CAUTION: Always replace this diaphragm with a new one as the material deteriorates on exposure to air. Install the cover and the four retaining screws and lockwashers. **CAUTION: Depress the accelerating pump lever slightly until the diaphragm is even (not wrinkled), and then tighten the screws evenly.**

㉓Assemble the choke housing, using a new vacuum-kick diaphragm. this assembled views shows the position of the various parts, and can be used for assembly purposes.

㉔Install the keyed end of the fast-idle rod into the keyed hole in the fast-idle lever. Position a new O-ring seal on the boss of the vacuum passageway, and then install the choke housing onto the main body with three screws and lockwashers. **CAUTION: If this O-ring seal is missing, there will be no vacuum signal to the vacuum-kick diaphragm, and the choke will remain closed too long, causing a decided drop in gas mileage, especially during short trips.**

㉕Install the gasket, with the lever, through the slotted hole, as shown, and then position the thermostatic housing and coolant cover over the choke housing. **CAUTION: Make sure that the tang of the thermostatic coil hooks onto the choke lever; otherwise, the choke will remain on too long and gas mileage will suffer greatly.** Install the three screws and lockwashers; tighten them securely.

㉖Install a new needle valve seat, with a new gasket under it. Replace the power valve economizer assembly. Depress the plunger slightly before tightening

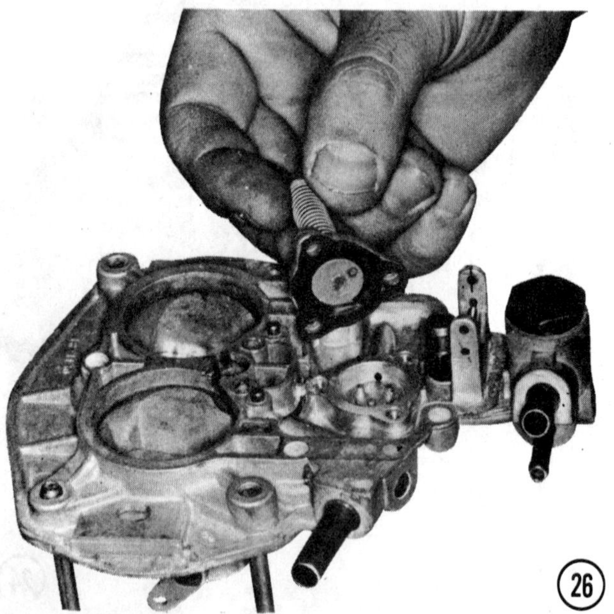
26

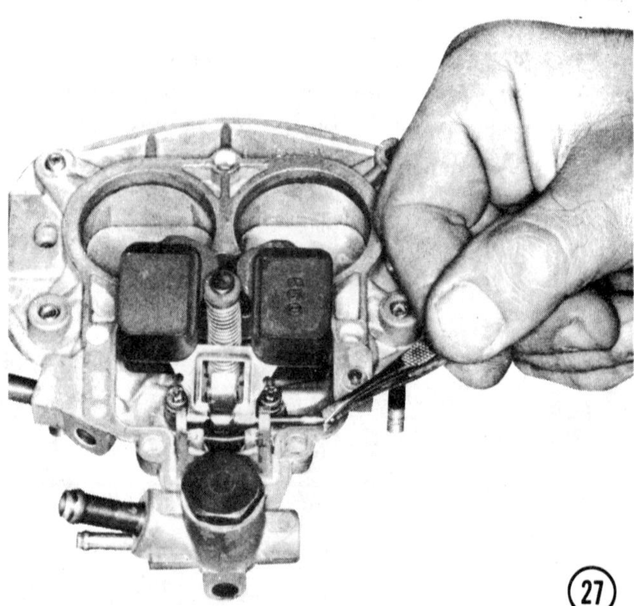
27

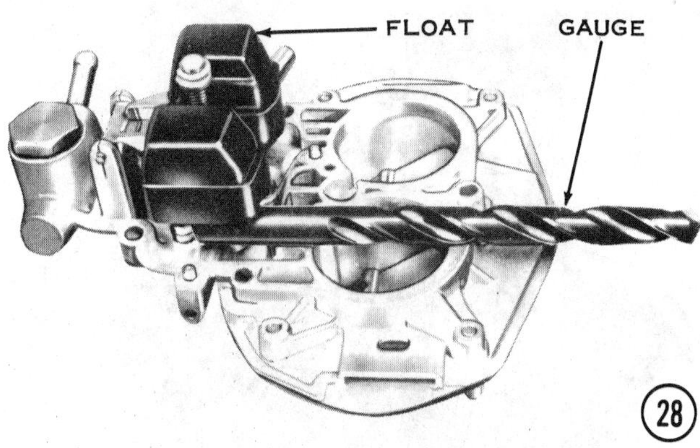

(28)

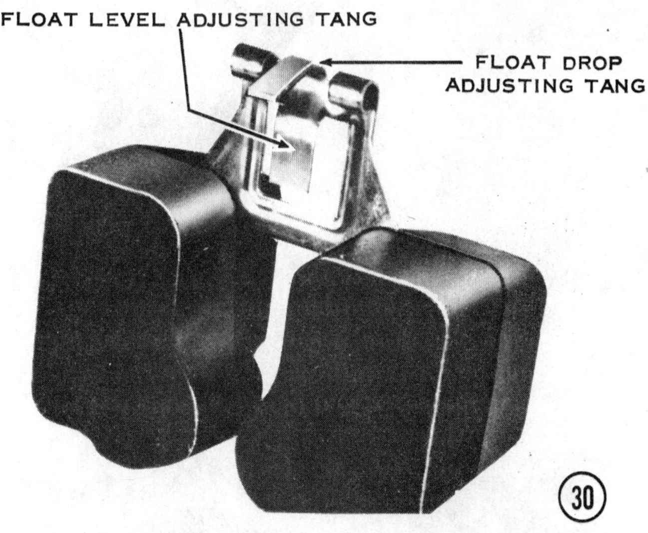

(30)

the screws and lockwashers. **CAUTION: This is important to keep the diaphragm from wrinkling.**

(27) Install the fuel inlet needle and the float assembly. Insert the float hinge pin, with the knurled end last, as shown.

(28) *To check the float level,* hold the air horn in this position, and then insert the specified gauge between each float and the casting surface. Check the specifications for the correct gauge.

(29) Invert the air horn, and then measure the float drop. The measurement must be made from the casting to the top edge of the float.

(30) This shows the tangs to be bent for a float level or float-drop adjustment.

(31) Position a new gasket on the bowl, and then carefully lower the air horn into place. Install and evenly tighten the five air horn attaching screws.

ADJUSTMENTS

Use the specifications in the parts kit for making the following adjustments:

(32) *To make the secondary throttle-stop adjustment,* back out the throttle-stop screw until the secondary throttle valve seats in the bore. Now, turn the secondary throttle stop screw in until it just contacts the throttle lever tab, and then turn the screw in an additional 1/4 turn.

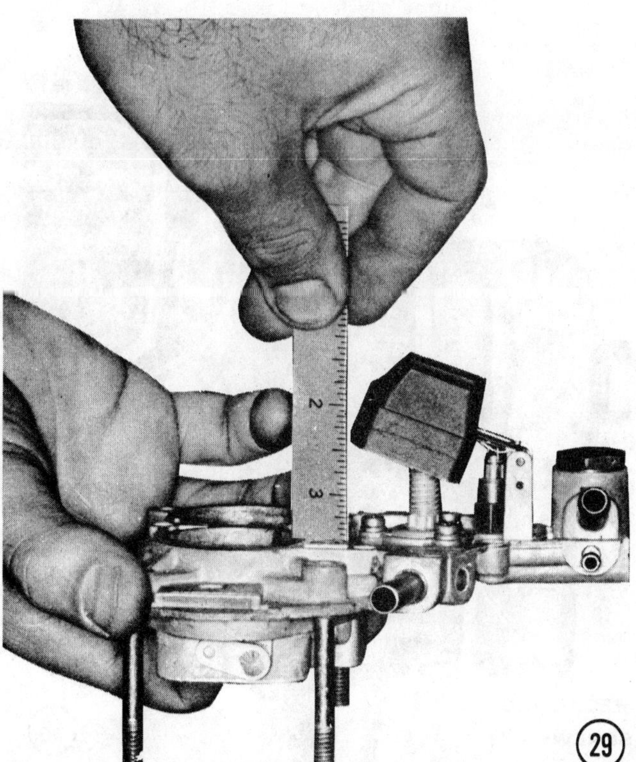

(29)

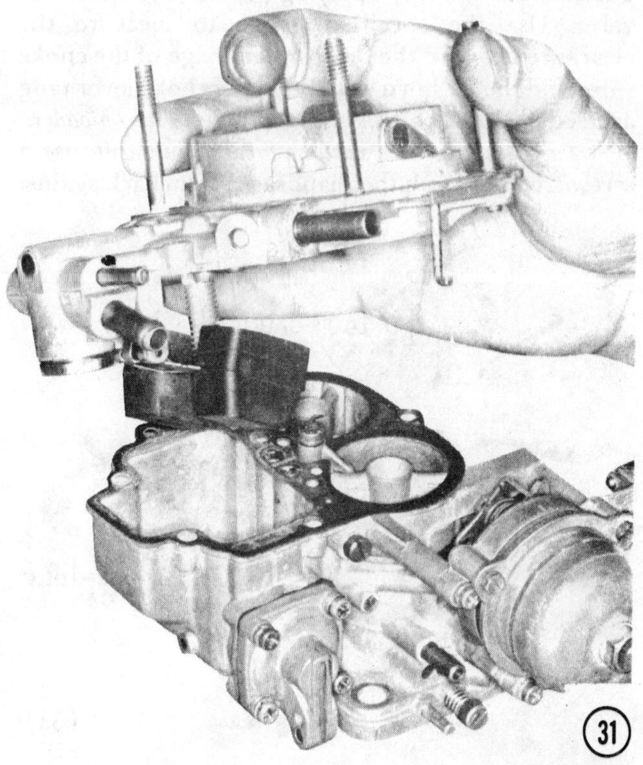

(31)

(33) *To make the fast-idle cam index adjustment,* place the fast-idle screw on the second step of the fast-idle cam, against the shoulder of the first step. Take the slack out of the linkage by applying pressure to the choke valve. Use the specified gauge to measure the clearance between the downstream edge of the choke valve and the air horn wall. Bend the choke lever tang as needed. *NOTE: This also adjusts the choke unloader.*

(34) *To check the choke vacuum-break adjustment,* use a screwdriver to push the diaphragm stem back against the stop. Take the slack out of the linkage, and then position the specified gauge between the downstream edge of the choke valve and the air horn wall. Use an Allen wrench to adjust the clearance until the gauge just fits between the choke valve and the air horn wall.

(35) *To make the choke index setting,* adjust the coolant cover to position the index line with the specified line on the housing. Tighten the three cover screws securely. Connect the wire to the electric choke terminal.

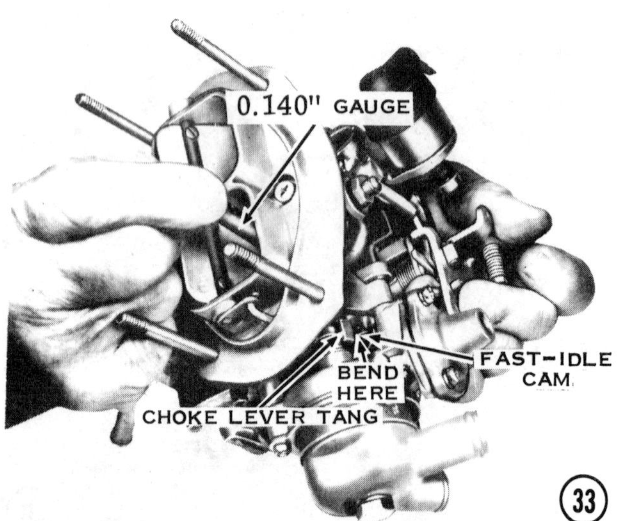

ON-THE-CAR ADJUSTMENTS

(36) *To make the idle adjustments,* the engine must be warmed to operating temperature, choke fully open, air cleaner installed, air conditioner turned off, fuel tank vapor hose disconnected at the charcoal canister, and distributor vacuum hose disconnected and the end plugged. *To make the low idle speed adjustment,* the idle-stop solenoid must be de-energized. Adjust the low-idle speed screw to obtain 500 rpm in neutral. Connect the solenoid, pull out on the stem, and then adjust the curb idle speed to the specification on the tuning decal.

(37) *To make the idle mixture adjustment,* turn the idle mixture adjusting screw to obtain the specified CO percentage, if an HC/CO analyzer is available.

(38) *To make the idle mixture adjustment by the "lean drop" method,* turn the idle speed adjusting screw to the specified idle rpm, **plus** the Artificial Enrichment rpm on the tuning decal. Now, turn the idle mixture adjusting screw **(not the idle speed screw)** in (lean) until you slow the engine to the curb-idle specification on the decal. Note that you are slowing engine speed about 50 rpm by **leaning** the air-fuel mixture, and this will result in as lean a mixture as possible, and the CO reading on an analyzer will generally be within specifications.

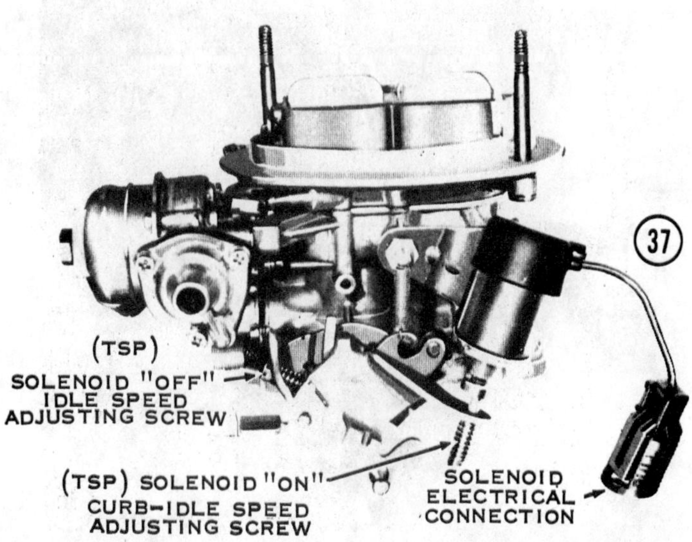

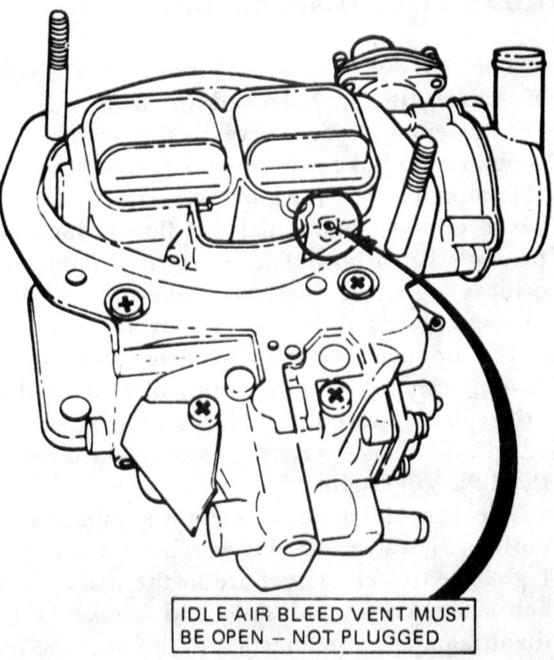

Poor fuel economy can result if the idle air bleed vent plugs up, as discussed in the text.

MODEL 5200 CARBURETOR SERVICE NOTE

POOR FUEL ECONOMY

The idle air vent, located adjacent and forward of the primary air bleed, is the only vent for the idle system. If it plugs up, fuel economy for stop-and-go type of driving will be significantly reduced.

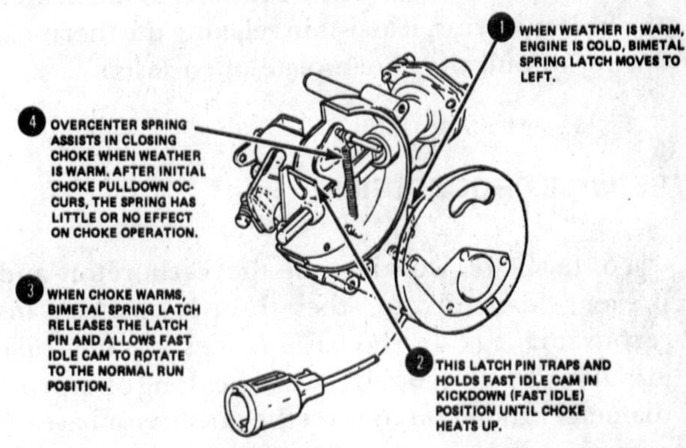

New fast-idle cam latch used on the 2.3 liter engine since 1975.

MODEL 2150-2V CARBURETOR

The Model 2150 carburetor has two main assemblies; the air horn and the main body. The air horn assembly, which serves as the main body cover, contains the choke plate and the fuel bowl vent valve.

It also contains the pull-over enrichment system, which provides additional fuel flow at high air flow through the air horn. Fuel is drawn through metering orifices from the fuel bowl and into the air flow through bleeds in the upper body air horn.

The air horn assembly also contains a fuel deceleration metering system, consisting of a metered pickup orifice in the fuel bowl and fuel/air mixing orifices and bleeds. This system is only used on carburetors with the 2.8L V-6 engine.

The throttle plate, accelerating pump assembly, enrichment valve assembly, fuel bowl, and mechanical high-speed bleed system are in the main body. The automatic choke housing and choke pull-down diaphragm are also attached to the main body.

Each bore contains a main and booster venturi, main fuel discharge, accelerating pump dishcarge, idle fuel discharge, and throttle plate.

The booster venturi contains high-speed bleed orifices, along with a mechanical high-speed bleed control system. This system consists of a mechanical lift rod that actuates reverse-tapered "ballbat" metering rods in the high-speed bleed orifices. This allows exacting control of the fuel/air mixture to the booster venturis for more precise high-speed operation and improved low-speed response.

The carburetor also uses an electric-assist automatic choke system, which consists of a choke cap, thermostatic spring, bimetallic temperature sensing disc (switch), and a ceramic heater, powered from the stator tap of the alternator. Voltage is constantly supplied to the temperature-sensing switch as long as the engine is running. The system is grounded through a strip connected to a carburetor body. At temperatures above approximately 60°F, the temperature-sensing switch closes, and current is supplied to the heater. As the heater warms, it assists in relaxing the thermostatic spring to pull the choke plate open faster.

SERVICE PROCEDURES

To facilitate working on the carburetor and to prevent damage to the throttle plates, install carburetor legs on the base. If legs are unavailable, install four bolts (about 2-1/4 inches long of the correct diameter) and eight nuts on the carburetor base. Use a separate container for the component parts of the

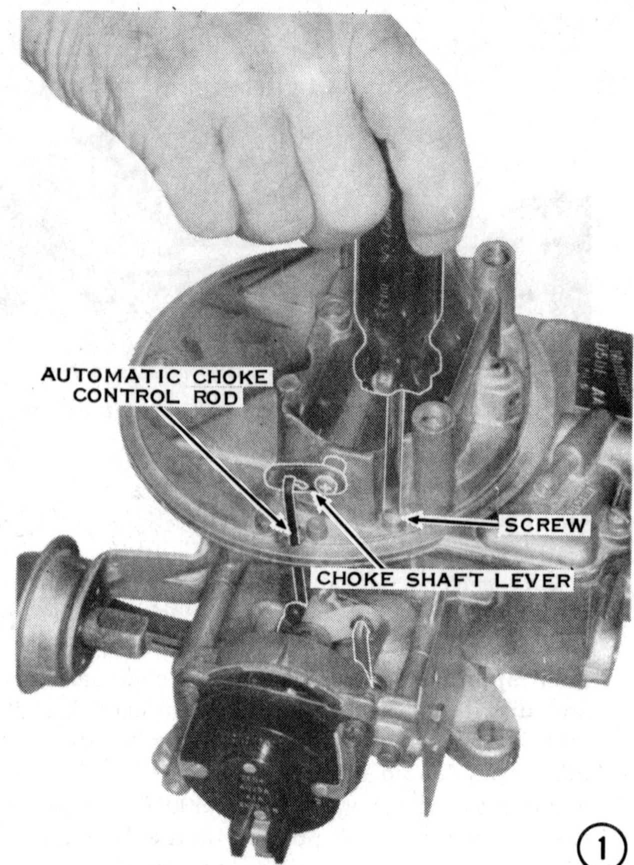

1

2

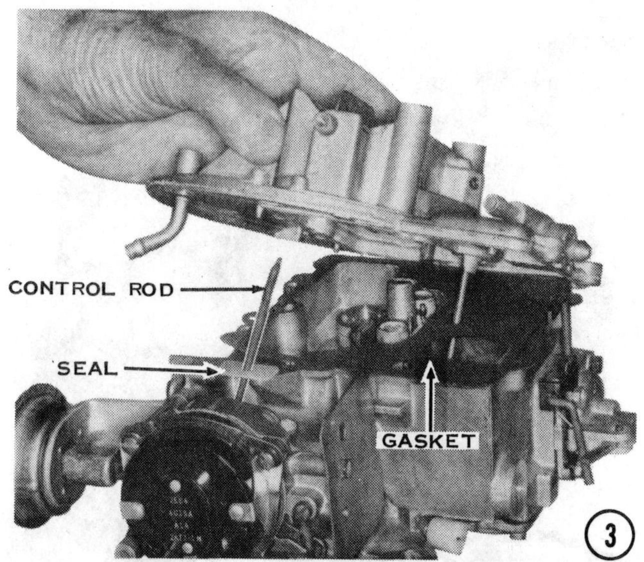

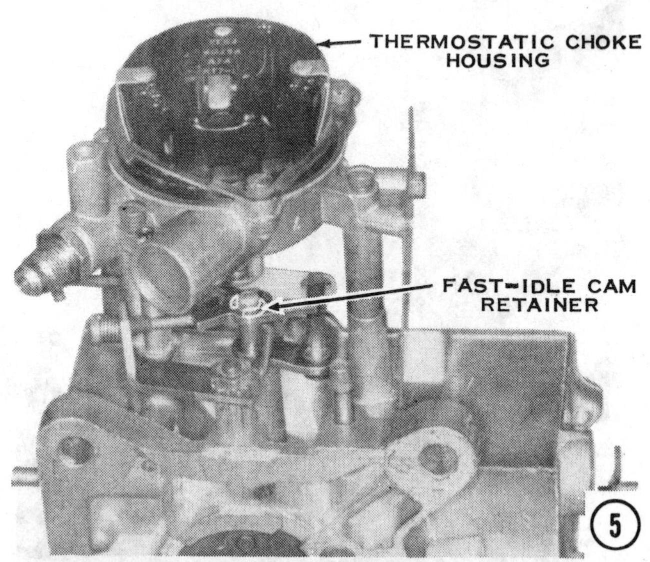

various assemblies to facilitate cleaning, inspection, and assembly.

The following is a step-by-step sequence of operations for completely overhauling the carburetor. However certain components of the carburetor may be serviced without a complete disassembly of the entire unit. For a complete carburetor overhaul, follow all of the steps. To partially overhaul a carburetor or to install a new gasket kit, follow only the applicable steps.

DISASSEMBLING

① Remove the air cleaner anchor screw. Remove the automatic choke control rod retainer at the bottom of the rod. Remove the air horn attaching screws, lockwashers, and carburetor identification tag.

Disassembling The Air Horn

② Remove the choke control rod by loosening the screw that secures the choke shaft lever to the choke shaft.

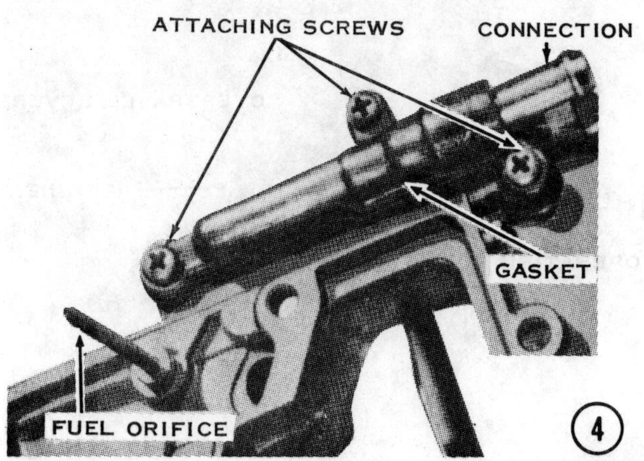

③ Lift off the air horn. Remove the rod from the air horn. Slide the plastic dust seal out of the air horn. If it is necessary to remove the choke plate, file off the staking marks on the choke plate attaching screws and remove the screws. Remove the choke plate by sliding it out of the shaft from the top of the air horn. Remove any burrs around the screw holes prior to removing the choke shaft. Slide the choke shaft out of the air horn.

④ Invert the air horn assembly and remove the three attaching screws from the decel metering assembly. Remove the metering assembly and gasket from the air horn. Discard the gasket.

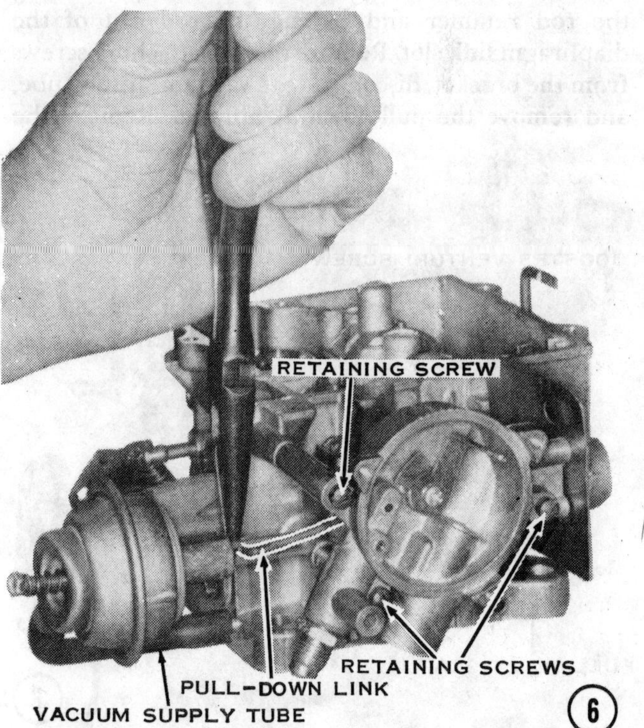

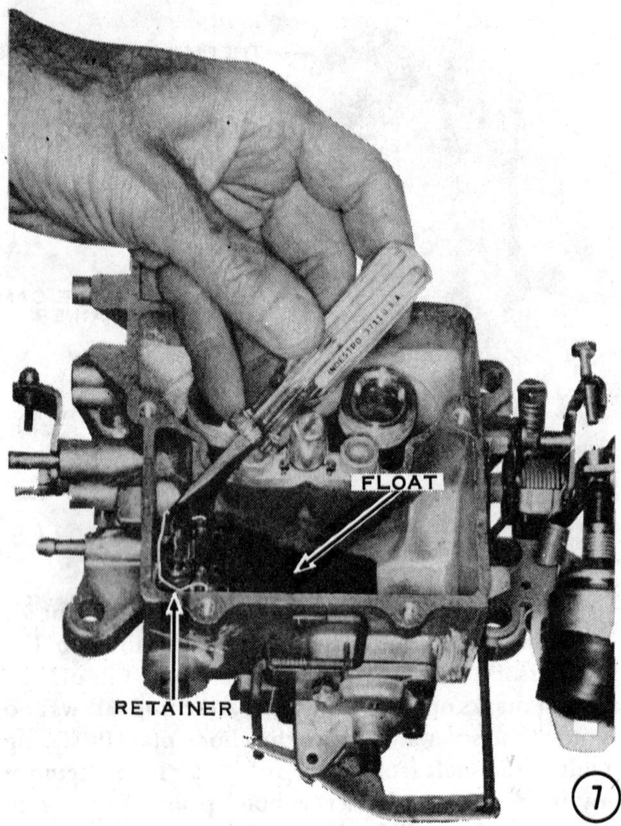

7

9

DISASSEMBLING THE CHOKE LINKAGE

⑤Remove the fast-idle cam retainer. Take out the thermostatic choke spring housing retaining screws, and then remove the clamp, housing, and gasket.

⑥Disconnect the choke pull-down link by removing the rod retainer and pulling the rod out of the diaphragm link slot. Remove the two attaching screws from the bracket, disconnect the vacuum supply tube, and remove the pull-down diaphragm. Remove the choke housing assembly retaining screws. Remove the choke control rod retainer, the choke housing assembly, gasket, and the fast-idle cam and rod from the fast-idle cam lever. Remove the choke lever retaining screw and washer. Disconnect the choke control rod from the choke lever. Remove the choke lever and fast-idle cam lever from the choke housing.

⑦With the use of a screwdriver, pry the float shaft retainer from the fuel inlet seat. Remove the float, float shaft retainer, and fuel inlet needle assembly. Remove the retainer and float shaft from the float lever.

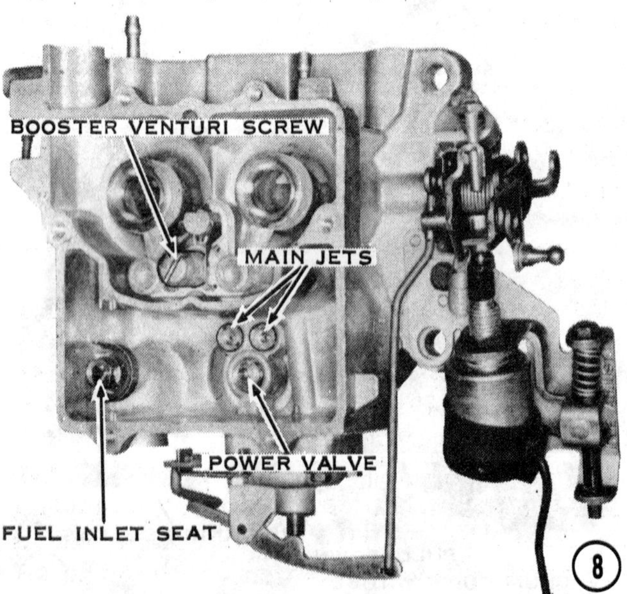

8

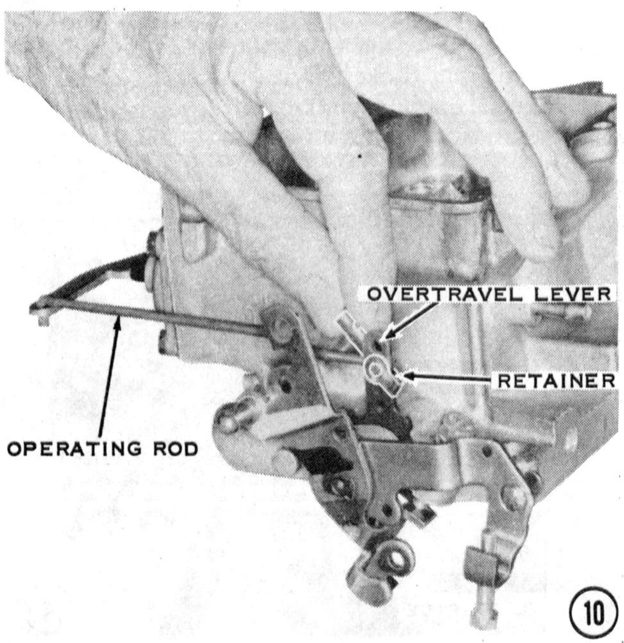

10

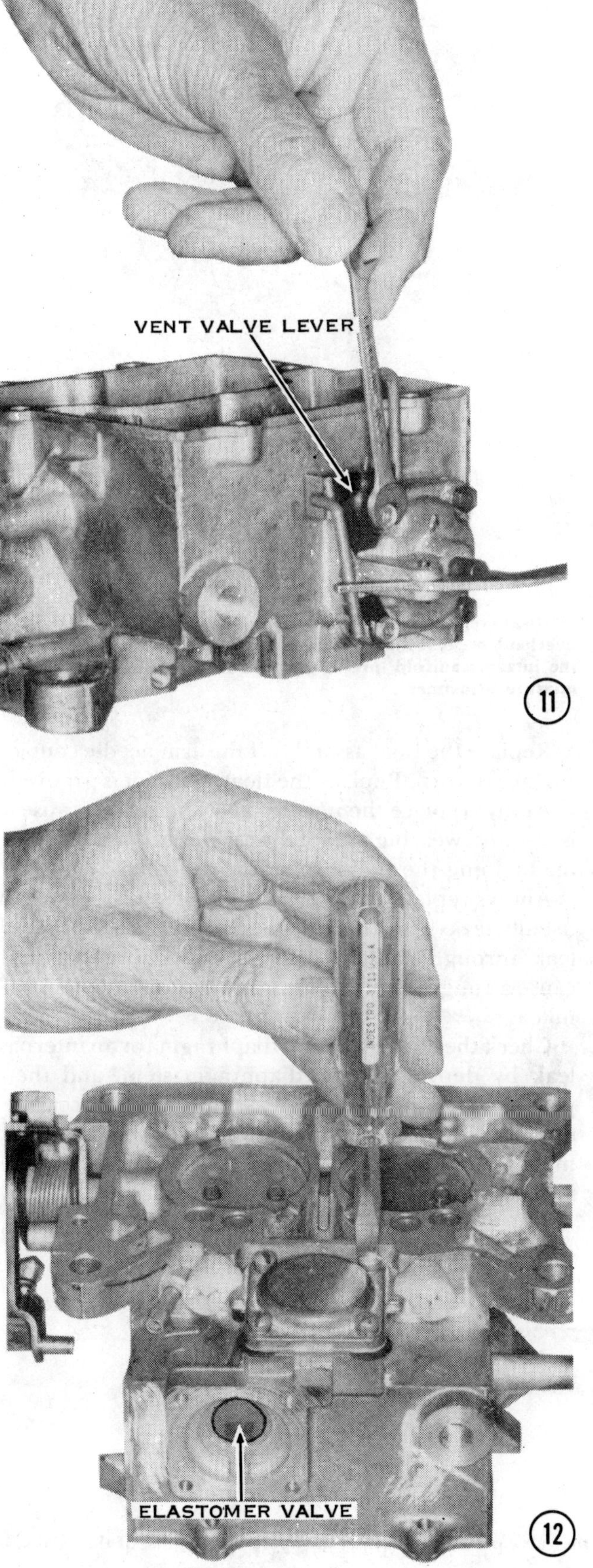

(11)
(12)

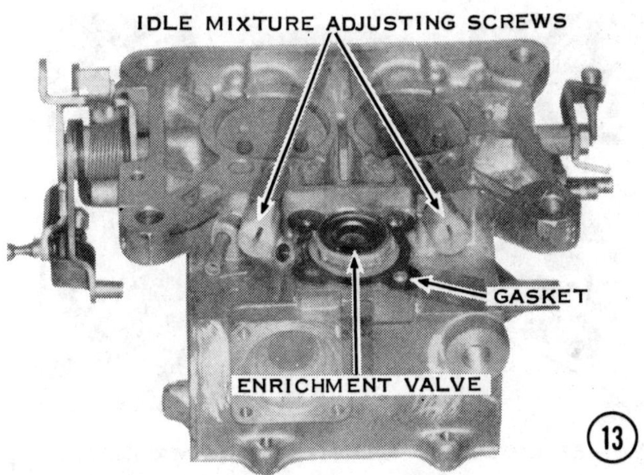

(13)

Dissassembling The Main Body

⑧ Remove the fuel inlet needle, seat, filter, screen, and the main jets with a jet wrench. Remove the booster venturi screw (accelerator pump discharge), booster venturi, metering rod assembly, and gasket. Invert the main body and let the accelerating pump discharge weight and ball fall into the hand.

⑨ Remove the solenoid-dashpot/throttle positioner.

⑩ Remove the accelerator pump operating rod from the overtravel lever and retainer. To release the operating rod from the overtravel lever retainer, press upward on the part of the retainer that snaps over the rod. Disengage the rod from the retainer, but be sure to make a note of the hole in which it was initially installed so that you can assemble it properly. Disengage the rod from the retainer and from the overtravel lever. Remove the rod and retainer.

⑪ Remove the accelerator pump cover attaching screws. Remove the accelerator pump cover, diaphragm assembly, spring, and the fuel bowl vent valve lever. If it is necessary to remove the Elastomer valve, grasp it firmly and pull it out. If the Elastomer valve tip broke off during removal, be sure to remove the tip from the fuel bowl. An Elastomer valve must be replaced whenever it has been removed from the carburetor.

⑫ Invert the main body and remove the enrichment valve cover and the gasket.

⑬ Remove the enrichment valve with a box or socket wrench. Remove the enrichment valve gasket. Discard the gasket. Remove the idle fuel mixture adjusting screws (needles) and the springs. Remove the limiters from the adjusting screws.

⑭ If it is necessary to remove the throttle shaft because of wear, lightly scribe the throttle plates along the throttle shaft, and mark each plate and its corresponding bore with a number or letter for proper

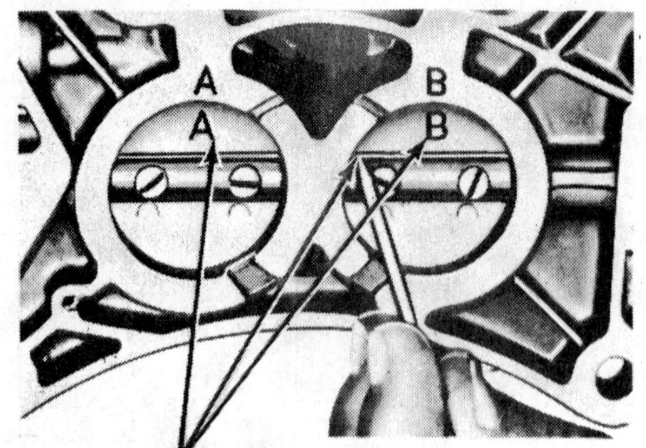

SCRIBE LINES AND IDENTIFICATION MARKS (14)

installation. Slide the throttle shaft out of the main body, making sure you catch the mechanical high-speed bleed actuator located on the throttle shaft between the throttle plates.

CLEANING AND INSPECTING

Wash all parts, except diaphragms and parts with rubber, in a commercial carburetor cleaning solvent. Lacquer thinner or denatured alcohol can also be used. Rinse parts in hot water to remove all traces of the cleaning solvent and dry them with compressed air. Direct compressed air through all passageways and jets to make sure that they are clean. **CAUTION: Don't use a wire or drill to clean jets or calibrated openings, or you may enlarge the holes.**

Check the choke and throttle shafts for excessive wear. Inspect the choke plate and throttle valve plate to be sure that they are not nicked. Replace the entire carburetor if the throttle shaft is worn excessively. During manufacture, the location of the idle transfer and spark advance control ports to the throttle valve is carefully established, and it would be very unlikely that the original relationships of the ports to the valve could be obtained if a new shaft were installed.

Always replace the power (enrichment) valve at each carburetor overhaul, because the diaphragm leaks and allows fuel to flow into the intake manifold, preventing you from leaning out the idle mixture adjustment.

Replace the float assembly if the arm needle contact surface is worn. Replace the float shaft if it is grooved.

Always replace the needle valve and seat, because it is the most wearing part of the carburetor and is vital in maintaining the fuel level at the designed height.

Always replace the power valve assembly because it usually leaks after long use and this will cause fuel to leak through the porous vacuum diaphragm and cause a rough engine idle as well as a reduction in gas mileage.

Check the choke vacuum diaphragm for an internal leak by depressing the diaphragm stem, and then placing your finger over the vacuum fitting to seal the opening. Release the diaphragm stem. If the stem moves out more than 1/16″ in ten seconds, the leakage is excessive and the unit must be replaced.

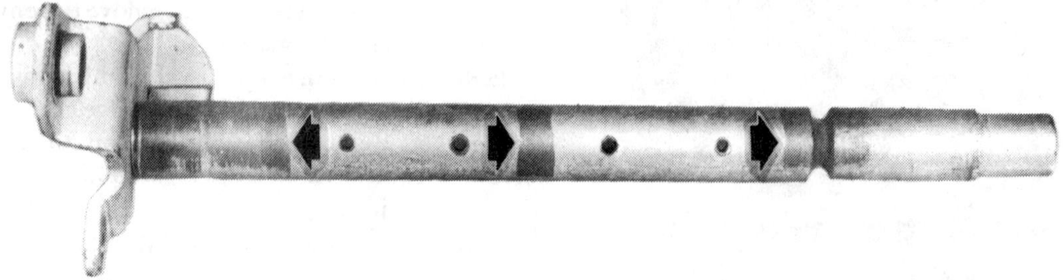

The throttle shaft wears in this fashion and this upsets the timing of the valve ports which affect the operation of some of the valves.

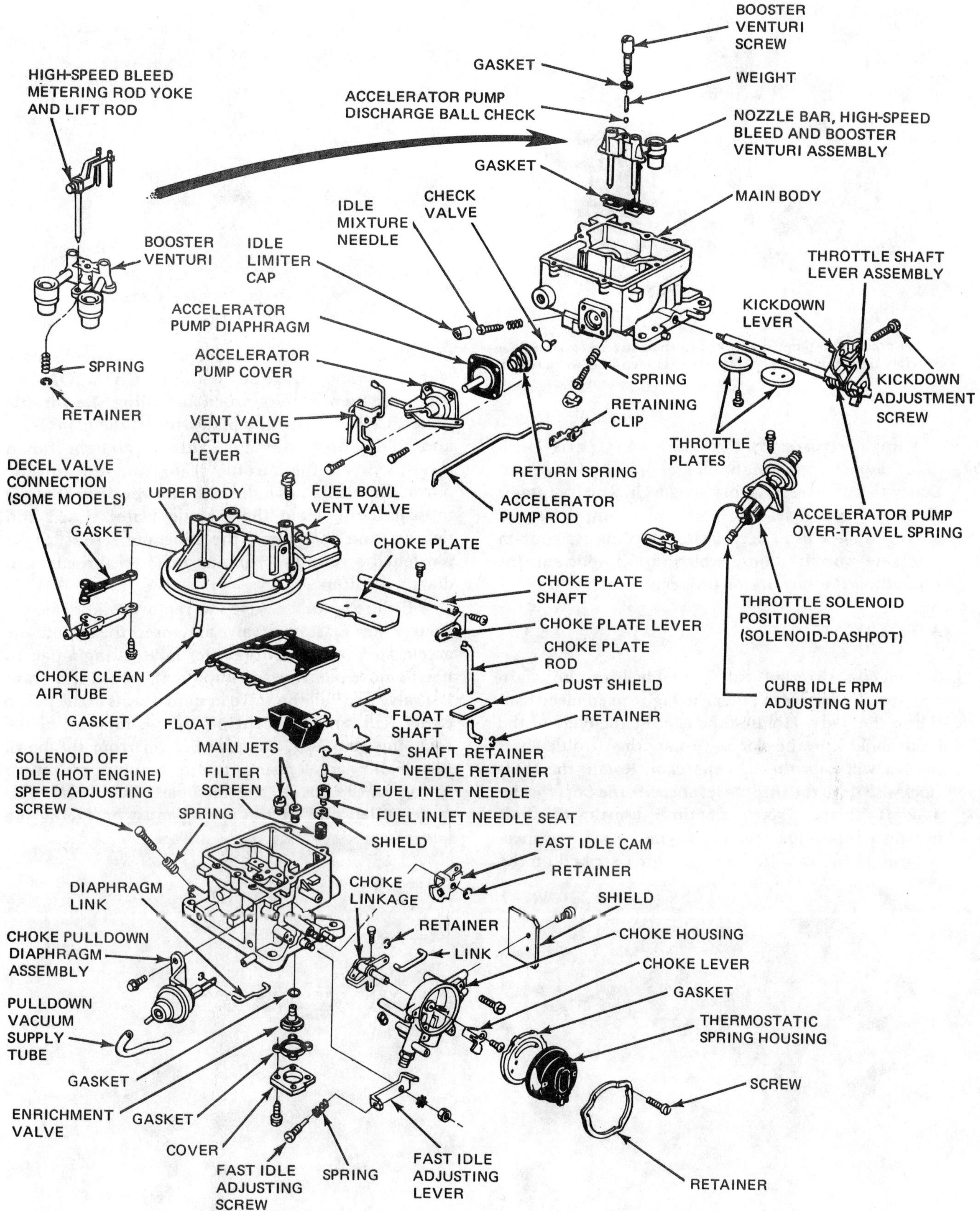

Motorcraft 2150-2V carburetor introduced in 1975 features a mechanical high-speed bleed system and new types of deceleration systems and throttle positioner/modulators.

The accelerator pump diaphragm must be stressed to straighten it before tightening the retaining screws to keep from wrinkling it.

Always replace all gaskets and parts with diaphragms because of the danger of leaks. It is a good policy to purchase a factory repair kit, which contains all of the parts that wear most and a complete set of gaskets and seals. These factory kits always contain complete specifications, which are important for rebuilding the carburetor properly.

ASSEMBLING

(15) Slide the throttle shaft assembly into the main body until it begins to enter the high-speed bleed cam slot in the body. Holding the cam by the edge of the point, hold it in the slot and rotate the throttle shaft until it will pass through the cam. Rotate the shaft clockwise until the throttle lever clears the boss for the TSP off-idle speed screw. Continue inserting the shaft into proper position, rotating it as necessary to properly position the cam. Refer to the lines scribed on the throttle plates and install them in their proper location with the screws snug, but not tight. **CAUTION: Always use new screws when installing the throttle plates.** Close the throttle plates, invert the main body and hold it up to the light. Little or no light should show between the throttle plates and the throttle bores. Tap the plates lightly with a screwdriver handle to seat them. Hold the throttle plates closed and tighten, and then stake the attaching screws. Stake hardened screws by crimping exposed threads with diagonal cutters.

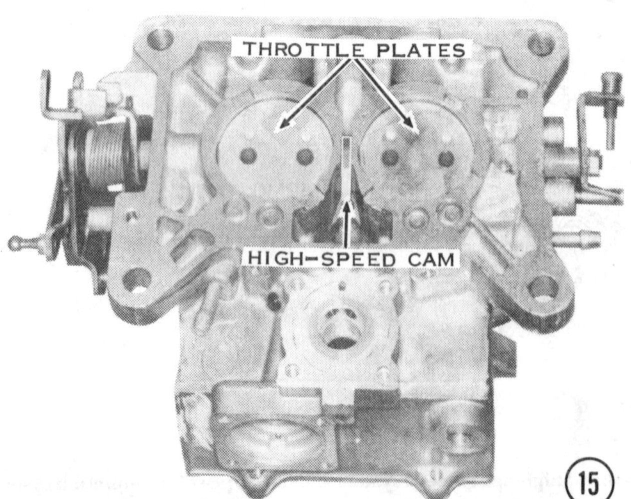

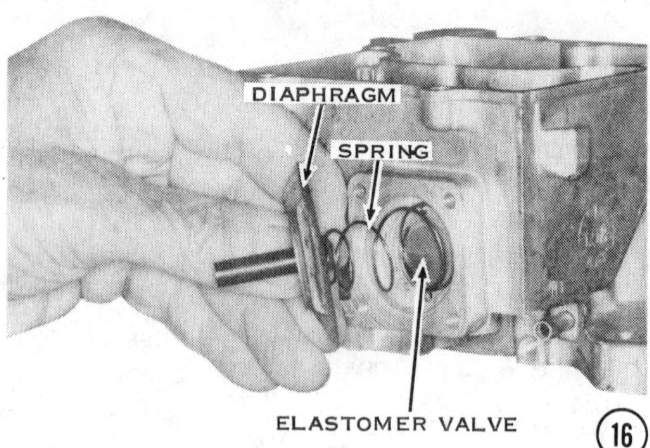

(16) If the Elastomer valve was removed, lubricate the tip of a new Elastomer valve and insert the tip into the accelerator pump cavity center hole. Using a pair of needle-nose pliers, reach into the fuel bowl and grasp the valve tip. Pull the valve in until it seats in the pump cavity wall, and then cut off the tip forward of the retaining shoulder. Remove the tip from the bowl. Install the accelerating pump diaphragm return spring on the boss in the chamber. **CAUTION: The large coiled end of the spring must be facing the**

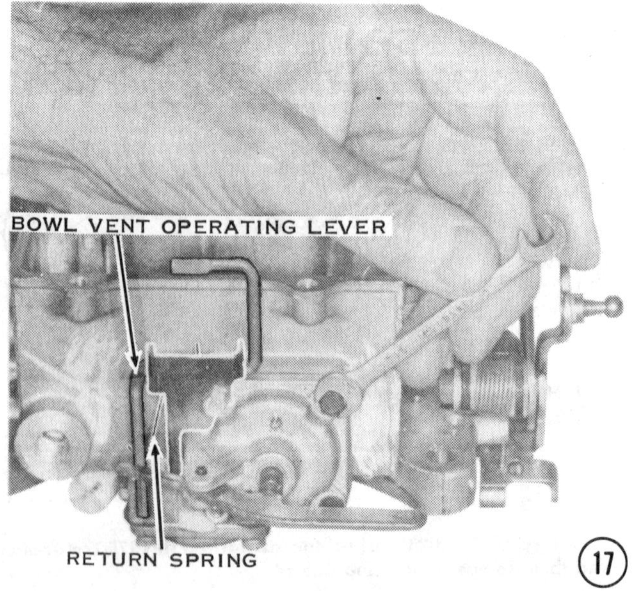

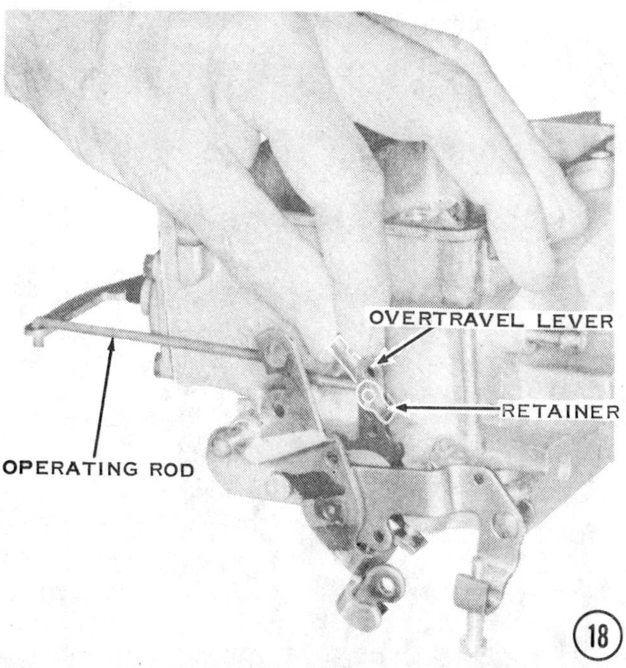

bowl, as shown. If installed in reverse, the Elastomer valve will be kept from operating and a flat spot on accleration will result. Insert the diaphragm assembly in the cover, and then place the cover-and-diaphragm assembly on the main body. Install and tighten the two outside cover screws. No lockwashers are used.

(17) Install the bowl vent operating lever under the pump operating rod with the return spring forcing it against the pump operating rod, and then insert the two inside cover screws. No lockwashers are needed.

GASKET

19

(18) Insert the accelerator pump operating rod into the hole in the accelerator pump actuating lever. Position the accelerator pump operating rod retainer over the overtravel lever. Insert the operating rod through the retainer and the hole in the overtravel lever, and then snap the retainer down over the rod to keep it in place. **CAUTION: Make sure that you have inserted the operating rod into the hole in the overtravel lever from which it was removed.**

(19) Invert the main body. Install a new enrichment valve and a new gasket. Tighten the valve securely with a wrench. **CAUTION: Always replace this valve; otherwise, exposure to the air will cause the diaphragm to become porous and leak.** When this occurs, fuel will be drawn through the diaphragm and into the intake manifold through the vacuum passageways. The gas mileage will drop drastically, and the engine will idle very rough because of the rich mixture.

(20) Install the idle mixture adjusting screws (needles) and springs. Turn the needles in gently with the fingers until they just touch the seat, then back them off 1-1/2 turns for a preliminary idle fuel mixture adjustment. Install the enrichment valve cover and new gasket. The cover must be installed with the limiter stops on the cover in position to provide a positive stop for the tabs on the idle mixture adjusting screws limiters.

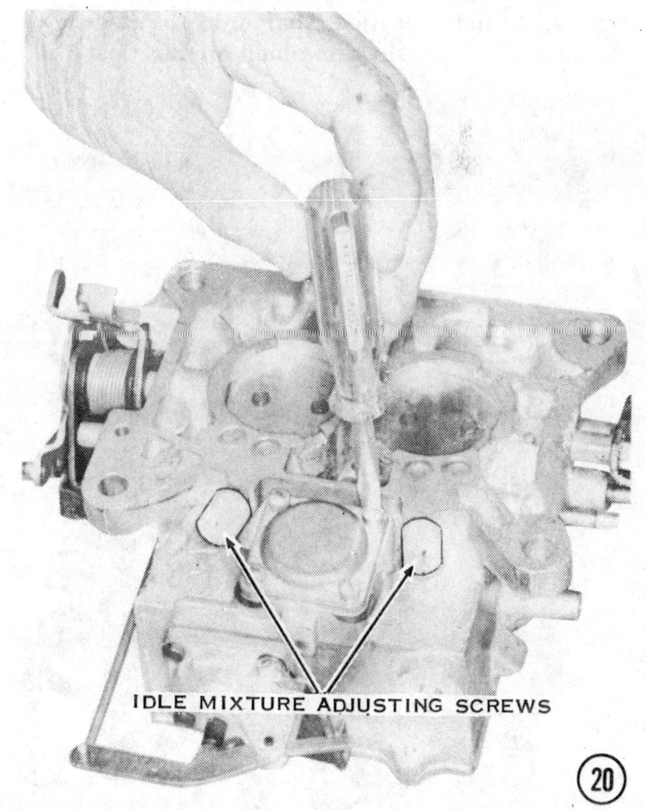

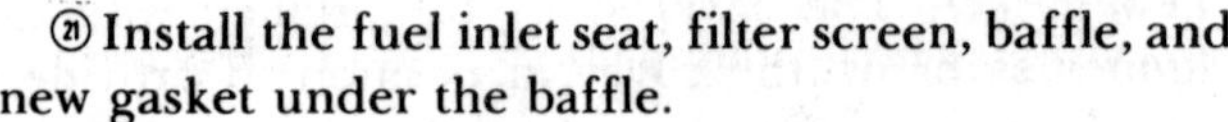

(21) Install the fuel inlet seat, filter screen, baffle, and new gasket under the baffle.

(22) Install the main jets. **CAUTION: Be sure the correct jets are installed according to specifications.**

(23) Install the fuel inlet needle assembly in the fuel inlet seat. Slide the float shaft into the float lever. Position the float shaft retainer on the float shaft.

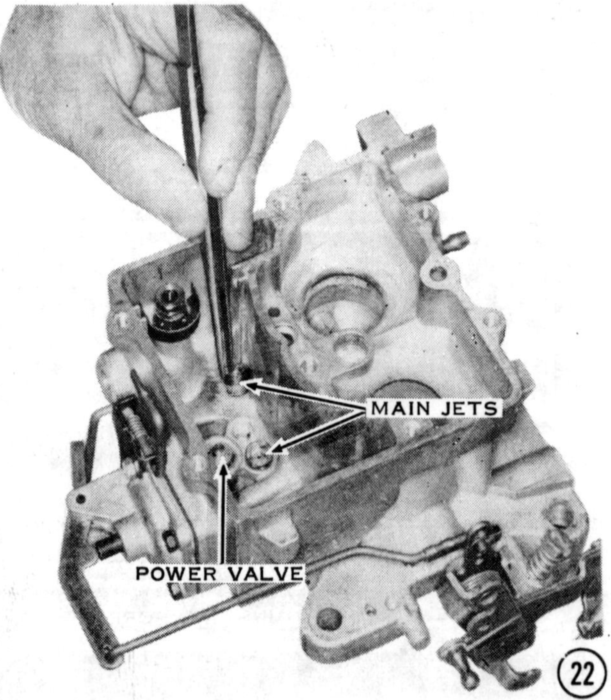

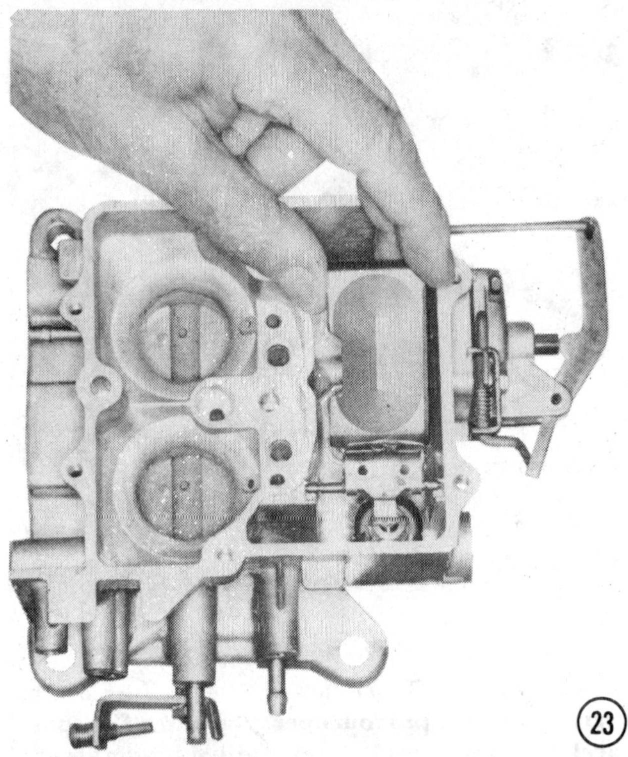

Insert the float assembly into the fuel bowl and hook the float lever tab under the fuel inlet needle assembly. Insert the float shaft into its guides at the sides of the fuel bowl. With a screwdriver, position the float shaft retainer in the groove on the fuel inlet needle seat.

(24) *To check the dry float level,* measure the distance between the top surface of the main body (without the gasket) and the top surface of the float. Depress the float tab to seat the fuel inlet needle. Take the measurement near the center of the float, at a point 1/8 inch from the free end of the float. **CAUTION: If the**

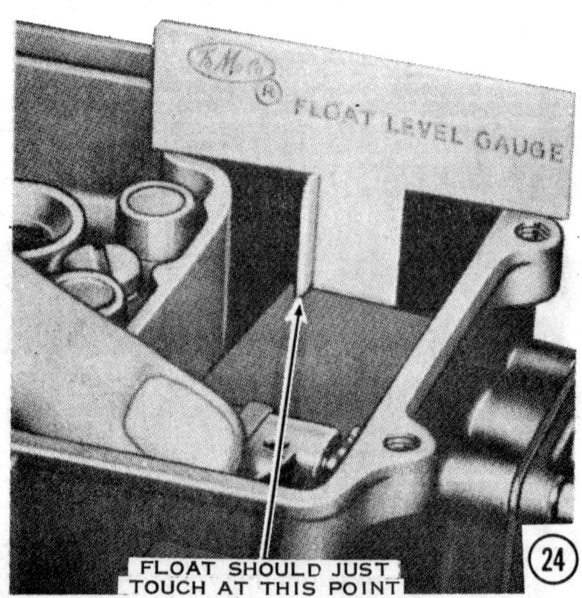

25

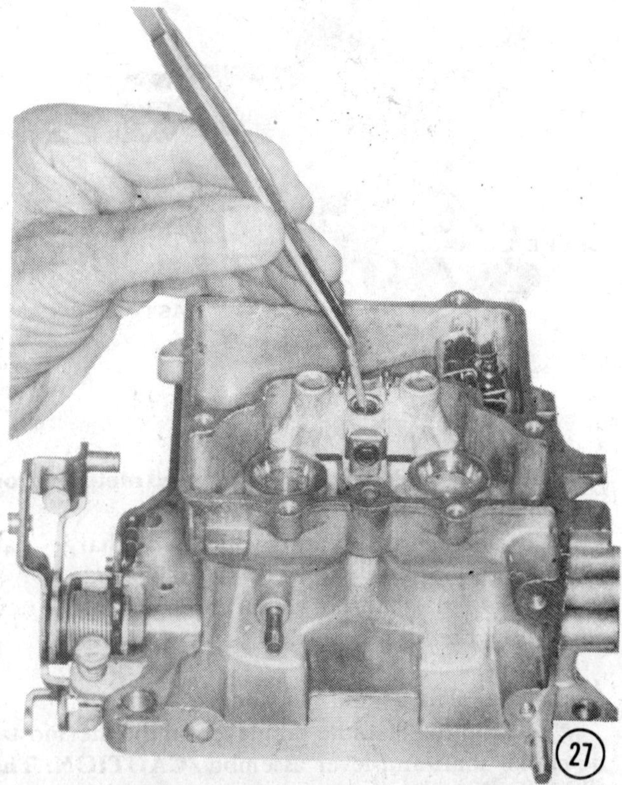
27

cardboard float gauge is used, place the gauge in the corner of the enlarged end section of the fuel bowl. The gauge should touch the float near the end, but not on the end radius. If necessary, bend the tab on the float to bring the setting within the specified limits. This should provide the proper preliminary fuel level setting. *NOTE: The dry float level adjustment is a preliminary one, and the final wet fuel adjustment must be made after the carburetor is mounted on the engine. However, the dry adjustment will suffice in most cases.*

(25) Drop the accelerator pump discharge ball into the passage in the main body.

(26) Position a new gasket, and then install the booster venturi assembly in the main body. **CAUTION: Make**

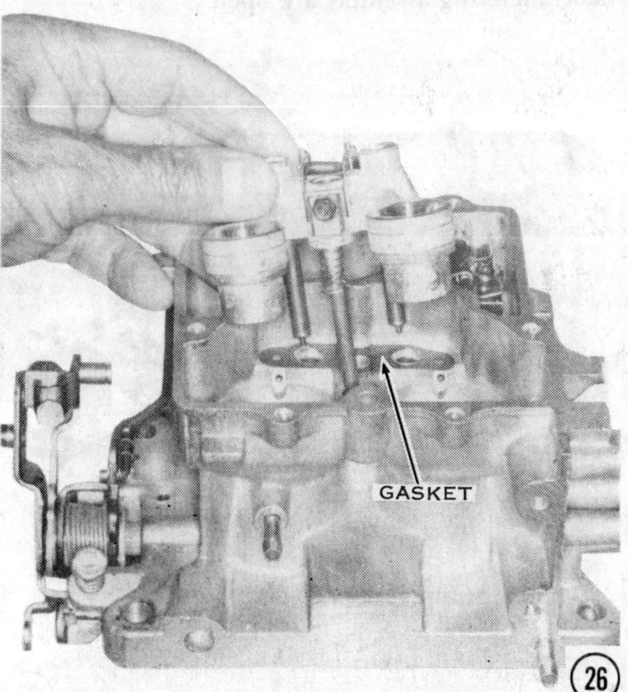

26

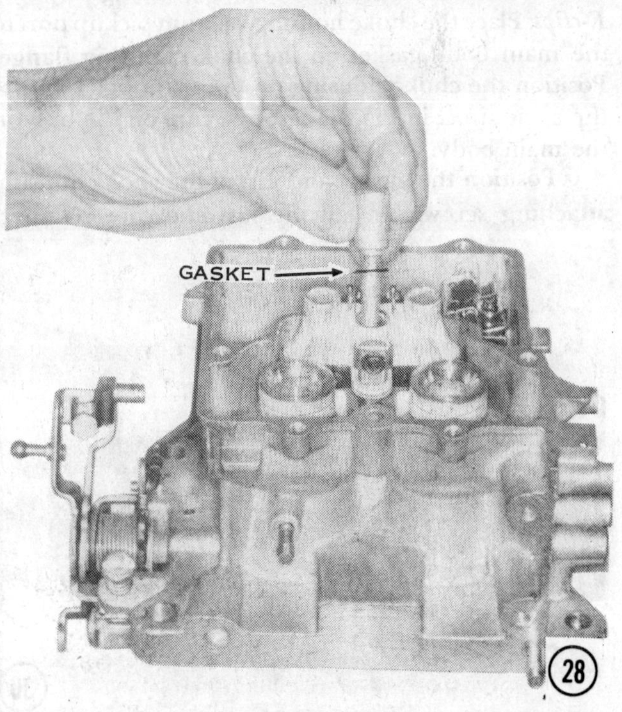

28

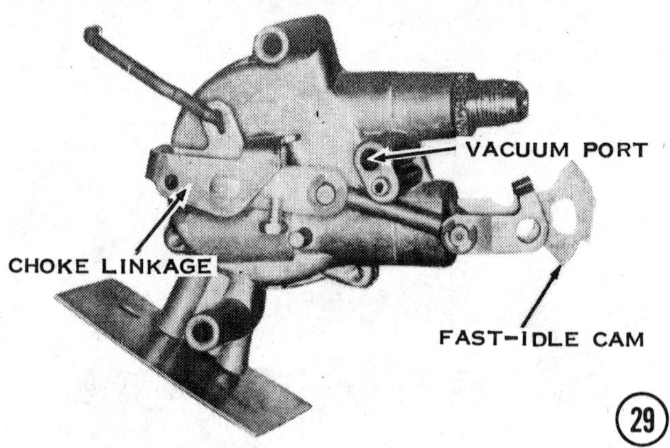

(29)

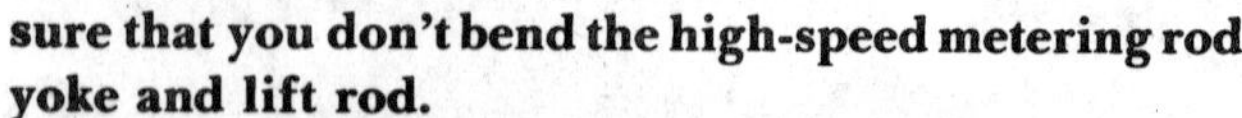

sure that you don't bend the high-speed metering rod yoke and lift rod.

(27) Install the accelerating pump discharge ball weight into place.

(28) Replace the booster venturi screw, using a new gasket. Tighten it securely.

Assembling The Choke Linkage

(29) Position the fast-idle cam lever on the thermostatic choke shaft-and-lever assembly. **CAUTION: The bottom of the fast-idle cam lever adjusting screw must rest against the tang on the choke lever.** Insert the choke lever into the rear of the choke housing. Position the choke lever so that the hole in the lever is to the left side of the choke housing. Install the fast-idle cam rod on the fast-idle cam lever.

(30) Place the fast-idle cam on the fast-idle cam rod and install the retainer. *NOTE: Use the largest of three E-clips.* Place the choke housing vacuum pickup port to the main body gasket on the choke housing flange. Position the choke housing on the main body and at the same time, install the fast-idle cam on the hub on the main body.

(31) Position the gasket and install the choke housing attaching screws. Install the fast-idle cam retainer.

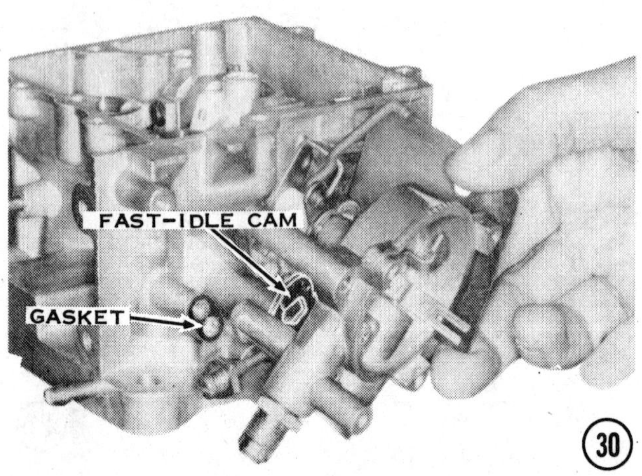

(30)

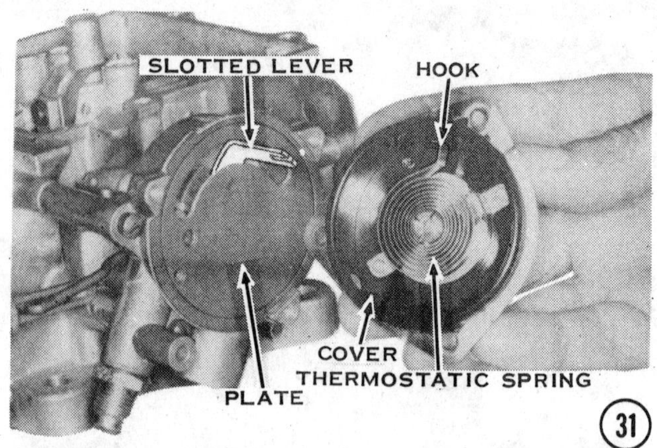

(31)

Install the choke plate and then the thermostatic spring housing. **CAUTION: Make sure that the hook of the thermostatic spring is engaged with the slot in the lever.** Install the cover screws.

(32) Position the choke pull-down diaphragm mounting bracket against the main body casting, and then install the two attaching screws. Connect the vacuum supply tube to the correct vacuum base tube connection. Insert the choke pull-down control rod through the slot in the diaphragm link, and then install the retainer clip over the end of the rod in the slot.

Assembling The Air Horn

(33) Using a new gasket, position the decel valve assembly to the bottom of the air horn. Install and torque the attaching screws evenly. After assembly, use shop air pressure to make sure all passages in the decel metering assembly are open.

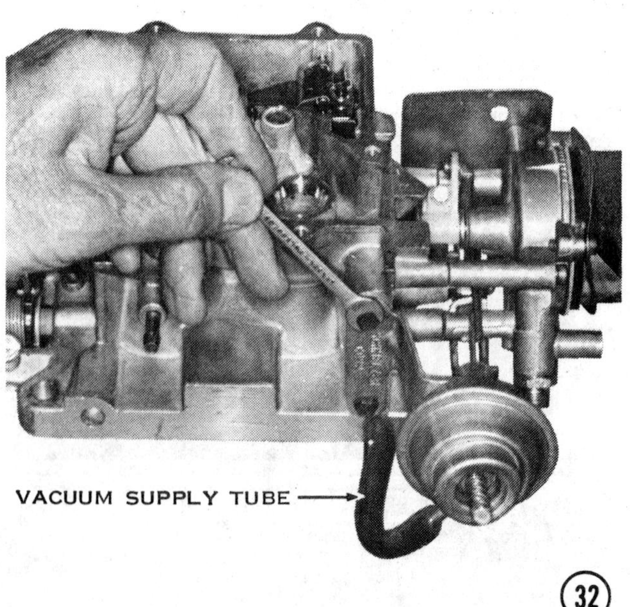

(32)

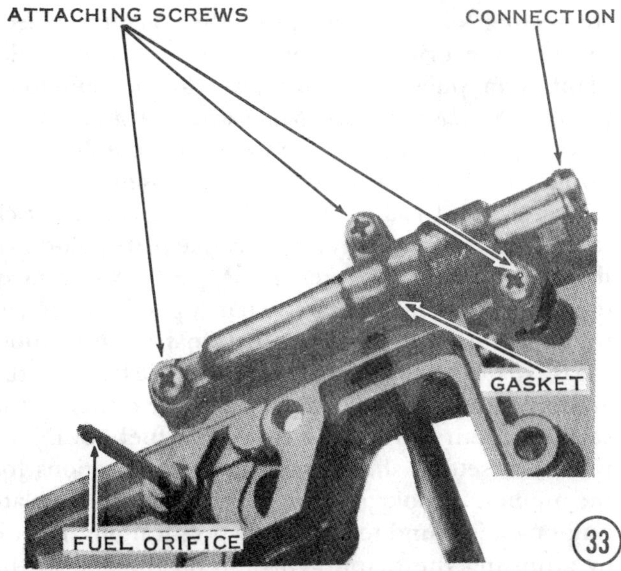

㉞If the choke plate shaft was removed, position the shaft in the air horn, then install the choke plate rod on the end of the choke shaft. Insert the choke plate into the choke plate shaft. Install the choke plate screws snug, but not tight. Check for the proper plate fit, binding in the air horn, and free rotation of the shaft by moving the plate from the closed to the open position. If necessary, remove the choke plate and grind or file the plate edge where it is binding or scraping on the air horn wall. If the choke plate-and-shaft assembly moves freely, tighten the choke plate screws while holding the choke in the fully closed position. Position the fuel bowl gasket and the choke rod plastic seal on the main body. Position the air horn on the main body and the gasket so that the choke plate rod fits through the seal and the opening in the main body.

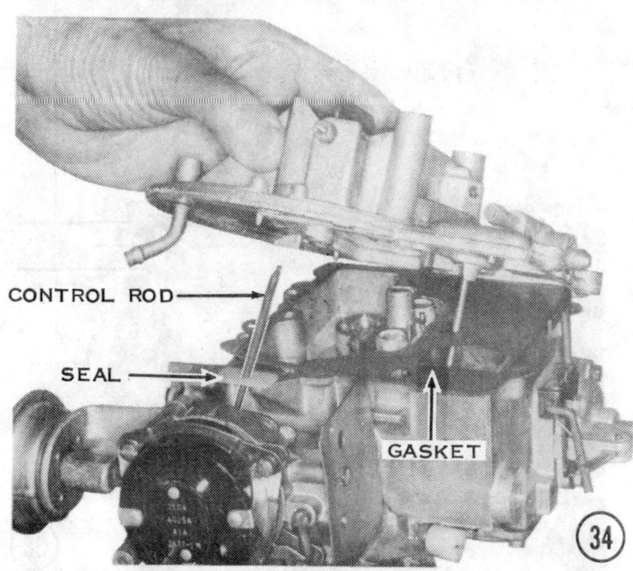

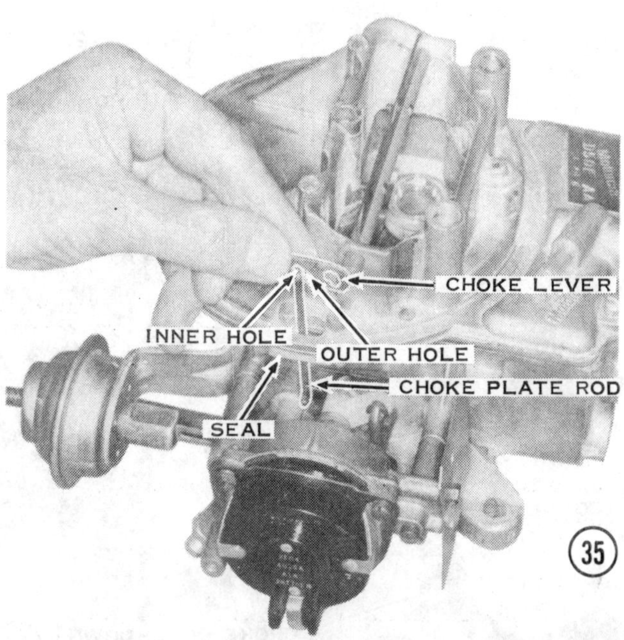

㉟Insert the end of the choke plate rod into the automatic choke lever. **CAUTION: Use the outer hole for elevations below 5,000 feet and the inner one above it.** Install the air horn attaching screws and the carburetor identification tag. Tighten the attaching screws. Install the choke plate rod retainer. Install the air cleaner anchor screw.

BENCH ADJUSTMENTS

The following bench adjustments must be made in the order given below. Always use the specifications in the factory repair kit of parts, which are always updated as revisions are made.

Accelerating Pump Stroke Adjustment

㊱*To make the accelerating pump stroke adjustment,*

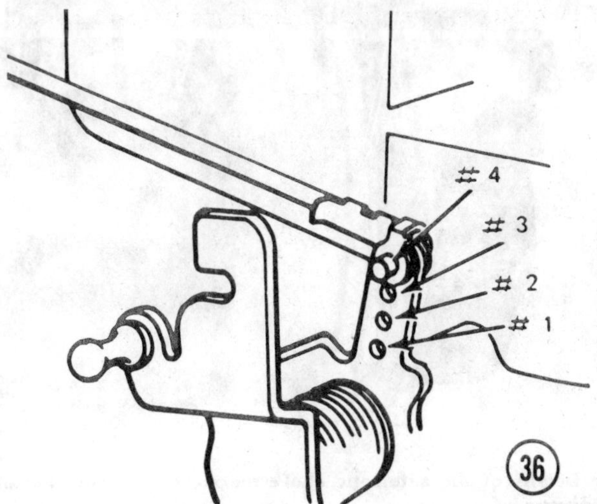

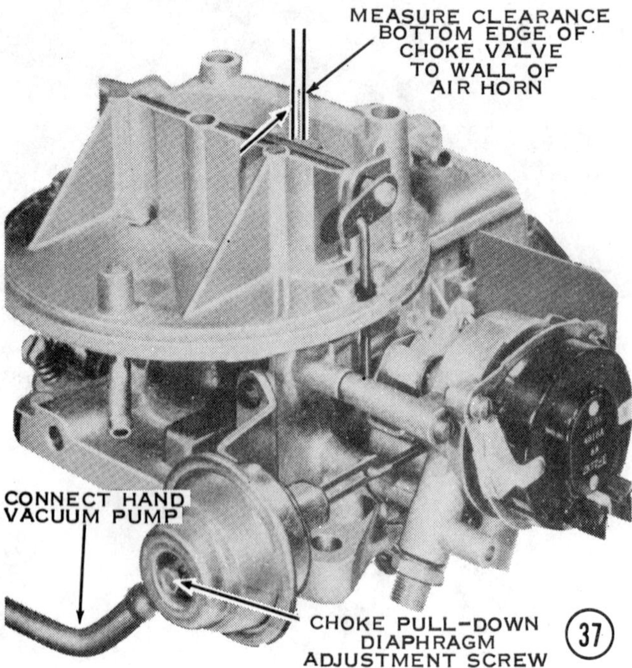

release the rod from the retaining clip, lift upward on the portion of the clip that snaps over the shaft, and then disengage the rod. Position the clip over the specified hole in the overtravel lever and insert the operating rod through the clip and the overtravel lever. Snap the end of the clip over the rod to secure.

Choke Plate Pulldown And Fast-Idle Cam Clearance Adjustment

(37) The Model 2150 2-V carburetor is equipped with a remotely-mounted choke pull-down diaphragm assembly. Vacuum is metered to the diaphragm through internal passages in the carburetor, through a connecting external tube. As the vacuum bleeds through the orifices in the carburetor, the choke diaphragm pulls the choke plate to the pull-down position. *To check the choke pull-down adjustment,* set the throttle on the fast-idle cam top step. Note the index position of the choke bimetallic cap. Loosen the retaining screws and rotate the cap 90 degrees in the rich (closing) direction. Activate the choke plate pull-down motor by manually forcing the pull-down control diaphragm link in the direction of applied vacuum, or by applying vacuum to the external vacuum tube. Measure the vertical hard gage clearance between the bottom edge of the choke plate and the center of the carburetor air horn wall nearest the fuel bowl. The pulldown setting should be within specifications for the minimum choke plate opening. If the choke plate pull-down is found to be out of specifications, reset it by adjusting the diaphragm stop on the end of the choke pull-down diaphragm. After the pull-down check is completed, reset the choke bi-metallic cap to the recommended index position.

Details of the automatic choke thermostatic spring housing adjustment.

Wet Fuel Level Adjustment

(38) Operate the engine to normalize temperatures, and place the vehicle on a flat surface as near level as possible. Stop the engine. Remove the air horn attaching screws and the carburetor identification tag. Temporarily leave the air horn and gasket in position on the carburetor main body and start the engine. Let the engine idle for a few minutes, then remove the air cleaner stud and the air horn and gasket to provide

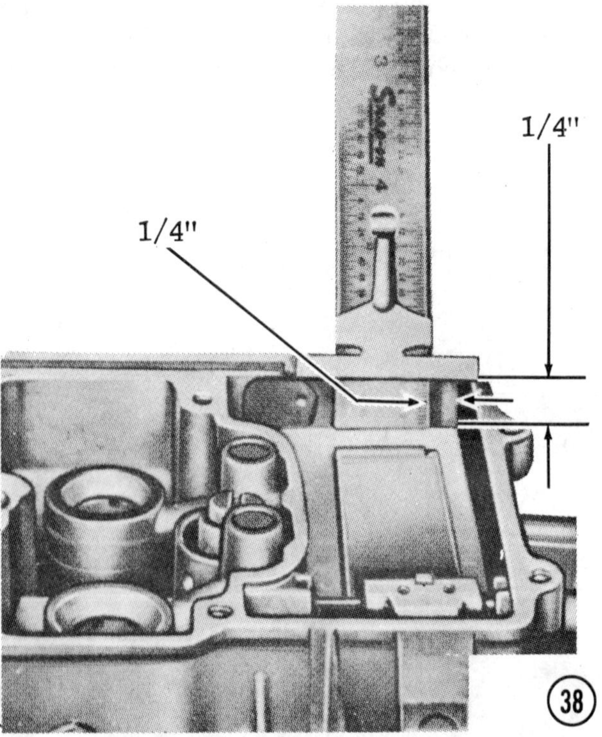

access to the float assembly. While the engine is idling, use a depth scale to measure the vertical distance from the top machined surface of the carburetor main body to the level of the fuel in the fuel bowl. **CAUTION: The measurement must be made at least 1/4 inch away from any vertical surface to assure an accurate reading, because the surface of the fuel is concave (higher at the edges than in the center). Care must be exercised to measure the fuel level at the point of contact with the gauge. CAUTION: If an adjustment is required, stop the engine to minimize the hazard of fire due to fuel spray when the float setting is disturbed.** To adjust the fuel level, bend the float tab (contacting the fuel inlet valve) upward in relation to the original position to raise the fuel level, and downward to lower it. **CAUTION: Each time an adjustment is made to the float tab to alter the fuel level, the air horn must be re-installed and held in place with the air cleaner assembly stud, the engine started and permitted to idle for a few minutes to stabilize the fuel level. Remove the air cleaner assembly stud and air horn and check the fuel level after each adjustment until the specified level is obtained.** Install a new air horn gasket, air horn assembly, carburetor identification tag, and attaching screws. **CAUTION: Be sure the plastic dust seal on the choke operating rod is positioned correctly and does not cause the rod to bind.** Tighten the screws. Install the air cleaner anchor stud.

ON-CAR ADJUSTMENTS

PRELIMINARY CONDITIONS

Remove the EGR and air cleaner vacuum lines and plug both vacuum lines. Connect a timing light (if necessary) and a tachometer to the engine. With the transmission in neutral and parking brake engaged, start the engine and bring it to a normal operating temperature. Check the initial timing and adjust to specifications. Remove the spark delay valve (if so equipped) and route the part-throttle vacuum signal directly to the advance side of the distributor. If the distributor is a dual-diaphragm model, leave the manifold vacuum line connected to the retard side of the distributor.

(39)

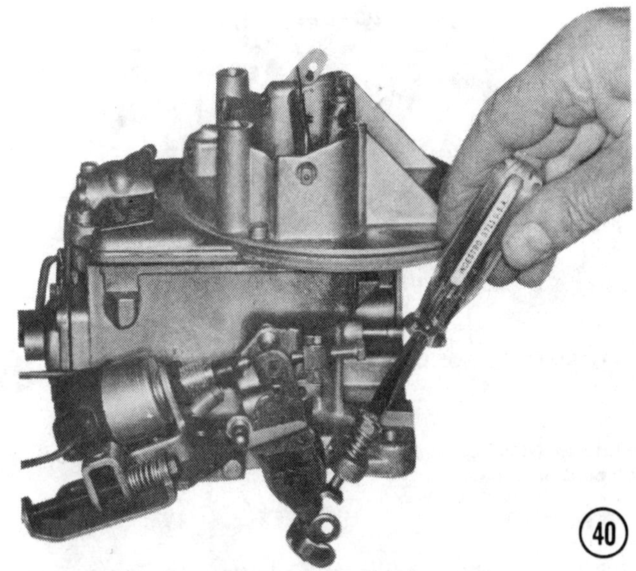
(40)

(39) *To make the fast-idle speed adjustment,* set the throttle to the kickdown step on the choke cam, making sure the adjusting screw is against the shoulder of the kick-down step, and then adjust the rpm to the specifications on the tuning decal.

(40) *To make the slow-idle speed (TSP-OFF) adjustment,* raise engine speed to 2,000 rpm for 10 seconds and allow it to return to idle. Collapse the solenoid plunger by forcing the throttle linkage against the solenoid stem. With the transmission in neutral, turn the throttle arm adjusting screw on the carburetor body to obtain the lower TSP-OFF idle speed.

(41)

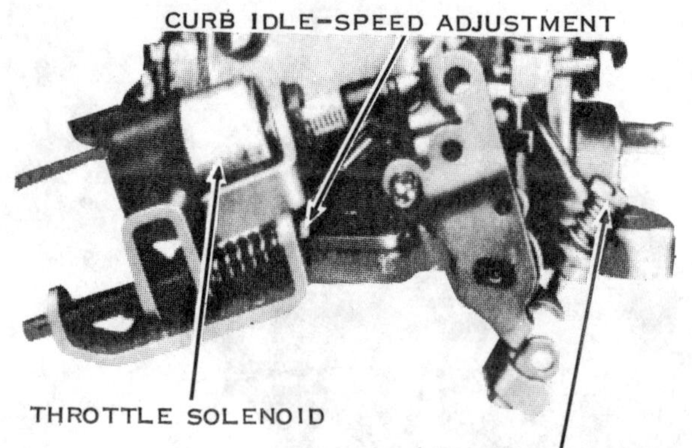

Idle speed adjustments on an engine equipped with a throttle solenoid positioner.

Making the idle fuel mixture adjustments. Note that the enrichment valve cover provides the stops for the idle mixture screw limiters.

(41) *To make the curb-idle speed adjustment,* raise engine speed to 2,000 rpm for 10 seconds and allow it to return to idle. If applicable, wait at least 5 seconds for the dashport to bottom out before checking the curb-idle speed. Place automatic transmission vehicles in drive and manual transmission vehicles in neutral. Turn the hex head adjusting screw on the TSP plunger to obtain the specified curb idle speed.

Reinstall the spark-delay valve (if removed) and reconnect the vacuum line to the EGR valve. Check the fuel decel valve (if so equipped) and adjust to specifications provided a gross curb idle speed adjustment of at least 100 rpm was required. Stop the engine, remove the test equipment, reinstall the air cleaner, and connect the vacuum line.

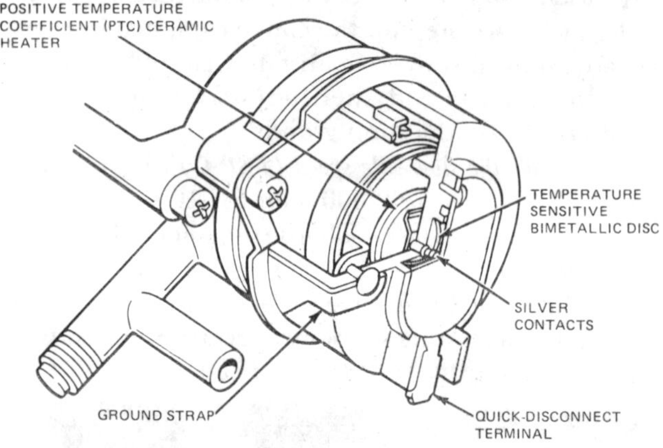

The new models have an electric-assist choke to provide for choke pull-off in a shorter time.

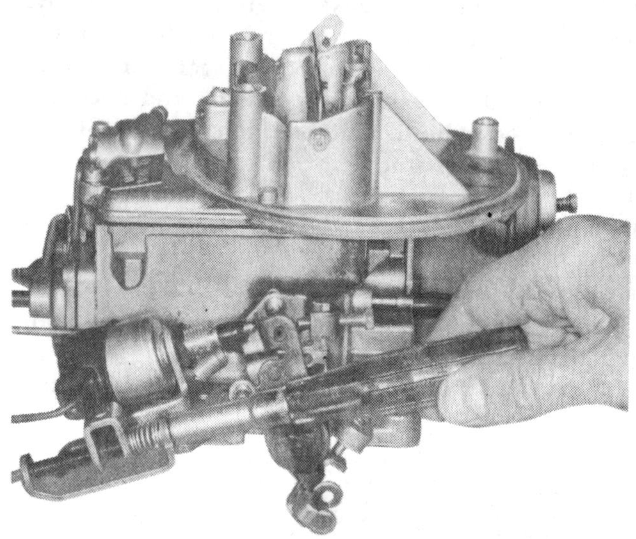

In some cases, the idle speed adjustment is made by shifting the entire solenoid. The bracket holding the solenoid has a long screw for making the adjustment.

6/engine service

All engines used in Ford passenger cars operate on the four-stroke cycle principle. During this cycle, the piston travels the length of its stroke four times. As the piston travels up or down, the crankshaft is rotated halfway (180 degrees). To accomplish one cycle, the crankshaft rotates two complete turns; the camshaft, which controls the valves, is driven by the crankshaft at half crankshaft speed. Valve action, intake and exhaust, occurs once in each four-stroke cycle, and the piston acts as an air pump during the two remaining strokes.

Intake Stroke

The intake valve is opened as the piston moves down the cylinder, and this creates an area of pressure lower than that of the surrounding atmosphere. Atmospheric pressure will cause air to flow into this low-pressure area. By directing the air flow through the carburetor, a measured amount of vaporized fuel is added. When the piston reaches the bottom of the intake stroke, the cylinder is filled with air and vaporized fuel. The exhaust valve is closed during the intake stroke.

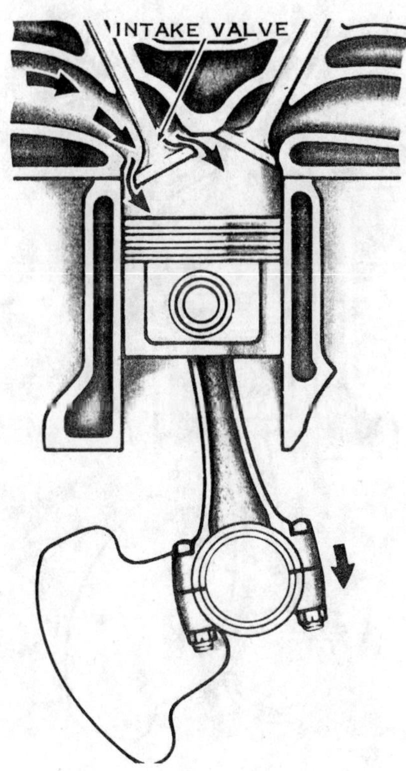

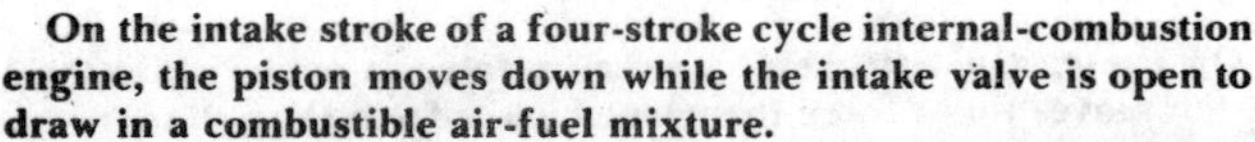

On the intake stroke of a four-stroke cycle internal-combustion engine, the piston moves down while the intake valve is open to draw in a combustible air-fuel mixture.

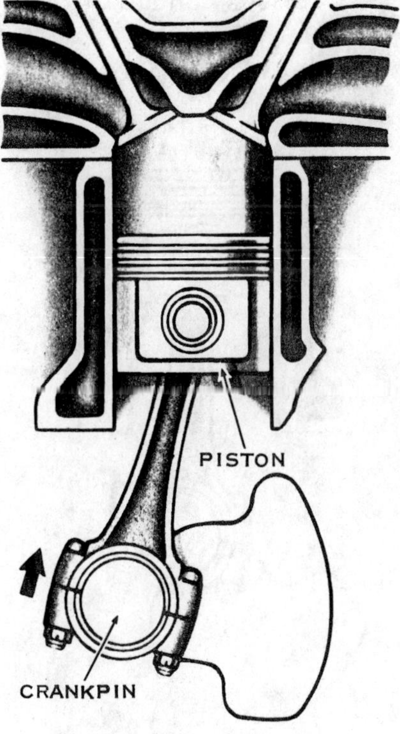

On the compression stroke, both valves are closed as the piston moves up to compress the air-fuel mixture.

Compression Stroke

When the piston starts to move upward, the compression stroke begins. The intake valve closes, trapping the air-fuel mixture in the cylinder. The upward movement of the piston compresses the mixture to a fraction of its original volume; exact pressure depends principally on the compression ratio of the engine.

Power Stroke

The power stroke is produced by igniting the compressed air-fuel mixture. When the spark plug arcs, the mixture ignites and burns very rapidly during the power stroke. The resulting high temperature expands the gases, creating very high pressure on top of the piston, which drives the piston down. This downward motion of the piston is transmitted through the connecting rod and is converted into rotary motion by the crankshaft. Both the intake and exhaust valves are closed during the power stroke.

Exhaust Stroke

The exhaust valve opens just before the piston completes the power stroke. Pressure in the cylinder at this time causes the exhaust gas to rush into the exhaust manifold (blowdown). The upward movement of the piston on its exhaust stroke expels most of the remaining exhaust gas.

As the piston pauses momentarily at the top of the exhaust stroke, the inertia of the exhausting gas tends to remove any remaining gas in the combustion chamber, however, a small amount always remains to dilute the incoming mixture. This unexpelled gas is captured in the clearance area between the piston and the cylinder head.

Combustion

The power delivered from the piston to the crankshaft is the result of a pressure increase in the gas mixture above the piston. This pressure increase occurs as the mixture is heated, first by compression, and then (on the down stroke) by burning. The burning fuel supplies heat that raises temperature and, at the same time, raises pressure. Actually, about 75 percent of the mixture in the cylinder is composed of nitrogen gas that does not burn but expands when heated by the burning of the combustible elements, and it is this expanding nitrogen that supplies most of the pressure on the piston.

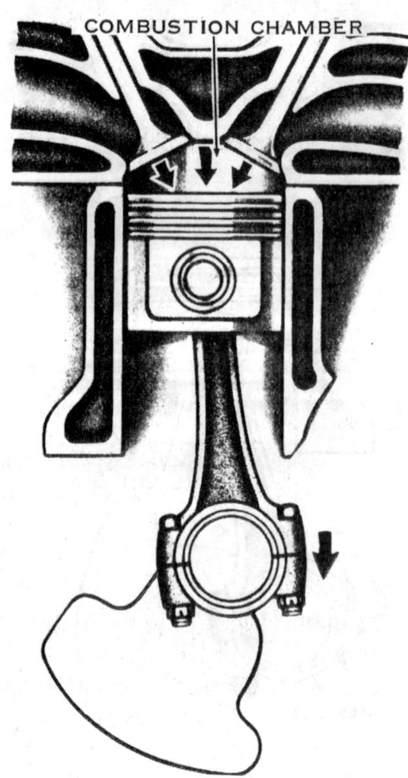

On the power stroke, the tightly compressed combustible mixture is ignited by the spark plug and the resulting burning of the fuel pushes the piston down the cylinder.

On the exhaust stroke, the exhaust valve is open, while the piston moves up to force the burned gases from the cylinder.

The fuel and oxygen must burn smoothly within the combustion chamber to take full advantage of this heating effect. Maximum power would not be delivered to the piston if an explosion took place, because the entire force would be spent in one sharp hammer-like blow, occurring too fast for the piston to follow.

Instead, burning takes place evenly as the flame moves across the combustion chamber. Burning must be completed by the time the piston is about half-way down so that maximum pressure will be developed in the cylinder at the time the piston applies its greatest force to the crankshaft. This will be when the mechanical advantage of the connecting rod and crankshaft is at a maximum.

At the beginning of the power stroke (as the piston is driven down by the pressure), the volume above the piston increases, which would normally allow the pressure in the cylinder to drop. However, combustion is still in progress, and this continues to raise the temperature of the gases, expanding them and maintaining a continuous pressure on the piston as it travels downward. This provides a smooth application of power throughout the effective part of the power stroke to make the most efficient use of the energy released by the burning fuel.

Valve Timing

On the power stroke, the exhaust valve opens before bottom dead center in order to get the exhaust gases started out of the combustion chamber under the remaining pressure (blowdown). On the exhaust stroke, the intake valve opens before top dead center in order to start the air-fuel mixture moving into the combustion chamber. These processes are functions of camshaft design and valve timing.

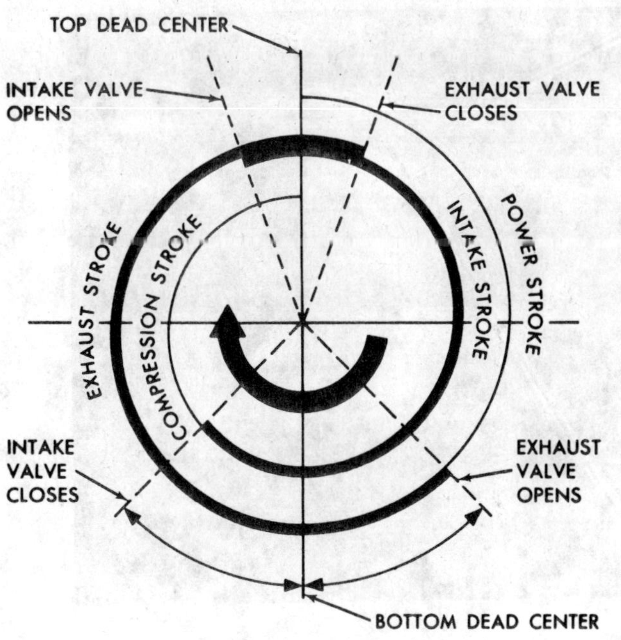

Typical valve timing diagram. Note that this represents two complete turns of the crankshaft (720°).

Valves always open and close at the same time in the cycle; the timing is not variable with speed and load as is ignition timing. There is, however, one particular speed for each given engine at which the air-fuel mixture will pack itself into the combustion chambers most effectively. This is the speed at which the engine puts out its peak torque. At low engine speeds, compression is somewhat suppressed due to the slight reverse flow of gases through the valves just as they open or close when the mixture is not moving fast enough to take advantage of the time lag. At high speeds, the valve timing does not allow enough time during the valve opening and closing periods for effective packing of the air-fuel mixture into the cylinders.

BOBCAT ENGINE TYPES

The Mercury Bobcat was introduced in 1975. This vehicle comes equipped with a 2300cc overhead-cam engine or an optional 2800cc V-6 type engine.

GENERAL ENGINE SERVICE PROCEDURES

The general service procedures that apply to all engines will be discussed in the section that follows, and this section should be referred to before doing any engine work. This general section is followed by specific service instructions that apply to each of the engine families.

Cylinder Block

The ring ridge must be removed before taking out the pistons; otherwise, the top ring will catch on the ledge and break a piston ring land. Inspect the cylinder walls for wear, scores, and evidence of scuffing. If the cylinder walls are worn over 0.012", it will be necessary to recondition the cylinder bores to the next oversize and install new oversize pistons. If the bores are not worn excessively, the cylinder walls should be honed to remove the glaze, which could prevent the new piston rings from seating quickly.

Cylinder Heads and Manifolds

Scrape all gasket materials from the manifolds and heads. Remove the deposits in the combustion

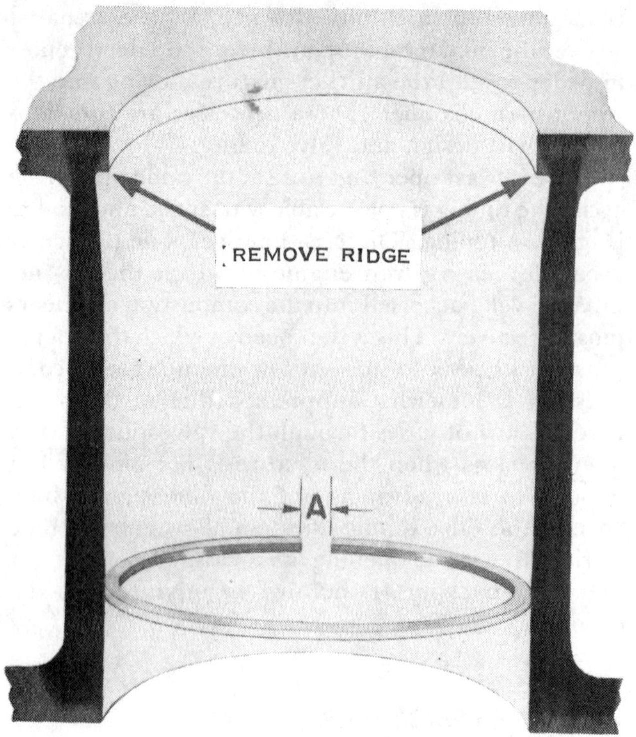

It is necessary to remove the ring ridge before taking the pistons out; otherwise, you will break the piston when a ring jams under the ledge. When measuring the piston ring end gap, it is essential to position the piston ring near the bottom of the cylinder in the unworn area, so that there will be sufficient clearance at all times.

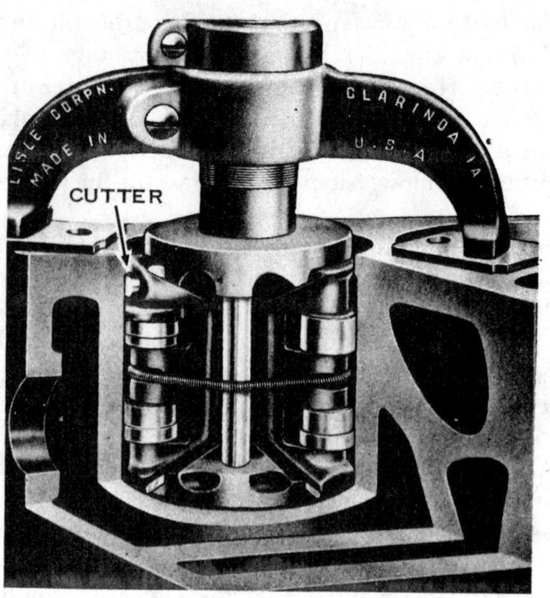

A ridge remover is needed to cut the ridge from the top of the cylinder walls. The stop under the blade keeps you from cutting into the walls too deeply. Don't cut more than 1/32" below the bottom of the ridge.

Cylinder Heads and Manifolds

Scrape all gasket materials from the manifolds and heads. Remove the deposits in the combustion

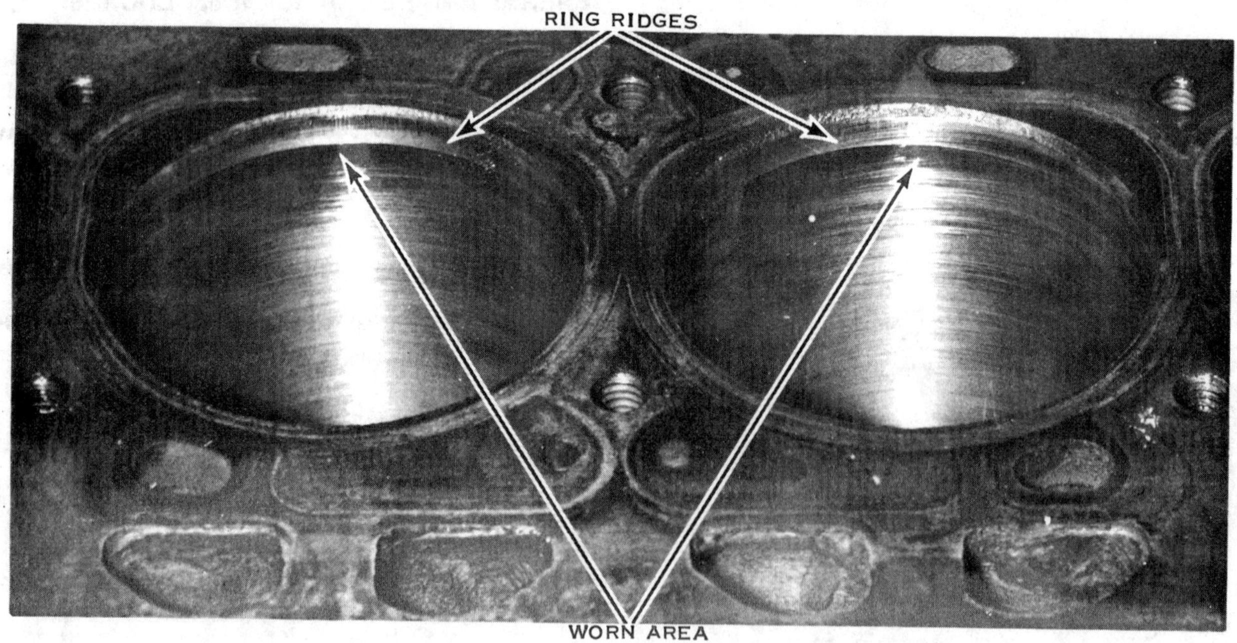

The cylinder walls wear the greatest amount at the top, due to the borderline lubrication conditions that exist. All measurements must be made in the worn area. This cylinder bore has been surfaced with a fine hone to remove the glaze for better piston ring seating.

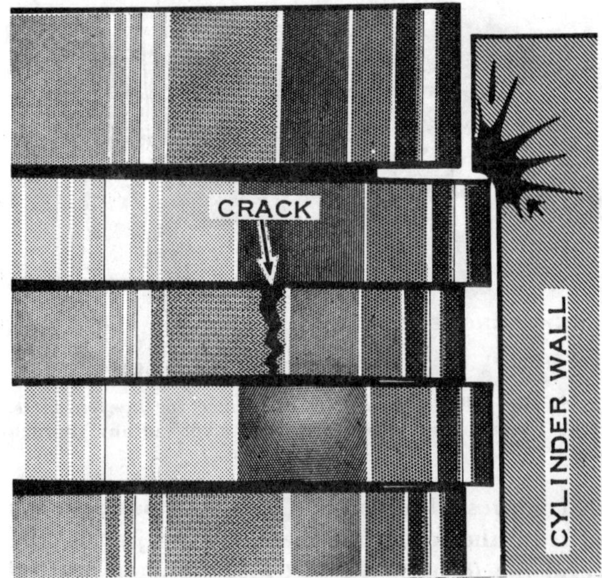

The ring ridge must be removed before the piston is pushed out of the top of the bore; otherwise, the top ring will strike it and break the piston ring land.

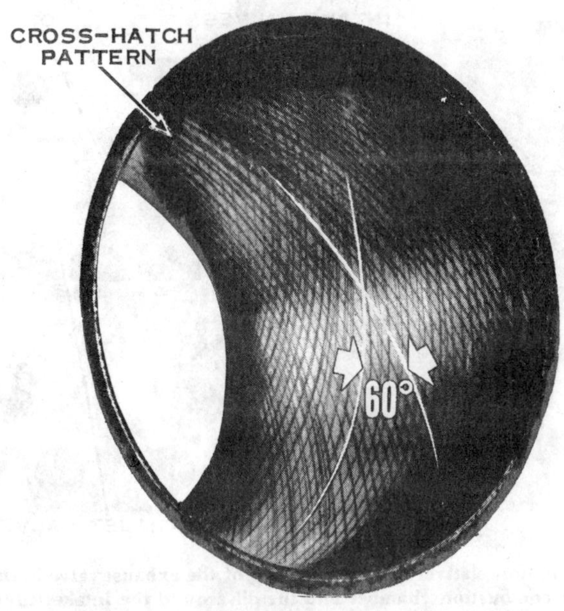

The cylinder walls should be honed to remove the glaze so that the new piston rings will seat quickly. The ideal crosshatch pattern is 60°.

chambers with a wire brush and scraper. **CAUTION: Be careful not to damage the gasket surfaces.** Clean the valve guides with a guide-cleaning brush. Apply some lacquer thinner to the revolving brush in order to dissolve the gum inside of the valve guides.

Check the gasket surface of the cylinder head for burrs and scratches, which could prevent the gasket from sealing properly. Check the flatness of the gasket surface with a straightedge and a feeler gauge. Surface irregularity must not exceed 0.003″ in any six-inch space, and the total must not exceed 0.007″ for the entire length of the head. If necessary, the cylinder head gasket surface can be machined. **CAUTION: Do not remove more than 0.010″ of stock.**

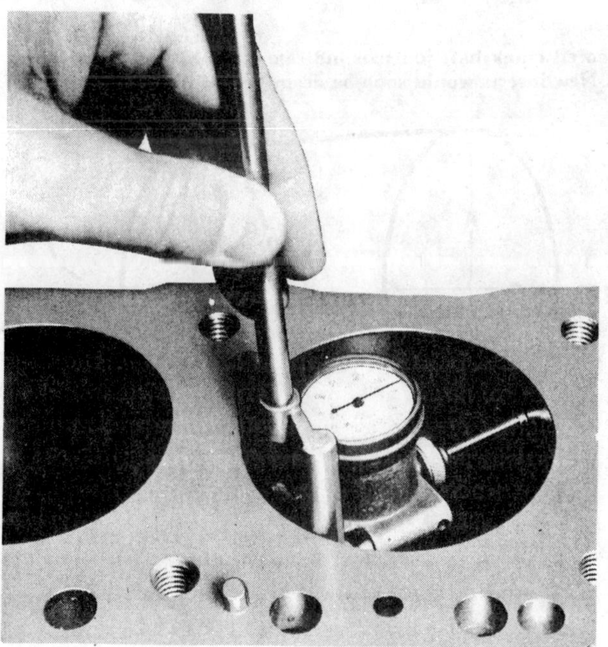

Measuring the cylinder wall taper and wear with a dial indicator.

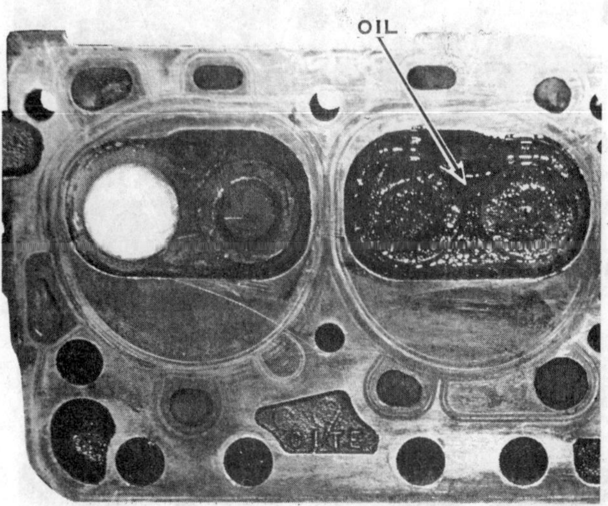

Always study the cylinder head when it is removed. The coloring of the valves tells a graphic story of the condition of the engine. In this case, the cylinder at the left was firing normally, as evidenced by the white (heated) exhaust valve. The cylinder at the right was pumping oil, possibly due to a scored cylinder wall or broken piston ring.

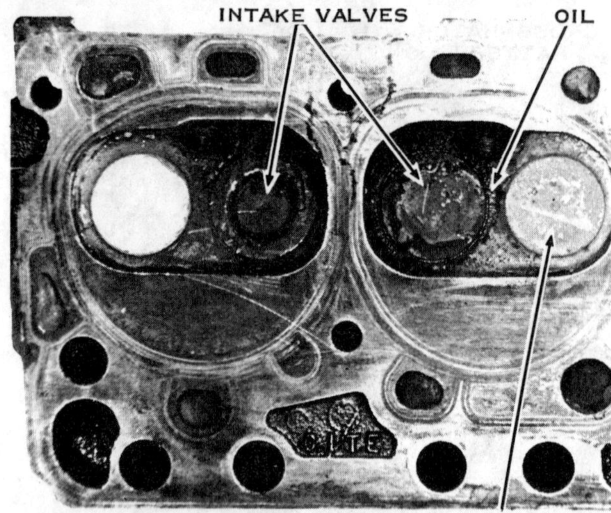

Note the relatively darker coloring of the exhaust valve in the right combustion chamber and the oil around the intake valve. This means that the compression in the right cylinder is lower than the compression in the left cylinder and that the intake valve guide and seal are defective and were allowing oil to leak into the combustion chamber.

Crankshaft

Clean the crankshaft with solvent and wipe the journals dry with a lint-free cloth. **CAUTION: Handle the shaft carefully to avoid damaging the highly finished journal surfaces.** Blow out all oil passages with compressed air. **CAUTION: Oil passageways lead from the rod to the main bearing journal. Be careful not to blow the dirt into the main bearing journal bore.**

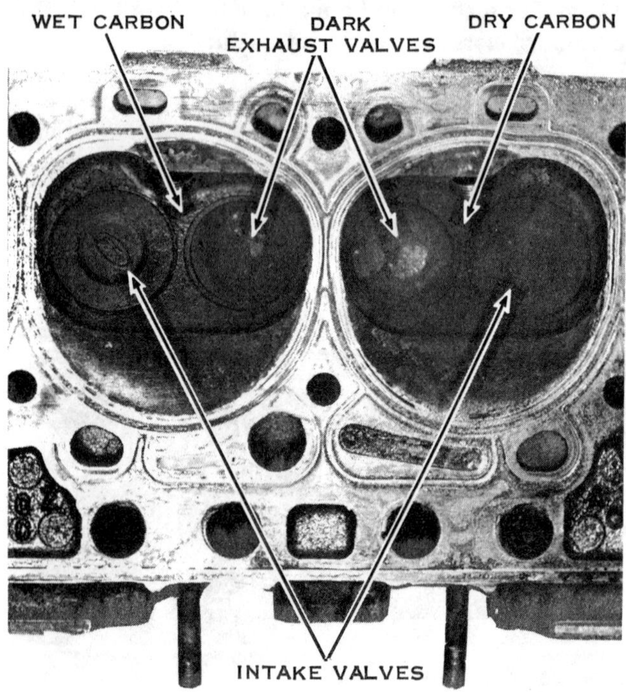

The sooty black appearance of these combustion chambers indicates an excessively rich air-fuel mixture. Note the wet carbon in the left combustion chamber which indicates that piston ring trouble is starting there.

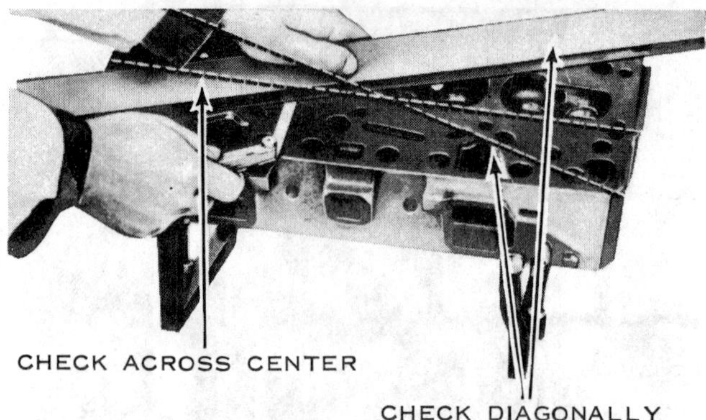

Check the cylinder head gasket surface for uneven spots. Surface irregularities must not exceed 0.003" in any six-inch space.

Scored crankshaft journals indicate the need for reconditioning. New inserts would soon be destroyed by this rough shaft.

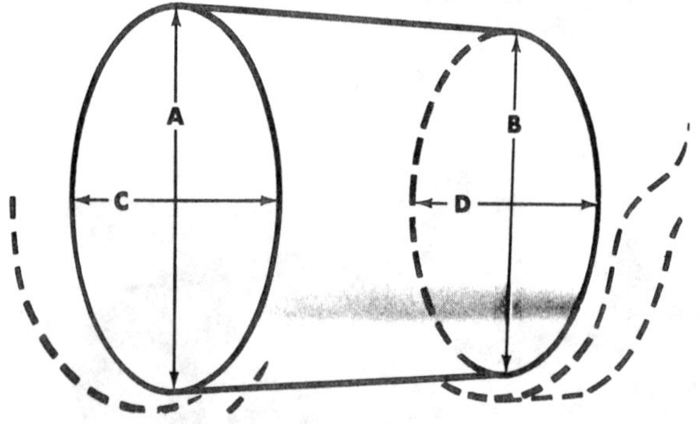

Measure the diameter of each journal at four places to determine the wear, taper, and out-of-roundness that exists.

The coloring of the old bearing inserts tells a story. Note the light gray coloring of the upper bearing insert, which indicates that the bearing was operating with the proper clearance. The dark coloring of the lower insert indicates excessive bearing clearance.

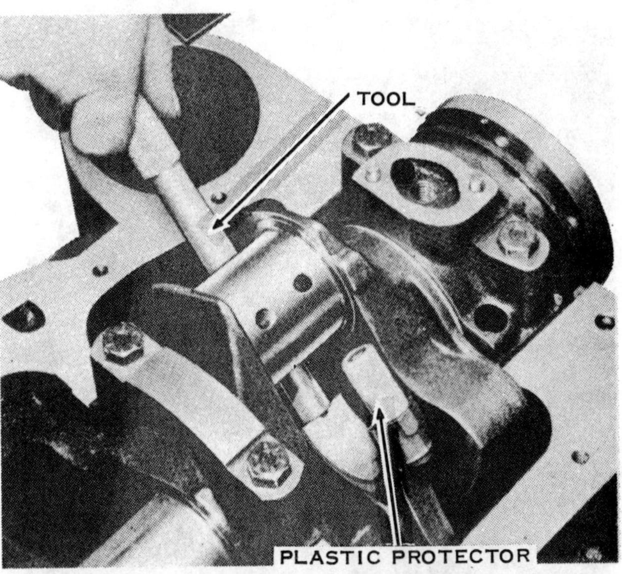

Always use a piece of rubber hose to cover the rod bolt threads when removing the piston and rod assembly; otherwise, you may damage the bearing surface by scraping the threads over it.

Measure the diameter of each journal at four places to determine the out-of-round, taper, and wear. The out-of-round limit is 0.001″; the taper must not exceed 0.001″; and the wear limit is 0.0025″. If any of these limits is exceeded, the crankshaft must be reground to an undersize, and undersized bearing inserts must be installed.

Main Bearings

Mark each bearing cap and the block so that the cap can be replaced in its proper position. Remove the main bearing cap and inspect the insert. If the upper half of the insert is to be removed, insert a bearing removal tool into the oil hole in the crankshaft, and then rotate the shaft in the direction of engine rotation to force the insert out of the block.

Clean the journal with solvent, and then wipe it dry with a lint-free cloth. If a new upper insert is to be installed, place the plain end over the shaft on the

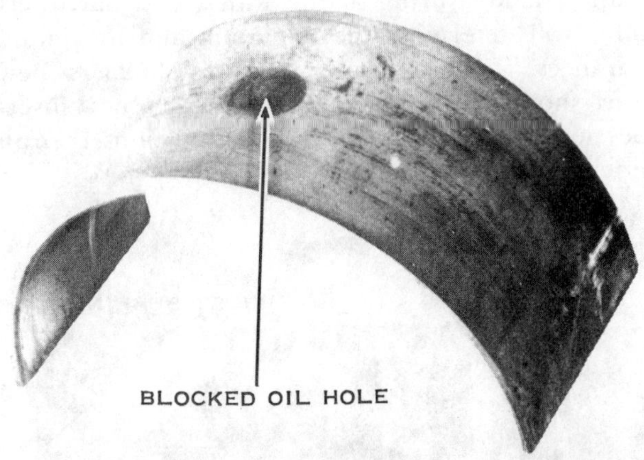

It is difficult to install a main bearing insert properly without removing the crankshaft because you can't see what you are doing. Be careful to check for oil holes and locking recesses before installing a new insert. A blocked oil hole will cause rapid destruction of the engine.

Bearing defects caused by improper installation. Carefully wipe each insert before installing it and make sure that your hands are reasonably clean.

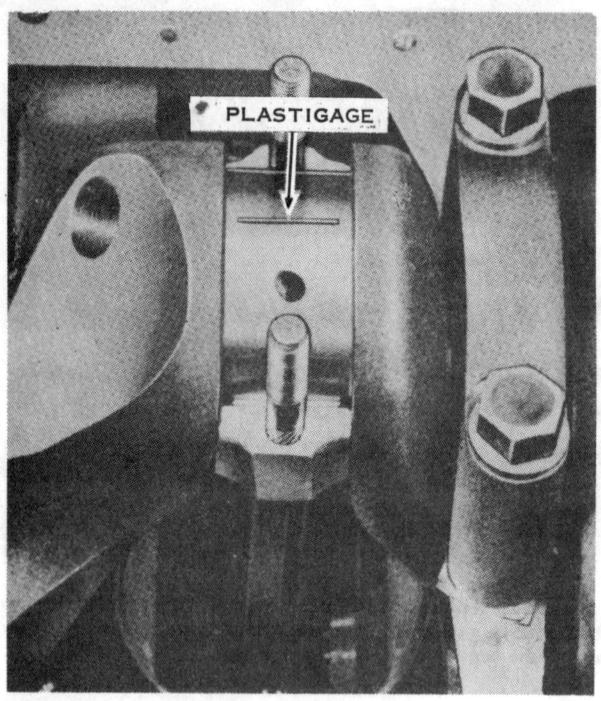

This shows how a piece of Plastigage is placed on the crankpin to measure the clearance. Then the cap is torqued to specifications.

This shows how the squeezed-out Plastigage strip looks after being compressed by the cap. Note the use of a scale on the side of the package to compare. New bearing insert clearance should be 0.001-0.003".

locking tang side and partially install it so that the inserting tool can be placed in the oil hole. Rotate the crankshaft in the direction opposite to engine rotation until the bearing is seated. Remove the tool.

Measuring the Oil Clearance

The clearance between the shaft and insert can be measured by using Plastigage. To check the clearance, support the crankshaft with a jack so that its weight will not compress the Plastigage and thereby provide an erroneous reading. Position the jack so that it bears against the counterweight adjoining the bearing to be checked.

Clean the journal thoroughly of all traces of oil, and then place a piece of Plastigage on the bearing surface, the full width of the cap. Install the cap and torque the retaining bolts to specifications. **CAUTION: Don't turn the crankshaft with the Plastigage in place or you will distort it.** Remove the cap. To determine the clearance, use the scale on the package to check the width of the squeezed-out piece in the bearing insert. If the squeezed-out plastic strip is tapered, the journal is tapered. Measuring at the widest and narrowest points will determine the minimum and maximum clearances. If the clearance exceeds 0.0025", a new insert should be installed. If installing a new insert does not return the clearance to specifications, then an undersized insert should be used.

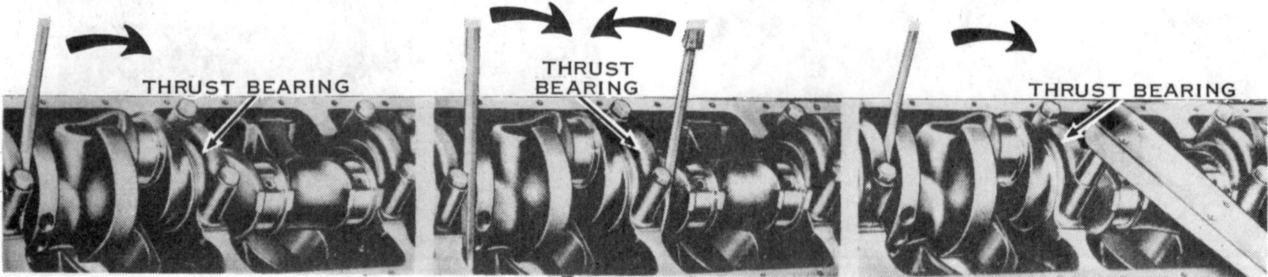

Before tightening the thrust bearing, it is essential to align it properly. This is done by prying the crankshaft forward and prying the main bearing cap backward, and then torquing the bolts to specifications.

This illustration shows how to remove and install an upper main bearing insert. The round body of the tool is inserted in the oil hole in the main bearing journal, and then the crankshaft is rotated in a direction to unlock the retaining lip. The same tool can be used to install a new insert as shown at the right. Clean the insert and the shaft carefully to avoid getting dirt behind the insert.

Connecting Rods

Remove the inserts from the rod and cap. Identify

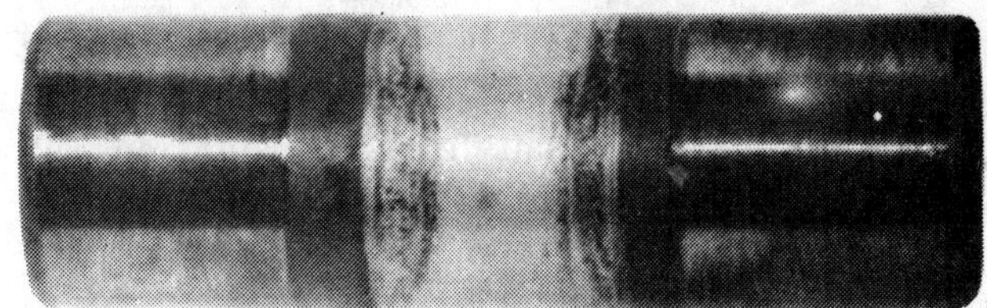

To measure the wear on a piston pin, it should be miked on an unworn section (center), and then on both ends for a comparative measurement.

the inserts if they are to be used again. Clean the parts in solvent and blow dry.

Check the rod bolts and nuts for defects in the threads. Inspect the inside of the rod bearing bore for evidence of galling, which indicates that the insert is loose enough to move around. Check the parting cheeks to be sure that the cap or rod has not been filed. Replace any defective rods.

Whenever servicing the piston and rod assembly, it is generally advisable to install new piston pins, especially if the mileage is over 50,000. Loose piston pins, coupled with tight piston assemblies because of new piston rings, will cause piston pin noises, which may disappear as the engine loosens but this is difficult to explain to a customer who has just paid the bill. Most mechanics have this work done by automotive

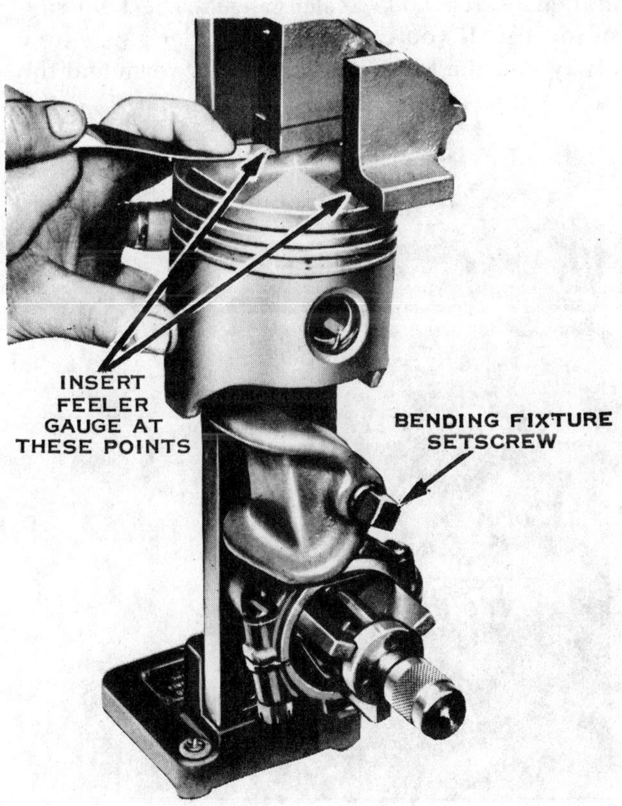

Showing the method of testing for, and correcting, a bent connecting rod.

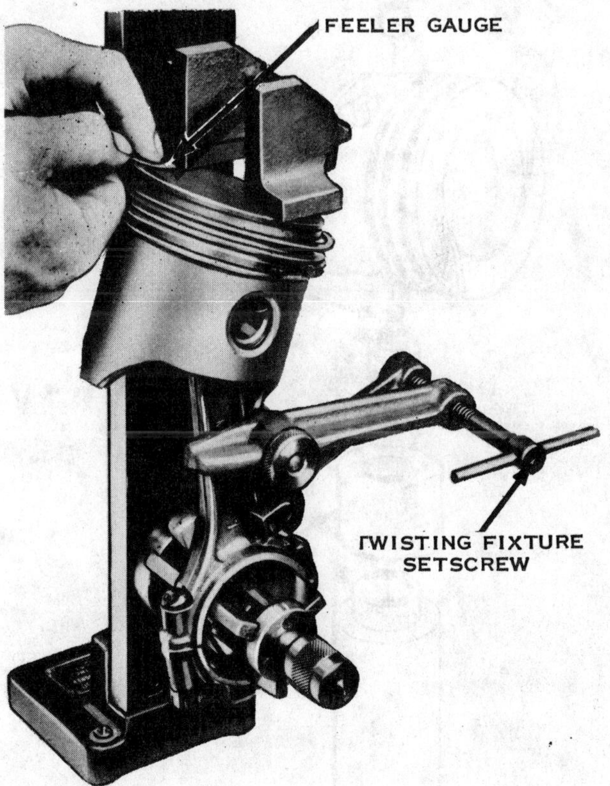

To check a connecting rod for twist, turn the piston as far as possible on its wrist pin, and then measure the clearance, as shown. The twisting jig can be used to straighten the rod.

machine shops, which have the neccessary equipment for a precision job. At the same time, the connecting rods will be aligned so that the pistons and rings will run true with the cylinder walls.

You can measure the connecting rod bearing clearance in the manner described in the previous section on main bearings.

Pistons

Remove deposits from the piston crown with a scraper. Clean the piston in solvent and blow dry. **CAUTION: Don't soak the pistons in a caustic solution because it will corrode the aluminim. CAUTION: Don't buff the pistons on a wire brush because it will deform the soft metal.** Clean the ring grooves with a ring groove cleaner or a piece of broken ring. **CAUTION: Don't scrape or nick the sides of the grooves, or you will damage the sealing surfaces.**

Inspect the piston for scuffed surfaces, cracks, and wear. Install a new compression ring in the top groove, and then insert a 0.006" feeler gauge to check for ring groove wear. If you can insert the feeler gauge over halfway into the top ring groove, it is worn, and the

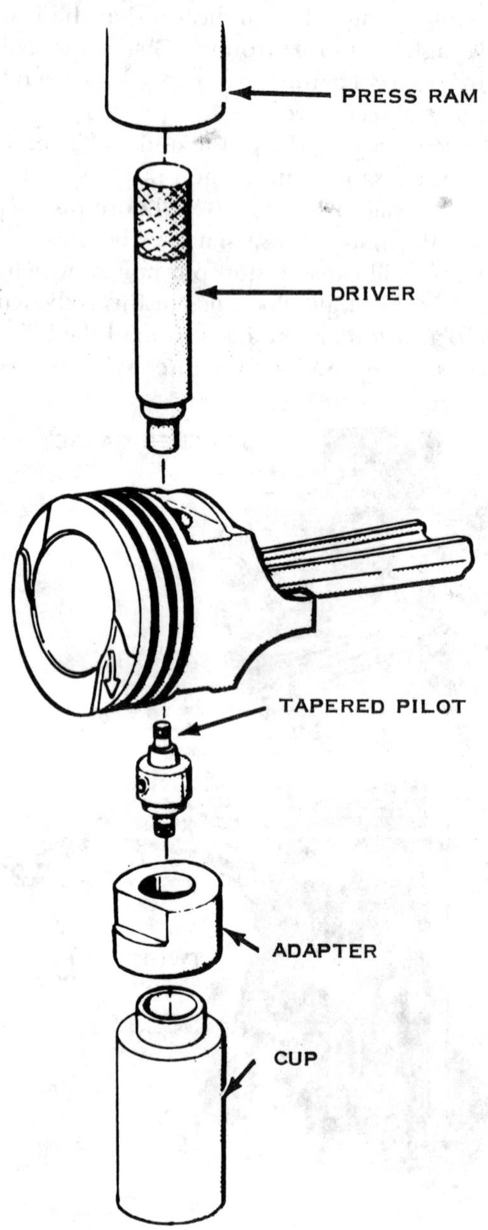

Details of the tool being used to press out a piston pin.

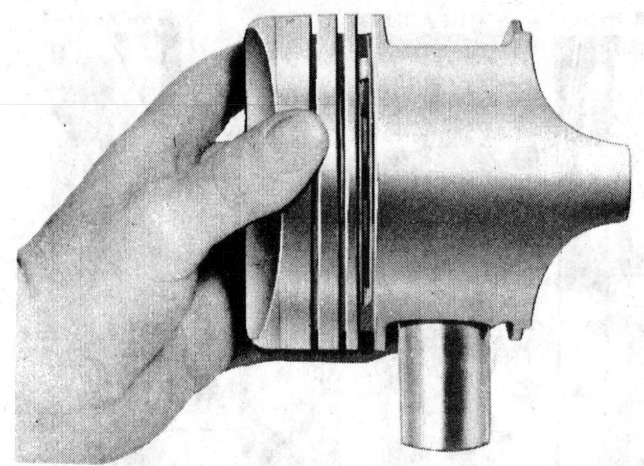

A properly fitted pin should support its own weight in either pin boss when coated with light engine oil at room temperature.

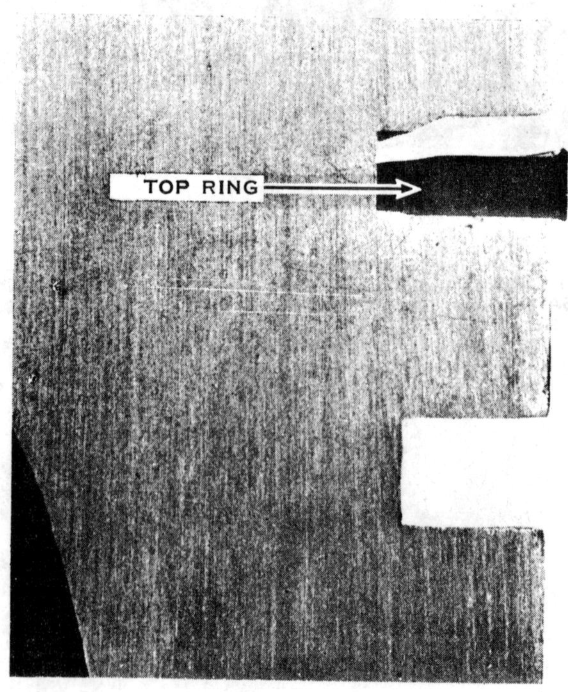

Top ring groove wear is commonplace, and this one requires that the groove be turned oversize and a steel spacer installed above the piston ring to restore production clearances.

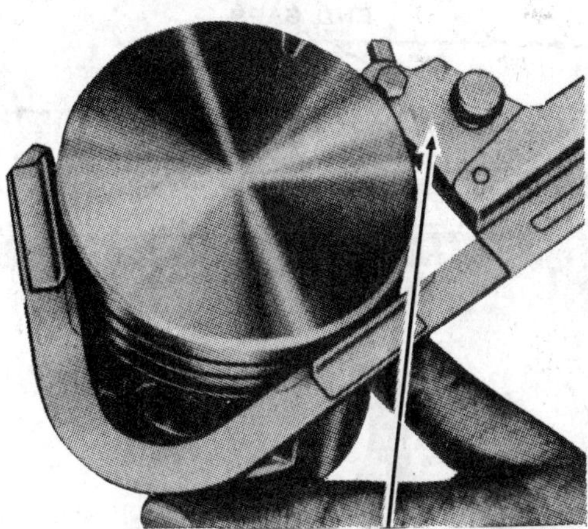

Always clean the ring grooves so that the new rings can seat properly. Be careful not to nick the sealing surfaces, or the ring will leak compression.

piston must be reconditioned by cutting the groove wide enough to accept a steel spacer.

Check the piston skirt-to-cylinder bore clearance by inserting the cleaned piston into the cylinder bore. If the cylinder walls have worn enough to form a ring ledge, the piston will be excessively loose. Generally, when installing new piston rings, it is considered good practice to have the pistons expanded in an automotive machine shop in order to compensate for this wear. The pistons can be expanded at the same time that the piston pins are fitted and the rods aligned.

Rings

Always install a new set of piston rings when overhauling an engine. Order the ring set according to the amount of cylinder wall wear. If the wear is less than 0.005", a standard set of piston rings can be used. If the cylinder wall wear is between 0.006" and 0.012", a set of piston rings with a special oil ring and expanders will be required to keep the engine from pumping oil. If the cylinder bore is worn over 0.012", it should be reconditioned by boring or honing in order to straighten the cylinder walls so that the new piston rings will make a better seal.

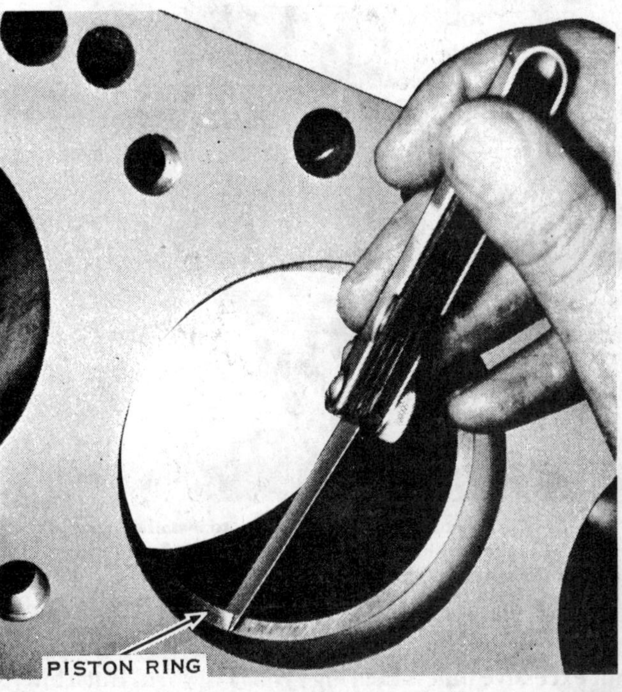

Check the piston ring end gap by pushing the ring into the cylinder bore. The end gap must not exceed specifications.

Before installing a set of piston rings, the end gaps and the side clearance between the piston ring groove and the ring must be checked. The correct side clearance should be 0.002"-0.004", with a wear limit of

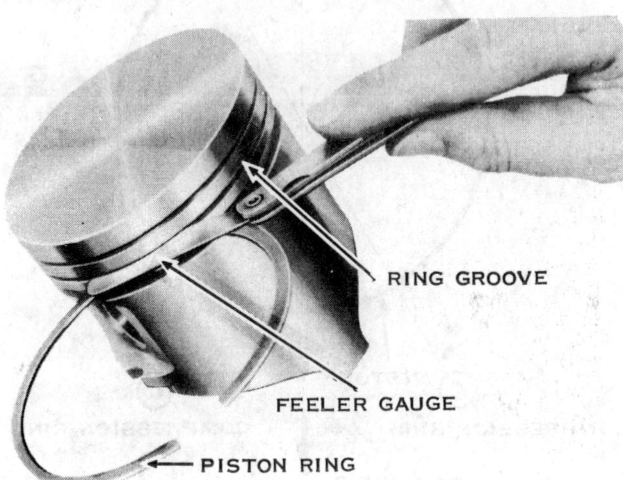

Measure the piston ring side clearance, which must not exceed 0.004".

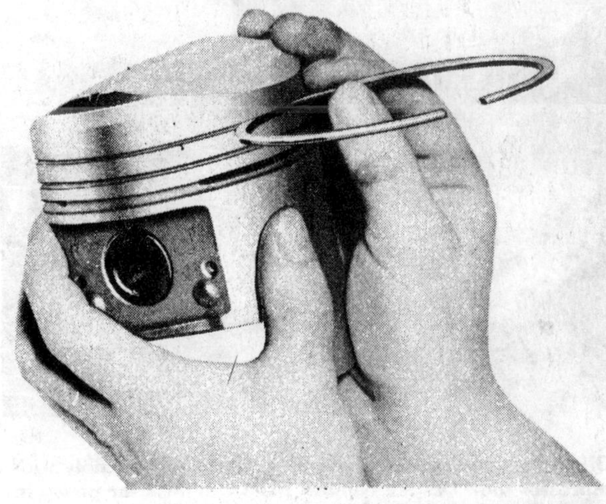

Roll each piston ring around its groove in this fashion to make sure that the groove is not nicked, which would keep the ring from "breathing" properly.

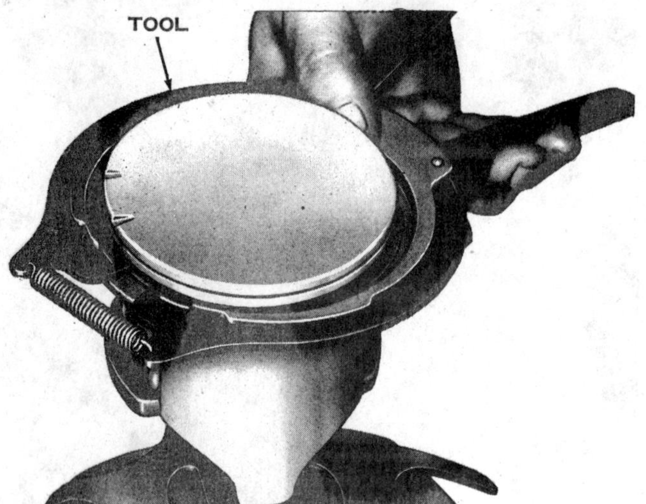

Always use a piston ring expanding tool to install the new piston rings. This tool avoids distorting a ring which could cause it to bind in the ring groove.

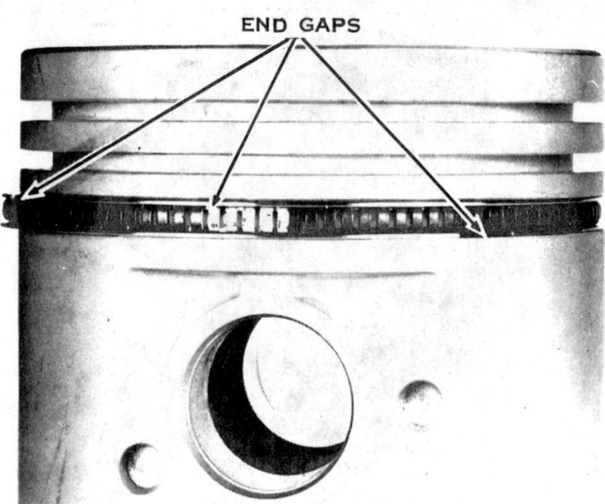

This picture shows how to space the rail gaps and the spacer gap on a compound oil ring.

0.002″. Generally, the side clearance of a new ring is not excessive unless the ring groove is worn. But a burr in the soft piston metal may cause the ring to bind.

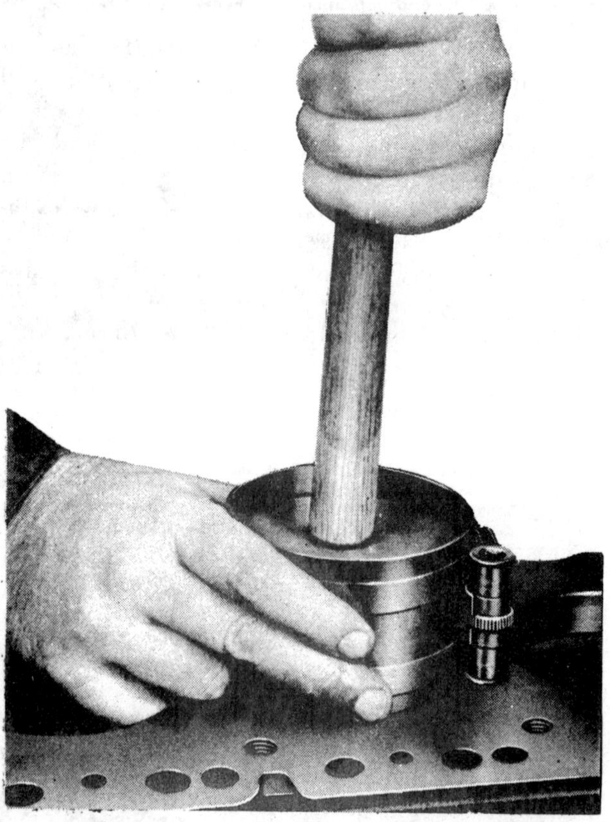

Oil the piston and rings, and then install the assembly with a compressor tool. Use the hammer handle to push the piston into the cylinder. Do not force it, because the edge of a ring may be caught on the top of the block. CAUTION: The side of the piston with the cast depression in the crown must be facing the front of the engine.

Rotate the back of each piston ring around the groove to make sure that it doesn't bind in any spot.

The end gaps must be checked by inserting each piston ring into its cylinder bore at the bottom, where very little wear exists, and then squaring up the ring by inserting the piston upside down. Measure the end gap, which generally must be 0.010″-0.020″, except for steel rails of the oil rings, which must be 0.015″-0.030″ unless specified differently in a specific engine family.

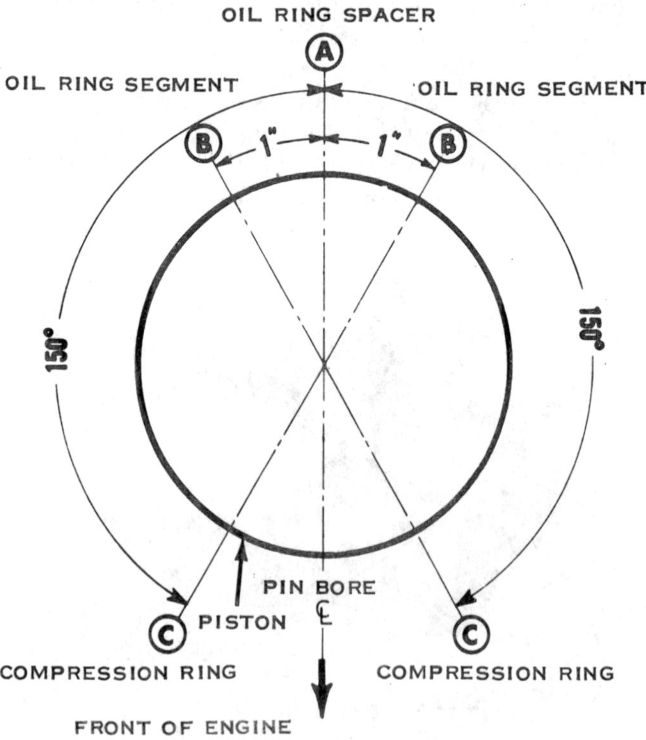

This diagram shows how to position the piston ring gaps for most efficient operation.

Localized heat areas on the valve face cause it to crack. Note how the small crack in the upper valve compares with the wider one in the lower valve face. This destructive process starts with a localized hot spot, possibly a piece of white-hot carbon on the seat.

If the end gap is too small, the ends of the ring can be filed to increase the gap.

When installing the rings on the piston, check the compression and scraper rings for the proper method of installation. Some rings have the word TOP stamped on the side that must face up. A compression

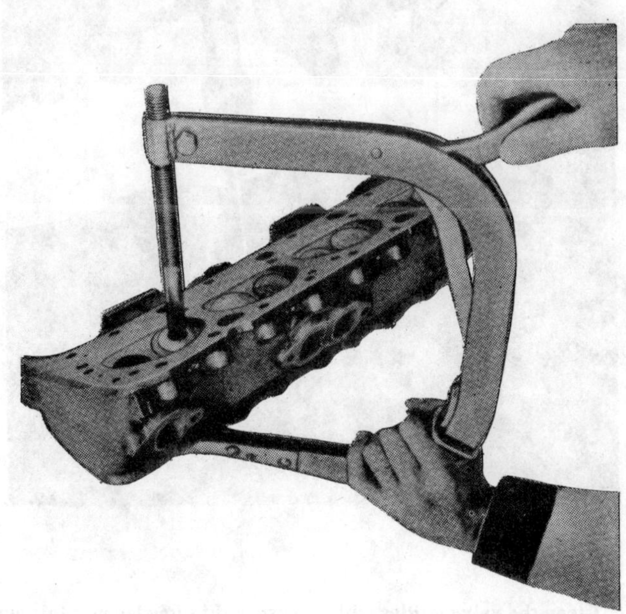

Use the illustrated tool to compress the valve spring, which will release the tapered keepers.

This exhaust valve face is severely burned. Note the gum on the neck of the valve stem, indicating that it was sticking in the guide. Be sure to clean the valve guide of all gum and carbon.

ring with a groove in its outer face must be installed with this groove facing down. If the groove is cut into the rear face of the ring, the groove must face up when installed. If a steel spacer is used in conjunction with a top compression ring in order to compensate for machine work on the groove, the steel spacer must be installed above the cast iron ring.

Valve Mechanism

Clean the valves, springs, spring retainers, locks, and sleeves in solvent, and the blow the parts dry. Inspect the valve face and the head for pits, grooves, and scores. Inspect the stem for wear and the end for grooves. The face must be trued on a valve grinding machine, which will remove minor pits and grooves. Valves with serious defects, or those having heads with a knife edge, must be replaced.

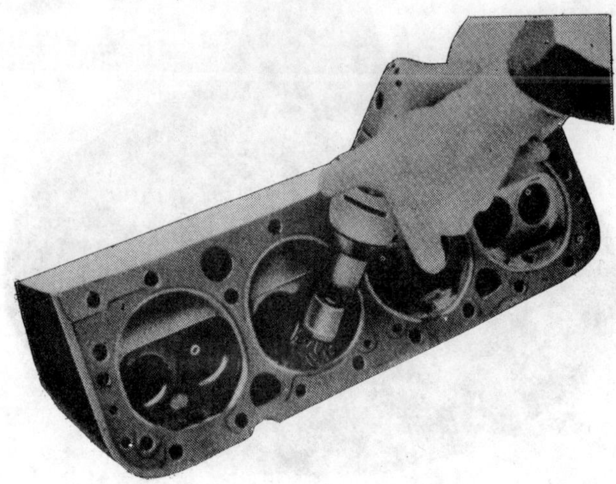

Use a wire brush to clean all carbon from the cylinder head.

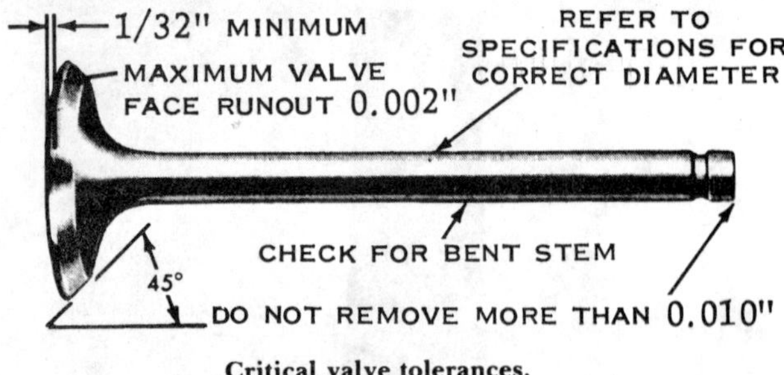

Critical valve tolerances.

Valve Guides

Clean the inside of the valve guides with a wire brush and lacquer thinner to remove all gum and carbon deposits, since such deposits could prevent the valve from closing properly.

If the valve guide is worn excessively, it can be reamed to an oversize for new valves with oversize stems of 0.015", and 0.030". When going from a standard size to an oversize, always use the reamers in sequence. After reaming a valve guide, always break the sharp ID corner at the top of the guide to prevent galling the valve stem. **CAUTION: Always reface the valve seat after reaming a valve guide in order to true it up with the new guide hole.**

To check the valve stem-to-guide clearance, insert the valve and measure its sideways movement with a dial indicator. The clearance must not exceed 0.0025". If the play is excessive, repeat the measurement with a new valve to determine whether the wear is in the valve guide or on the valve stem.

Checking the valve stem clearance with a dial indicator. Total indicator reading with a new valve installed must not exceed 0.0025" for an in.take valve or 00035" for an exhaust.

Valve Springs

Check the valve spring for the correct tension

Loose intake valve guides, or defective oil seals, can cause an oil leak onto the top of the intake valve.

Clean the valve guides with a brush. Add some lacquer thinner to remove the gum that causes valve sticking. Worn valve guides can be reamed oversize and valves with oversize stems used to restore production clearances.

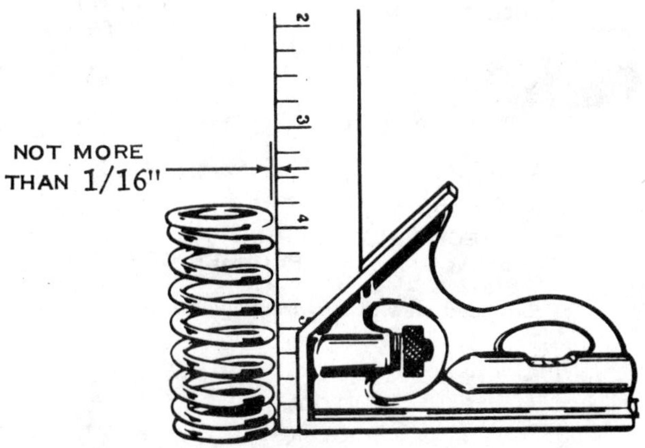

For a rough check on a valve spring, determine whether or not it is square with the end coils.

against specifications. A quick check can be made by laying all of the springs on a flat surface and comparing the heights, which must be even. Also, the ends must be square or the spring will tend to cock the valve stem. Weak valve springs cause poor engine performance; therefore, if any spring is weak or out of square more than 1/16", replace it.

Valves

Grind a 45° valve face to a 44° angle, and a 30° valve face to 29° for a 1° interference angle. Remove only enough stock to correct runout or to dress off the pits and grooves. If the edge of the valve head is less than 1/32" after grinding, replace the valve as it will run too hot in the engine. **CAUTION: Don't lap the valves together with grinding compound, or you will remove the interference angle.**

Valve Seats

The valve seat must be reground so that the pits and grooves are removed. Grind the seats to a 45° or 30°

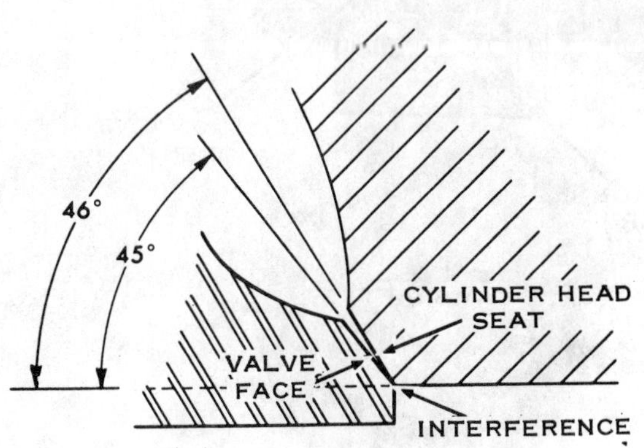

An interference angle of 1° should be ground into the valve or seat so that the seal is at the outer edge. This prevents carbon from being blown into the seating surfaces.

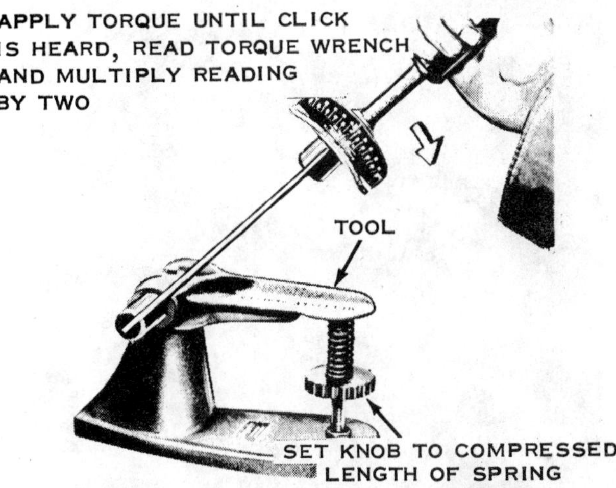

Accurate equipment is available to measure spring pressure, as shown.

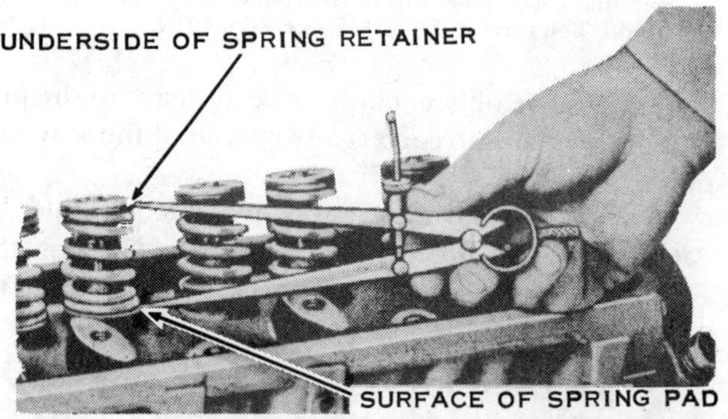

Always measure the valve spring height and compare it with specifications. This measurement must be made from the underside of the retainer to the machined surface of the head. Spacers are available for adjusting the compressed height.

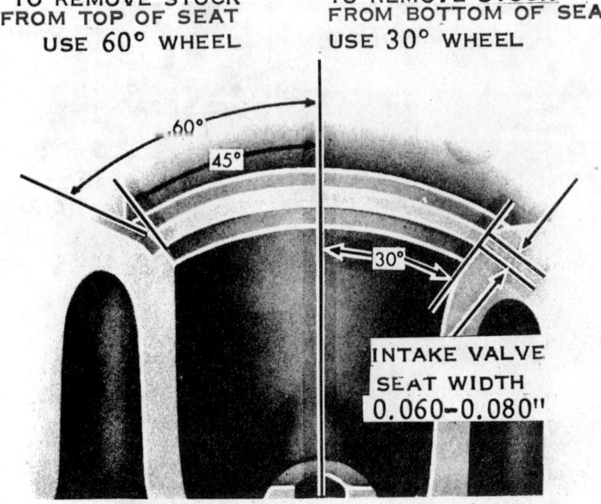

If it is necessary to narrow the valve seat, use a 60° grinding wheel to remove stock from the top.

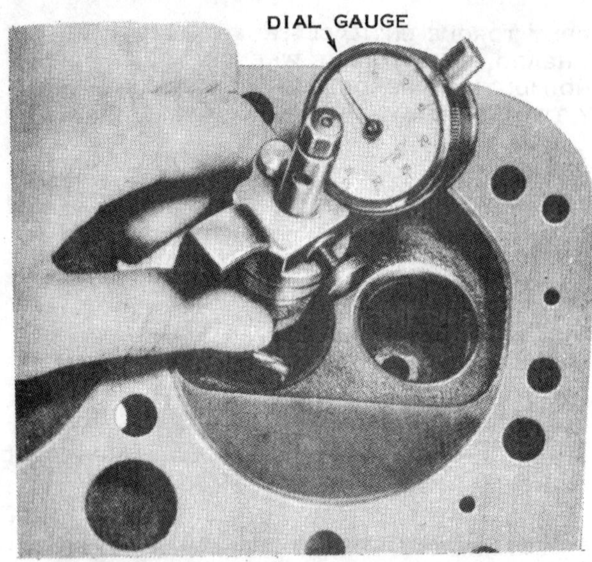

Use a dial gauge to see that the reground seat is concentric with the guide. The runout should not exceed 0.002".

angle. Remove only enough stock to clean up the pits and grooves and to correct any runout of the seat and guide.

Measure the valve seat widths, which should be 3/64-1/16" for the intake and 5/64-3/32" for the exhaust or as specified. The seats can be narrowed by

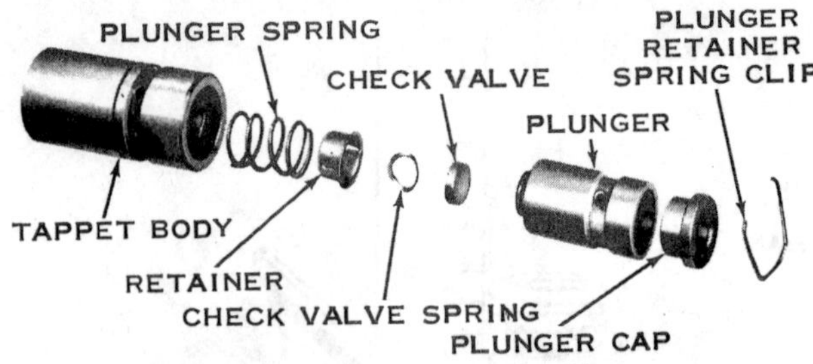

Exploded view of a hydraulic valve lifter.

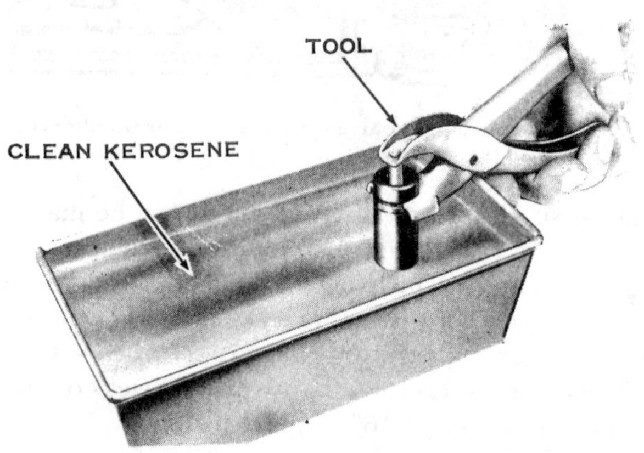

Testing a hydraulic tappet with a pair of special pliers. A good tappet will have considerable resistance to movement of the parts.

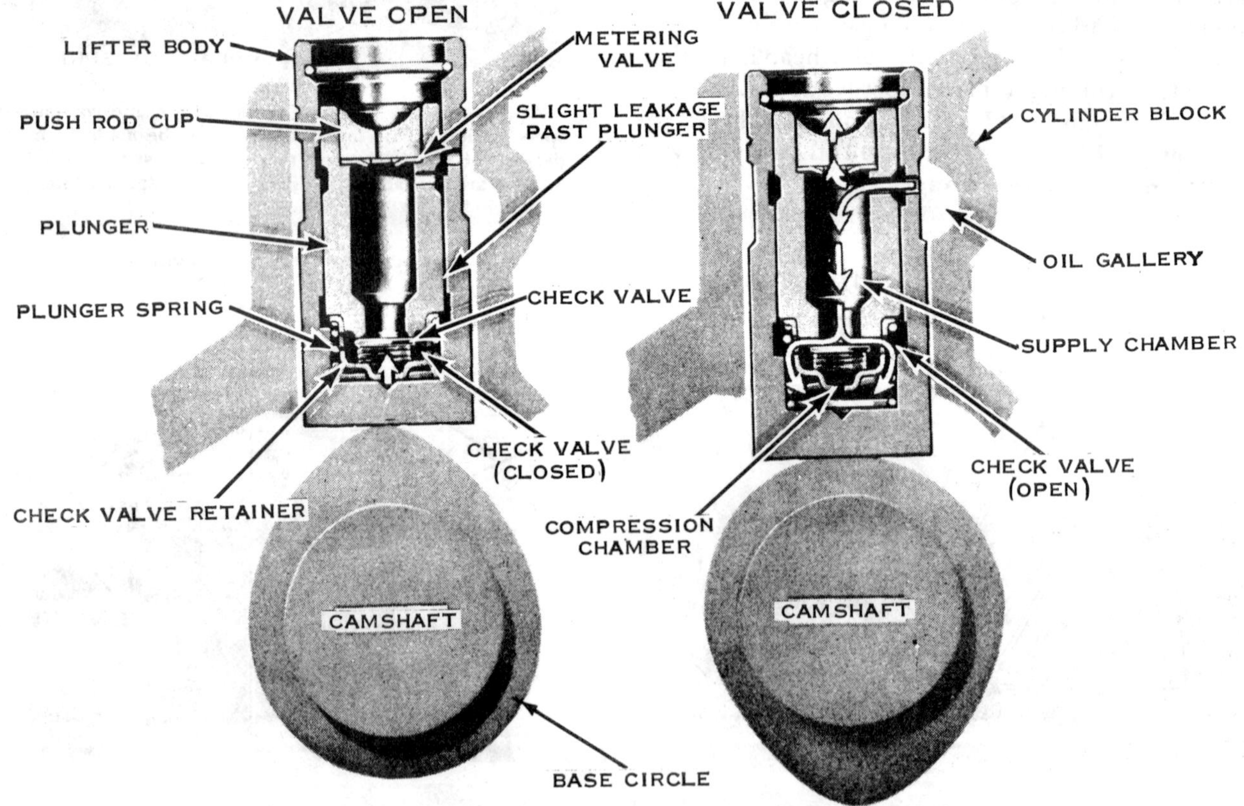

Operation of the hydraulic valve lifter.

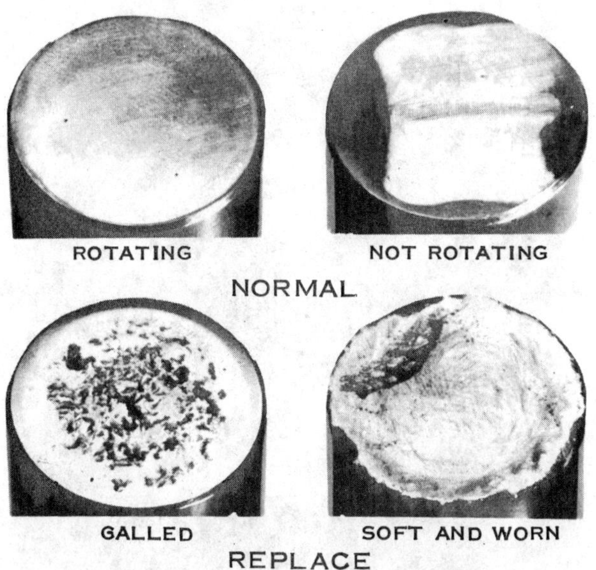

Details of the wear pattern to expect on the base of a tappet or hydraulic lifter.

removing stock from the top and bottom edges by using a 30° stone and a 60° stone.

The finished seat should contact the approximate center of the valve face. To determine the position of the seat on the valve face, coat the seat with Prussian blue, and then rotate the valve in place with light pressure. The blue pattern on the valve face will show the position of the seat.

Hydraulic Valve Lifters

Dirt, deposits of gum, and air bubbles in the lubricating oil can cause the hydraulic lifters to wear enough to cause failure. The dirt and gum can keep a check valve from seating, which will cause the oil to return to the reservoir during the time that the push rod is being lifted. Excessive movement of the parts of the lifter causes wear, which soon destroys its effectiveness.

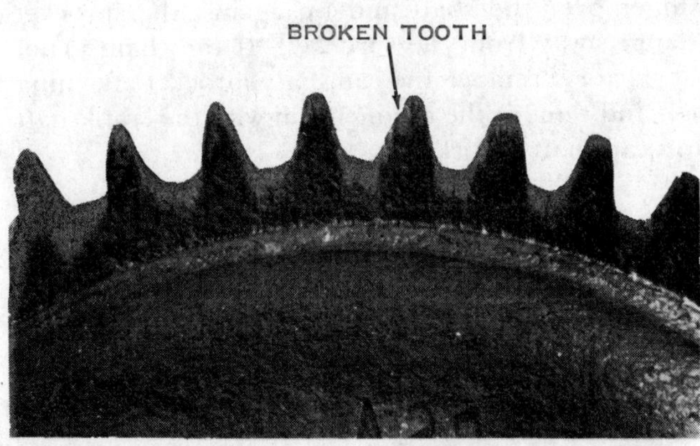

Timing gear wear is spotty. Note that the teeth at the right are fairly well formed, while those on the left are badly worn.

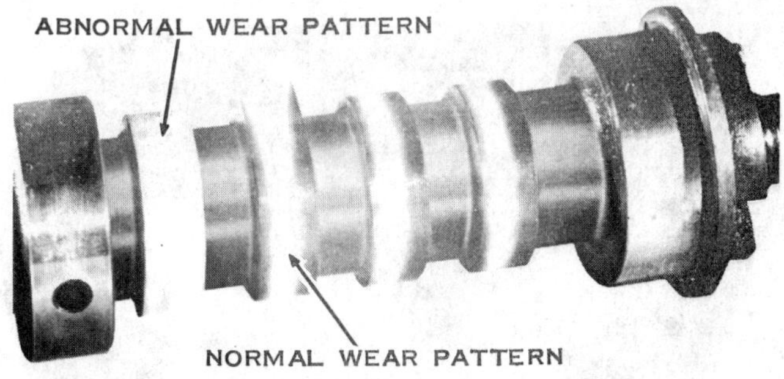

Typical wear patterns on the cam lobes of a camshaft.

The backlash between the timing gear teeth should be between 0.004-0.006".

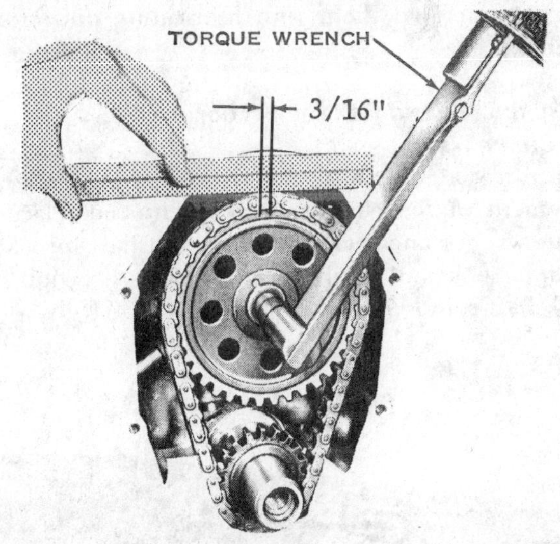

Measuring the timing chain stretch. With the crankshaft kept from rotating, tighten the sprocket attaching bolt to 15 ft-lbs of torque, and apply the same torque in a reverse direction. Replace the timing chain if its movement exceeds 3/16".

Timing sprocket wear caused by the teeth of the chain. This type of wear causes noise from the front of the engine.

With the timing chain properly installed, the timing marks on the crankshaft and camshaft sprockets must be in alignment, as shown.

The valve lifter assemblies must be kept in the proper sequence so that they can be re-installed in their original position. Clean, inspect, and test each lifter separately so as not to intermix the internal parts. If any one part of a lifter needs to be replaced, replace the entire assembly.

To test a cleaned lifter, assemble the parts dry, and then quickly depress the plunger with your finger. The trapped air should partially return the plunger if the lifter is operating properly. If the lifter is worn, or if the check valve is not seating, the plunger will not return.

Install the assembled lifters in the engine dry. They will bleed to their correct operating position quicker than if you filled them with lubricating oil before installing.

Measuring Timing Gear or Sprocket and Chain Wear

Place a scale next to the timing chain so any movement of the chain may be measured. Place a torque wrench and socket over the camshaft sprocket attaching bolt and apply torque in the direction of crankshaft rotation to take up the slack; 30 ft-lbs with the cylinder heads installed or 15 ft-lbs with the cylinder heads removed. With torque applied to the camshaft sprocket bolt, the crankshaft must not be permitted to move. *NOTE: It may be necessary to block the crankshaft to prevent rotation.*

Holding a scale with the dimensional reading even with the edge of a chain link, apply the same torque in the reverse direction and note the amount of chain movement. Install a new timing chain if its movement exceeds 3/16″.

If the chain is satisfactory, slide the crankshaft oil slinger over the shaft and up against the sprocket (flange away from the sprocket). If the chain is not satisfactory, remove the camshaft sprocket attaching bolt and remove the timing chain with the crankshaft and camshaft sprockets.

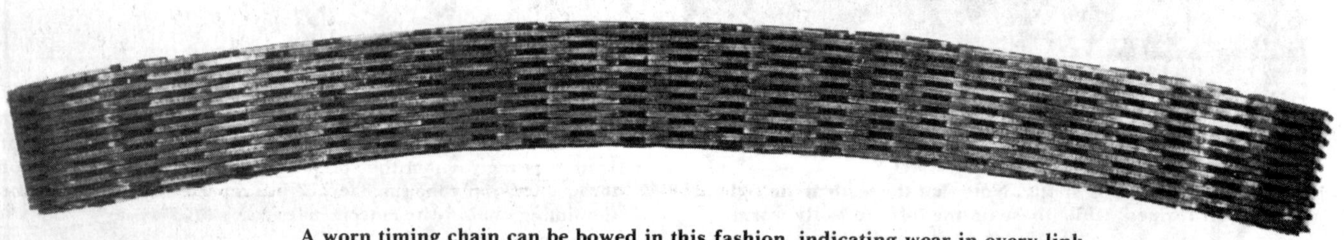

A worn timing chain can be bowed in this fashion, indicating wear in every link.

2,000/2,300CC ENGINES

The 2,000cc engine was produced from 1971-74, and has been superseded by the 2,300cc engine in 1974. Both engines have a great deal in common, but there are some procedural differences due to design simplification and to the use of hydraulic lash adjusters in place of the valve clearance adjusting screws used on the 2,000cc engine.

The service procedures for the 2,000cc engine are given first, and this is followed by a section on the 2,300cc engine, discussing the special service instructions or modified procedures needed.

2300CC ENGINE

The 4-cylinder 2300cc overhead cam engine is of lightweight iron construction. The crankshaft is supported on five main bearings and the camshaft by four. Main, connecting rod, camshaft, and auxiliary shaft bearings are all replaceable.

The camshaft is driven from the crankshaft by a cogged belt, which also operates the auxiliary shaft, and through this shaft, the oil pump, fuel pump, and distributor. Tension on the cam drive belt is maintained by a pre-loaded and locked idler pulley bearing on the outside of the belt.

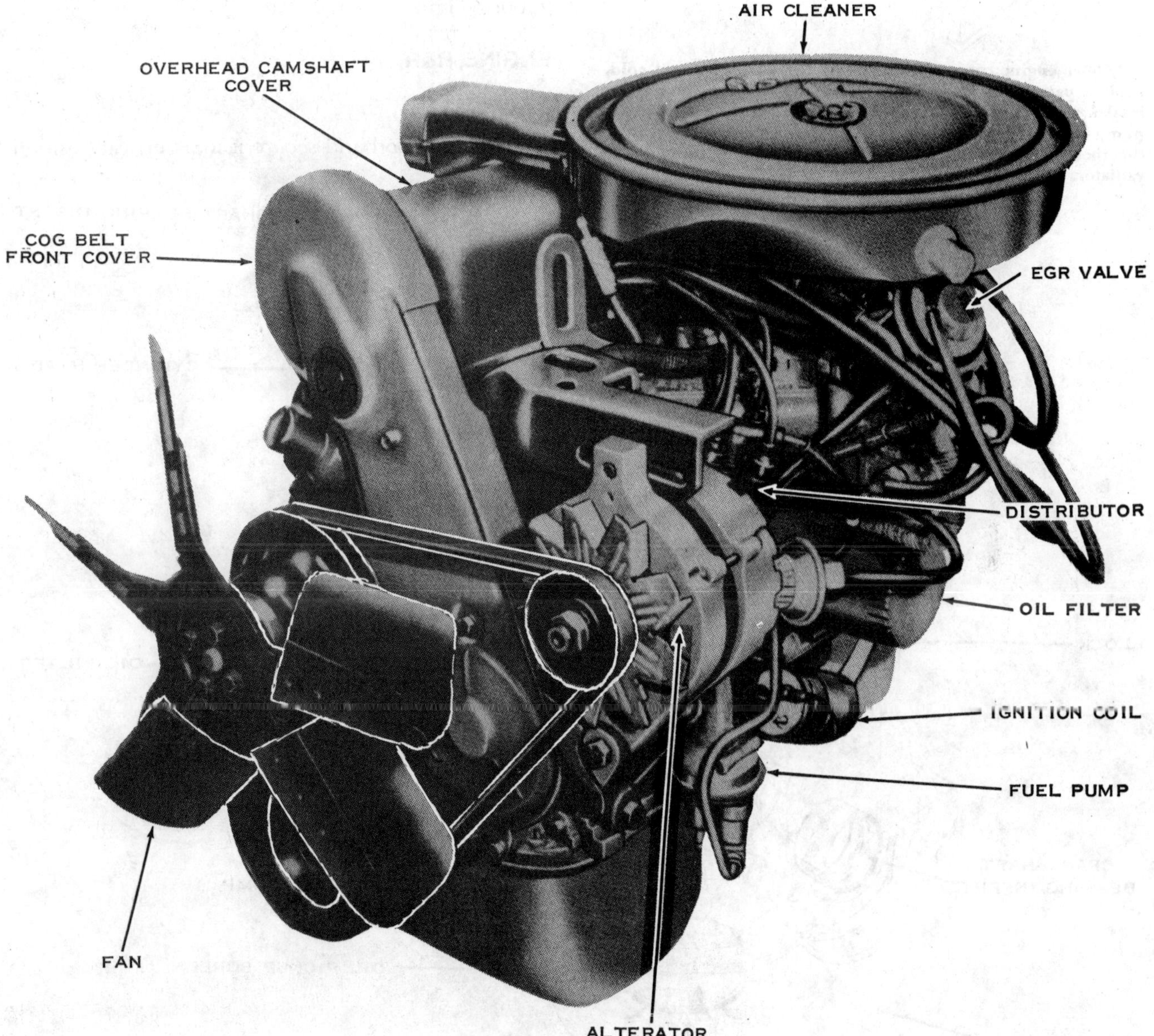

2,300cc overhead-cam engine. This engine differs from the 2,000cc engine in several respects, the most of important of which are the hydraulic lash adjusters in place of the rocker arm adjusting screws.

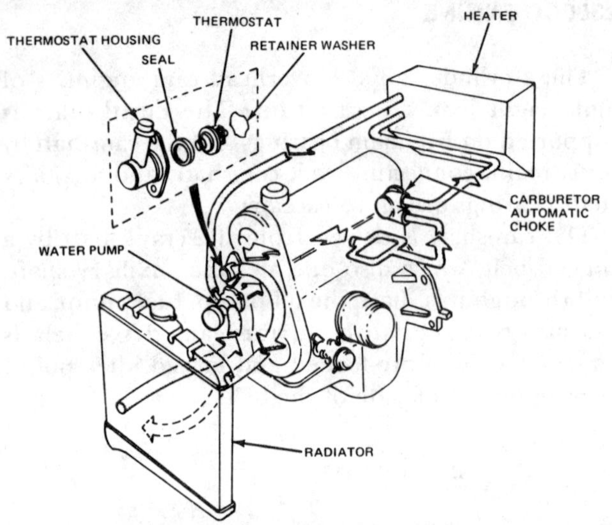

2,000cc engine coolant system. As long as the engine is cold, coolant passes only from the water pump through the engine, intake manifold, automatic choke, and heater core, back to the pump to ensure a quick warm up. When the coolant reaches 190° F, the thermostat opens and allows coolant to flow through the radiator.

The water pump and fan are separately driven from the crankshaft by a conventional V-belt, which also drives the alternator.

Hydraulic valve lash adjusters are used in the valve train. These units are placed at the fulcrum point of the cam followers (or rocker arms). Their action is similar to the hydraulic valve lifters used in push-rod engines; they are constructed and serviced in the same manner. The cylinder head has drilled oil passages to provide engine oil pressure to the lash adjusters.

Although similar in design to the 2000cc overhead cam 4-cylinder engine, the 2300cc engine is different in several details, and few parts will interchange.

A set of metric wrenches is required to service the 2300cc engine.

ENGINE, R&R

REMOVING

Raise the hood and secure it in a vertical position.

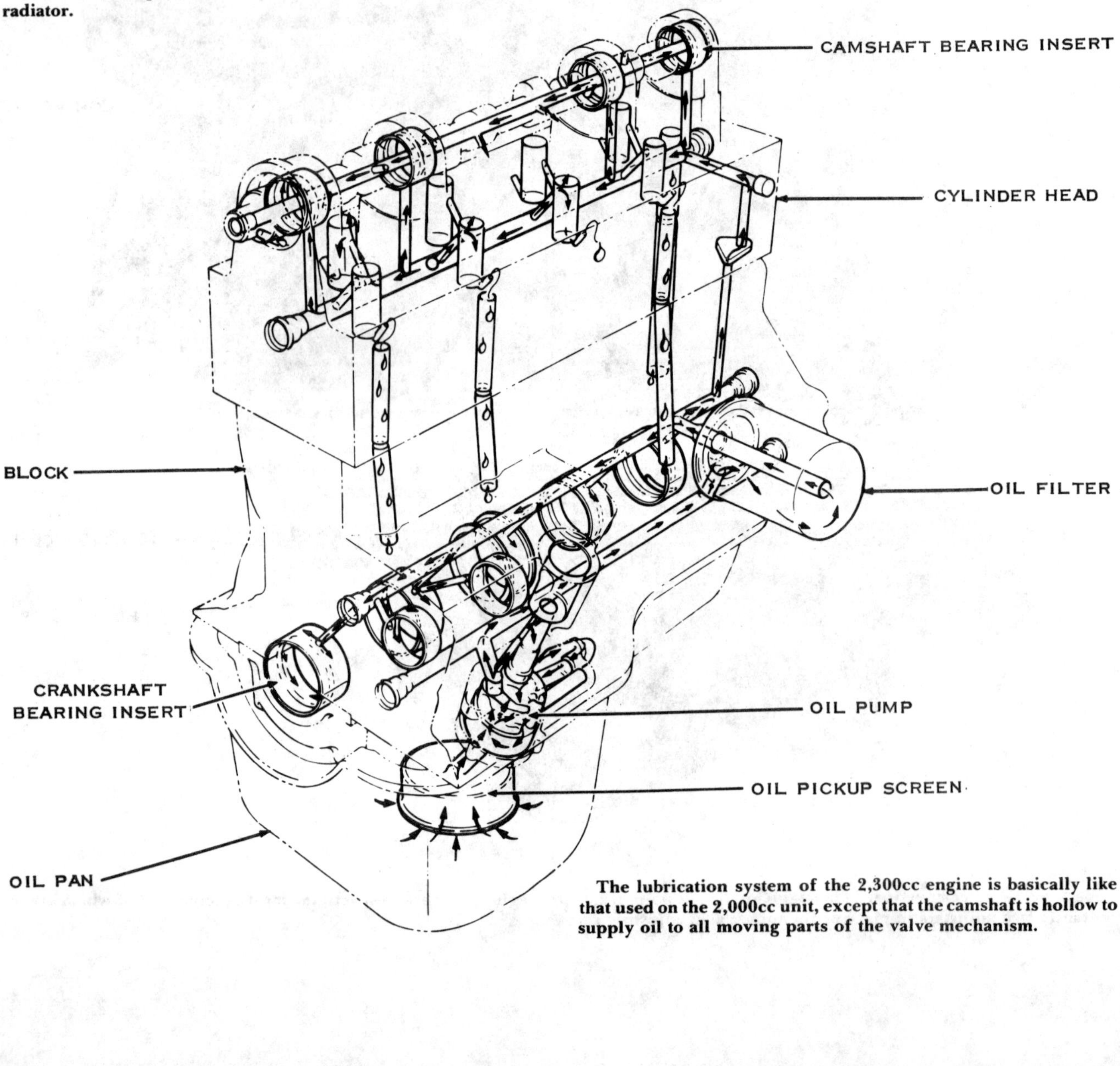

The lubrication system of the 2,300cc engine is basically like that used on the 2,000cc unit, except that the camshaft is hollow to supply oil to all moving parts of the valve mechanism.

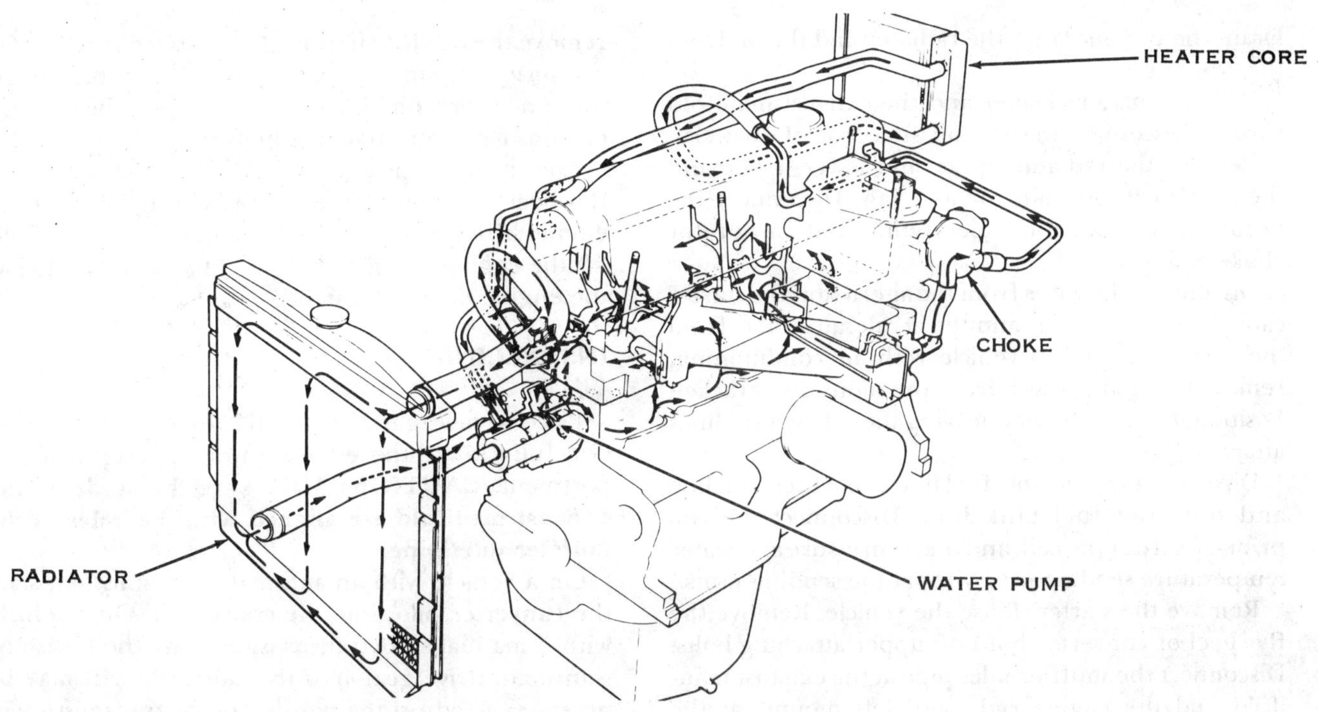

The cooling system of the 2,300cc engine is basically like the one used on the 2,000cc engine.

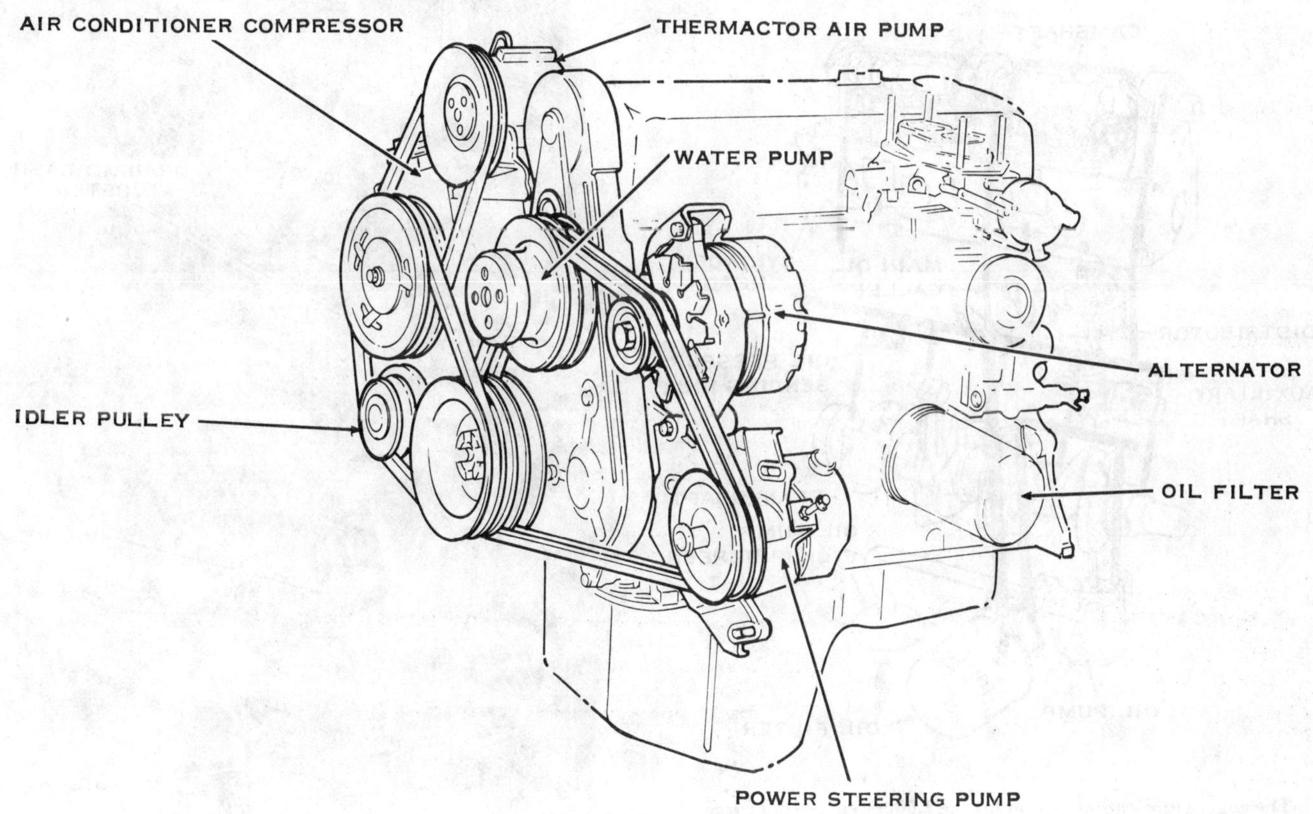

2,300cc engine with all optional accessories installed.

Drain the coolant from the radiator and the oil from the crankcase.

Remove the air cleaner and the exhaust manifold shroud. Disconnect the ground cable from the battery.

Remove the radiator upper and lower hoses, and then take off the radiator and fan. Disconnect the heater hose from the water pump and carburetor choke fitting.

Disconnect the wires from the alternator, the starter cable from the starter, and the accelerator cable from the carburetor. On a vehicle with air conditioning, remove the compressor from the mounting bracket. Position it out of the way, leaving the refrigerant lines attached.

Disconnect the flexible fuel line at the fuel tank line and plug the fuel tank line. Disconnect the coil primary wire at the coil, and the oil pressure and water temperature sending unit wires at the sending units.

Remove the starter. Raise the vehicle. Remove the flywheel or converter housing upper attaching bolts. Disconnect the muffler inlet pipe at the exhaust manifold and the engine right and left mounts at the underbody bracket. Remove the flywheel or converter housing cover.

On a vehicle with a manual-shift transmission, remove the flywheel housing lower attaching bolts. On a vehicle with an automatic transmission, disconnect the converter from the flywheel. Remove the converter housing lower attaching bolts.

Lower the vehicle. Support the transmission and flywheel or converter housing with a jack. Attach engine lifting hooks to the lifting brackets. Carefully lift the engine out of the engine compartment. Install the engine on a work stand.

INSTALLING

Place a new gasket over the exhaust inlet pipe. Carefully lower the engine into the engine compartment. **CAUTION: Make sure the studs on the exhaust manifold are aligned with the holes in the muffler inlet pipe.**

On a vehicle with an automatic transmission, start the converter pilot into the crankshaft. On a vehicle with a manual-shift transmission, start the transmission main drive gear into the clutch disc. It may be necessary to adjust the position of the transmission in

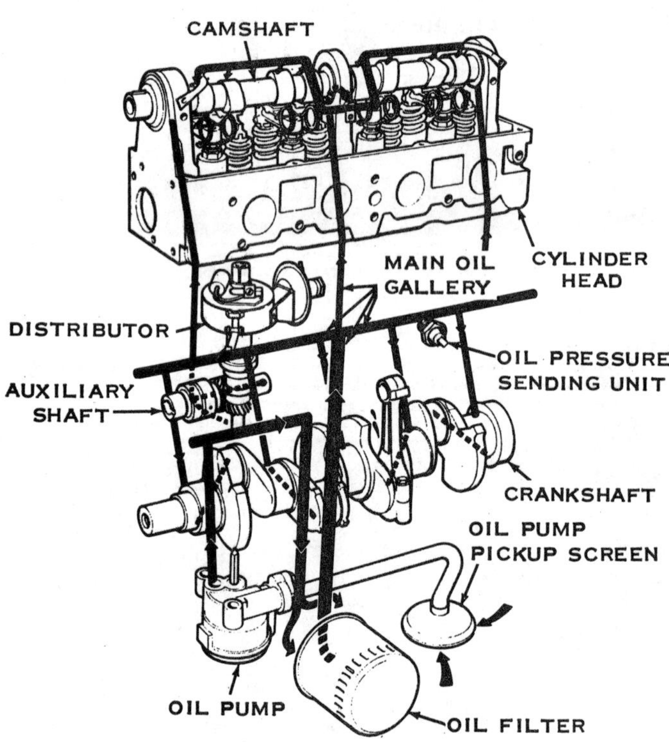

The engine lubrication system for the 2,000cc engine is a force-feed type. The five crankshaft main bearings and the three camshaft bearings are in direct connection with the main oil gallery.

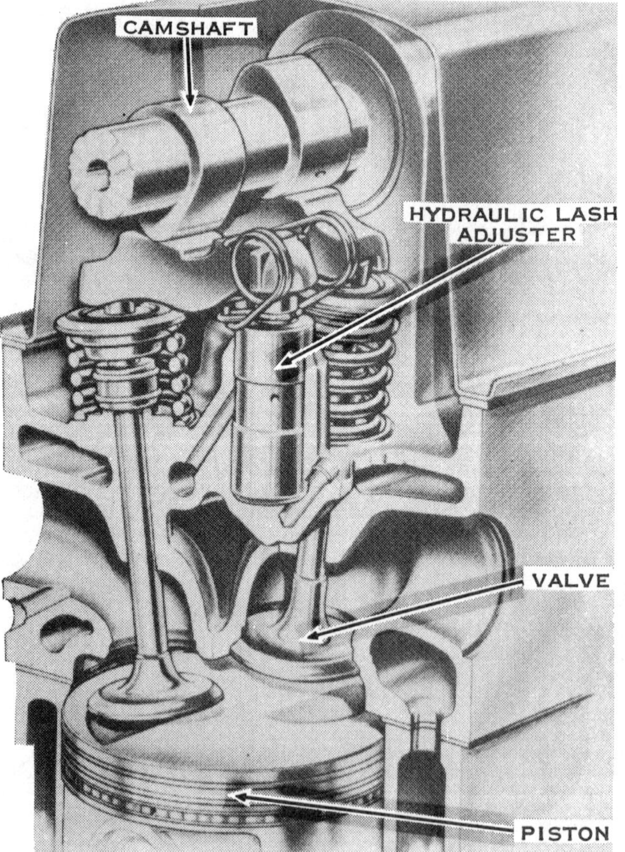

The 2,300cc engine uses hydraulic lash adjusters in place of an adjusting screw.

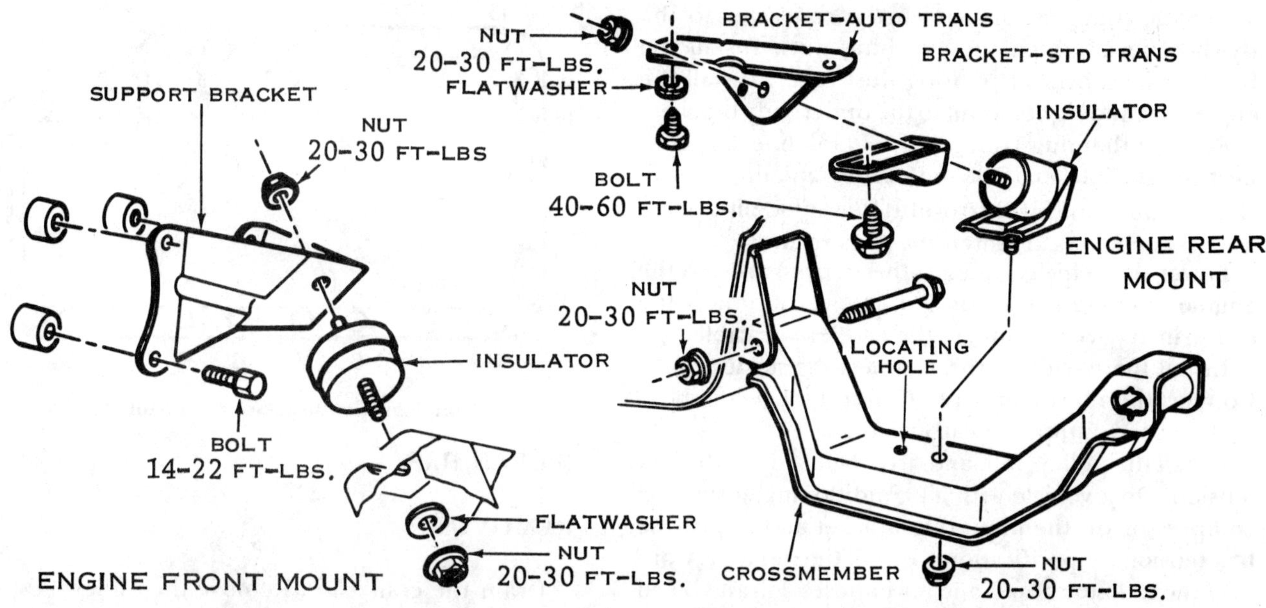

2,000cc engine mounts and torque values.

relation to the engine if the input shaft will not enter the clutch disc. If the engine hangs up after the shaft enters, turn the crankshaft in the clockwise direction slowly, (transmission in gear) until the shaft splines mesh with the clutch splines.

Remove the engine lifting sling hooks. Install the flywheel or converter housing upper attaching bolts. Remove the jack from the transmission.

Raise the vehicle. Install the flywheel converter housing lower attaching bolts. On a vehicle with an

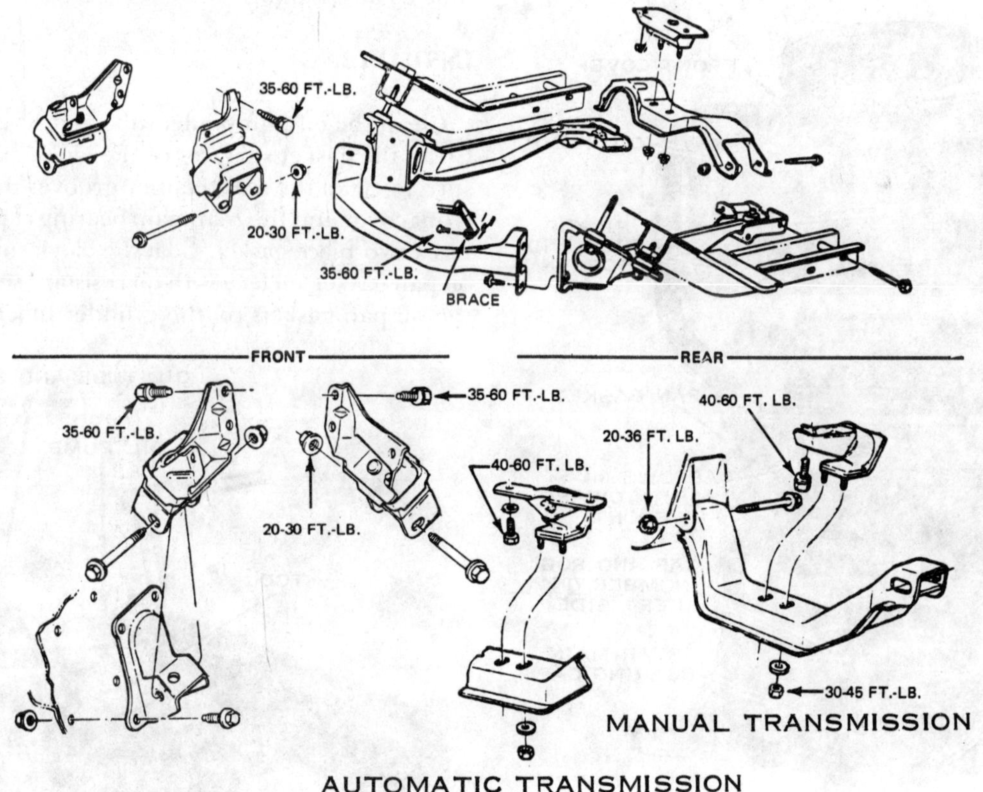

2,300cc engine mounts and torque values.

automatic transmission, attach the converter to the flywheel and tighten the attaching nuts. Install the flywheel or converter housing dust cover. Install the engine left and right mount to the underbody bracket.

Remove the plug from the fuel tank line and connect the flexible fuel line to the fuel tank line. Install the exhaust manifold-to-muffler inlet pipe lockwashers and nuts. Tighten the nuts securely.

Lower the vehicle. Connect the oil pressure and the engine temperature sending unit wires. Connect the coil primary wire. Connect the accelerator cable.

Install the starter motor. Connect the starter cable. Connect the alternator wires. Connect the heater hose at the water pump and carburetor.

Install the pulley, fan, and drive belt. Adjust the belt tension. On a vehicle with air conditioning, install the compressor on the mounting bracket and adjust the belt tension to specifications. Install the radiator. Connect the radiator upper and lower hoses. Fill and bleed the cooling system. Fill the crankcase with the proper grade and quantity of engine oil.

Connect the battery ground cable. Install the air cleaner and connect the positive closed-type crankcase ventilation hose. Operate the engine at fast idle and check all gaskets and hose connections for leaks.

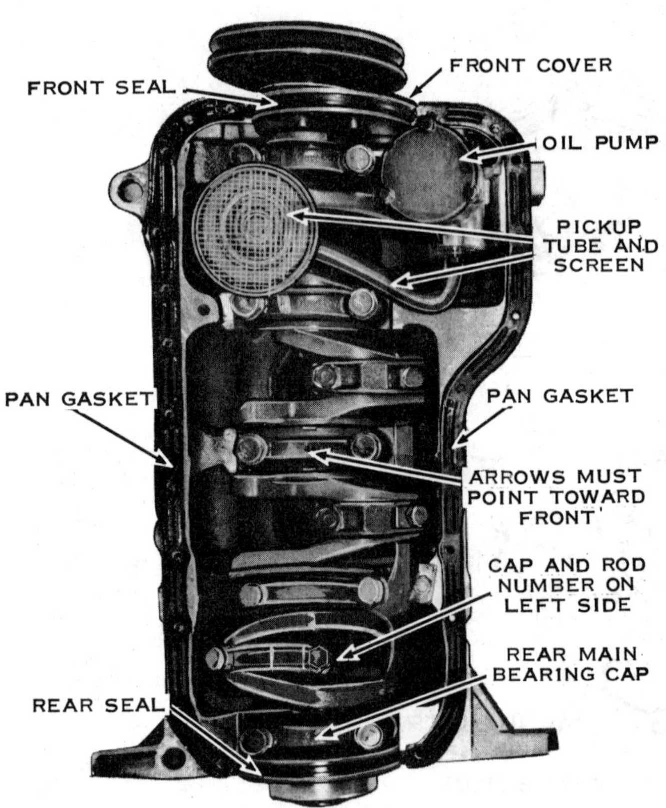

Position of the oil pan gaskets and seals.

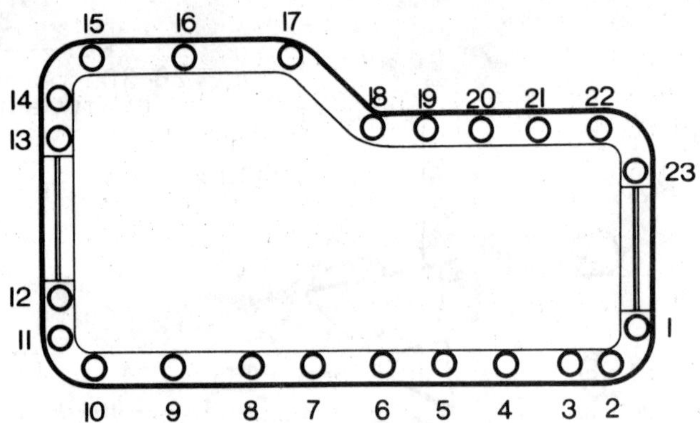

Bolt tightening sequence for the oil pan.

OIL PAN, R&R

REMOVING

Drain the crankcase. Remove the oil level dipstick and the flywheel housing inspection cover.

Disconnect the steering cable from the rack and pinion. Disconnect the rack and pinion from the crossmember and move it forward to provide clearance for the oil pan.

Remove the oil pan attaching bolts, and then remove the pan and gasket. Remove the oil pump and inlet tube as an assembly.

INSTALLING

Clean the oil pump inlet tube and screen assembly. Clean the gasket surfaces of the block and oil pan. Be sure to clean the seal retainer grooves in the cylinder front cover and the rear main bearing cap. The oil pan has a two-piece gasket. Coat the block surface and the oil pan gasket surface with oil resistant sealer. Position the oil pan gaskets on the cylinder block.

Removing the oil pump assembly from the 2,000cc engine.

Position the oil pan front seal on the cylinder front cover. **CAUTION: Be sure the ends of the seal are contacting the oil pan gasket.** Install the rear seal on the rear main bearing cap. Coat all gaskets and joints with sealer.

Prime the pump and install it and the tube and screen on the engine. Torque the two attaching bolts to 12-15 ft-lbs with Tool T71P-6603-A.

Position the oil pan and torque the bolts in two steps: (1) 1-2 ft-lbs., and (2) 4-6 ft-lbs.

Position the rack and pinion and tighten the attaching bolts. Connect the steering cable to the rack and pinion.

Fill the crankcase to the correct level with the specified oil. Start the engine and check for leaks.

CHECKING THE CAMSHAFT TIMING 2,000CC ENGINE

Remove the three bolts retaining the camshaft belt shield, and then remove the shield. Take out the camshaft sprocket retaining bolt.

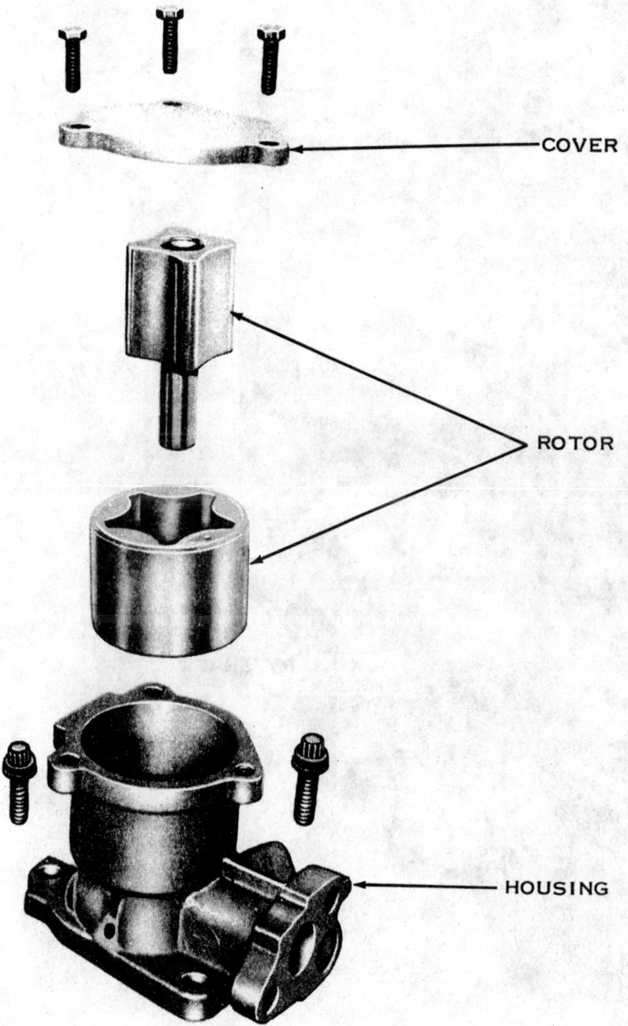

Disassembled view of the oil pump used on the 2,000cc engine.

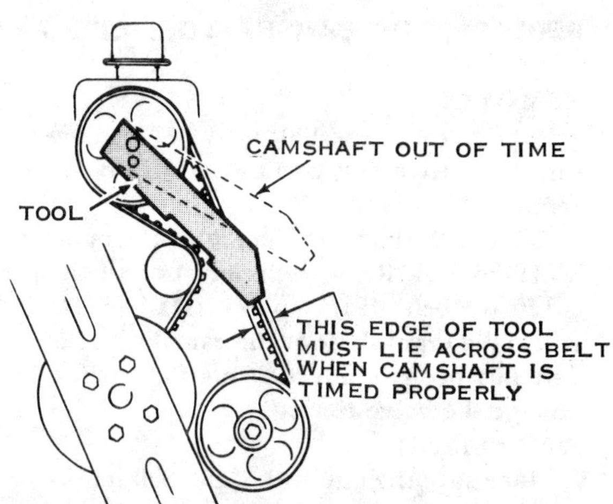

Using tool No. T71P-8620-A to check the camshaft timing, as discussed in the text.

Set the crankshaft to TDC by aligning the timing mark on the engine front cover with the "O" mark on the crankshaft damper. **CAUTION: If the crankshaft is to be turned by hand, always turn it in the direction of normal rotation. Backward rotation will cause the belt to jump time due to the arrangement of the belt tensioner.**

Install Tool T71P-8620-A on the engine, with the large pin inserted in the camshaft sprocket bolt hole. The tool should be to the left of the thermostat housing. Rotate the tool in a clockwise direction until the small pin can be inserted into the large keyway near the bottom of the gear. Since the camshaft rotates at 1/2 engine speed it may be necessary to turn the crankshaft one full turn to bring the large keyway to the bottom edge of the sprocket. Check the point where the bottom edge of the tool lies across the belt. If the bottom edge of the tool does not lie across the belt, the timing is incorrect.

If the timing is incorrect, inspect the camshaft belt for wear or damage. If the belt is damaged, replace it.

If the belt is not damaged, mark the position of a cam sprocket tooth and also make an index mark on the belt. Then remove the belt. Turn the cam sprocket slightly and install the belt so that the sprocket teeth engage the belt one tooth away from the original position. Install tool T71P-8620-A and recheck the timing. Repeat until the belt is timed correctly.

When the timing is correct, install the cam sprocket retaining bolt and torque it to 32-36 ft-lbs.

Install the camshaft belt shield, and then install the three retaining bolts with rubber grommets.

REPLACING THE CAMSHAFT DRIVE BELT

REMOVING

Position the crankshaft on TDC. Remove the three camshaft drive belt cover attaching bolts, and then remove the cover.

Remove the belt tensioner adjustment bolt with tool T71P-6603-A. Remove the pivot bolt end spring.

Lift the belt off the sprockets. **CAUTION: Do not rotate the crankshaft or the camshaft after the drive belt has been removed. Rotating either one will change the valve timing.**

INSTALLING

Make sure the one end of the belt tensioner spring engages the groove in the anchor stud which is behind the pin of the back plate. Rotate the tensioner clockwise as far as possible, then tighten the adjustment bolt snugly with tool T71P-6603-A. Align the timing marks as shown. Then position the drive belt on the sprockets. Loosen the tensioner adjustment bolt. Rotate the crankshaft two complete turns to remove all slack from the belt and allow the tensioner to move tightly against the belt. Torque the tensioner adjustment and pivot bolts to 32-36 ft-lbs. Recheck the timing marks.

Postition the camshaft drive belt cover and torque the three attaching bolts to 7-9 ft-lbs. Start the engine and check the ignition timing. Adjust it as required.

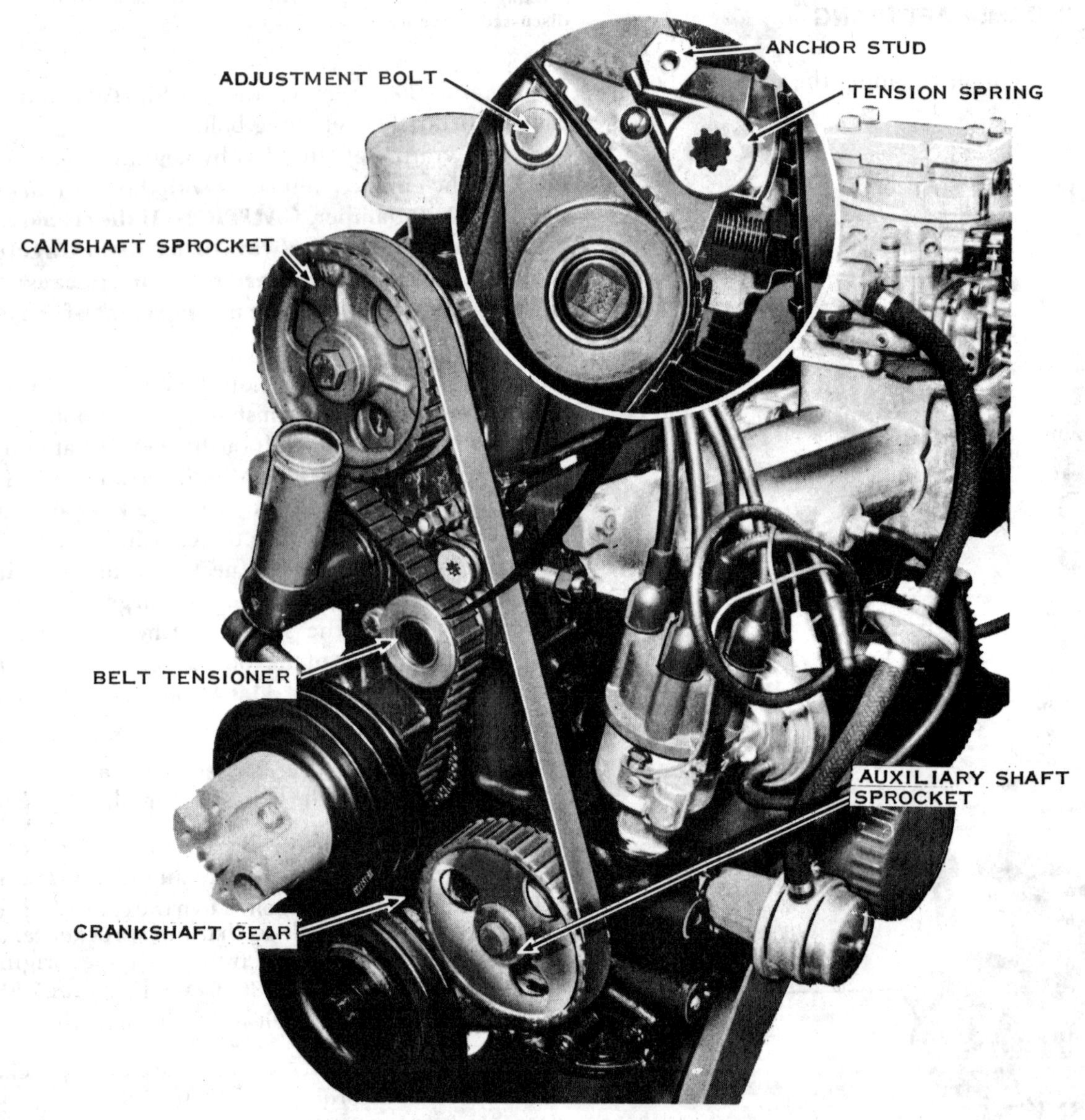

Camshaft drive train for the 2,000cc engine.

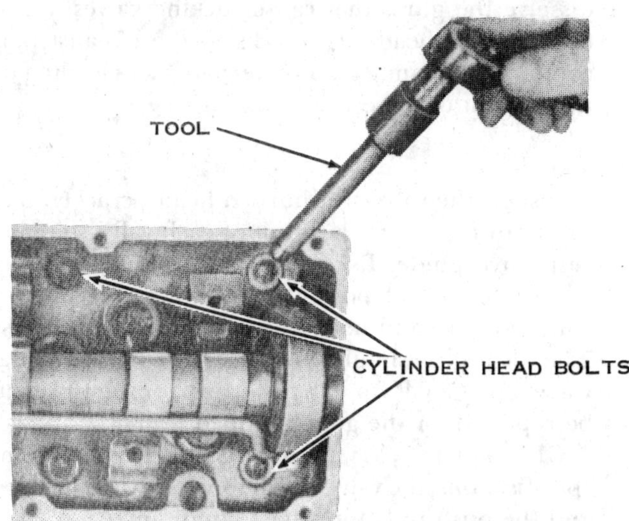

Using special tool T71P-6065-A to remove the cylinder head bolts from the 2,000cc engine.

CYLINDER HEAD SERVICE

The condition of the cylinder head and valve mechanism, more than anything else, determines the performance and economy of an engine. Extreme care should be exercised when reconditioning the cylinder head and valves to maintain correct valve stem-to-guide clearance, correctly ground valves, valve seats of the correct width, and correct valve adjustment.

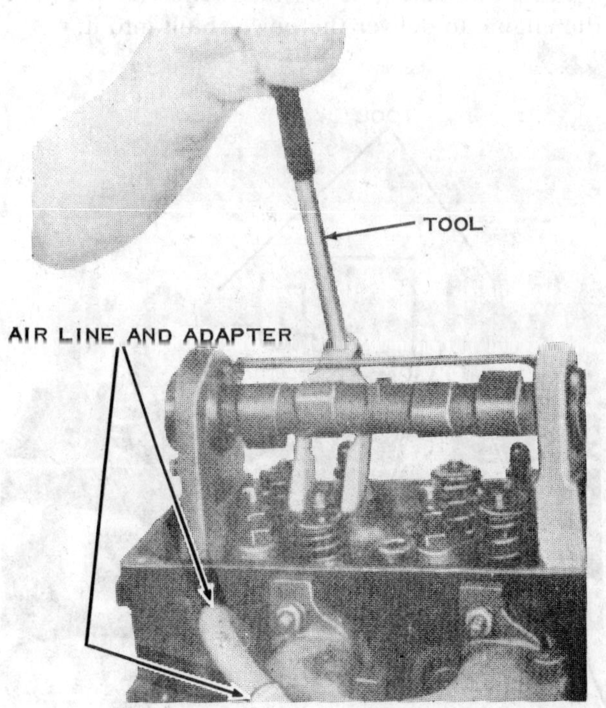

Use the illustrated tool to compress the valve spring just enough to slide the rocker arm off the valve tip and toward the hydraulic lash adjuster. CAUTION: Use compressed air in the combustion chamber to keep the valve from dropping down.

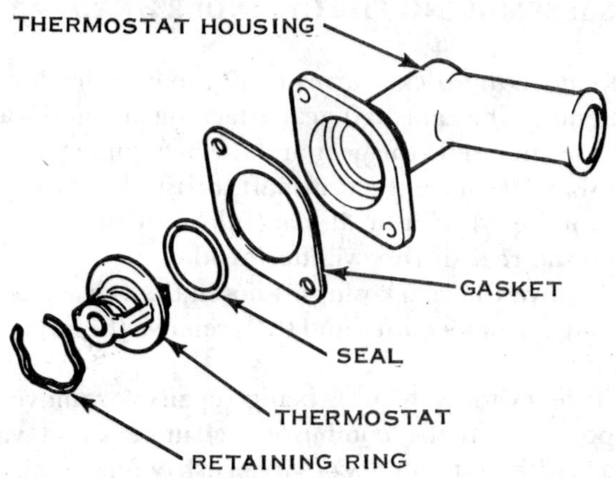

Removing the thermostat from the water outlet housing.

REMOVING THE CYLINDER HEAD

Drain the cooling system. Remove the air cleaner. Remove the valve rocker arm cover and the exhaust manifold. Remove the intake manifold, carburetor, and decel valve as an assembly.

Remove the camshaft drive belt cover. **CAUTION: Do not lose the rubber grommets from the attaching screws.** Loosen the drive belt tensioner, and then remove the drive belt.

Remove the water outlet elbow from the cylinder head. Take out the ten cylinder head attaching bolts with tool T71P-6065-A, as shown. Lift the cylinder head and camshaft assembly from the engine.

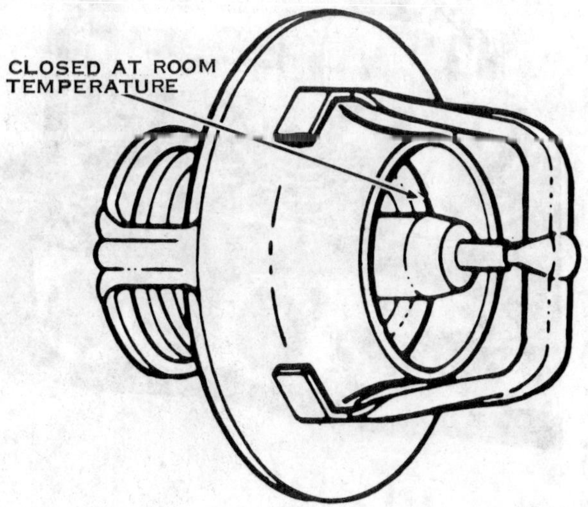

Check the cold thermostat for leakage by holding it up to a lighted background. No light should be visible at the point shown. Immerse the thermostat in boiling water and it must open at least ¼" if it is good.

DISASSEMBLING THE CYLINDER HEAD

Remove the rocker arms from the cylinder head.

Remove the camshaft gear attaching bolt and washer, and then slide the gear and the belt guide plate off the shaft. Remove the camshaft thrust plate from the rear of the cylinder head. Carefully slide the camshaft from the rear of the cylinder head.

Remove the spark plugs. Loosen the valve lash adjusting screw locknuts, and then remove the adjusting screws.

If the cylinder head is being repaired, remove the deposits from the combustion chambers and valve heads with a scraper and a wire brush before removing the valves. **CAUTION: Be careful not to scratch the cylinder head gasket surface.**

Compress the valve springs with a spring compressor. Remove the retainer locks, retainers, springs, and seals. Remove the valves from the guides and tag them so that they can be installed in the guides from which they were removed.

Remove the camshaft bearings as shown. **CAUTION: Do not remove the bearings if they are in a serviceable condition.**

CLEANING AND INSPECTING

Scrape and buff all carbon from the head, valve ports, valves, and the tops of the pistons. Clean the valve guides, using a brush and lacquer thinner to dissolve the gums that cause sticking valves. Insp‹ the cylinder heads for cracks in the exhaust ports, combustion chambers, or external cracks leading into the coolant chamber.

VALVES

Inspect the valves for burned heads, cracked faces, or worn stems. Check the fit of each valve stem in its respective guide. Excessive valve-to-guide clearance will cause lack of power, rough idling, excessive oil consumption, and noisy valve-operating mechanism. The clearance should not exceed 0.003″ for intake valves and 0.004″ for exhaust valves, or the valve must be replaced, or the guide reamed oversize.

Check the valve spring tension against specifications, the valve lifters for a free fit in the block, and the push rods for a bent condition.

VALVE FACES

Valves that are pitted can be refaced to the proper angle, insuring correct relation between the head and stem, on a valve-refacing machine. Dress the valve-refacing machine grinding wheel to make sure it is smooth and true. Set the chuck at the 45° mark for grinding all valve faces.

VALVE SEATS

Reconditioning the valve seats is very important, because the seating of the valves must be perfect for the engine to deliver the power built into it.

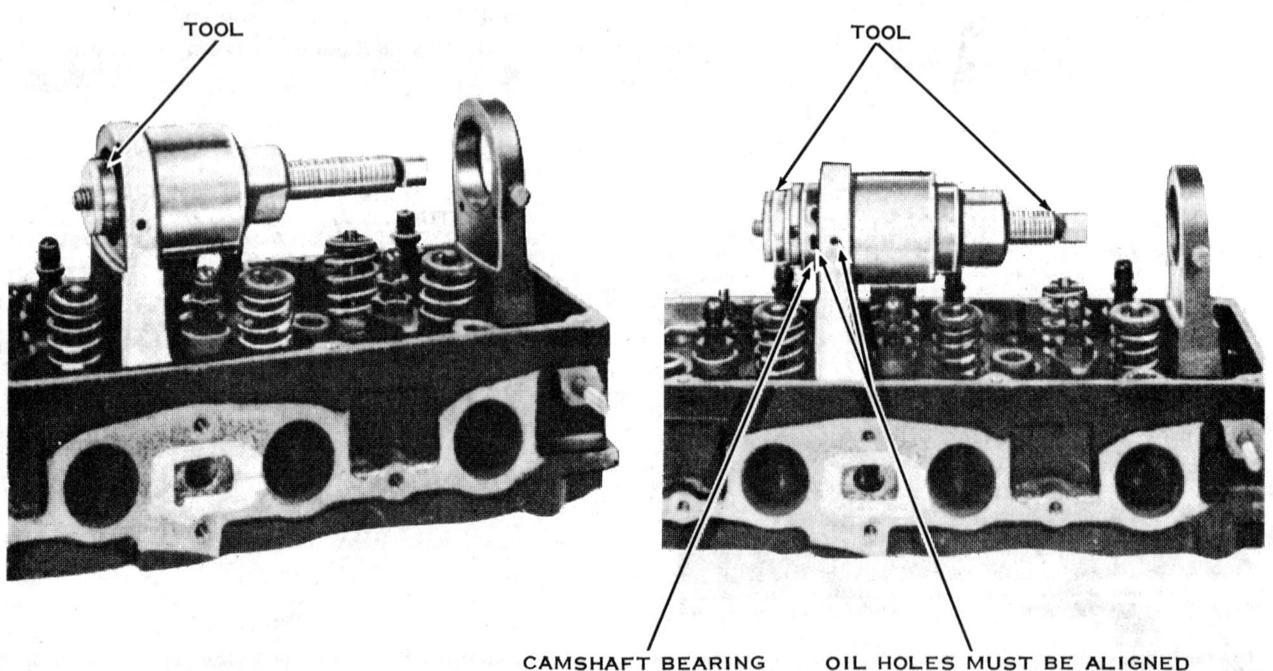

Using tool 71P-6250-A to remove a camshaft bushing on the 2,000cc engine (left) and installing it (right).

spring engages the groove in the anchor stud, which is behind the pin of the back plate. Rotate the tensioner clockwise as far as possible, then tighten the adjustment bolt snugly with Tool T71P-6603-A. Align the timing marks as shown. Then position the drive belt on the sprockets. Loosen the tensioner adjustment bolt. Rotate the crankshaft two complete turns to remove the slack from the belt and to allow the tensioner to move tighter against the belt. Tighten the tensioner adjustment and pivot bolts to 32-36 ft-lbs. Recheck the timing marks.

Position the camshaft drive belt cover. Install the attaching bolts and grommets. Torque the bolts to 7-9 ft-lbs.

ASSEMBLING THE ENGINE

Position the water outlet elbow and new gasket, then install and tighten the attaching screws. Connect the water outlet hose to the elbow.

Position a new intake manifold gasket on the studs. Position the manifold, carburetor, and decel valve assembly on the studs, and then install the attaching nuts. Torque the nuts to 12-15 ft-lbs. in the sequence shown.

Apply a film of graphite grease to the mating surfaces, then position the exhaust manifold. Install and torque the attaching nuts to 12-15 ft-lbs. Using a new inlet pipe gasket, connect the inlet pipe and install the attaching nuts.

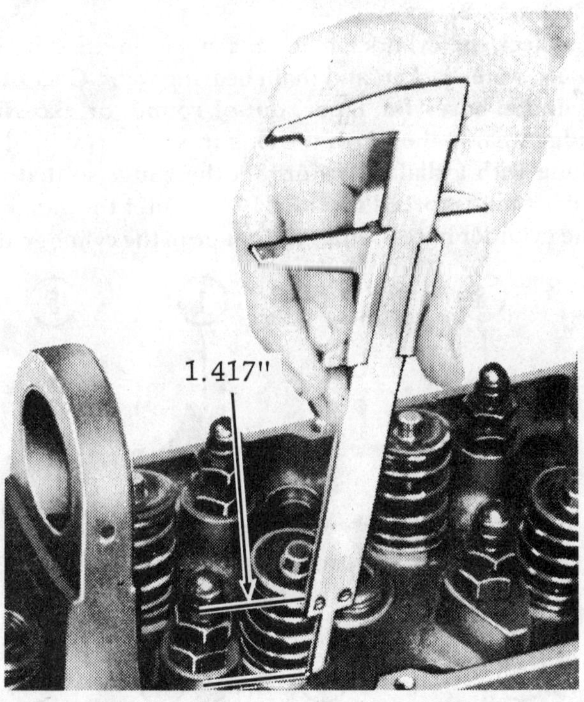

Checking the valve spring height, which should be 1.417" for the 2,000cc engine and 1-35/64 to 1-37/64" for the 2,300cc engine.

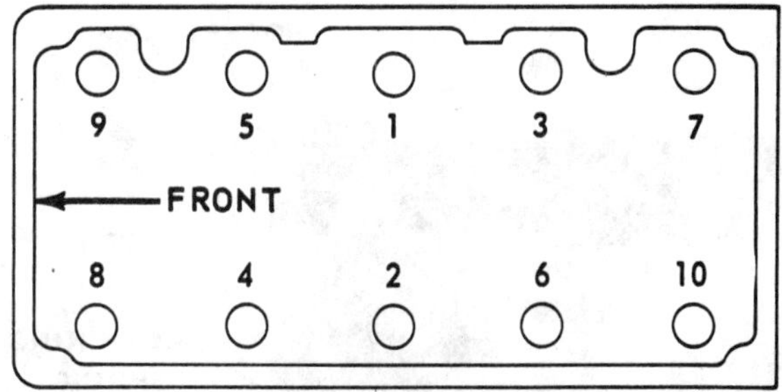

Cylinder bolt tightening sequence for the 2,000cc engine.

ADJUSTING THE VALVE LASH—2,000CC ENGINE

Adjust the valve clearance cold to 0.008" for the intake and 0.010" for the exhaust. To do this, rotate the crankshaft clockwise until the high point of No. 1 cam lobe is pointing down (valve spring depressed). Check the clearance between the cam lobe and the rocker arm on valves 6 and 7.*NOTE: The valve clearance is checked with the feeler gauge inserted from the valve side.*

In order to accurately check the clearance between the cam lobe and rocker arm, you must first remove the rocker arm retaining spring. To do this, use a flat-bladed screwdriver to reach under the spring at the rocker arm, and then snap the spring up and off. The spring should now hang loosely.

If the clearance is incorrect, loosen the locknut and use a 15mm open-end wrench to turn the adjustment screw in to increase the clearance or out to decrease it. When you've completed this adjustment, tighten the locknut securely with a 3/4 inch open-end wrench.

Turn the crankshaft so that the valve spring for valve No.2 is fully depressed. Valves 3 and 8 can be adjusted at this time. Turn the crankshaft so that the

No. 1 valve spring depressed for adjusting the valve lash for Nos. 6 and 7 valves.

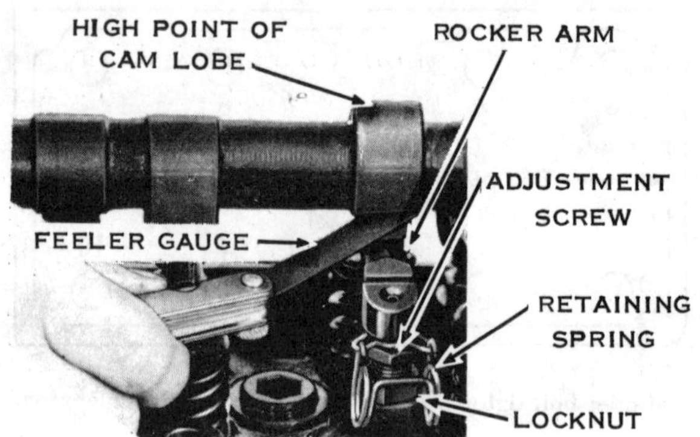

Checking the clearance between the cam lobe and rocker arm.

valve spring for valve No. 3 is fully depressed. Valves 2 and 5 can be adjusted at this time.

Snap the rocker arm retaining springs back in place. If a spring has fallen completely off, snap it into place the same way the other springs are set.

Clean all gasket material from the cylinder head and valve rocker arm cover. Straighten the valve cover flange, if necessary.

Install the valve cover and new gasket. Torque the attaching screws in the sequence shown. **CAUTION: Make sure that the two screws with rubber-coated washers are installed at the front and at the vertical attaching surface.**

Install the air cleaner and the crankcase ventilation hose. Replace the spark plugs. Fill the cooling system to the correct level with the specified coolant.

PISTONS, RINGS, AND RODS: SERVICE

REMOVING

Drain the cooling system and the crankcase. Remove the cylinder head and manifold assemblies as a unit.

Remove the oil pan and related parts. Remove the

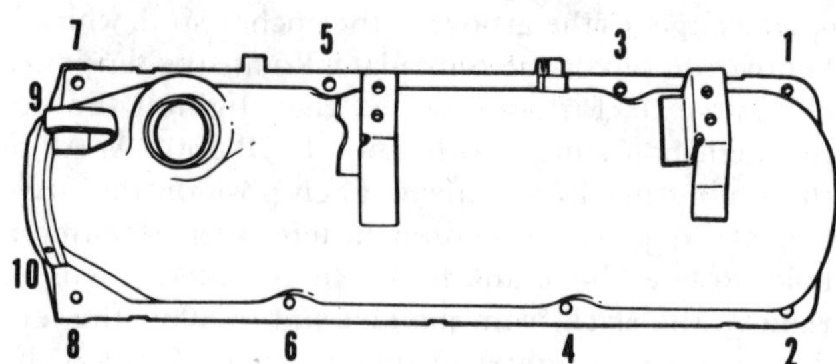

Rocker arm cover bolt tightening sequence for the 2,000cc engine.

oil pump inlet tube and the oil pump.

Turn the crankshaft until the piston to be removed is at the bottom of the stroke. Place a cloth on the head of the piston being worked on, then remove the ridge or deposits at the upper end of the cylinder bore with a ridge reamer. **CAUTION: Never cut into the ring travel area in excess of 1/32 inch when removing ridges.**

Make certain that all the connecting rod caps are marked so that they can be installed in their original positions. Remove the connecting rod cap. Push the connecting rod and piston assembly out the top of the cylinder with the handle end of a hammer. **CAUTION: Avoid damage to the crankpin or the cylinder wall when removing the piston and rod.**

CLEANING AND INSPECTING

Cylinder Block

Check the cylinder block for cracks in the cylinder walls, water jacket, and main bearing webs. Check the cylinder bores for taper, out-of-round, or excessive ridge wear at the top of the ring travel. This should be done with a dial indicator. Set the gauge so that the thrust pin is forced in about 1/4" to enter the gauge in the cylinder bore. Center the gauge in the cylinder and

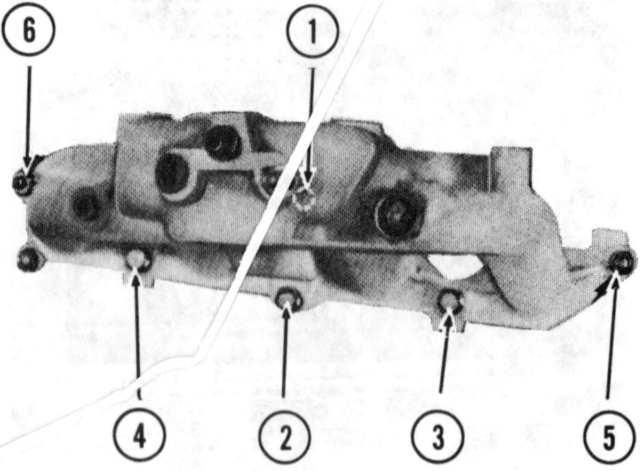

Intake bolt tightening sequence for both engines.

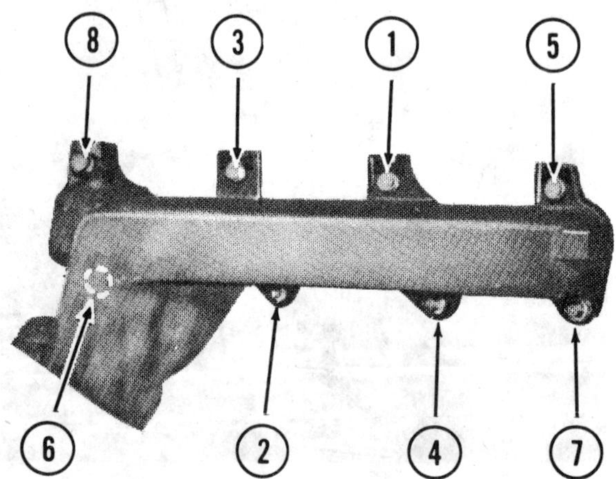

Exhaust bolt tightening sequence for both engines.

turn the dial to "0". Carefully work the gauge up and down the cylinder to determine the amount of taper. Turn it to different points around the cylinder wall to determine the out-of-round condition. If the cylinders have more than 0.002" out-of-round, boring will be necessary. If the cylinder bores are not worn excessively, use a 220-grit stone to remove the wall glaze so that the new rings will seat quickly. **CAUTION: Use a solution of soap and hot water to remove all traces of abrasives to prevent excessive engine wear.**

Pistons and Pins

Wash the connecting rods in cleaning solvent and dry with compressed air. Check for twisted or bent rods and inspect for nicks or cracks. Replace any connecting rods that are damaged.

Clean varnish from the piston skirts and pins with a cleaning solvent. **CAUTION: Do not wire brush any part of the piston.** Clean the ring grooves with a groove cleaner and make sure the oil ring holes and slots are clean. Inspect the pistons for cracked ring land, skirts, or pin bosses; wavy or worn ring lands; scuffed or damaged skirts; and eroded areas at the top of the pistons. Replace pistons that are damaged or show signs of excessive wear. Inspect the grooves for nicks or burrs that might cause the rings to hang up. Measure the piston skirt (across the center line of the piston pin) and check the clearance, which should not exceed 0.0025".

Inspect the piston bores and piston pins for wear. Piston pin bores and piston pins must be free of varnish or scuffing when being measured. The piston pin should be measured with a micrometer, and the piston pin bore should be measured with a dial bore gauge or an inside micrometer. If the clearance is in excess of 0.001", the piston and/or piston pin should be replaced.

Piston Rings

Check the end gap of the two compression rings by inserting them into the proper cylinder bore and pushing them down with a piston held upside down. This squares the ring with the walls. Measure the end gaps, which should be between 0.015-0.023" for both compression rings. Check the side clearance of each piston ring in its groove on the piston. The compression ring side clearance is specified as 0.019-0.038". The oil ring side clearance is 0.000-0.005". All compression rings are marked on the upper side of the ring. When installing compression rings, make sure the marked side is toward the top of the piston.

Install the oil ring spacer in the groove with the gap in line with the piston pin hole. Hold the spacer ends butted, and then install the lower oil ring steel rail, with the gap located one inch to the left of the spacer gap. Install the upper oil ring steel rail, with the gap one inch to the right of the spacer gap. Install the second compression ring expander, and then the ring. Install the top compression ring. Adjust the location of the gaps of the two top rings so that each is 1/3 of the way around the piston and no gaps are aligned.

INSTALLING THE PISTON AND ROD ASSEMBLY

Oil the piston rings and cylinder walls with light engine oil. **CAUTION: Be sure to install the pistons in the same cylinders from which they were removed, or to which they were fitted. The connecting rod and bearing caps are numbered on the left side from 1 to 4, beginning at the front of the engine. The numbers on the connecting rod and bearing cap must be on the same side when installed in the cylinder bore.**

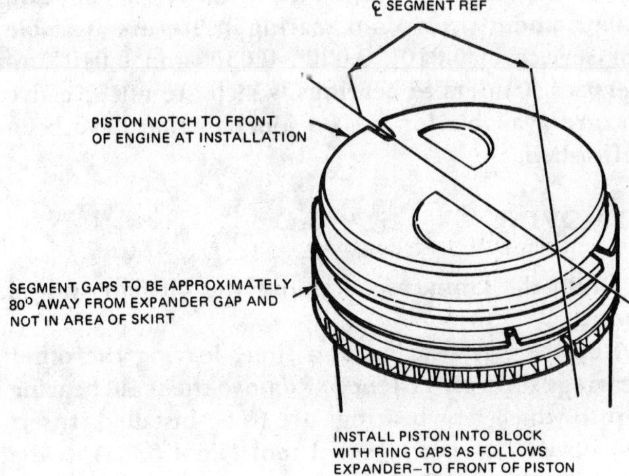

Ring and piston installation for the 2,300cc engine.

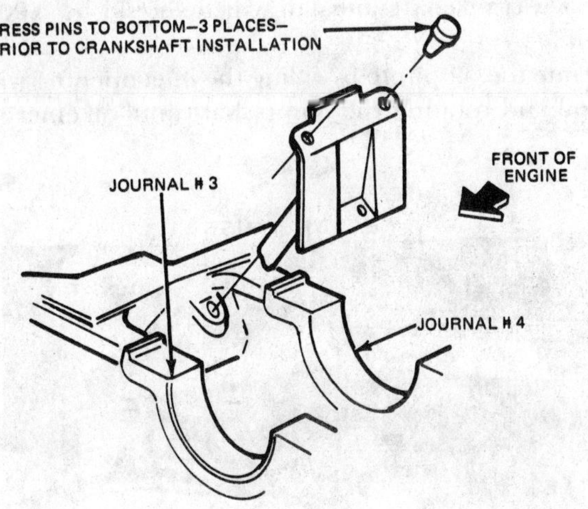

Details of the 2,300cc engine PCV baffle installation between Nos. 3 and 4 crankcase webs.

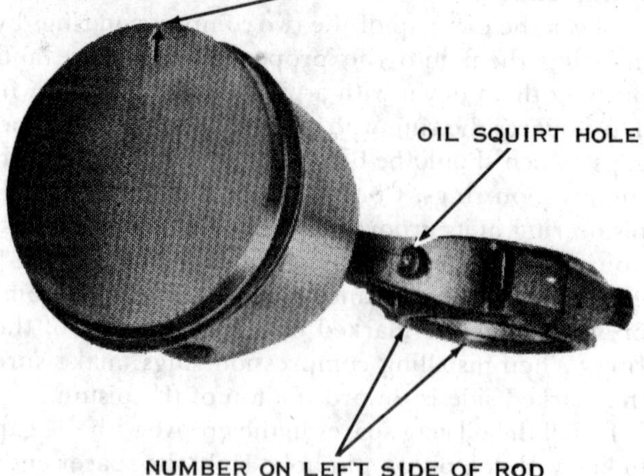

Piston and rod positions for the 2,000cc engine.

Piston and rod positions for the 2,300cc engine.

Make sure the ring gaps are properly spaced around the circumference of the piston. Install a piston ring compressor and push the piston in with a hammer handle until it is slightly below the top of the cylinder. **CAUTION: Be sure to guide the connecting rods to avoid damaging the crankshaft journals. CAUTION: Install the piston with the arrow in the piston head toward the front of the engine.**

Check the clearance of each bearing, following the procedures in the general service procedures in the first part of this chapter.

After the bearings have been fitted, apply a light coat of engine oil to the journals and bearings. Turn the crankshaft throw to the bottom of the stroke, then push the piston all the way down until the connecting rod bearing seats on the crankshaft journal. Install the connecting rod cap. Torque the nuts to 29-34 ft-lbs.

After the piston and connecting rod assemblies have been installed, check the connecting rod side clearance on each crankshaft journal, which should be 0.004-0.010″.

Prime the oil pump by filling the inlet opening with the oil and rotating the pump shaft until oil emerges from the outlet opening. Install the oil pump and the oil pump inlet tube. Install the oil pan and related parts.

Install the cylinder head.

Fill the crankcase and the cooling system. Install the air cleaner.

Start the engine and check for oil pressure. Operate the engine at fast idle and check for oil and coolant leaks.

Check and adjust the ignition timing, engine idle speed, and the fuel mixture.

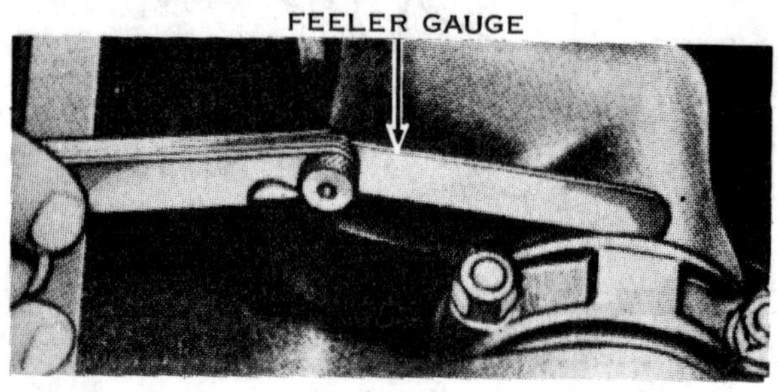

Measuring the connecting rod side clearance.

MAIN BEARINGS

The main and connecting rod bearing inserts are selectively fitted. **CAUTION: Do not file or lap bearing caps or use shims to obtain the proper bearing clearance.**

Selective fit connecting bearings are available for service in standard sizes, 0.002″, 0.010″, 0.030″ and 0.040″ under sizes. Main bearing inserts are available for service in 0.010″, 0.020″, 0.030″ and 0.040″ undersizes. Undersize bearings, which are not selective fit, are available for use on journals that have been refinished.

REMOVING

Drain the crankcase. Remove the oil pan and oil pump.

Replace one bearing at a time, leaving the other bearings securely fastened. Remove the main bearing cap to which new bearings are to be installed. Insert the upper bearing removal tool (Tool 6331) in the journal oil hole. Rotate the crankshaft slowly in the direction of engine rotation to force the bearing insert out of the block.

INSTALLING

Clean each crankshaft journal before installing the main bearing insert. Inspect the journals for nicks, burrs, or bearing pickup that would cause premature bearing wear. Make sure that the four thrust washers are in place on the center main bearing.

To install the upper main bearing, lubricate the bearing with heavy engine oil. Then place the plain end of the bearing over the shaft on the locking tang side of the block and partially install the bearing so the Tool 6331 can be inserted in the journal oil hole. With the tool installed, rotate the crankshaft slowly in the opposite direction of engine rotation until the bearing tang is seated. Remove the bearing tool.

Install the dry insert into the main bearing cap, and then measure the oil clearance with Plastigage, as discussed in the General Service Procedures at the first part of this chapter. Remove the Plastigage, coat the bearing insert and journal with heavy engine oil, and then install the bearing cap. Tighten the cap bolt to 65-75 ft-lbs. Install the remaining bearings in the same manner.

Clean all oil pan gasket surfaces thoroughly. Straighten the oil pan flange if deformed. Clean the oil pump inlet tube screen. Prime the pump by filling the inlet opening with oil while rotating the shaft until oil emerges from the outlet opening. Install the pump and torque the attaching bolts with tool T71P-6603-A.

Coat the cylinder block oil pan surfaces and oil pan gasket surface with oil resistant sealer. Position the gaskets on the block. Install the end seal in the rear main bearing cap and the other in the cylinder block front cover. Position the oil pan and install the attaching bolts. Torque the bolts to 4-6 ft-lbs.

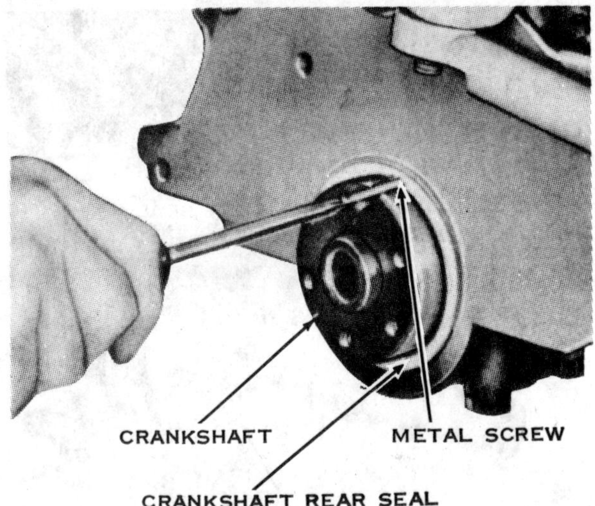

Removing the crankshaft rear oil seal on the 2,000cc engine.

Install the steering linkage. Fill the crankcase to the correct level with the specified oil. Start the engine and check for leaks.

CRANKSHAFT REAR OIL SEAL, REPLACE

REMOVING

Remove the transmission, clutch, and flywheel; or the automatic transmission, converter, and flywheel. Remove the crankshaft rear seal which is held in place by a sheet metal screw.

INSTALLING

Install a new crankshaft rear seal with tool T71P-6701-A.

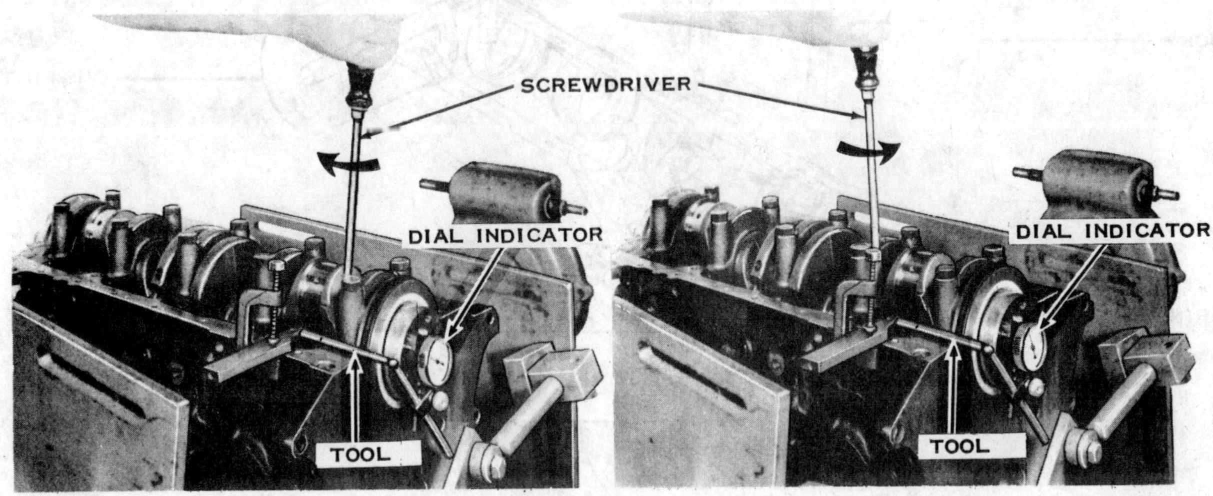

Checking the crankshaft and play. First pry the shaft forward (left), zero the dial indicator, and then pry the shaft to the rear. The total crankshaft end play will register on the dial indicator, which should be 0.003-0.011" for the 2,000cc engine and 0.004-0.008" for the 2,300cc engine.

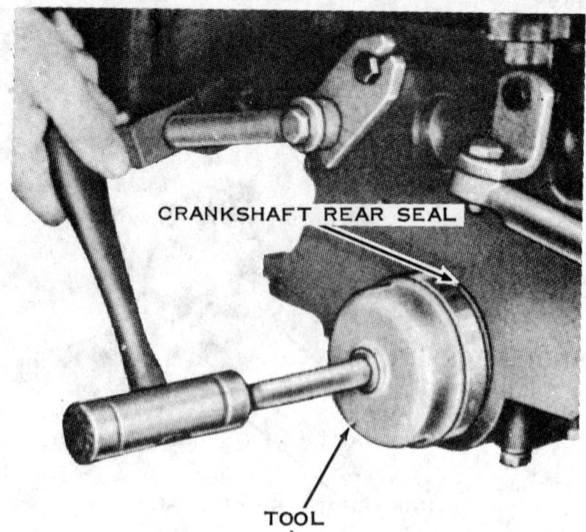

Installing the oil seal on the 2,000cc engine.

Install the flywheel, clutch, and transmission; or the flywheel, converter, and automatic transmission.

Start the engine and check for oil leaks.

2000CC ENGINE SERVICE SPECIFICATIONS

Block

The nominal bore and stroke are 3.575" x 3.029". The actual bore measurement can be between 3.5748-3.5763", with a wear limit of 0.005". The standard piston size is 3.5746-3.5760", measured at the piston pin bore centerline at 90° to the pin holes.

Crankshaft

The main bearing journals should measure 2.2432-2.2440", and the crankpins should be 2.0464-2.0472", both with a wear limit of 0.002". The crankshaft end play should be 0.003-0.011

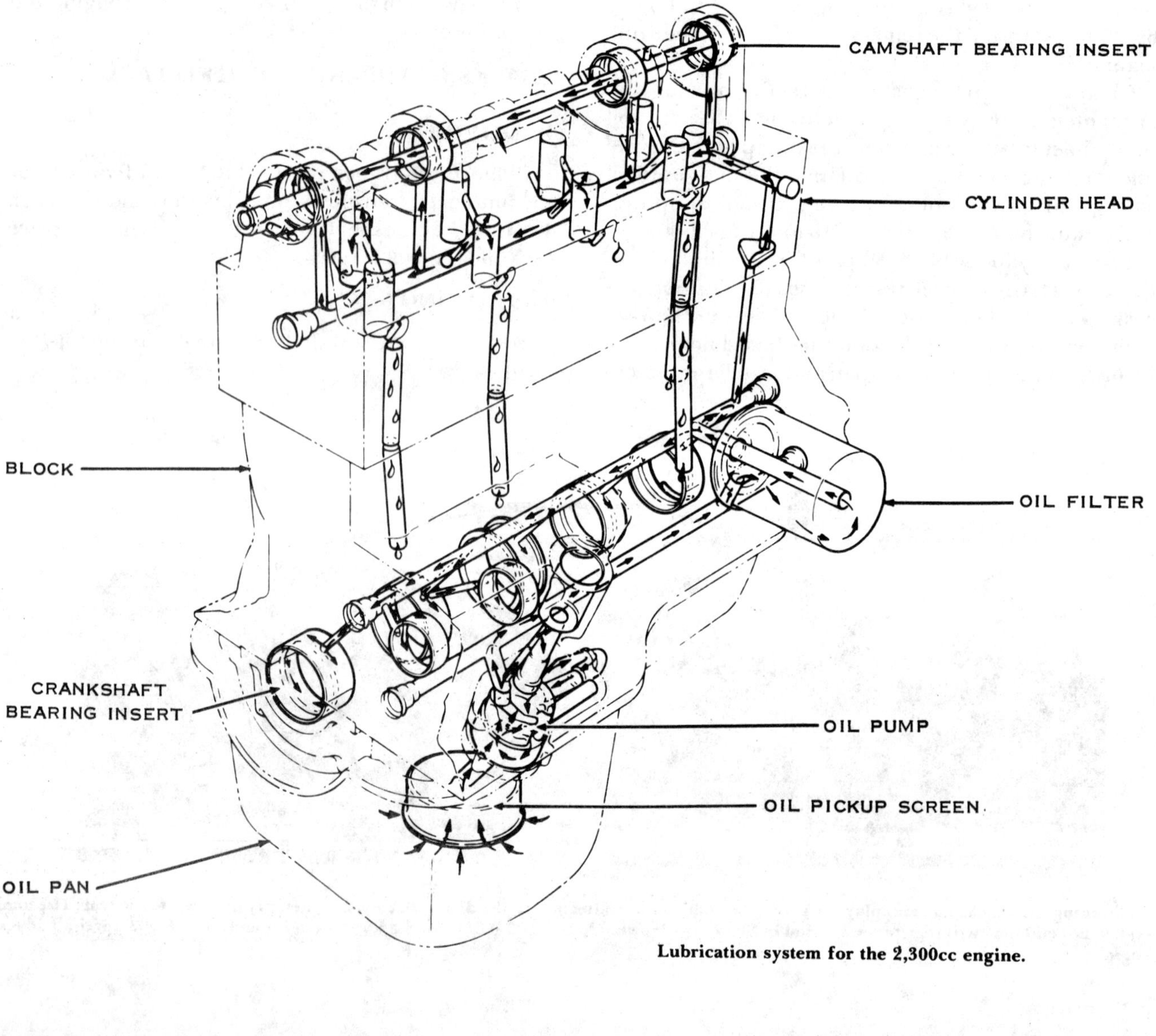

Lubrication system for the 2,300cc engine.

VALVES

The intake valve stem should measure 0.3159-0.3167″ and 0.3149-0.3156″ for the exhaust. The intake valve stem-to-guide clearance should measure 0.0008-0.0025″, and 0.0018-0.0035″ for the exhaust. The valve face angle should be 44° and the seat angle 45°. Both valve springs should measure 170-183 lbs. at a compressed height of 1.02″.

2300CC ENGINE SERVICE PROCEDURES

Service procedures for the 2300cc engine are similar to those for the 2000cc engine just described. However, there are some procedural differences due to simplification of some service operations and the use of hydraulic lash adjusters in place of the adjustable screws used on the smaller engine. Where the service procedures differ from the 2000cc engine, they will be provided in this section. Where they are modified, these differences will be covered in this part by special service notes. Where the procedures are the same, no mention will be made; use the service procedures in the 2000cc engine section.

OIL PAN SERVICE NOTES

The oil pan retaining screws and washers are different in size and torque specifications. Four large screws, two at each end of the pan, are used to apply

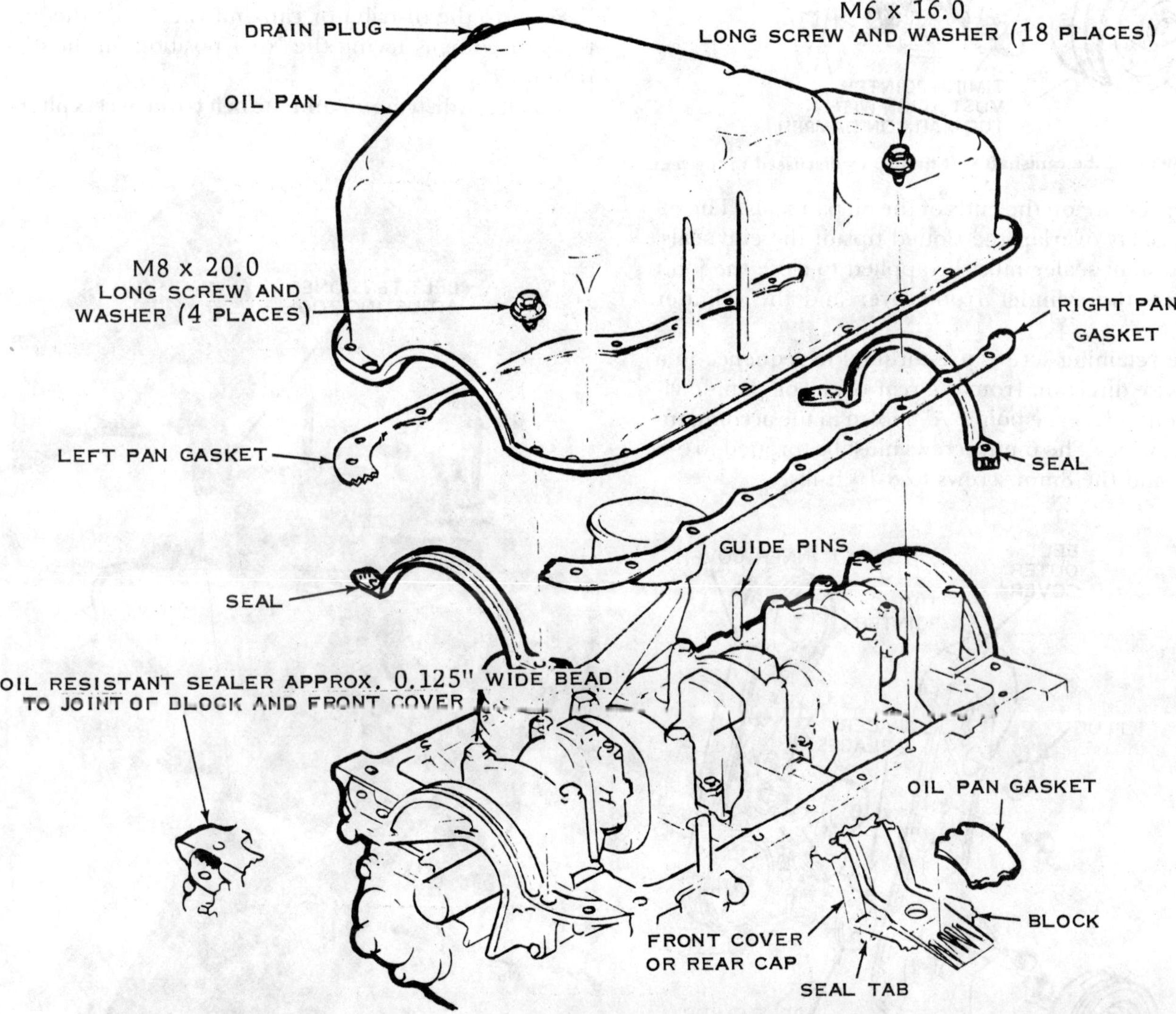

To install the oil pan on the 2,300cc engine, first apply gasket adhesive evenly to the flanges and to the side gaskets. Allow the adhesive to dry past the wet stage, and then install the gaskets to the oil pan. Apply sealer to the joint of the block and front cover. Install the seals and press them firmly to the block. CAUTION: Be sure to install the rear seal before the rear main bearing cap sealer has cured. Position the two guide pins, and then install the oil pan. Secure the pan with the four 8mm bolts, one at each corner. Remove the guide pins and install and torque the eighteen 6mm bolts, working clockwise around the pan.

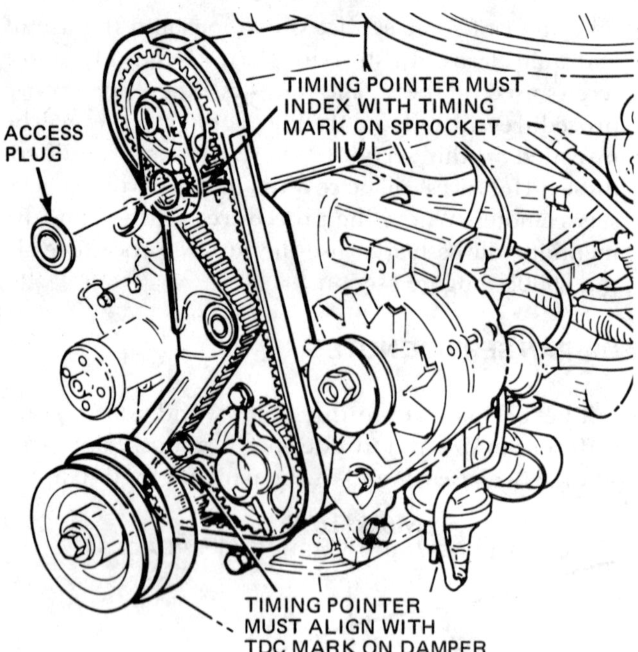

Checking the camshaft belt timing, as discussed in the text.

extra pressure on the ends of the oil pan seals. The oil pan gaskets overlap the slotted tips of the end seals. Oil-resistant sealer must be applied to close the joint between the cylinder front cover and the cylinder block.

The retaining screws are torqued in sequence in a clockwise direction from the rear of the oil pan, starting from reference point "A" shown in the accompanying drawing. The 6mm screws must be torqued to 6-8 ft-lbs. and the 8mm screws to 8-10 ft-lbs.

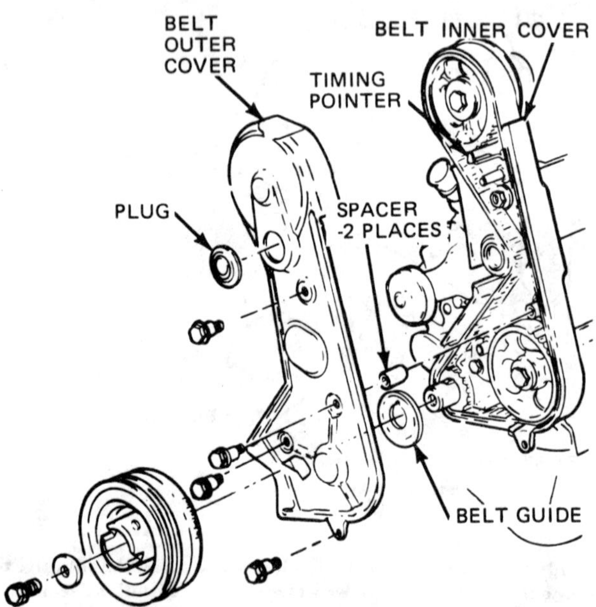

Timing belt covers, inner and outer.

CHECKING THE CAMSHAFT TIMING

An access plug is provided in the cam drive belt cover so that camshaft timing can be checked without removal of the cover or any other parts. To check the timing, remove the access plug from the cam drive belt cover.

Set the crankshaft to TDC by aligning the timing pointer on the belt cover with the 0-mark on the crankshaft damper. **CAUTION: Always turn the engine in the direction of normal rotation. Backward rotation may cause the timing belt to jump time, due to the arrangement of the belt tensioner.**

Look through the access hole in the belt cover to be sure that the timing mark on the cam drive sprocket is lined up with the pointer on the inner belt cover.

Remove the distributor cap and check that the distributor rotor is facing the No.1 position on the distributor cap.

Install the distributor and the belt cover access plug.

Releasing belt tension, as discussed in the text.

ADJUSTING THE CAMSHAFT TIMING

Remove the timing belt outer cover.

If the belt timing is incorrect, loosen the belt tensioner adjustment screw, position the tension adjusting tool shown on the tension spring rollpin, and release the belt tensioner. Tighten the adjustment screw to hold the tensioner in the released position.

Remove the crankshaft damper and belt guide. Remove the drive belt and inspect it for wear or damage. If the belt is damaged, replace it.

Position the crankshaft sprocket, camshaft sprocket, and auxiliary shaft sprocket as shown, with the crankshaft and camshaft at TDC, No 1 cylinder firing position.

Install the timing belt over the crankshaft sprocket and then counterclockwise over the auxiliary and camshaft sprockets. Align the belt fore and aft on the sprockets. Loosen the tension adjustment bolt to allow the tensioner to move against the belt.

To be sure that the belt does not jump time, remove the spark plugs. Rotate the crankshaft two complete turns in normal rotation to remove the slack from the belt. Torque the tensioner adjustment bolt to 14-21 ft-lbs. and the pivot bolt to 28-40 ft-lbs. Re-check the alignment of the timing marks.

Install the crankshaft damper and belt guide. Install the timing belt outer cover and the spark plugs.

REPLACING THE CAMSHAFT DRIVE BELT

The cogged, rubber belt is wider and heavier than that used on the 2000cc engine. The belt is enclosed within an inner and outer cover, separated by rubber gaskets and spacers. These covers prevent the accumulation of dirt and ice around the drive belt area that can cause the cogged belt to jump out of the grooves in the drive sprockets. When this occurs, the timing is upset and poor engine performance will result, such as rough engine idle.

REMOVING

Remove the belt outer cover and spacers. Loosen the tensioner adjustment bolt and the spring pivot bolt.

Position the tensioner adjusting tool as shown, and then move the tensioner toward the left of the engine to release the belt tension by pulling to the right on the tool. With the tensioner held in this position against spring pressure, tighten the tensioner adjustment bolt to hold it in this position.

Slide the timing belt off the drive sprockets.

INSTALLING

Position the crankshaft drive sprocket so that the sprocket key faces straight up. Rotate the camshaft

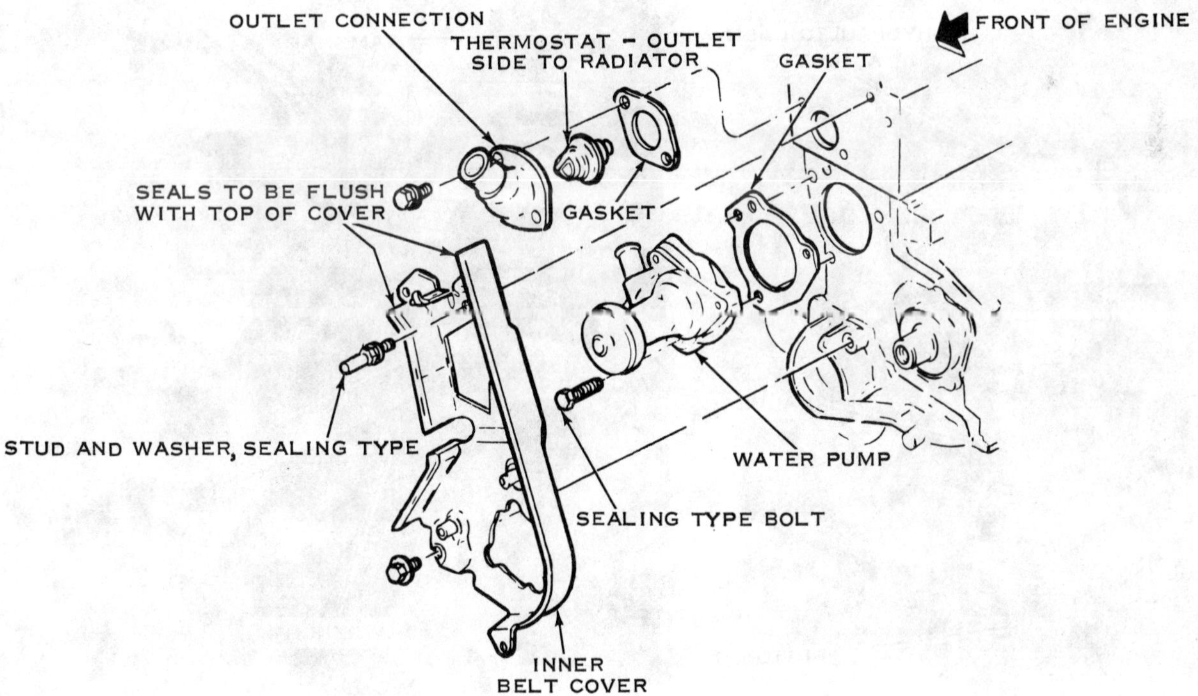

Installing the water pump, thermostat, and inner timing belt cover on the 2,300cc engine.

drive sprocket to align the timing mark on the sprocket with the timing pointer on the belt inner cover. Remove the distributor cap and set the distributor rotor in the No. 1 position.

Carefully position and seat the belt on the crankshaft sprocket, then counterclockwise over the auxiliary sprocket and camshaft sprocket. **CAUTION: The belt must not overhang the front edge of the crankshaft drive sprocket. Be sure the crankshaft belt guide is installed with the cupped (dished) side facing away from the cylinder block. Be sure the camshaft belt guide is installed with the cupped (dished) side facing the cylinder block.**

Place the tensioner adjusting tool in position and allow the tensioner to move slowly toward the smooth side of the belt as the adjustment bolt is gradually loosened. Rotate the crankshaft two complete revolutions to remove the slack from the belt and to allow the tensioner to move tighter against the belt. Torque the tensioner bolt to 14-21 ft-lbs. and the spring pivot bolt to 28-40 ft-lbs.

Before installing the belt outer cover, check that the timing marks are still in proper alignment. After the belt cover is installed, start the engine and check the ignition timing. Adjust if necessary.

VALVE TRAIN SERVICE NOTES

The combination of the overhead camshaft and the cross-flow cylinder head is basically the same as the 2000cc engine. The main difference is that hydraulic lash adjusters are used instead of the adjustable screws. The cylinder head contains rifle-drilled oil galleries to feed the hydraulic lash adjusters and to lubricate the cam lobes, bearings, and rocker arms. The rocker arm springs shown will be installed on early production engines only. It will not be incorporated in later engines. Make note of this running change so that you'll be aware that the spring was not omitted in error.

CAMSHAFT SERVICE NOTES

The camshaft service procedures are basically the same as for the 2000cc engine with these exceptions: (1) The camshaft is removed and installed from the

Valve train lubrication system and the hydraulic lash adjuster.

Using a puller to remove the front camshaft seal, as discussed in the text.

front of the cylinder head. This makes in-chassis replacement much easier because it does not require removal of the cylinder head assembly. (2) Camshaft seal removal from the front pedestal of the cylinder head is accomplished by using the seal remover (T74P-6700-B). (3) Camshaft seal installation is performed with the replacer tool (T74P-6150-A). (4) Camshaft sprocket removal requires the use of a special remover (T74P-6256-A). Simply remove the sprocket bolt, position the tool to hold the sprocket, and then screw in the center arbor to remove the sprocket. (5) Camshaft sprocket installation is performed using the same tool with the center arbor removed. Position the sprocket on the camshaft with the timing mark facing outward, and then install the washer and bolt. Next, position the tool on the sprocket to hold the sprocket while the bolt is screwed in to drive the sprocket on the camshaft. **CAUTION: Use teflon tape on the threads of a "used" sprocket retaining bolt or use a "new" sealing bolt (metric). This is a very important step in order to prevent leaks at the bolt because it screws into the oil gallery in the camshaft.**

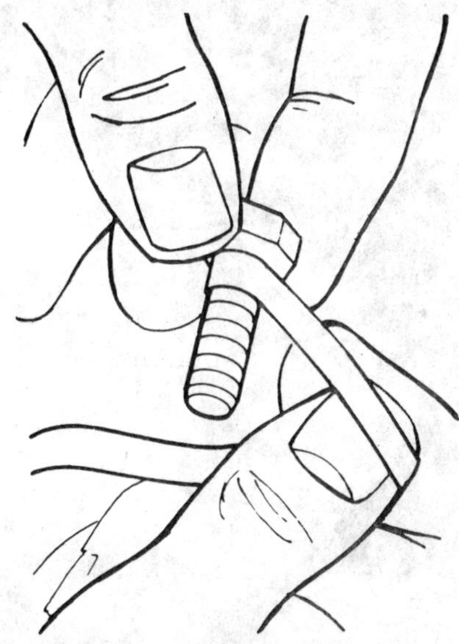

It is essential to wrap teflon tape around the threads of a used sprocket retaining bolt to prevent oil leaks because it screws into the camshaft oil gallery.

REPLACING A ROCKER ARM

Servicing the rocker arm is entirely different from

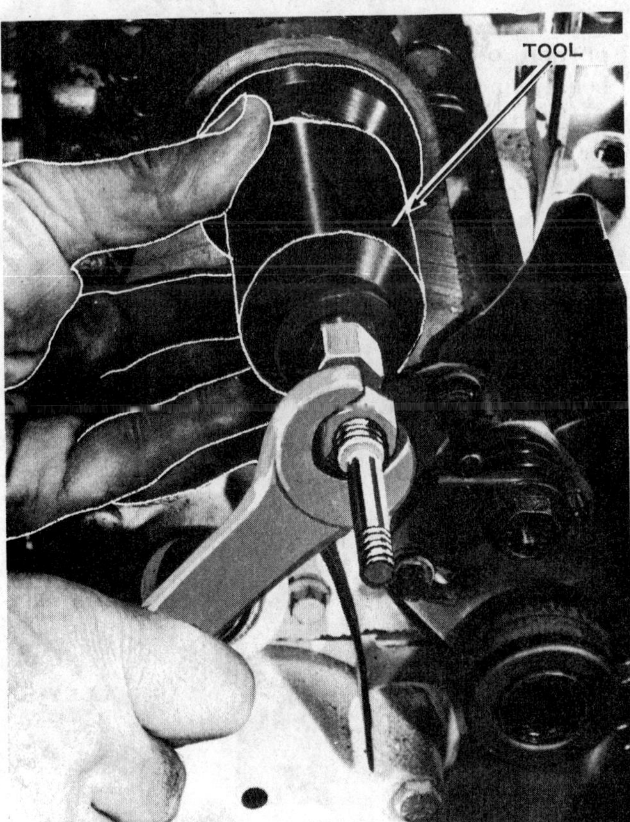

Installing a new seal.

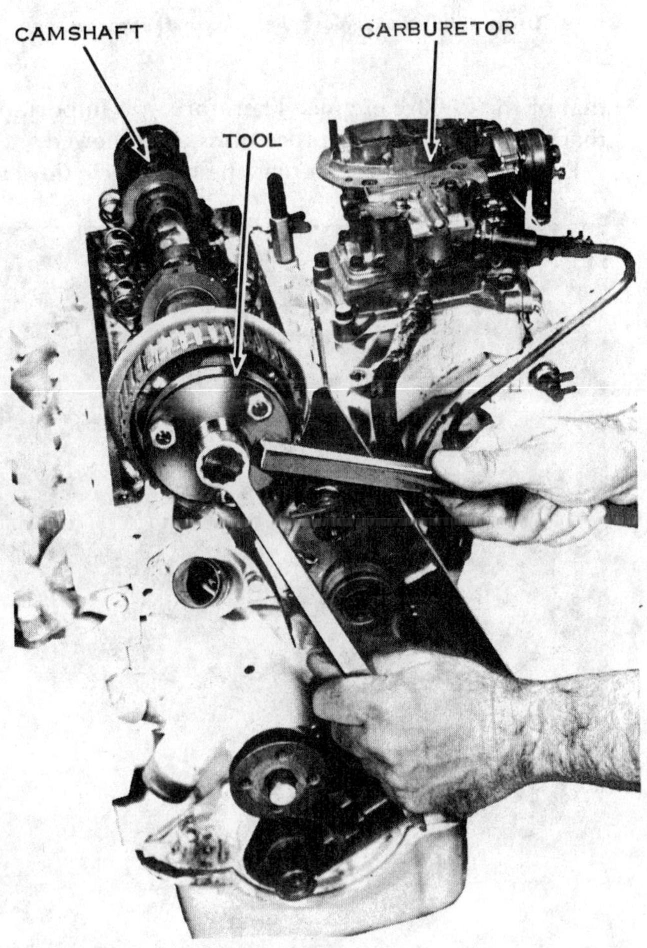

Removing the camshaft drive sprocket.

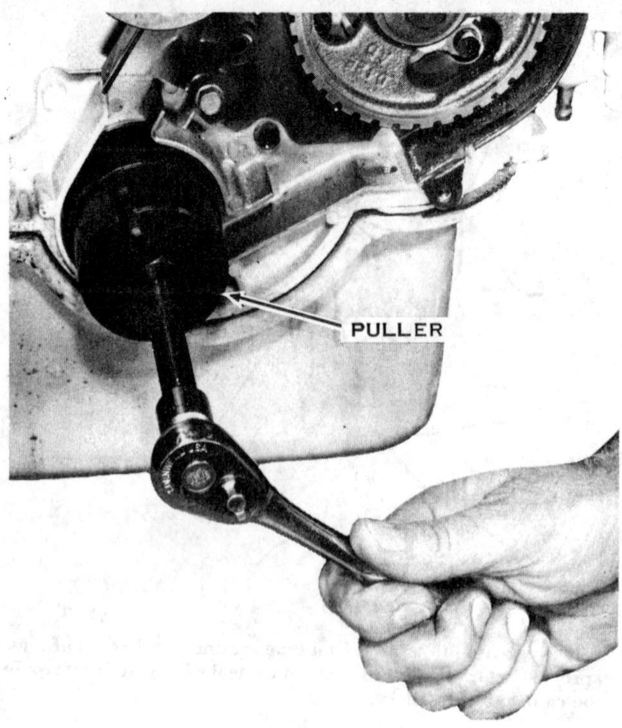

Using a puller to remove the crankshaft sprocket.

Installing the camshaft sprocket.

that of the 2000cc engine. Therefore, it is important that the recommended procedures are followed.

Rotate the camshaft so that the base circle (lowest portion) of the camshaft lobe faces the rocker arm being removed. Position the valve spring compressor under the camshaft and over the valve spring as shown. Use the camshaft as a fulcrum to compress the valve spring.

Using a puller to remove the cylinder front cover oil seal.

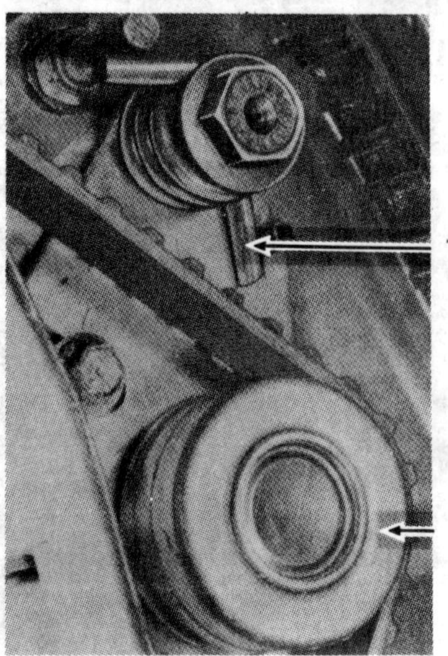

Details of the belt tensioner used on the 2,300cc engine.

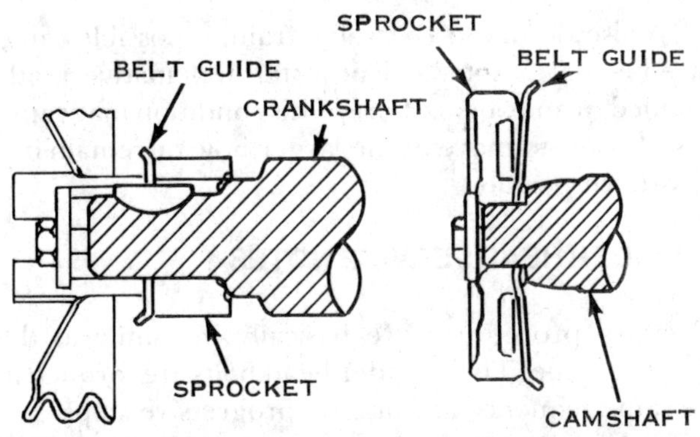

Details of the crankshaft and camshaft belt guide installation.

Remove the rocker arm spring on units so equipped. Compress the valve spring just enough to slide the rocker arm off the valve tip and toward the hydraulic lash adjuster to clear the adjuster. **CAUTION: Use compressed air at the applicable cylinder (spark plug removed) when performing this operation in-chassis. Otherwise, the valve may drop into the combustion chamber and removal of the cylinder head will be necessary.**

To install the rocker arm, be sure the base circle of the camshaft faces the cylinder head. Then partially compress the valve spring to position the rocker arm over the valve tip and hydraulic lash adjuster (from the adjuster side). Install the rocker arm spring if so equipped. **CAUTION: For any repair that requires the removal of a rocker arm, each affected lash adjuster must be fully collapsed after the rocker arm is installed and then released. This step must be taken before any rotation of the camshaft is attempted. Otherwise, valve train damage will occur.**

CHECKING THE VALVE CLEARANCE

Measuring the gap (valve clearance) between the camshaft base circle and the rocker arm is only an audit check after a cylinder head overhaul to be sure the valve train meets specifications. *NOTE: This is not a scheduled maintenance check.*

The camshaft must be rotated so that the base circle of the lobe rests on the rocker arm. Position the valve spring compressor under the camshaft and over the rocker arm end on the hydraulic lash adjuster of the valve being checked. Compress the lash adjuster to the fully collapsed position and insert a feeler gauge (from the valve side) between the cam lobe and rocker arm.

A 0.035-0.055 inch gap is within the specified limits. Replace the hydraulic adjuster if it does not meet the limits.

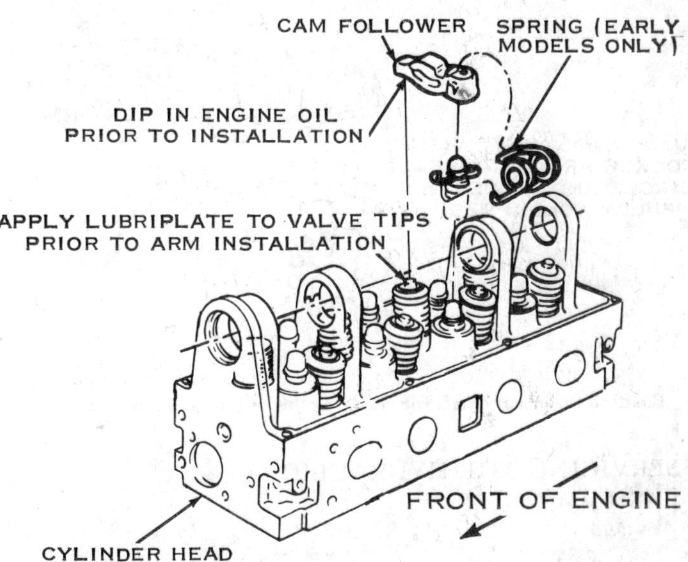

Details of the rocker arm and spring (used only on early models) for the 2,300cc engine.

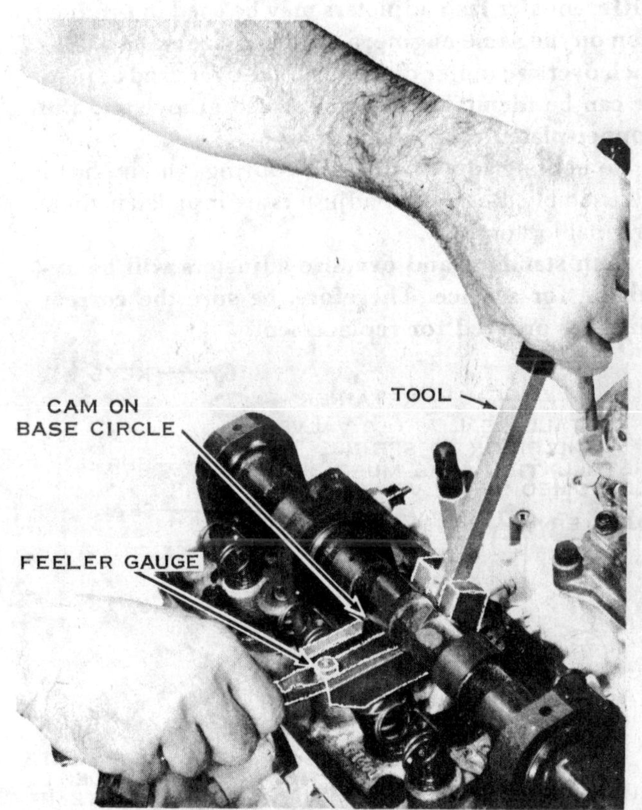

To measure the hydraulic lash adjuster clearance, compress the adjuster until it is fully collapsed, and then insert a feeler gauge between the cam lobe and rocker arm from the valve side. This is not a maintenance check, but only should be performed after refacing or grinding valves, which always changes the valve operating mechanism dimensions.

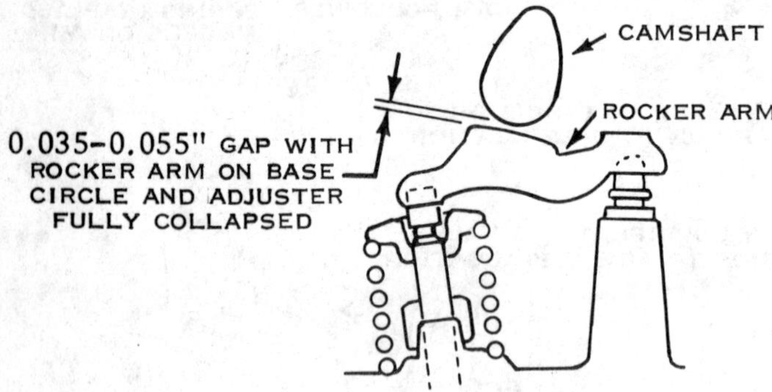

Position of the camshaft for checking the collapsed valve lash.

SERVICING THE HYDRAULIC LASH ADJUSTER

The hydraulic lash adjusters are cleaned and tested in the same manner as hydraulic valve lifters on conventional engines. However, they are more accessible on the 2300cc engine, which simplifies in-chassis repairs for this component. **CAUTION: Two different-size lash adjusters may be used in production on the same engine; a standard size and a 0.020-inch oversize (outer diameter). The oversized adjuster can be identified by a machined groove and the copper-plated retaining ring.**

Do not intermix the adjusters during cylinder head disassembly. Be sure the adjusters are installed in their original locations.

Both standard and oversize adjusters will be available for service. Therefore, be sure the correct sizes are ordered for replacement.

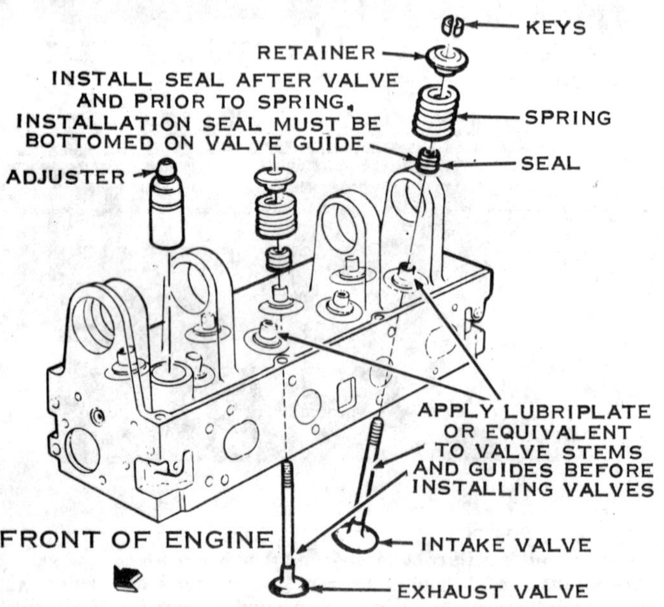

Valve assembly details for the 2,300cc engine.

If noise occurs in the valve train, a possible cause may be that a standard adjuster was inadvertently installed in an oversize bore. This condition may cause the adjuster to move in the larger hole or remain in a leak-down position.

CYLINDER HEAD SERVICE NOTES

Service procedures are basically the same as the 2000cc engine. The cylinder head bolts are torqued in the same sequence and in two progressive steps.

Other important features are: (1) The rifle-drilled oil galleries in the cylinder may require cleaning to maintain optimum lubrication to the lash adjusters, can lobes, and bearings. (2) The cylinder head gasket is imprinted with instructions to ensure proper installation. (3) When installing the cylinder head as an assembly, the camshaft must be positioned as shown to protect the valves protruding underneath the cylinder head. *NOTE: This camshaft position minimizes the amount the valves stick out from the cylinder head.*

ROCKER ARM COVER REPLACEMENT

The rocker arm cover replacement procedures and

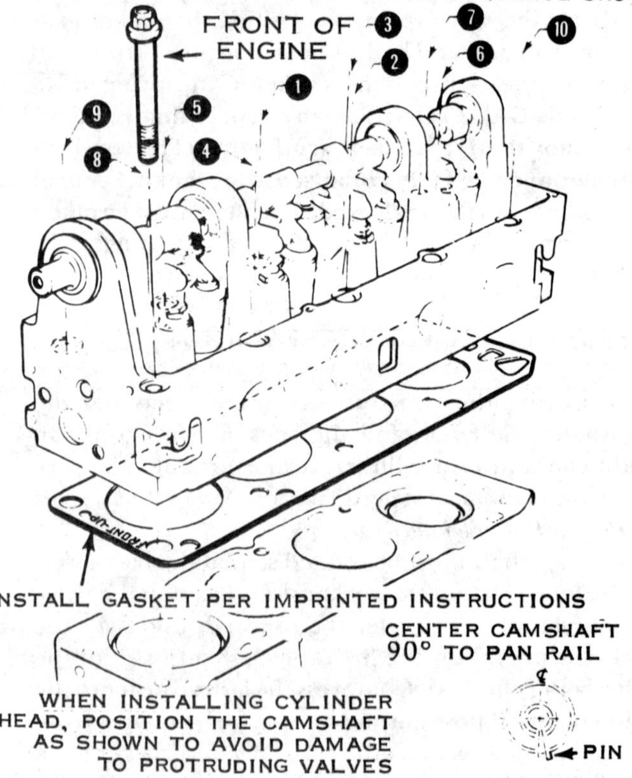

Cylinder head gasket installation and bolt tightening sequence for the 2,300cc engine.

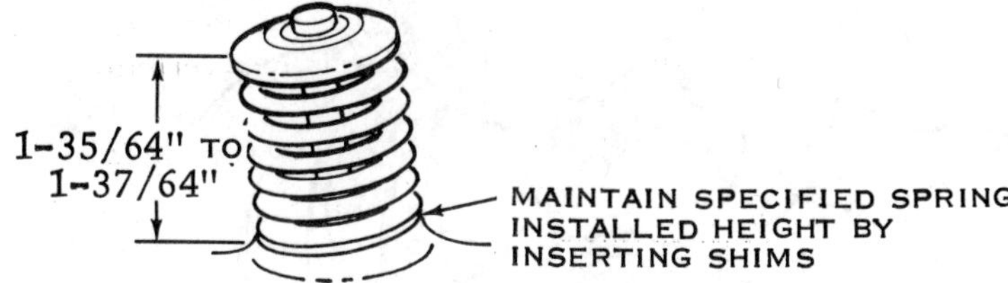

The valve spring height for the 2,300cc engine must be 1-35/64 to 1-37/64" and 1.417" for the 2,000cc engine. Insert shims as needed.

sealant recommendations are the same as for the 2000cc engine. However, the following procedure must be adhered to when installing the cover to assure proper sealing between the cylinder head and cover. (1) Install and torque the eight vertical screws first. (2) Then install and torque the two angled screws into the front pedestal.

INTAKE MANIFOLD SERVICE NOTES

The floor of the intake manifold is corrugated to assist in heat transfer. Coolant from the cylinder head enters through a port under the manifold to provide a heat stove to ensure proper fuel-and-air mixing temperatures. The coolant is then directed through a connection to the carburetor choke mechanism and out to the heater.

The intake manifold is made of die-cast aluminum and, therefore, it cannot be overemphasized that tor-

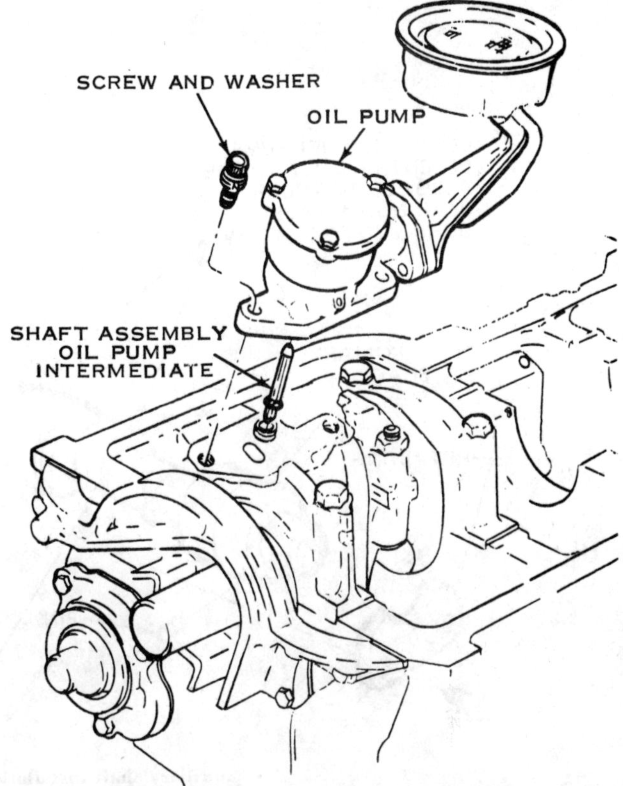

Oil pump installation for the 2,300cc engine.

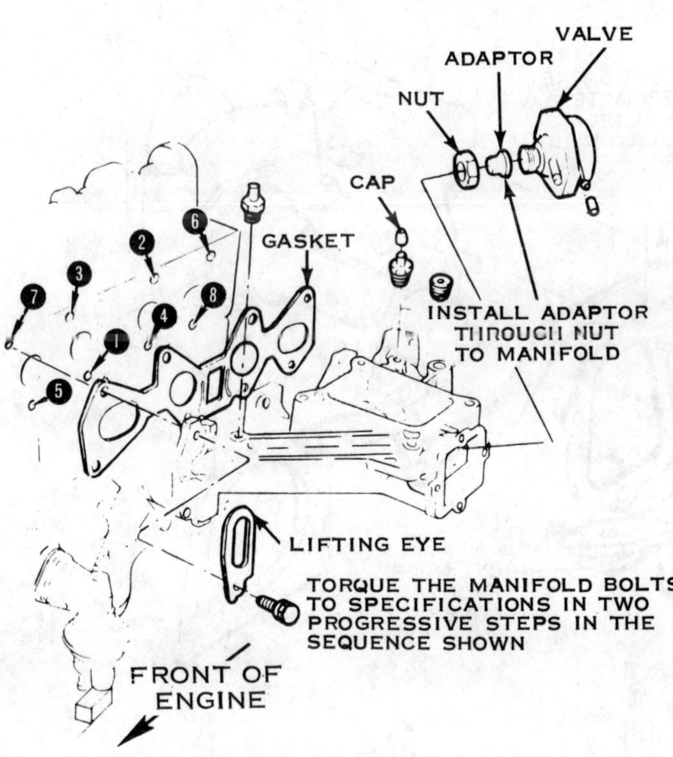

Intake manifold installation.

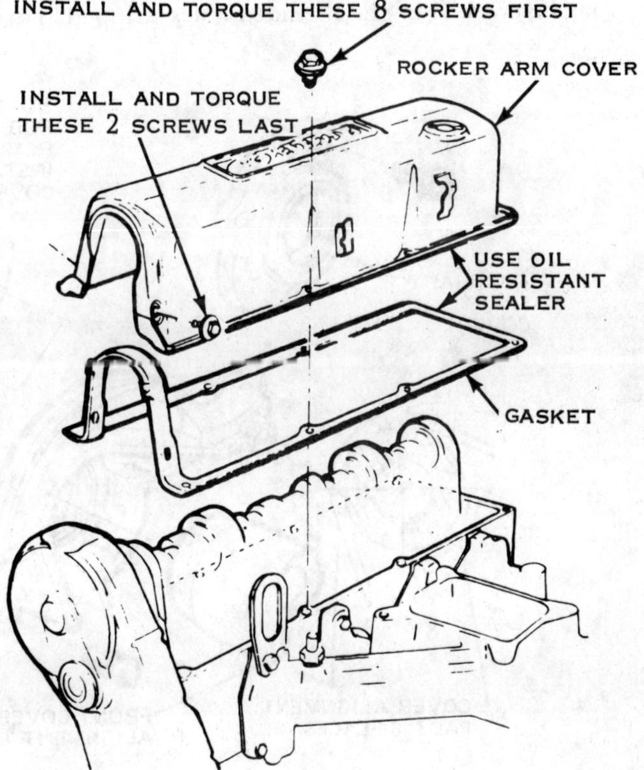

Rocker arm cover bolt tightening sequence for the 2,300cc engine.

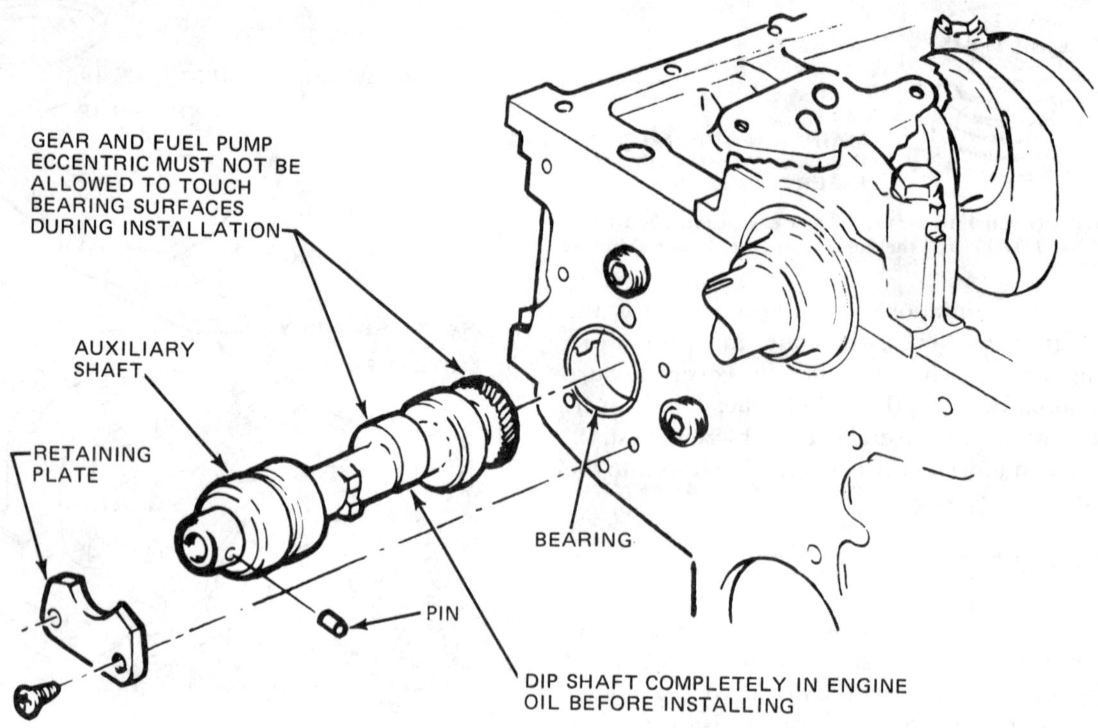

Auxiliary shaft installation for the 2,300cc engine.

que specifications must be adhered to for all attaching or retaining screws and bolts. Otherwise, the manifold may be cracked or the threaded holes stripped. Torque the manifold bolts in two steps and in the sequence shown first to 8 ft-lbs, and then a second time to 16-23 ft-lbs.

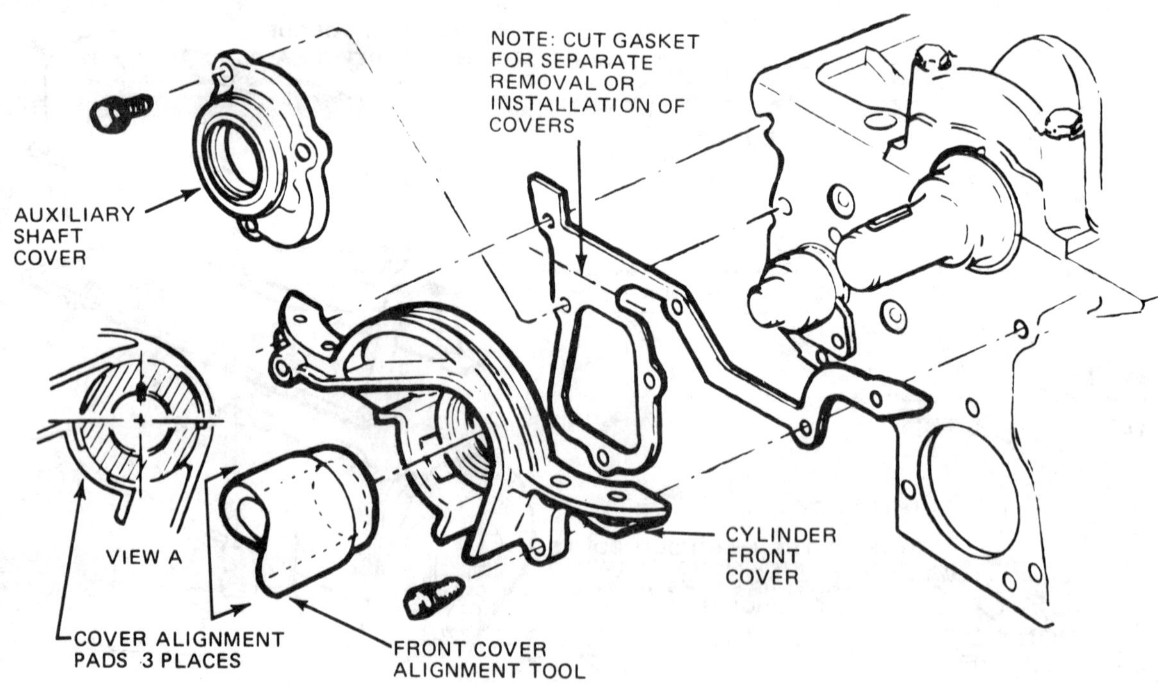

Auxiliary shaft cover and cylinder front cover installation.

SERVICING THE AUXILIARY SHAFT

Two replaceable bearings support the auxiliary shaft in the 2000cc engine, instead of a single bearing as in the 2000cc engine. Replacement procedures for the bearings are the same for both engines, using the same tools. **CAUTION: Care must be exercised when installing the shaft to be sure the distributor drive gear and fuel pump eccentric are not allowed to touch the bearing surfaces.**

AUXILIARY SHAFT COVER

A one-piece gasket is used to seat the auxiliary shaft cover and cylinder front cover to the cylinder block. The covers can be removed and installed separately by cutting the one-piece gasket as shown. Then remove the appropriate cover and its portion of the gasket. Cut a new gasket in the same manner and carefully fit it to the cylinder block and cover. This eliminates the need to remove the cover not affected by the repair being performed, resulting in a savings of labor and time.

A front cover alignment tool (T74P-6019-B) is available for proper installation of the cover. The aligner is positioned on the crankshaft and bears against the alignment pads in the cover. It is left in place while the cover attaching bolts are torqued to be sure that there will be sufficient operating clearance for the drive belt when assembly is complete.

2300CC ENGINE SERVICE SPECIFICATIONS

Block

The nominal bore and stroke are 3.78" x 3.216". The bore measurement should be 3.7795-3.7831". The piston size is 3.7777-3.7781", and the clearance should be 0.0013-0.0021".

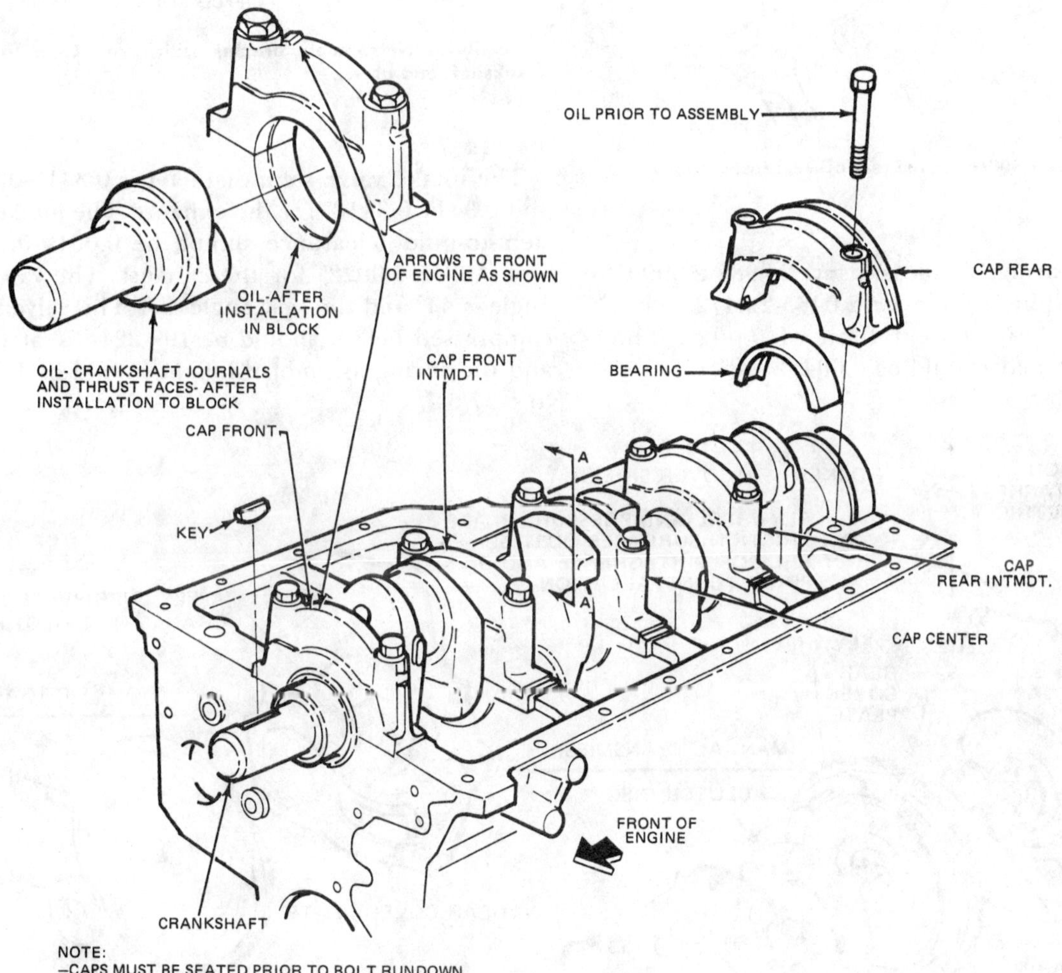

Crankshaft installation instructions for the 2,300cc engine.

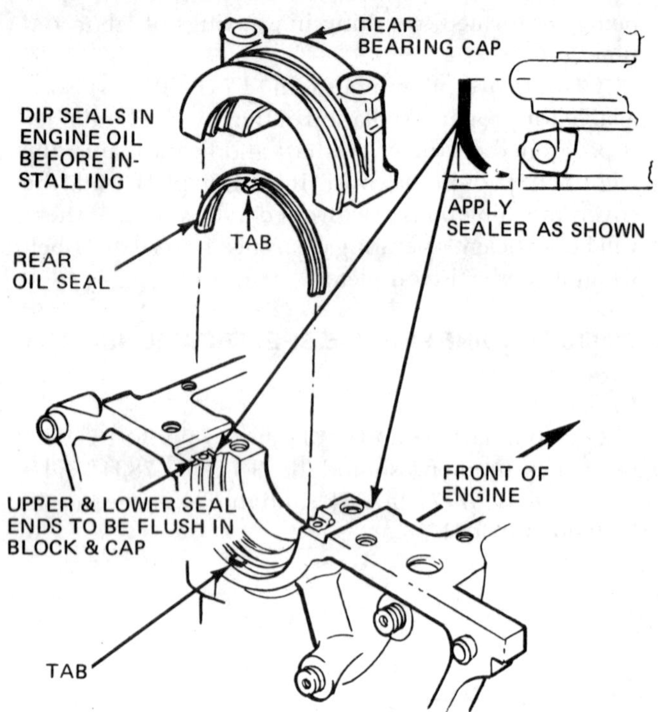

Details of the 2,300cc engine rear oil seal installation.

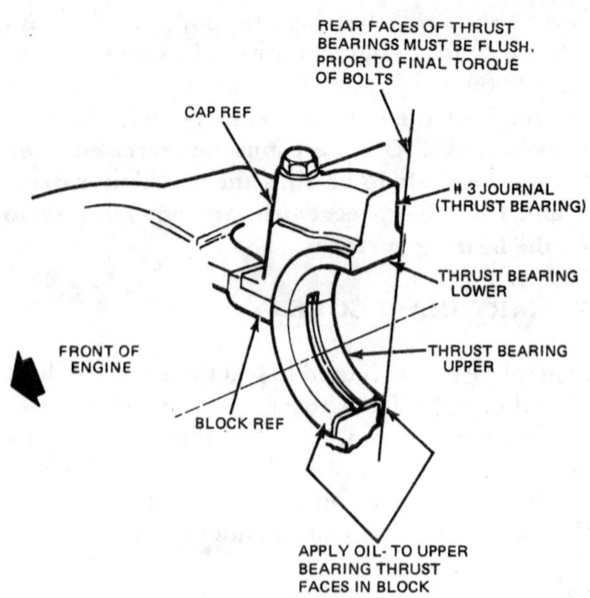

Details of No. 3 main bearing with thrust faces to control crankshaft end play.

Crankshaft

The main bearings should measure 2.3982-2.3990", and the crankpins should be 2.0465-2.0472", both measurements have a wear limit of 0.002". The crankshaft end play should be 0.004-0.008".

Valves

The intake valve stem diameter is 0.3416-0.3423", and 0.3411-0.3418" for the exhaust. The intake valve stem-to-guide clearance should be 0.0010-0.0027", and 0.0015-0.0022" for the exhaust. The valve face angle is 44° and the seat angle 45°. The valve spring compressed height should be 199-221 lbs. at 1.160", and the spring assembled height should be 1-35/64" to 1-37/64".

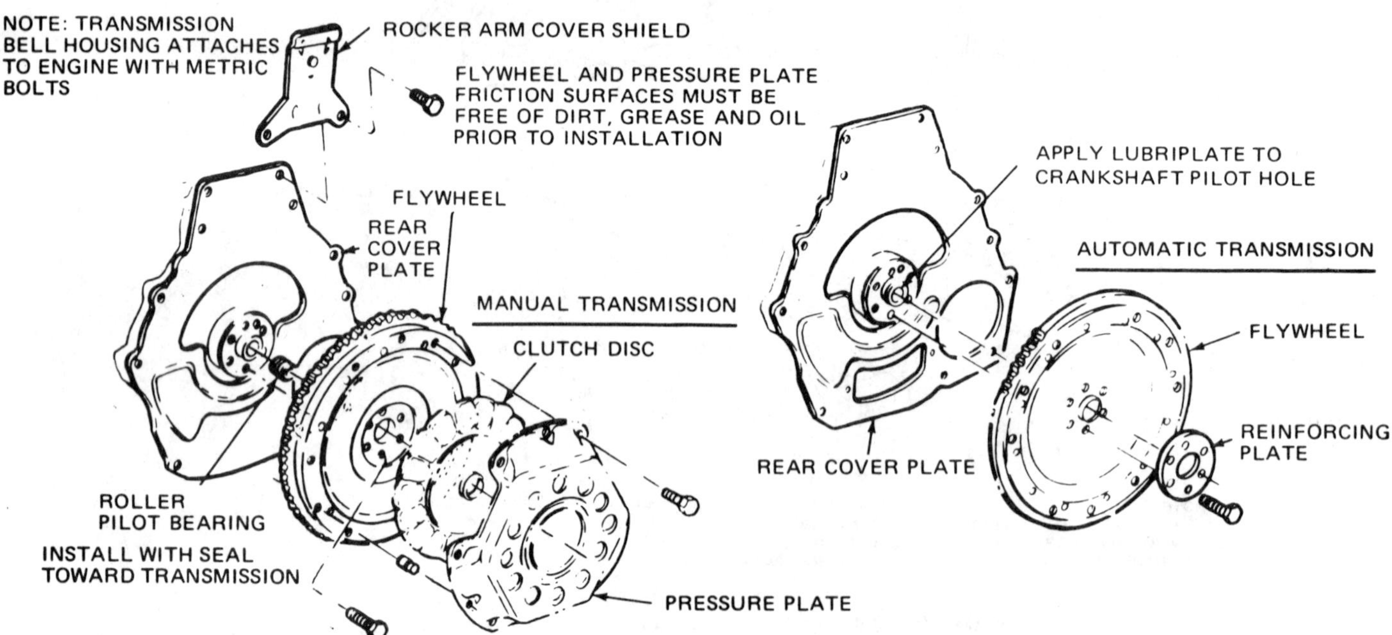

Details of the flywheel and clutch for the 2,300cc engine.

2600/2800CC ENGINES

This compact V-6 engine is of light-weight design. Except for the 60-degree block inclination, it is similar to V-8 engines in construction and service accessibility. The 2800cc engine is essentailly the same as the 2600cc engine that it replaces, except for an increase in bore and stroke.

Timing gears are used in place of a timing chain. The valve arrangement for the left cylinder head (from front to rear) is I-E-E-I-E-I and for the right head I-E-I-E-E-I. The firing order is 1-4-2-5-3-6.

ENGINE, R&R

REMOVING

Disconnect the battery, drain the cooling system and remove the hood. Remove the air cleaner and intake duct assembly. If the engine is equipped with the Thermactor system, remove or disconnect parts that will interfere with removal or installation of the engine. Disconnect the upper and lower hoses at the radiator.

Remove the fan shroud attaching bolts and position the shroud over the fan. Remove the radiator and shroud. Remove the alternator and bracket. Position the alternator out of the way. Disconnect the alternator ground wire from the cylinder block.

Disconnect the heater hoses at the block and water pump. Remove the ground wires from the cylinder block. Disconnect the fuel line at the fuel pump. Plug the fuel tank line.

Disconnect the accelerator cable or linkage at the carburetor and intake manifold. Disconnect the transmission downshift linkage, if so equipped. Disconnect the engine wire loom at the ignition coil. Disconnect the brake booster line.

Raise the vehicle and secure it with safety stands. Disconnect the muffler inlet pipes at the exhaust manifolds. Disconnect the starter cable, and then remove

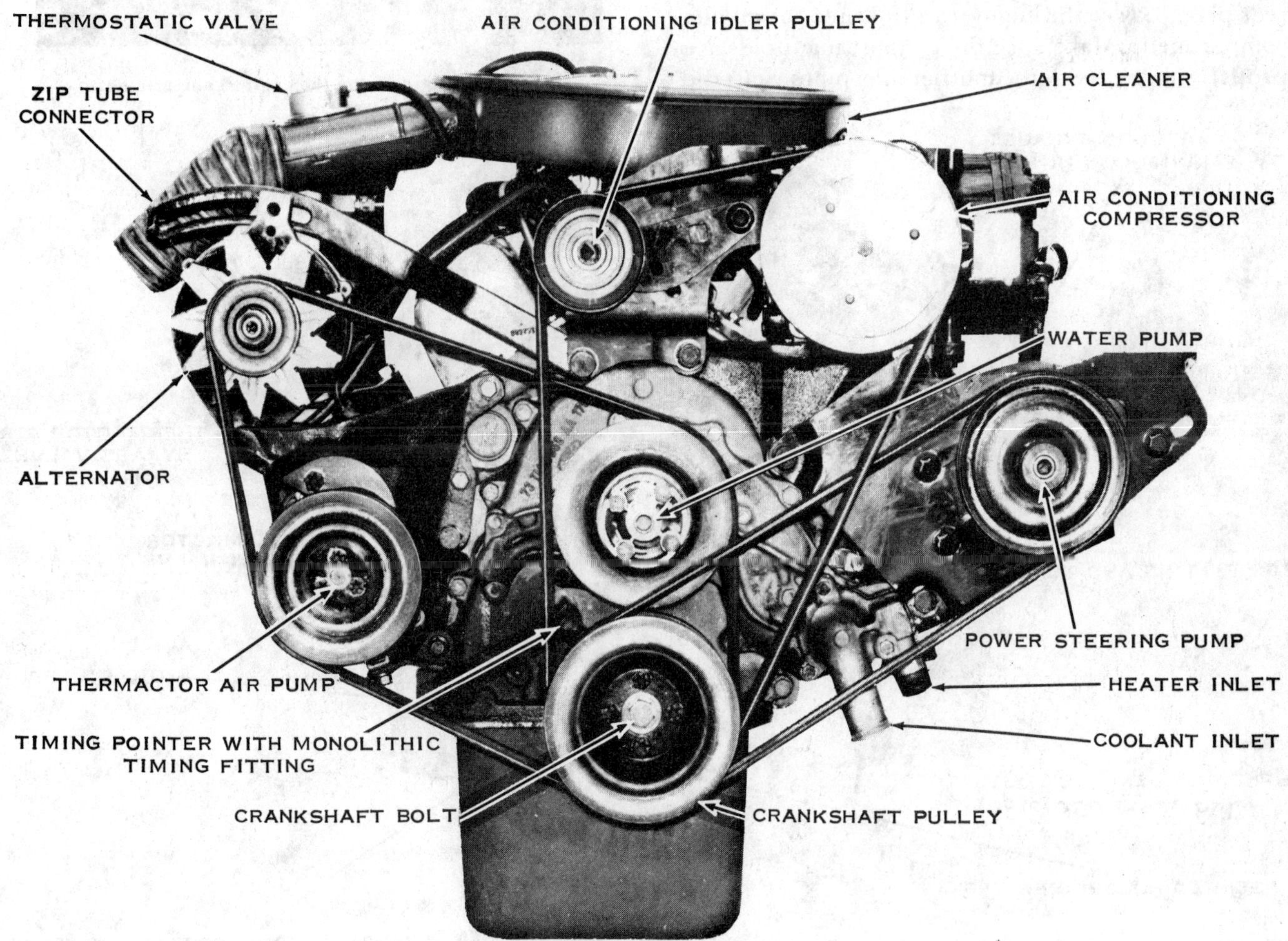

The 2,800cc V-6 engine. It is basically the 2,600cc engine, except for a slight increase in bore and stroke.

the starter. Remove the engine front support throughbolts.

If equipped with an automatic transmission, remove the converter inspection cover and disconnect the flywheel from the converter. Remove the downshift rod, converter housing-to-engine block bolts, and adapter plate-to-converter housing bolt.

On vehicles equipped with a manual transmission, remove the clutch linkage and the bell housing-to-engine block bolts. Lower the vehicle.

Attach an engine lifting sling to the lifting brackets at the exhaust manifolds. Position a jack under the transmission. Raise the engine slightly and carefully pull it from the transmission. Carefully lift the engine out of the engine compartment so that the rear cover plate is not bent or components damaged. Install the engine on a work stand.

INSTALLING

On a vehicle with a manual-shift transmission, align the clutch disc. Install the rear plate pilot studs and the rear plate. Lower the engine carefully into the engine compartment. Make sure the exhaust manifolds are properly aligned with the muffler inlet pipes. Start the

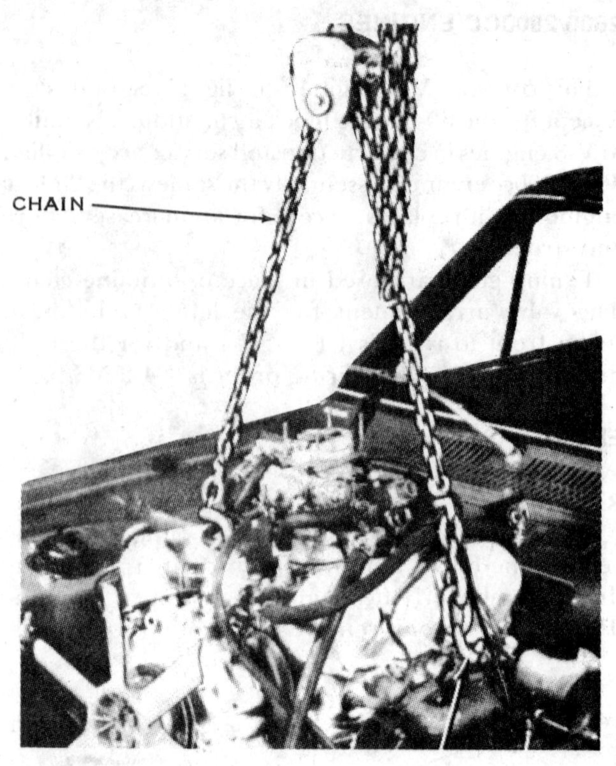

Lifting the engine from the engine compartment.

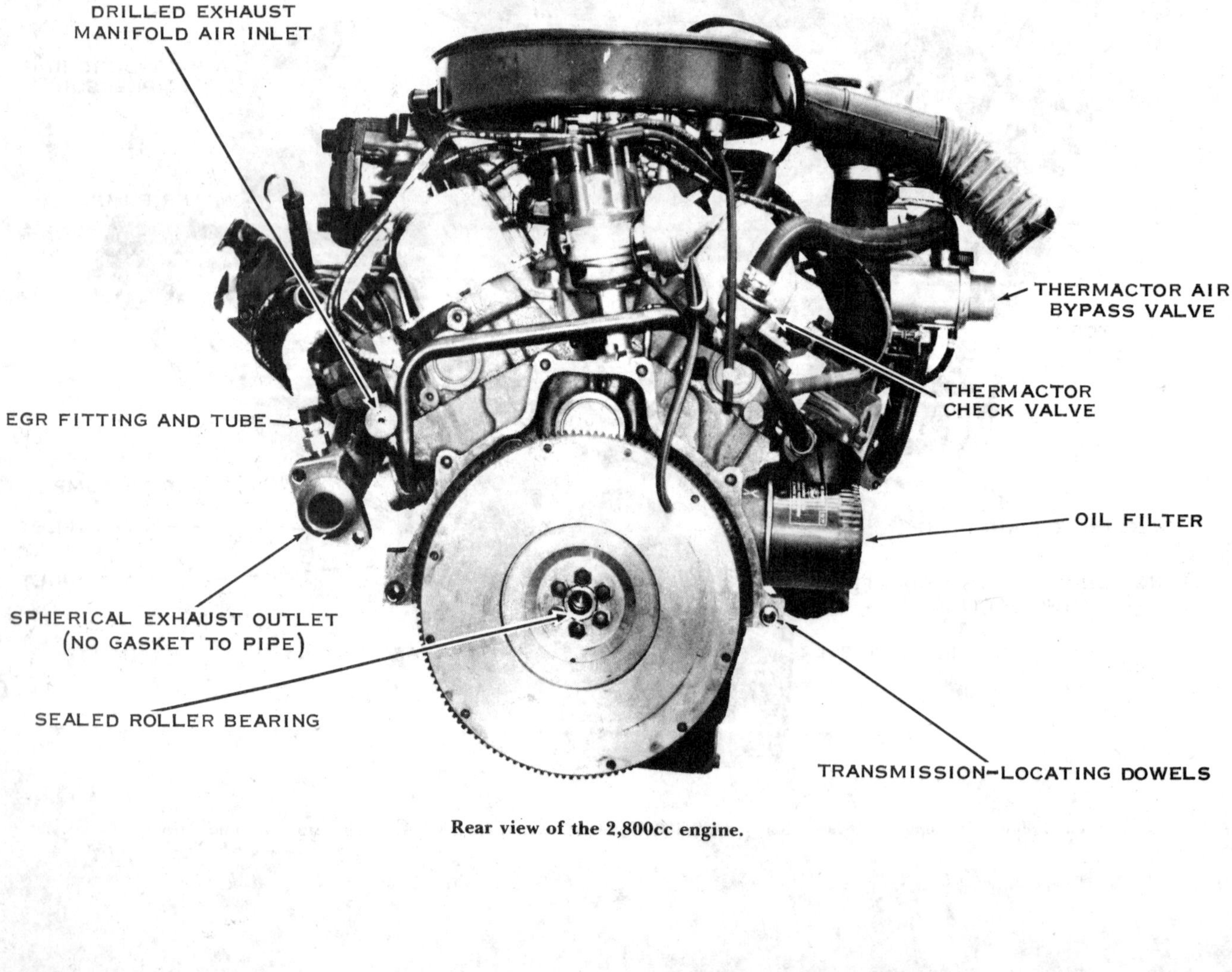

Rear view of the 2,800cc engine.

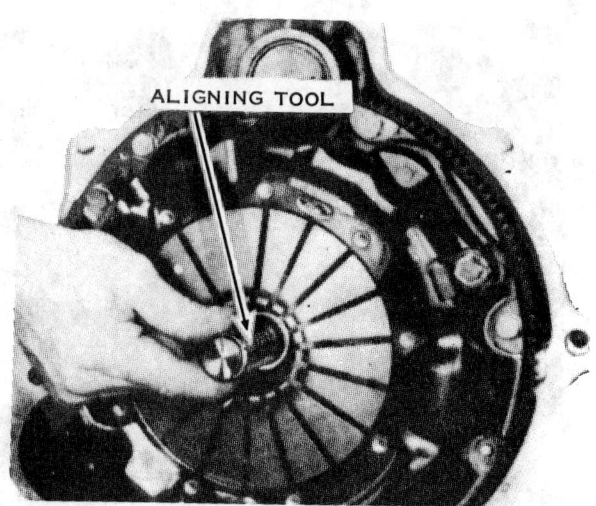

Aligning the clutch disc.

transmission main drive shaft into the clutch disc. It may be necessary to adjust the position of the transmission in relation to the engine if the input shaft does not enter the clutch disc. If the engine hangs up after the shaft enters, turn the crankshaft slowly (transmission in gear) until the shaft splines mesh with the clutch disc splines.

On a vehicle with an automatic transmission, start the converter pilot into the crankshaft. Install the bell housing or converter housing upper bolts, making sure that the dowels in the cylinder block engage the flywheel housing. Remove the jack from under the transmission. Remove the lifting sling. Position the downshift rod on the transmission and engine.

Raise the vehicle and secure it with safety stands. On a vehicle with an automatic transmission, position the transmission linkage bracket, and then install the remaining converter housing bolts. Install the adapter plate-to-converter housing bolt. Install the converter-to-flywheel nuts and install the inspection cover. Connect the downshift rod on the transmission.

On a vehicle with a manual-shift transmission, remove the pilot studs, and then install the lower bell housing bolts. Connect the clutch linkage to the engine block. Install the starter and connect the cable. Connect the muffler inlet pipes at the exhaust manifolds. Install the engine front support through-bolts.

Lower the vehicle. Install the ground wire and the engine wire loom. Connect it to the ignition coil, then install the water temperature sending unit and oil pressure sending unit. Connect the brake booster line.

Install the accelerator linkage and connect the downshift rod, if so equipped. Connect the vacuum lines and the fuel tank line at the fuel pump. Connect the ground wire at the cylinder block.

Install the heater hoses at the water pump and cylinder block. Install the alternator and bracket. Connect the alternator ground wire to the cylinder block. Install the drive belt and adjust the belt tension.

Position the fan shroud over the fan. Install the radiator and connect the upper and lower radiator hoses. Install the fan shroud attaching bolts. Fill and bleed the cooling system. Fill the crankcase with the proper grade and quantity of oil Adjust the transmission downshift linkage, if so equipped. Connect the battery.

Operate the engine at a fast-idle speed until it reaches normal operating temperature and check all gaskets and hose connections for leaks. Adjust the ignition timing and idle speed. Install the air cleaner and intake duct. Install and adjust the hood.

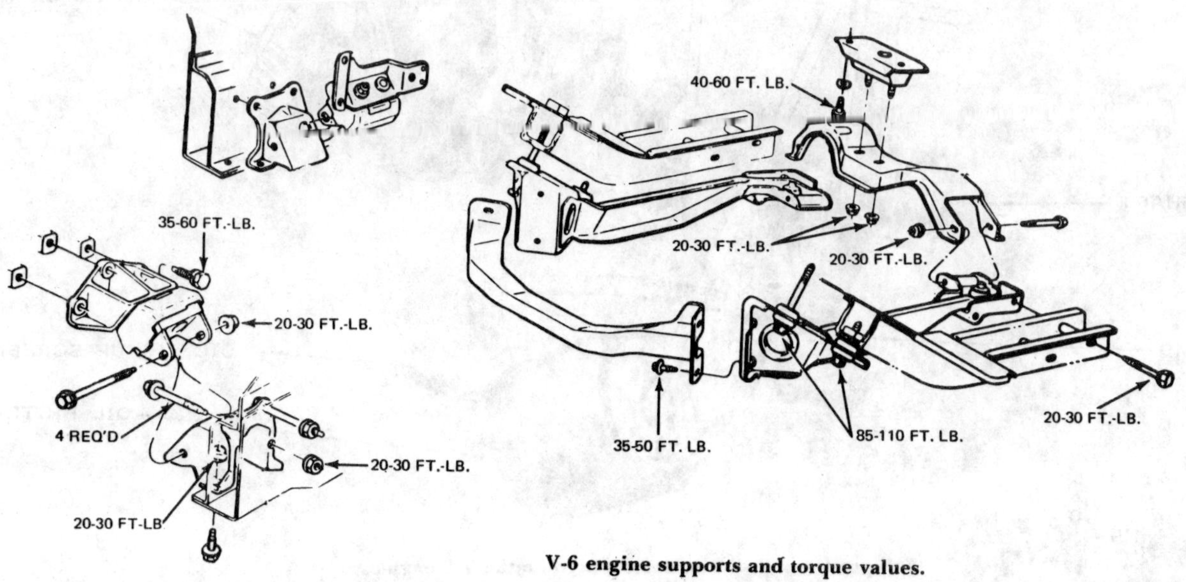

V-6 engine supports and torque values.

OIL PAN, R&R

REMOVING

Remove the oil level dipstick. Remove the bolts attaching the fan shroud to the radiator. Position the shroud over the fan. Disconnect the battery ground wire at the battery. Loosen the alternator bracket and adjusting bolts.

Raise the vehicle. Drain the crankcase. Remove the splash shield and starter. Remove the engine front support nuts. Raise the engine and place wood blocks between the engine front supports and chassis brackets.

Remove the clutch or converter housing cover. Take out the oil pan attaching bolts and remove the oil pan.

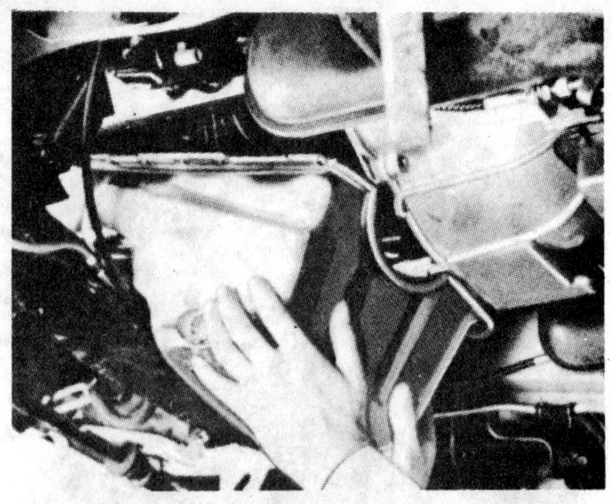

Removing the oil pan.

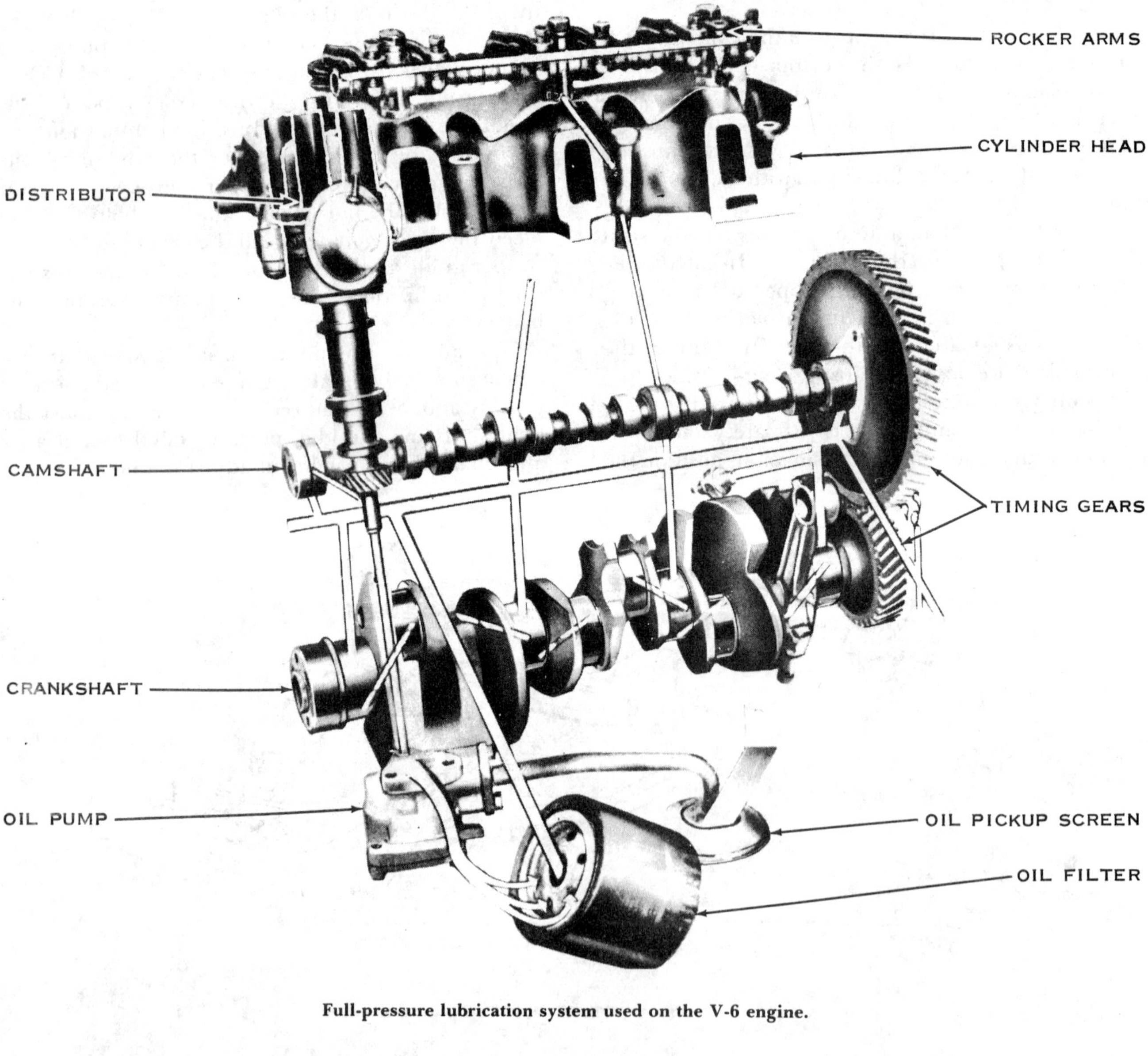

ROCKER ARMS
CYLINDER HEAD
DISTRIBUTOR
CAMSHAFT
TIMING GEARS
CRANKSHAFT
OIL PUMP
OIL PICKUP SCREEN
OIL FILTER

Full-pressure lubrication system used on the V-6 engine.

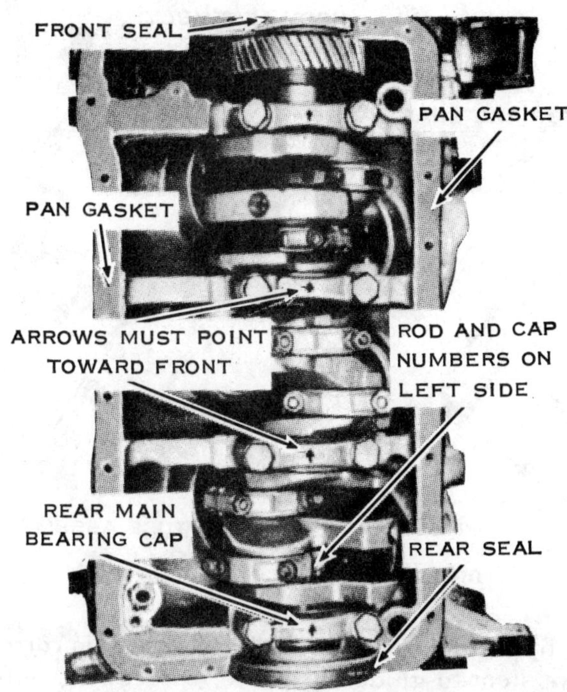

Oil pan gaskets and seals installed.

INSTALLING

Clean the gasket surfaces of the block and oil pan. *NOTE: The oil pan has a two-piece gasket.* Coat the block surface and the oil pan gaskets on the cylinder block. Position the oil pan front seal on the cylinder front cover. **CAUTION: Be sure the tabs on the seal are over the oil pan gasket.** Place the end seals in position flush with the cylinder block oil pan rail. Position the oil pan rear seal on the rear main bearing cap. **CAUTION: Be sure the tabs on the seal are over the oil pan gasket.**

Position the oil pan centered on the cylinder block. Install four bolts, as shown, to secure the front and rear ends of the oil pan. Install the remaining bolts and torque them to 5-7 ft-lbs. in the sequence shown.

Replace the converter housing or clutch cover. Raise the engine and remove the wood blocks from between the engine supports and chassis brackets. Lower the engine and install the engine support nuts. Tighten the nuts to the specifications shown in the accompanying drawing. Replace the starter and splash shield.

Lower the vehicle. Position the alternator and tighten the bolts. Adjust the belt tension. Connect the battery ground wire. Install the fan shroud. Install the oil level dipstick. Fill the crankcase with the proper grade and quantity of engine oil. Start the engine and check for oil leaks.

OIL PUMP, R&R

REMOVING

Remove the oil pan as previously described. Remove the bolt that attaches the oil pickup screen to the main bearing cap. Remove oil pump and withdraw the oil pump driveshaft.

INSTALLING

Prime the oil pump by filling either the inlet or outlet port with engine oil. Rotate the pump shaft to distribute the oil within the pump body.

Insert the oil pump driveshaft into the block with the pointed end facing inward. *NOTE: The pointed end is closest to the pressed-on flange.* Place the oil pump in position with a new gasket and install the attaching

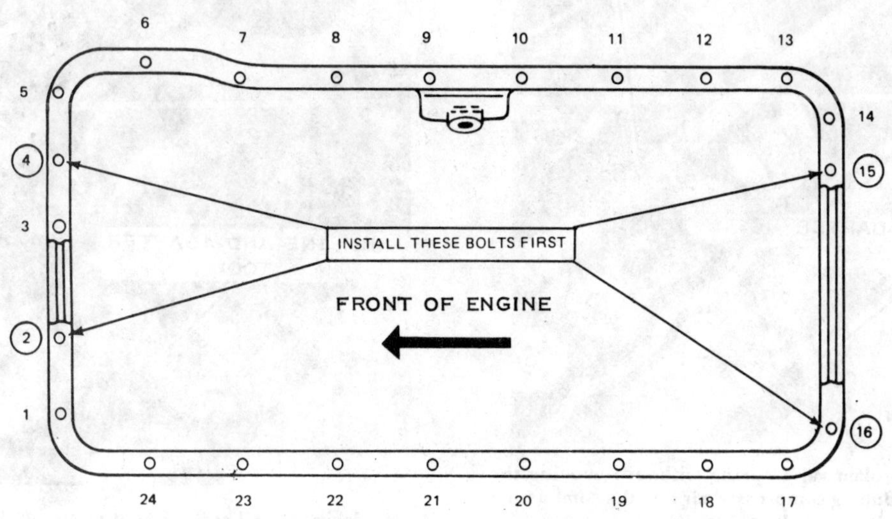

Oil pan bolt tightening sequence for the V-6 engine.

Oil pump and inlet tube details.

screws. Tighten the screws securely.

Clean and install the oil pump inlet tube-and-screen assembly with a new gasket. Torque the bolts to 12-15 ft-lbs.

Install the oil pan. Operate the engine at a fast-idle speed and check for oil leaks.

CYLINDER HEAD SERVICE

The condition of the cylinder head and valve mechanism, more than anything else, determines the power, performance, and economy of an engine. Extreme care should be exercised when recondition-

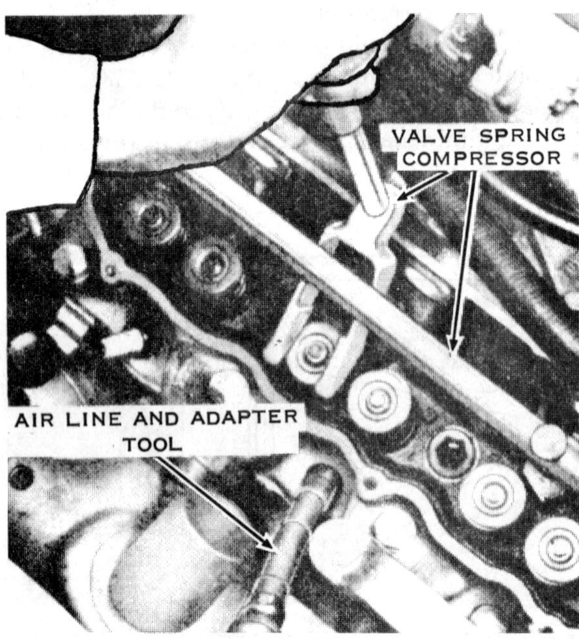

You can replace a broken valve spring without removing the cylinder head by introducing compressed air into the combustion chamber to keep the valve from dropping down.

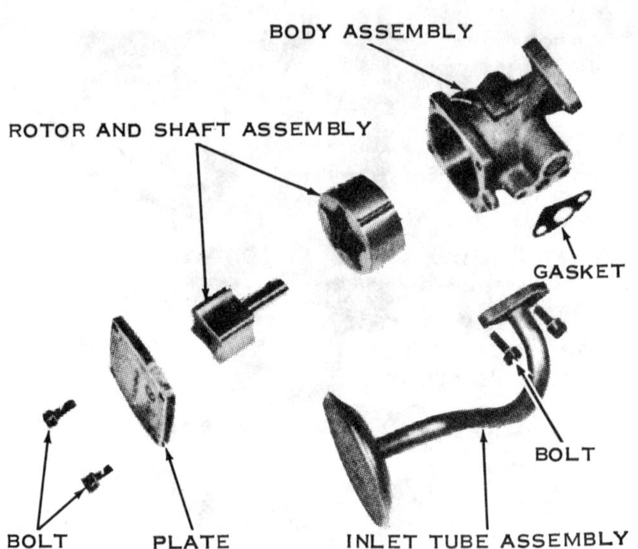

Disassembled view of the oil pump.

ing the cylinder head and valves to maintain correct valve stem-to-guide clearance, correctly ground valves, valve seats of the correct width, and correct valve adjustment.

REMOVING

Remove the air cleaner from the carburetor. Disconnect the negative battery cable.

Disconnect the linkage. Drain the coolant. Remove the distributor cap with the spark plug wires as an assembly. Remove the distributor vacuum line, distributor, coolant outlet hose, coolant hose from the

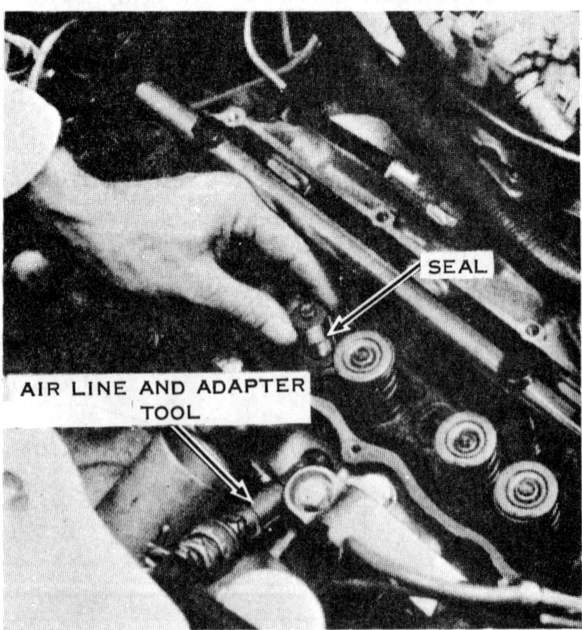

Replacing an oil seal without removing the cylinder head.

pump to the water outlet, rocker arm covers, fuel line, filter, carburetor and intake manifold.

Remove the rocker arm shaft by loosening two bolts at a time (in sequence) and the oil baffles. Remove the push rods and keep them in the same sequence for proper assembly.

Remove the exhaust manifold. Remove the cylinder head retaining bolts and lift off the heads. Remove and discard the head gaskets.

CLEANING AND INSPECTING

Scrape and buff all carbon from the head, valve ports, valves, and the tops of the pistons. Clean the valve guides, using a brush and lacquer thinner to dissolve the gums that cause sticking valves. Inspect the cylinder heads for cracks in the exhaust ports, combustion chambers, or external cracks leading into the coolant chamber.

VALVES

Inspect the valves for burned heads, cracked faces, or worn stems. Check the fit of each valve stem in its respective guide. Excessive valve-to-guide clearance will cause lack of power, rough idling, oil comsumption, and noisy valve-operating mechanism. The Clearance should not exceed 0.0035″ for intake valves and 0.0045″ for exhaust valves, or the valves must be replaced.

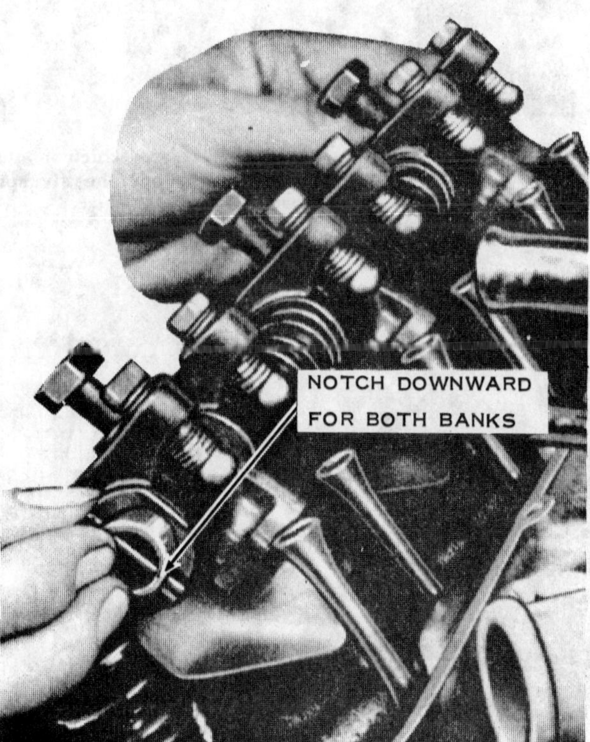

Removing the rocker arm assemblv.

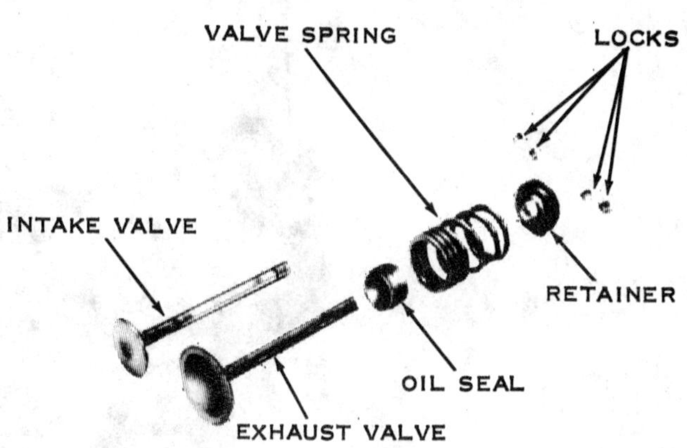

Valve and spring details for the V-6 engine.

Check the valve spring tension against specifications, the valve lifters for a free fit in the block, and the push rods for a bent condition.

VALVE FACES

Valves that are pitted can be refaced to the proper angle, insuring correct relation between the head and stem, on a valve-refacing machine. Dress the valve-refacing machine grinding wheel to make sure it is smooth and true. Set the chuck at the 44° mark for grinding all valve faces. **CAUTION: Only the extreme end of the valve stem is hardened to resist wear. Do not grind the end of the stem excessively.**

VALVE SEATS

Reconditioning the valve seats is very important, because the seating of the valves must be perfect for the engine to deliver the power built into it. Another important factor is the cooling of the valve heads. Good contact between each valve and its seat in the head is imperative to insure that the heat in the valve

Removing a valve lifter.

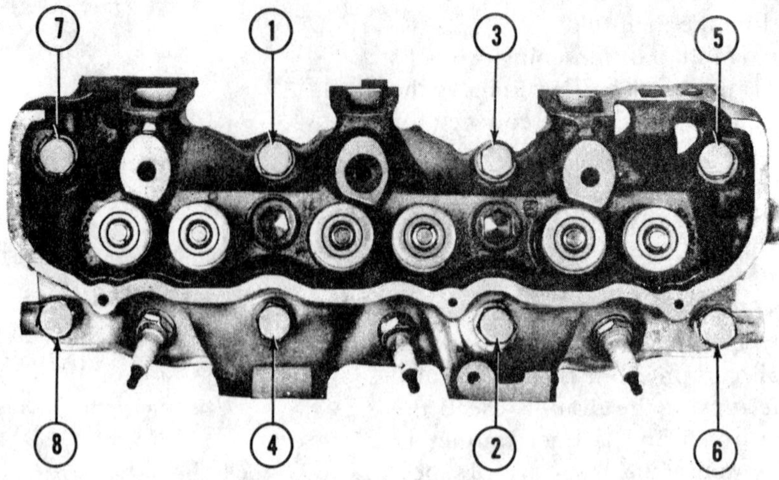

Cylinder head bolt tightening sequence.

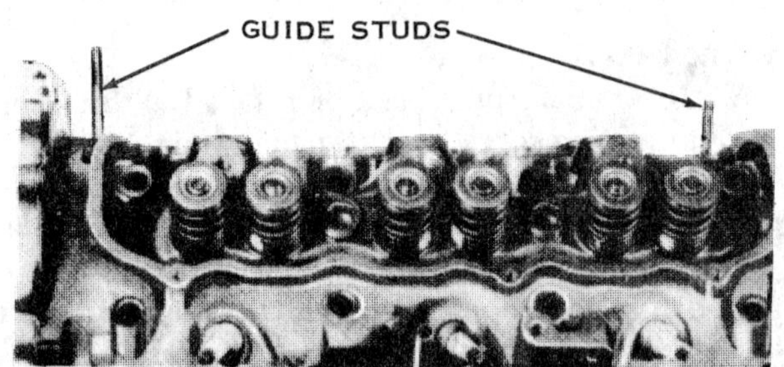

Guide studs should be used to assist in installing the cylinder head without shifting the gasket.

head will be properly carried away.

Use a 45° stone on the valve seats. Use a forming cutter of 30° and 60° at the top and bottom of the seat to narrow it to 0.030-0.060″ for an intake seat and 0.060-0.090″ for an exhaust seat. Check the valve seat with a dial indicator; it must be concentric within 0.002″ total indicator reading.

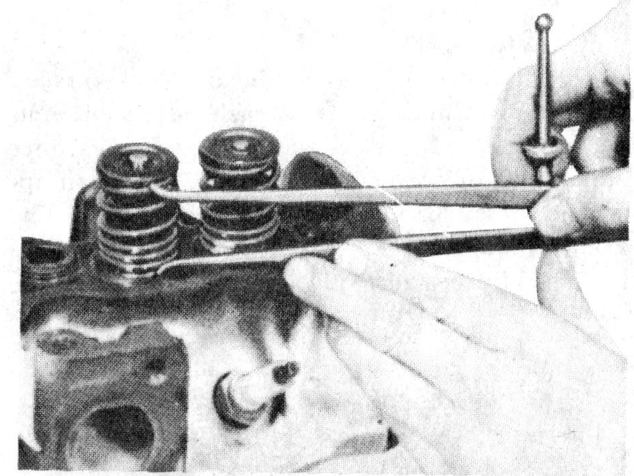
Measuring the valve spring installed height, which should be 1-37/64 to 1-39/64″. Shims can be positioned under the valve spring to decrease the valve spring installed height.

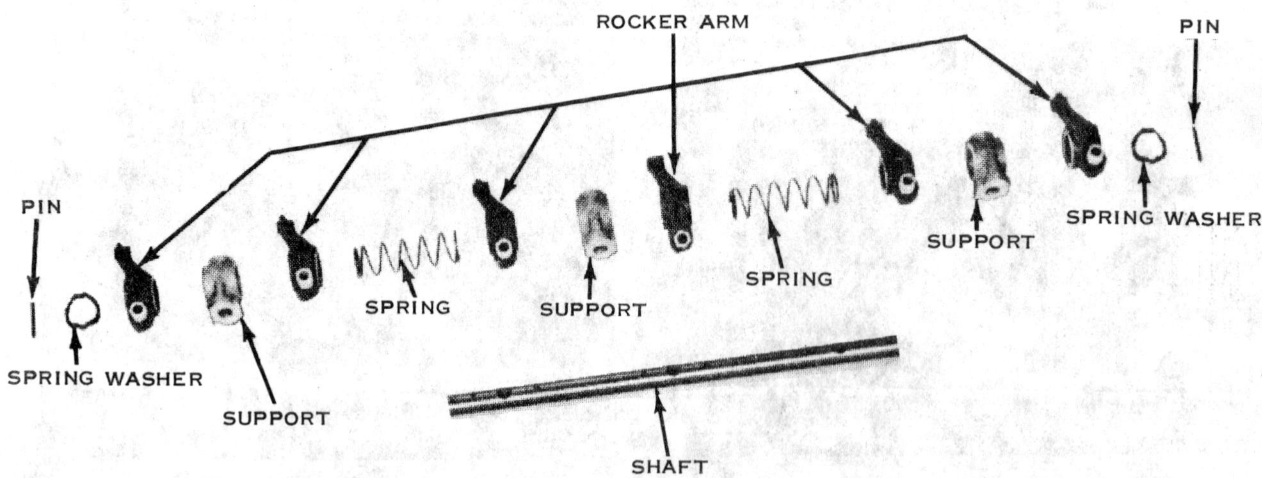

Exploded view of the rocker arms and shaft.

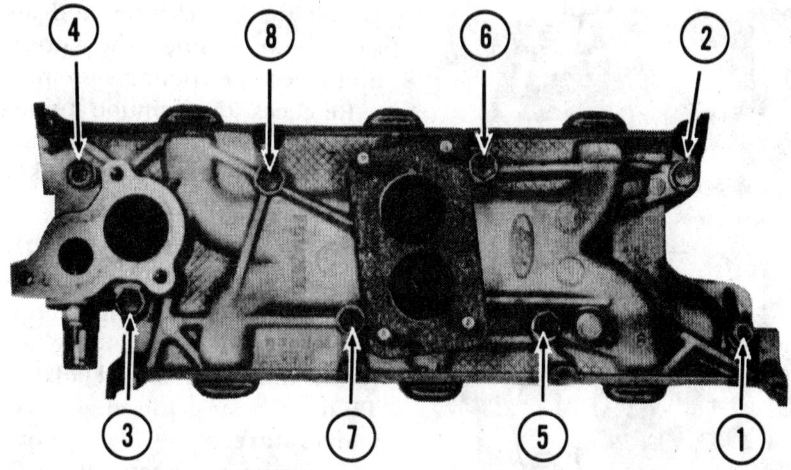

Intake manifold bolt tightening sequence.

ASSEMBLING THE CYLINDER HEAD

Clean the cylinder head, intake manifold, valve rocker arm cover, and cylinder block gasket surfaces. Place the cylinder head gaskets in position on the cylinder block. The gaskets are marked with the words FRONT and TOP for correct positioning. **CAUTION: The left and right cylinder head gaskets are different and non-interchangeable.**

Install the cylinder head assemblies on the cylinder block one at a time. Guide carefully it over the positioning studs. Tighten the attaching bolts in the sequence shown in three separate steps: (1) 40 ft-lbs., (2) 50 ft-lbs., and (3) 65-80 ft-lbs.

Install the intake manifold. **CAUTION: Be sure to use sealing compound on the gasket surfaces and to position the gasket correctly.** Torque the attaching bolts to 10-12 ft-lbs. in the sequence shown.

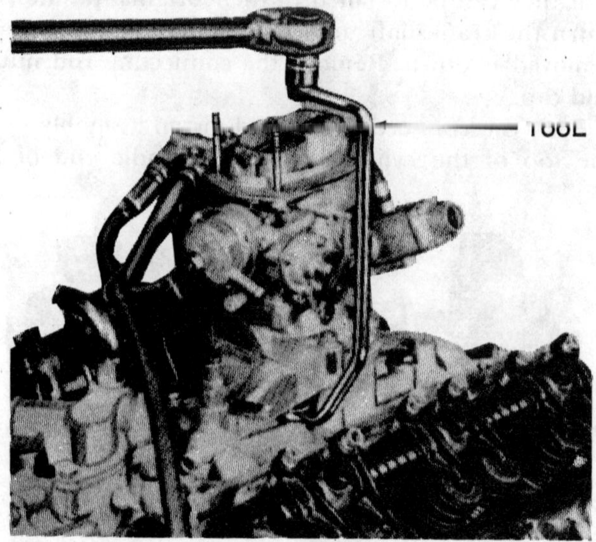

A special wrench is needed to tighten the intake manifold bolts.

Install the exhaust manifold and torque the nuts and bolts to 14-18 ft-lbs.

Apply Lubriplate to both ends of the push rods. Install the push rods, oil baffles, and rocker arm-and-shaft assemblies. Install the distributor, hold-down bolt, and clamp.

MAKING A VALVE LASH ADJUSTMENT (COLD)

If some component of the valve train is replaced, it will be necessary to make a preliminary (cold) valve lash adjustment before starting the engine to prevent damage. If the valve lash adjustment is made for an engine tune-up, the hot adjustment procedure can be used instead.

The valves are adjusted by positioning each piston at TDC on the compression stroke in the firing order sequence, 1-4-2-5-3-6. Rotate the crankshaft until No. 1 piston is on TDC at the end of the compression stroke. With the crankshaft in the correct position, loosen the locknut and set the valve lash to 0.018" for all valves. The valve adjusting nuts are self-locking and will remain at the set position.

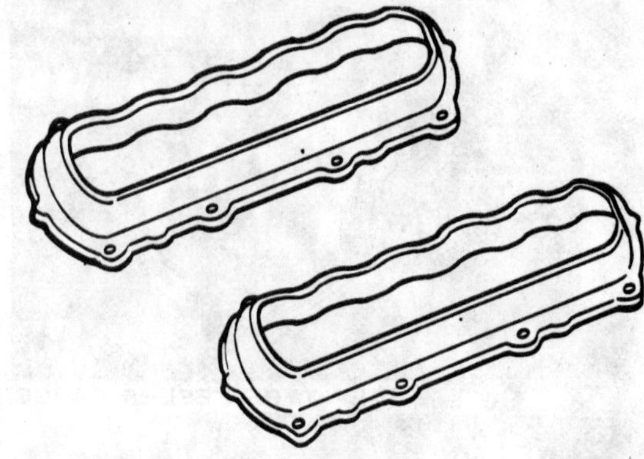

To make a hot valve lash adjustment, you should use dummy rocker covers to avoid oil running down the side of the engine.

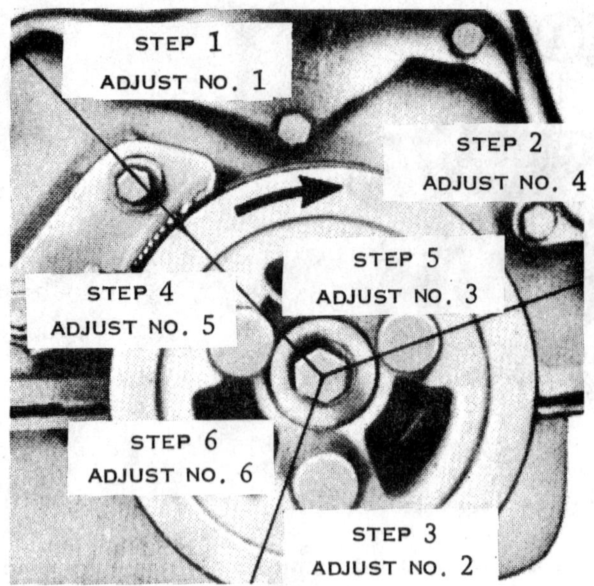

Rotating the crankshaft in increments of 120° for making the valve adjustment, as discussed in the text.

Adjust the valves in the remaining cylinders following the firing order sequence. This can be accomplished by rotating the crankshaft in increments of 1/3 revolution (120 degrees). After two complete revolutions, all the cylinders will have been at their TDC position at the top of the compression stroke. After the valves are adjusted, clean the rocker arm covers, replace the gaskets, and install on the engine. Tighten the bolts to 3-5 ft-lbs.

Install the carburetor and distributor cap with the spark plug wires. If necessary, adjust the linkage. Install the fuel line with the filter and the vacuum line.

Making the valve lash adjustment on the V-6 engine.

Install the air cleaner and air cleaner tube at the carburetor. Connect the battery negative cable. Refill and bleed the cooling system.

Re-check the ignition timing after the engine is started. Operate the engine at a fast-idle speed and check for coolant and oil leaks.

MAKING A VALVE LASH ADJUSTMENT (HOT)

With the engine idling, set the hot valve lash, using a step-type feeler gauge only (go and no/go) to 0.014″ for the intake valves and 0.016″ for the exhaust. **CAUTION: Be sure the engine is at normal operating temperature.**

The valve arrangement for the left cylinder head is I-E-E-I-E-I and for the right, I-E-I-E-E-I, both from the front of the engine. The valve adjusting nuts are self-locking and will remain at the set position.

PISTONS AND RODS, R&R

REMOVING

Drain the cooling system and the crankcase. Remove the intake manifold, cylinder heads, oil pan, and oil pump.

Remove the ridges and/or deposits from the upper end of the cylinder bores as follows: Turn the crankshaft until the piston to be removed is at the bottom of its travel and place a cloth on the piston head to collect the cuttings. Remove the ridge from the upper end of the cylinder bore. **CAUTION: Never cut into the ring travel area in excess of 1/32 inch when removing ridges.**

Make sure all connecting rod caps are marked so that they can be installed in their original positions. Turn the crankshaft until the connecting rod being removed is down. Remove the connecting rod nuts and cap.

Push the connecting rod-and-piston assembly out the top of the cylinder with the handle end of a

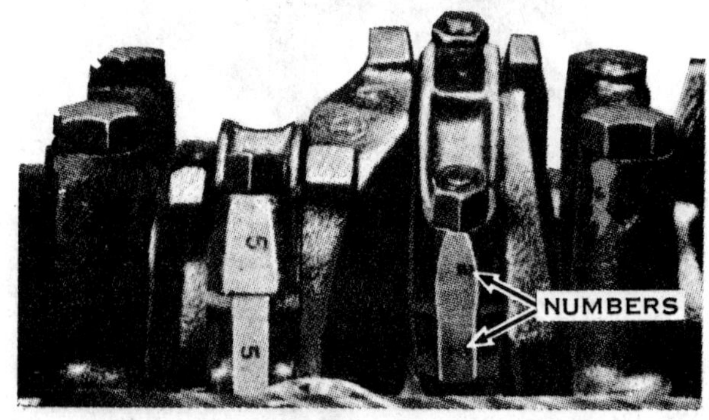

The connecting rods are numbered in this manner.

hammer. **CAUTION: Avoid damage to the crankshaft journal or the cylinder wall when removing the piston and rod.** Remove the bearing inserts from the connecting rod and cap. Install the cap on the connecting rod from which it was removed.

CLEANING AND INSPECTING

Cylinder Bores

If the cylinder bores are worn excessively, they must be bored to the next oversize. Pistons and rings are available in 0.010", 0.020", 0.030", and 0.040" oversizes. If the cylinder bores are not worn too much, the glazed surfaces must be removed by honing with a 220-grit stone. **CAUTION: Clean all traces of abrasives with soap and hot water to prevent excessive wear after the engine is placed back in service.**

Piston Rings

Compression rings in all engines are the deep-section twist type. This type of compression ring takes its name from its installed position which is cocked or twisted. It assumes and maintains this position for life because the upper edge of the top ring and the lower edge of the second ring is chamfered, making the rings unbalanced in cross section. All compression rings are marked on the upper side of the ring. When installing compression rings, make sure the marked side faces the top of the piston.

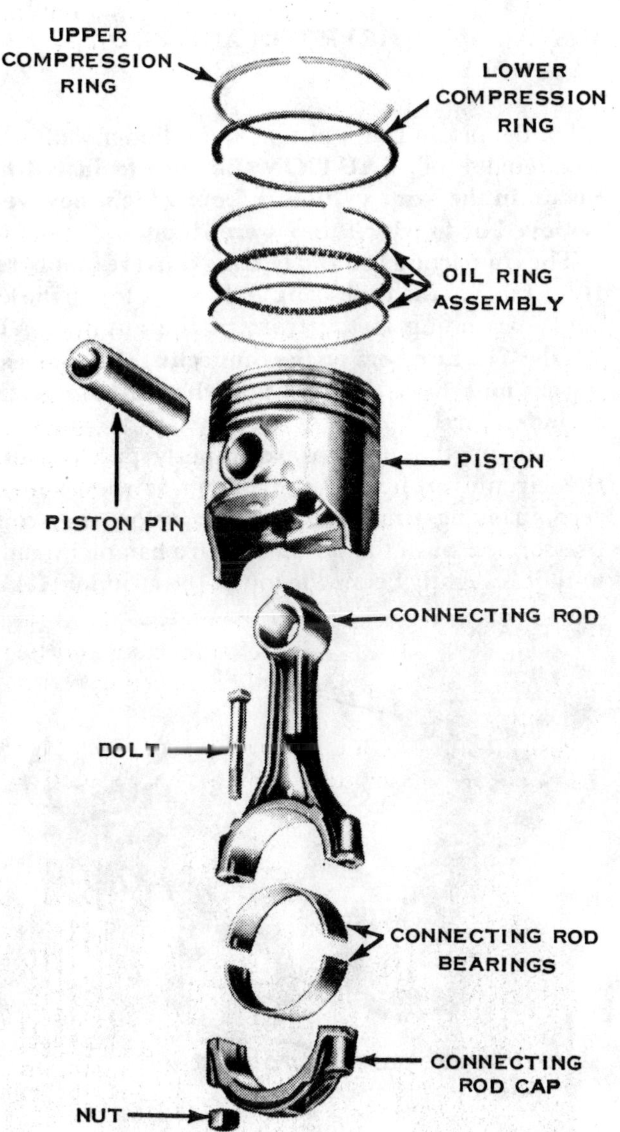

Piston, rod, and rings for the V-6 engine.

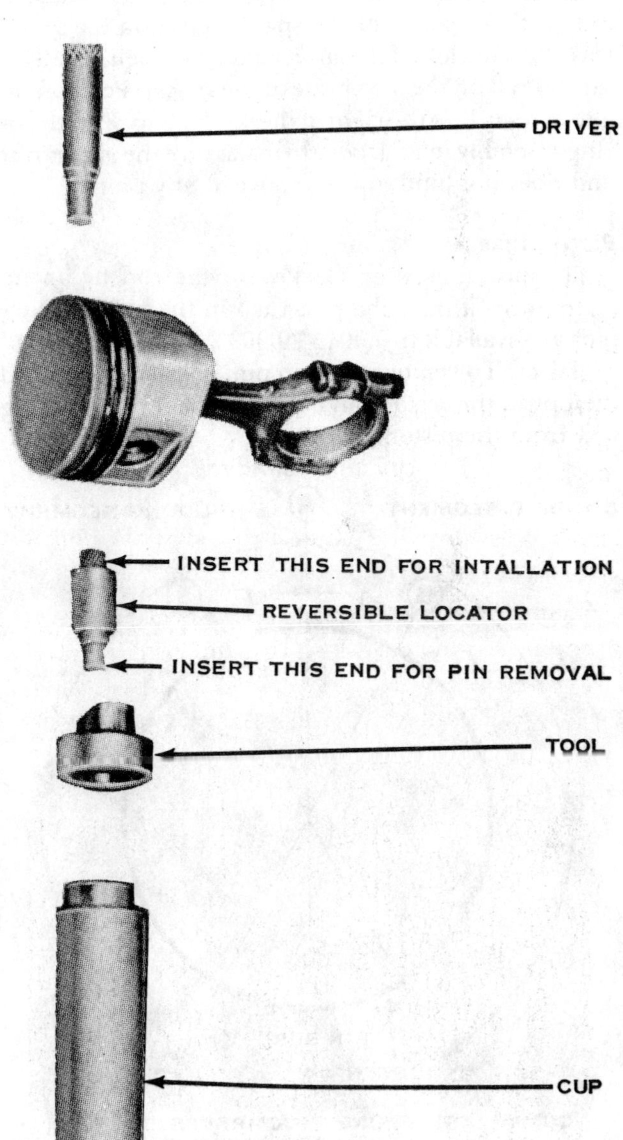

Removing or installing a piston pin, which is a press-fit in the rod.

The oil-control rings consist of two segments (rails) and a spacer. Piston rings are furnished in standard sizes as well as 0.020", 0.030", and 0.040" oversizes. Check the space or gap between the ends of the compression rings with a feeler gauge, which should be 0.015-0.023" for both rings. The oil ring rail gap should be 0.015-0.055".

Slip the outer surface of each ring into the piston ring groove and roll the ring entirely around the groove to make sure that it is free and does not bind in the groove at any point. The compression ring side clearance should be 0.0020" to 0.0032". The assembled oil ring side clearance should be 0.0005-0.0065".

Install the oil ring spacer in the oil ring groove, and then position the gap in line with the piston pin hole. Hold the spacer ends butted, and then install a steel rail on the top side of the spacer. Position the gap at least 1" to the left of the spacer gap, and then install the second rail on the lower side of the spacer. Position the gap at least 1" to the right of the spacer gap. Flex the oil ring assembly in its groove to make sure the ring is free and does not bind in the groove at any point.

Piston Pins

The piston pins are locked in the rod by an interference fit, and the pins turn in the pistons. New pins are available in 0.0015", 0.003", 0.005", and 0.010" oversizes. To remove a piston pin, install the tool, and then push the piston pin out. Remove the connecting rod from the piston.

OIL RING SPACER
OIL RING SEGMENT (A) OIL RING SEGMENT
(B) 1" 1" (B)
150° 150°
PIN BORE
PISTON ℄
(C) (C)
COMPRESSION RING COMPRESSION RING
FRONT OF ENGINE

Piston ring gap spacing.

To assemble a fitted piston pin to its rod, lubricate the piston pin holes in the piston and connecting rod to facilitate installation. Position the connecting rod in its respective piston so that the numbered side of the rod, at the bearing end, will be toward the left and the cast depression in the crown of the piston faces the front of the engine.

Install the piston pin on the installer and the spring and pilot into the support. Install the piston and rod on the support, indexing the pilot through the piston and rod. Place the assembly on an arbor press, start the pin into the piston, and press on the installer until the pilot bottoms. Remove the installer-and-support assembly from the piston-and-connecting rod assembly. Check the piston pin for freedom of movement in the piston bores.

INSTALLING THE PISTON-AND-ROD ASSEMBLY

Oil the piston rings, piston, and cylinder walls with light engine oil. **CAUTION: Be sure to install the piston in the same cylinders from which they were removed or to which they were fitted.**

The connecting rod and bearing caps are numbered from 1 to 3 in the right bank and from 4 to 6 in the left bank, beginning at the front of the engine. **CAUTION: The numbers on the connecting rod and bearing cap must be on the same side when installed in the cylinder bore.**

Make sure the ring gaps are properly spaced around the circumference of the piston as shown in an accompanying drawing. Install a piston ring compressor and push the piston in with a hammer handle until it is slightly below the top of the cylinder. **CAU-**

RIGHT BANK LEFT BANK

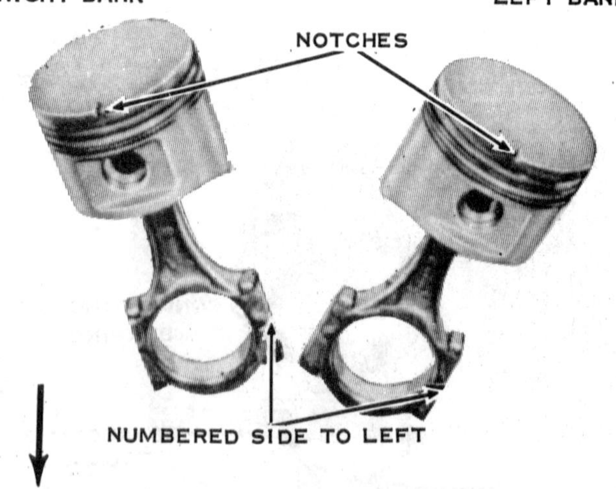

FRONT OF ENGINE

Correct piston and rod assembly.

TION: Be sure to guide the connecting rods to avoid damaging the crankshaft journals. Install the piston with the indentation notch in the piston head toward the front of the engine.

Check the clearance of each bearing. After the bearings have been fitted, apply a light coat of engine oil to the journals and bearings. Turn the crankshaft throw to the bottom of its stroke. Push the piston all the way down until the connecting rod bearing seats on the crankshaft journal. Install the connecting rod cap. Tighten the nuts to 21-25 ft-lbs.

After the piston and connecting rod assemblies have been installed, check the side clearance between the connecting rods on each crankshaft journal, which should be 0.004-0.011".

Disassemble, clean, and assemble the oil pump. Clean the oil pump inlet tube screen and the oil pan and block gasket surfaces. Prime the oil pump by filling either the inlet port or outlet port with engine oil and rotating the pump shaft to distribute the oil within the housing. Install the oil pump and the oil pan.

Install the cylinder heads and intake manifold.

Fill and bleed the cooling system. Fill the crankcase with the proper grade and quantity of engine oil.

Start the engine. Check and adjust the ignition timing. Connect the distributor vacuum hoses at the carburetor.

Operate the engine at a fast-idle speed and check for oil and coolant leaks. When the engine temperature has stabilized, adjust the valve clearance, the engine idle speed and the idle fuel mixture. Install the air cleaner and intake duct assembly.

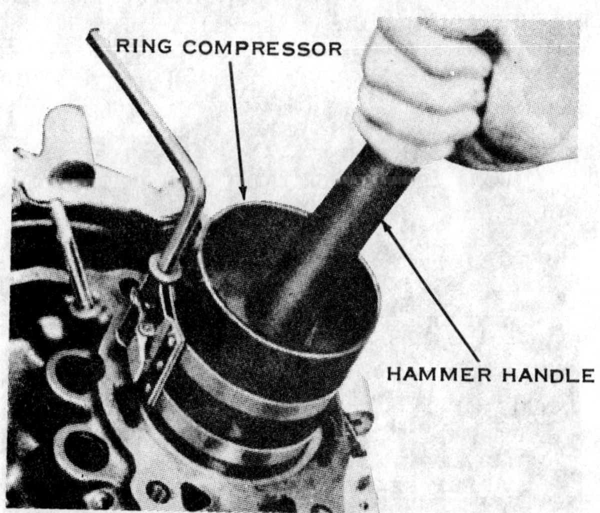

Use a piston ring compressor and hammer handle to push down the piston. CAUTION: Don't hammer on the piston if it sticks. Remove the compressor to determine if one of the piston rings has popped out of a groove.

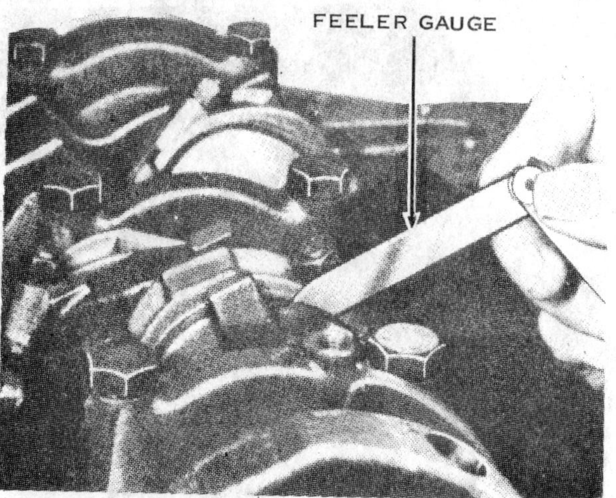

Using a feeler gauge to determine the connecting rod side clearance, which should be 0.004-0.011".

MAIN BEARINGS, R&R

The main and connecting rod bearing inserts are a selective fit. **CAUTION: Do not file or lap the bearing caps or use shims to obtain the proper bearing clearance.** Selective fit main bearings are available for service in standard and undersizes. Undersize bearings, which are not selective fit, are available for use on journals that have been refinished.

If the rear main bearing is to be replaced, remove the engine and place it in a work stand.

CRANKSHAFT REAR OIL SEAL, R&R

REMOVING

Remove the transmission assembly. Remove the

Align the thrust bearing by moving the crankshaft back and forth before tightening the cap.

Removing the crankshaft rear oil seal.

clutch pressure plate and clutch disc. Remove the flywheel, flywheel housing, and rear plate.

Use an awl to punch two holes in the crankshaft rear oil seal. Punch the holes on opposite sides of the crankshaft and just above the bearing cap to the cylinder block split line. Install a sheet metal screw in each hole. Use two large screwdrivers to pry against both screws at the same time to remove the crankshaft rear oil seal. It may be necessary to place small blocks of wood against the cylinder block to provide a fulcrum point for the pry bars. **CAUTION: Use caution throughout this procedure to avoid scratching or damaging the crankshaft oil seal surface.**

Replacing the rear main bearing cap wedge seals.

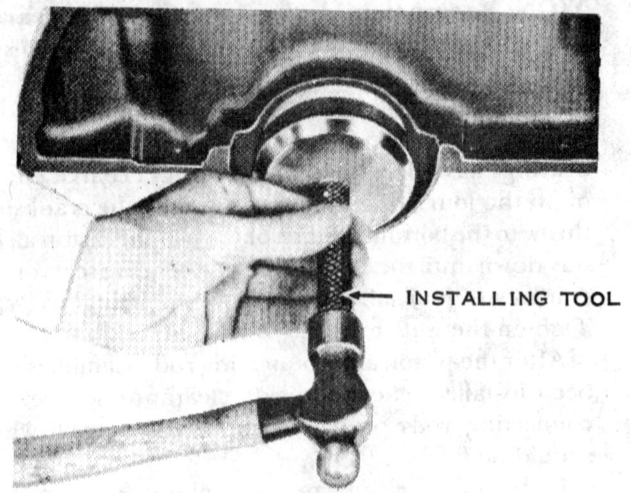

Installing the crankshaft rear oil seal.

Clean the oil seal recess in the cylinder block and main bearing cap. Inspect and clean the oil seal contact surface on the crankshaft.

INSTALLING

Coat the oil seal-to-cylinder block surface of the oil seal with oil. Coat the seal contact surface of the oil seal and crankshaft with Lubriplate. Start the seal in the recess and install it with the tool as shown. Drive the seal into position until it is firmly seated.

Install the rear plate, flywheel housing, and flywheel. Tighten the flywheel bolts to 47-51 ft-lbs. Install the clutch disc and clutch pressure plate. Align the clutch disc before tightening the pressure plate retaining screws. Install the transmission.

Apply sealer where shown before replacing the rear main bearing cap.

Removing the front cover plate.

Tightening the front cover retaining bolts.

TIMING GEARS, REPLACE

REMOVING

Drain the cooling system and crankcase. Remove the oil pan and radiator.

Remove the water pump, drive belt, and camshaft front cover.

Use a gear puller to remove the crankshaft gear. Remove the key from the crankshaft and the gear from the camshaft. Remove the thrust plate, spacer and key.

Pulling off the crankshaft gear.

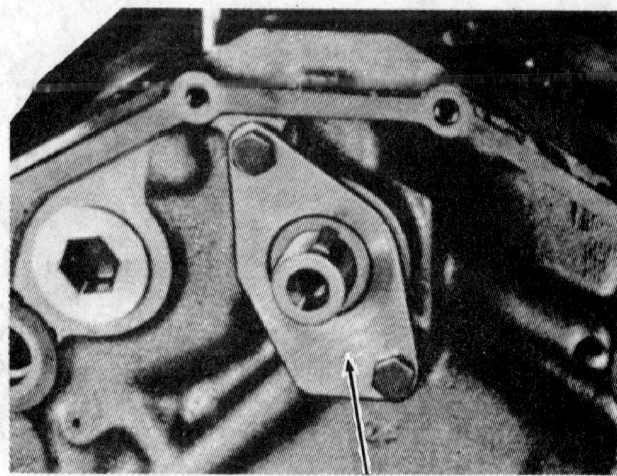

The camshaft spacer plate is available in two thicknesses to keep the end play within specifications (0.0008-0.0040").

Installing a new crankshaft gear.

Installing new guide sleeves.

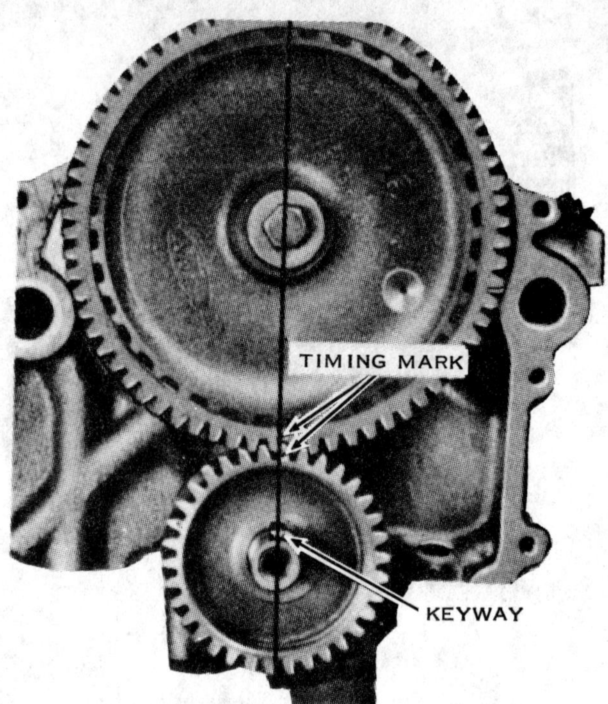

The timing marks must align through the center of the shafts on the V-6 engine.

INSTALLING

Place the spacer and thrust plate on the camshaft. Install the key in the camshaft. Align the keyway in the gear with the keyway, and then press the gear onto the shaft, making sure that it seats tight against the spacer. Check the camshaft end play, which should be 0.0008-0.0040". If it is not within specifications, replace the thrust plate.

Position the key in the crankshaft. Align the keyway and install the gear.

Install the cylinder front cover. Replace the oil pan and radiator. Fill the cooling system and crankcase. Start the engine and adjust the ignition timing. Operate at a fast idle and check all hose connections and gaskets for leaks.

2600CC ENGINE SPECIFICATIONS

Block

The nominal bore and stroke are 3.545" x 2.63". The cylinder bore standard diameter should be 3.543-3.546". The piston should measure 3.542-3.545", and the clearance should be 0.001-0.003".

Crankshaft

The main bearing journals should measure 2.243-2.244", and the crankpins 2.125-2.126", both with a wear limit of 0.002". The oil clearance should be 0.0005-0.0020". The crankshaft end play should be 0.004-0.008".

Valves

The intake valve stem should measure 0.316" and the exhaust 0.315". The valve stem-to-guide clearance for intake valves should be 0.002" and 0.003" for the exhaust. The valve face angle is 44° and the seat angle 45°. The valve clearance cold should be 0.014" for the intake and 0.016" for the exhaust.

2800CC ENGINE SPECIFICATIONS

Block

The nominal bore and stroke are 3.66" x 2.70". The actual bore diameter should measure 3.6614-3.6630". The piston diameter should be 3.6599-3.6615". The piston-to-cylinder bore clearance should be 0.001-0.002".

Crankshaft

The main bearing journals should measure 2.2433-2.2441" and the crankpins should be 2.0464-2.0472", both with a wear limit of 0.002". The crankshaft end play should be 0.003-0.011".

Valves

The intake valve stem diameter should measure 0.3159-0.3167", and the exhaust 0.3149-0.3156". The intake valve stem-to-guide clearance is 0.0008-0.0025" and 0.0018-0.0035" for the exhaust. The valve face angle is 44° and the seat angle 45°. The valve spring pressure should measure 138-149 lbs. at a compressed height of 1.22". The valve spring assembled height should be 1-37/64" to 1-39/64".

7 | driveline service

The driveline consists of a clutch, transmission (manual and automatic), and rear axle. The service procedures in this chapter will follow this order.

CLUTCH

REMOVING

Open the hood and disconnect the battery.

Loosen the gearshift lever knob locknut and remove the knob and locknut. Remove the two front attaching screws from each step plate. Remove the attaching screws from each kick pad and remove the pads.

Working from the front, fold the carpet up against the shift lever. Remove the four shift lever boot retaining ring screws. Remove the boot through the opening in the floor mat. Compress the spring on the lower end of the shift lever and remove the snap ring. Bend the lock tabs up on the shift lever where necessary, then remove the plastic dome nut. Lift the shift lever from the transmission.

Working from under the hood, remove the two clutch housing upper bolts. Raise the vehicle and position safety stands.

Mark the driveshaft and companion flange so that it can be installed in the same relative position. Remove the driveshaft and insert Tool T70P-7095 in the extension housing to prevent lubricant leakage.

Remove the speedometer cable retainer attaching bolt. Lift the cable and driven gear from the extension housing. Disconnect the back-up light switch wires at the switch.

Lift the boot from the clutch housing. Loosen the locknut and the adjusting nut just enough to disconnect the cable from the release lever. *NOTE: Early models will have a C-clip to retain the cable instead of a locknut and adjustment nut.*

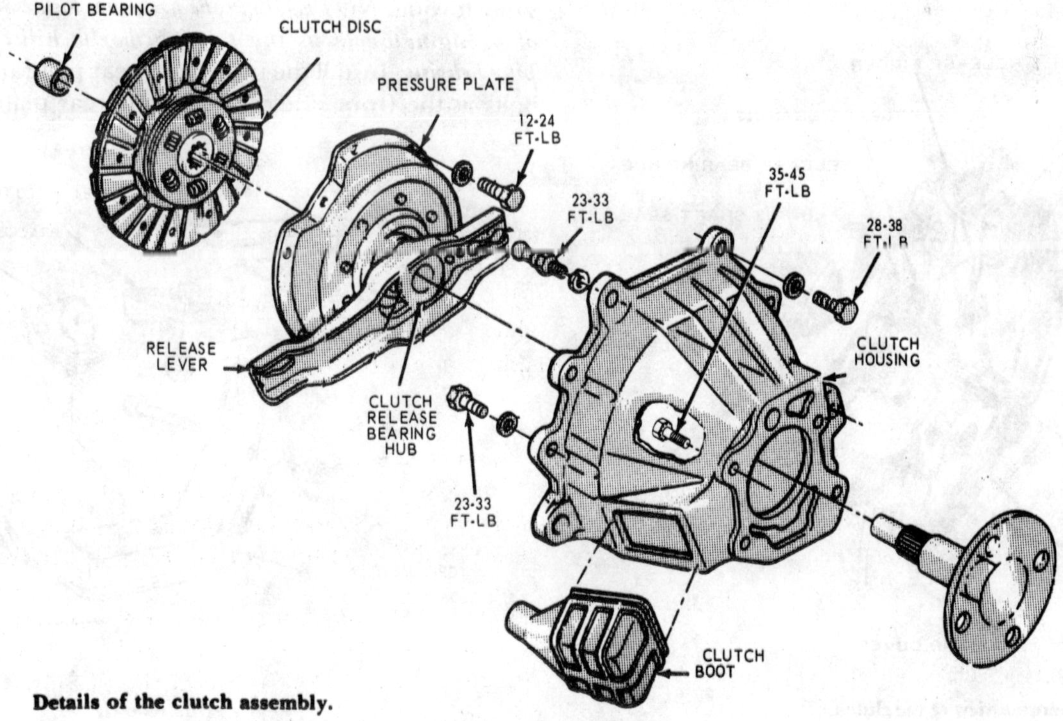

Details of the clutch assembly.

Remove the three starter attaching bolts and position it to one side.

Remove the engine rear plate attaching bolts from each side of the engine. Remove the insulator-to-crossmember attaching nut. Place a wood block and jack under the oil pan. Raise the engine just high enough to remove all weight from the crossmember attaching bolts and then take off the member.

Remove the transmission drain plug and allow the lubricant to drain into a container. Lower the engine and remove the remaining clutch housing attaching bolts. Separate the transmission and clutch housing from the engine.

Mark the clutch pressure plate and flywheel for alignment during assembly, and then loosen the pressure plate bolts one turn at a time to avoid distorting the plate. Remove the pressure plate and clutch disc.

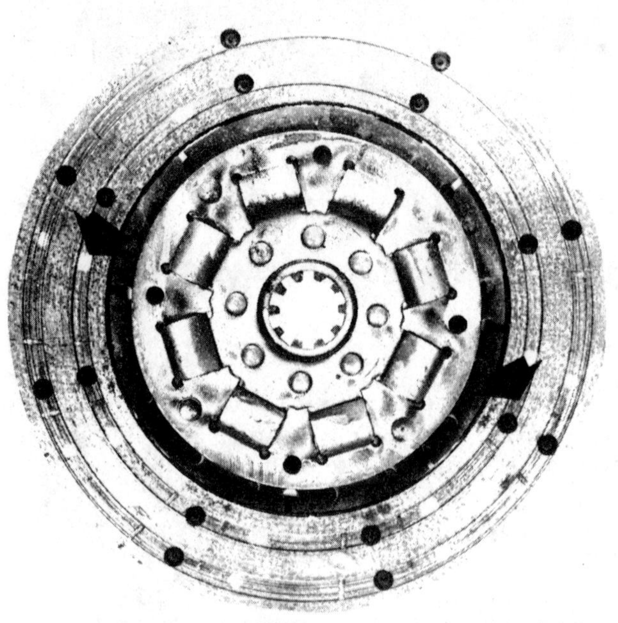

Scored clutch facings indicate that the pressure plate is likewise scored.

INSTALLING

Place a light coating of molybdnium-based grease in the pilot bearing in the flywheel and the splines of the clutch disc. Align the clutch disc with a tool, and then install the pressure plate assembly, locating it properly on the dowels. Tighten the screws evenly and alternately to 12-15 ft-lbs. Remove the locator tool.

Clean the machined surfaces of the engine and the clutch housing. Apply a light film of lubricant to the input shaft splines. **CAUTION: Excessive lubrication can damage the clutch disc.** Make sure that the release bearing and lever are installed properly.

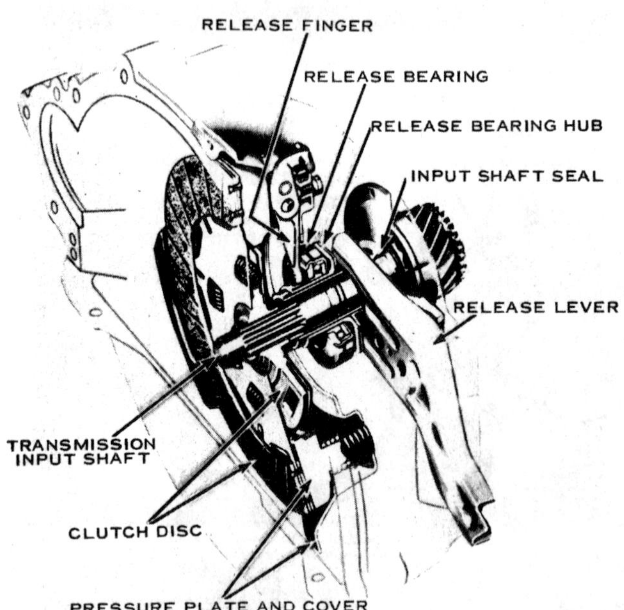

Phantom view of the clutch.

Align the splines on the input shaft with the splines in the clutch disc. Move the transmission forward until the input shaft enters the bearing in the crankshaft. Make certain that the clutch housing is seated in the two dowels, then install the attaching bolts. Torque the two dowel pins through-bolts to 23-33 ft-lbs. Torque the remaining clutch housing-to-engine bolts to the same torque. *NOTE: It may be necassary to raise the front of the engine to enter the input shaft in the clutch disc hub and pilot bearing.* Install the two engine rear plate attaching bolts at the front side of the engine rear plate.

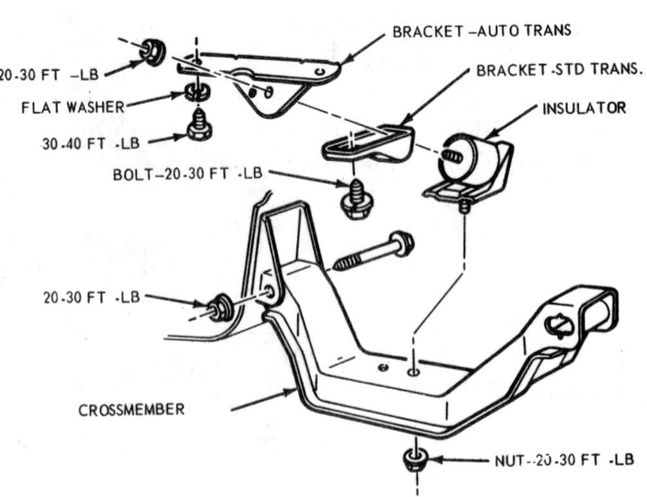

Rear engine mount.

After positioning the clutch disc, it must be aligned to the pilot bearing in the flywheel with this special tool so that you can install the transmission.

Raise the engine and transmission assembly into its normal operating position and secure the crossmember to the extension housing and to the body. Torque all attaching bolts. Remove the jack.

Insert the speedometer cable in the extension housing and secure it with the cap screw. Install the starter motor.

Apply a film of grease on the ball end of the clutch release cable and fit the cable to the clutch release lever. Adjust the clutch pedal free play. Install the release lever dust cover.

Remove Tool T70P-7095-A from the extension housing. Install the driveshaft, align the mating marks, and assemble the driveshaft to the rear U-joint flange.

Fill the transmission to the bottom of the filler hole with the specified lubricant. Raise the vehicle, remove the stands, and lower the vehicle to the ground. Working through the hood opening, install the flywheel uppermost housing-to-engine bolts.

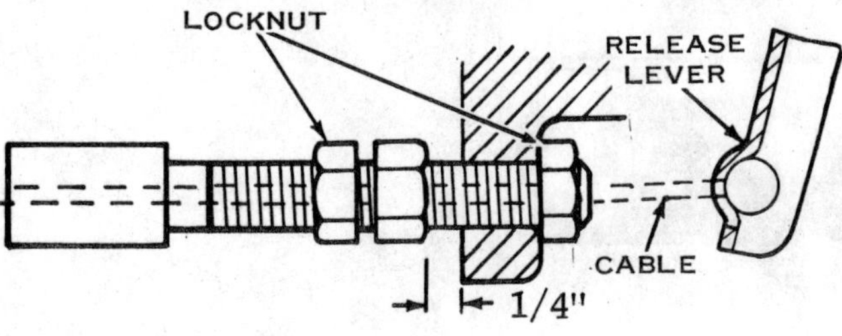

Details of the clutch cable adjustment.

Install the floor mounted shift lever. Position the floor mat, then install the two front attaching screws in each step plate. Install the two kick pads. Check the gearshift lever operation.

CLUTCH PEDAL FREE PLAY ADJUSTMENT

From under the car, release the cable locknut and adjusting nut at the flywheel housing boss. Pull the cable toward the front of the car until free movement of the release lever is eliminated.

Holding the cable in this position, place a 1/4-inch spacer against the flywheel housing boss (on the engine side). Run the adjusting nut against the spacer finger-tight. Tighten the locknut against the adjusting nut, being careful not to disturb the adjustment. Torque the locknut to 40-60 ft-lbs and remove the spacer.

FOUR-SPEED TRANSMISSION

These 4-speed transmissions are of the fully synchronized type with all gears, except the reverse gear, being in constant mesh. All forward speed changes are accomplished through forged blocker ring synchronized units.

The constant mesh gears, that is the input shaft gear, the three other forward gears on the output

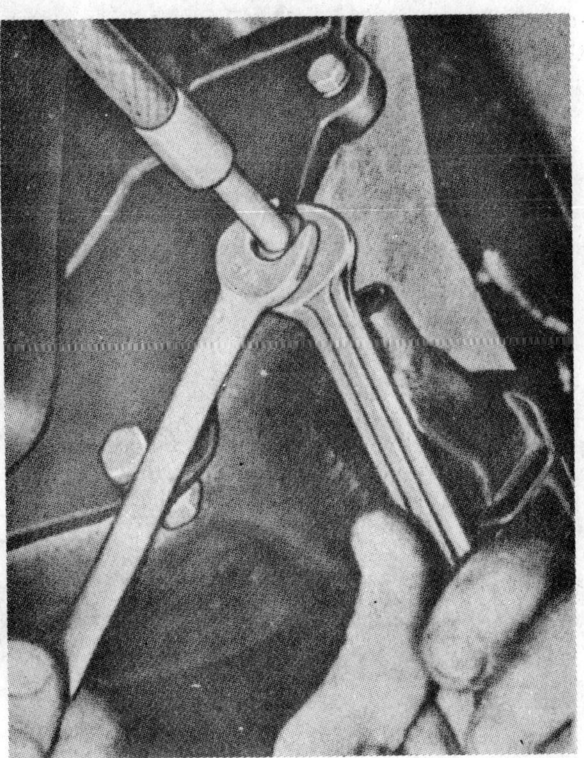

Adjusting the clutch cable.

shaft, and the corresponding gears on the countershaft gear, are helically cut. The reverse gear on the countershaft gear has straight-cut spur teeth which mesh, through an idler gear, with spur teeth on the outside of the first-second gear synchronizer sleeve.

Gear selection is by means of a floor shift lever. The shift lever is attached directly to a single selector rail, internally mounted in the transmission, which has assembled to it a selector lever. Movement of the shift lever, and thereby the selector rail, causes the selector lever to locate in the appropriate selector fork and move it to the required position. Movement of the first-second or third-fourth selector fork causes the appropriate synchronizer sleeve to move as necessary to engage with the dog teeth on the required gear. When reverse gear is required, movement of the reverse selector relay lever draws the reverse idler gear into mesh with both the reverse gear on the countershaft gear and on the output shaft.

Engagement of two gears at once is prevented by means of a selector interlock plate pivoted in the transmission case, (German). This plate engages with the selector forks which are not in use and holds them positively in the disengaged position. In the English version, engagement of two gears at once is prevented by a C-cam pivoted in the transmission top cover on the right-hand side. This engages with the shift forks which are not in use and holds them positively in the disengaged position. The selector forks are not attached to the selector rail. The first-second and third-fourth forks, while they are mounted on the rail, are free to slide. Gear engagement only takes place when the selector lever locates in the appropriate fork and moves it into the required position.

Selective snap rings compensate for tolerances which must be allowed in manufacture. Excessive end play or backlash can be eliminated without unnecessarily close, and thus expensive, tolerances and fits. Whenever overhauling the gear case, or a part of the case that involves removing a snap ring, always install new snap rings, never install snap rings that have been used Every care should be taken to ensure that the correct size snap ring is selected and properly installed.

REMOVING THE TRANSMISSION

See the clutch section of this chapter.

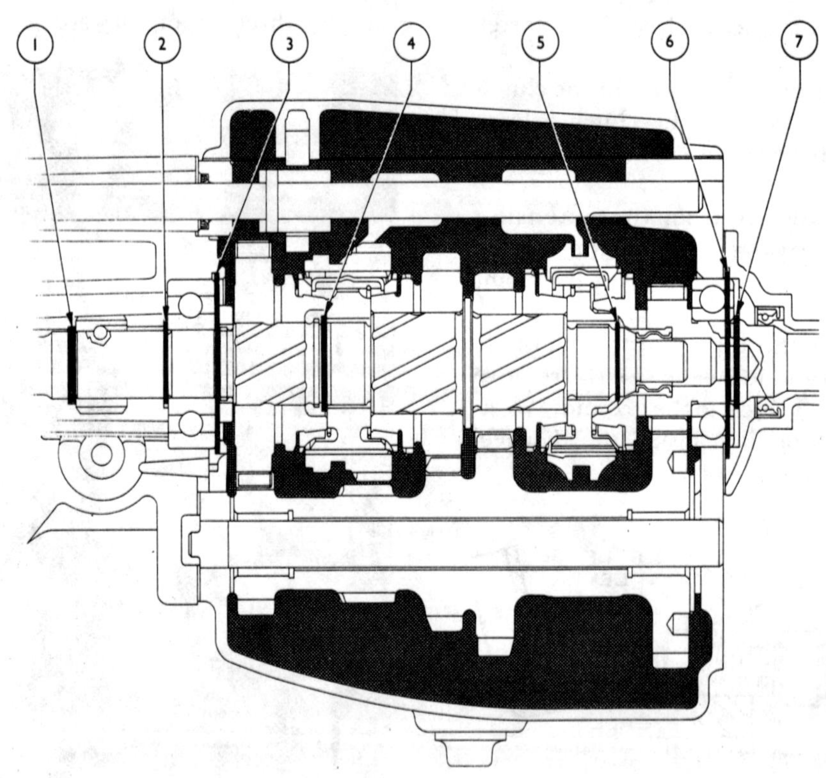

Snap ring locations.

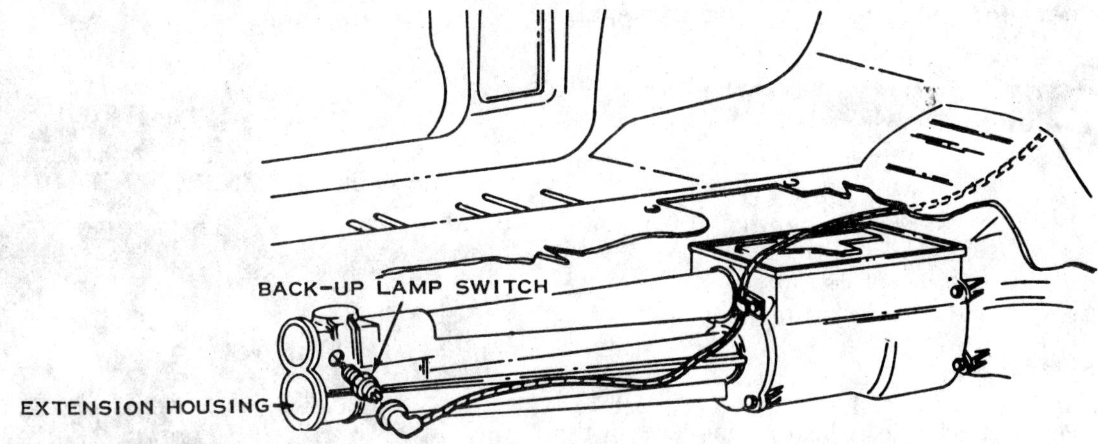

Position of the back-up light switch.

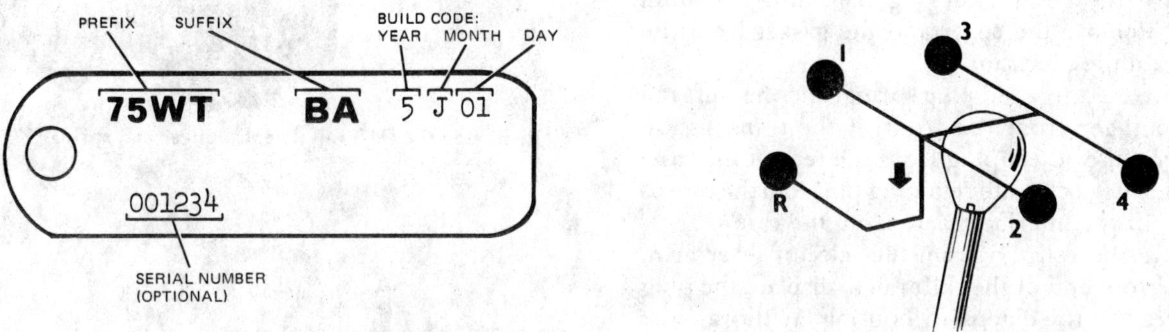

Transmission code plate.

Gear shift pattern for the four-speed transmission.

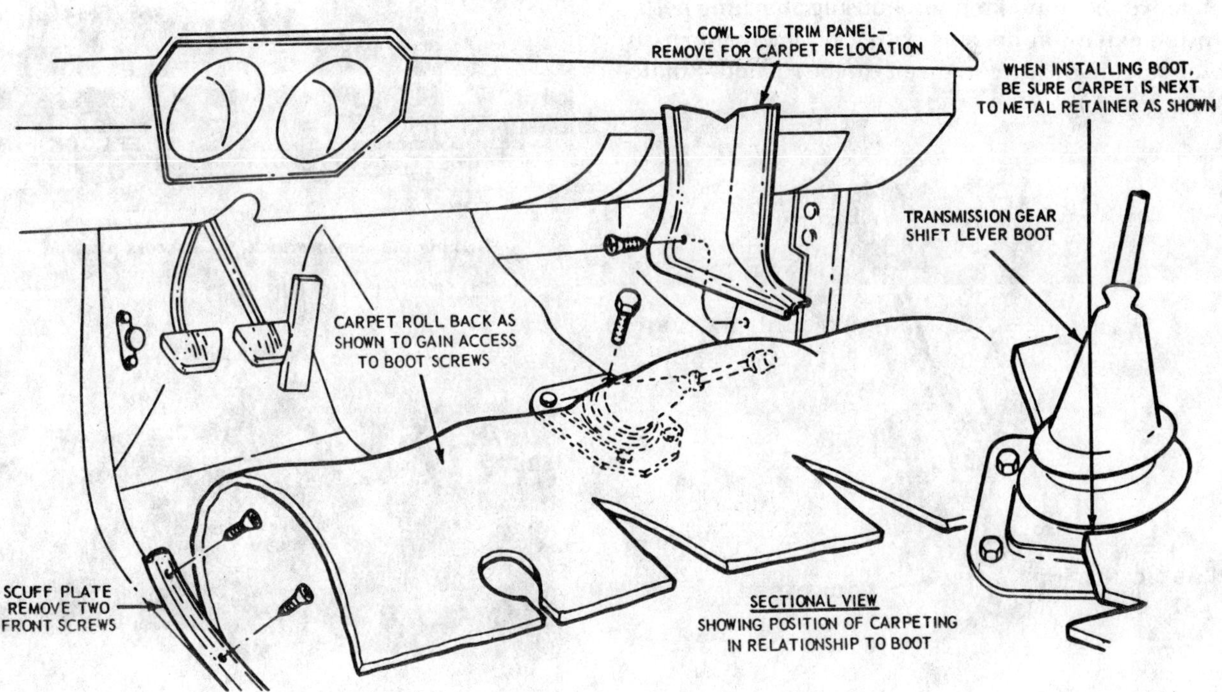

Details of transmission removal.

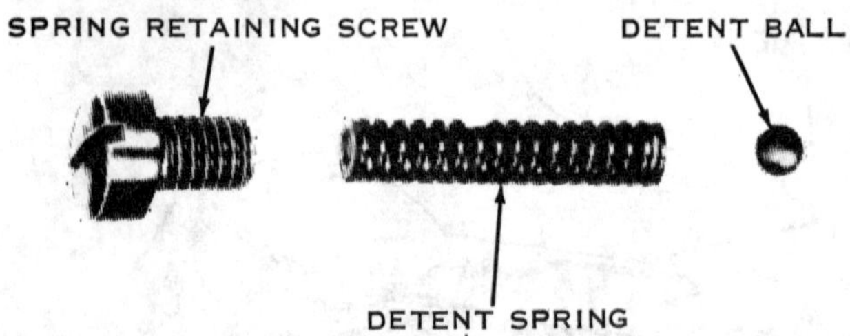

Detent ball and spring.

DISASSEMBLING

Remove the clutch release bearing and lever or the converter. Remove the clutch or converter housing attaching bolts and remove the housing.

Remove the cover attaching bolts with a 10mm wrench. Remove the cover and the gasket from the case. Drain the lubricant.

Remove the threaded plug spring, and the shift rail detent plunger from the front of the transmission case. Drive the access plug from the rear of the case. Drive the interlock plate retaining pin from the case as shown. Lift the interlock plate from the case.

Remove the roll pin from the selector lever arm. Tap the front end of the shift rail to displace the plug at the rear of the extension housing. Withdraw the shift rail from the extension housing and case as shown. Lift the selector arm and the shift fork from the case.

Remove the four extension housing attaching bolts. Tap the extension housing with a plastic hammer to loosen it from the case so that it can be rotated. Rotate

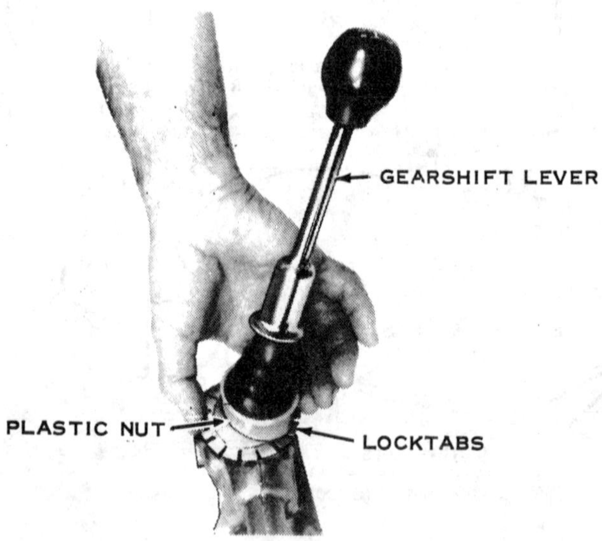

Removing the shift lever.

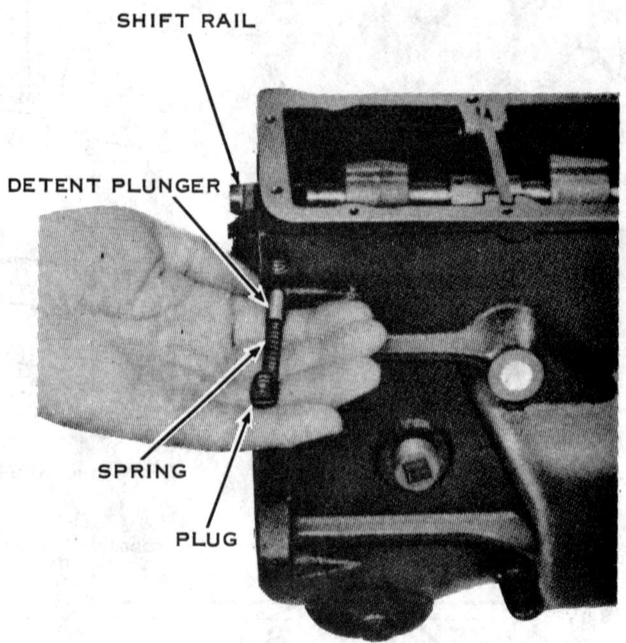

Removing the shift rail detent plunger and spring.

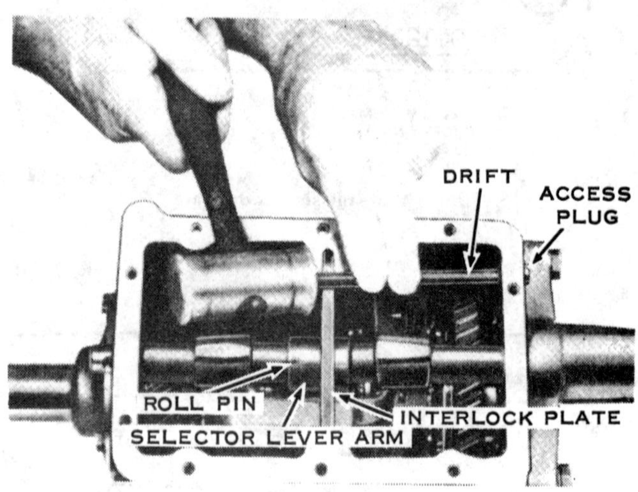

Driving out the interlock plate access plug.

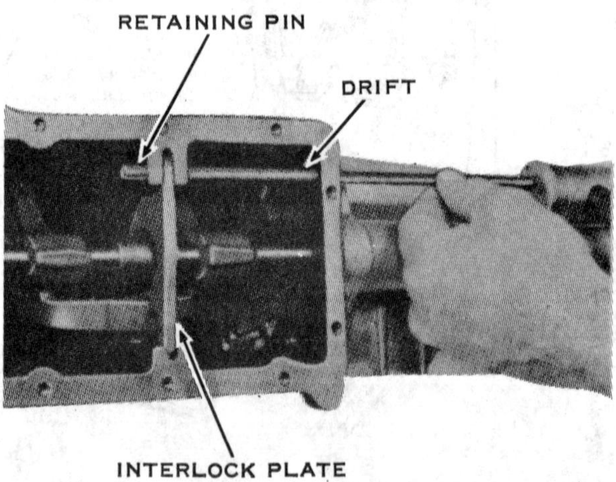

Removing the interlock plate retaining pin.

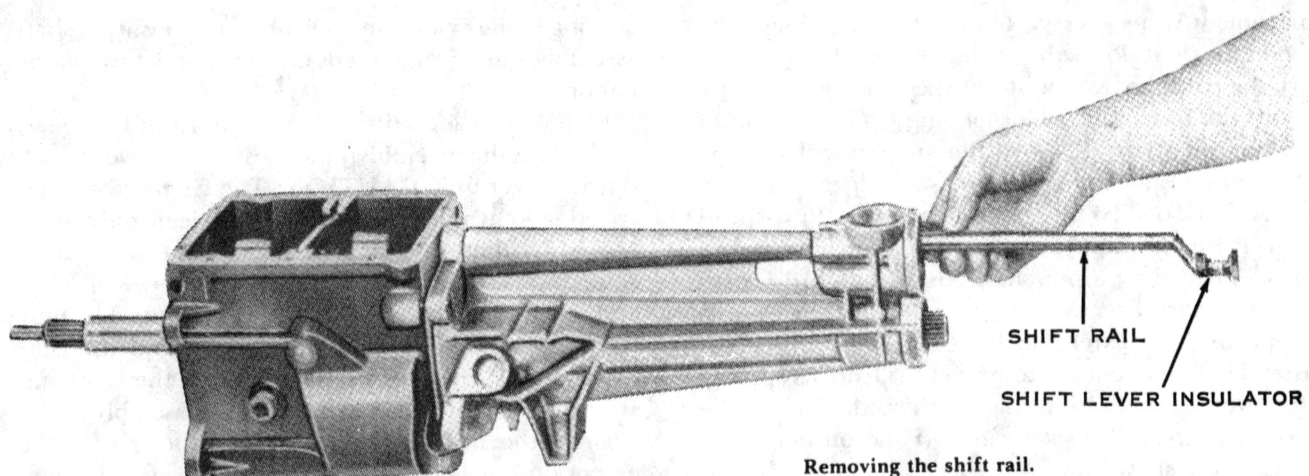

Removing the shift rail.

the housing to align the countershaft with the cutaway in the extension housing flange. Using a brass drift, drive the countershft rearward until it just clears the front of the case. Install a dummy shaft in the case and gear until the countershaft gear can be lowered to the bottom of the case, then remove the countershaft.

Using a slide hammer to pull out the reverse idler gear shaft.

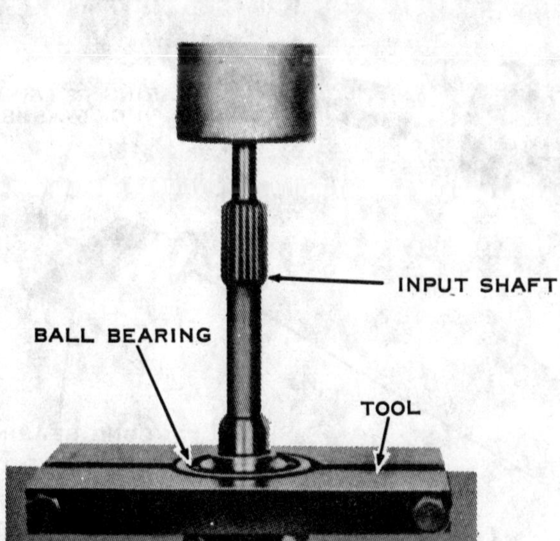

Removing the input shaft bearing in a press.

Lift the extension housing and mainshaft from the case as an assembly.

Remove the four 10mm input shaft bearing retainer attaching bolts. Remove the input shaft and bearing retainer from the case as an assembly.

Remove the reverse idler gear shaft from the rear of the case. Remove the reverse idler gear.

Remove the bearing retaining washers, bearings (19 each end) dummy shaft, and spacer rom the countershaft gear.

Remove the bearing retainer and the pilot bearing from the input shaft gear. **CAUTION: Do not remove the ball bearing from the input shaft unless re-**

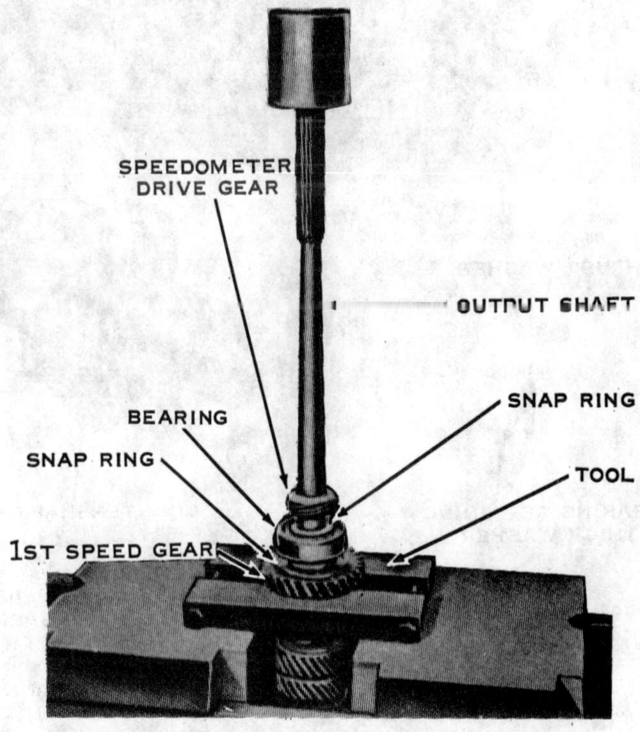

Removing the 1-2 synchronizer unit from the output shaft.

placement is necessary. Remove the snap ring from the input shaft. Press the shaft out of the ball bearing. Pry the input shaft seal out of the bearing retainer.

Lift the fourth-gear blocker ring from the front of the output shaft. Remove the snap ring from the forward end of the output shaft and discard it.

Position Tool T69P-4621-A behind the third-speed gear. Place the output shaft and extension housing in a press. Press the output shaft out of the third-fourth speed synchronizer assembly and the third gear, while supporting the extension housing and output shaft assembly from beneath to prevent it from dropping. Remove the snap ring and washer, then slide the second gear and blocker ring off the output shaft. Discard the snap ring.

Disassemble the synchronizer assembly by pulling the sleeve off the hub and removing the inserts and springs.

Remove the snap ring that retains the output shaft bearing in the extension housing. Tap the output shaft assembly out of the extension housing with a plastic hammer.

Position Tool T69P-4621-A behind the first gear, then place the assembly in a press to remove the 1-2 synchronizer unit. **CAUTION: The first-and-second speed synchronizer and hub is serviced only as an assembly, therefore no attempt should be made to separate the hub from the shaft.** The sleeve, springs, and inserts may be removed from the hub. The only parts that can be serviced are the springs and inserts. If the hub or sleeve is worn or damaged, the shaft and synchronizer must be replaced as an assembly.

Drive the shift rail bushing from the rear of the extension housing with a 9/16 inch socket and extension. **CAUTION: Do not remove the bushing if serviceable.** Pry the shift rail seal from the rear of the transmission case. Remove the remaining shift linkage from the case.

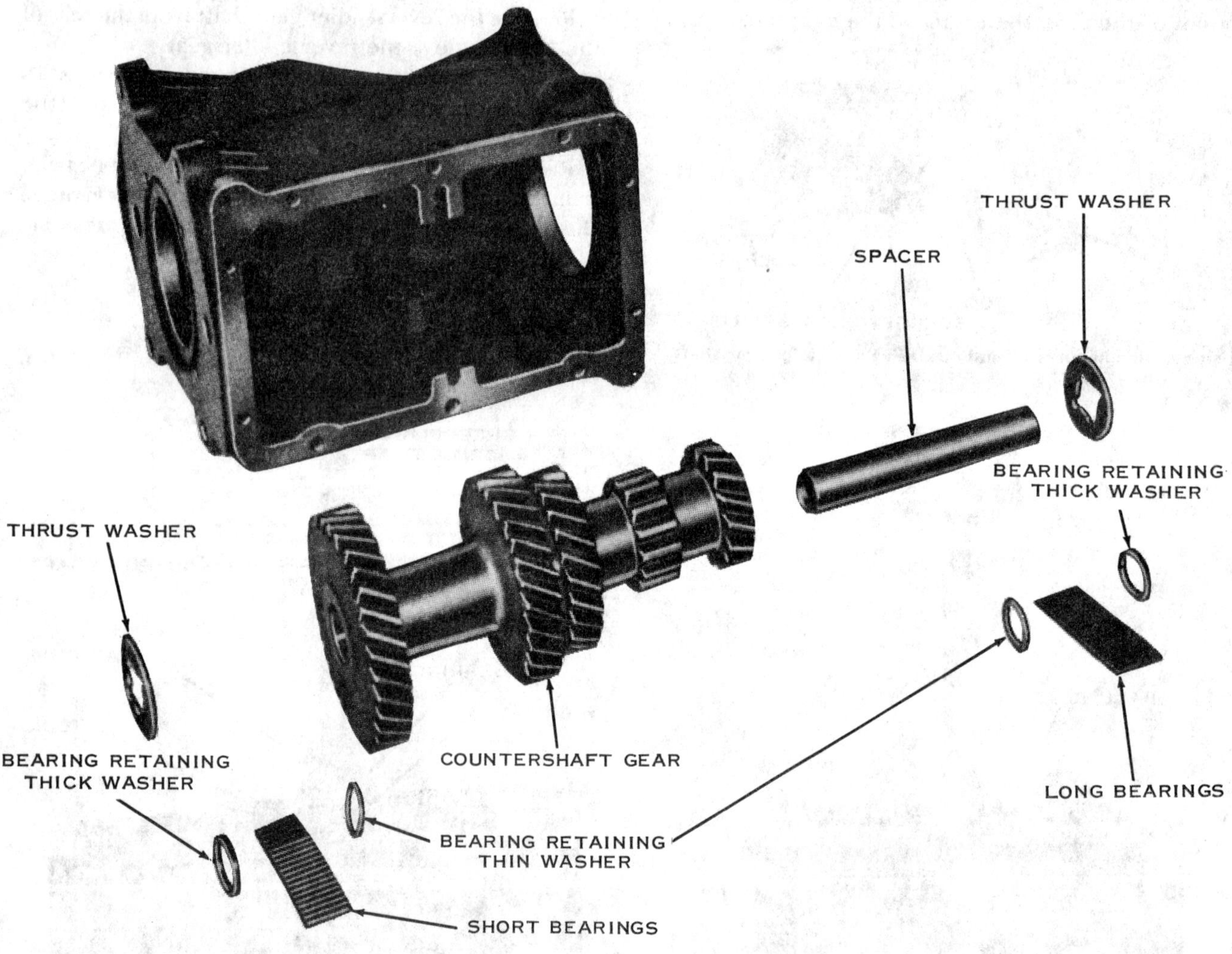

Disassembled view of the countershaft gear parts.

CLEANING AND INSPECTING

Cleaning

Wash all parts, except the ball bearings and seals, in a suitable cleaning solvent. Brush or scrape all foreign matter from the parts. Be careful not to damage any parts with the scraper. **CAUTION: Do not clean, wash or soak transmission seals in cleaning solvents.** Dry all parts with compressed air.

Rotate the ball bearings in a cleaning solvent until all lubricant is removed. Hold the bearing assembly to prevent it from rotating and dry it with compressed air. Lubricate the bearings with approved transmission lubricant and wrap them in a clean, lint-free cloth or paper until ready for use.

Clean the magnet welded to the bottom of the case with kerosene or mineral spirits.

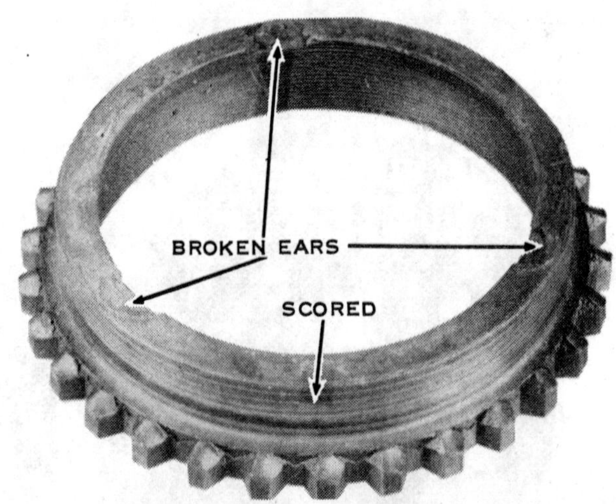

The synchronizer blocking ring should be inspected for wear, and discarded if any of the tangs are cracked or broken off.

Inspecting

Inspect the transmission case for cracks, worn or damaged bearings bores, damaged threads, or other damage that could affect the operation of the transmission. Inspect the front face of the case for small nicks or burrs that could cause misalignment of the transmission with the flywheel housing. Remove all small nicks or burrs with a fine stone.

Replace a cover that is bent or distorted. Make sure that the vent hole in the cover is open.

Check the condition of the shift levers, forks, shift rails and the lever and shafts.

Examine the ball bearing races for cracks, wear, or roughness. Inspect the balls for looseness, wear, end play, or other damage. Check the bearings for looseness in the bores. If any of these conditions exist, replace the bearings. Replace roller bearings that are broken, worn, or rough.

Replace the countershaft (cluster) gear if the teeth are chipped, broken, or worn. Replace the countershaft if it is bent, scored, or worn.

Replace the reverse idler gear or sliding gear if the teeth are chipped, worn, or broken. Replace the idler gear shaft if bent, worn, or scored.

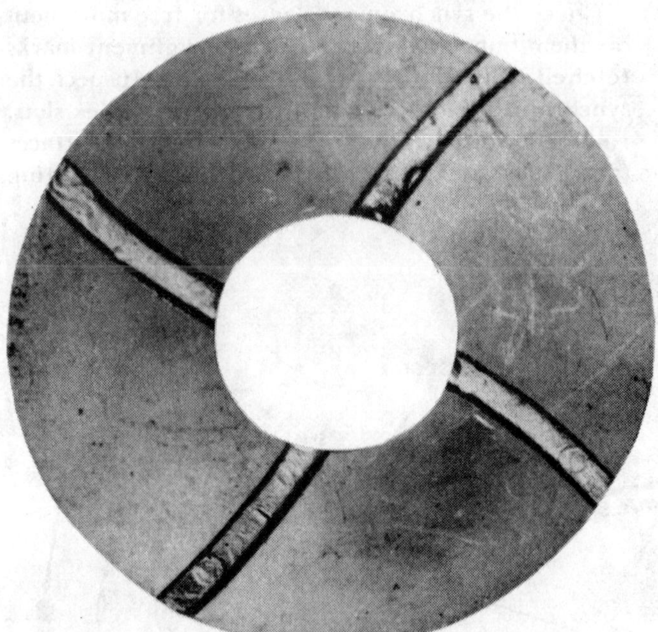

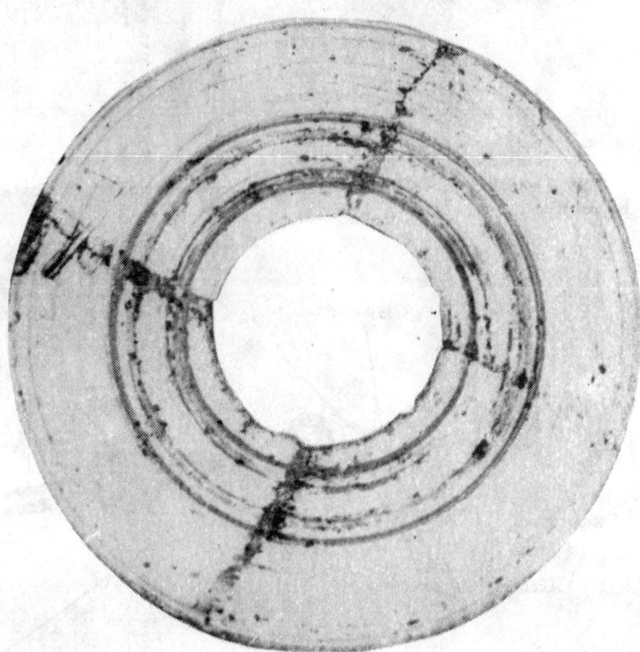

The cluster gear thrust washers wear (right), and must be replaced to maintain the correct end play. The washer at the left is a new one for comparison.

The bearing at the left has turned on the shaft, causing the inner race to gall. The bearing race at the right shows an indentation from one defective ball bearing.

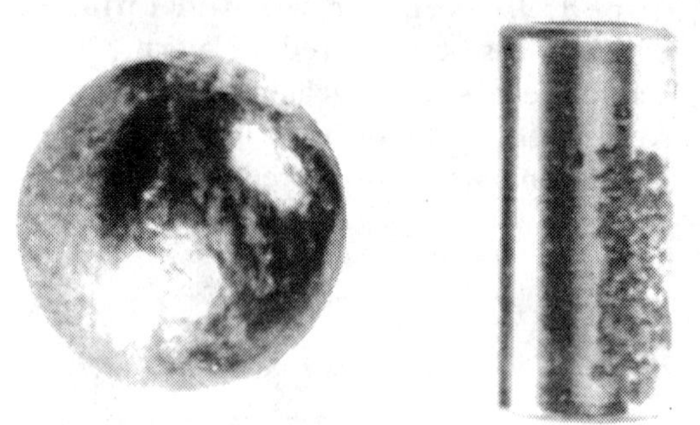

Galled ball (left) and roller bearings. Such defective parts must be replaced.

Replace the input shaft and gear if the splines are damaged or if the teeth are chipped, worn, or broken. If the roller bearing surface in the bore of the bearing is worn or rough, or if the cone surface is damaged, replace the gear and the gear rollers. Replace all other gears that are chipped, broken or worn.

Check the synchronizer sleeves for free movement on their hubs. Make sure that the alignment marks (etched marks) are properly indexed. Inspect the synchronizer blocking rings for widened index slots, rounded clutch teeth, and smooth internal surfaces (must have machined grooves). With the blocker ring

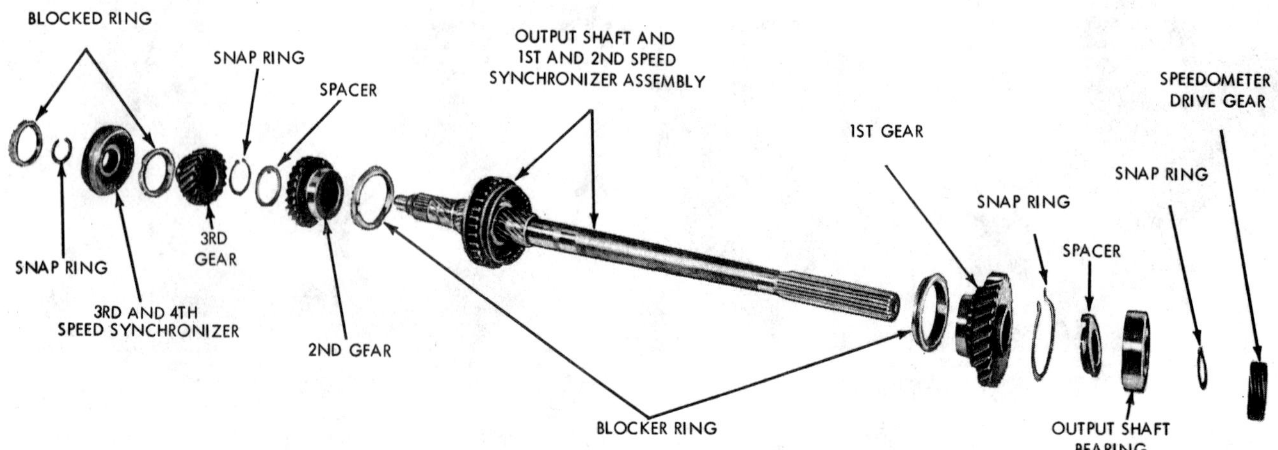

Exploded view of the output shaft.

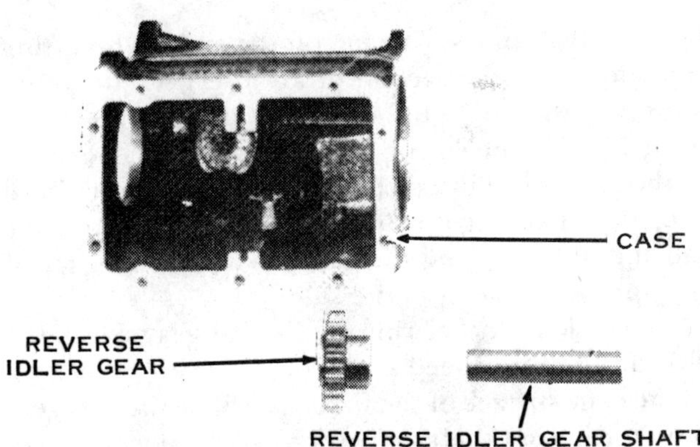

Disassembled view of the idler gear and shaft.

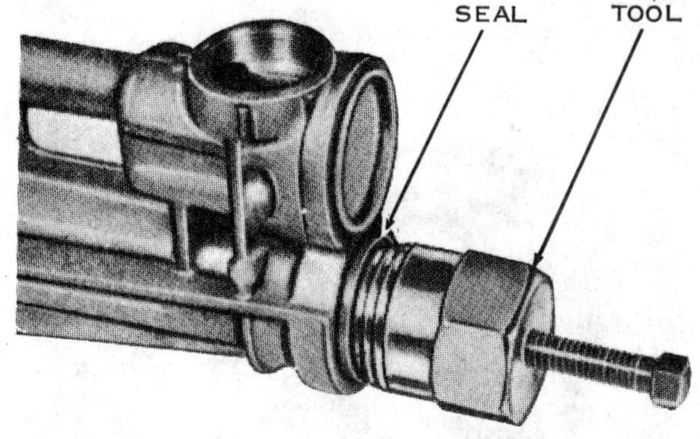

Removing the seal from the extension housing.

on the cone, the distance between the face of the blocker ring and the clutch teeth on the gear must not be less than 0.010 inches.

Replace the speedometer drive gear if the teeth are damaged. Make certain to install the correct size replacement gear.

Replace the output shaft if there is evidence of wear or if any of the splines are damaged.

Inspect the bushing and the seal in the extension housing. Replace them if they are worn or damaged. The bushing and/or seal should be replaced after the extension housing has been installed on the transmission.

Replace the seal in the input shaft bearing retainer. Replace the seals on the cam and shafts.

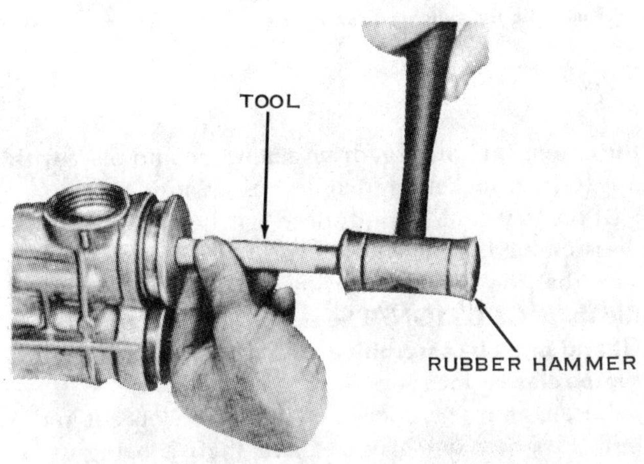

Installing a new shift rail bushing and seal.

ASSEMBLING THE TRANSMISSION

Seat the new shift rail seal in the rear of the transmission case. If the shift rail bushing was removed from

Installing a new seal in the extension housing.

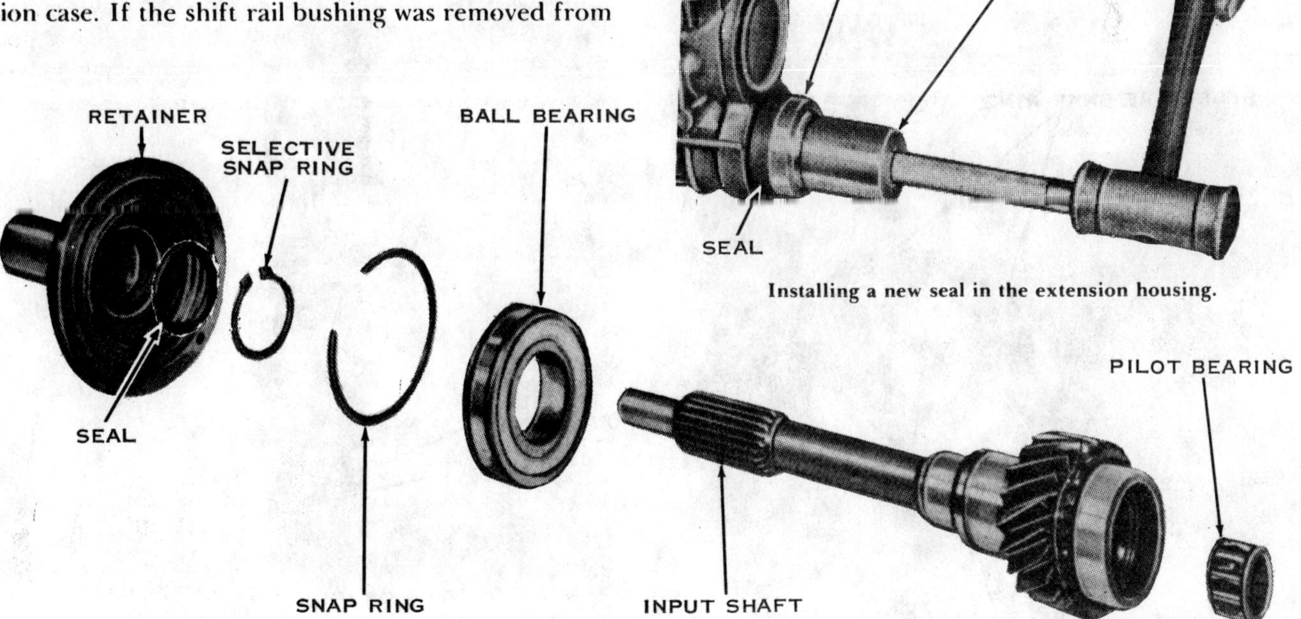

Exploded view of the input shaft.

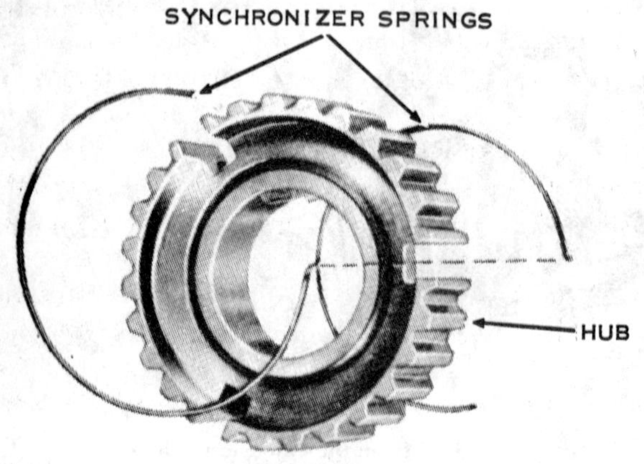

Installing the synchronizer spring, as discussed in the text.

the extension housing, drive a new one into place with a 9/16-inch socket wrench and extension.

If the first-and-second speed synchronizer has been disassembled, slide the sleeve over the hub making sure that the shift fork groove is toward the front of the shaft. **CAUTION: The sleeve and hub are a select fit and must be assembled with the etch marks in the same relative location.**

Locate an insert in each of the three slots cut in the hub. If a new synchronizer and shaft is being used, clean all traces of preservative from the hub, sleeve, inserts and springs. Oil all parts at time of assembly. Install an insert spring inside the synchronizer sleeve beneath the inserts. The tab on the end of the spring must locate in the section of an insert. Fit the other spring to the opposite face of the synchronizer unit, ensuring that the spring tab locates in the same insert as the spring just installed and is in the same rotational direction. Looking down at the synchronizer unit, the tab end of one spring should be in line with the tab of the spring on the opposite side.

Assemble a blocker ring on the first gear side of the first-and-second speed synchronizer. Apply lubricant to the cone surface of the first gear. Slide the first gear onto the output shaft so that the cone surface engages the blocker ring. Position the spacer on the shaft making certain that the larger diameter is toward the rear of the shaft.

Place the master spacer, Tool T70P-7154, in the output shaft bearing bore of the extension housing. Determine the thickness of the snap ring required to remove all end play from the master gauge. Then measure the width of the output shaft bearing outer race with a micrometer. The difference in thickness between the master gauge and the bearing outer race will determine the thickness of the selective snap ring which will finally be used to eliminate end play. If the bearing race thickness is more than that stamped on the master gauge, the snap ring thickness must be decreased by that closest to the available snap ring. If the thickness is less, the snap ring thickness must be increased.

Position the selected snap ring and the bearing on the output shaft. Position Tool T69P-4621-A on the

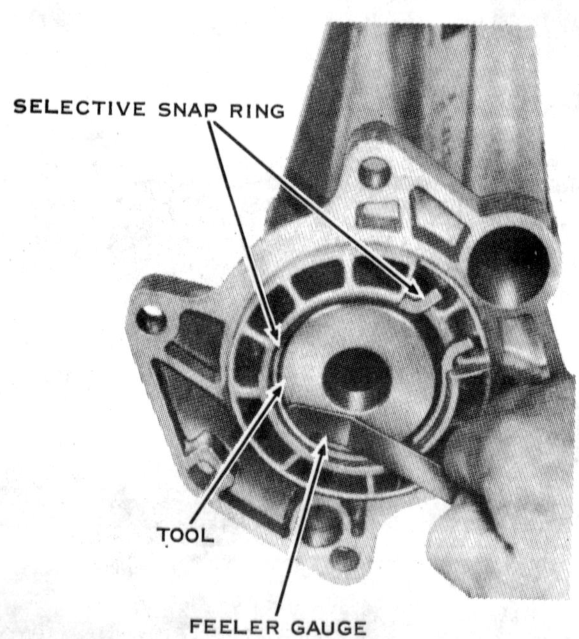

To determine the size of the snap ring needed, place the master spacer in the output shaft bearing bore, as shown, and then measure the clearance.

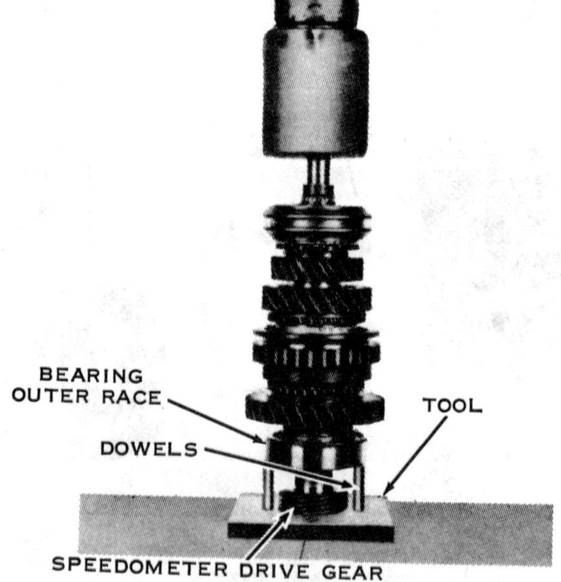

Pressing on the speedometer gear, using the special tool shown to position the gear properly.

shaft, then place the assembly in a press. Press the bearing into place. Secure the bearing with the thickest snap ring that will fit the groove in the output shaft.

Slide the synchronizer sleeve over the hub and locate an insert in each of the three slots cut in the sleeve. The sleeve and hub are a select fit and must be assembled with the etch marks in the same relative location. If a new synchronizer assembly is being installed, slide the sleeve off the hub and clean all traces of preservative from the hub, sleeve, inserts, and springs. Lightly oil all parts.

Install an insert spring, inside the synchronizer sleeve beneath the inserts. The tab on the end of the spring must locate in the U-section of an insert. Fit the other spring to the opposite face of the synchronizer unit, ensuring that the spring tab locates in the same insert as the spring just installed and is in the same rotational direction. Looking down at the synchronizer unit, the tab end of one spring should be in line with the tab of the spring on the opposite side.

Position the second gear and blocker ring on the output shaft so that the dog teeth face rearward. Install the washer and snap ring. Position the third gear on the output shaft so that the dog teeth face forward. Apply lubricant to the cones of the gears. Assemble the blocker ring on the third-gear cone.

Position the third-fourth synchronizer assembly on the output shaft, with the hub boss facing forward. Position Tool T69P-4621-A so that it butts against the boss on the synchronizer hub. Place the entire unit, extension end up, in a press and push the synchronizer assembly onto the output shaft as far as possible.

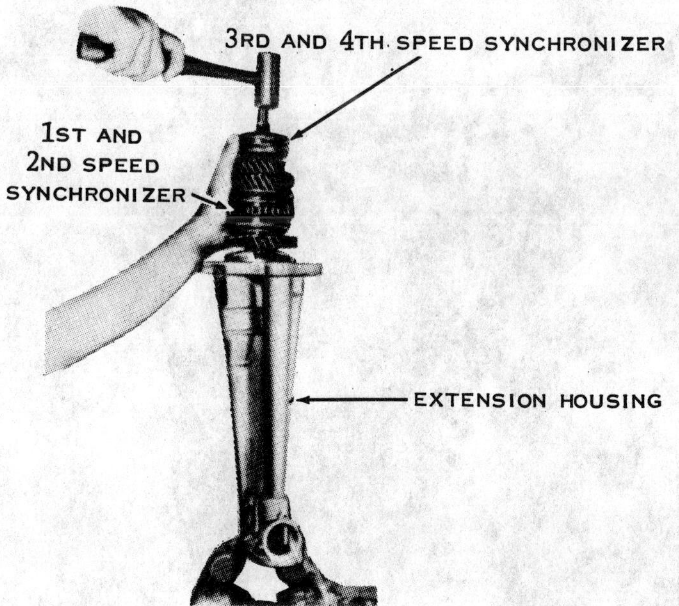

Installing the output shaft assembly into the extension housing.

Retain the third-fourth synchronizer assembly to the output shaft with a snap ring. Pull up on the synchronizer assembly so that the snap ring is tight in its groove.

Prior to assembling the output shaft and extension housing assembly into the transmission case, apply lubricant to the cone of the gear and place the fourth-gear blocker ring on the input shaft gear cone.

Press the speedometer drive gear onto the shaft until the dowels of the tool just contact the bearing outer race. **CAUTION: The dowels must contact the bearing outer race to properly locate the speedometer drive gear on the shaft.**

Coat the bearing bore of the extension housing with grease. Install the output shaft in the housing. It may be necessary to tap the shaft with a plastic hammer while holding the two synchronizer sleeves firmly to prevent sleeve separation from the hubs. Secure it to the extension housing with the selective snap ring that was previously installed.

Press the bearing on the input shaft, making sure that the snap ring groove is toward the front end of the shaft. Secure the bearing to the shaft with the thickest selective snap ring.

Slide the spacer and Tool T71P-7111-A into the countershaft gear. Position a thin bearing retaining washer, one at each end of the dummy shaft. Coat the 38 bearings with lubricant. Load the 19 long bearings in the snall end of the gear and the 19 short bearings in the large end of gear. Fit a thick retaining washer over each end of dummy shaft. Coat each thrust washer with grease and position one on each end of the dummy shaft. Make sure that the tabs are in the same relative position so they can engage the slots provided in the case when the gear is lowered into place. Loop a piece of rope or wire around each end of the gear. Carefully install the countershaft gear and rope

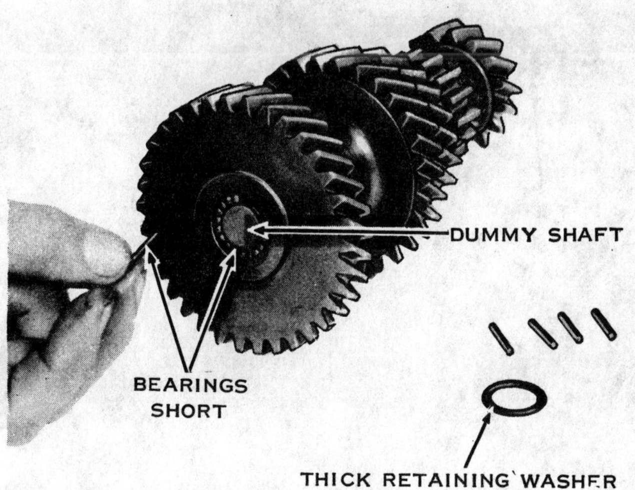

Assembling the countershaft gear.

through the rear end of the case. Lower the gear into place, being careful not to disturb the thrust washers and making sure that the tabs engage the slots in the case.

Apply lubricant to the reverse idler gear shaft. If the selector lever relay was removed, position it on the pivot pin. Secure the lever on the pin with a spring clip. Hold the gear in the lever with the long hub toward the rear of the case. Slide the reverse idler gear shaft into place. Seat the shaft in the case with a copper hammer.

Install a new seal in the input shaft bearing retainer. Assemble the input shaft to the transmission case using a new bearing retainer O-ring. If necessary, tap the outer race of the bearing with a copper hammer evenly and alternately until the outer snap ring is seated against the case. **CAUTION: Do not tap on the input shaft. Tapping the input shaft will result in the load passing through the bearings and may damage the races and/or bearings.**

Carefully slide the third-and-fourth speed synchronizer sleeve into the fourth-speed position (forward) to provide clearance.

Position a new gasket on the extension housing. Make certain that the input shaft pilot bearing is lubricated and installed in the shaft. Slide the extension housing and output shaft into place, being careful not to disturb the third-and-fourth speed synchronizer. Align the cutaway in the extension housing flange with the countershaft bore in the rear of the transmission case.

Lift the countershaft gear into place with the cord or wire previously installed, then slip the countershaft into place making sure that both thrust washers are n place. Make sure that the flat on the countershaft is toward the top of the case and in a horizontal position, then tap it into the case with a brass hammer until the front of the shaft is flush with the case.

Use a piece of rope to lower the countershaft gear assembly into the housing. The rope is needed to lift the assembly into position when installing the countershaft.

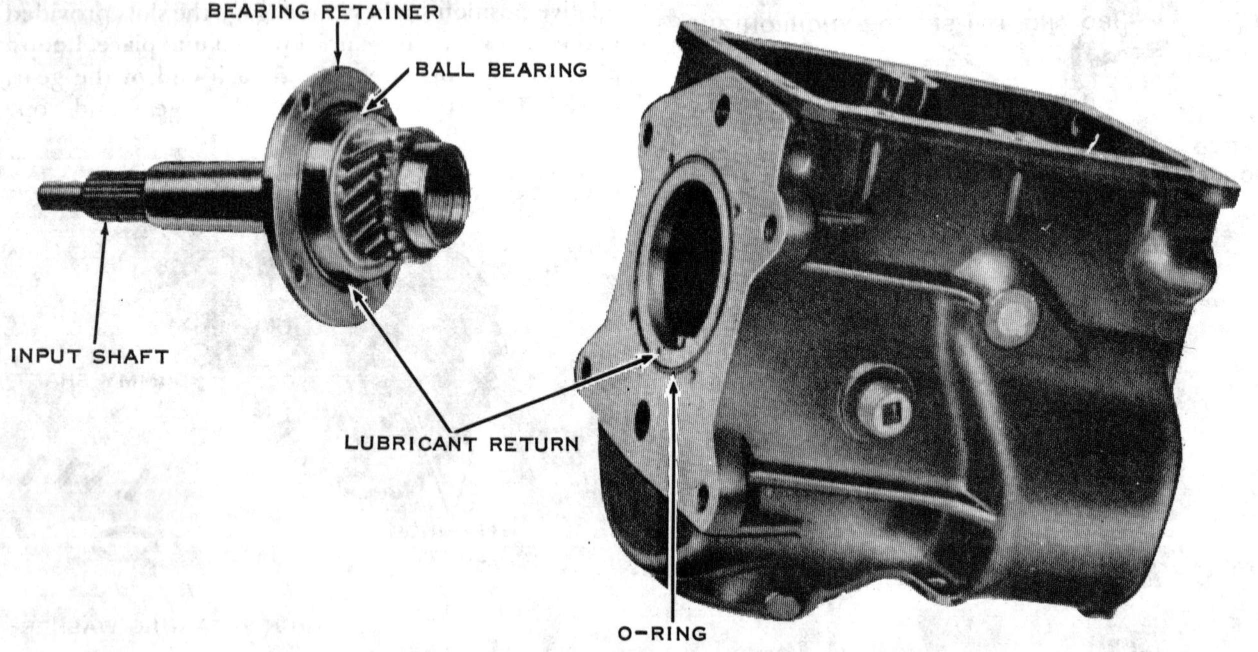

Installing the input shaft assembly into the transmission case.

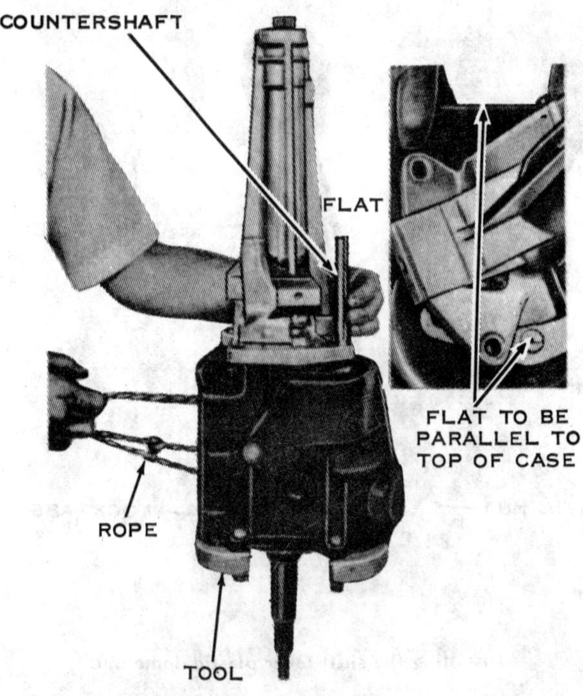

Installing the countershaft, as discussed in the text.

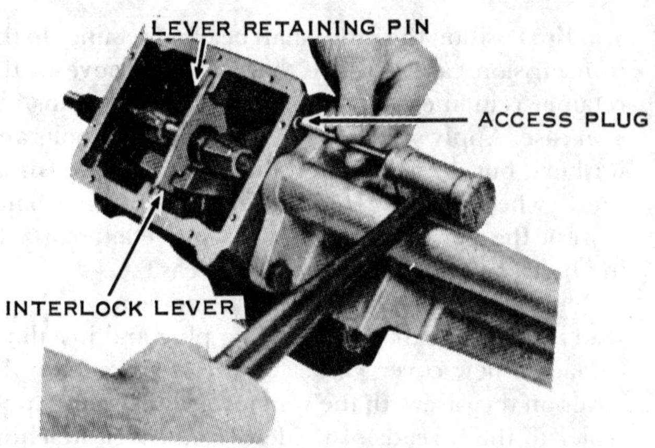

Installing the interlock lever access plug.

Place the shift forks in the synchronizer sleeves. Position the interlock lever and install a new retaining pin. Lubricate the shift rail oil seal and slide the shift rail through the extension housing, transmission case, and the first-and-second speed shift fork. Position the selector arm on the rail, then slide the rail through the third-and-fourth speed shift fork, then through the front of the case until the center detent is aligned with the detent plunger bore. Install a new retaining pin in the selector arm. Install the detent plunger and spring. Install the plug with sealer. Install a new access plug in the rear of the case.

Rotate the extension housing to align the bolt holes, hen install the attaching bolts loosely. Prior to tightening the extension housing bolts, make sure that the shift rail slides freely in the bore. If it binds, rotate the extension housing slightly to free the rail, then push the housing into the case. Apply sealer to the four attaching bolts. Torque the bolts, making sure that the housing does not interfere with the reverse idler or countershafts.

Position a new oil seal so that the tension spring and the lip of the sealing element face in the direction of the transmission case. Drive the seal into the retainer until it bottoms.

Position a new O-ring in the groove provided in the face of the transmission case. Apply grease to the input shaft seal journal area. **CAUTION: Exercise care when installing the retainer to prevent damage to the**

Sliding the mainshaft and extension housing assembly into the transmission case.

seal lip. Position the input shaft bearing retainer to the transmission case. Ensure that the oil groove in the retainer is in line with the oil passage in the transmission case. Apply sealer to the four attaching bolts and washers, but do not tighten them at this time. Install the flywheel housing and torque the attaching bolts. Torque the transmission front bearing retainer attaching bolts. Coat the retainer with grease.

Reinstall the clutch release arm and bearing. Apply sealer to a new extension housing plug and install it.

Place a new cover gasket on the case. Position the cover on the case with the vent toward the rear. Apply sealer to the threads of the left-front cover attaching bolt to seal the bolt hole which communicates with the detent plunger hole. Attach the three T.R.S. switch wire retaining clips to the cover, using the cover bolts and a lockwasher between each clip and the cover. Install and torque the ten attaching bolts.

Install a new T.R.S. switch in the case bore if the old switch was damaged.

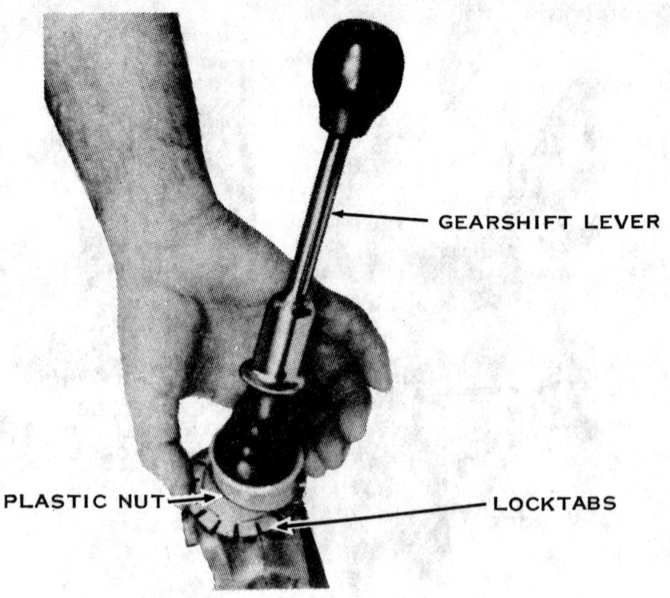

Installing the shift lever plastic dome nut.

SPECIFICATIONS

MODEL 75 WT TRANSMISSION

Transmission Lubricant		
Type	**Level**	**Capacity**
ESW-M2C83-C	To Bottom of Filler Hole	2.8 Pints

Torque Specifications	
Description	**Ft-Lb**
Input Shaft Bearing Retainer to Case Bolt	8-10
Extension Housing to Case Bolt	33-36
Cover to Case Screw	8-10
Filler Plug to Case	24-27
Seat Belt Warning Switch	15-20
Detent Plug	12-14

GEAR RATIOS – 1975

Engine	Transmission Model	1st	2nd	3rd	4th	Rev.
2.3 Liter S/W	75WT-7003-BA	3.358:1	1.809:1	1.258:1	1:1	3.365:1
2.3 Liter Sedan	75WT-7003-AA	3.651:1	1.968:1	1.368:1	1:1	3.66:1

GEAR RATIOS – 1976

Engine	Transmission Model	1st	2nd	3rd	4th	Rev.
2.3 Liter S/W ①	75WT-7003-BB	4.07:1	2.57:1	1.66:1	1:1	3.795:1
2.3 Liter Sedan ①	75WT-7003-AB	3.651:1	1.968:1	1.368:1	1:1	3.66:1
2.3 Liter S/W ②	75WT-7003-EB	3.358:1	1.809:1	1.258:1	1:1	3.365:1
2.3 Liter Sedan ②	75WT-7003-DB	3.651:1	1.968:1	1.368:1	1:1	3.66:1

① With 3.40/3.18 Axle
② With 2.79 Axle

Transmission Component End Play

Component	In Inches
Cluster Gear To Case	.006-.018

AUTOMATIC TRANSMISSION

Because of the complexity of an automatic transmission, only troubleshooting and external adjustments are discussed in this chapter.

TROUBLESHOOTING

The routine for diagnosing troubles in an automatic transmission requires you to follow certain procedures. Before any repairs or adjustments are made, certain checks must be made, and then the vehicle must be taken for a road test. For example, the transmission fluid level and the throttle linkage adjustment must be checked before any road test is undertaken.

The sequence in which the diagnosis is performed is most important. It must follow the recommended procedures of the Diagnosis Guide, which lists the steps in the order in which they must be taken. The Guide covers the likeliest causes of troubles first, especially those which do not require opening the transmission.

AUTOMATIC TRANSMISSION DIAGNOSIS GUIDE

1. Transmission fluid. Check the transmission fluid level. ☐ Full ☐ Overfull ☐ Low

The very first test to make of any automatic transmission complaint is that of the level and condition of the fluid. Too little fluid starves the hydraulic system and causes delay in clutch application, causing slippage. There's also danger of the pump taking in air and causing the fluid to foam, resulting in mushy application of clutches and bands and excessive wear. Too much fluid can be just as bad as too little. The gear train churns it up with the same results as the pump sucking air.

Certain fluid conditions are important to watch for, such as varnish on the dipstick, black fluid with the odor of a burned electrical coil, and friction material in the fluid. Varnish on the dipstick indicates the control valves, clutches, and gears are coated with varnish. Burned, black fluid means overheating and a clutch or band burned out.

Before checking the fluid be sure that it is warmed to operating temperature. Move the selector lever through all ranges to fill the clutches and servos. Then, with the engine idling and the selector lever in PARK, check the fluid level. It should be ¼" below the FULL mark on the dipstick, but never higher than the FULL mark. If there's too much fluid, take some out. If it's low, add some.

2. Engine idle. Too high an engine idle can cause rough initial shifts because of too much control pressure in applying the clutches. Be sure the engine idle speed is set to specifications. ☐ Performed

3. Linkage. Check the kickdown linkage by driving the vehicle at a road speed of approximately 40 mph and then depressing the accelerator to the floorboard. The transmission should shift back to second gear. ☐ O.K. ☐ Other

SHIFT SPEEDS — ACTUAL MPH
C3 AUTOMATIC TRANSMISSION — 2.3L-2V

Throttle	Range	Shift	OPS—RPM	SHIFT SPEEDS — ACTUAL MPH			
				1	2	3	4
Minimum (10"-15" Vacuum)	D	1-2	580-760	12-16	11-16	11-15	11-14
	D	2-3	700-990	17-21	16-21	15-20	15-19
	D	3-2	620-860	13-16	12-16	12-15	11-14
	D	2-1	340-450	7-9	7-9	6-9	6-8
	1	2-1	1060-1570	22-34	21-33	21-31	20-30
To Detent (Torque Demand)	D	1-2	750-1150	16-25	15-24	14-23	14-22
	D	2-3	1350-2050	29-45	27-43	26-41	25-40
	D	3-2	1700-Max.	37	36	34	33
Through Detent (W.O.T.)	D	1-2	1760-2130	38-47	35-45	34-43	33-41
	D	2-3	3100-3425	66-76	63-73	61-70	59-67
	D	3-2	3175-Max.	70	67	64	62
	D	3-1	1200-Max.	26	25	24	23

Axle Ratio	Tire Size	Use Column No.	Axle Ratio	Tire Size	Use Column No.
3.18:1	195 x 13, 70R x 13, CR70 x 13, BR70 x 13, 175 x 13, B78 x 13	1	3.40:1	B78 x 13	2
	B78 x 13	2		BR70 x 13, BR78 x 13	3
3.40:1	175 x 13, 70R x 13, CR70 x 13, 175 x 13	2	3.55:1	175 x 13, B78 x 13, B78 x 13, BR70 x 13	4

Shift speeds for the automatic transmission.

Converter Part Number	Nominal Size	Stall Ratio	Ident. No. ①	Transmission Model	Engine CID	Stall Speed
D1MP-7902-AA	10-1/4	2.64:1	BU	PEJ-B6	2000 cc	2400-2700
				PEJ-G	2300 cc	2625-2925
D4ZP-7902-BA	10-1/4	2.56:1	CL	PEJ-H	2300 cc	2225-2525
D4ZP-7902-AA	10-1/4	2.56:1	CJ	PEJ-J, E	2800 cc	2525-2825

① Converter identification is stamped on the converter cover adjacent to the converter drive stud.

Converter identification and stall speeds for the automatic transmission.

4. Stall test. Perform a stall test to check engine performance and for any sign of transmission slippage. A stall test is made in DRIVE position at full throttle to check engine performance, converter clutch operation, and the holding ability of the clutches and bands. To make a stall test, apply both the parking and service brakes. Connect a tachometer. Start the engine (thoroughly warmed), shift into DRIVE, and then open the accelerator wide. **CAUTION: While making this severe test, don't hold the throttle open for more than five seconds at a time.** After each test, move the selector lever to NEUTRAL and run the engine at about 1000 rpm for 20 seconds in order to cool the converter before making the next test. **CAUTION: If the engine speed exceeds the maximum specified limit, release the accelerator immediately because clutch or band slippage is indicated.** Additional abuse will destroy the slipping unit. If the stall speed is too high, band or clutch slippage is indicated and the transmission must be removed for service. When the stall test speeds are too low, the engine needs turning. ☐ Performed

5. Road test. Drive the car in each range and through all shifts, including forced downshifts, observing any irregularities of performance. The transmission should shift automatically at approximately the speeds shown. The shifts may occur at somewhat different speeds due to production tolerances and rear axle ratios, but this is not as important as the quality of the shifts, which must be smooth, responsive, and made with little noticeable engine speed-up. ☐ Road test completed

6. Pressure tests. CAUTION: The transmission must be at operating temperature. When the linkage is adjusted properly, all of the transmission shifts should occur within or close to the specified speeds. If the shifts do not occur within limits or if the transmission slips during shifts, it is necessary to attach testers to check the pressures. Attach a tachometer gauge to the engine and pressure gauges to the control pressure outlets at the transmission. Firmly apply the parking brake, and then start the engine. Make the tests as indicated according to the type of transmission.

SERVICE PROCEDURES

KICKDOWN LINKAGE ADJUSTMENTS

With the carburetor throttle held at wide-open throttle and the kickdown rod held against the "through detent" stop, adjust the kickdown adjusting screw to obtain 0.010-0.080" clearance between the screw and the throttle arm.

NEUTRAL-START SWITCH ADJUSTMENT

The neutral-start switch is designed to allow the engine to be cranked only when the selector lever is in NEUTRAL or PARK. If an adjustment is necessary, loosen the two switch attaching bolts, with the selector lever in NEUTRAL, rotate the switch body until you can insert a gauge pin (No. 43 drill) into the gauge pin holes as shown. **CAUTION: The gauge has to be inserted a full 31/64"** into the three holes of the switch.

Transmission	Range	Manifold Vacuum						
		Engine Idle Speed						Wide Open Throttle Thru Detent
		15" & Above	14"	13"	12"	11"	10" ①	
C4	D	55-86	55-91	55-97	55-102	55-107	98-110	143-164
	2, 1	55-122	55-117	55-117	55-116	55-116	90-115	143-164
	R	55-197	55-196	55-195	55-194	55-193		239-272
	P, N	55-86	55-91	55-97	55-102	55-107		

① On units equipped with EGR type dual area diaphragm, the front port of diaphragm must be vented to atmosphere (hose disconnected and plugged) during this check only.

Control pressures at zero governor speed for the automatic transmission.

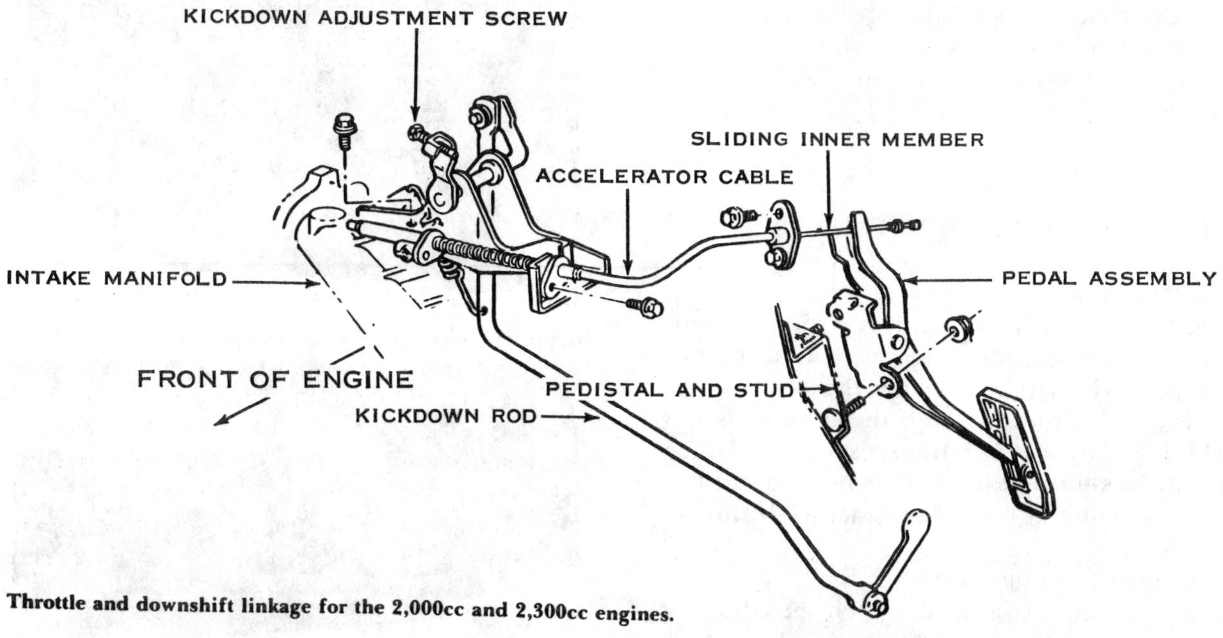

Throttle and downshift linkage for the 2,000cc and 2,300cc engines.

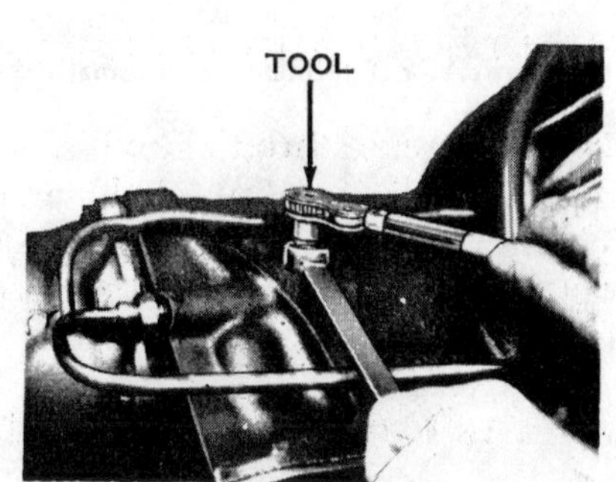

Adjusting the band.

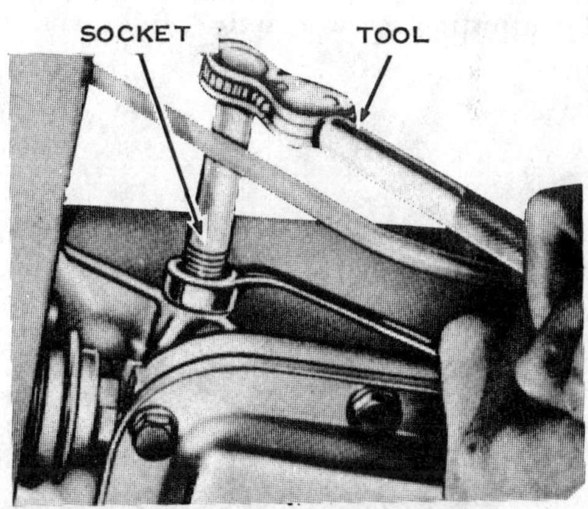

Adjusting the low-reverse band.

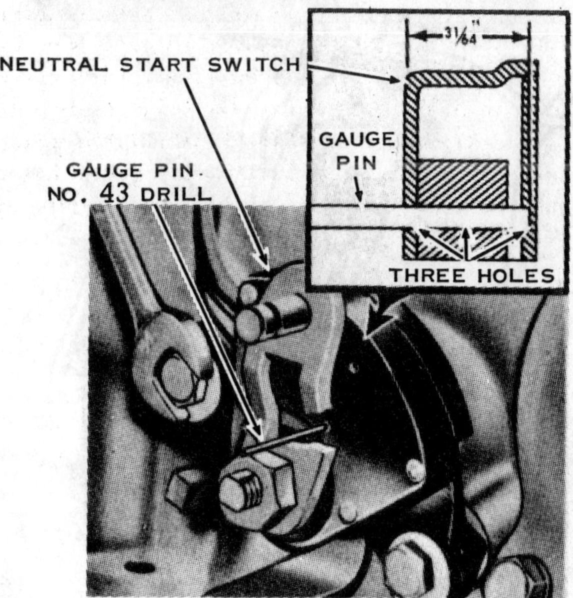

Details of the neutral-start switch adjustment, as discussed in the text.

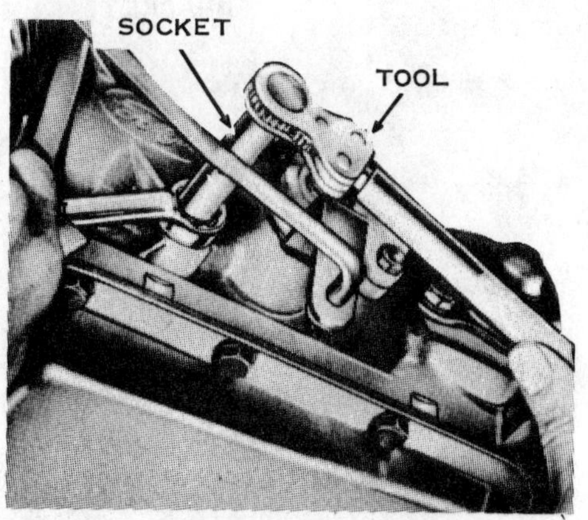

Adjusting the intermediate band.

Tighten the attaching bolts and remove the gauge. Check the operation of the switch to be sure that the cranking motor operates only in NEUTRAL or PARK.

TRANSMISSION BAND ADJUSTMENTS

Intermediate Band Adjustment

Using tool 71P-77370H (which is a special torque wrench), tighten the adjusting screw until the tool handle clicks, which will occur when the torque on the screw reaches 10 ft-lbs. Back off the adjusting screw **exactly** 1-3/4 turns, (C-4 transmission), and then tighten the locknut. The band adjustment for the C-3 transmission should be backed off **exactly** 1-1/2 turns.

Low-Reverse Band Adjustment

Using the same special tool, tighten the adjusting screw until the handle clicks (10 ft-lbs.), and then back off the adjusting screw **exactly** 3 full turns. Tighten the locknut.

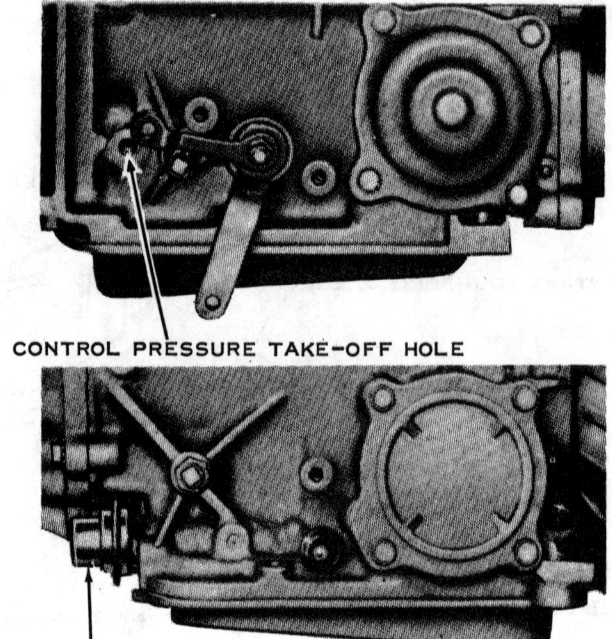

Control pressure take-off point on the automatic transmission.

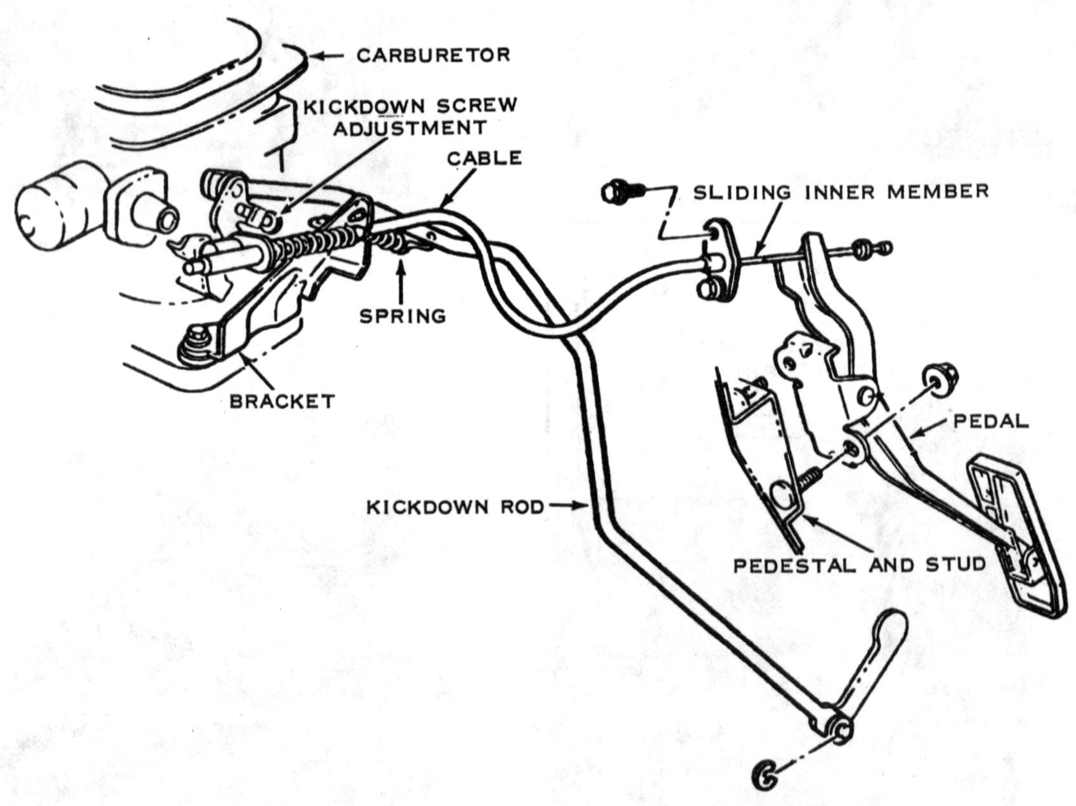

Throttle and downshift linkage for the 2,800cc engine.

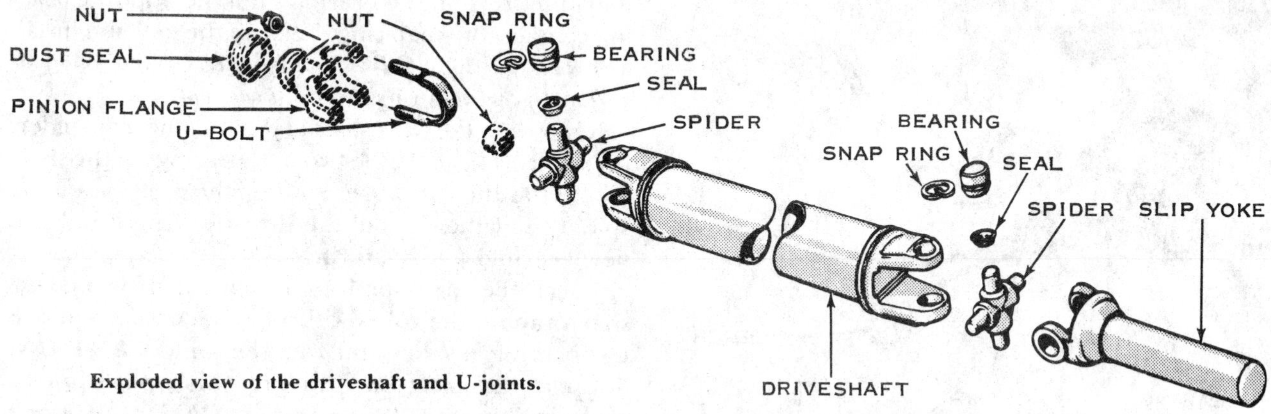

Exploded view of the driveshaft and U-joints.

DRIVESHAFT

The driveshaft receives the power from the engine, through the clutch and transmission, and transfers it to the differential in the rear axle, and then to the rear wheels. The driveshaft incorporates two universal joints and a slip yoke. The splines in the yoke and those on the transmission output shaft permit the driveshaft to move forward and rearward as the axle moves up and down. All driveshafts are balanced. If the vehicle is to be undercoated, cover the driveshaft and the universal joints to protect them from the undercoating material.

REMOVING

Whenever a driveshaft is to be removed, be sure to mark it for correct assembly in order to preserve the balance. Disconnect the rear universal joint from the axle drive pinion flange. Wrap tape around the loose bearing caps to keep them from falling off. Pull the driveshaft toward the rear of the vehicle until the slip yoke clears the transmission extension housing and the seal.

UNIVERSAL JOINT REPLACEMENT

Place the driveshaft in a vise. Remove the snap rings that retain the bearings. Press the bearing out of the slip yoke. Reposition the tool to press on the spider in order to remove the bearing from the opposite side of the yoke, and then take off the yoke.

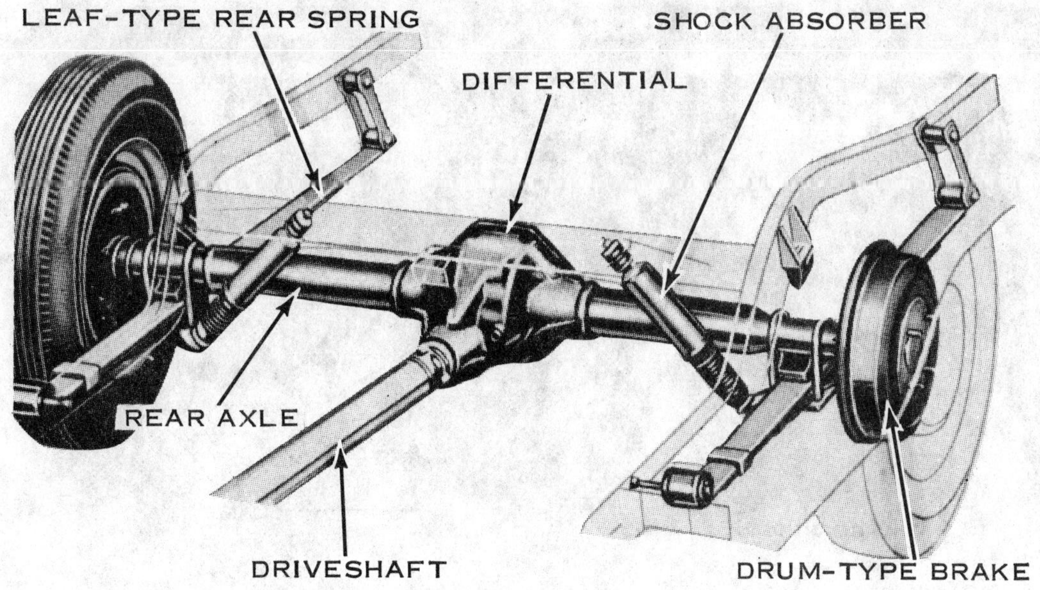

Details of the rear axle and suspension system.

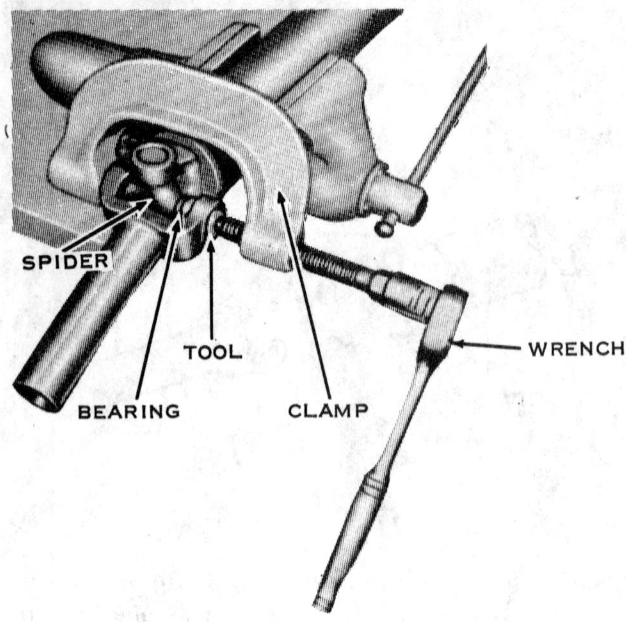

Removing the universal joint bearing.

ASSEMBLING

Start a new bearing into the yoke at the rear of the driveshaft. Insert the thrust bearings into the end of the spider. Position the spider in the rear yoke, and then press the bearing in 1/4" below the surface. Remove the tool and install a new snap ring. Insert the thrust bearings into the end of the spider. Start a new bearing into the opposite side of the yoke. Install the tool and press on the bearing until the opposite bearing contacts the snap ring. Remove the tool and install a new snap ring. *NOTE: It may be necessary to dress off the surface of the snap ring to permit easy entry.*

Reposition the driveshaft and install the new spider, thrust bearings, and the two new bearings in the same manner as the rear yoke. Position the slip yoke on the spider, and then install the thrust bearings and two new bearings and snap rings.

Check the joint for free movement. If it binds, a sharp rap on the yokes with a brass hammer will seat the bearing needles and free the joint. **CAUTION: Support the shaft end during this operation to prevent damage to the driveshaft. CAUTION: Don't install the driveshaft assembly in the vehicle unless the universal joints move freely.**

DRIVELINE VIBRATION

If detailed parts of the driveshaft are replaced and shaft vibration is encountered after installation, disconnect the shaft at the slip yoke. Rotate the slip yoke 180 degrees then, reconnect the shaft to the slip yoke. If the vibration persists, disconnect the shaft at the rear axle companion flange. Rotate the companion flange 180 degrees and reconnect the shaft to the flange.

DRIVE LINE ANGLE CHECK

Vibration or shudder which is noticeable either on

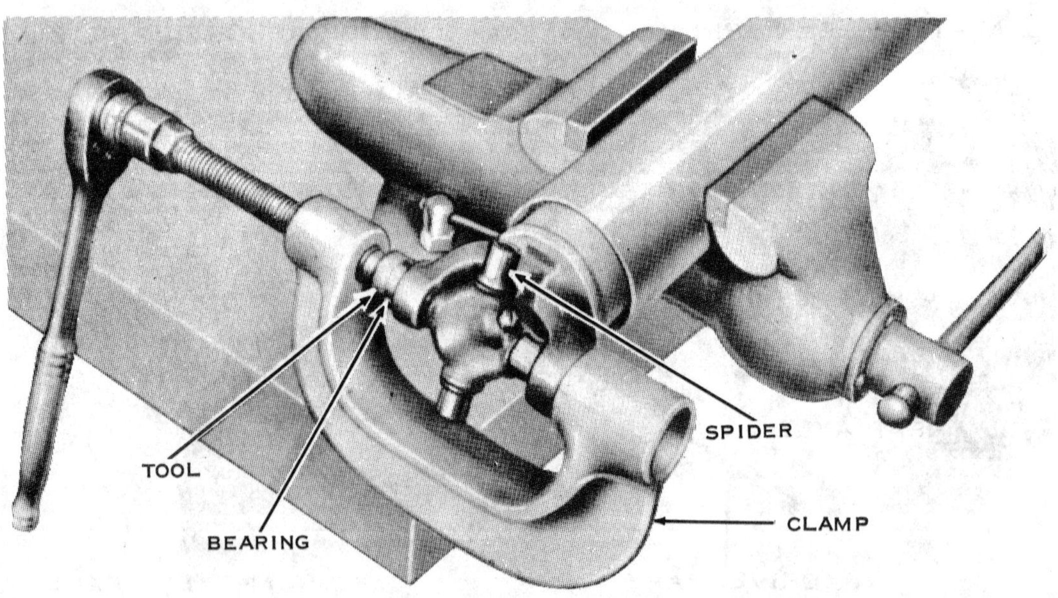

Installing a universal joint bearing with a C-clamp, as discussed in the text.

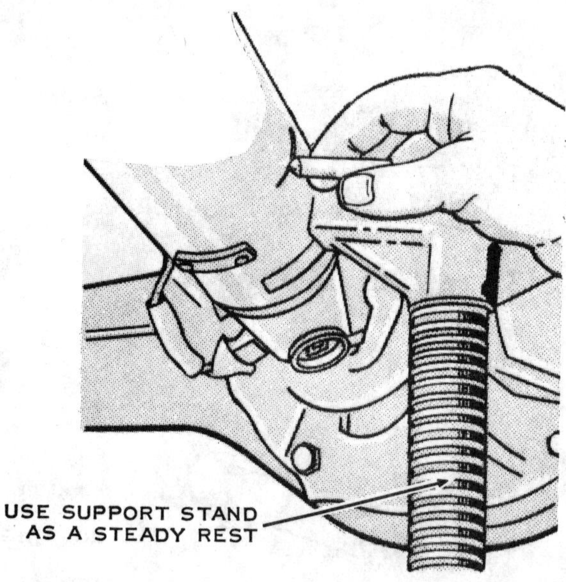

Marking the high point of driveshaft run-out, as discussed in the text.

fast acceleration, when coasting, or when using the engine for braking, may be caused by the rear axle housing being loose on the rear springs or by an improper pinion angle.

DRIVESHAFT RUNOUT CHECK

Using a dial indicator, check the runout at each end and in the middle of the driveshaft. The rear check should be made on the small tube section of the shaft between the balance weights and the yoke welds.

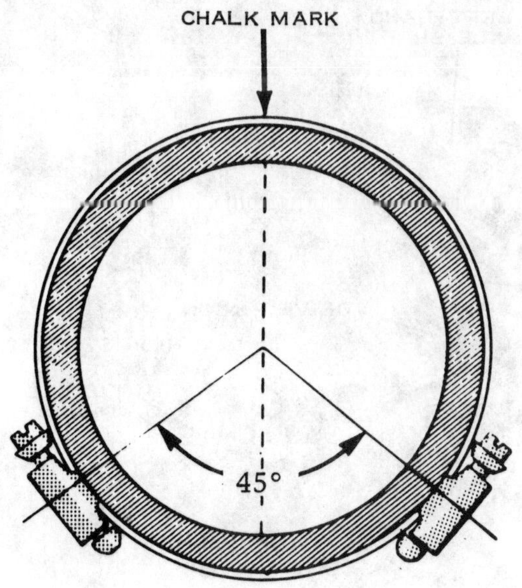

Rotating the clamps to obtain balance, as discussed in the text.

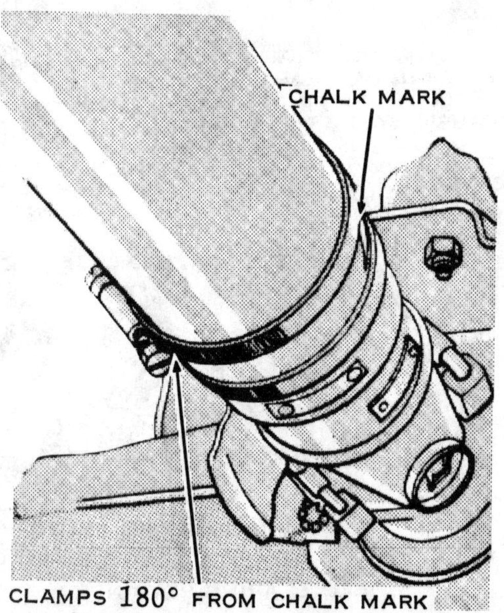

Installing Whittek clamps.

Driveshaft runout should not exceed 0.035 inch at any one point.

DRIVESHAFT BALANCING

If rotating the driveshaft 180 degrees does not eliminate the vibration, the driveshaft may be balanced using the following procedure: Place the vehicle on a twin-post hoist so that the rear of the vehicle is supported on the rear axle housing with the wheels free to rotate.

With the driveshaft rotating at a speedometer speed of 40-50 mph, carefully bring a crayon or colored pencil up until it just barely contacts the rear end of driveshaft. The mark made by the crayon or pencil will indicate the heavy side of the shaft. **CAUTION: Care should be exercised when working near the balance weights to prevent injury to the hands.**

Install two Whittek-type hose clamps on the driveshaft so that the heads are located 180 degrees from the crayon marking. Tighten the clamps.

Run the vehicle up to 65-70 mph speedometer speed. If no vibration is felt, lower the vehicle and road test. If unbalance still exists, rotate the clamp heads approximately 45 degrees away from each other and test for vibration.

Continue to rotate the clamp heads apart in smaller amounts until vibration is eliminated. **CAUTION: To prevent overheating, do not run the vehicle on the hoist for an extended period.** Road test the vehicle.

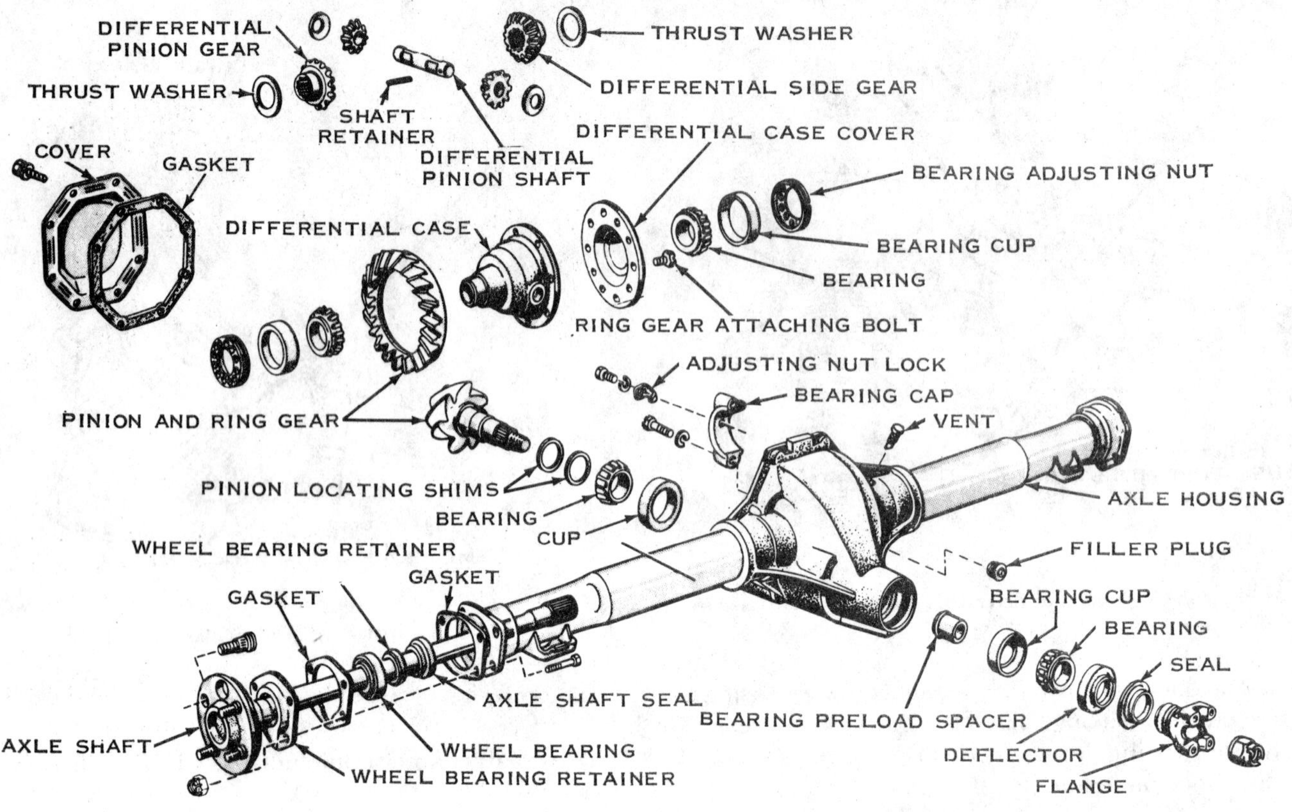

Exploded view of the integral-type rear axle.

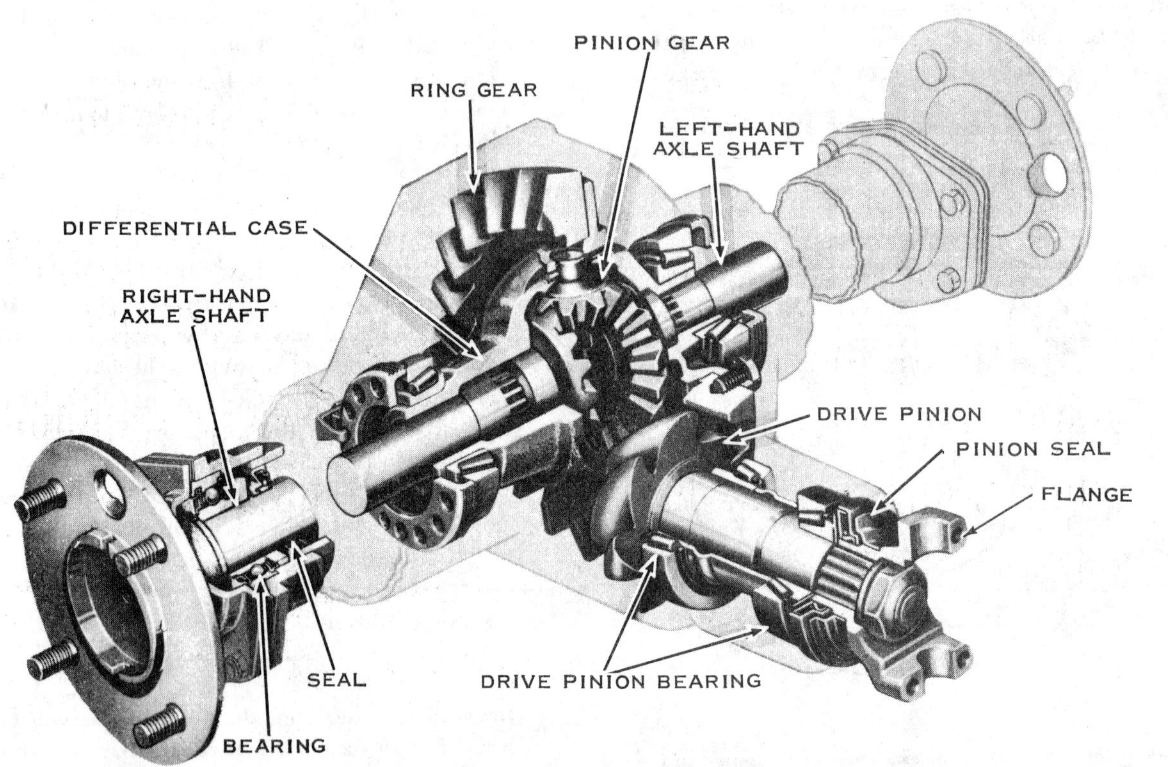

Exploded view of a removable-carrier type differential unit.

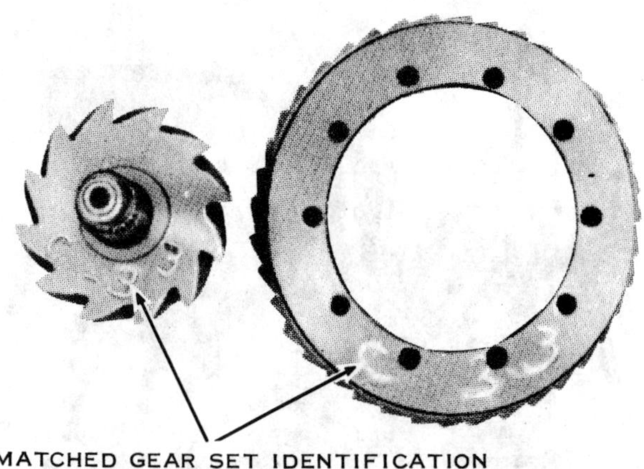

The pinion and ring gears are marked to be used as matched sets.

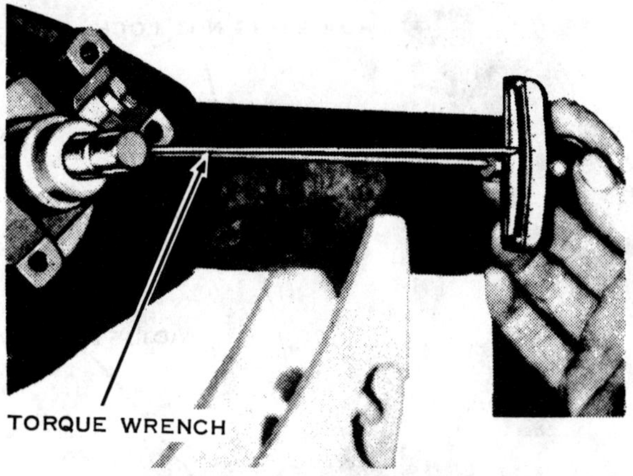

Checking the pinion bearing preload adjustment.

REAR AXLE

Pinion-Positioning Shim

The pinion-positioning shim is installed just behind the pinion gear, between it and the cone of the rear roller bearing. Changing the thickness of this shim moves the pinion gear in or out in relation to the centerline of the ring gear, which has a decided effect on the gear tooth pattern.

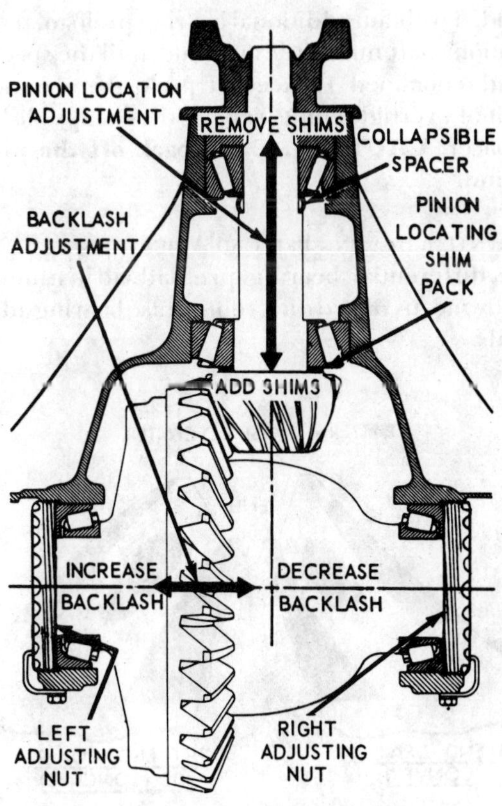

Pinion and ring gear tooth contact adjustments.

Generally, it requires special tools to determine the correct pinion-positioning shim when starting from scratch. However, the marks on the heads of the old and the replacement pinion gears can be used for selecting the correct shim. If the mark on the replacement pinion gear head is the same as on the one it is to replace, use the original shim. If the mark is more positive (i.e., if it changes from + 1 to + 4), use a 0.003″ thinner shim. If the mark is more negative (i.e., changes from + 1 to -1), use a 0.002″ thicker shim.

Pinion Bearing Preload Adjustment

A collapsible spacer is used to obtain the proper

Paint marks must be aligned to assure quiet operation.

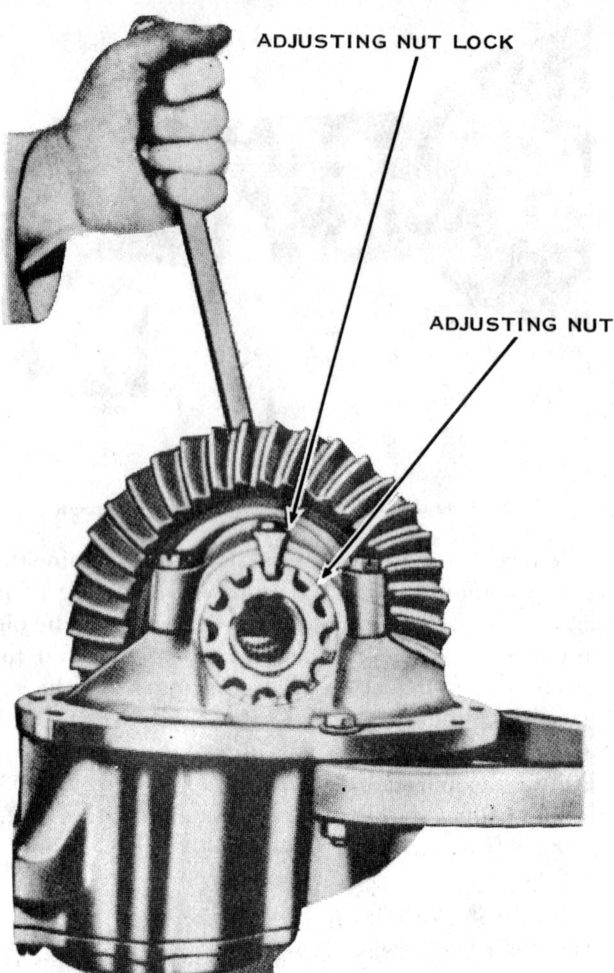

Making the differential bearing adjustment.

Checking the backlash.

preload. To obtain additional bearing preload, tighten the pinion shaft nut a little at a time until the specified preload is obtained. If excessive preload is obtained as a result of overtightening, replace the collapsible bearing spacer. **CAUTION: Don't back off the pinion shaft nut.**

Differential Bearing Preload Adjustment

The differential bearing preload adjustment is made by means of two differential case bearing adjusting nuts.

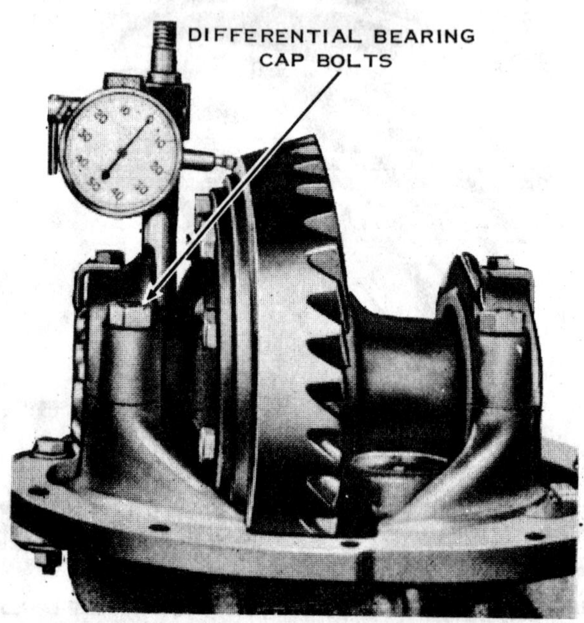

Checking the ring gear run-out with a dial indicator.

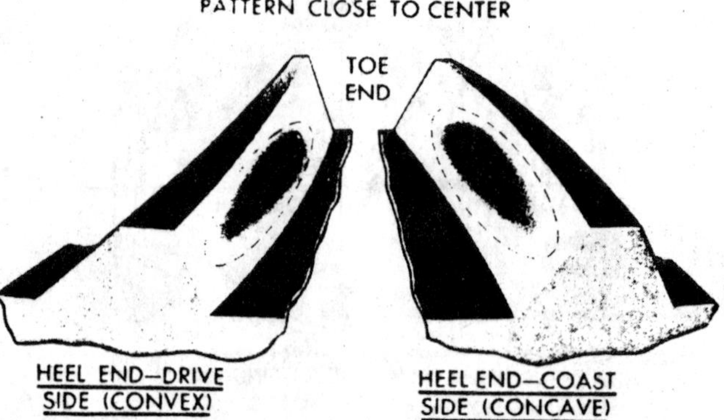

Desired ring gear tooth contact patterns under light loading.

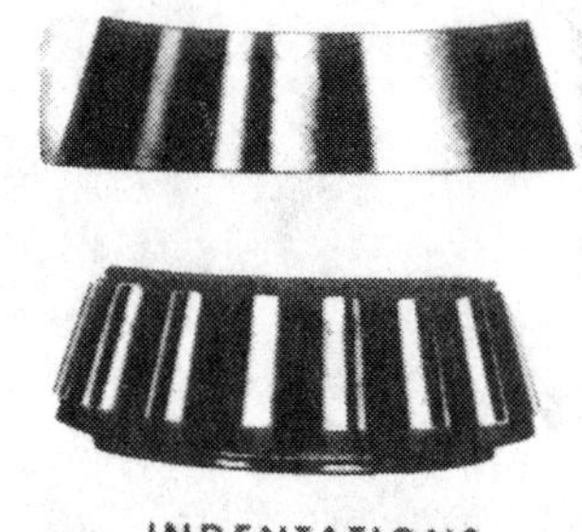

INDENTATIONS

SURFACE DEPRESSIONS ON RACE AND ROLLERS CAUSED BY HARD PARTICLES OF FOREIGN MATERIAL.

CLEAN ALL PARTS AND HOUSINGS. CHECK SEALS AND REPLACE BEARINGS IF ROUGH OR NOISY.

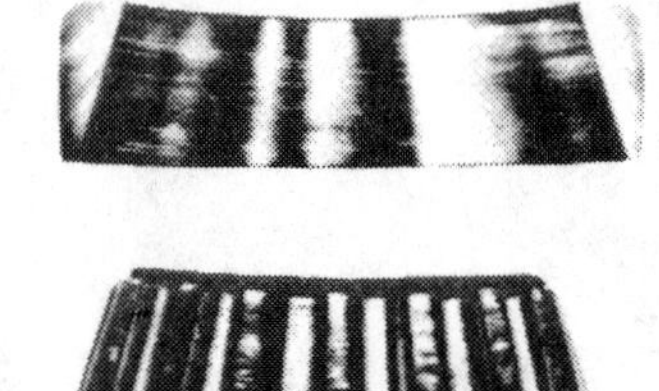

CAGE WEAR

WEAR AROUND OUTSIDE DIAMETER OF CAGE AND ROLLER POCKETS CAUSED BY ABRASIVE MATERIAL AND INEFFICIENT LUBRICATION.

CLEAN RELATED PARTS AND HOUSINGS. CHECK SEALS AND REPLACE BEARINGS.

MISALIGNMENT

OUTER RACE MISALIGNMENT DUE TO FOREIGN OBJECT.

CLEAN RELATED PARTS AND REPLACE BEARING. MAKE SURE RACES ARE PROPERLY SEATED.

Types of roller bearing failure.

Tooth Contact Adjustments

Two separate adjustments affect the pinion and ring gear tooth contact; they are the location of the pinion and the backlash between the gear teeth. When rolling a tooth pattern, use the special compound (tube) packed with each service ring gear and pinion set. Paint all gear teeth and roll a pattern. After diagnosing the tooth pattern as explained here, make the appropriate adjustments.

The drive pattern is rolled on the convex side of the tooth, and the coast pattern is rolled on the concave side. The movement of tooth contact patterns with changes in shimming can be summarized as follows: (1.) Thinner shim with the backlash set to specifications moves the pinion farther from the ring gear. (2.) Thicker shim with the backlash set to specifications moves the pinion closer to the ring gear.

If the patterns are not correct, make the changes as indicated. The differential case and drive pinion will have to be removed from the carrier casting to change a shim.

PATTERN MOVES TOWARD CENTER AND DOWN

TOE END

HEEL END—DRIVE SIDE (CONVEX)

HEEL END—COAST SIDE (CONCAVE)

PATTERN MOVES INWARD AND UP

TOE END

HEEL END—DRIVE SIDE (CONVEX)

HEEL END—COAST SIDE (CONCAVE)

The drawing at the left shows the effect of increasing the thickness of the pinion-positioning shim. The pattern at the right shows the effect of decreasing the shim thickness.

8 | running gear service

WHEEL SUSPENSION

The front wheels are suspended on coil springs, which are attached to a long-and-short arm type suspension system. The front end incorporates ball joints, which allow the front wheels to move up and down with changes in the road surface. A direct-action shock absorber is bolted to the arm and to the top of the spring housing on each side.

The rear wheels are bolted to axle shafts, which are supported by the rear axle housing by means of wheel bearings. The rear axle housing assembly is supported by two leaf-type springs, the rear of which are shackled to the frame. Two angularly-mounted shock absorbers cushion the ride.

REPACKING THE FRONT WHEEL BEARINGS

Raise the vehicle until the wheel and tire clear the floor. Remove the wheel cover or hub cap from the wheel. Remove the wheel and tire from the hub and rotor.

Remove 2 bolts and washers that attach the caliper to the spindle. Remove the caliper from the rotor and wire it to the underbody to prevent damage to the brake hose.

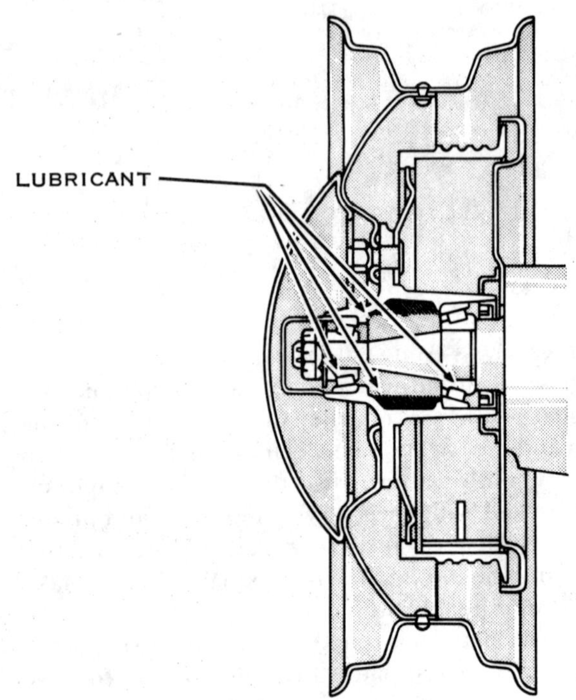

When repacking the bearings, add some lubricant between the bearings to act as a reservoir.

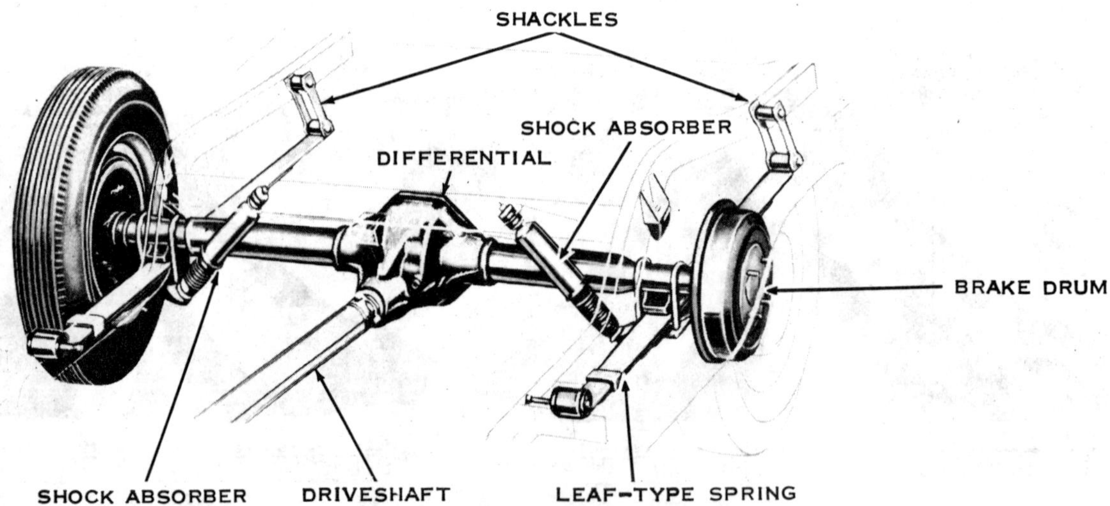

Details of the rear axle suspension. Note the straddle-mounted shock absorbers.

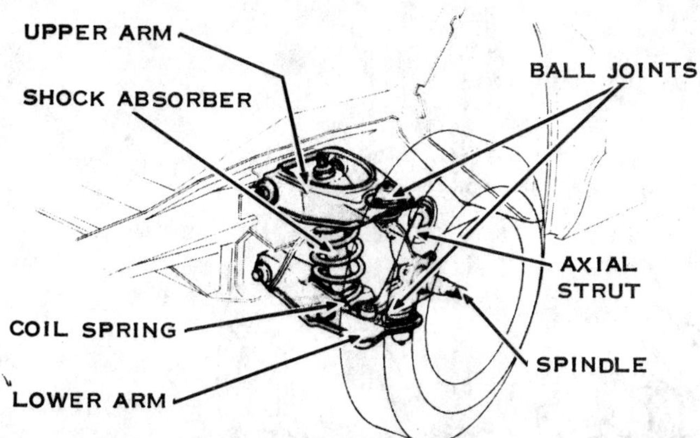

The 1976 front suspension has been redesigned to minimize toe-in change during front wheel turning to prevent tire scuffing. The suspension has also been improved to minimize nose-diving that can occur upon braking. Pinto/Bobcat.

Remove the grease cap from the hub. Remove the cotter pin, nut lock, adjusting nut, and flat washer from the spindle. Remove the outer bearing cone-and-roller assembly.

Pull the hub and rotor assembly off the wheel spindle. Remove and discard the old grease retainer. Remove the inner bearing cone and roller assembly from the hub.

CLEANING AND INSPECTING

Clean the lubricant off the inner and outer bearing cups with solvent and inspect the cups for scratches,

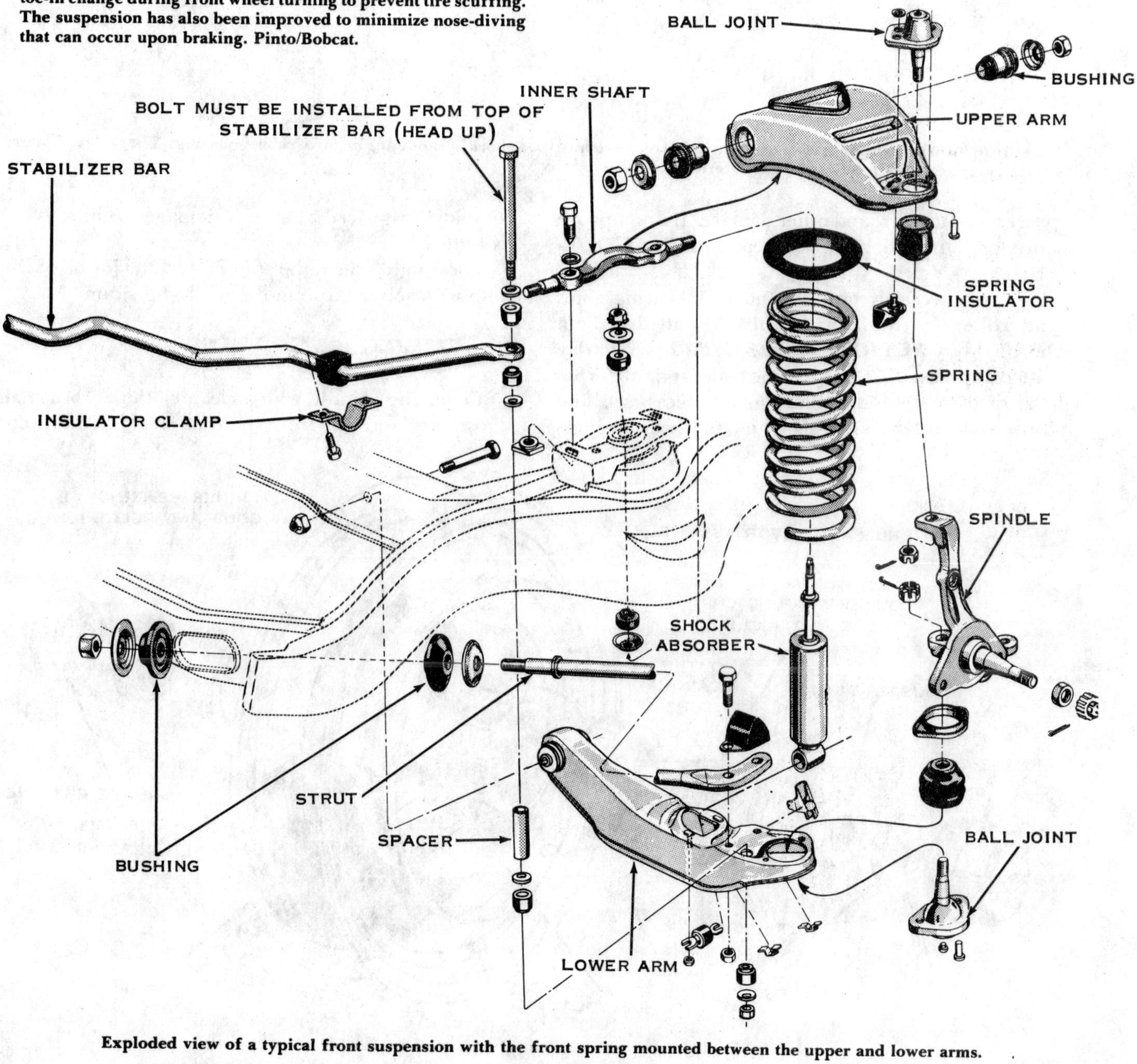

Exploded view of a typical front suspension with the front spring mounted between the upper and lower arms.

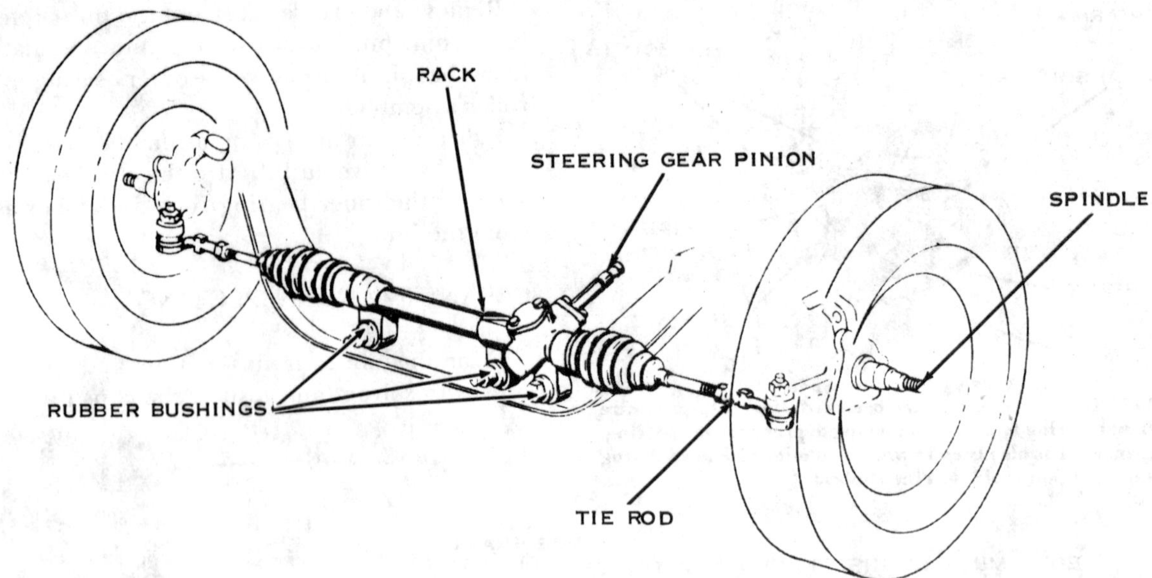

The 1976 front suspension system has been improved to reduce road shock by mounting on three rubber bushings. The rack-and-pinion steering gear assembly provides precise steering response.

pits, excessive wear, and other damage. If the cups are worn or damaged, remove them with Tool T69L-1102-A.

Thoroughly clean the inner and outer bearing cones and rollers with cleaning solvent, and dry them thoroughly. **CAUTION: Do not spin the bearings dry with compressed air.** Inspect the cones and rollers for wear or damage, and replace them if necessary. The cone and roller assemblies and the bearing cups should be replaced as a set if damage to either is encountered.

Thoroughly clean the spindle and the inside of the hub with solvent to remove all old lubricant.

INSTALLING

Cover the spindle with a clean cloth and brush all loose dust and dirt from the dust shield. To prevent

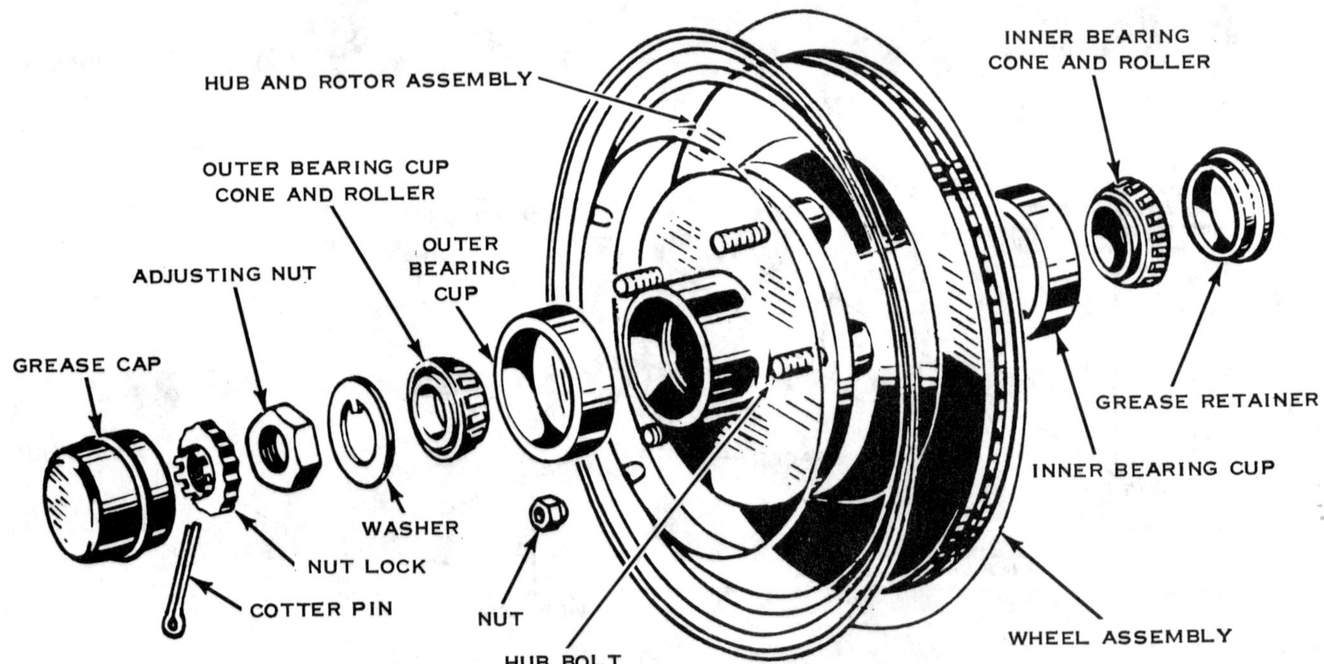

Exploded view of the front wheel and disc assembly.

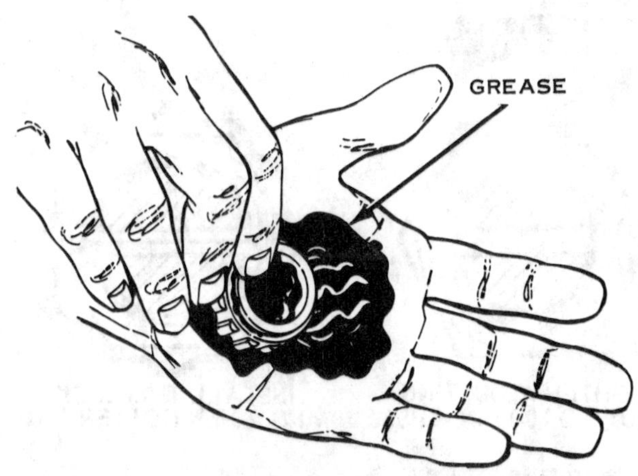

Repacking a wheel bearing, as discussed in the text.

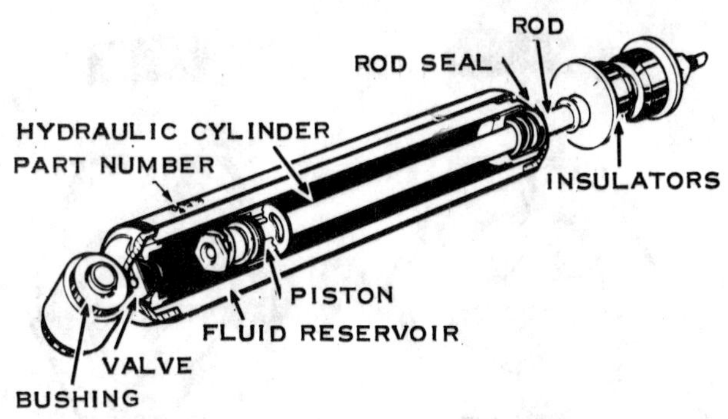

Details of the shock absorber. Check the action by pushing down on a fender, and then release the pressure suddenly. The car should rebound once or twice, but if it continues to bob up and down, the shock absorbers are weak and need to be replaced. CAUTION: A light film of oil on the shaft is normal.

getting dirt on the spindle, carefully remove the cloth from the spindle.

If the inner and/or outer bearing cup(s) were removed, install the replacement cup(s) in the hub with the tools shown. **CAUTION: Be sure to seat the cups properly in the hub.**

Pack the inside of the hub with the specified wheel bearing grease. Add lubricant to the hub only until the grease is flush with the inside diameter of both bearing cups. **CAUTION: It is important that all old grease be removed from the wheel bearings and surrounding surfaces because the new Lithium base grease C1AZ19590-B is not compatible with Sodium base grease which may already be present on the bearing surfaces.**

Pack the bearing cone and roller assemblies with wheel bearing grease. A bearing packer is desirable for this operation. If a packer is not available, work as much lubricant as possible between the rollers and cages. Lubricate the cone surfaces with grease.

Place the inner bearing cone-and-roller assembly in the inner cup. Apply a light film of grease to the lips of the grease retainer and install the new grease retainer with the tool shown. **CAUTION: Be sure the retainer is properly seated.**

Install the hub-and-rotor assembly on the wheel spindle. **CAUTION: Keep the hub centered on the spindle to prevent damage to the grease retainer or the spindle threads.** Install the outer bearing cone-and-roller assembly and the flat washer on the spindle, then install the adjusting nut finger-tight. Do not attempt to adjust the wheel bearings at this time.

Install the caliper to the spindle using new bolts, and torque the top attaching bolt, first to 90-120 ft-lbs. and the bottom one to 55-70 ft-lbs. Install the wheel and tire on the hub.

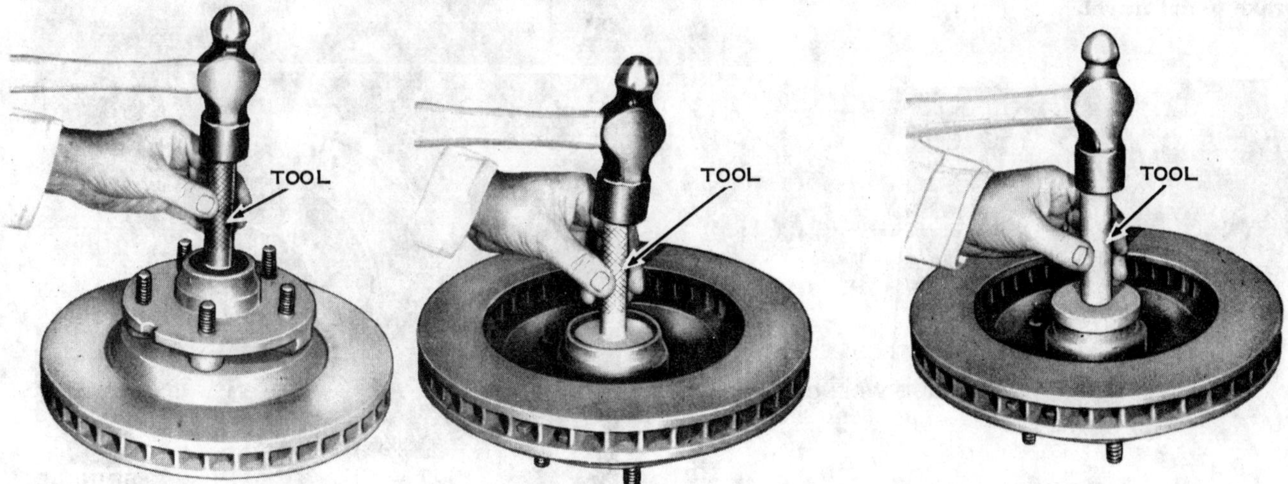

Installing the front wheel bearing cups, outer (left view) and inner (center view). The right view shows the grease retainer being installed.

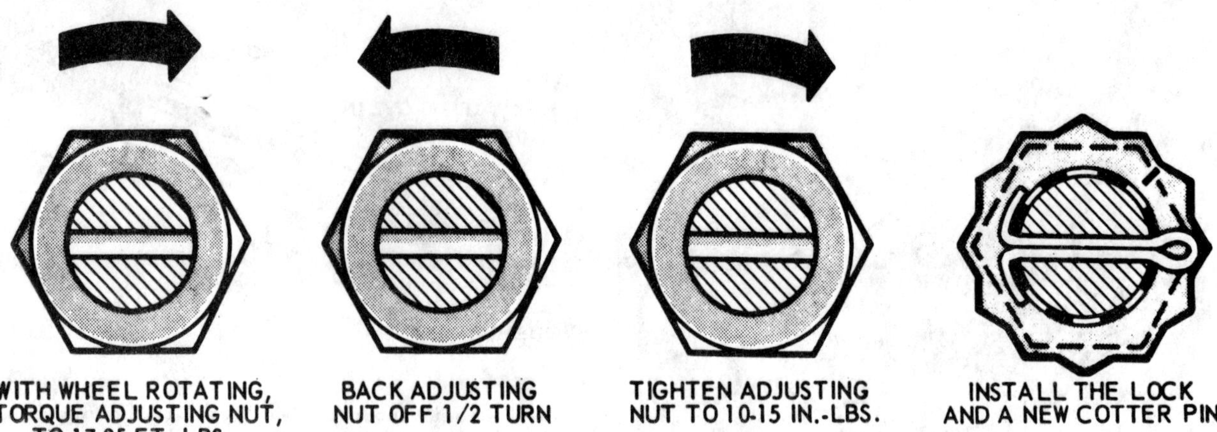

Details for making the front wheel bearing adjustments.

ADJUSTING THE WHEEL BEARINGS

Rock the wheel, hub, and rotor assembly in and out several times to push the shoe and linings away from the rotor.

While rotating the wheel, hub, and rotor assembly, torque the adjusting nut to 17-25 ft-lbs to seat the bearings. Back the adjusting nut off one half turn. Retighten the adjusting nut to 10-15 **in-lbs** with a torque wrench or just finger-tight.

Locate the nut lock on the adjusting nut so that the castellations on the lock are aligned with the cotter pin hole in the spindle, as shown. Install a new cotter pin, and bend the ends of the cotter pin around the castellated flange of the nut lock.

Check the front wheel rotation. If the wheel rotates properly, install the grease cap and the hub cap or wheel cover. **CAUTION: Before driving the vehicle, pump the brake pedal several times to obtain normal brake lining to rotor clearance and restore normal brake pedal travel.**

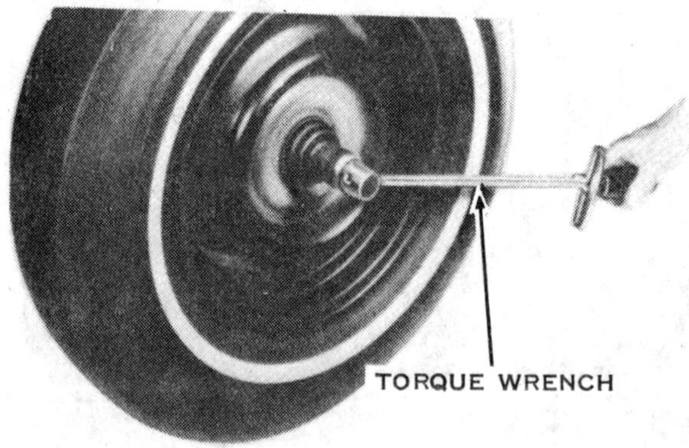

Adjust the front wheel bearings with a torque wrench. CAUTION: Don't overtighten. The correct torque value is 10-15 inch-lbs.

WHEEL ALIGNMENT

Front wheel alignment is the proper adjustment of all the interrelated suspension angles affecting the running and steering of the front wheels of the vehicle. The importance of wheel alignment and wheel balancing is considered essential in order to maintain ease of steering and good directional stability and to prevent abnormal tire wear.

The six basic factors which are the foundation of front wheel alignment are: height, caster, camber, toe-in, steering axis inclination, and turning radius. All of the angles, except steering axis inclination and turning radius, are adjustable. The two unadjustable angles are valuable in determining if parts are bent, especially so when the other angles cannot be adjusted to specifications.

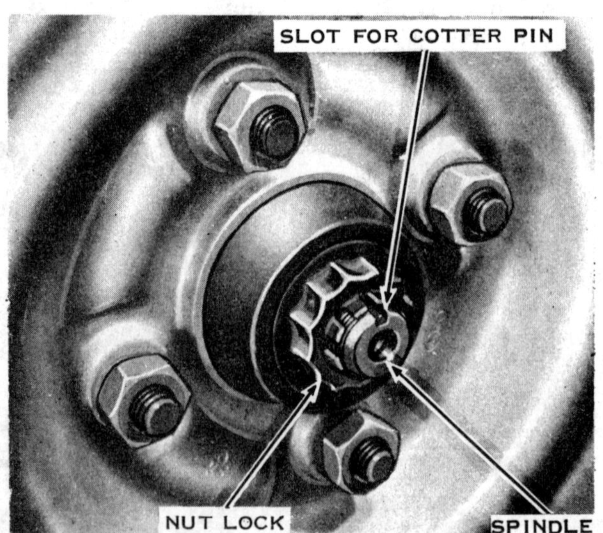

Illustration to show the correct position of the nut lock aligned with the adjusting nut.

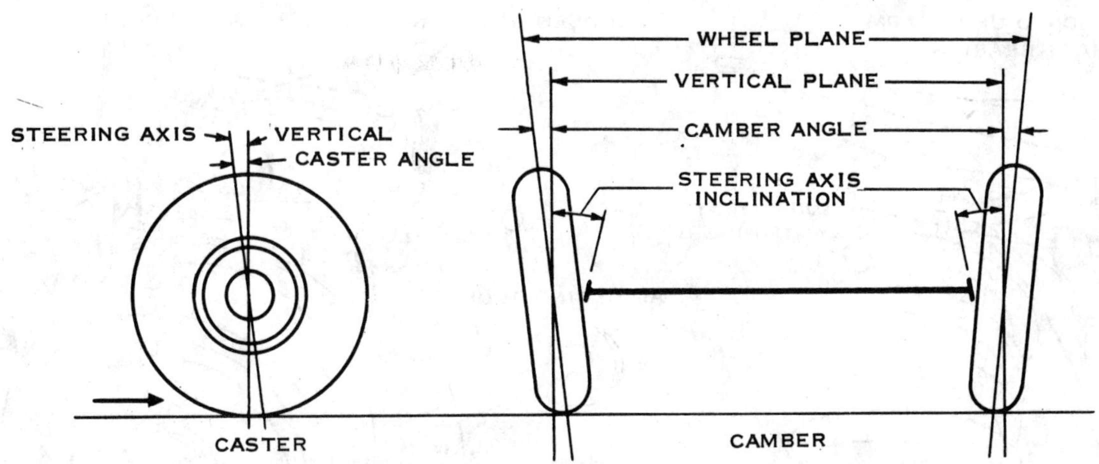

Caster and camber angles of the front suspension.

HEIGHT

The front suspension height must be held to specifications for a satisfactory ride, correct appearance, proper front wheel alignment, and reduced tire wear. The heights must be measured only after the vehicle has the recommended tire pressures, a full tank of fuel, no passengers, no luggage, and is on a level floor.

Jounce the vehicle several times and release it on a downward motion. Measure the distance from the lowest point on one adjusting blade to the floor to obtain measurement "A" and from the lowest point of the steering knuckle arm to the floor to obtain measurement "B". The difference between measurements "A" and "B" is the front suspension height, and the maximum allowable difference between sides is 1/8". Replace the front springs, if necessary, to establish the correct heights.

CASTER AND CAMBER

Caster is the forward (negative) or rearward (positive) tilt of the top of the wheel spindle. Camber is the amount that the front wheels are tilted outward (positive) or inward (negative) at the top. The

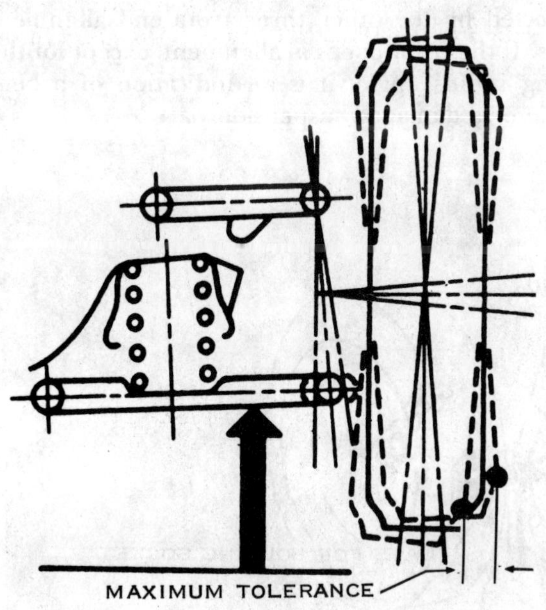

The front end ball joints must not be worn, or the front end alignment will be adversely affected. To measure the lower ball joint radial play, support the front end under the lower suspension arm, as indicated by the black arrow.

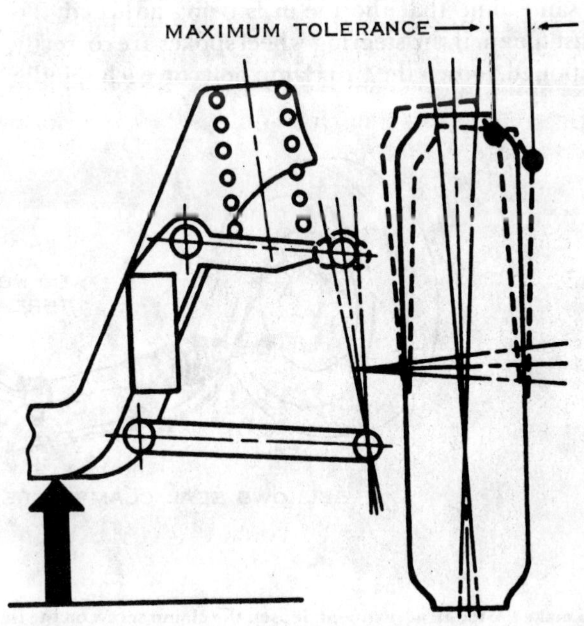

To measure the upper ball joint wear radial play, support the vehicle at the frame, as indicated by the black arrow.

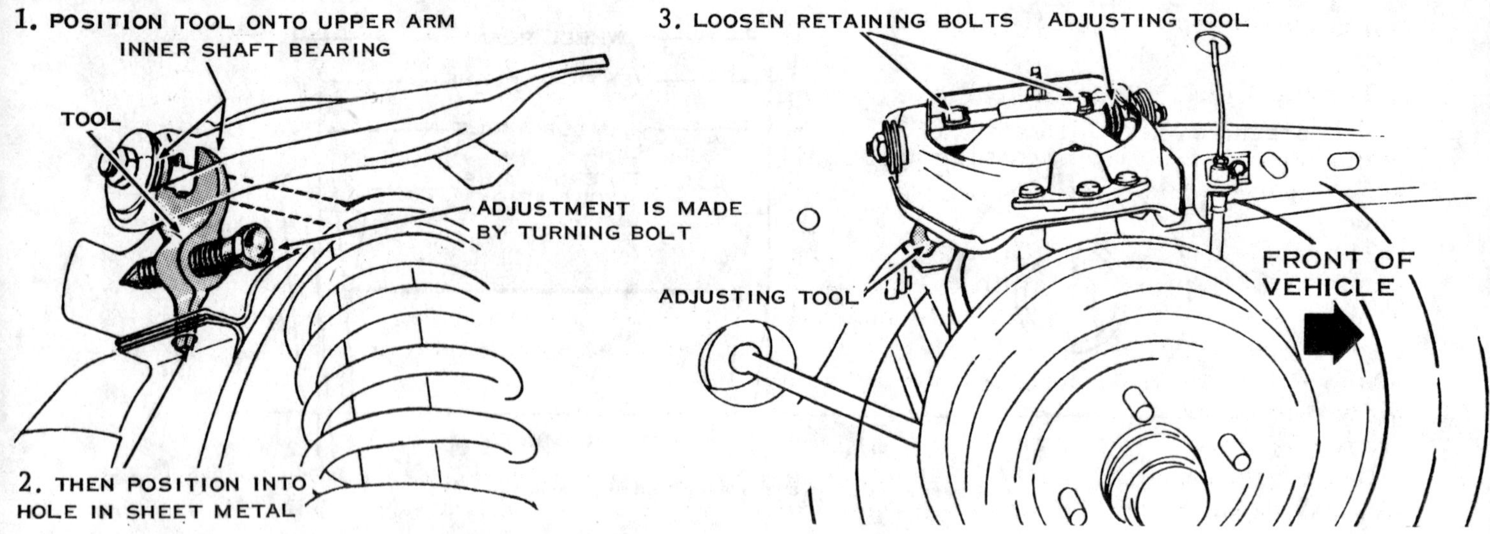

It requires a special tool to make the camber and caster adjustment, as discussed in the text.

maximum difference between the front wheel caster angles or the front wheel camber angles should not exceed 1/2°.

TOE-IN

Toe-in is the difference between the distance at the extreme front and rear of both front wheels. It must be measured only after you have corrected the caster and camber angles, as these angles affect the toe-in reading.

Check the steering wheel spoke position when the front wheels are pointed straight ahead. If the spokes are not correctly positioned, they can be adjusted at the same time that the toe-in is being adjusted. To adjust toe-in, if the steering wheel spokes are correctly positioned, loosen the two clamp bolts on each spindle connecting rod sleeve and lengthen or shorten both rods equally. If the spokes are not correctly positioned, make the necessary rod adjustments as indicated in the accompanying illustrations.

When the correct alignment is obtained, tighten the clamp bolts on both connecting rod sleeves. **CAUTION: The sleeve clamp bolts must be at the bottom.**

TURNING RADIUS

When the front wheels are turned so that the inside wheel on a curve is turned 20°, the outside wheel should turn 18-3/4°. This angle is not adjustable, but it is affected by the other three front-end alignment angles. If the front-end is in alignment, except for the turning radius angle, it is an indication of a bent spindle or a damaged suspension part.

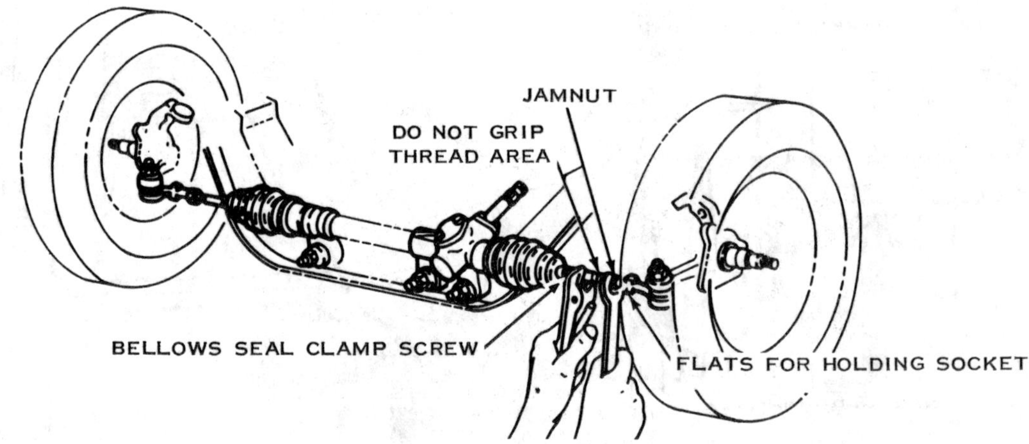

To make the toe-in adjustment, loosen the clamp screw on the tie rod bellows and free the seal on the rod to prevent twisting the bellows. Use an open-end wrench on the flats of the tie rod socket to keep it from turning when while loosening the jam nut. Use a pair of pliers to turn the tie rod inner end to adjust the toe-in. CAUTION: Don't clamp the pliers on the tie rod threads. This procedure applies to both the left and right tie rod ends.

RACK AND PINION STEERING GEAR

The gear input shaft is connected to the steering shaft by a U-joint shaft and flexible coupling. A pinion gear, machined on the input shaft, engages the rack, and rotation of the input shaft pinion causes the rack to move laterally.

Tie rods, attached at each end of the rack joint, move with the action of the front suspension. The gear is sealed at each end with a rubber bellows. The steering gear is filled with approximately 7 oz. of lubricant D2AZ-19580-B at initial assembly and need not be checked unless leakage is evident or the unit is drained for repair.

Couplings attaching the tie rods are pinned to the rack and can be disassembled for service. Damage to the inner tie rods, rack, housing or upper pinion bearing, necessitates installation of a new steering gear assembly. With the front suspension and linkage in good condition and the gear in proper adjustment, there should be no more than 3/8 inch of free play at the rim of the steering wheel.

In a stationary vehicle, there should be no knock in the steering gear when the steering wheel is turned from stop to stop. If a knock is experienced, check adjustment of rack preload and pinion bearing preload. A faint knock produced by the steering gear while driving on an extremely rough road is acceptable, and in no way affects the proper functioning of the gear. **CAUTION: Do not turn the steering wheel quickly or forcefully from lock to lock when the front wheels of the vehicle are off the ground. This could cause a buildup of pressure within the gear, which could damage or blow off the bellows.**

ADJUSTMENTS

The rack-and-pinion gear provides two means of service adjustment. The gear must be removed from the vehicle to perform both adjustments.

Support Yoke To Rack

Clean the exterior of the steering gear thoroughly and mount the gear by installing two long bolts and washers through the mounting boss bushings and attaching it to a bench-mounted holding fixture.

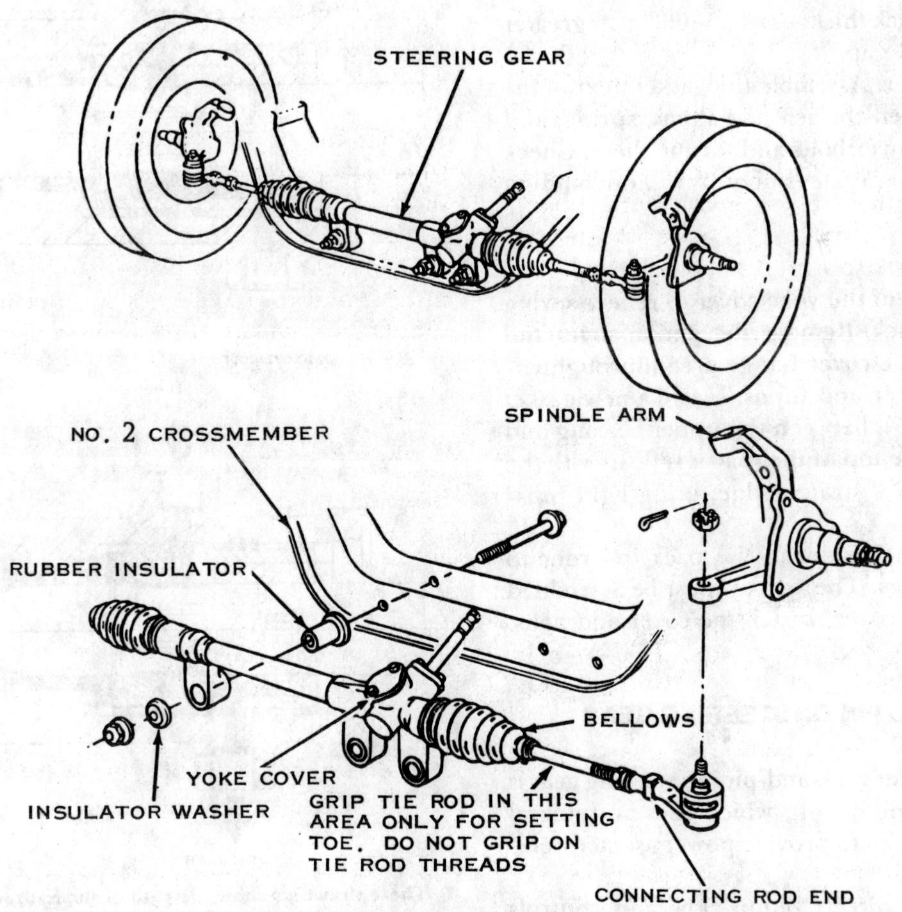

Details of the steering linkage.

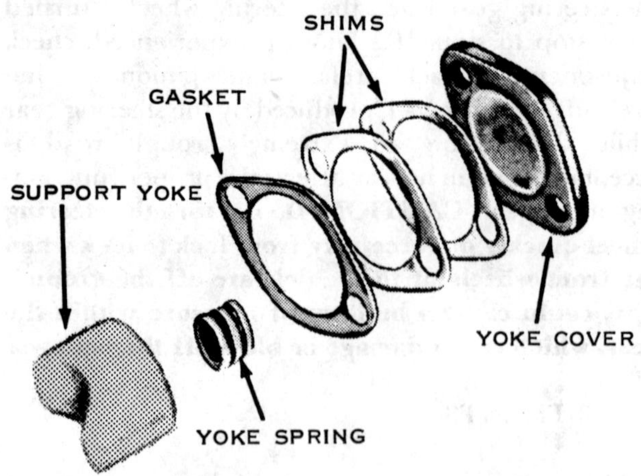

Support yoke arrangement.

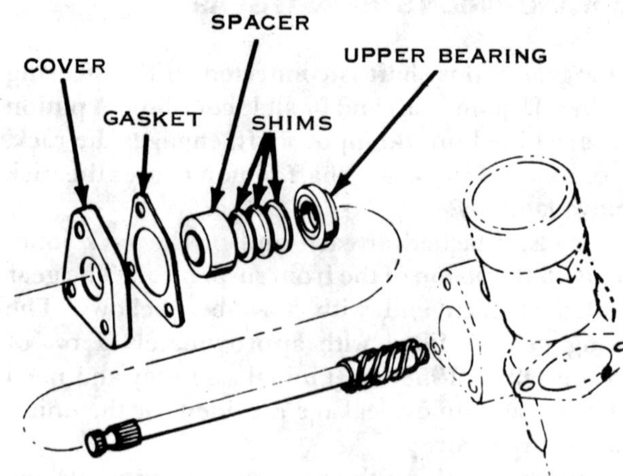

Pinion bearing cover and shim arrangement.

Remove the yoke cover, gasket, shims, and yoke spring. Clean the cover and housing flange areas thoroughly. Reinstall the yoke and cover, omitting the gasket, shims, and the spring. Torque the cover bolts lightly until the cover just touches the yoke.

Measure the gap between the cover and the housing flange. With the gasket, add selected shims (3F518) to give a combined pack thickness .005-.006 inch greater than the measured gap.

Remove the cover. Assemble the gasket next to the housing flange, then the selected shims, spring, and cover. Install the cover bolts and torque them. Check to see that the gear operates smoothly without binding or slackness.

Pinion Bearing Preload

Loosen the bolts of the yoke cover to relieve spring pressure on the rack. Remove the pinion cover and gasket and clean the cover flange area thoroughly.

Remove the spacer and shims. Install a new gasket and fit shims (3595), between the upper bearing and the spacer, until the top of the spacer is flush with the gasket. Check with a straightedge, using light pressure.

Add one .005-inch shim to the pack in order to preload the bearings. The spacer must be assembled next to the pinion cover. Install the cover and bolts. Torque the bolts.

POWER RACK AND PINION STEERING GEAR

The integral power rack-and-pinion steering gear is a hydraulic-mechanical unit, which uses an integral piston and rack design to provide power assisted vehicle steering control.

Internal valving directs pump flow and controls pressure, as required, to reduce steering effort during operation. The unit contains a rotary hydraulic fluid control valve integrated to the input shaft and a boost cylinder integrated with the rack.

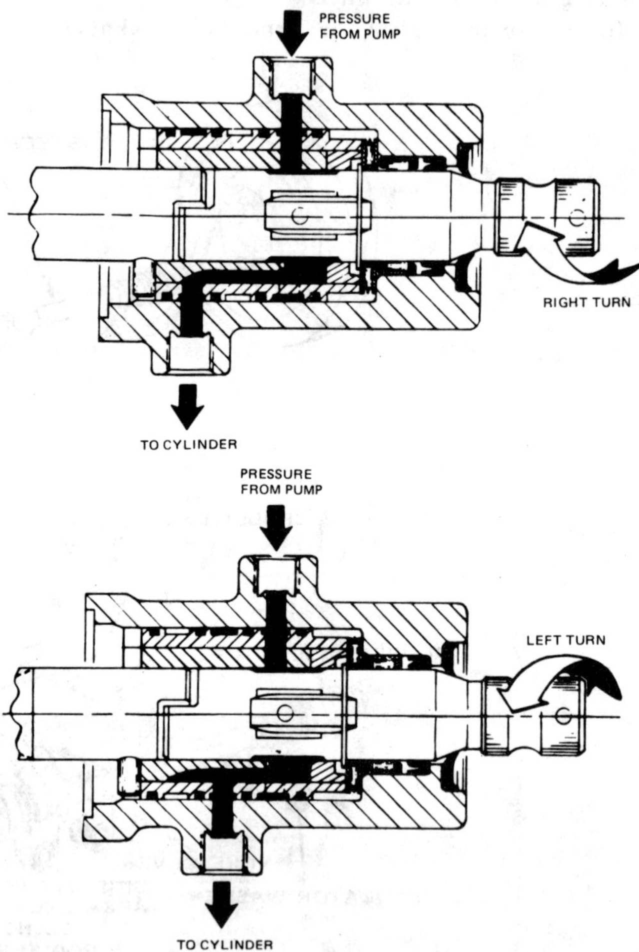

These drawings show the path of the hydraulic fluid from the pressure port to the left and right turn passages. NOTE: The pressure fittings are shown out of position for clarity.

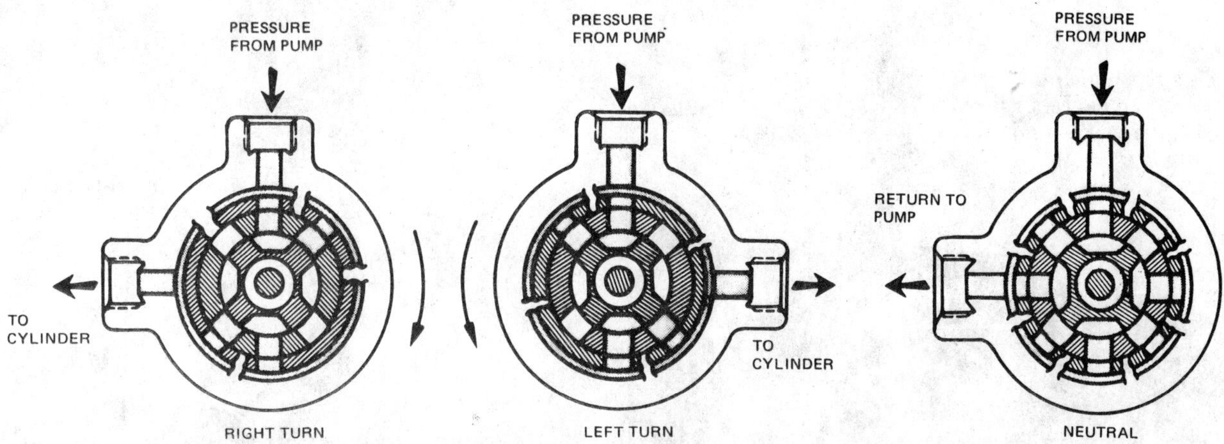

These drawings show the relative position of the input shaft to the sleeve to achieve right, left, and straight ahead maneuvers.

OPERATION

The rotary design control valve uses relative rotational motion of the input shaft and valve sleeve to direct fluid flow. When the steering wheel is turned, resistance of the wheels and the weight of the vehicle cause a torsion bar to deflect. This deflection changes the position of the valve spool and sleeve ports, directing fluid under pressure to the appropriate end of the power cylinder. The difference in pressure forces on the piston helps move the rack to assist turning effort. The piston is attached directly to the rack, and the housing tube functions as the power cylinder. The oil in the opposite end of the power cylinder is forced to the control valve and back to the pump reservoir.

When the driver stops applying steering effort, the valve is forced back to a centered position by the torsion bar. When this occurs, pressure is equalized on both sides of the piston and the front wheels tend to return to a straight ahead position.

In normal operation, steering effort should be considerably less than with the manual gear. There may be some *apparent* loss of assist (a hesitation) at engine hot

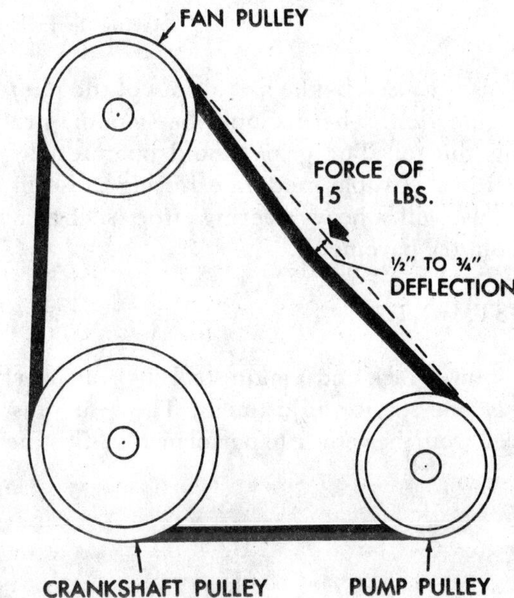

The power steering pump drive belt should deflect 1/2-3/4" under a force of 15 lbs.

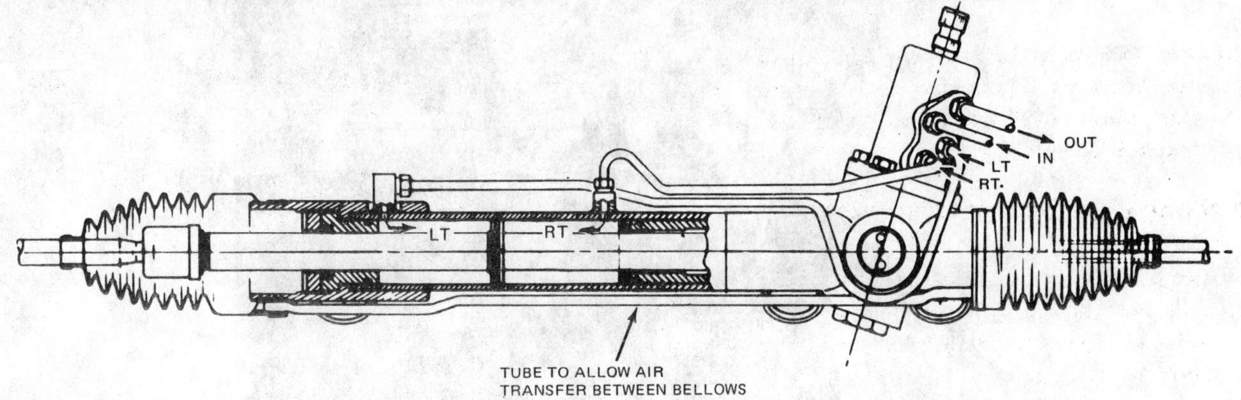

Power steering gear assembly used since 1974.

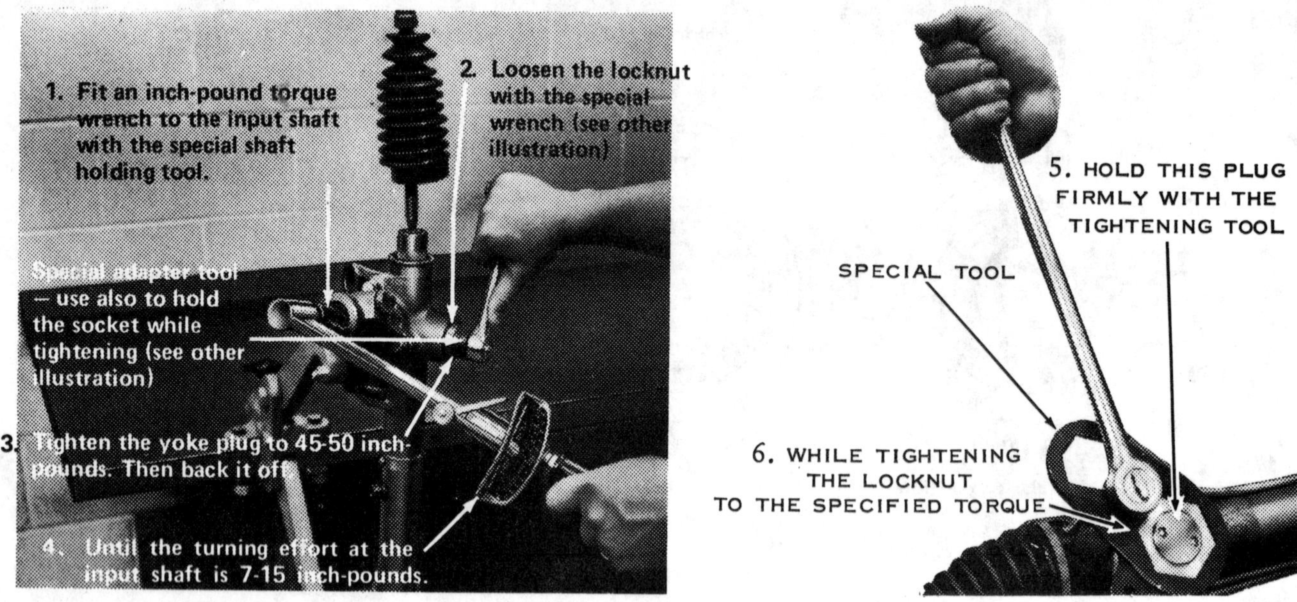

Making the rack yoke bearing preload adjustment.

idle. This is caused by the low output of the pump at low engine rpm. There should be smooth, straight steering control. The gear should operate silently except for a possible moderate hissing noise in the rotary valve with a heavy steering effort (such as at low speed on dry pavement).

ADJUSTMENTS

The power rack and pinion steering gear provides for only one service adjustment. The gear must be removed from the vehicle to perform this adjustment.

Rack Yoke Bearing Preload

Clean the exterior of the steering gear thoroughly. Remove the external pressure line assemblies from the gear and drain the power steering fluid out through the openings into a container. Install two long bolts and washers through the bushings and attach to the bench-mounted holding fixture.

Insert an in-lb torque wrench (max. capacity 30-60 in-lbs) into the input shaft torque adapter, Tool T74P-3504-R. Position the adapter and wrench on the input shaft splines. Loosen the yoke plug locknut with

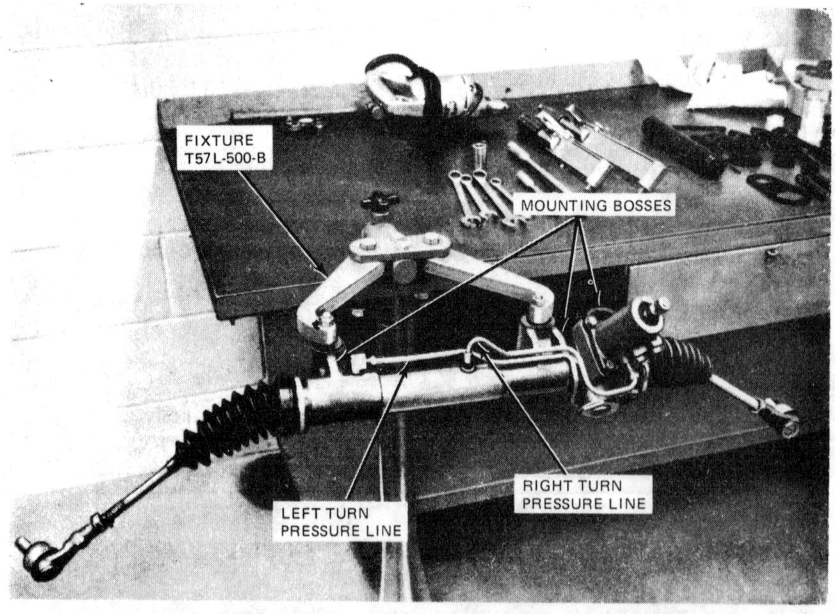

Holding fixture for working on the power steering unit.

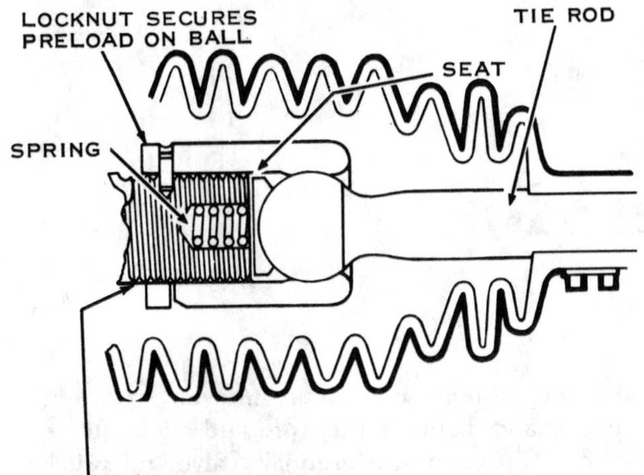

Sectioned view through the tie rod ball socket.

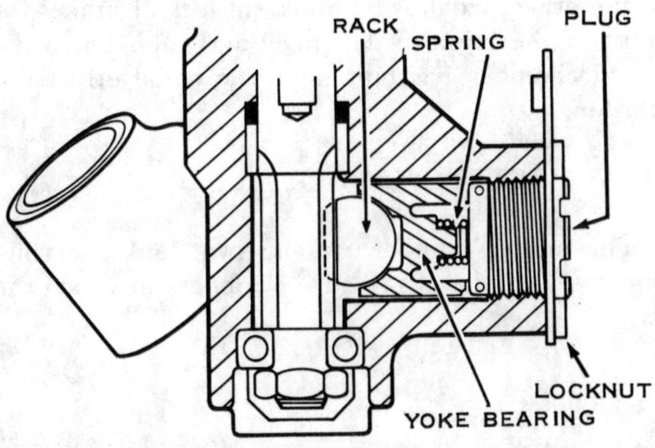

Sectioned view through the yoke bearing and adjuster plug.

a wrench, Tool T74P-3504-U. Insert the yoke spanner wrench, Tool T74P-3504-U , with an in-lb torque wrench into the drilled holes in the yoke plug.

With the rack at the center of travel, tighten the yoke plug to 45-50 in-lb. **CAUTION: Clean the threads of the yoke plug prior to torquing to prevent a false reading.** Back off the yoke plug (a maximum of 45 degrees) until the torque required to initiate and sustain rotation of the input shaft is 7-15 in-lb.

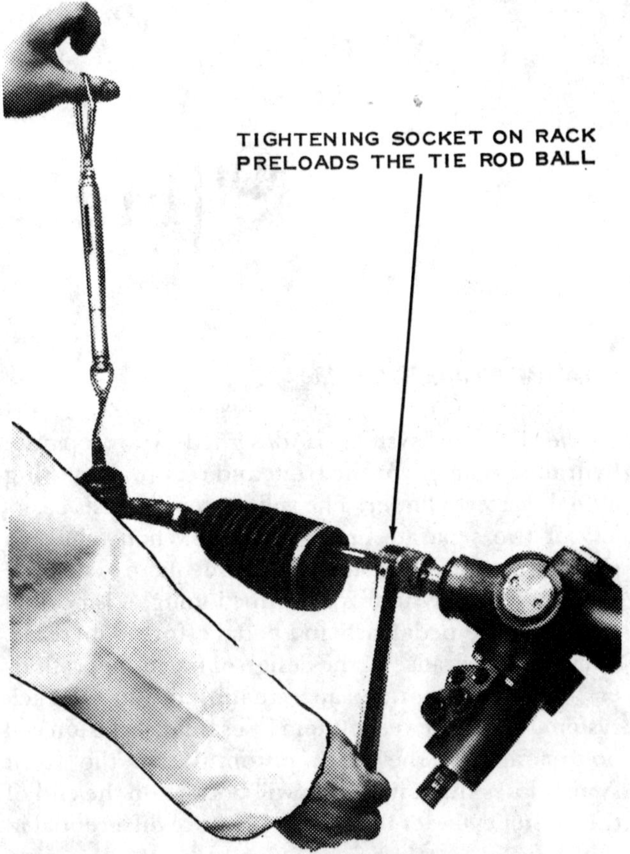

Making the tie rod ball socket preload adjustment.

Place Tool T74P-3504-U on the yoke plug locknut. While holding the yoke plug firmly with spanner wrench, Tool T74P-3504-W, torque the locknut to 44-66 ft-lbs. **CAUTION: Do not allow the yoke plug to move while torquing, or the pre-load will be affected.** Recheck the input shaft torque after tightening the locknut.

Remove all tools and reinstall the external pressure line assemblies, using new copper flare gaskets. Torque the pressure line fitting to 10-25 ft-lbs. and the return line fitting to 25-34 ft-lbs. Install the gear assembly on the vehicle.

9 | brake service

DUAL BRAKING SYSTEM

The braking system is designed with separate hydraulic systems for the front and rear brakes, using a dual master cylinder. The split system consists basically of two separate brake systems. When failure is encountered in either, the other is adequate to stop the vehicle. If one system is not functioning, it is normal for the brake pedal lash and pedal effort to increase. This occurs because of the design of the master cylinder, which incorporates an actuating piston for each system. When the rear system loses fluid, its piston will bottom against the front piston. When the front system loses fluid, its piston will bottom on the end of the master cylinder body. The pressure differential in one of the systems causes an uneven hydraulic pressure balance between the front and rear systems. The brake pressure-differential valve-and-switch assembly, near the master cylinder, detects the loss of pressure and illuminates the brake alarm indicator light on the instrument panel. The pressure loss is felt at the brake pedal by an apparent lack of brakes for most of the brake pedal travel and then, when the failed chamber has bottomed, the pedal effort will harden.

DUAL MASTER CYLINDER

The master cylinder contains two fluid reservoirs and two cylindrical pressure chambers in which the

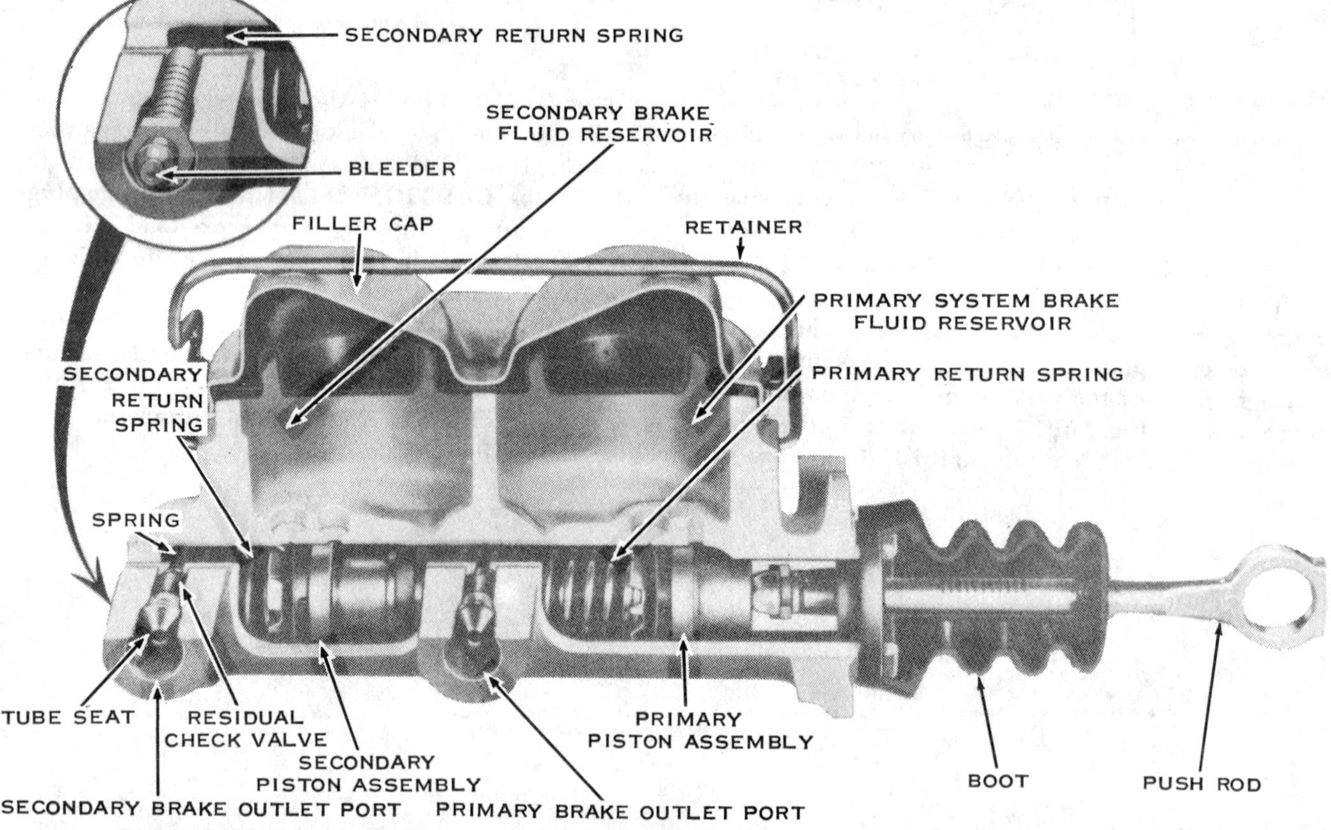

Sectioned view through a dual master cylinder. The left section directs hydraulic pressure to the rear-wheel brakes.

brake pedal force is transmitted to the fluid to actuate the brake shoes. Breather ports and compensating ports permit passage of the fluid between each of the pressure chambers and its fluid reservoir during certain operating conditions. A vented cover and flexible rubber diaphragm at the top seal the hydraulic system against the entrance of dirt and, at the same time, permit expansion and contraction of the hydraulic fluid within the system without direct venting to the atmosphere. The forward reservoir is used to supply hydraulic pressure to the rear brake wheel cylinders and the reservoir closest to the dash panel supplies the front wheel cylinders.

BRAKE BOOSTER

The diaphragm-type brake booster is a self-contained vacuum-hydraulic braking unit mounted on the engine side of the dash panel. The brake booster is of the vacuum suspended-type which utilizes engine intake manifold vacuum and atmospheric pressure for its power.

PRESSURE-DIFFERENTIAL VALVE AND BRAKE WARNING LIGHT SWITCH

A self-centering pressure-differential valve assembly is used. The valve body is step-bored to accommodate a sleeve and seal installed over the piston and into the larger valve body bore in the front brake system area. The brake warning light switch is mounted at the center of the valve body and the spring-loaded switch plunger fits into a tapered shoulder groove in the center of the piston. In this position, the electrical continuity through the switch is interrupted and the brake warning lamp on the instrument panel is out.

If there should be a pressure loss in either the front or rear brake system, the valve will be moved off center. The electrical circuit through the switch will be completed and the warning light will be on. After repairs are made, and the brake system properly bled, the valve will center itself and the warning light will be out.

CONTROL VALVE ASSEMBLY

The brake control valve assembly used on many vehicles with disc brakes in the front consists of a pressure-differential valve, metering valve, and proportioning valve. These valves are housed within a single cast-iron valve body (housing). The pressure-differential and metering valves are located in the central bore of the valve body. The proportioning valve is located in a separate angular vertical bore.

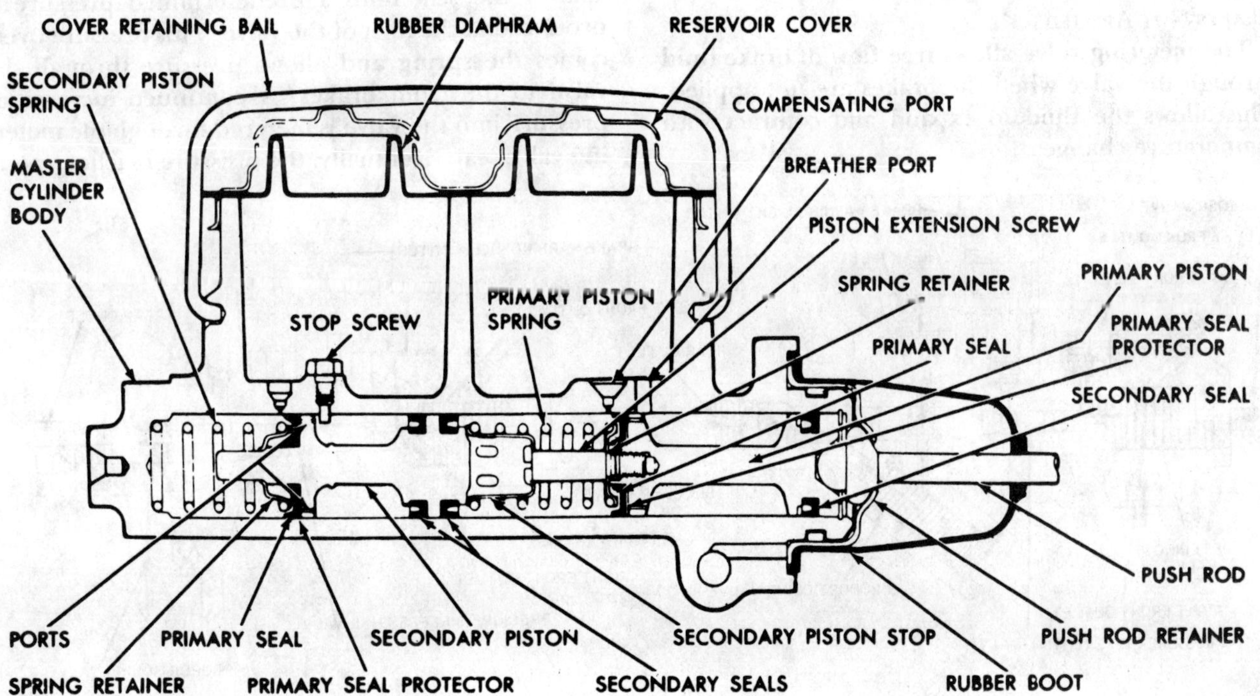

The dual master cylinder used with modern braking systems has two reservoirs and two pistons to develop pressure in each of the braking systems. A vented cover and flexible rubber diaphragm at the top of the reservoirs seal the system from contamination.

PRESSURE-DIFFERENTIAL VALVE

The pressure-differential valve in the center of the control valve senses unbalanced pressure between the front and rear brakes. A pressure loss in either the front or rear brake system, upon pedal application, will move the valve off-center, causing the warning light to come on. After repairs are made, and the brake system properly bled, the valve will center itself and the warning light will shut off.

The brake warning light switch is mounted on the top of the valve body casting, above the piston tapered shoulder groove. When the piston is in the centralized position, the spring-loaded switch plunger fits into the tapered shoulder groove, and the switch contacts are open.

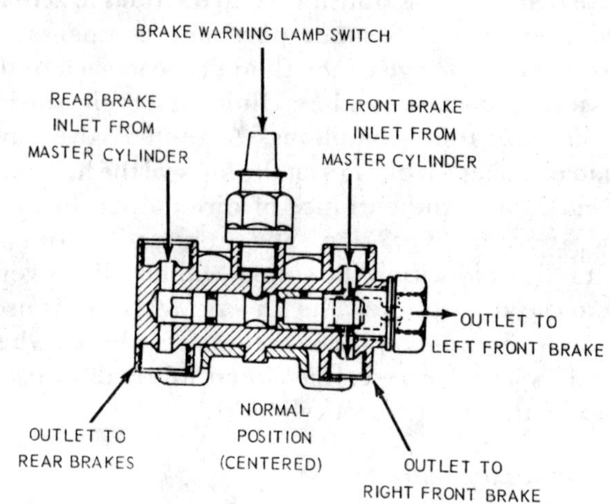

Sectioned view through a pressure-differential valve with a brake warning light switch.

METERING VALVE

The metering valve is located in the front end of the control valve central bore, between the front brake system inlet port and the right and left front brake outlet ports. This valve delays front disc brake application until the shoes of the rear drum brakes contact the drum. The action is needed because of the return springs on the rear wheel brake shoes. Disc brake shoes have no return springs.

Brakes Not Applied

The metering valve allows free flow of brake fluid through the valve when the brakes are not applied. This allows the fluid to expand and contract with temperature changes.

Shut -Off Point (Initial Brake Apply)

The metering valve stem moves to the left and, at 4 to 30 psi, the smooth end of the stem is in a sealing position with the metering valve seal lip, and this is the shut-off point.

Hold -Off Bend Pressure

The metering valve stem continues to the left on initial brake apply and stops on the knurl at the metal retainer. The metering valve spring holds the retainer against the seal until a predetermined pressure is produced at the inlet of the valve. This pressure overcomes the spring and allows pressure through the valve to the front brakes. A continued increase of pressure into the valve is metered through the metering valve seal. Eventually, the pressure reaches a point

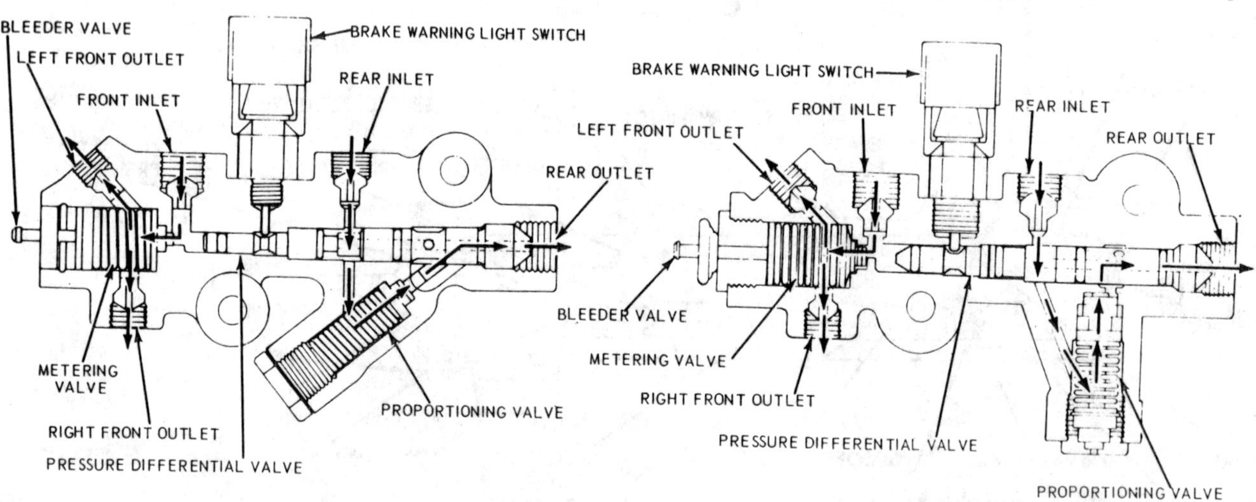

Sectioned view through a control valve assembly used for metering the hydraulic pressure to the front wheel system and proportioning it to the rear wheels. The brake warning light switch is in the center section of the control valve.

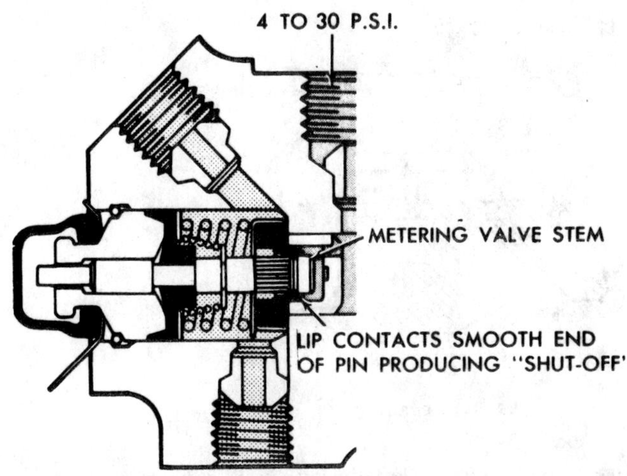

On initial brake apply, the metering valve stem moves to the left and shuts off hydraulic pressure to the front disc brakes.

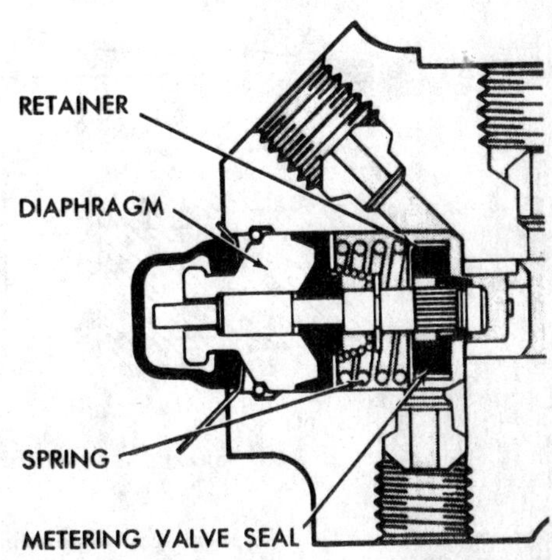

As pressure builds up in the system, the metering valve allows pressure through the valve to the front disc braking system.

where the spring is completely pulled away by the diaphragm pin and retainer, leaving the metering valve seal free to pass unrestricted pressure through the valve.

PROPORTIONING VALVE

The proportioning valve assembly is installed in a separate angular or vertical bore at the bottom of the valve body casting, between the rear brake system inlet and outlet ports. The proportioner improves front-to-rear brake balance at high deceleration. During quick stops, a percentage of the rear weight is transferred to the front wheels. Compensation must be made for the resultant loss of weight to the rear wheels to avoid early rear wheel skid. The proportioner part of the control valve reduces the rear brake pressure and so delays a rear wheel skid. The proportioner is not repairable; it must be replaced if defective.

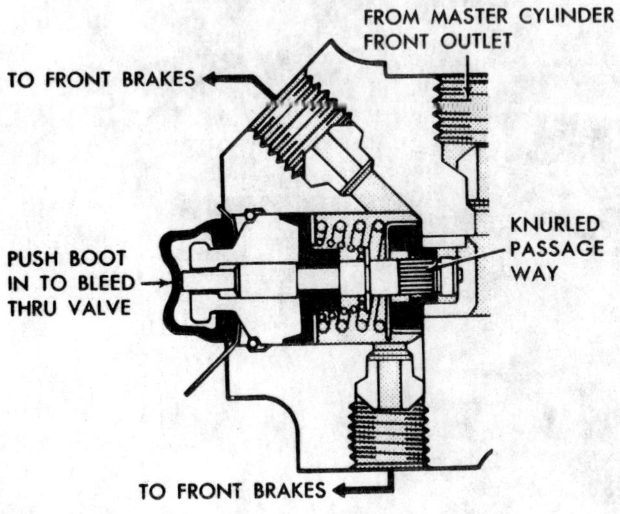

FROM MASTER CYLINDER FRONT OUTLET
TO FRONT BRAKES
KNURLED PASSAGE WAY
PUSH BOOT IN TO BLEED THRU VALVE
TO FRONT BRAKES

The metering valve keeps the disc brake pads from operating until the shoes of the rear drum brake contact the drum. In this non-applied position, free passage of brake fluid is allowed through the knurled passageway.

Normal Brake Stops

The proportioner does not operate during normal brake stops. Fluid normally flows into the proportioner through the space between the piston center hole and valve stem, through the stop plate, and out to the rear brakes. The spring loads the piston so that it rests against the stop plate during normal brake pressures.

Proportioning Action

Pressure developed within the valve pushes against the large end of the piston and, when sufficient to overcome the spring load, moves the piston to the left. The piston contacts the spherical stem seat and starts proportioning by restricting pressure through the valve.

FRONT WHEEL DISC BRAKES

The disc brake consists of a ventilated rotor and caliper assembly. The caliper used is a single piston, sliding caliper, mounted on an anchor plate which is attached to the spindle arms. A pressure differential valve provides balanced braking action between front and rear brakes.

The caliper assembly is made up of a sliding caliper housing assembly and an anchor plate. The anchor plate is bolted to the wheel spindle arm by two bolts. Two angular machined surfaces on the upper end of

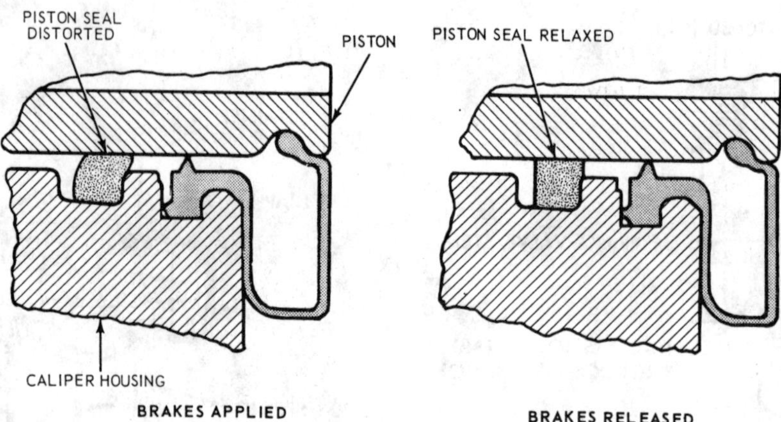

Caliper disc brakes are self-adjusting because of distortion and slippage of the piston seal (left) during a brake application. When the lining wears, the seal slips slightly, allowing the piston to move out farther. When the brake pedal pressure is released, (right), the seal assumes its normal relaxed position to pull the piston slightly back from contact with the rotor to provide a slight running clearance.

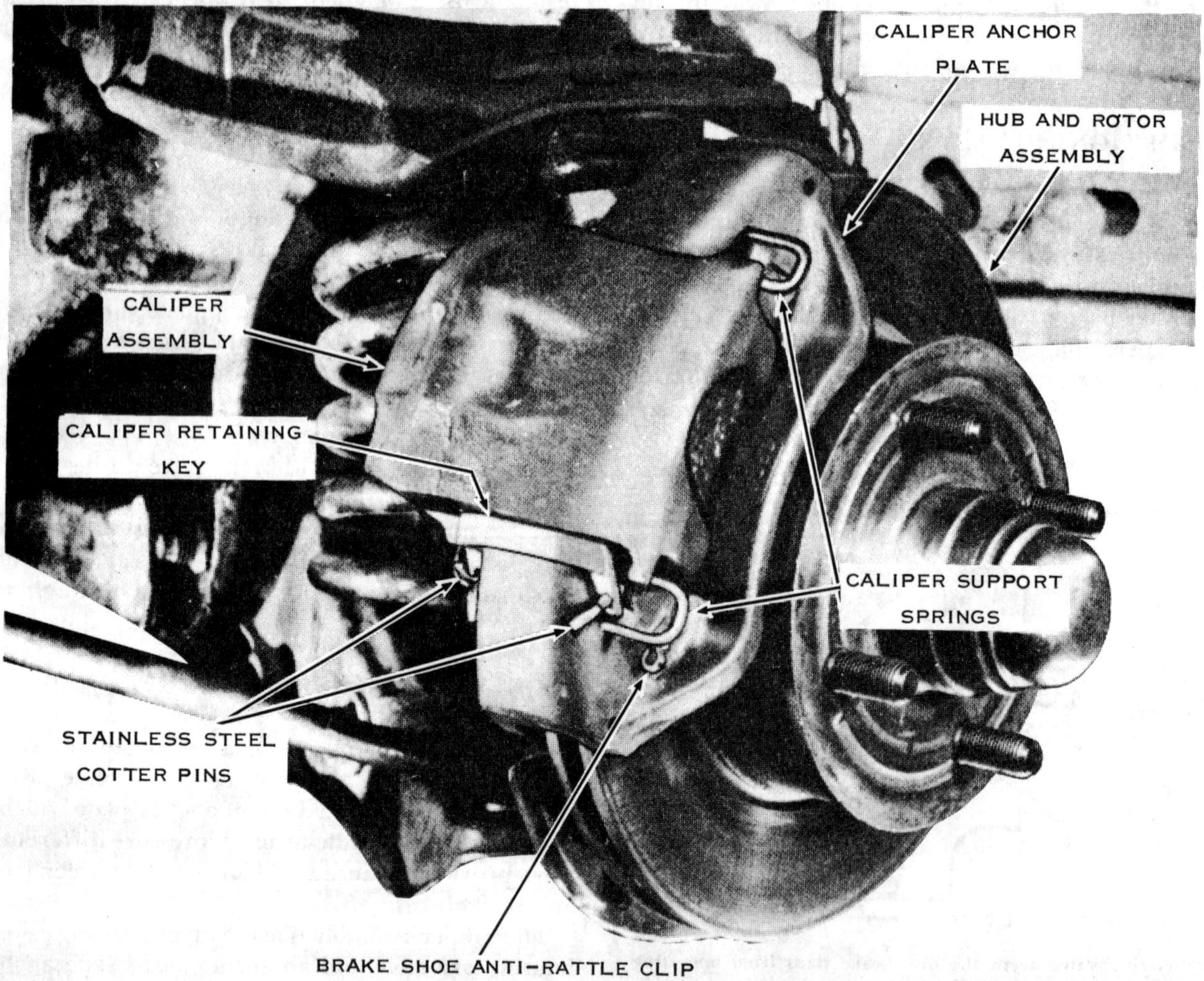

Details of the sliding-caliper type front disc brake assembly.

the caliper housing contact mating machined surfaces of the anchor plate. A steel key is fitted between the angular machined surfaces of the lower end of the caliper and the machined surfaces of the anchor plate. The key is retained with two stainless steel cotter pins through holes near each end of the key. The caliper is held in position against the mating surfaces of the anchor plate by two caliper support springs. A brake shoe anti-rattle spring clip is provided at the lower end of each brake shoe and lining assembly. The brake linings are riveted to the brake shoes and insulator gaskets are bonded on the back of each brake shoe. Both the outer and inner brake shoe and lining assemblies are the same size.

The sliding caliper contains a single cylinder and piston assembly. The cylinder bore contains a piston with a molded rubber dust boot to seal the cylinder bore from contamination. A square section rubber piston seal is positioned in a groove in the cylinder bore to provide sealing between the cylinder and piston.

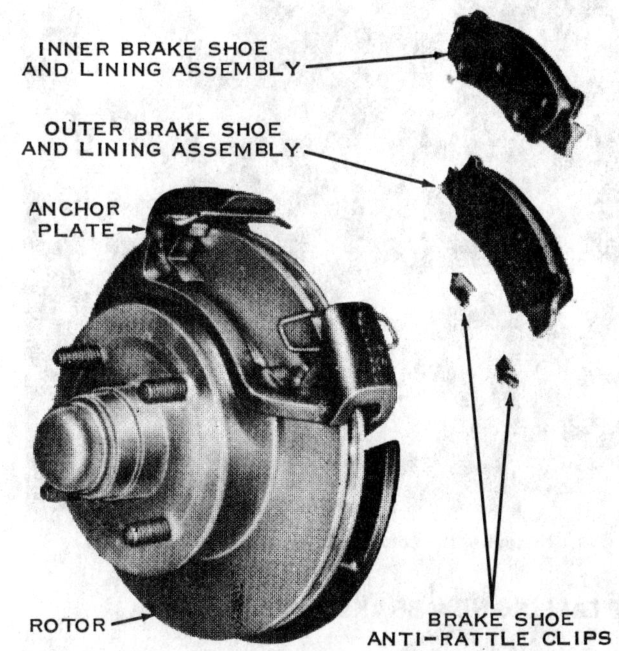

The brake shoe assemblies can be replaced without removing the caliper.

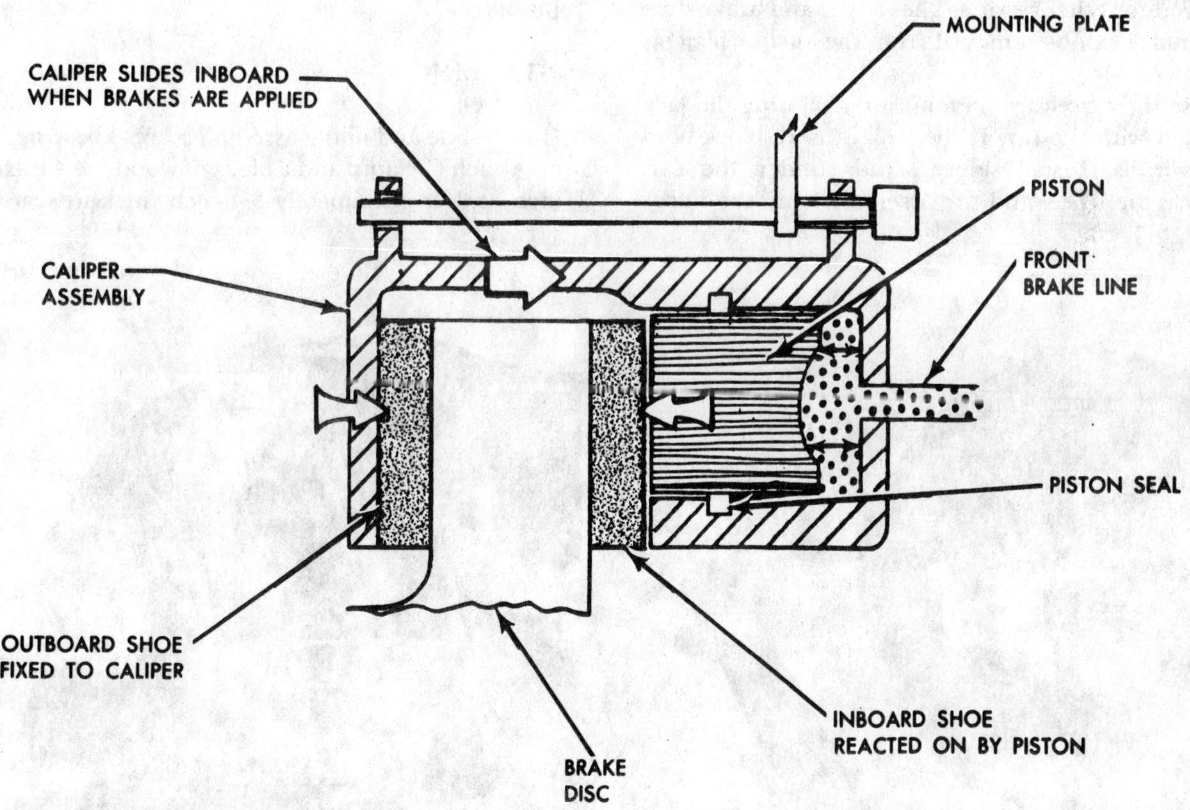

When fluid is contained in a closed system and pressure is applied, it is exerted equally in all directions and, in the single-piston assembly, it acts on two surfaces: (1) the piston, and (2) in the opposite direction against the caliper housing, which pulls the housing inboard, sliding on the four rubber bushings.

Removing the cotter pins from the retaining key.

INSTALLING NEW BRAKE PADS

REMOVING

It is not necessary to remove the caliper and anchor plate to replace the brake shoes, although they can be easily replaced if the caliper and anchor plate are removed for other repairs. The caliper and brake shoe and linings can be removed from the anchor plate as follows:

Raise the car either on a hoist or by using the jack supplied with the car. If the jack is used, block both rear wheels. Install safety stands under the car. Remove the wheel and tire assembly from the hub.

Remove the two stainless steel cotter pins from the caliper retaining key. Slide the caliper retaining key either inward or outward from the anchor plate. Use a hammer and drift, if necessary, to remove the key. Use care to avoid damaging the key.

Press the caliper assembly inward and upward against the caliper support springs and lift the assembly away fron the anchor plate. **CAUTION: Use care so that the flexible brake hose is not stretched or twisted.** Use mechanic's wire to temporarily suspend the caliper assembly from the upper suspension arms.

If the brake shoe and lining assemblies are to be re-used, mark them for identification so that they can be replaced in their original positions. Remove the shoe and lining assemblies from the anchor plate. The brake shoe anti-rattle clips may come out of place when the shoe and lining assemblies are removed.

CLEANING AND INSPECTING

Clean the caliper, anchor plate, and rotor assembly. Inspect them for signs of brake fluid leakage, excess wear, or damage. Inspect the brake shoe and lining assemblies for wear. If either lining is worn to within 1/32-inch of any rivet head, both shoes and linings must be replaced. Any other damaged parts must be replaced.

INSTALLING

If new shoe and lining assemblies are to be installed, use a 4-inch C-clamp and a block of wood 1-3/4 inch by 1 inch and approximately 3/4 inch thick to seat the

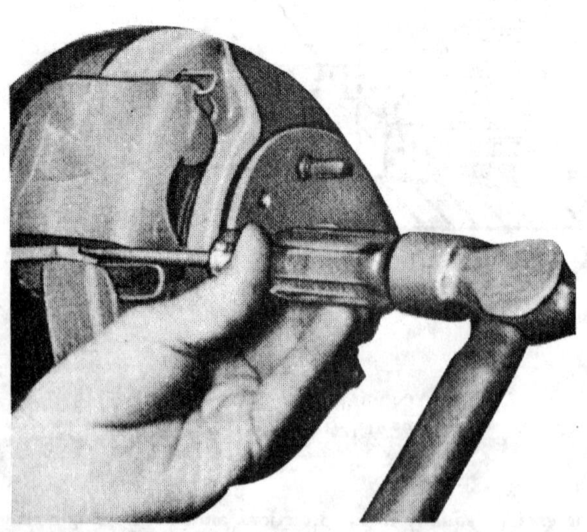

Driving out the caliper retaining key.

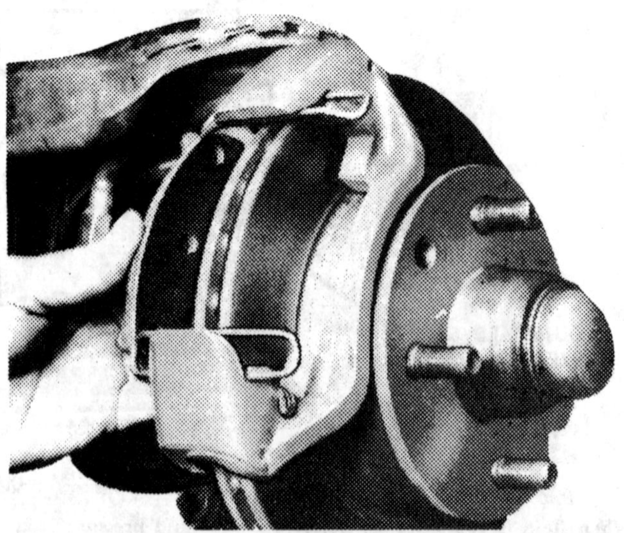

Removing the brake shoes.

caliper hydraulic piston in its bore as shown. This must be done to provide clearance for the caliper to fit over the shoes when installed.

Be sure that the brake shoe anti-rattle clips are in place, and then position the shoe and lining assemblies in the anchor plate. **CAUTION: If re-using the old shoes, install them in the position from which they were removed.** If installing new shoe and lining assemblies, they can be placed in either the inner or outer position as they are both of the same size and material.

Remove the C-clamp from the caliper (the caliper piston will remain seated in its bore). While holding the caliper with one hand, remove the mechanic's wire used to support the caliper.

Install the caliper assembly on the anchor plate as follows: Position the caliper to the anchor plate, with the lower beveled edge of the caliper on top of the rearward caliper support spring. Carefully slide the caliper on over the shoes in a pivoting motion until the caliper upper beveled edge can be pushed over the forward caliper support spring.

Use a heavy screwdriver as shown to hold the caliper over the upper caliper support spring and against the anchor plate; then, insert the caliper retaining key as shown. Remove the screwdriver and lightly tap the caliper key into position.

Install two **new** stainless steel cotter pins in the caliper retaining key.

Depress the brake pedal several times to position the caliper and brake shoe assemblies properly. Also, at this point, again check for signs of brake fluid leaks around the caliper and flexible brake hose. Perform repairs, if necessary.

Install the wheel and tire assembly. Torque the wheel lug nuts to 70-115 ft-lbs. Install the wheel cover. Road test the car to insure proper brake operation.

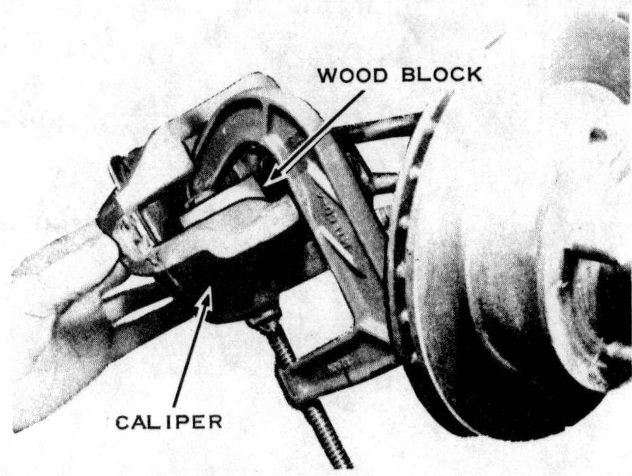

Using a C-clamp to force the piston back into the caliper.

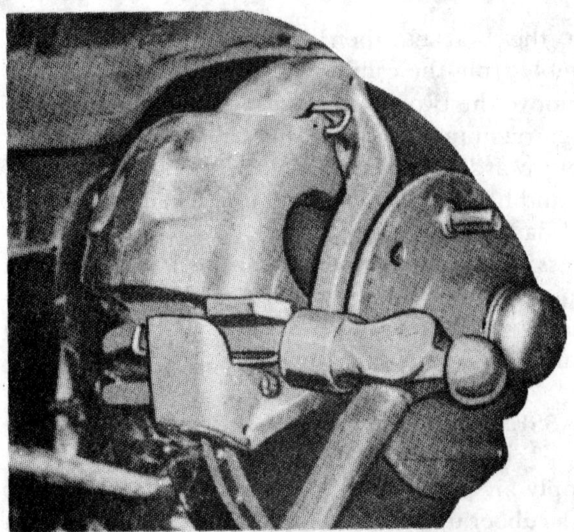

Installing the caliper retaining key on the anchor plate.

OVERHAULING THE CALIPER

REMOVING

Raise the car either on a hoist or by using a jack. If the jack is used, block both rear wheels. Install safety stands under the car. Remove the wheel and tire assembly from the hub.

Disconnect the flexible brake hose from the caliper. To do this, loosen the tube fitting that connects the opposite end of the hose to the brake tube at a bracket on the frame. Remove the horseshoe-type retaining clip from the hose and bracket and disengage the hose

Installing the caliper retaining key cotter pin.

from the bracket, then unscrew the entire hose assembly from the caliper.

Remove the two stainless steel cotter pins from the caliper retaining key. Slide the caliper retaining key either inward or outward from the anchor plate. Use a drift and hammer to remove the key, being careful to avoid damaging the key.

Press the caliper assembly inward and upward against the caliper support springs, and then lift the assembly away from the anchor plate. Place the assembly on a bench.

DISASSEMBLING

Apply air pressure to the fluid port in the caliper with a rubber tipped nozzle. **CAUTION: Place a cloth over the piston before applying air pressure to prevent damage to the piston.** If the piston is seized and cannot be forced from the caliper, tap lightly around the piston while applying air pressure. **CAUTION: Care should be taken because the piston can develop considerable force due to pressure build-up.**

Remove the dust boot from the caliper assembly. Remove the rubber piston seal fron the cylinder and discard it.

CLEANING AND INSPECTING

Clean all metal parts with alcohol or a suitable solvent. Use clean, dry, compressed air to clean out and dry the grooves and passageways. **CAUTION: Make sure that the caliper bore and component parts are completely free of any foreign material.**

Check the cylinder bore and piston for damage or excessive wear. Replace the piston if it is pitted, scored, or the chrome plating is worn off.

If a new caliper is to be used, transfer the bleeder screw from the old caliper.

ASSEMBLING

Apply a film of clean brake fluid to the new caliper piston seal and install it in the cylinder bore. **CAUTION: Make sure the seal does not become twisted and that it is seated fully in the groove.**

Install a new dust boot by setting the flange squarely in the outer groove of the caliper bore.

Coat the piston with brake fluid and install the piston in the cylinder bore. Spread the dust boot over the piston as it is installed. Seat the dust boot in the piston groove and push the piston on into its bore.

INSTALLING

Install the caliper assembly on the anchor plate as follows: Position the caliper to the anchor plate with the lower beveled edge of the caliper on top of the rearward caliper support spring. Carefully slide the caliper on over the shoes in a pivoting motion until the caliper upper beveled edge can be pushed over the forward caliper support spring.

Use a heavy screwdriver as shown to hold the caliper over the upper caliper support spring and against the anchor plate; then, insert the caliper retaining key. Remove the screwdriver and lightly tap the caliper retaining key into position.

Install two **new** stainless steel cotter pins in the caliper retaining key. **CAUTION: Make sure that the cotter pins are spread open at least 150°.**

Connect the flexible brake hose to the caliper. Install a new copper gasket over the hose fitting. Thread the hose into the caliper and tighten it. Engage the opposite end of the hose to the bracket on the frame. Install the horseshoe-type retaining clip and connect the brake tube to the hose with the tube fitting nut. Tighten the nut.

Bleed the brake system. Install the wheel and tire assembly. Remove the safety stand(s) and lower the car.

Depress the brake pedal several times before driving the car to position the brake shoes properly and establish the pedal height. Test the car to insure proper brake operation.

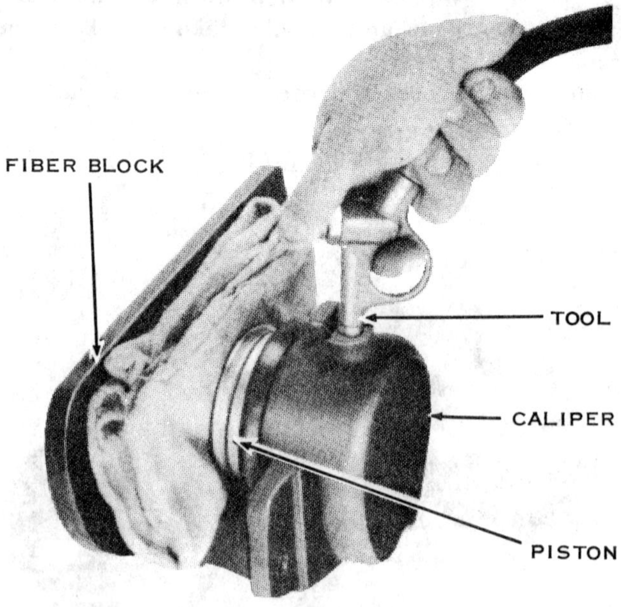

Air pressure can be used to force the piston out of the caliper, if the seals need to be replaced.

SERVICING DRUM BRAKES

REMOVING THE BRAKE DRUM

Raise the vehicle so that the tire is clear of the floor. Remove the hub cap and wheel.

Remove the three drum retainer nuts and remove the brake drum. If the drum will not come off, pry the rubber cover from the backing plate. Insert a narrow screwdriver through the hole in the backing plate, and disengage the adjusting lever from the adjusting screw. While holding the adjusting lever away from the adjusting screw, back off the adjusting screw with the brake adjusting tool. **CAUTION: Be very careful not to burr, chip or damage the notches in the adjusting screw; otherwise, the self-adjusting mechanism will not function properly.**

REMOVING THE BRAKE SHOES

With the wheel and drum removed, install a clamp over the ends of the brake cylinder as shown.

Remove the shoe to anchor springs and then unhook the cable eye from the anchor pin. Remove the shoe guide (anchor pin) plate when so equipped. Remove the shoe hold-down springs, shoes, adjusting screw, pivot nut, socket, and automatic adjustment parts.

If you cannot pull off the wheel and drum assembly, it may be necessary to release the automatic adjuster. This rubber cover must be pried out to gain access to the adjuster mechanism.

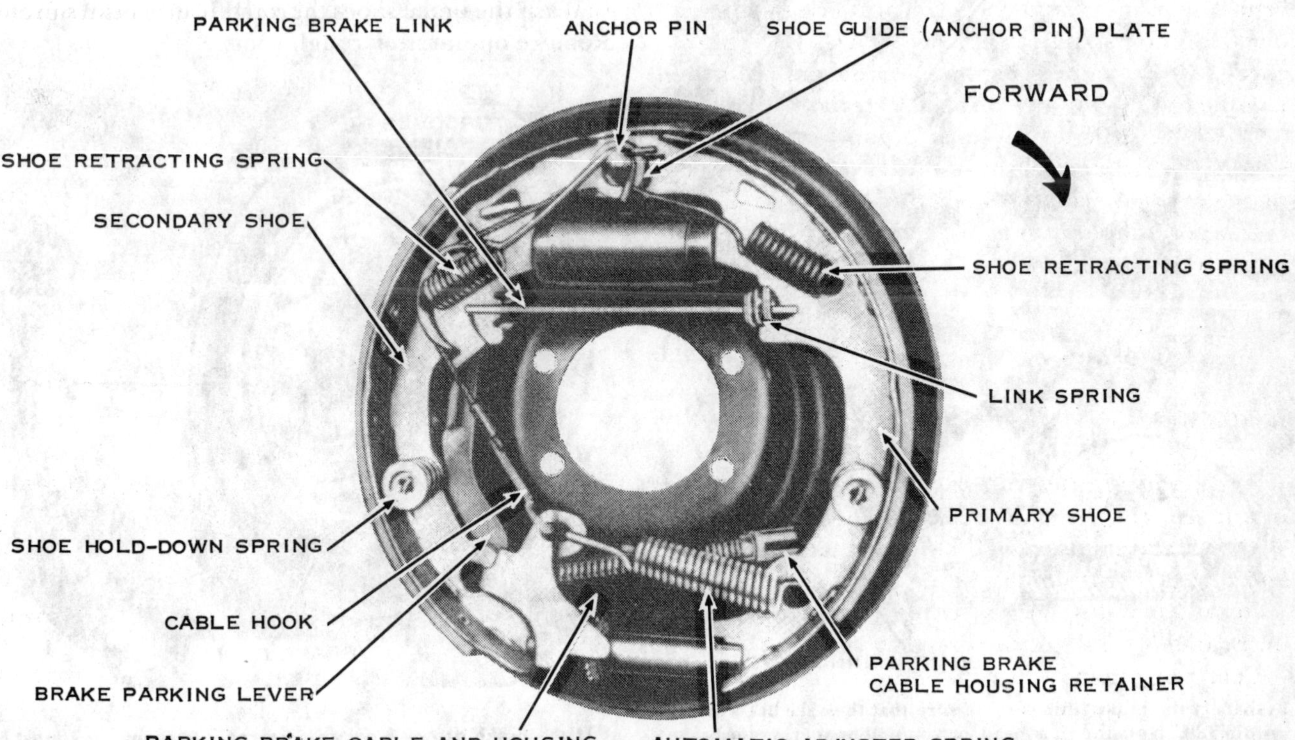

Details of the self-adjusting brake mechanism and brake shoe mounting.

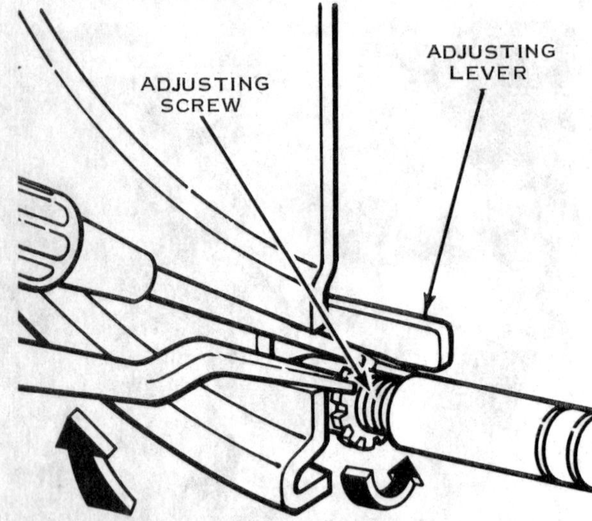

Lift the adjusting lever and turn the adjusting screw to retract the mechanism.

On rear brakes, remove the parking brake link, spring, and retainer. Disconnect the parking brake cable from the parking brake lever. After removing the rear brake secondary shoe, disassemble the parking brake lever from the shoe by removing the retaining clip and spring washer.

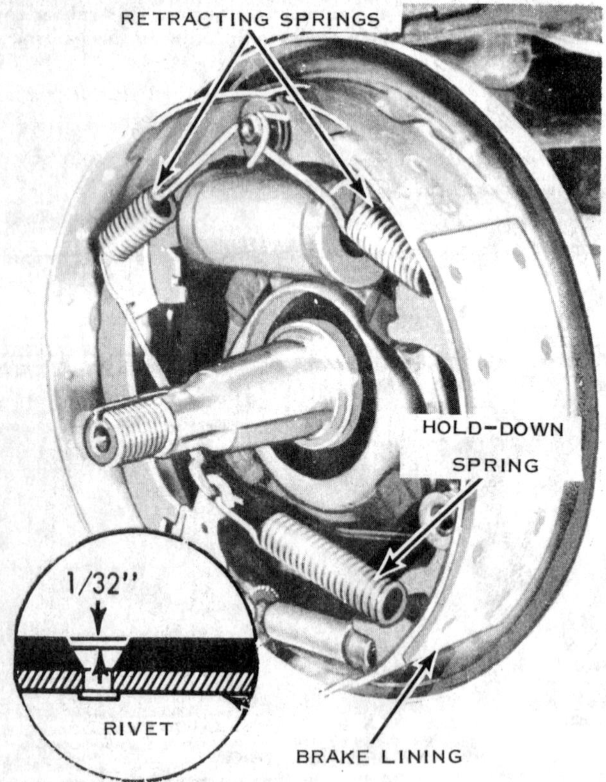

Inspect the brake linings to be sure that they are not worn to within 1/32" from the rivet head, or you will be scoring the brake drums. Check the retracting springs for evidence of distortion and stretching.

Cover the spindle with a clean cloth, and then brush all dust and dirt from the brake mechanism.

CLEANING AND INSPECTING

Relining The Brake Shoes

Brake linings that are worn to within 1/32 inch of the rivet head or are less than 0.030 inch thick (bonded lining) or have been contaminated with brake fluid, grease, or oil must be replaced. Failure to replace worn linings will result in a scored drum. **CAUTION: When it is necessary to replace linings, they must also be replaced on the wheel on the opposite side of the vehicle.**

Inspect brake shoes for distortion, cracks, or looseness. If this condition exists, the shoe must be discarded. **CAUTION: Do not attempt to repair a damaged brake shoe.**

Wash the brake shoes thoroughly in a clean solvent. Remove all burrs or rough spots.

If the brake drums have grooves cut into them, they must be turned in a drum lathe.

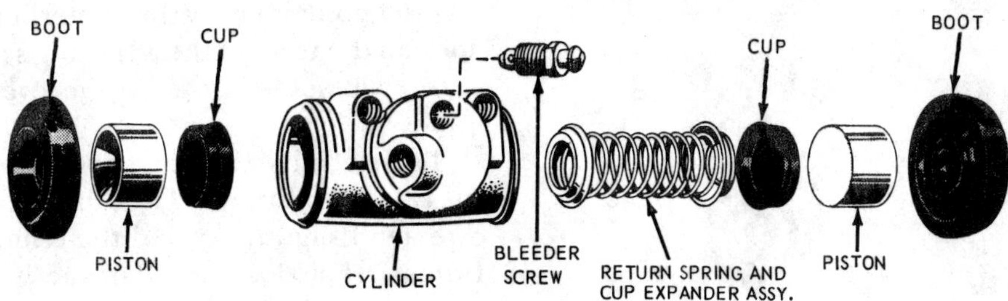

Exploded view of the wheel cylinder.

WHEEL CYLINDERS

Wheel cylinders should not be disassembled unless they are leaking or unless new cups and boots are to be installed. It is not necessary to remove the brake cylinder from the backing plate to disassemble, inspect, or hone and overhaul the cylinder. Removal is necessary only if the cylinder is damaged or scored beyond repair.

INSTALLING THE RELINED BRAKE SHOES

Before installing the rear brake shoes, assemble the parking brake lever to the secondary shoe and secure it with the spring washer and retaining clip.

Apply a light coating of high-temperature grease at the points where the brake shoes contact the backing plate. Position the brake shoes on the backing plate and secure the assembly with the hold-down springs. On the rear brake, install the parking brake link, spring, and retainer. Back off the parking brake adjustment, then connect the parking brake cable to the parking brake lever.

Install the shoe guide (anchor pin) plate on the anchor pin, when so equipped. Place the cable eye over the anchor pin, with the crimped-side toward the backing plate (11-inch brakes) or drum (9 and 10-inch brakes).

Install the cable guide on the secondary shoe web, with the flanged hole fitted into the hole in the secondary shoe web. Thread the cable around the cable guide groove. **CAUTION: It is imperative that the cable be positioned in this groove and not between the guide and the shoe web.**

Install the secondary shoe-to-anchor spring (9 and 10-inch brakes) or the primary shoe-to-anchor spring (on 11-inch brakes) with the tool shown. **CAUTION: Be certain that the eye is not cocked or binding on the anchor pin when installed. All parts should be flat on the anchor pin.** Remove the brake cylinder clamp.

Apply the high-temperature grease (ESA-M1C75-B) to the threads and the socket end of the adjusting screw. Turn the adjusting screw into the adjusting pivot nut to the limit of the threads and then back it off 1/2 turn. **CAUTION: Interchanging the brake shoe adjusting screw assemblies from one side of the vehicle to the other would cause the brake shoes to**

If brake service is delayed too long, the grooves can cut the drum in two, with disastrous results.

Replacing the brake shoe retracting spring.

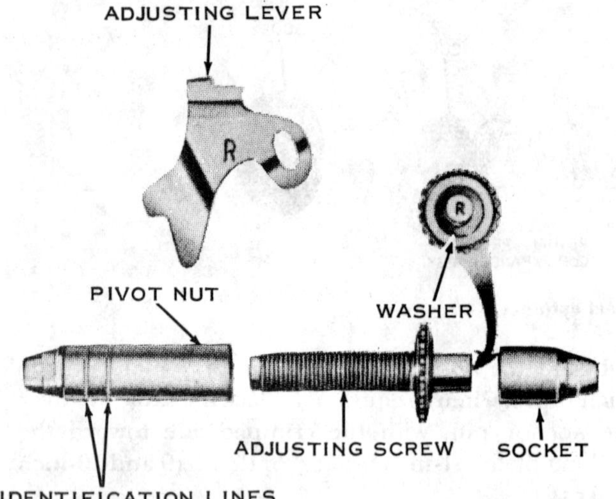

Details of the adjusting lever, pivot nut, adjusting screw, and socket, with identifying marks for right or left side installation.

retract rather than expand each time the automatic adjusting mechanism operated. To prevent installation on the wrong side of the vehicle, the socket end of the adjusting screw is stamped with an R or L for identifying the right and left side parts.

Place the adjusting socket on the screw and install this assembly between the shoe ends with the adjusting screw toothed wheel nearest the secondary shoe. Hook the cable hook into the hole in the adjusting lever. The adjusting levers are stamped with an R or L to indicate their installation on a right or left brake assembly.

Position the hooked end of the adjuster spring completely into the large hole in the primary shoe web. The last coil of the spring should be at the edge of the hole. Connect the loop end of the spring to the adjuster lever hole. Pull the adjuster lever, cable and automatic adjuster spring down and toward the rear to engage the pivot hook in the large hole in the secondary shoe web.

After installation, check the action of the adjuster by pulling the section of the cable between the cable guide and the anchor pin toward the secondary shoe web far enough to lift the lever past a tooth on the adjusting screw wheel. The lever should snap into position behind the next tooth, and release of the cable should cause the adjuster spring to return the lever to its original position. This return action of the lever will turn the adjusting screw one tooth.

If pulling the cable does not produce the action described, or if the lever action is sluggish instead of positive and sharp, check the position of the lever on the adjusting screw toothed wheel. With the brake in a vertical position (anchor at the top), the lever should contact the adjusting wheel 3/16 inch (plus or minus 1/32 inch) above the centerline of the screw. If the contact point is below this centerline, the lever will not lock on the teeth in the adjusting screw wheel, and the screw will not be turned as the lever is actuated by the cable.

To determine the cause of this condition: (a) Check the cable end fittings. The cable should completely fill or extend slightly beyond the crimped section of the fittings. If it does not, damage is indicated and the cable assembly should be replaced. (b) Check the cable length. On models equipped with 11-inch brakes, the cable should measure 11⅛ inches (plus or minus 1/64 inch) from the end of the cable anchor to the end of the cable hook. On models equipped with 9-inch brakes, the cable should measure 8-7/16 inches. On models equipped with 10-inch brakes, the cable should measure 9-3/4 inches from the end of the cable anchor to the end of the cable hook. (c) Check the cable guide for damage. The cable groove should be parallel to the shoe web, and the body of the guide should lie flat against the web. Replace the guide if it shows damage. (d) Check the pivot hook on the lever. The hook surfaces should be square with the body of the lever for proper pivoting. Replace the lever if the hook shows damage. (e) See that the adjusting screw socket is properly seated in the notch in the shoe web.

INSTALLING THE BRAKE DRUM

The hydraulic drum brakes are self-adjusting and require a manual adjustment only after the brake

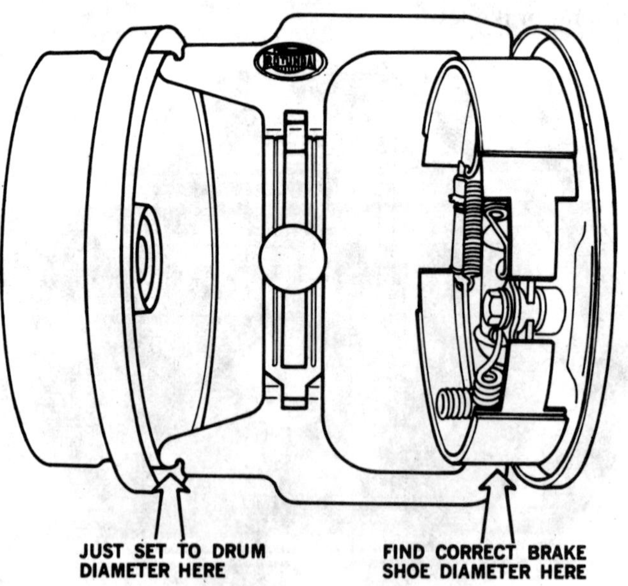

Using a special brake caliper to measure the inside drum diameter and setting tool for adjusting the position of the brake shoes to match the drum.

shoes have been relined, replaced, or when the length of the adjusting screw has been changed while performing some other service operation. The manual adjustment is performed with the drums removed, using the tool and the procedure detailed below. **CAUTION: When adjusting the rear brake shoes, check the parking brake cables for the proper adjustment. Make sure that the equalizer operates freely.**

To adjust the brake shoes, use the illustrated gauge to determine the inside diameter of the drum braking surface. Use the tool as shown and adjust the brake shoe diameter to fit the gauge. *NOTE: Hold the automatic adjusting lever out of engagement while rotating the adjusting screw to prevent burring the screw slots.* **CAUTION: Make sure the adjusting screw rotates freely. If necessary, lubricate the adjusting screw threads with a thin uniform coating of lubricant (ESA-M1C75-B).** Rotate the tool around the brake shoes to be sure of the setting.

Apply a small quantity of high temperature grease to the points where the shoes contact the backing plate, being careful not to get the lubricant on the linings. Place the drum over the brake assembly and into position. Install the three drum retainer nuts and tighten them securely. Install the wheel on the axle shaft flange studs against the drum and tighten the attaching nuts. Bleed the brakes.

Complete the adjustment by applying the brakes several times with a minimum of 50 lbs pressure on the pedal (non-power brakes) or 25 lbs pressure (power brakes) while backing the vehicle. **CAUTION: After each stop, the vehicle must be moved forward. CAUTION: After any brake service work, obtain a firm brake pedal before moving the vehicle. Riding the brake pedal (common on left foot application) should be avoided when driving the vehicle.**

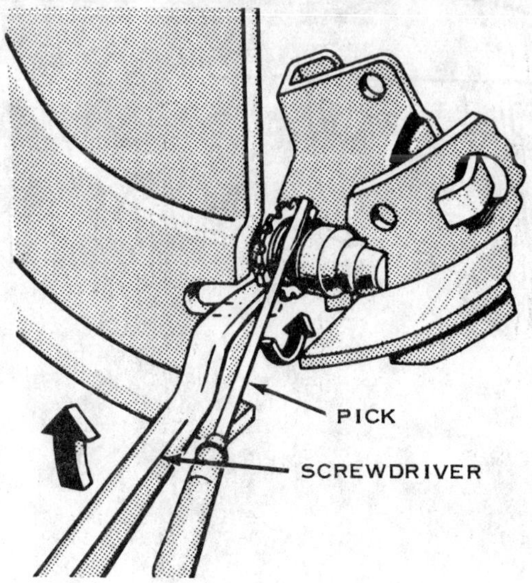

Making the brake shoe adjustment from the backing plate side of the brake assembly.

BLEEDING THE HYDRAULIC SYSTEM

The hydraulic system must be bled of all entrained air whenever any parts have been replaced which required draining of the hydraulic fluid. Also, the system must be bled to remove trapped air whenever the brake pedal feels spongy on application.

The primary and secondary (front and rear) hydraulic brake systems are individual systems and are bled separately. Bleed the longest line first on the individual system being serviced. **CAUTION: During the complete bleeding operation, do not allow the reservoir to run dry.** Keep the master cylinder reservoirs filled with Brake Fluid—Extra Heavy Duty (ESA-M6C25-A). **CAUTION: The extra heavy duty brake fluid is colored blue for identification purposes. Never re-use brake fluid that has drained from the hydraulic system or has been allowed to stand in an open container for an extended period of time; it will absorb moisture from the air. CAUTION: Do not use the secondary piston stop screw (located on the bottom of some master cylinders) to bleed the brake system. Loosening or removing this**

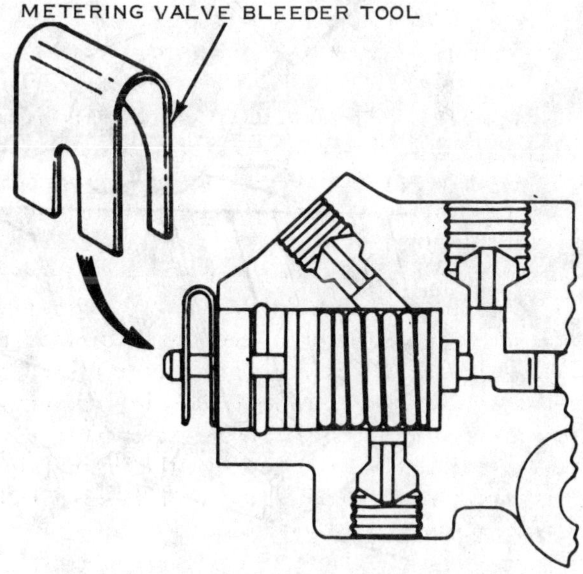

When pressure-bleeding the hydraulic brake system, it is necessary to pull out the pin extending through the metering valve so that brake fluid can flow to the front disc brakes. This is not necessary when manually bleeding the system because the pressure developed by depressing the brake pedal is enough to force the metering valve open. CAUTION: Make sure to remove the valve bleeder tool when you have finished bleeding the system.

screw could result in damage to the secondary piston by the stop screw.

To bleed the brake system, position a suitable box wrench on the bleeder fitting on the brake wheel cylinder. Attach a rubber drain tube to the bleeder fitting. **CAUTION: The end of the tube must fit snugly around the bleeder fitting.** Submerge the free end of the tube in a container partially filled with clean brake fluid, and loosen the bleeder fitting approximately ¾ turn.

Have a second person push the brake pedal down slowly through its full travel. Close the bleeder fitting, then return the pedal to the full-released position. Repeat this operation until air bubbles cease to appear at the submerged end of the bleeder tube. When the fluid is completely free of air bubbles, secure the bleeder fitting and remove the bleeder tube.

Repeat this procedure at the brake wheel cylinder on the opposite side. Refill the master cylinder reservoir after each wheel cylinder is bled and install the master cylinder cover and gasket. **CAUTION: Be sure the diaphragm-type gasket is properly positioned in the master cylinder cover.** When the bleeding operation is completed, the fluid level should be filled to FULL or within ¼ inch of the top of the reservoirs.

If the primary (front brake) system is to be bled, repeat the bleeding process at the right front brake caliper or cylinder and ending at the left front brake caliper or cylinder. **CAUTION: On disc-brake equipped models, be sure that the front brake pistons are returned to their normal positions, and that shoe-and-lining assemblies are properly seated by depressing the brake pedal several times until normal pedal travel is established.**

CENTRALIZING THE PRESSURE-DIFFERENTIAL VALVE

After any repair or bleeding of the primary (front brake) or secondary (rear brake) system, the dual-brake warning light switch in the pressure-differential valve should be centralized. To centralize the valve and turn off the warning light after a repair operation: (a) Turn the ignition switch to the ACC or ON position. (b) Depress the brake pedal and the piston will center itself, causing the brake warning light to go out (if it was illuminated). (c) Turn the ignition switch to the OFF position. **CAUTION: Before driving the vehicle, check the operation of the brakes to be sure that a firm pedal is obtained.**

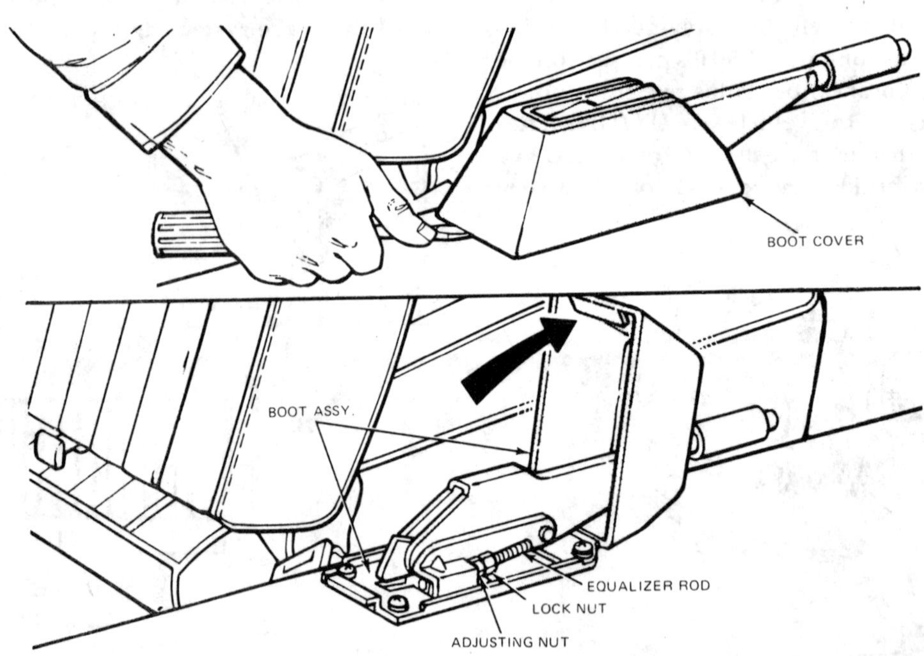

Adjusting the parking brakes.

10 | electrical system service

The service procedures covered in this chapter are: battery, charging, cranking, ignition, and lighting systems. A great deal of ignition system service procedures can be found in Chapter 2, with detailed conventional ignition service troubleshooting tests in Chapter 1. Electronic ignition troubleshooting and service procedures are covered in this chapter. The sections will be covered in the above order.

BATTERY

The battery is made up of a number of separate elements, each located in an individual cell in a hard-rubber case. Each element consists of an assembly of positive plates and negative plates containing dissimilar active materials and kept apart by separators. The elements are immersed in an electrolyte composed of dilute sulfuric acid. Plate straps, located on the top of each element, connect all the positive plates and all the negative plates into groups. The elements are connected in series electrically by connectors that pass directly through the case partitions between the cells. The top is a one-piece cover. The cell connectors, passing through the cell partitions, connect the elements along the shortest practical path. With the length of the electrical circuit inside the battery reduced to a minimum, the internal voltage drop is decreased, resulting in improved performance, particularly during engine cranking at low temperatures.

RATINGS

A battery has two classifications of ratings: (1) a 20-hour rating at 80° F and, (2) a cold rating at 0° F which indicates the cranking load capacity. The ampere-hour rating found on older batteries was based on the 20-hour rating. That is, a battery capable of furnishing three amperes for 20 hours, while maintaining a specified average individual cell voltage, would be classified as a 60-ampere hour battery (e.g., 3 amperes x 20 hours = 60 A.H.). A Peak Watt Rating

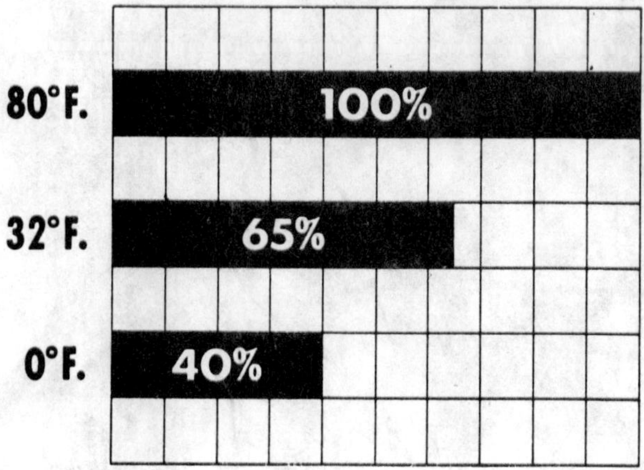

The capacity of a battery falls off rapidly with low temperatures, and this makes starting much more difficult in cold weather. At 0° F, a battery has only 40% of its 80° capacity.

A battery cell group consists of a set of positive plates, nestled together with a set of negative plates and kept apart by separators, which are porous to allow a free flow of electrolyte.

(PWR) has been developed as a measure of the battery's cold-cranking ability. The numerical rating is embossed on each case at the base. This value is determined by multiplying the maximum current by the maximum voltage. The PWR should not be confused with the ampere-hour rating since two batteries with the same ampere-hour rating can have quite different PWR ratings. For battery replacement, a unit of at least equal power rating must be selected.

NEW BATTERY RATINGS

The method of rating batteries has been recently revised by the Society of Automotive Engineers. The new rating system provides information which defines a battery's ability to deliver a given amount of usable cranking power.

A "Reserve Capacity Rating" represents the approximate time in minutes it is possible to travel at night with battery ignition and minimum electrical load, but without a charging system in operation. The time in minutes is based on a current draw of 25 amperes while maintaining a minimum battery terminal voltage of 10.2 volts at 80° F. This rating replaces the previous 20-hour capacity (ampere hour) rating and more accurately represents the electrical load which must be supplied by the battery in the event of a charging system failure. The ampere hour rating will eventually be dropped.

A "Cold Cranking Rating" specifies the minimum amps available at 0° F. and at -20° F. This rating replaces the old method of relating voltage and time as measures of cranking and starting ability. It is much more accurate because it allows cranking capacity to be related to such significant variables as engine displacement, compression ratio, temperature, cranking time, condition of the engine and electrical system, and the lowest practical voltage for cranking and ignition (the old tests do not take these factors into account). The new test relates a discharge rating in amperes that a fully charged battery will maintain for 30 seconds without the terminal voltage falling below 7.2 v. for a 12 v. battery.

To provide enough starting power under adverse conditions, a 12 volt system generally requires one ampere for each cubic inch of engine displacement. In other words, a 350 cu. in. engine requires a battery with a "Cold Cranking Rating" of at least 350 amps. Some manufacturers still provide the ampere-hour ratings while others do not.

BATTERY SERVICE

Since the battery is a perishable item which requires periodic servicing, a good maintenance program will insure the longest possible life. If the unit tests good but fails to perform satisfactorily in service for no

Sulfation results from a low water level. The top plate area is removed from active service by the insulating sulfated coating, cutting the battery capacity in half. This process cannot be reversed.

The results of overcharging are bent plates, crushed separators, and powdered out tops of the positive plates.

apparent reason, the following are some of the more important factors that may point to the cause of the trouble. (1) Vehicle accessories inadvertently left on overnight to cause a discharged condition. (2) Slow speed driving of short duration to cause an undercharged condition. (3) The vehicle electrical load exceeding the generator capacity. (4) A defect in the charging system such as high resistance, slipping fan belt, faulty generator, or voltage regulator. (5) Battery abuse, including failure to keep the battery top clean, cable ends clean and tight, and improper addition of water to the cells.

ELECTROLYTE LEVEL

Keep the fluid level up to the level of the level of the ring in the bottom of the filler well. **CAUTION: Hydrogen and oxygen gases are produced during normal battery operation. This combustible gas mixture can explode if flames or sparks are brought near the vent openings of the battery. The sulphuric acid in the battery electrolyte can cause a serious burn if spilled on the skin or spattered in the eyes. It should be flushed away with large quantities of clear water. Medical assistance should be called for immediately if acid is splashed into the eyes.**

The electrolyte level should be checked regularly. In hot weather, particularly during trip driving, checking should be more frequent because of more rapid loss of water. If the electrolyte level is found to be low, then colorless, odorless, drinking water should be added to each cell until the liquid level rises to the split vent located in the bottom of the vent well. **CAUTION: Do not overfill because this will cause loss of electrolyte, which will result in poor performance, short life, and excessive corrosion. CAUTION: Only water should be added to the battery, never electrolyte.**

The liquid level in the cells should never be allowed to drop below the top of the plates, as the portion of the plates exposed to air may be permanently damaged with a resulting loss in performance. Excessive usage of water indicates the battery is being overcharged. The most common causes of overcharge are high battery operating temperatures, too high a voltage regulator setting, or a poor regulator ground wire connection. Normal battery water usage is approximately one to two ounces per month per battery.

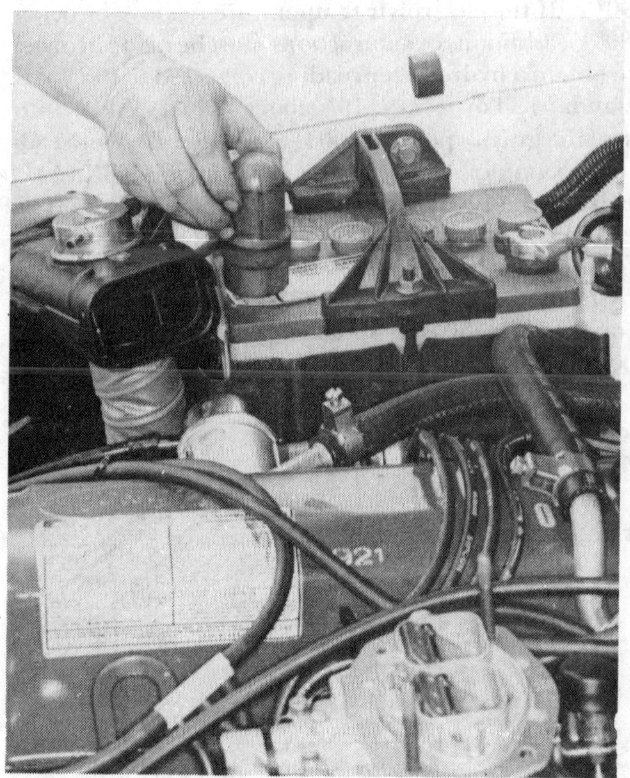

One of the greatest difficulties in the electric system is the maintenance of the correct operating voltage, and this, in turn, is dependent on minimizing resistance between connections in the charging circuit. One of the most important service procedures is the cleaning of the battery terminal posts and cable connections.

CLEANING

The external condition of the battery should be checked periodically for damage or for the presence of dirt and corrosion. The battery should be kept clean. An accumulation of acid film and dirt can permit current to flow between the terminals, which will slowly discharge the battery. For best results when cleaning a battery, wash it first with a diluted ammonia or a soda solution to neutralize any acid present, then flush it with clean water. Care must be taken to keep the vent plugs tight so that the neutralizing solution does not enter the cells.

Clean the battery posts by scraping with a sharp-bladed tool or with a wire brush. Clean the inside of the cable clamps to make sure that they do not cause resistance. This is very important since a poor contact at the terminals adds resistance to the charging circuit and causes the voltage regulator to be "looking" at a fully charged battery; therefore, it calls for a reduced generator output to compound a battery problem.

TESTING

A hydrometer can be used to measure the specific gravity of the electrolyte in each cell. It measures the percentage of sulfuric acid in the battery electrolyte in terms of specific gravity. As a battery drops from a charged to a discharged condition, the acid leaves the solution and enters the plates, causing a decrease in specific gravity of the electrolyte.

When using a hydrometer, observe the following points: (1) The hydrometer must be clean, inside and out, to insure an accurate reading. (2) Hydrometer readings must never be taken immediately after water has been added. The water must be thoroughly mixed with the electrolyte by charging for at least 15 minutes at a rate high enough to cause vigorous gassing. (3) If the hydrometer has a built-in thermometer, draw liquid into it several times to insure correct temperature before taking a reading. (4) Hold the hydrometer vertically and draw in just enough liquid so that the float is free floating. (5) Hold the hydrometer at eye level so that the float is vertical and free of the outer tube, then take a reading at the surface of the liquid. Disregard the curvature where the liquid rises against the float stem due to surface tension. (6) Avoid dropping battery fluid on the car or your clothing as it is extremely corrosive. Any fluid that drops should be washed off immediately with water and neutralized with a baking soda solution.

The specific gravity of the elctrolyte varies with the percentage of acid in the liquid and also with temperature. As temperature increases, the electrolyte expands so that the specific gravity is reduced. Unless these variations in specific gravity are taken into account, the specific gravity obtained by the hydrometer may not give a true indication of the concentration of acid in the electrolyte. A fully charged battery will have a specific gravity reading of approximtately 1.270 at an electrolyte temperature of 80° F. If the electrolyte temperature is above or below 80° F., additions or subtractions must be made in order to obtain a hydrometer reading corrected to the 80° F. standard. For every 10° above 80° F., add four specific gravity points (0.004) to the hydrometer reading. Example: A hydrometer reading of 1.260 at 110° F. would be 1.272 corrected to 80° F., indicating a fully charged battery. For every 10° below 80° F., subtract four points (0.004) from the reading. Example: A hydrometer reading of 1.272 at 0° F. would be 1.240 corrected to 80° F., indicating a partially charged battery.

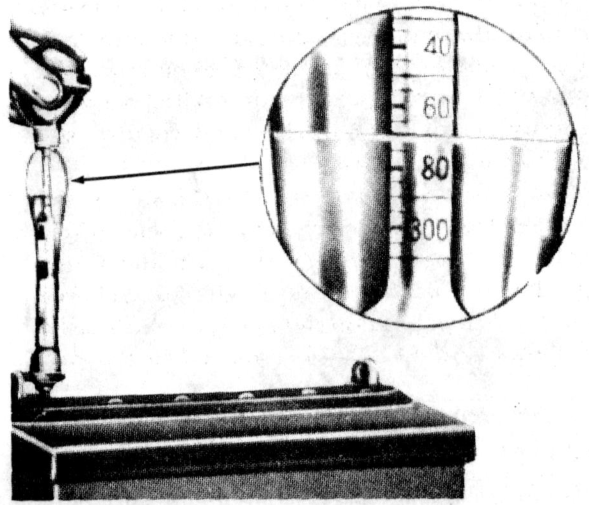

Checking the specific gravity with a hydrometer, as discussed in the text.

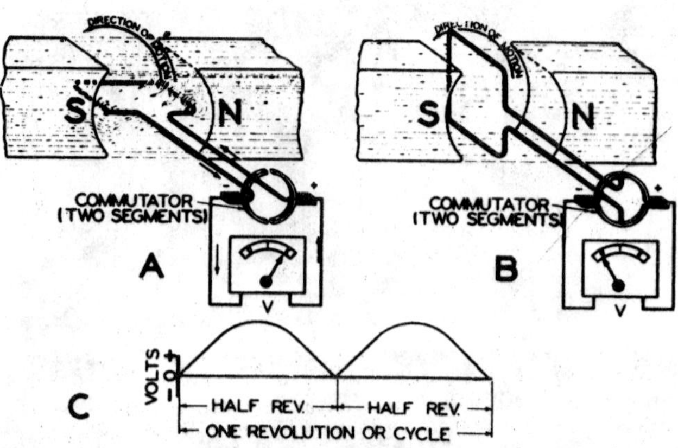

Generation of pulsating DC current, as discussed in the text.

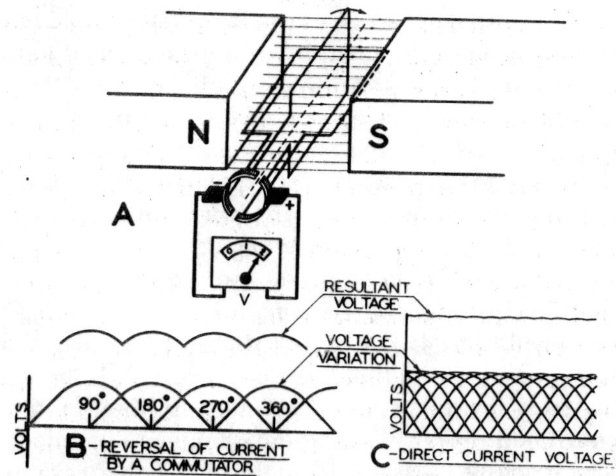

By increasing the number of rotating loops, the voltage variations can be minimized.

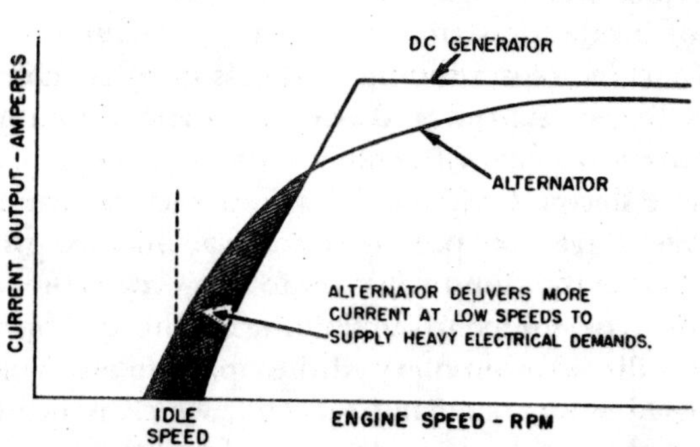

Alternator output curve as compared with that of a conventional DC generator. Note the improved output of the alternator at low speeds.

CHARGING SYSTEM

The charging system generates electric current for the ignition system, lights, and any accessories that may be in operation. The excess current is used to charge the battery.

GENERATORS

A generator produces electricity because a coil of wire is moved across a magnetic field. The coil is in the armature and the field is produced by the pole pieces located in the generator housing. As the coil rotates, one side of the loop passes a *north* magnetic pole.

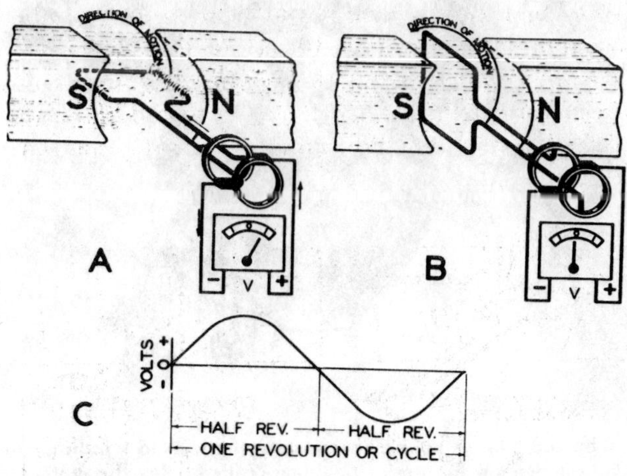

Generation of AC voltage. In its most basic form, the stator is a coil of wire, which is shown here as a single loop. (Naturally, in the alternator, there are many such coils.) As the magnetic field from the spinning rotor cuts across this wire, an electrical voltage is produced in the loop. The faster the rotor turns, the greater will be the generated voltage.

During the second half of the rotating cycle, it passes a *south* magnetic pole.

The direction of current flow in the loop is reversed at each half turn. If the current is taken from the rotating loop by means of slip rings, the generator produces AC current; if it is removed by a commutator, it produces DC current.

ALTERNATORS

The alternator is an AC generator used in place of the conventional DC generator. Its advantages include a higher charging rate, lower cut-in charging speed, lighter weight, and longer trouble-free service. The alternator differs from the conventional generator in that the armature is the stationary member, called the stator, while the field is the rotating member, called the rotor. An advantage of this type of construction is that the higher current values carried by the stator are conducted to the external circuit through fixed leads, rather than through a rotating commutator and brushes, as must be done in the DC generator. The relatively small current supplied to the fields can be conducted through small brushes and rotating slip rings with trouble-free ease.

The alternator charging circuit consists of the battery, alternator, voltage regulator, ignition switch, ammeter, and charging circuit wiring, with the return through the vehicle frame. Many models use a charge indicator lamp in place of the ammeter, in which case a charge indicator light relay is required in the regulator.

The alternator employs a three-phase stator winding in which the windings are phased electrically 120° apart. The rotor consists of a field coil encased between two four- or six-pole, interleaved sections, producing an eight- or twelve-pole magnetic field with alternate north and south poles. The rotation of the rotor inside the stator induces an alternating current (AC) in the stator windings, which is rectified (changed into DC) by six silicon diodes and brought out to the output terminal of the alternator.

The silicon diode rectifiers act as electrical one-way valves. Three are polarized one way and are pressed into an aluminum heat sink (to carry away the heat), which is grounded to the slip ring end head. The other three diodes are polarized the opposite way and are pressed into a similar heat sink, which is insulated from the end head and connected to the alternator output terminal. Since a diode has high resistance to the flow of electricity in one direction and passes current with very little resistance in the opposite direction, it is connected in a manner which allows current to flow from the alternator to the battery in the low-resistance direction. The high resistance in the opposite direction prevents the battery current from flowing to the alternator, therefore no circuit breaker (cutout) is required between the alternator and the battery.

Residual magnetism in the rotor field poles is negligible and, therefore, the field must be excited by an external source, the battery, which is connected to the field winding through the ignition switch and regulator. As in the DC shunt-type generator, the alternator charging voltage is regulated by varying the field strength. This is accomplished through the use of a voltage regulator unit. No current regulator is required since the alternator has self-limiting current characteristics.

SERVICE PROCEDURES

Because of the complexity of the alternator test and service equipment, most mechanics replace the defective alternator with a new or rebuilt one. Therefore, this section will discuss the general charging system tests that can be made with minimum equipment to determine the problem: alternator, regulator, fusible link, charge indicator, or wiring.

SERVICE PRECAUTIONS

(1) Reversed battery connections will damage the diodes. Battery polarity must be checked with a voltmeter before any connections are made to make sure that the connections correspond to the vehicle battery ground polarity. (2) The field circuit between the alternator and the regulator must never be grounded; otherwise, the regulator will be damaged. (3) Grounding the alternator output terminal will damage the alternator and/or wiring. This is true even when the engine is not in operation since no circuit breaker is used, and battery current is applied to the alternator output terminal at all times. (4) The alternator must not be operated on an open circuit with the field winding energized, or the unit will be damaged. (5) Do not attempt to polarize the alternator as it is never required. Any attempt to do so will result in damage to the alternator, regulator, or wiring. (6) Do not short the bending tool to the regulator base when adjusting the voltage, or the unit will be damaged. The bending tool should be insulated by tape, or an insulating plastic sleeve. (7) If booster batteries are to be used for starting, they must be connected properly to prevent damage to the diodes. The negative (—) cable from the booster battery must be connected to the negative terminal of the vehicle battery, and the positive (+) booster cable to the positive terminal. Always disconnect the battery ground strap before replacing an alternator or connecting any meter to it. (8) When a fast charger is to be used to charge the battery, the vehicle battery cables must be disconnected. The fast charger must never be used as a booster for starting the engine. Failure to observe these precautions will result in damage to the diodes.

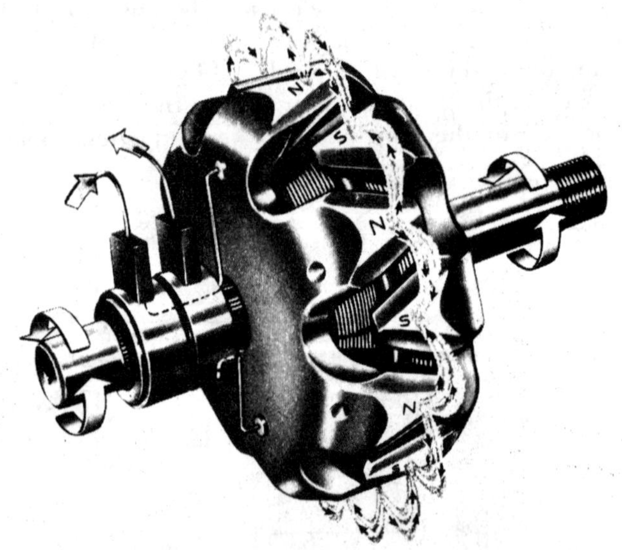

The rotor of an alternator consists of the field winding, two iron segments with interlacing fingers called poles, the shaft, and two slip rings. The slip rings, on which the brushes ride, are connected to the leads from the field coil. When the ignition switch is first closed, current from the battery passes through one brush through the slip ring, and then through the field coil from whence it returns to the battery through the other slip ring, brush, and ground circuit. This flow of current forms a north magnetic pole at each pole of one rotor segment and a south magnetic pole at each pole of the other segment. As the rotor turns, a spinning magnetic field is produced.

ON-VEHICLE TESTS

Before performing charging system tests on the vehicle, note the complaint such as: slow cranking, battery dead or using an excessive amount of water, top of battery wet, ammeter shows charge at all times and/or no charge, alternator warning lamp does not come on and/or never goes out. This information will aid in isolating the part of the system causing the problem. **CAUTION: The battery must be in proper state of charge (at least 1,200 specific gravity).**

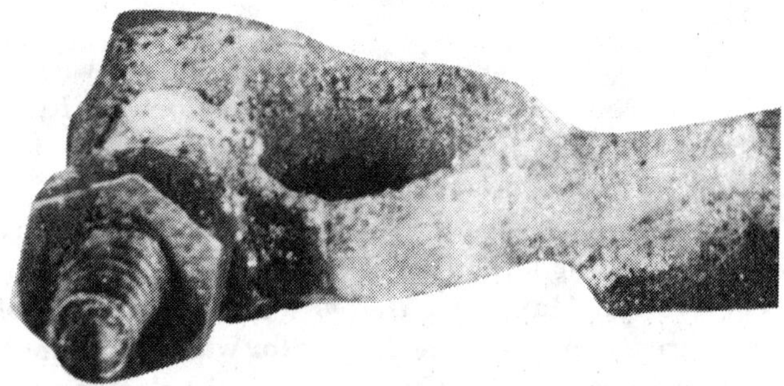

A corroded battery cable causes a high-resistance connection, which creates problems in the charging circuit as discussed in the text.

Visual Inspection

Check the fuse link located between the starter relay and the alternator. Replace the fuse link, if burned. Check the battery posts and battery cable terminals for clean and tight connections. Remove the battery cables (if corroded), clean and install them securely. Check for clean and tight wiring connections at the alternator, regulator and engine. Check the alternator belt tension and tighten to specification (if necessary).

Normal Charge Indication

With Ignition switch **off**—Alternator lamp is **off**. With ignition switch **on** (engine not running)—Alternator lamp is **on.** With ignition switch **on** (engine running)—Alternator lamp is **off.**

If the charge indicator lamp does not light with the ignition key in the **on** position and the engine not running, check the I (Ignition) wiring circuit for an open circuit or burned-out charge indicator lamp (ignition switch to regulator I terminal).

If the charge indicator lamp does not light, disconnect the wiring plug connector at the regulator and connect a jumper wire from the I terminal of the regulator wiring plug to the negative battery post cable clamp to by-pass the switch connections. The charge indicator lamp should now light with the ignition key turned to the **on** position.

If the charge indicator bulb does not light, check the bulb for continuity and replace (if burned out). If the bulb is not burned out, an open circuit exists between the ignition switch and the regulator.

A good indication of a problem in the I wiring circuit (ignition switch to regulator I terminal) will show when the charge indicator light goes out with high engine rpm. This is caused by an open circuit in the 15-ohm resistor wire (connected in parallel with the indicator light), generally at the terminal point (either end of the resistor wire).

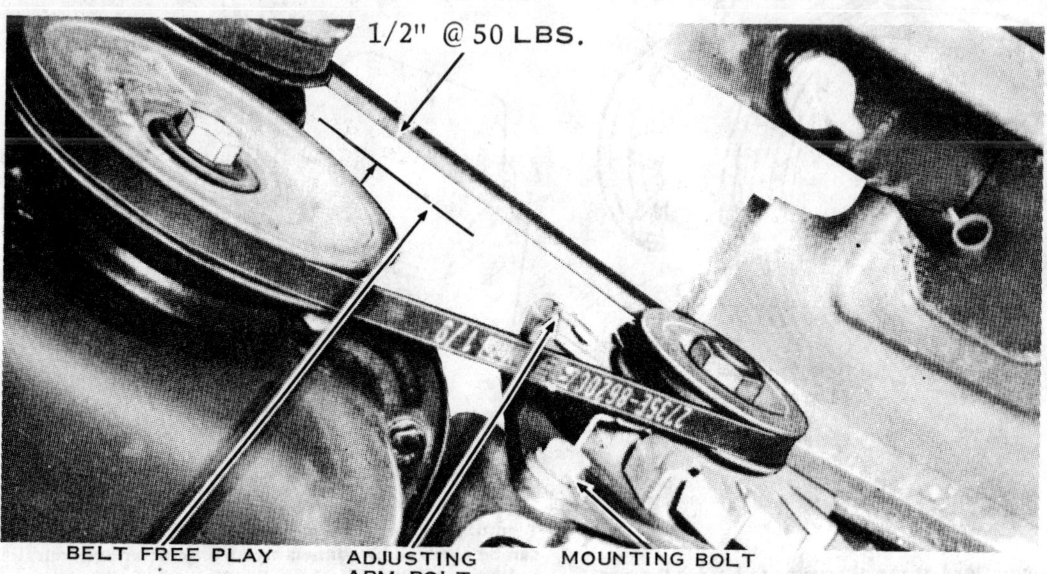

Adjust the fan belt so that you have ½" free play between the longest span with a 50-lb. deflection. This view shows the belt and alternator mountings from below the engine.

ISOLATING THE TROUBLE

Charging system troubles can be in the wiring, alternator, or regulator. If the system does not function properly, you can isolate the trouble by a few simple tests as follows:

To make a rough test of the field excitation circuit, hold a screwdriver against the back end of the alternator. **CAUTION: Make sure that you don't touch any of the bare terminals on the alternator which are "hot", because sparks will fly, and you will damage the diodes and fusible link.** If you have magnetism at the rear of the alternator with the ignition switch turned ON, then you know that current is passing through the field circuit. This means that the field excitation circuit and regulator are in good condition. If you don't get magnetism, then you know you have trouble in the field excitation circuit (through the ignition switch) or the regulator contacts are burned. Make a voltmeter test at the field excitation wire at the wiring plug to check this out, and you must have 12 volts here with the ignition switch turned ON.

To check the efficiency of the regulator, you can disconnect the wiring plug at the regulator and connect a jumper wire between the field and battery terminals of the regulator plug, as shown. Now start the engine and, if the charging system functions properly with the jumper wire in place (regulator by-passed), and did not operate properly with the regulator connected, then replace the regulator. If the charging system does not function with the jumper wire in place (regulator by-passed), then replace the alternator.

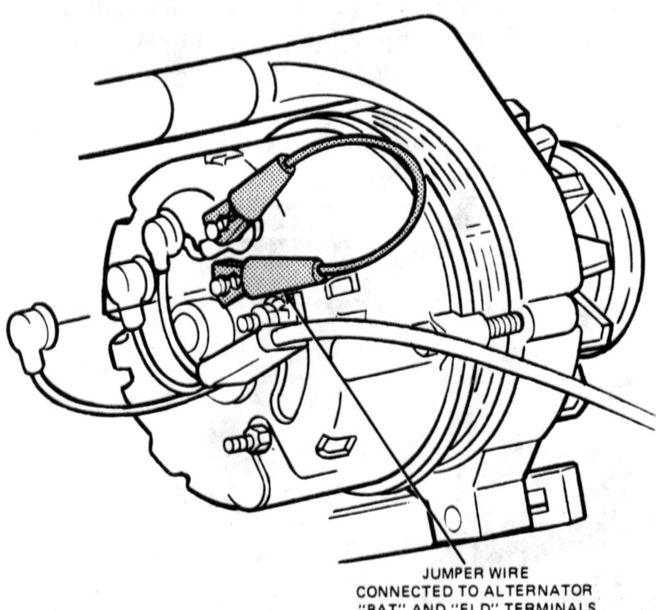

Jumper wire connections at the alternator to bypass the regulator. If an inoperative alternator charges with this jumper in place, then the regulator is defective.

SERVICE NOTES

In any case where the alternator is burned up, always check for the cause. **CAUTION: Unless the basic trouble is eliminated, the new alternator will soon burn out, too.**

Alternator problems are almost always caused by overloading the unit, and this is generally caused by making it work at an excessively high voltage which is always caused by high resistance connections in the

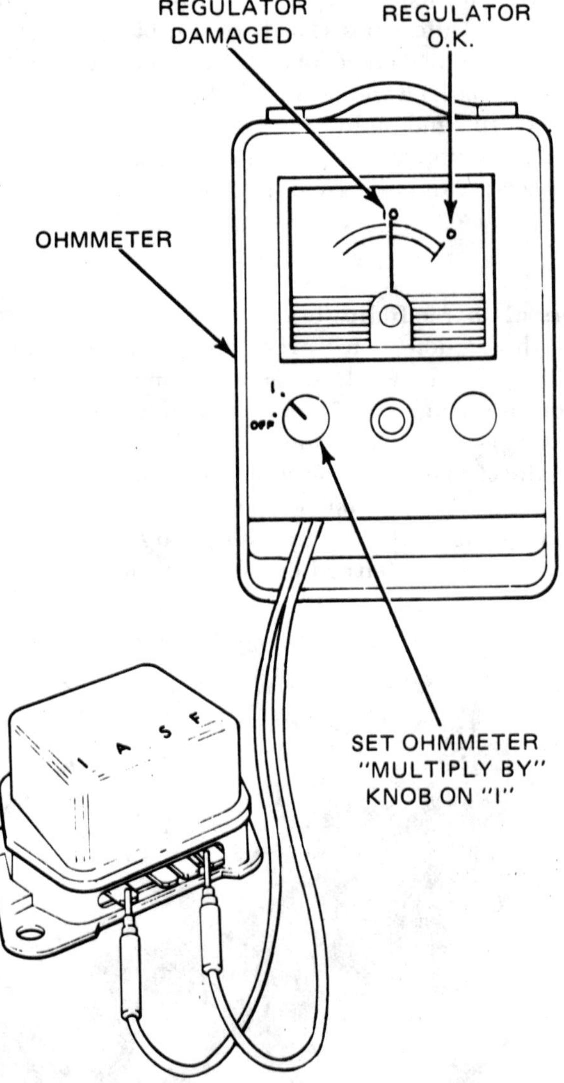

The contact points of the regulator frequently oxidize and eventually the unit fails. The resistance of the regulator contacts can be checked by connecting an ohmmeter between field (F) and indicator circuit (I) terminals. There must be no resistance between these two connections, or the regulator is defective and must be replaced.

charging circuit, generally at the battery terminals, where the acid corrodes the battery cable clamps and forms high-resistance connections.

The alternator "sees" this added resistance as something to overcome and increases the system's voltage to get across these poor connections. Because this condition is one which is progressive, the initial overload is easily controlled by the voltage regulator, which works harder and harder to keep the charging system voltage within the specified limits. Eventually, the voltage regulator fails and, without control, the alternator also fails, burning up in a vain attempt to push current across the corroded battery terminals. **CAUTION: Whenever you replace an alternator that is burned out, always replace the regulator, and clean the battery cable connections, where the problem originally started.**

Before the alternator burns up, there are warning signs. The headlights will burn dimly with the engine idling, and brighten considerably when the engine speed is increased. This is due to the higher voltage under which the charging system is operating. Another indication of trouble is short bulb life. The higher operating voltages cause the bulb filiments to burn out relatively fast. If you have to replace bulbs frequently, and note the telltale headlight flare, then remove the battery cables and scrape the inside of the terminals and the battery posts until you can see only bright and clean surfaces. Replace the terminals, and tighten the bolts securely.

FUSIBLE LINKS

The fuse link is a short length of insulated wire integral with the engine compartment wiring harness. It is several wire gages smaller than the circuit which it protects. Production fuse links are the color of the circuit being supplied by the fuse link. Service fuse links are green or black, depending on usage. All fuse links have a flag moulded on the wire or on the terminal insulator. Color identification of the flag or connector is Red—18 Ga. wire, Orange—16 Ga. wire, or Green—14 Ga. wire.

When heavy current flows, such as when a booster battery is connected incorrectly or when a short to ground occurs in the wiring harness, the fuse link burns out and protects the alternator and wiring.

A burned-out link may have bare wire ends protruding from the insulation, or it may only have expanded or bubbled insulation with illegible identification. When it is hard to determine if the link is burned out, perform a continuity test with an ohmmeter.

REPAIRING A FUSE LINK

To repair a blown fuse link, determine which circuit is damaged, its location, and the cause of the open fuse link. If the damaged fuse link is one of three fed by a common number 10 or 12 gauge feed wire, determine the specific affected circuit. **CAUTION: Do not mistake a resistor wire for a fuse link. The resistor wire is generally longer and has print stating, "Resistor—do not cut or splice."**

Disconnect the negative battery cable. Cut the damaged fuse link from the wiring harness and discard it. If the fuse link is one of three circuits fed by a single feed wire, cut it out of the harness at each splice end and discard it. Identify and procure the proper fuse link and butt connectors for attaching the fuse link to the harness.

To repair any fuse link in a 3-link group with one feed: (a) After cutting the open link out of the harness cut each of the remaining undamaged fuse links clos€

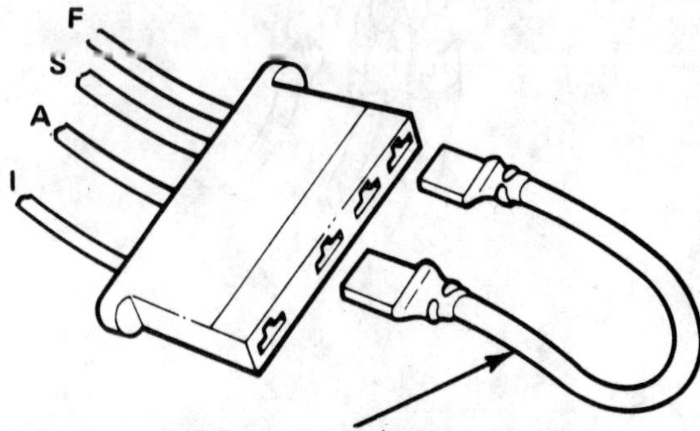

To isolate the Ford regulator from the circuit, for testing purposes, by-pass it with a jumper wire which connects the A (armature) and F (field) wires together. This feeds field excitation current directly from the armature, and the alternator should charge unless it is defective.

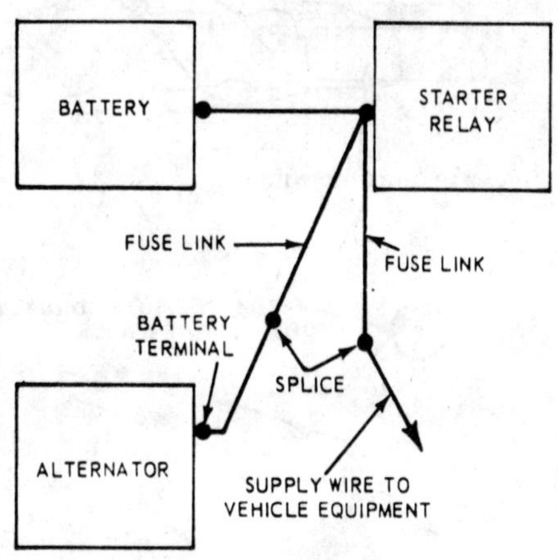

Charging system fuse link.

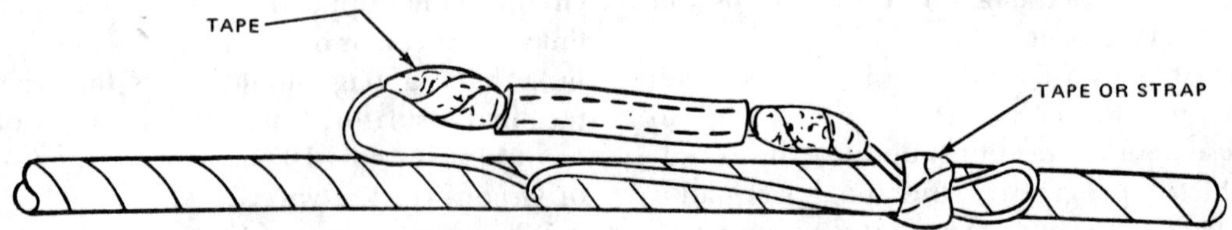

TYPICAL REPAIR USING THE SPECIAL #17 GA. (9.00" LONG-YELLOW) FUSE LINK REQUIRED FOR THE AIR/COND. CIRCUITS (2) # 687E AND# 261A LOCATED IN THE ENGINE COMPARTMENT

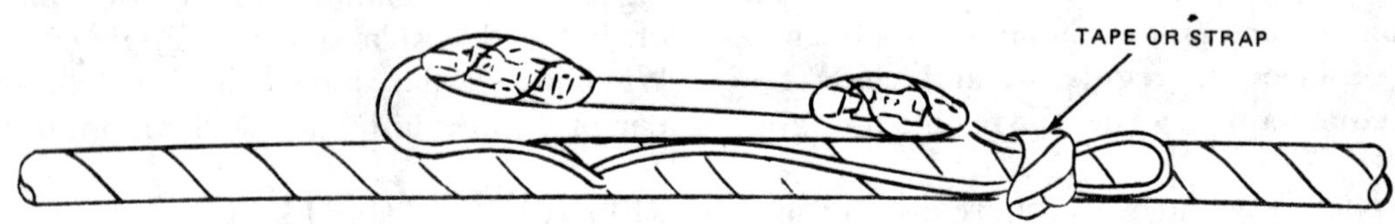

TYPICAL REPAIR FOR ANY IN-LINE FUSE LINK USING THE SPECIFIED GAGE FUSE LINK FOR THE SPECIFIC CIRCUIT

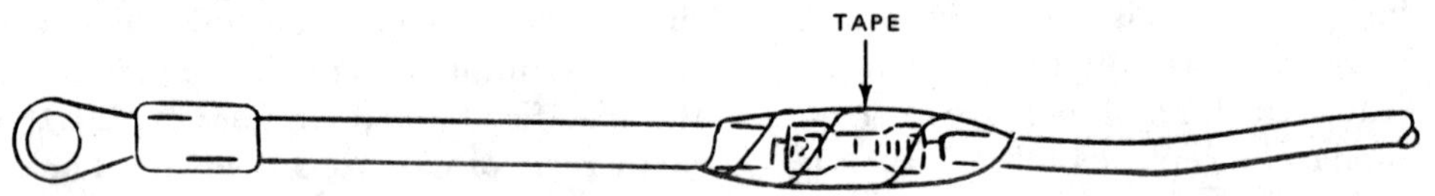

TYPICAL REPAIR USING THE EYELET TERMINAL FUSE LINK OF THE SPECIFIED GAGE FOR ATTACHMENT TO A CIRCUIT WIRE END

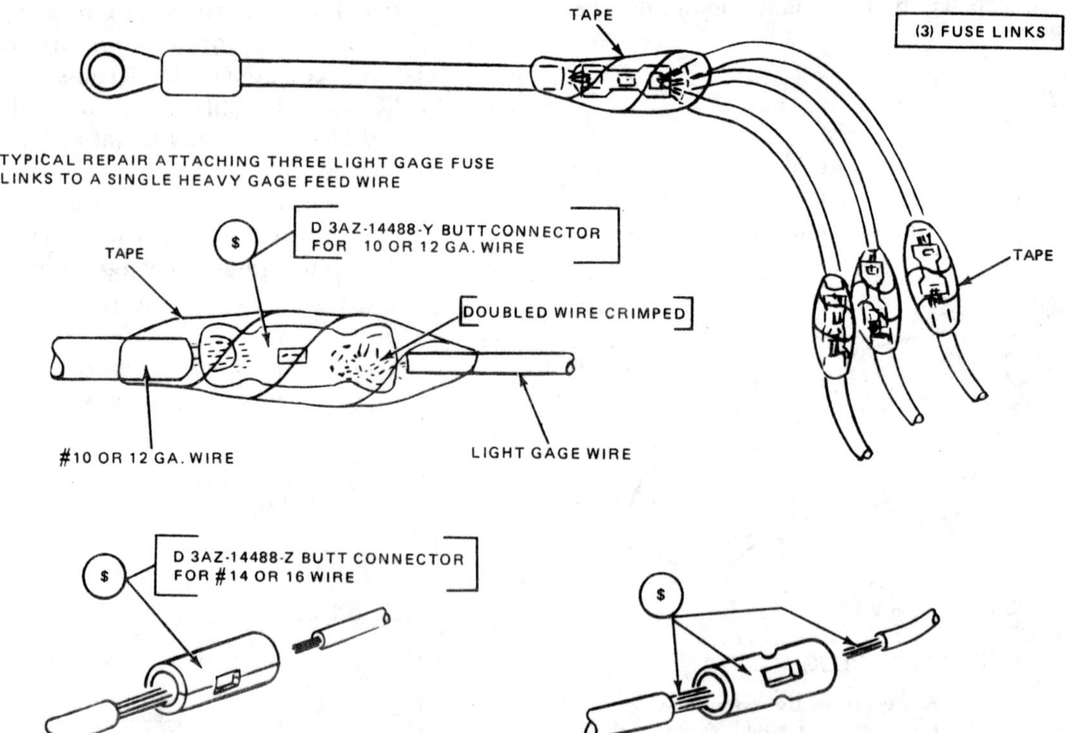

TYPICAL REPAIR ATTACHING THREE LIGHT GAGE FUSE LINKS TO A SINGLE HEAVY GAGE FEED WIRE

Procedures for making a fusible link repair, as discussed in the text.

D3AZ–14A526–D	# 14 GAGE WIRE - 9.00" ± .50 LENGTH (GREEN INSULATION) AS REQ'D.
D3AZ–14A526-E	# 16 GAGE WIRE - 9.00" ± .50 LENGTH (ORANGE INSULATION) AS REQ'D.
D3AZ–14A526-F	# 18 GAGE WIRE – 9.00" ± .50 LENGTH (RED INSULATION) AS REQ'D.
D3AZ–14A526-G	# 20 GAGE WIRE-9.00 ± .50 LENGTH (BLUE INSULATION) AS REQ'D.

Wiring assembly fuse link with an eyelet at one end.

to the feed wire weld. (b) Strip approximately ½ inch of insulation from the detached ends of the two good fuse links. Then, insert the wire ends into one end of a D3AZ-14488-Y or Z Butt Connector. Carefully push one stripped end of the replacement fuse link into the same end of the butt connector and crimp all three together firmly. **CAUTION: Care must be taken when fitting the three fuse links into the butt connector as the internal diameter is a snug fit for three wires. Make sure to use a proper crimping tool as pliers, side cutters, etc. will not apply the proper crimp to retain the wires and withstand a pull test. CAUTION: When attaching a single number 16, 17, 18 or 20 gauge fuse link to a heavy gauge wire, always double the stripped wire end of the fuse link before inserting and crimping it into the butt connector for positive wire retention.** (c) After crimping the butt connector to the three fuse links, cut the weld portion from the feed wire and strip approximately ½ inch of insulation from the cut end. Insert the stripped end into the open end of the butt connector and crimp very firmly. (d) To attach the remaining end of the replacement fuse link, strip approximately ½ inch of insulation from the wire end of the circuit from which the blown fuse link was removed, and firmly crimp a D3AZ-14488-Y or -Z Butt Connector to the stripped wire. Then, insert the end of the replacement link into the other end of the butt connector and crimp firmly. (e) Using rosin-core solder with a consistency of 60

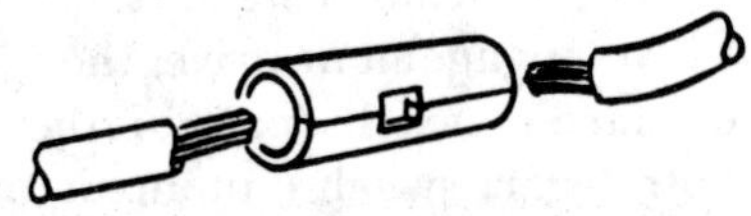

D3AZ–14488-Y	FOR # 10 AND 12 GA. WIRE (LOAD CIRCUIT) AS REQ'D.
D3AZ–14488-Z	FOR # 14 AND 16 GA. WIRE (LOAD CIRCUIT) AS REQ'D.

Butt connector used for a wiring splice, as discussed in the text.

percent tin and 40 percent lead, solder the connectors and the wires at the repairs and insulate with electrical tape.

To replace a fuse link on a single circuit in a harness, cut out the damaged portion, strip approximately ½ inch of insulation from the two wire ends, and attach the appropriate replacement fuse link to the stripped wire ends with two proper size butt connectors. Solder the connectors and wires and insulate with tape.

To repair a fuse link which has an eyelet terminal on one end, such as the charging circuit, cut off the open fuse link behind the weld, strip approximately ½ inch of insulation from the cut end, and attach the appropriate new eyelet fuse link to the cut stripped wire with an appropriate size butt connector. Solder the connectors and wires at the repair and insulate with tape.

Connect the negative battery cable to the battery and test the system for proper operation.

D3AZ–14A526-H	# 14 GAGE WIRE - 9.00" ± .50 LENGTH (GREEN INSULATION)
D3AZ–14A526-J	# 16 GAGE WIRE - 9.00" ± .50 LENGTH (ORANGE INSULATION) AS REQ'D.
D3AZ–14526-K	# 17 GAGE WIRE - 9.00" ± .50 LENGTH(YELLOW INSULATION) AS REQ'D. (SPECIAL USED WITH AIR CONDITIONING SYSTEM)
D3AZ14A526-L	# 18 GAGE WIRE - 9.00" ± .50 LENGTH (RED INSULATION) AS REQ'D
D3AZ–14A526-M	# 20 GAGE WIRE – 9.00" ± .50 LENGTH (BLUE INSULATION) AS REQ'D.

Fuse link with insulation stripped at both ends, which is used in the wiring assembly.

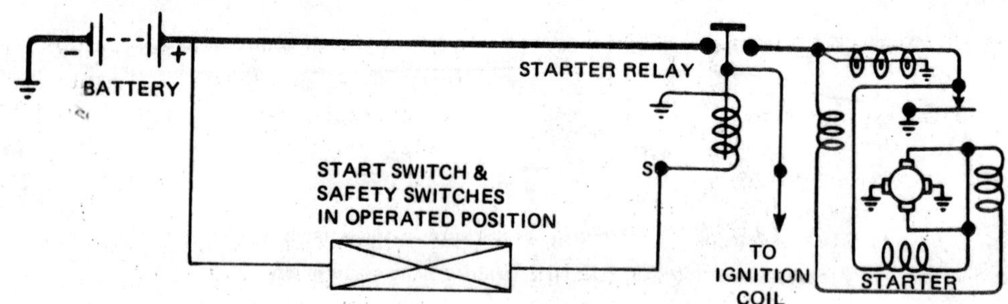

Cranking motor circuit used on Ford engines.

CRANKING SYSTEM

The cranking system includes the starter motor with an integral positive-engagement drive, the battery, a remote control starter switch (part of the ignition switch), the neutral-start switch (automatic transmission with floor shift only), the starter relay, and heavy circuit wiring.

Turning of the ignition key to the START position actuates the starter relay, through the starter control circuit. The starter relay then connects the battery to the starter.

Vehicles equipped with an automatic transmission, and a console or floor mounted shift lever, have a neutral-start switch in the starter control circuit, which prevents operation of the starter if the selector lever is not in the N (neutral) or P (park) position.

Vehicles equipped with an automatic transmission and a column shift do not use a neutral-start switch. The ignition switch mechanism in the steering column is designed so that the ignition switch can be turned to the start position only when the selector lever is in NEUTRAL or PARK.

When the starter is not in use, one of the field coils is connected directly to ground through a set of contacts. When the starter is first connected to the battery, a large current flows through the grounded field coil, actuating a movable pole shoe. The pole shoe is attached to the starter drive plunger lever and thus the drive is forced into engagement with the flywheel ring gear.

When the movable pole shoe is fully seated, it opens the field coil grounding contacts, and the starter is then in normal operation. A holding coil is used to maintain the movable pole shoe in the fully seated position during the time that the starter is turning the engine.

CRANKING SYSTEM PROBLEMS

The function of the starting system is to crank the engine at a speed fast enough to permit the engine to start. Heavy cables, connectors, and switches are used in the starting system because of the large current required by the starter while it is cranking the engine. **CAUTION: The amount of resistance in the starting circuit must be kept to an absolute minimum to provide maximum current for starter operation.** Loose or corroded connections, relay contacts, or partially broken cables will result in slower than normal cranking speeds, and may even prevent the starter from cranking the engine.

CRANKING MOTOR VOLTAGE TESTS

Although the cranking motor cannot be checked accurately on the engine, a check can be made for excessive resistance in the cranking motor circuit by making the five voltmeter connections as shown in the

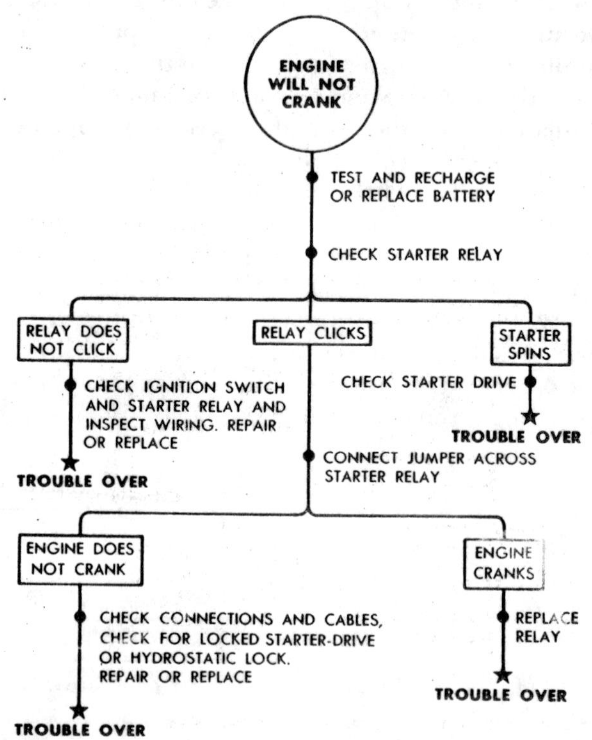

Roadmap for troubleshooting a cranking motor that does not crank the engine.

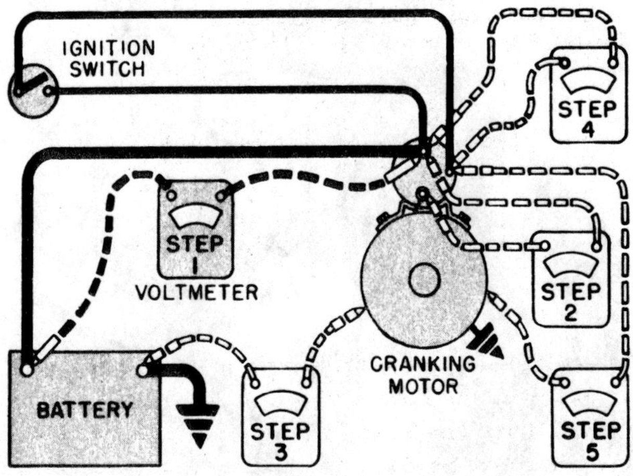

Cranking motor voltage test that are discussed in the text.

accompanying illustration. **CAUTION: Before making these checks, ground the primary lead to the distributor to keep the engine from starting.** Then measure the voltage drop across each part of the circuit with the engine being cranked as follows:

Step 1

Connect the voltmeter across the insulated battery post and the solenoid battery terminal. The voltage (loss) must not exceed 0.2 volt, or there is a high-resistance connection at the battery terminal or the cable is too thin.

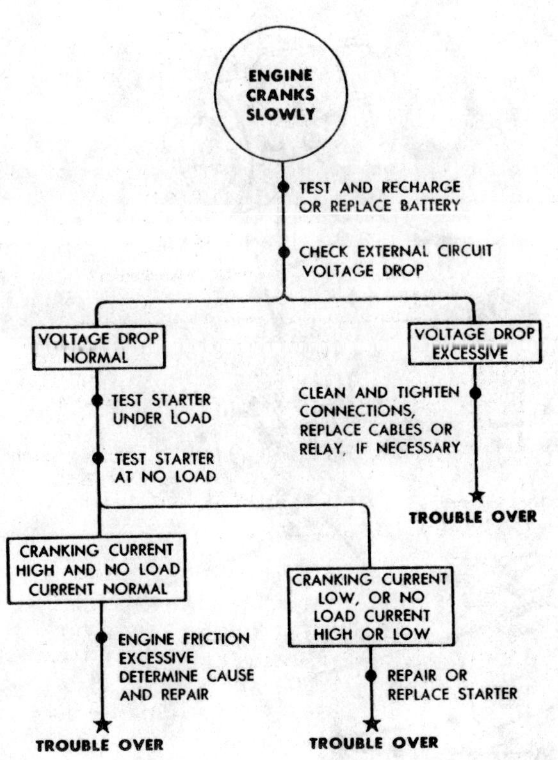

Roadmap for troubleshooting a cranking motor that cranks the engine too slowly.

Step 2

Connect the voltmeter across the solenoid battery terminal and the solenoid motor terminal. The voltage (loss) must not exceed 0.2 volt, or the solenoid contacts have high resistance.

Step 3

Connect the voltmeter across the grounded battery post and the cranking motor frame. The voltage (loss) must not exceed 0.2 volt, or there is a high-resistance connection at the battery ground terminal or ground strap.

If the solenoid fails to pull in, the trouble can be due to excessive resistance in the solenoid-control circuit, which can be checked with two addition tests, as follows:

Step 4

Connect the voltmeter across the solenoid battery terminal and the solenoid switch terminal. The voltage (loss) must not exceed 2.4 volts on a 12-volt system, or excessive resistance is indicated in the solenoid-control circuit.

Step 5

If the voltage loss in the previous test did not exceed 2.4 volts and the solenoid did not pull in, connect the voltmeter across the solenoid switch terminal and ground. The solenoid should pull in if the voltmeter reading is 7.7 volts or more; if it doesn't, replace the solenoid.

CRANKING MOTOR SERVICE PROCEDURES

Because the cranking motor drive-end bushing is inaccessible, it receives no lubrication while the commutator-end bushing sometimes receives too much. The result is that the drive-end bushing wears, allowing the armature to drop down and rub against the field pole pieces, causing internal drag which lowers the output torque. Overlubrication of the commutator-end bushing results in an oil-covered commutator, insulating it from the brushes. The added resistance lowers the efficiency of the cranking system greatly.

Cranking motor service consists of replacing defective switches, bushings, brushes, and turning the commutator to true it up.

REMOVING THE STARTER

Raise the vehicle on a hoist and install stands.

On 2.0 and 2.3L engines, remove the engine mounting bracket bolts to the frame and engine and remove the bracket. Raise the engine to provide the necessary clearance to remove the starter motor. Disconnect the starter cable from the starter terminal. Remove the three starter attaching bolts and remove the starter. With the 2000cc engine, it may be necessary to turn the steering gear bellows clamp to remove the starter.

INSTALLING

Position the starter to the vehicle and start the three attaching bolts. Snug the bolts while holding the starter squarely against its mounting surface and fully inserted into the pilot hole. Tighten the bolts.

Connect the starter cable to the starter terminal. Tighten the steering gear bellows clamp on 2000cc engine models. Remove the stands and lower the vehicle.

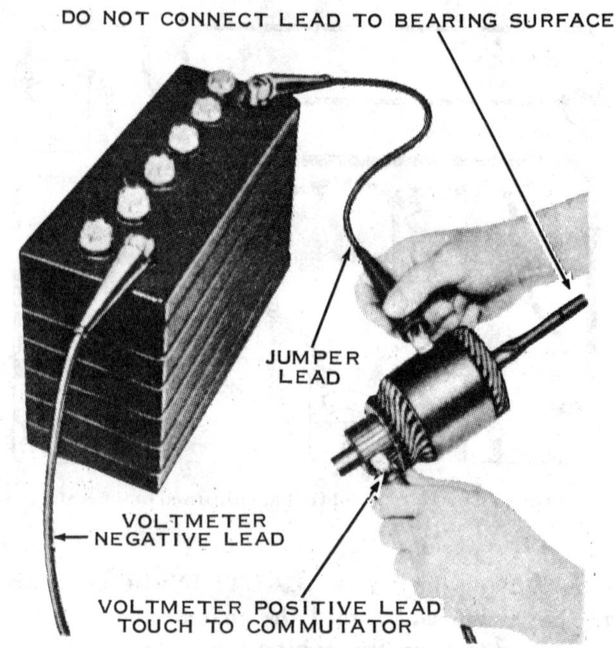

Checking the armature for a ground. There must be no indication of current flowing from the commutator to the armature core.

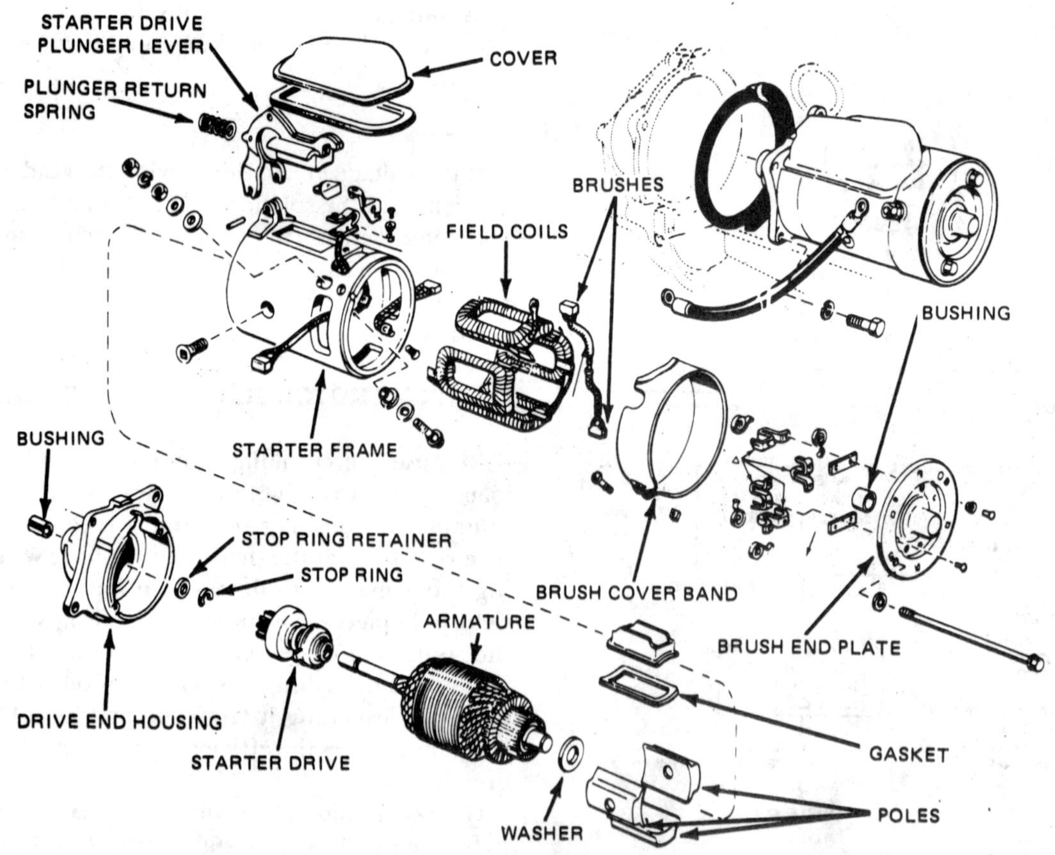

Disassembled view of the starter.

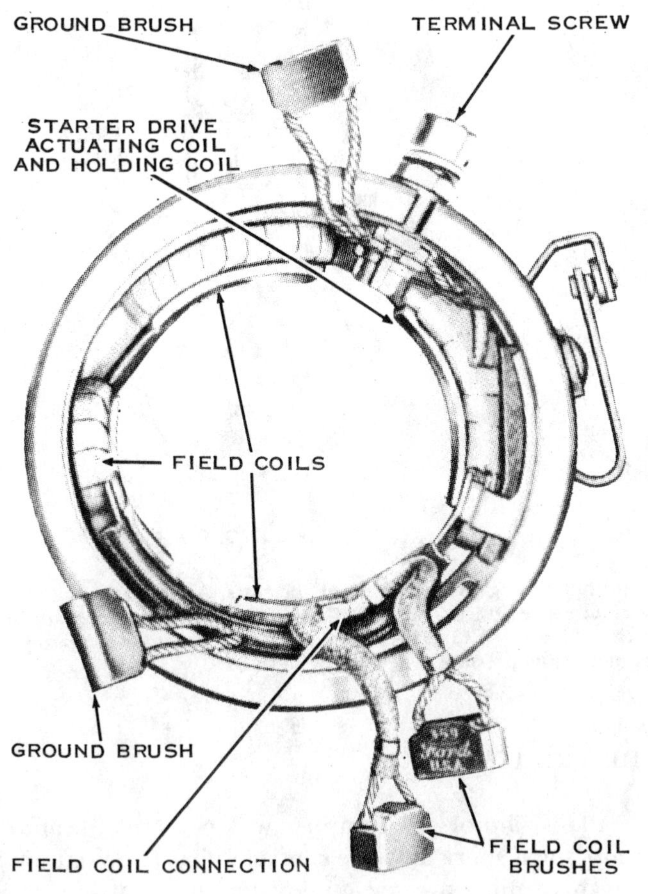

Details of the field coil and brushes used on the starter.

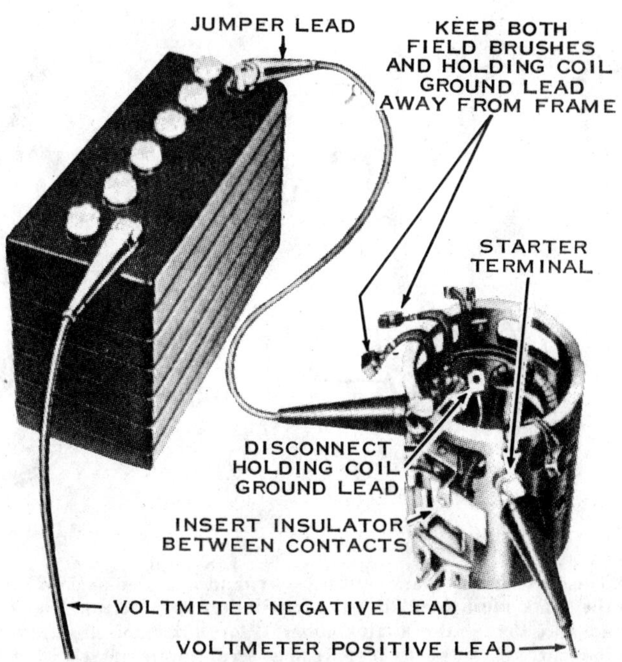

Checking the field coils for ground. There must be no indication of current flowing from the starter terminal to ground.

IGNITION SYSTEM

Basic ignition system isolation tests are covered in Chapter 1, Troubleshooting. Tuning is covered in Chapter 2, Tuning for Performance, and detailed tests are provided in this chapter to isolate the trouble, and to service or replace the defective part.

The breakerless-type ignition system retains most of the features of the conventional system, but employs a unique armature and magnetic pickup coil assembly in the distributor and a solid-state amplifier module.

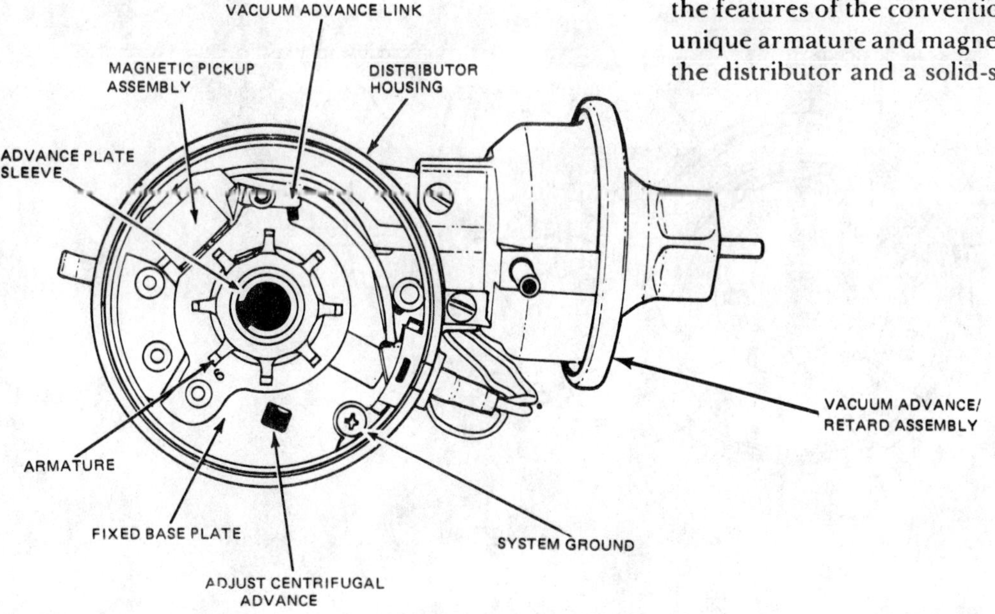

Details of the electronic (breakerless) ignition system distributor. The armature comes with four teeth for a four-cylinder engine, six teeth for a six-cylinder engine, or eight teeth for a V-8 engine.

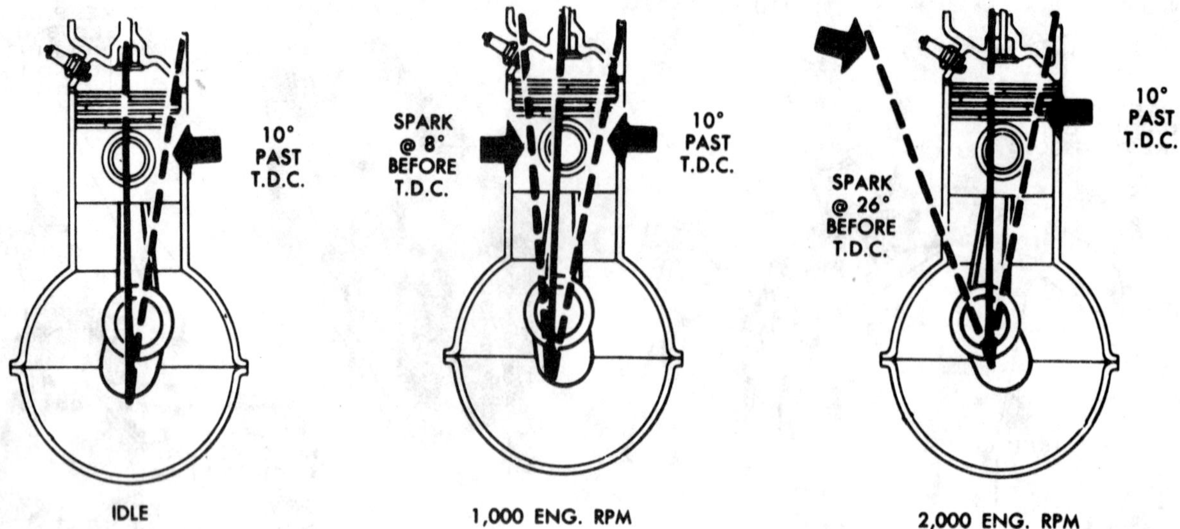

The mechanical spark advance mechanism is designed to advance ignition timing as engine speed increases. At idle speeds (left), the spark must occur at TDC for the burning fuel to develop its maximum pressure by 10° ATDC. At 1,000 rpm, it is necessary to advance the ignition timing about 8° for maximum pressure to be developed by 10° ATDC because of the time it takes for combustion to occur. At 2,000 rpm, the spark must occur approximately 26° BTDC for maximum pressure to develop by 10° ATDC.

The armature turns with the distributor shaft, causing fluctuations in the magnetic field generated by the pickup coil assembly. These fluctuations cause the amplifier to turn the ignition coil current off and on, causing the high-tension spark needed to fire the spark plugs. The distributor is equipped with a standard rotor and cap.

DISTRIBUTOR

All distributors are equipped with both vacuum and centrifugal spark advance control units. The vacuum advance unit governs ignition timing according to engine load, while the centrifugal advance unit governs ignition timing according to engine speed (rpm).

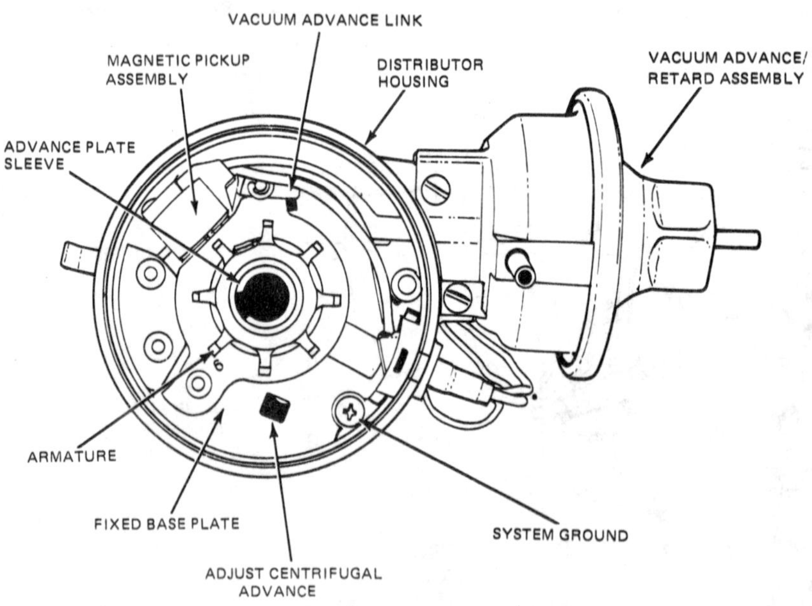

Details of the electronic (breakerless) ignition system distributor. The armature comes with four teeth for a four-cylinder engine, six teeth for a six-cylinder engine, or eight teeth for a V-8 engine.

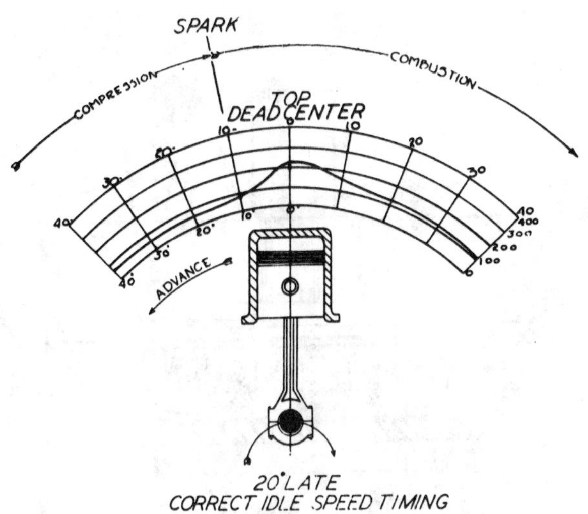

This graph shows the pressure rise in the combustion chamber during compression and after the air-fuel mixture is ignited. With the engine idling, ignition occurs at 10° BTDC, and maximum pressure is developed just as the piston passes TDC. The 10° timing advance compensates for the 1/350th of a second that it takes for combustion to be completed.

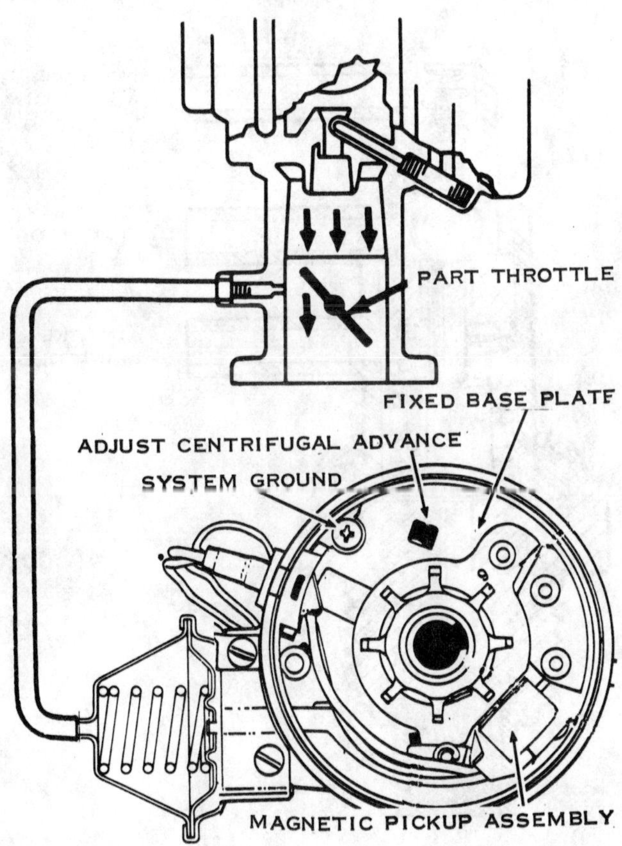

The vacuum-advance mechanism consists of a diaphragm unit which receives its vacuum supply from the manifold side of the throttle valve. Generally, this tap is above the throttle blade at idle speed so that there is no vacuum advance; this is especially true on emission-controlled engines.

A dual-diaphragm vacuum advance unit is used on some engines to provide additional ignition timing retard during engine closed-throttle operation. This occurs both at curb idle and during engine coast-down with closed throttle. Retarding the timing during these periods helps control engine emissions.

Centrifugal-Advance Mechanism

When the engine is idling, the spark is timed to occur just before the piston reaches top dead center, so that combustion can be completed by the time the piston reaches a little past top dead center. At higher engine speeds, there is less time for the mixture to ignite, burn, and deliver its power to the piston. Consequently, at higher engine speeds, the spark must be delivered earlier in the cycle. This is accomplished by a centrifugal advance mechanism designed about two governor weights, which throw out against spring tension as engine speed increases. This motion is transmitted to the breaker cam, which is advanced with regard to the distributor driveshaft.

Vacuum-Advance Mechanism

Under light engine load conditions, there is a high vacuum in the intake manifold caused by the restriction of the partially closed throttle valve; consequently, there is a smaller amount of air-fuel mixture delivered to the combustion chambers. Because of the fewer particles, the mixture will not burn as rapidly; therefore, ignition must take place earlier in the cycle.

To provide additional spark advance control, based on intake manifold pressures, a vacuum advance mechanism is incorporated in the distributor. It contains a spring-loaded diaphragm which rotates the breaker plate assembly. The diaphragm is connected

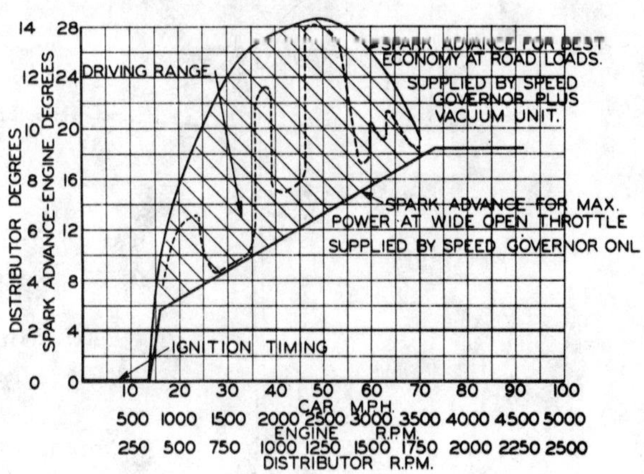

In operation, the ignition timing may be at any point in the shaded section of this graph, due to the action of the centrifugal advance, modified by the vacuum-advance.

to a vacuum passageway in the carburetor bore, located on the atmospheric side of the throttle valve when the engine is idling. In this position, no vacuum is applied to the diaphragm, and the breaker plate is retarded by spring pressure. As the throttle is opened, it swings past the vacuum port, applying vacuum to the diaphragm, moving it against spring pressure to advance the breaker plate.

When the engine is accelerated, intake manifold vacuum drops according to the degree of throttle advance, retarding the position of the breaker plate assembly accordingly.

Dual-Diaphragm Vacuum-Advance Mechanism

The dual-diaphragm unit consists of two diaphragms that operate from two independent sources of vacuum. The outer (primary) diaphragm operates from carburetor venturi vacuum to provide timing advance during normal off-idle driving conditions. This diaphragm is connected to the distributor point plate or magnetic pickup coil assembly by the vacuum advance link.

The inner (secondary) diaphragm operates from intake manifold vacuum and acts to retard ignition timing. This retard diaphragm is connected to the outer diaphragm by means of a sliding linkage. Since intake manifold vacuum is stronger than carburetor venturi vacuum during closed-throttle operation, the

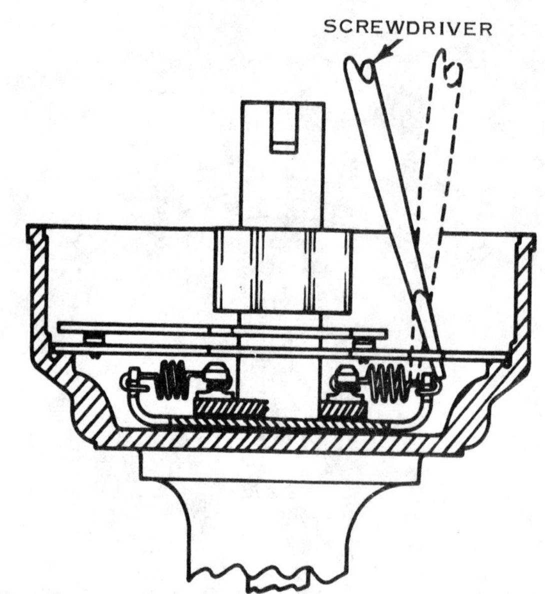

The centrifugal advance can be adjusted by inserting a screwdriver through an access hole in the distributor plate and then bending the spring tab as necessary.

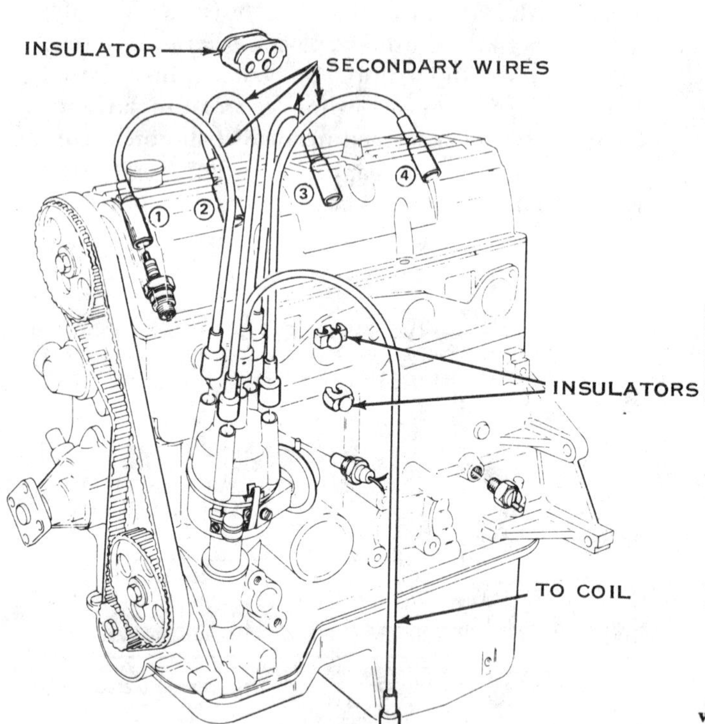

Typical four-cylinder engine secondary wiring.

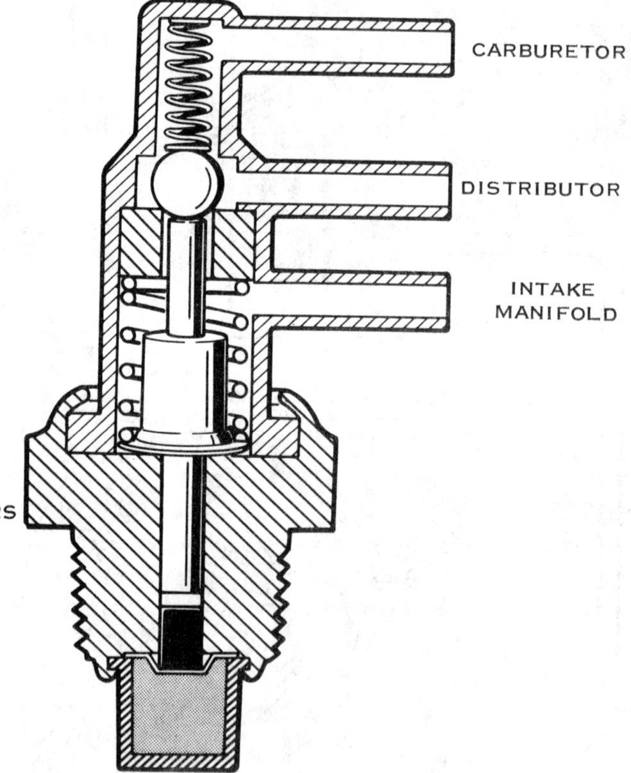

The Ported Vacuum-Switching (PVS) valve is used to change the vacuum supply to the distributor actuator from a ported supply above the throttle plate to full intake manifold vacuum when the engine overheats. This advances the ignition timing, thus speeding up coolant flow and reducing engine temperature.

secondary diaphragm will retard the spark during these periods. In all other phases, the larger primary diaphragm operates from venturi vacuum and pulls the base plate against distributor rotation, advancing the spark timing.

Return springs in both the advance and retard portions center the diaphragms when vacuum drops.

Vacuum modulators installed in the vacuum supply lines from the carburetor and intake manifold will vary the operation of the advance and retard diaphragms. These modulators are covered in Chapter 4, Emission-Control Systems.

SERVICING THE DISTRIBUTOR

REMOVING

Remove the air cleaner. Disconnect the distributor wiring connector from the vehicle wiring harness. Disconnect the vacuum advance lines at the distributor. Remove the distributor cap and place it and the wires to one side.

Scribe a mark on the distributor body and the cylinder block indicating the position of the rotor in the distributor and the distributor in the block. These marks will be used as guides when installing the distributor.

Remove the distributor hold-down bolt and clamp. Lift the distributor out of the block. **CAUTION: Do not rotate the crankshaft while the distributor is out of the block, or it will be necessary to retime the engine.**

INSTALLING THE DISTRIBUTOR

If the crankshaft has not been moved, position the distributor in the block with the rotor aligned with the mark previously scribed on the distributor body and the marks on the distributor body and cylinder block in alignment. Tighten the hold-down bolt.

If the crankshaft was rotated while the distributor was removed from the engine, it will be necessary to time the engine as follows: Rotate the crankshaft until No. 1 piston is on TDC after the compression stroke. Align the correct initial timing mark on the timing tab with the timing pointer.

Position the distributor in the block with one of the armature segments as shown and the rotor at number one firing position. **CAUTION: Make sure the oil pump intermediate shaft properly engages the distributor shaft. It may be necessary to crank the engine with the starter, after the distributor drive gear is partially engaged, in order to engage the oil pump intermediate shaft. Install, but do not tighten, the retaining clamp and bolt. Rotate the distributor to**

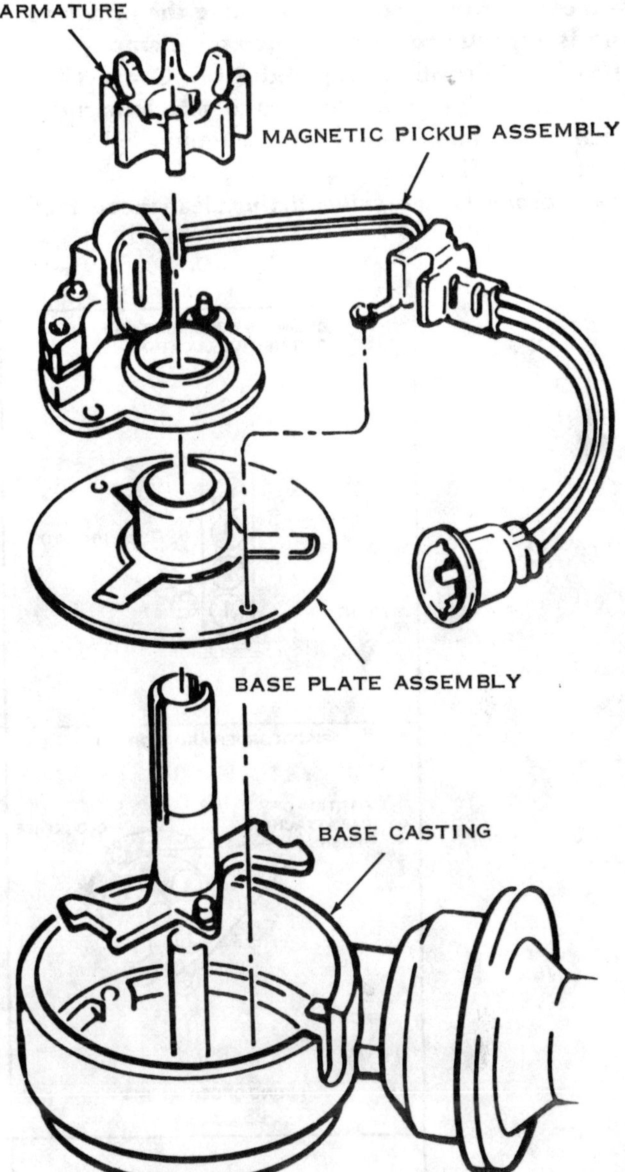

Exploded view of the distributor.

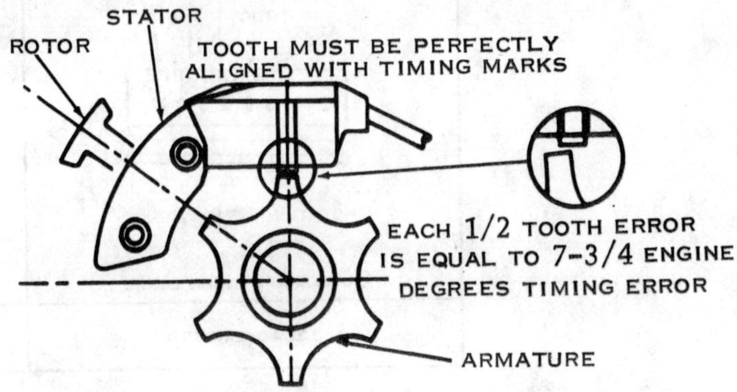

Static timing position of the rotor and armature when the ignition spark occurs in the electronic ignition system.

advance the timing to a point where the armature tooth is aligned properly. Tighten the clamp.

Install the distributor cap and wires. Connect the distributor wiring connector to the vehicle harness. Check the ignition timing with a timing light and adjust to specifications.

To check or adjust the ignition timing, clean the surface and place a white mark on the proper degree line on the front damper and pointer according to the specification on the engine decal. Disconnect the vacuum line(s) at the distributor and plug the hose(s). Connect a timing light to Number 1 cylinder spark plug wire. Install a tachometer. Loosen the distributor hold-down bolt. Start the engine and warm it up; then

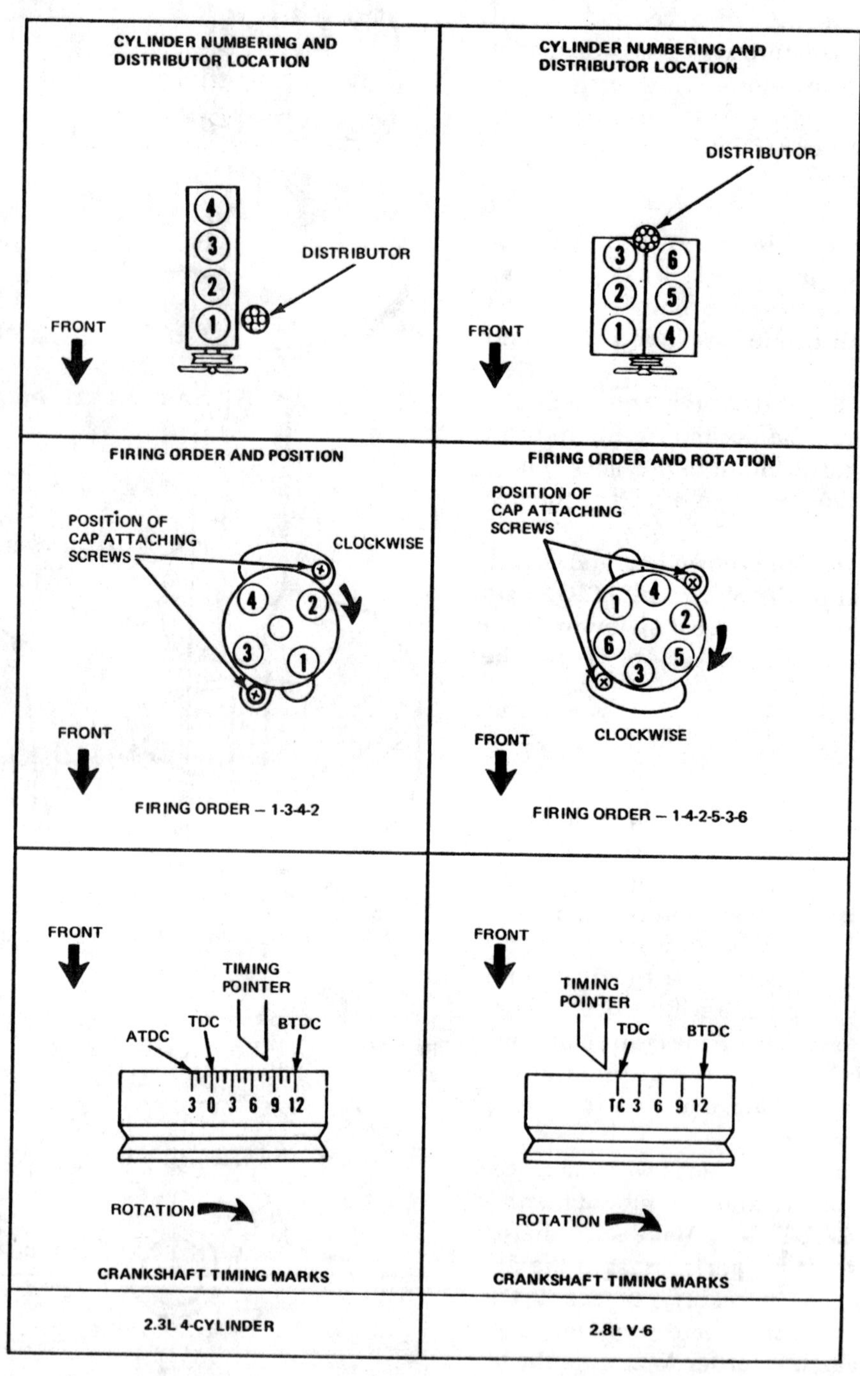

Engine and ignition timing details for the four and V-6 engines.

reduce idle speed to 600 rpm. Adjust the initial timing to specifications by rotating the distributor against rotor rotation to advance the timing. When the white mark is directly in line with the pointer, the ignition timing is correct. Tighten the hold-down bolt. Recheck the timing when the hold-down bolt is tightened.

To check the centrifugal advance, accelerate the engine to 2500 rpm. If timing advance is noted during acceleration, the centrifugal advance mechanism is functioning properly.

To check the vacuum advance, reconnect the carburetor source vacuum hose to the distributor vacuum unit (outer fitting on dual-diaphragm units). Accelerate the engine to 2500 rpm. Total advance should now be greater than in the prior step (centrifugal only), if the advance mechanism is functional. If no additional advance is observed and vacuum is noted at the line to the diaphragm, remove the distributor and make the required repairs. To check the vacuum-retard operation (dual diaphragm), connect the intake manifold vacuum line to the inner diaphragm side of the distributor. With the engine at normal curb idle, a 6 degree or 12 degree retard should now be noted. If the retard is not evident, remove the distributor and make the required repairs.

With all distributor lines properly connected, check the curb idle and reset the speed, if necessary. Remove the timing light and tachometer.

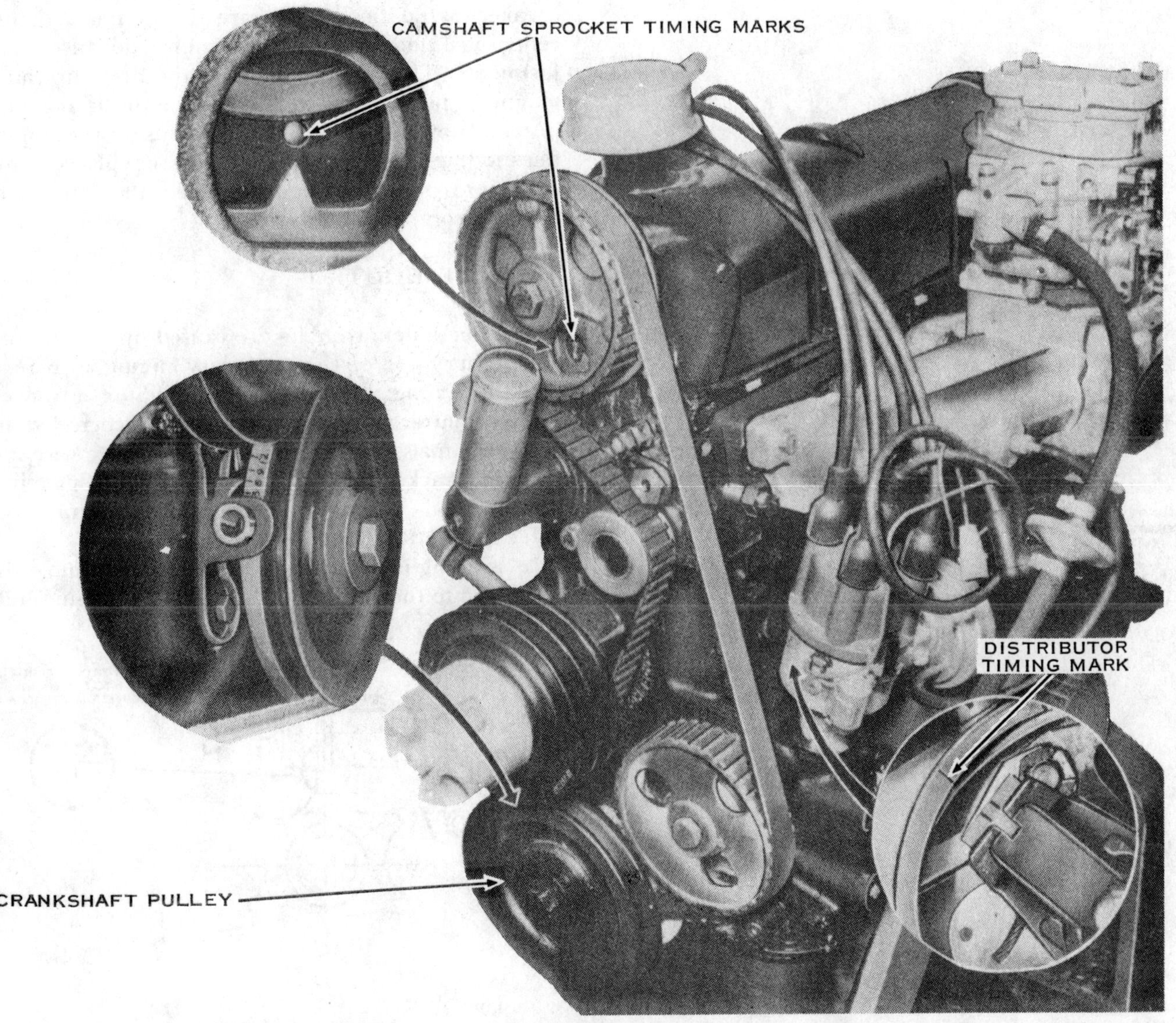

Timing marks for the 2,000/2,300cc engines.

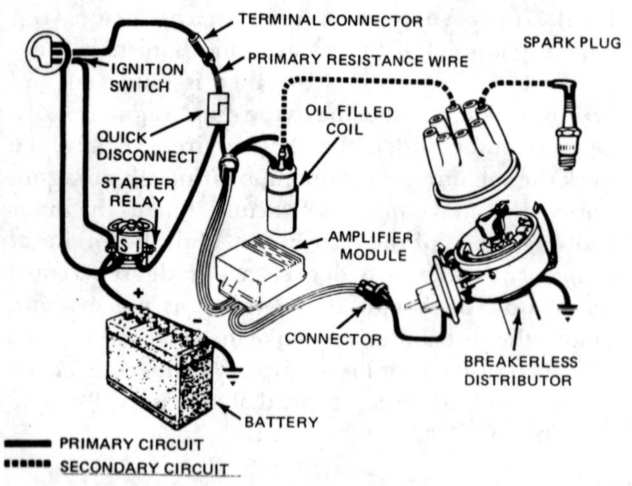

Schematic diagram for the electronic ignition system used since 1975.

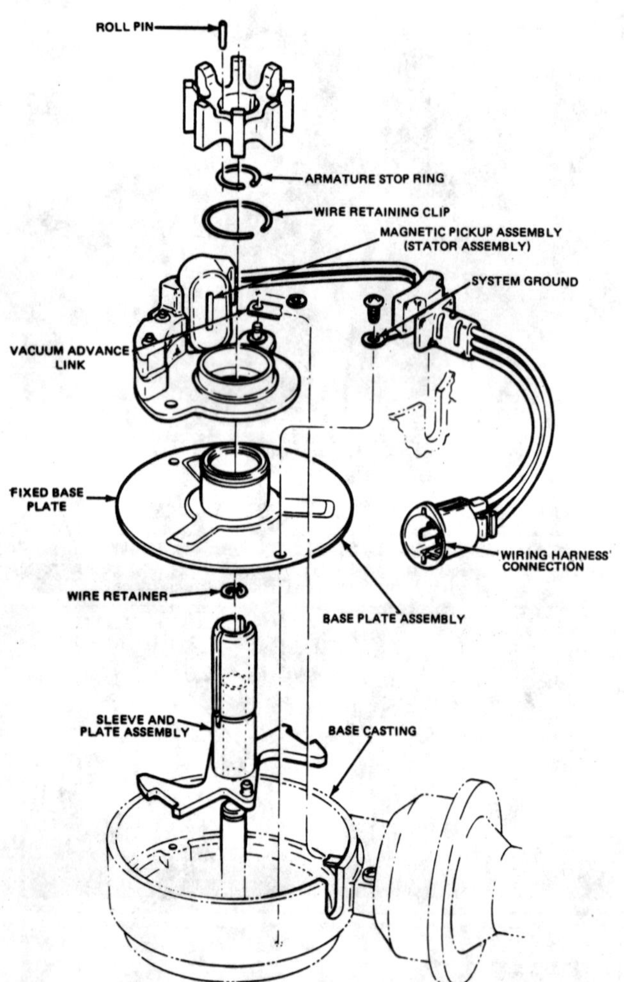

Disassembled view of the breakerless ignition system distributor.

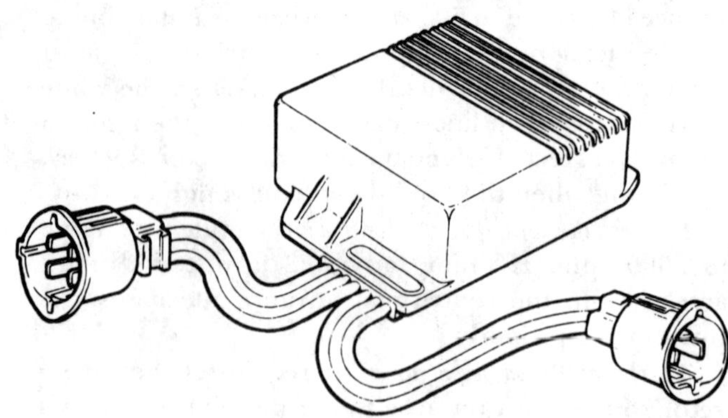

Amplifier module used with the electronic ignition system.

ELECTRONIC (BREAKERLESS) IGNITION SYSTEM

The only adjustments that can be made to the breakerless ignition system are the timing and the centrifugal advance and vacuum advance adjustments. The air gap between the armature and magnetic pickup coil in the distributor is not adjustable, nor are there any adjustments for the amplifier module. Defective components are replaced. Any attempt to connect components outside the vehicle can result in component failure.

TROUBLESHOOTING

Ignition system troubles are caused by a failure in the primary and/or the secondary circuit; incorrect ignition timing; or incorrect distributor advance. Circuit failures may be caused by shorts, corroded or dirty terminals, loose connections, defective wire insulation, cracked distributor cap or rotor, defective pick-up coil assembly or amplifier module, or defective spark plugs.

If an engine starting or operating trouble is attributed to the ignition system, start the engine and

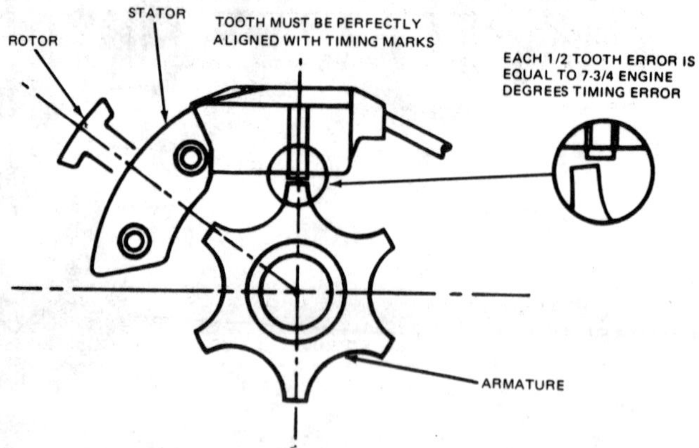

Static timing position of the rotor and armature when the ignition spark occurs in an electronic ignition system.

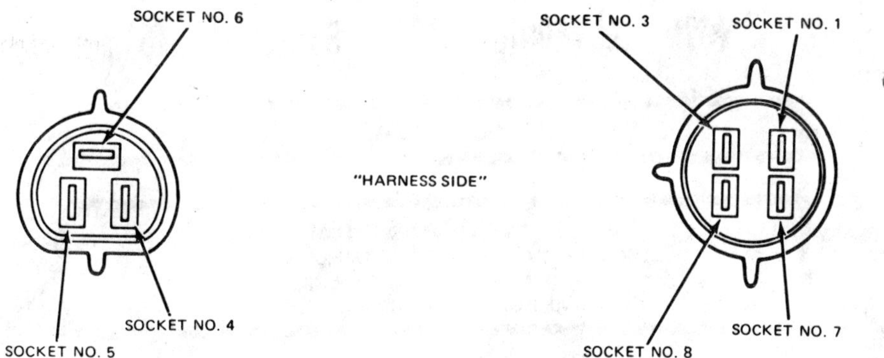

Details of the electronic module connectors on the harness side.

SOLID-STATE MODULE

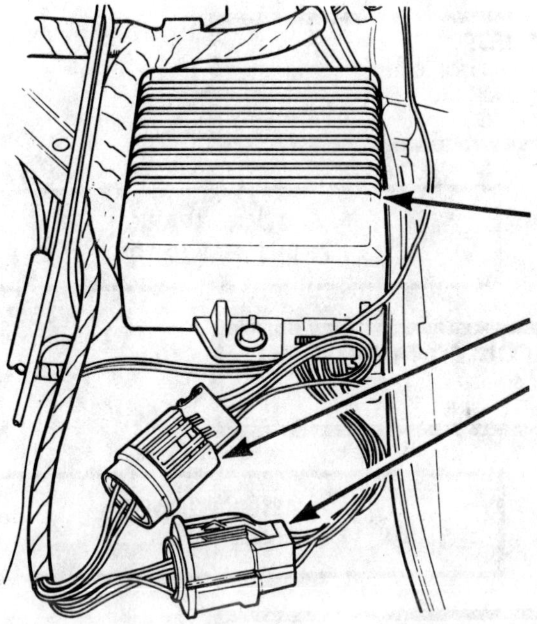

- Module is located on left fender apron in the engine compartment.
- Three-terminal connector.
- Four-terminal connector.

verify the complaint. On engines that will not start, be sure there is gasoline in the fuel tank and that fuel is reaching the carburetor. Then locate the ignition system problem by making the sequential tests in the following Roadmap.

WIRING

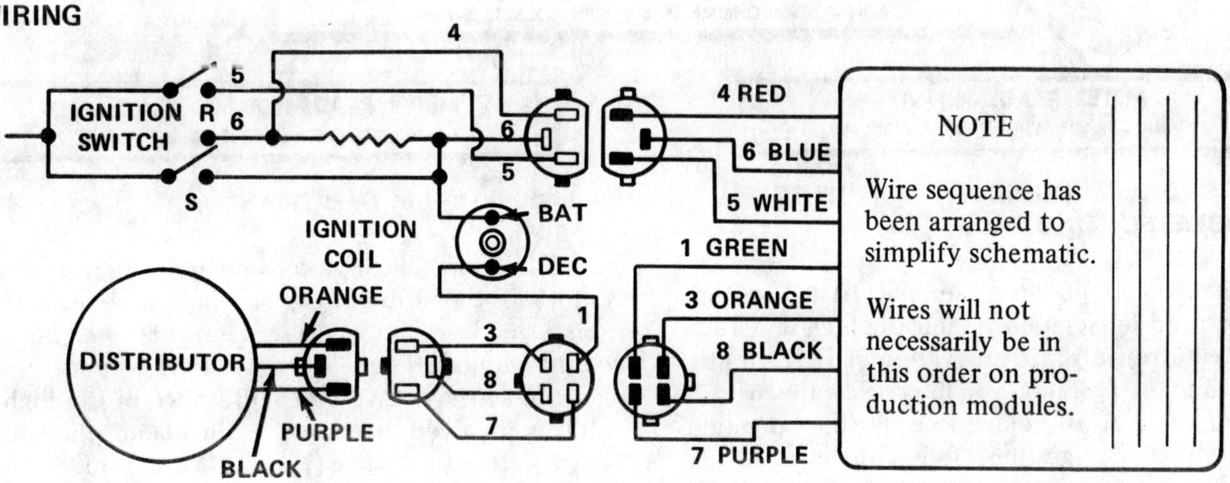

IGNITION SWITCH R S 5 6 4 5 6 4 RED 6 BLUE 5 WHITE BAT IGNITION COIL DEC 1 GREEN ORANGE 3 ORANGE 1 3 8 7 DISTRIBUTOR 8 BLACK PURPLE BLACK 7 PURPLE

NOTE

Wire sequence has been arranged to simplify schematic.

Wires will not necessarily be in this order on production modules.

Placement of the parts (top) and the schematic wiring diagram for the 1975 electronic ignition system.

1975 ELECTRONIC IGNITION SYSTEM TESTS

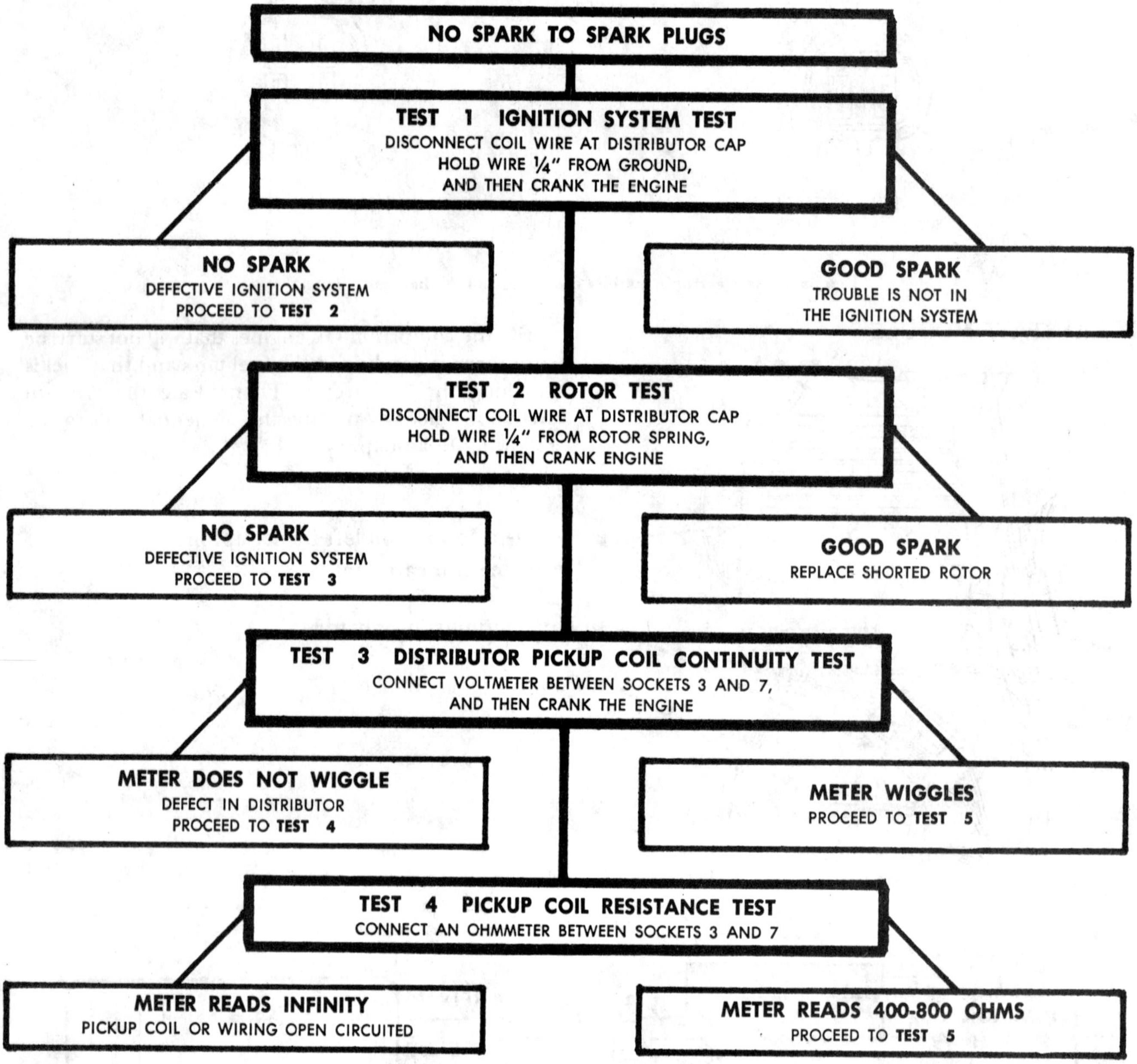

NO SPARK TO SPARK PLUGS

TEST 1 IGNITION SYSTEM TEST
DISCONNECT COIL WIRE AT DISTRIBUTOR CAP
HOLD WIRE 1/4" FROM GROUND,
AND THEN CRANK THE ENGINE

NO SPARK
DEFECTIVE IGNITION SYSTEM
PROCEED TO **TEST 2**

GOOD SPARK
TROUBLE IS NOT IN
THE IGNITION SYSTEM

TEST 2 ROTOR TEST
DISCONNECT COIL WIRE AT DISTRIBUTOR CAP
HOLD WIRE 1/4" FROM ROTOR SPRING,
AND THEN CRANK ENGINE

NO SPARK
DEFECTIVE IGNITION SYSTEM
PROCEED TO **TEST 3**

GOOD SPARK
REPLACE SHORTED ROTOR

TEST 3 DISTRIBUTOR PICKUP COIL CONTINUITY TEST
CONNECT VOLTMETER BETWEEN SOCKETS 3 AND 7,
AND THEN CRANK THE ENGINE

METER DOES NOT WIGGLE
DEFECT IN DISTRIBUTOR
PROCEED TO **TEST 4**

METER WIGGLES
PROCEED TO **TEST 5**

TEST 4 PICKUP COIL RESISTANCE TEST
CONNECT AN OHMMETER BETWEEN SOCKETS 3 AND 7

METER READS INFINITY
PICKUP COIL OR WIRING OPEN CIRCUITED

METER READS 400-800 OHMS
PROCEED TO **TEST 5**

1975 FORD ELECTRONIC IGNITION SYSTEM TROUBLESHOOTING CHART

This roadmap provides a series of basic tests that can be used to isolate common troubles in a 1975 Ford electronic ignition system. To arrive at a solution to the problem, you must make the tests in the sequence given below. Because the operation of an electronic ignition system depends on an adequate voltage supply to the components, it is essential that voltage and resistance measurements be made to determine the source of trouble.

ENGINE CRANKS BUT DOES NOT START

① Disconnect the high-tension coil wire from the center of the distributor cap and hold it about 1/4" from a good ground. *NOTE: If the rubber boot cannot be pushed back enough, insert a paper clip or a screwdriver.* **CAUTION: Because of the high voltages involved, use a pair of insulated pliers to avoid getting a shock.** Have a helper turn the ignition switch to the START position to crank the engine. If there is a good spark here, you can have trouble in the secondary circuit, a shorted rotor, or a

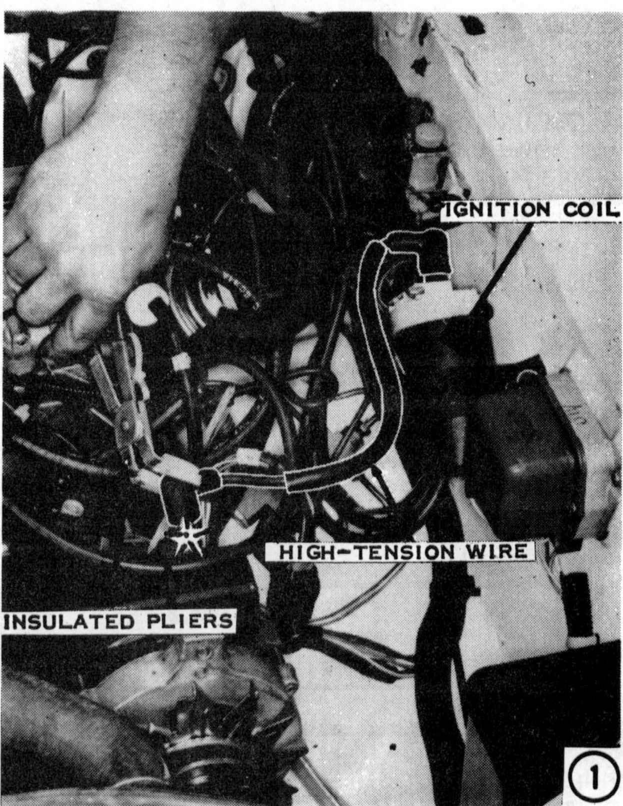

cracked distributor cap. To make the rotor test, proceed to Test ②.

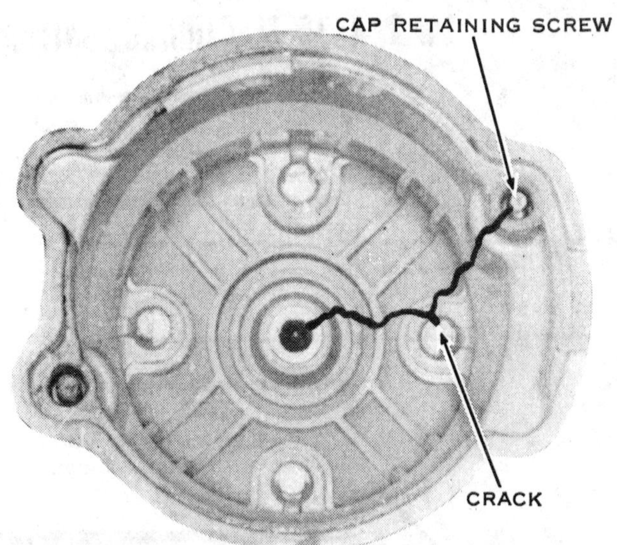

A cracked distributor cap can keep the engine from running.

Rotor Test

② Hold the high-tension coil wire about 1/4" from the rotor spring, and then crank the engine. If a spark jumps to the rotor, then it is shorted to ground and must be replaced. If no spark jumps to the rotor, then check the distributor cap for a crack, which can short the voltage to ground. If the cap is not defective, then you have trouble in other than the secondary circuit, and this must be checked by a series of voltage and resistance tests to determine the exact cause as follows:

Armature And Pickup Coil In The Distributor

③ To check the distributor circuits, unplug the four-wire connector at the module, and then connect a voltmeter between sockets Nos. 3 and 7. Have a helper crank the engine with the key switch, and the voltmeter (set to the lowest scale) should wiggle slightly (approximately 1/2 volt) as each tooth of the armature moves past the permanent magnet pickup. If the meter wiggles slightly, then the arma-

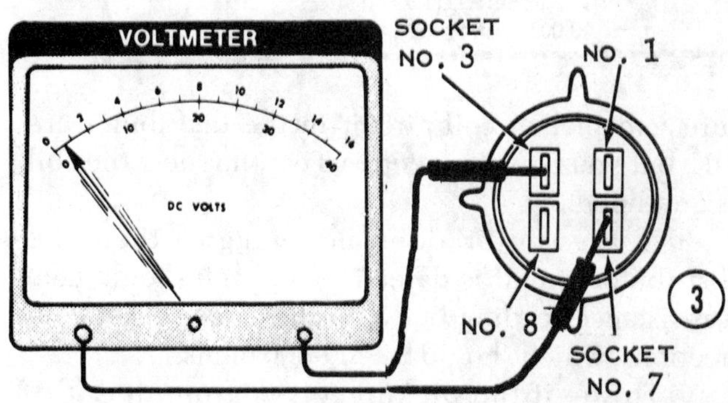

1975 ELECTRONIC IGNITION SYSTEM TESTS (CONTINUED)

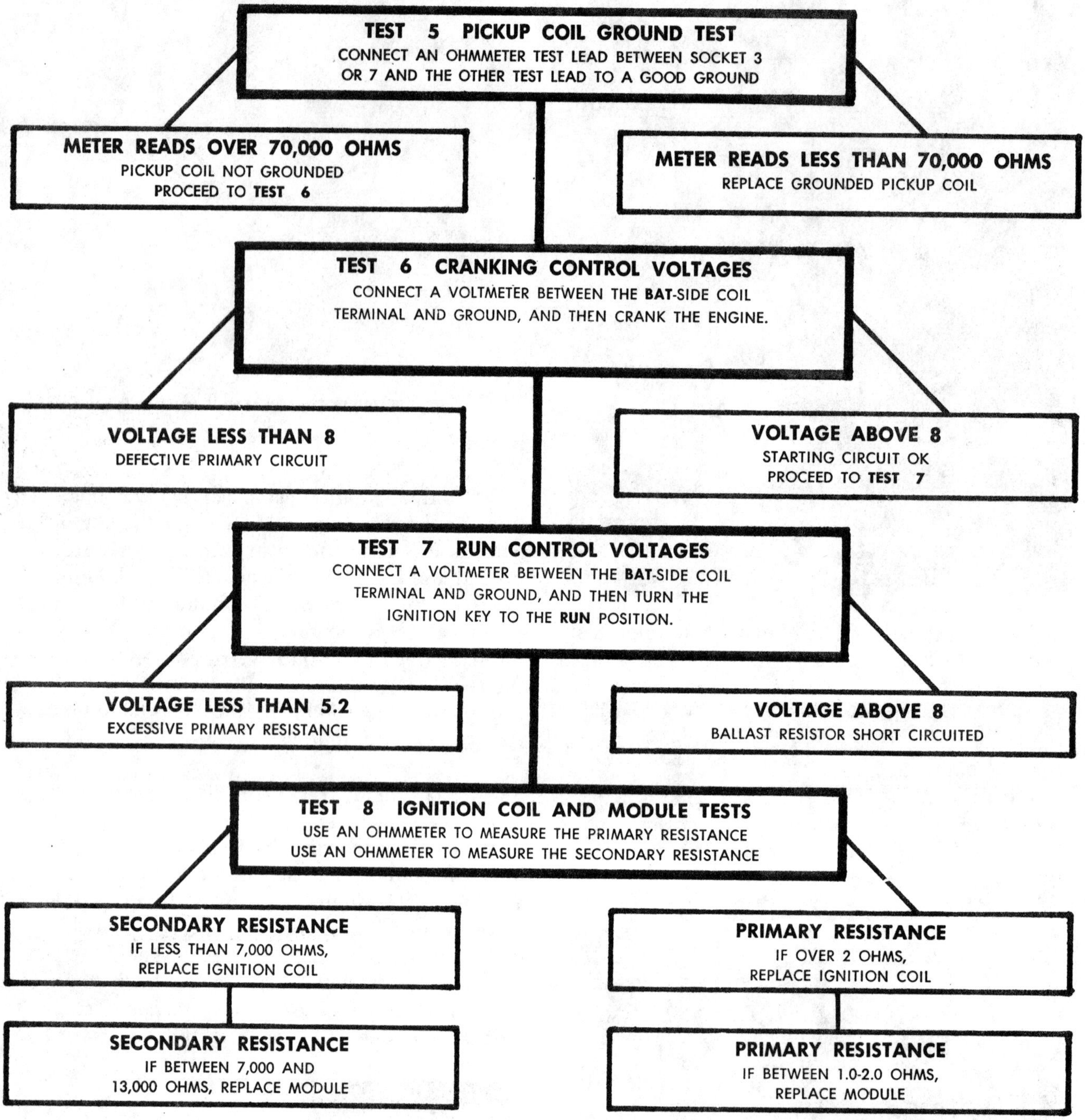

TEST 5 PICKUP COIL GROUND TEST
CONNECT AN OHMMETER TEST LEAD BETWEEN SOCKET 3 OR 7 AND THE OTHER TEST LEAD TO A GOOD GROUND

METER READS OVER 70,000 OHMS
PICKUP COIL NOT GROUNDED
PROCEED TO **TEST 6**

METER READS LESS THAN 70,000 OHMS
REPLACE GROUNDED PICKUP COIL

TEST 6 CRANKING CONTROL VOLTAGES
CONNECT A VOLTMETER BETWEEN THE **BAT**-SIDE COIL TERMINAL AND GROUND, AND THEN CRANK THE ENGINE.

VOLTAGE LESS THAN 8
DEFECTIVE PRIMARY CIRCUIT

VOLTAGE ABOVE 8
STARTING CIRCUIT OK
PROCEED TO **TEST 7**

TEST 7 RUN CONTROL VOLTAGES
CONNECT A VOLTMETER BETWEEN THE **BAT**-SIDE COIL TERMINAL AND GROUND, AND THEN TURN THE IGNITION KEY TO THE **RUN** POSITION.

VOLTAGE LESS THAN 5.2
EXCESSIVE PRIMARY RESISTANCE

VOLTAGE ABOVE 8
BALLAST RESISTOR SHORT CIRCUITED

TEST 8 IGNITION COIL AND MODULE TESTS
USE AN OHMMETER TO MEASURE THE PRIMARY RESISTANCE
USE AN OHMMETER TO MEASURE THE SECONDARY RESISTANCE

SECONDARY RESISTANCE
IF LESS THAN 7,000 OHMS, REPLACE IGNITION COIL

SECONDARY RESISTANCE
IF BETWEEN 7,000 AND 13,000 OHMS, REPLACE MODULE

PRIMARY RESISTANCE
IF OVER 2 OHMS, REPLACE IGNITION COIL

PRIMARY RESISTANCE
IF BETWEEN 1.0-2.0 OHMS, REPLACE MODULE

ture and pickup coil circuit in the distributor are OK, but you must proceed to Test⑤to see if the coil is grounded.

④If the meter does not wiggle, then the distributor circuit is defective, and you should take a resistance reading between the same socket connections, which should be 400-800 ohms.

⑤To see if the pickup coil is grounded (defective), connect the ohmmeter between socket 3 or 7 and a good ground. You must have a reading of over 70,000 ohms; otherwise, the coil is grounded. If not, proceed to Test⑥.

Control Voltages To The Module

⑥If the distributor is OK, then you must make sure that the module is receiving the correct

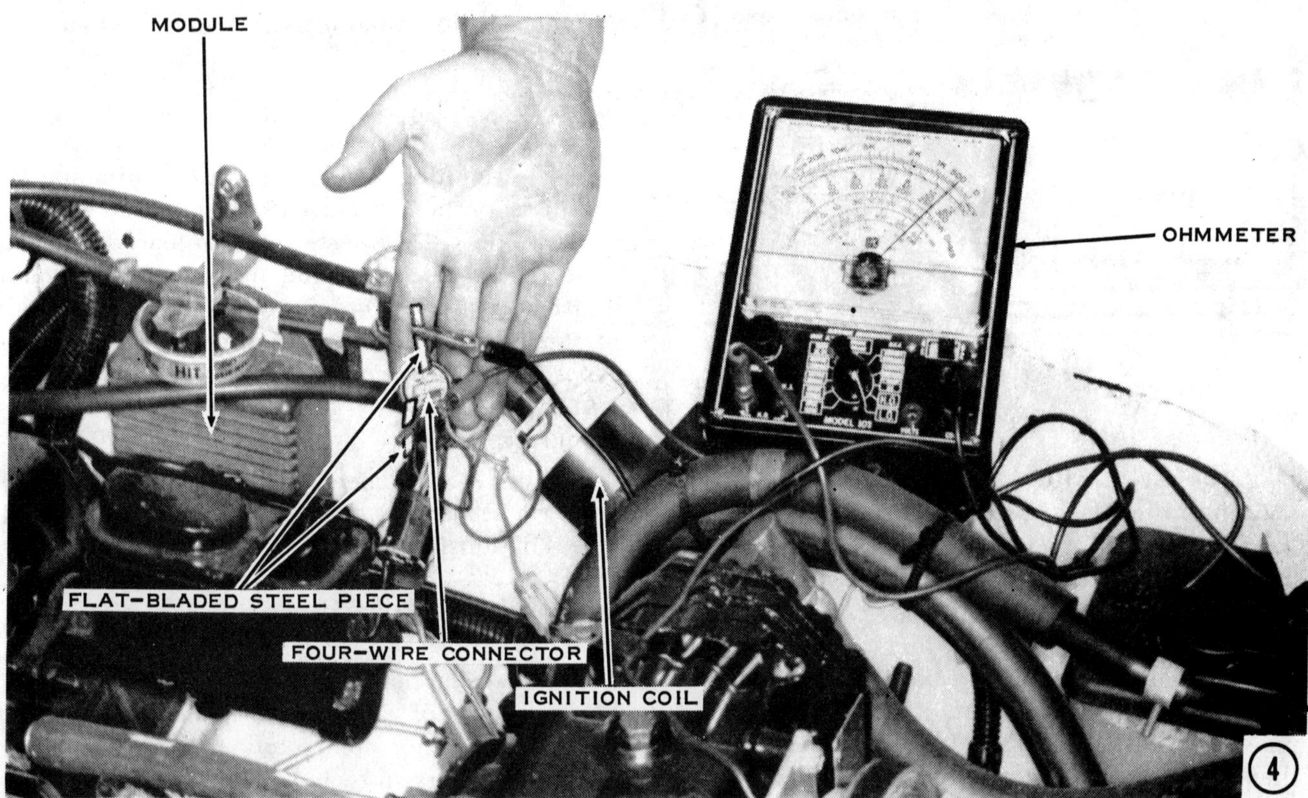

voltages from the ignition switch in both the START and RUN positions. To make these tests, connect a jumper wire from the "DEC" terminal of the ignition coil to a good ground. *NOTE: Some late-model coils have a white plastic coil connector cover, which can be slid off. In these cases, it is a simple matter to connect the jumper wire between sockets 1 and 8 of the four-wire connector to replace the jumper from the "DEC" terminal of the ignition coil to ground.* Connect a voltmeter between socket 6 of the three-wire connector and ground. With all lights and accessories off, turn the ignition key to the START position, and the voltage should be no lower than 7.9 volts, which indicates that the primary circuit from the battery through the ignition coil is satisfactory. If the voltage is less than 7.9, check the primary circuit for defects: corroded ignition switch contacts, connections of the three-wire connector, or an excessive current draw in the starter.

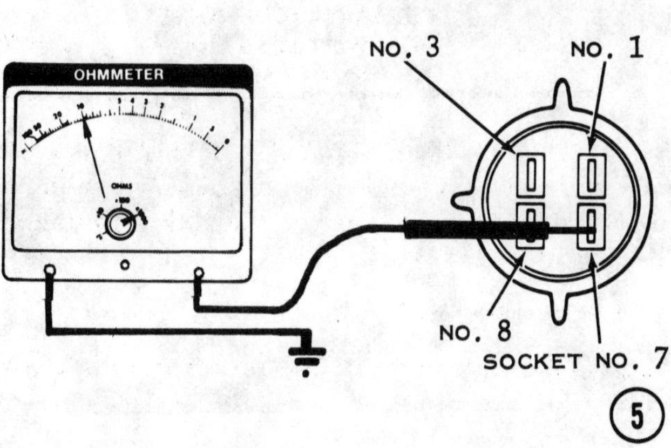

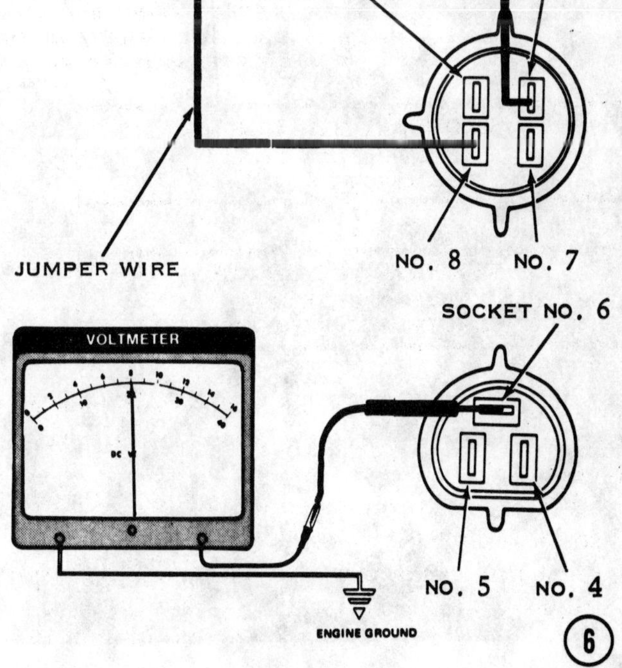

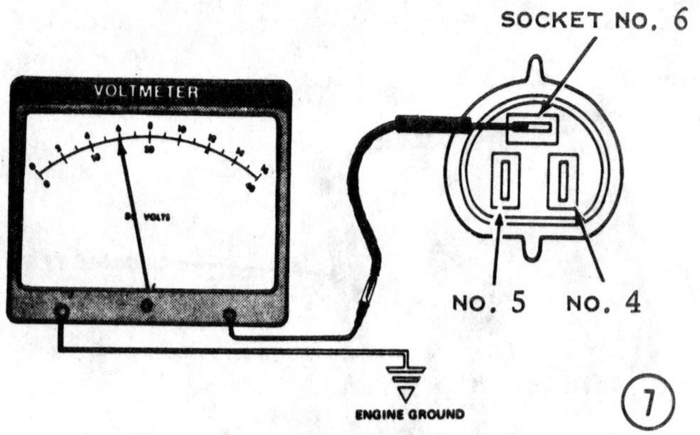

⑦ To test the RUN circuit, turn the ignition switch to the RUN position while checking the voltage between socket 6 and ground with the jumper wire still connected from the "DEC" terminal of the ignition coil to a good ground (or between sockets 1 and 8 of the four-wire connector). The voltage reading should be 5.2–7.9 volts, indicating that the primary circuit through the ballast resistor is satisfactory. If the reading is over 8 volts, then the ballast resistor is short circuited. If the voltage is less than 5.2, then the primary circuit has excessive resistance, or the ballast resistor is open circuited. Remove the jumper wire from the "DEC" terminal of the ignition coil or from the four-wire connector.

Ignition Coil Test

⑧ The ignition coil can be tested on a special coil tester or the resistance can be checked with the coil terminals disconnected. The primary resistance must be 1.0-2.0 ohms, and the secondary should register 7,000-13,000 ohms. *NOTE: It is necessary to slide the white cover-insulator from the coil to expose the primary contacts.*

Module Test

If all of the other checks are OK to this point, then replace the module, because it cannot be checked except by substitution.

Assembling The Connectors

As a final step before plugging in the connectors, dip both sides of each in Lubriplate D.S. so as to coat the connector completely with grease. Plug in the connectors and wipe all surplus grease from the outside of the connectors. **CAUTION: It is essential to use this grease to prevent the entrance of moisture, which will cause corrosion.**

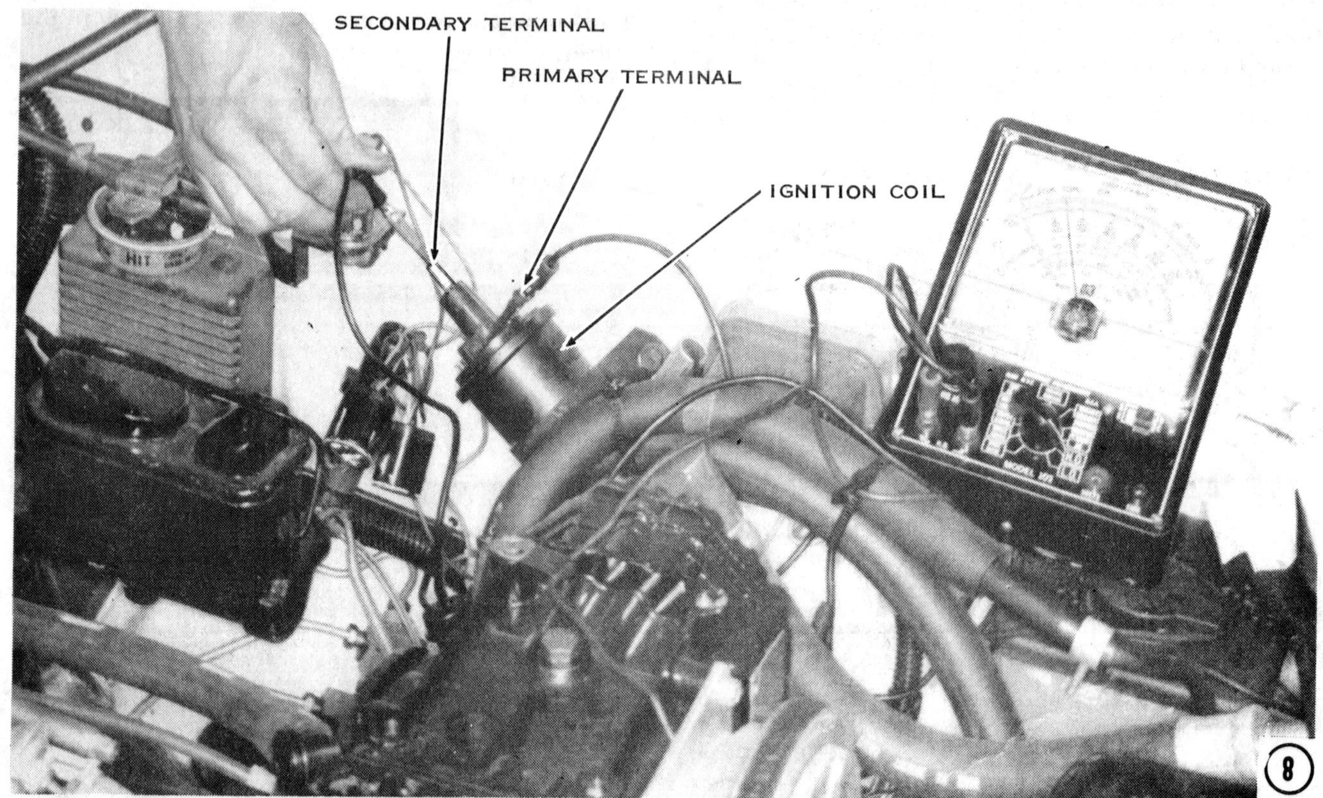

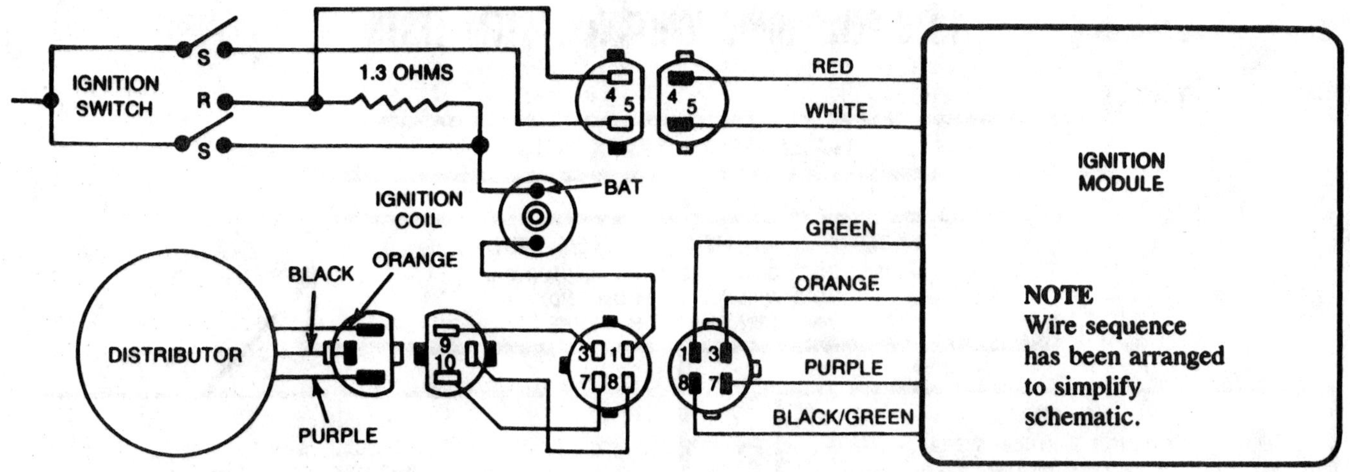

Schematic wiring diagram for troubleshooting the 1976 electronic ignition system.

1976 FORD ELECTRONIC IGNITION SYSTEM TROUBLESHOOTING CHART

In 1976, the Ford Motor Company made wiring changes again, with the module having a two-terminal connector and a four-terminal connector. The 1975 three-terminal connector center terminal 6 (blue wire) is not used in 1976. The 1976 four-terminal connector terminals 7 (purple wire) and 8 (black-green wire) changed positions from 1975. This rewiring affects the meter connections for troubleshooting, and these changes will be covered in the following series of tests.

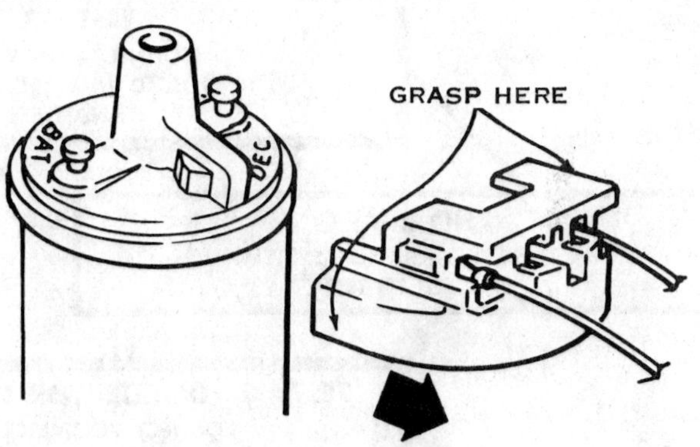

If it is necessary to remove the ceramic insulator from the top of a 1975-76 ignition coil, grasp it at the sides, as shown, and then pull it firmly away from the coil.

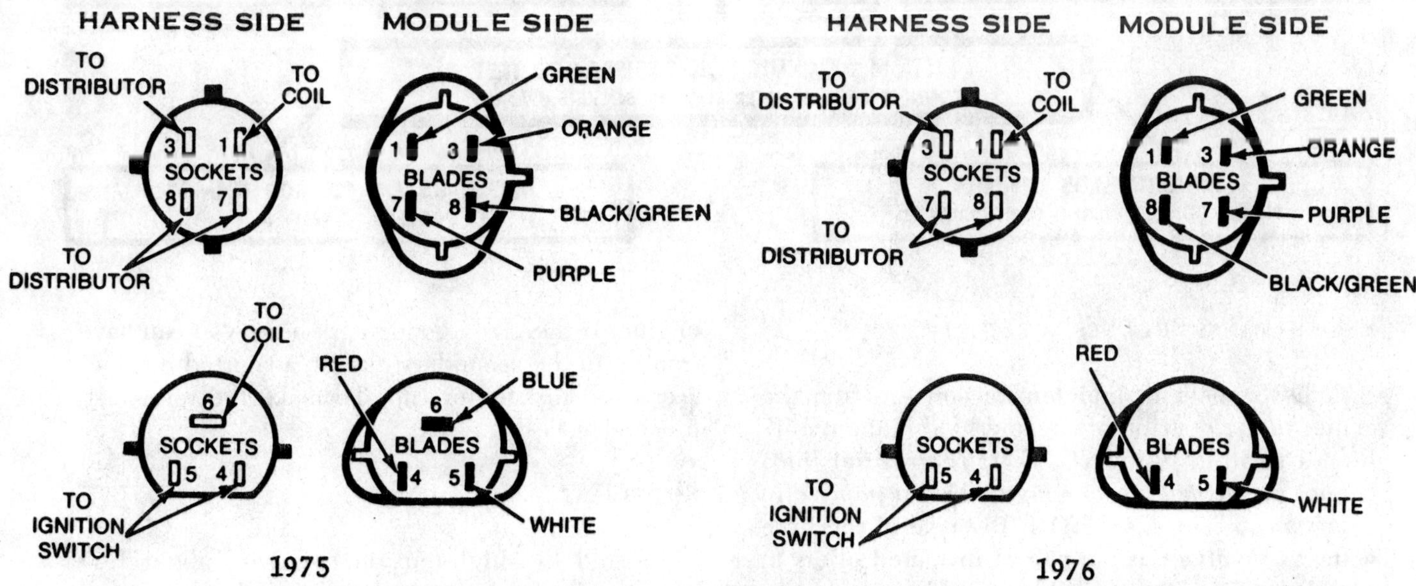

Comparison of the 1975 (left) and 1976 module connectors. The 1976 rewiring affects the meter connections for diagnosis.

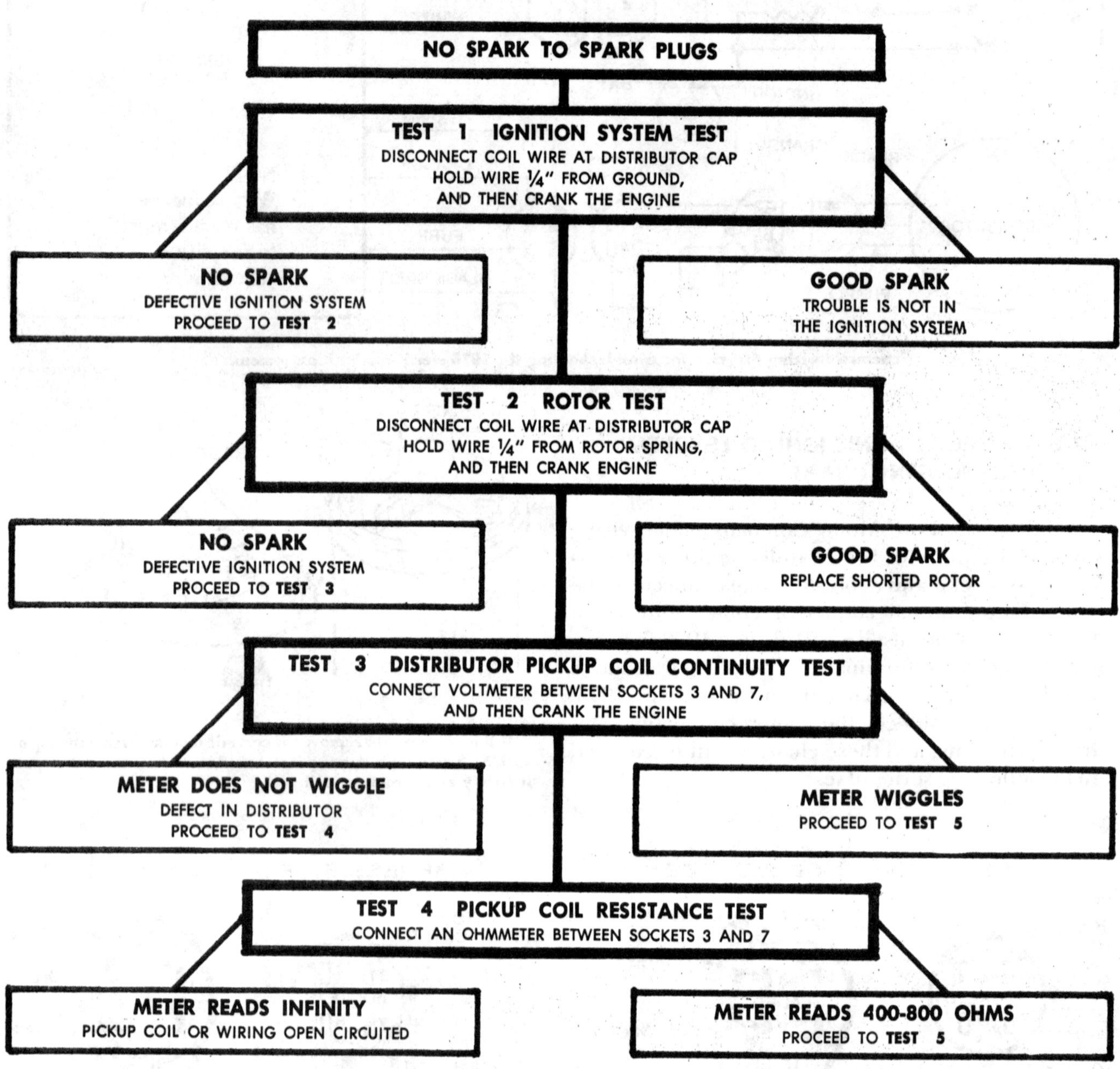

Engine Cranks But Does Not Start

① Disconnect the high-tension coil wire from the center of the distributor cap and hold it about 1/4" from a good ground. *NOTE: If the rubber boot cannot be pushed back enough, insert a paper clip or a screwdriver.* **CAUTION: Because of the high voltages involved, use a pair of insulated pliers to avoid getting a shock.** Have a helper turn the ignition switch to the START position to crank the engine. If there is a good spark here, you can have trouble in the secondary circuit, a shorted rotor, or a cracked distributor cap. To make the rotor test, proceed to Test ②.

Rotor Test

② Hold the high-tension coil wire about 1/4" from the rotor spring, and then crank the engine. If a spark jumps to the rotor, then it is shorted to

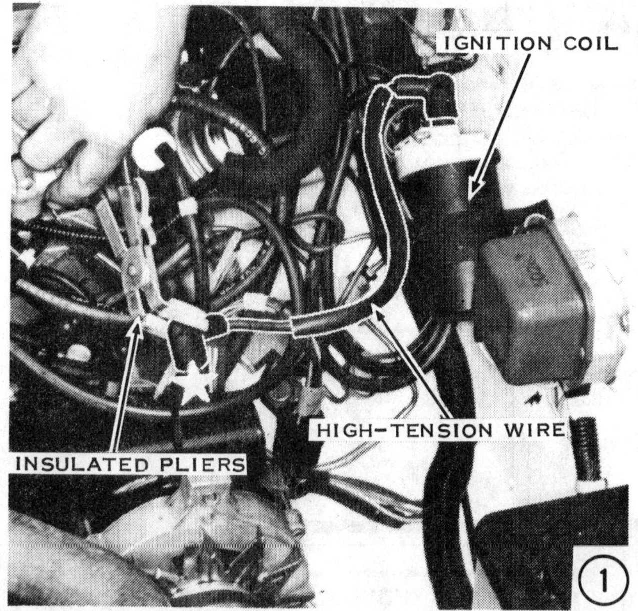

ground and must be replaced. If no spark jumps to the rotor, then check the distributor cap for a crack, which can short the voltage to ground. If the cap is not defective, then you have trouble in other than the secondary circuit, and this must be checked by a series of voltage and resistance tests to determine the exact cause as follows:

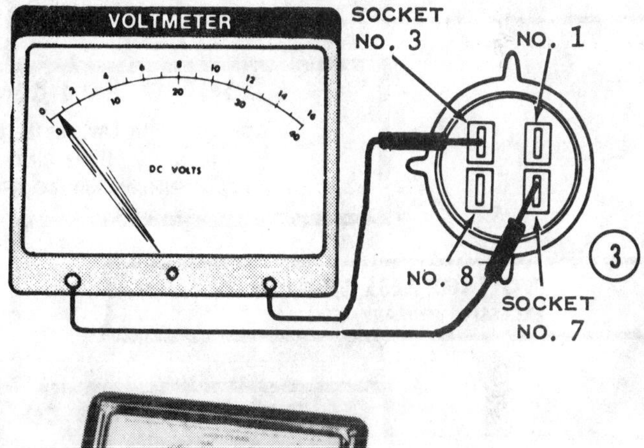

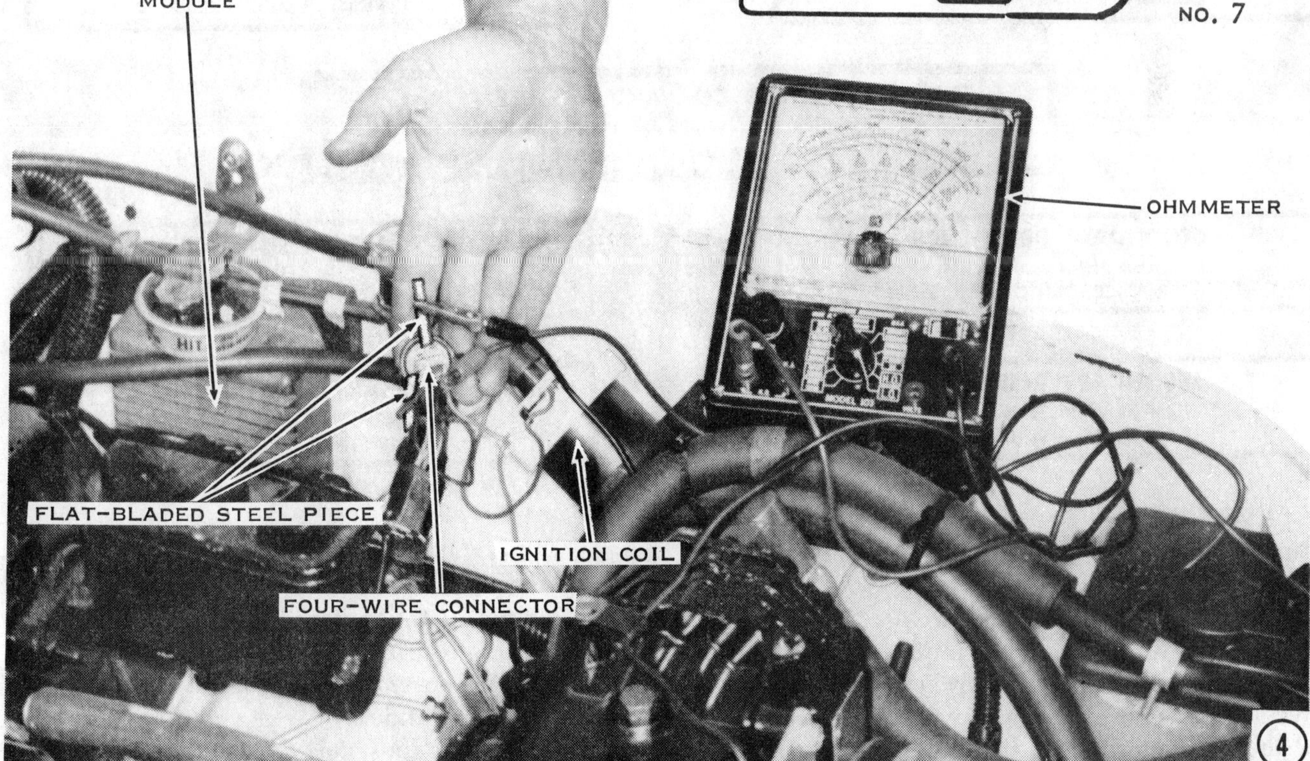

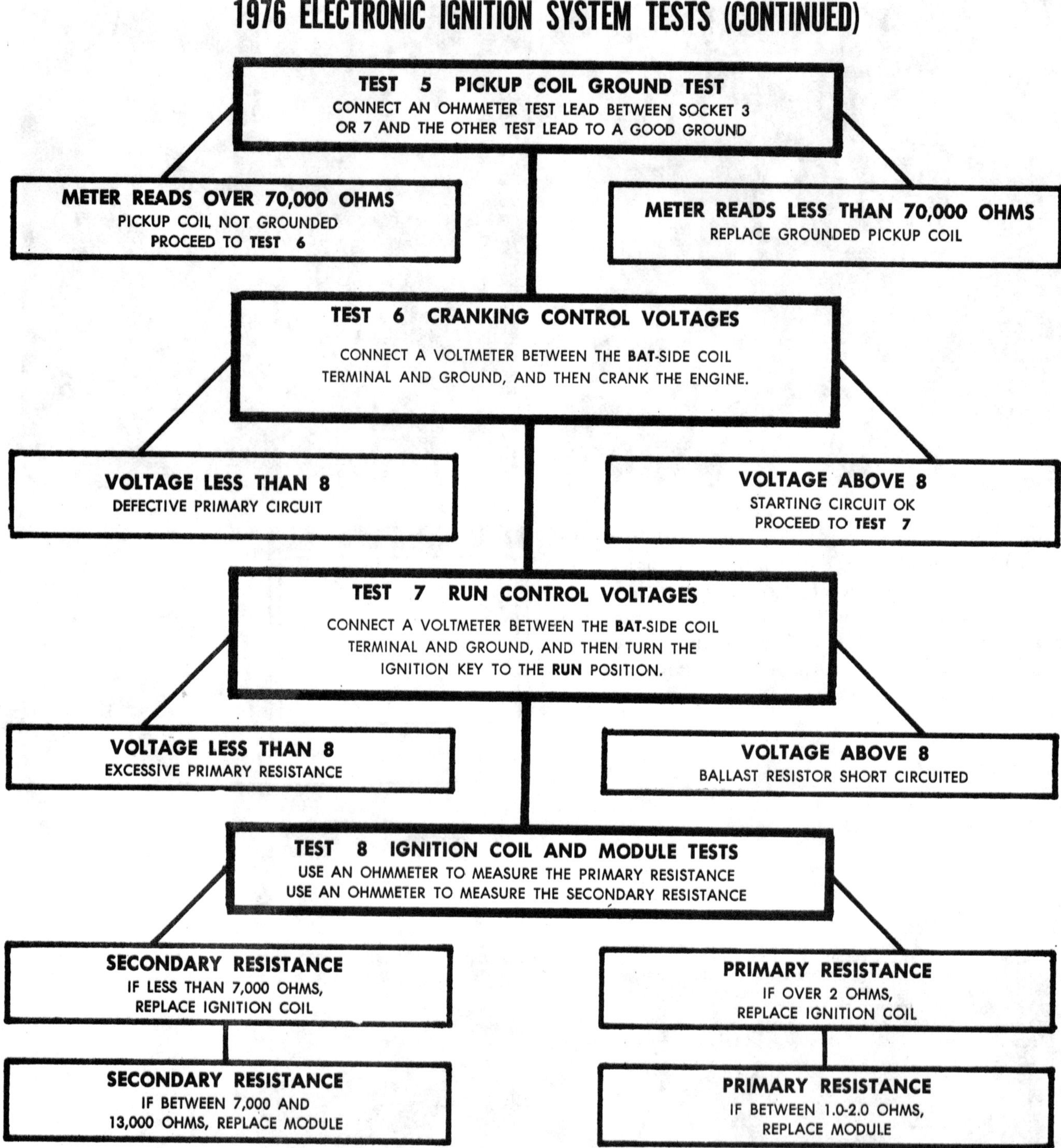

Armature and Pickup Coil In The Distributor

③ To check the distributor circuits, unplug the four-wire connector at the module, and then connect a voltmeter between sockets Nos. 3 and 7. Have a helper crank the engine with the key switch, and the voltmeter (set to the lowest scale) should wiggle slightly (approximately 1/2 volt) as each tooth of the armature moves past the permanent magnet pickup. If the meter wiggles slightly, then the armature and pickup coil circuit in the distributor are OK, but you must proceed to Test ⑤ to see if the coil is grounded.

④ If the meter does not wiggle, then the dis-

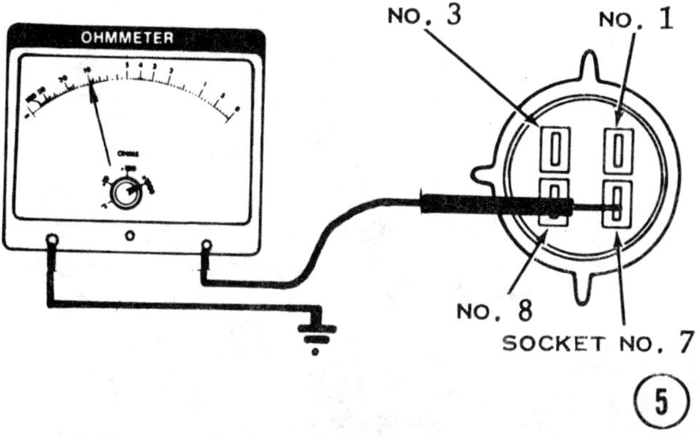

tributor circuit is defective, and you should take a resistance reading between the same socket connections, which should be 400-800 ohms.

⑤ To see if the pickup coil is grounded (defective), connect the ohmmeter between the same four-wire connector socket 3 or 7 and a good ground. You must have a reading of over 70,000 ohms; otherwise, the coil is grounded. If it is not grounded, proceed to Test ⑥.

CONTROL VOLTAGES

⑥ If the distributor is OK, then you must check to see that the ignition coil is receiving the correct voltages through the system. To do this, reconnect all of the disconnected connectors to the module, and then measure the voltage at the BAT side of the ignition coil by inserting a flat metallic probe between the ceramic shield and the ignition coil until it makes contact with the BAT-side coil terminal. Connect a voltmeter between the probe and a good engine ground. Turn the ignition switch to the CRANKING position; the voltage should be above 7.9 volts. If the voltage is low, check the supply wire and/or connectors through the ignition switch and also the starter current draw to be sure that it is not drawing down the cranking voltage excessively.

⑦ To test the RUN circuit, turn the key switch to the RUN position (without starting the engine) while checking the voltage between the probe and a good engine ground as in the previous test. The reading should be 4.9 – 7.9 volts, indicating that the primary circuit through the ballast resistor is satisfactory. If the reading is over 8 volts, then the ballast resistor is short circuited. If the voltage is less than 8 volts, then the ballast resistor is open circuited, or the primary circuit has excessive resistance. Remove the metallic probe from between the ceramic shield and the ignition coil.

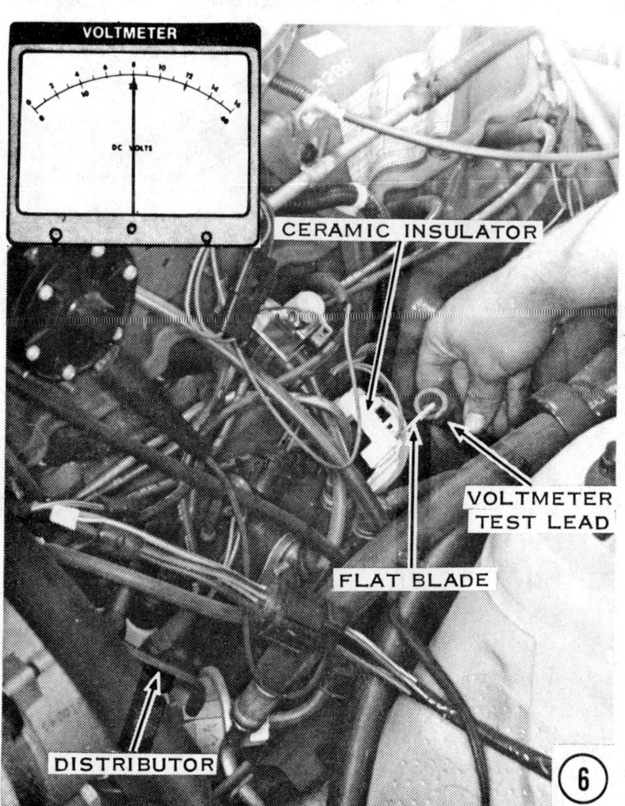

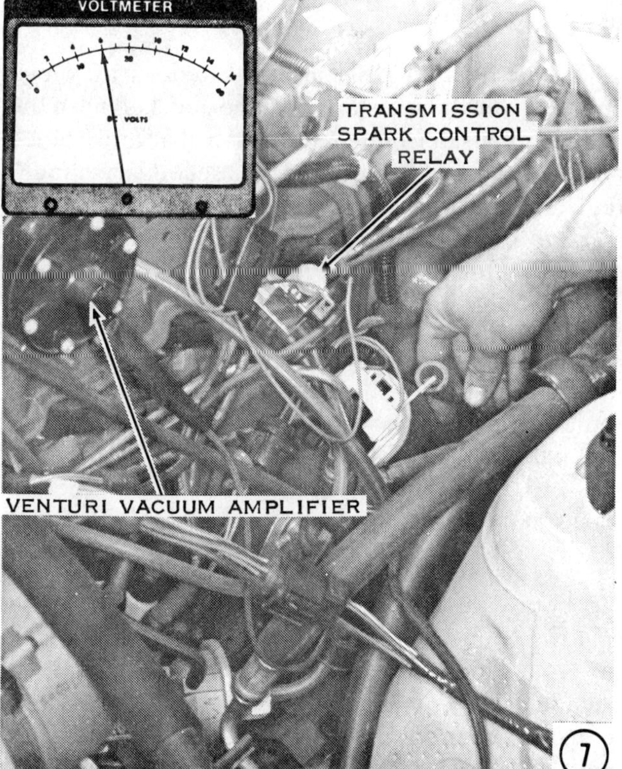

Ignition Coil Test

⑧ The ignition coil can be tested on a special coil tester or the resistance can be checked with the coil terminals disconnected. The primary resistance must be 1.0 – 2.0 ohms, and the secondary should register 7,000 – 13,000 ohms. *NOTE: It is necessary to slide the white cover-insulator from the coil to expose the primary contacts.*

Module Test

If all of the other checks are OK to this point, then replace the module, because it cannot be checked except by substitution.

Assembling The Connectors

As a final step before plugging in the connectors, dip both sides of each in Lubriplate D.S. so as to coat the connector completely with grease. Plug in the connectors and wipe all surplus grease from the outside of the connectors. **CAUTION: It is essential to use this grease to prevent the entrance of moisture, which can cause corrosion.**

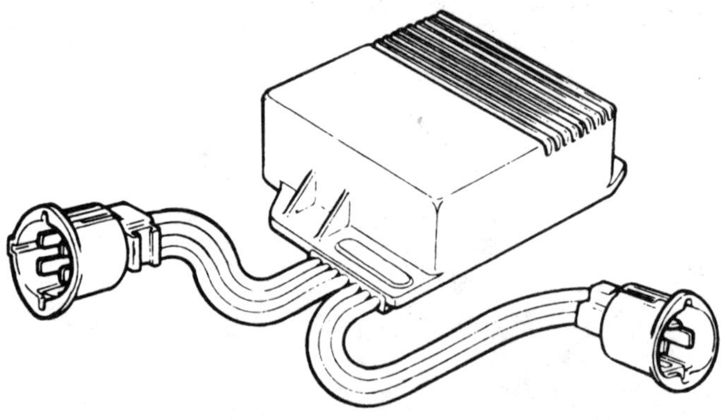

Amplifier module used with the electronic ignition system.

LIGHTING CIRCUIT

The lighting and accessory circuits of modern automobiles are exceedingly complex because of the maze of circuits' switches, and controls. However, most problems concern burned-out bulbs, which are easily replaceable. More difficult problems revolve about locating open and short circuits.

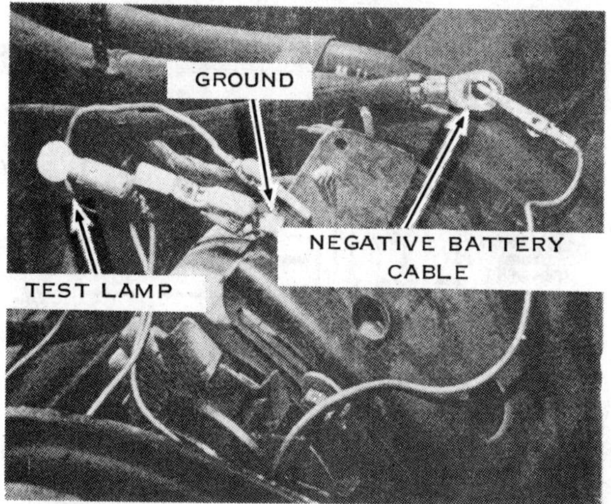

To check for a short circuit, connect a test lamp between the disconnected battery cable and a good ground, as discussed in the text.

CHECKING FOR A SHORT CIRCUIT

The first step is to disconnect the battery ground cable at the engine and connect a 12-volt test lamp between the end of the disconnected cable and a good ground as shown. If there is a short circuit, the test lamp will glow with all accessories turned off. If the vehicle is equipped with an electric clock, make the battery connection for a few seconds to wind the clock so that you can have a two-minute test period before the clock runs down and needs to be energized again. **CAUTION: Make sure that all vehicle doors are closed so that the courtesy lights are not lit, which would cause the bulb to glow dimly in some cases.** It is not a good idea to use a voltmeter in place of the suggested test lamp because, in late-model vehicles with diodes in the charging circuit, some voltmeter reading will be obtained under normal conditions.

To check for a short, disconnect and reconnect each electrical circuit, one at a time. When a disconnect causes the test lamp to go out, you have found the shorted circuit and each section of it can be tested in a like manner.

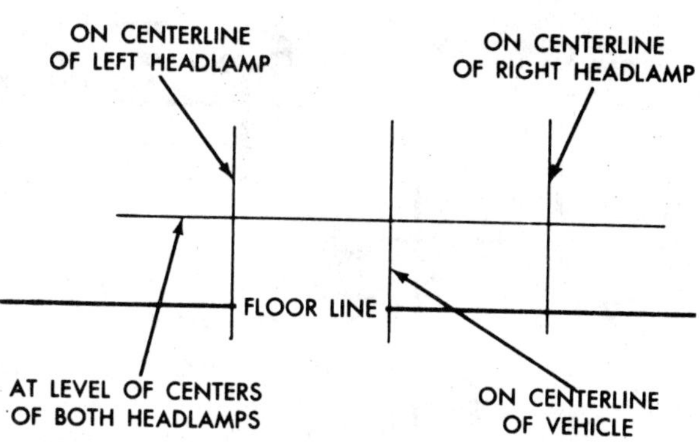

Headlamp screen aiming pattern discussed in the text.

CHECKING FOR AN OPEN CIRCUIT

If a unit does not function, the first check is to see that the unit in question is getting current. Use a test lamp or voltmeter for these tests. If there is no current, check the fuse, fusible links, and harness connectors. A loose, bent, corroded, or damaged connector can cause this trouble. Loose connections and corroded or loose-fitting fuses can cause intermittent operation.

HEADLAMP AIMING

If it becomes necessary to adjust the headlamps, the following screen method will give accurate results. Position the vehicle on a level floor, 25' from a light-colored wall. Make four lines on the wall, as shown in the accompanying drawing. (1) A horizontal line at the level of the centers of the headlights. (2) a center vertical line, which must be aligned with the vehicle center line. *NOTE: A good method of doing this is to sight through the rear window and align the center of the rear window molding through the mirror bracket or hood center line.* (3) A vertical line aligned with the center line of the left headlamp. (4) A vertical line aligned with the center line of the right headlamp.

Adjust the low beam and high beam patterns as shown in the accompanying drawings.

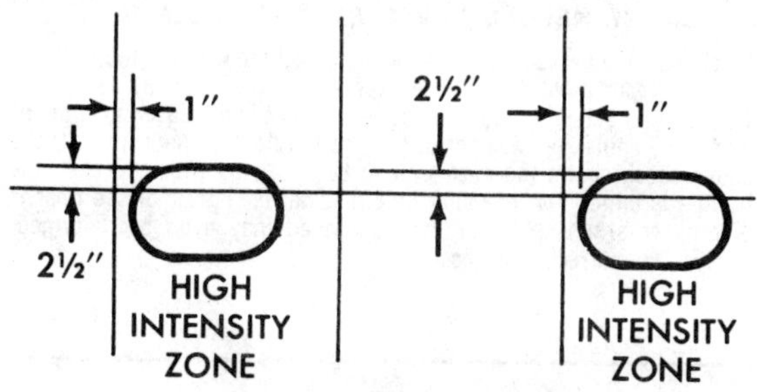

Low beam adjustment pattern.

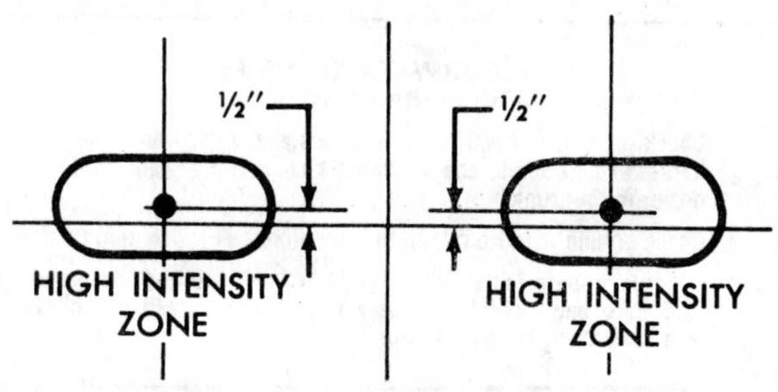

High beam adjustment pattern.

Directional signal lamp circuit. The stop lights are lit, but no turn is indicated.

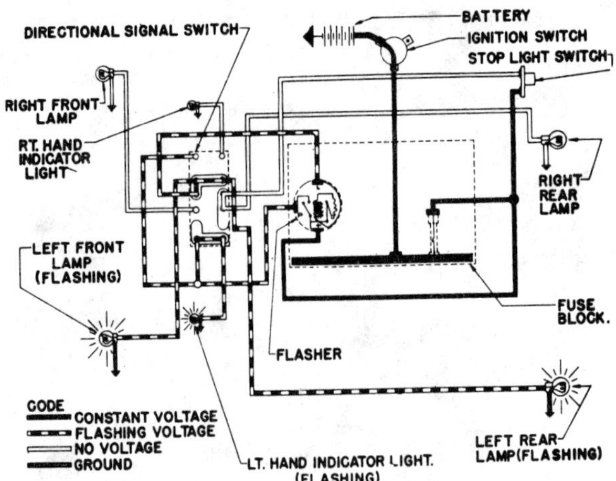

The stop lights are out, with a left turn indicated.

FUEL GAUGES

These gauges work on a lowered voltage, and the voltage is dropped by a CV (constant voltage) regulator, which provides pulsating voltage at an average value of 5 volts. Care must be taken when working around the CV regulator because of the delicate nature of its contacts. Always disconnect the battery cable before doing any work in that area.

FUEL GAUGE TROUBLESHOOTING CHART

The following checks of this circuit will assist you to determine quickly whether incorrect fuel gauge readings are the result of an improperly operating gauge, fuel tank sending unit, or circuit wiring. Similar tests can be performed on the other gauge circuits in the event of a malfunction.

ERRATIC FUEL GAUGE READINGS

Inspect all circuit wiring for damage to insulation and conductor, also carefully check to assure good electrical connections are provided at the following locations:

1. Ground connections at dash unit mounting.
2. Harness connector to dash unit.
3. Body harness connector to chassis harness.
4. Ground connection from tank unit to trunk floor pan.
5. Feed wire connection at tank unit.

GAUGE ALWAYS READS EMPTY (With Ignition Switch On)

Disconnect tank unit feed wire and do not allow wire terminal to ground. Dash unit should now read full.

Gauge Reads Empty

1. Remotely connect a spare dash unit into the dash unit harness connector and provide ground for unit. If full reading shown, dash unit shorted. Replace.
2. If still reads empty, short in harness between tank unit and dash unit.

Gauge Now Reads Full

1. Connect a spare tank unit to tank feed wire and the ground lead.
2. Raise and lower float while observing dash unit. If dash unit follows float movement, replace tank unit.

GAUGE ALWAYS READS FULL (With Ignition Switch On)

1. Check for proper electrical connections at the dash unit, the body harness connector to chassis harness connector or tank unit connector in the trunk.
2. Check ground wire from tank to trunk floor pan for continuity.
3. Connect a spare tank unit to the tank feed wire and the ground lead. Raise and lower float, observing dash unit. If dash unit follows arm movement, replace tank unit.

GAUGE NEEDLE NEVER REACHES FULL MARK

Disconnect feed wire to tank unit and connect the wire to ground thru a variable resistor in shop test equipment or thru a spare tank unit. The dash unit should read full when resistance is increased to approximately 90 ohms (equivalent to fully raised float on tank unit). If the above check shows the dash unit to be operating properly, then the trouble is either that the tank unit rheostat is shorter or the float is binding or arm is bent, or the tank itself may even be deformed. Inspect and correct as necessary.

Fuel gauge troubleshooting chart.

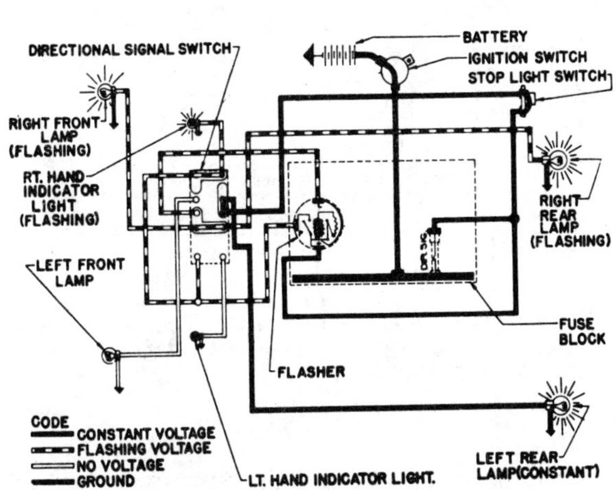

The stop lights are lit, with a right turn indicated.

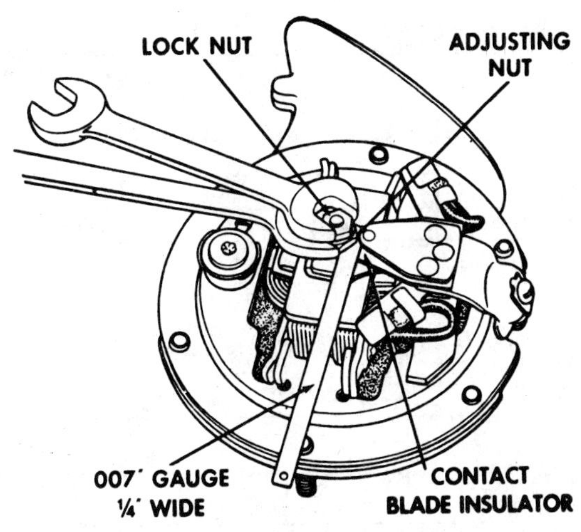

Using a 0.007" feeler gauge to make an adjustment to the horn, as discussed in the text.

HORNS

Generally, a horn is serviced because it does not operate or because it is out of tune. An inoperative horn can usually be traced to an open circuit in the wiring or a defective relay. To check the relay and horn wiring, connect a jumper from the battery to the horn terminal. If the horn now operates, the trouble is in the relay or horn wiring; otherwise, the horn itself is defective. As a further check, connect a second jumper from the horn frame to a ground to check the ground connection.

The contact points should be cleaned with crocus cloth and carbon tetrachloride. Do not force the contacts apart or you will bend the contact spring and change the operating tension. Test the winding for an open circuit, faulty insulation, and ground. Check the resistor with an ohmmeter, or test the condenser for capacity, ground, and leakage. Inspect the diaphragm for cracks and the horn parts for loose rivets.

To adjust the tone, it is necessary to loosen the locknut, and then turn the adjustment screw until the desired tone is obtained. On dual horns, disconnect one horn so that only one will blow at a time. A simple way to make the contact point adjustment is to insert a 0.007" feeler gauge blade between the adjusting nut and the contact blade insulator. **CAUTION: Make sure that the gauge does not touch the metallic parts of the contact points, because it will short them out.** Loosen the locknut and turn the adjusting nut down until the horn does not blow. Then loosen the adjusting nut slowly until the horn barely blows. **CAUTION: The locknut must be tightened after each trial adjustment.** Without the feeler gauge in place, the horn will operate satisfactorily and the current draw will be within specifications.

APPENDIX

GENERAL SPECIFICATIONS

Engine	Compression Ratio	Bore and Stroke	Compression Pressure PSI (Sea Level) @ Cranking Speed	Oil Pressure-Hot @ 2000 R P M	Firing Order	Belt Tension (Ft-Lbs)①
2000cc	N.A.	3.575 x 3.029	Lowest Reading within 75% of highest	45-65	1-3-4-2	New 140, Used 110
2300cc	N.A.	3.78 x 3.126		40-60		

① All belts except camshaft drive belt: used belt is any in operation 10 minutes. Except thermactor and camshaft drive belts. Thermactor drive belt tension—New-80 lb.;Used-60 lb.

CYLINDER HEAD

Engine	Combustion Chamber Volume	Valve Guide Bore Diameter (Standard Intake and Exhaust)	Valve Seat Width		Valve Seat Angle	Valve Seat Runout (Maximum)	Valve Arrangement (Front to Rear)	Gasket Surface Flatness ①
			Intake	Exhaust				
2000cc	48.6-50.1	0.3174-0.3184	0.060-0.079		45°	0.002	EIEIEIEI	0.003 in any 6 inches, 0.006 overall
2300cc	63.7-66.7	0.3443-0.3433	0.060-0.090	0.070-0.090		0.0016		

①Head Gasket Surface Finish R.M.S. 60-150

VALVE SPRINGS

Engine	Valve Spring Pressure Lbs @ Specified Length Pressure	Valve Spring Free Length Approximate	Valve Spring Assembled Height Pad to Retainer	Valve Spring Out-of-Square (Maximum)
2000 cc	64-73 @ 1.418 170-183 @ 1.02	1.73	1 25/64 - 1 27/64	5/64
2300cc	78-86 @ 1.56 199-221 @ 1.16	1.816	1 35/64 - 1 37/64	

Wear Limit . . . . 58 @ 1.418

VALVES

Engine	Valve Stem To Valve Guide Clearance ①		Follower to Cam Clearance		Valve Head Diameter		Valve Face Angle ②	Rocker Arm Follower Ratio
	Intake	Exhaust	Intake	Exhaust	Intake	Exhaust		
2000 cc	0.0008- 0.0025	0.0018- 0.0035	0.008 Cold	0.010 Cold	1.661 1.646	1.425 1.409	44°	1.6:1
2300cc	0.0010 0.0027	0.0015 0.0022			1.728 1.744	1.492 1.508		1.65:1

①Wear Limit 0.0055

②Valve face runout . . . . Maximum 0.0020

VALVES (Continued)

Engine	Valve Stem Diameter							
	Standard		0.008 Oversize		0.016 Oversize		0.032 Oversize	
	Intake	Exhaust	Intake	Exhaust	Intake	Exhaust	Intake	Exhaust
2000 cc	0.3159- 0.3167	0.3149- 0.3156	0.3237- 0.3244	0.3227- 0.3234	0.3234- 0.3394	0.3306- 0.3313	0.3473- 0.3480	0.3463- 0.3470
2300cc	0.3416- 0.3423	0.3411- 0.3418	0.3446- 0.3453	0.3441- 0.3448	0.3566- 0.3573	0.3561- 0.3568	0.3716- 0.3723	0.3711- 0.3718

CYLINDER BLOCK

Engine	Cylinder Bore Diameter①	Cylinder Bore Diameter 0.003 OS	Main Bearing Bore Diameter	Head Gasket Surface Flatness②
2000 cc	3.5748-3.5763	3.5778-3.5793	2.3866- 2.3874	0.003 in 6" 0.006 overall
2300cc	3.7795-3.7831	3.7825-3.7861	2.5902 2.5910	

①Maximum out-of-round 0.001
Wear Limit 0.005
Cylinder bore surface finish RMS . 15-38
Maximum Taper 0.001
Wear Limit 0.010
②Head gasket surface finish RMS . 60-150

2,000, 2,300cc engine specifications.

CAMSHAFT

Engine	Lobe Lift ①		Theoretical Valve Lift @ Zero Lash		Camshaft	Camshaft Journal To Bearing Clearance ③
	Intake	Exhaust	Intake	Exhaust	End Play ②	Clearance
2300cc	0.2493		0.3993		0.0016-0.0047	0.0010-0.0025
	0.2437		0.4000		0.001-0.007	0.001-0.0029

① Maximum allowable-lobe lift loss – 0.005. ② Wear Limit – 0.009. ③ Wear Limit – 0.006.

CAMSHAFT (Continued)

Item	Bearing	2000 cc
Camshaft Journal Diameter Standard①	(No. 1)	1.6531-1.6539
	(No. 2)	1.7563-1.7571
	(No. 3)	1.7713-1.7720
Camshaft Bearings Inside Diameter	(No. 1)	1.655-1.657
	(No. 2)	1.758-1.760
	(No. 3)	1.773-1.775
Camshaft Bearing Location ②	(No. 1)	0.059

①Camshaft journal maximum runout 0.005. Camshaft journal maximum out-of-round 0.0005.
②Distance in inches that the front edge of the bearing is installed towards the rear from the front of the cylinder block or pedestal.

CAMSHAFT DRIVE MECHANISM

Engine	CAMSHAFT GEAR OR SPROCKET Assembled Face Runout TIR Max	CRANKSHAFT GEAR OR SPROCKET Assembled Face Runout TIR Max
2000 cc	0.007	0.005
2300cc		

AUXILARY SHAFT

End Play ①	Bearing Clearance ②
0.0015-0.005	0.001-0.0025

① 2300cc-0.001-0.007 ② 2300cc-0.001-0.0028

CRANKSHAFT AND FLYWHEEL

Engine	Main Bearing Journal Diameter①	Main Bearing Journal Runout-Maximum ②	Main Bearing Journal Thrust Face Runout	Main Bearing Journal Taper Max	Thrust Bearing Journal Length	Main Bearing Surface Finish RMS Maximum	
						Journal	Thrust Face
2000 cc	2.2432-2.2440	0.002	0.0017	0.0003	1.259-1.261	12	20
2300cc	2.3982-2.3990				1.199-1.201		25 Rear 35 Front

①Connecting rod and main bearing journal out-of-rount maximum 0.0004. ② Wear Limit – 0.005

CRANKSHAFT AND FLYWHEEL (Continued)

Engine	Connecting Rod Journal Diameter ①	Connecting Rod Bearing Journal Maximum Taper	Crankshaft Free End Play ②	Flywheel Clutch Face Runout	Flywheel Ring Gear Lateral Runout	
					Standard	Automatic
2000 cc	2.0464-2.0472	0.0003	0.003-0.011	0.005	0.025	
2300cc	2.0465-2.0472		0.004-0.008		0.025	0.060

1 Connecting rod bearing journal out-of-round maximim 0.0006
②Wear Limit 0.012

CRANKSHAFT BEARINGS

Engine	Connecting Rod Bearings To Crankshaft Clearance Desired	Connecting Rod Bearings To Crankshaft Clearance Allowable	Connecting Rod Bearings Wall Thickness Standard①	Main Bearings To Crankshaft Clearance Desired	Main Bearings To Crankshaft Clearance Allowable	Main Bearings Wall Thickness Standard②
2000 cc	0.0006-0.0015	0.0006-0.0026	Red 0.0585-0.0588 Blue 0.0589-0.05892	0.0006-0.0016	0.0006-0.0016	Red 0.07071-0.07098 Blue 0.07110-0.07138
2300cc	0.0006-0.0015	0.0009-0.0027	0.0619-0.0624	0.0008-0.0015	0.0008-0.0015	0.0951-0.0956

①0.002 U.S. Thickness Add 0.001 to Standard Thickness. ②0.002 U.S. Thickness Add 0.0010 to Standard Thickness.

2,000/2,300cc engine specifications.

CONNECTING ROD

Engine	Piston Pin Bore Or Bushing ID	Connecting Rod Bearing Bore Diameter①	Connecting Rod Length Center To Center	Connecting Rod Alignment Maximum Total Difference②		Connecting Rod Assembly (Assembled To Crankshaft) ③
				Twist	Bend	Side Clearance
2000 cc	0.9435-0.9439	2.1654-2.1661	4.9986-5.0012	0.004	0.004	0.004- 0.011
2300cc	0.9104-0.9112	2.1720-2.1728	5.2031-5.2063	0.012		0.0008-0.0026

①Connecting rod bearing bore maximum out-of-round and taper 0.0004

②Pin bushing and crankshaft bearing bore must be parallel and in the same vertical plane within the specified total difference at ends of 8-inch long bar measured 4 inches on each side of rod.

③ Wear Limit – 0.014

PISTON

Engine	Diameter①		Piston To Cylinder Bore Clearance	Piston Pin Bore Diameter	Ring Groove Width	2000 cc
	Standard	0.020 Oversize				
2000 cc	3.5746-3.5730	3.5931-3.5943	0.001-0.002	0.9448-0.9451	Upper Compression Ring	0.0803 0.0811
					Lower Compression Ring	0.1000-0.1008
					Oil Ring	0.1579-0.1687
2300cc	3.7777-3.7781	3.7801 3.7805	0.0013-0.0021	0.9123-0.9127	Upper Compression Ring	0.0800-0.0810
					Lower Compression Ring	0.0800-0.0810
					Oil Ring	0.1880-0.1890

①Measured at the piston pin bore centerline at 90° to the pin bore.

PISTON PIN

Engine	Diameter		To Piston Clearance	To Connecting Rod Bushing Clearance
	Length	Standard		
2000 cc	2.834-2.866	0.9446-0.9450	0.0002-0.0004	Interference Fit
2300cc	3.010-3.040	0.9120-0.9123		

PISTON RINGS

Engine	Ring Width: Compression Ring Top	Ring Width: Compression Ring Bottom	Side Clearance: Compression Ring① Top	Side Clearance: Compression Ring① Bottom	Side Clearance: Oil Ring	Ring Gap Width: Compression Ring Top	Ring Gap Width: Compression Ring Bottom	Ring Gap Width: Oil Ring
2000 cc	0.0779-0.0784	0.0976-0.0981	0.0019-0.0038		Snug	0.0150-0.0229		0.016-0.055②
2300cc	0.0770-0.080	0.0770-0.080	0.002-0.004			0.010-0.020		0.015-0.055

①Wear Limit . . . . 0.006 ②Steel Rail

OIL PUMP

Engine	Rotor Type Oil Pump Relief Valve Spring Tension Lbs @ Specified Length	Drive Shaft To Housing Bearing Clearance	Relief Valve Clearance	Rotor Assembly End Clearance	Outer Race To Housing (Radial Clearance)
2000 cc	13.6-14.7 @ 1.39	0.001-0.002	0.001-0.002	0.001-0.004	0.005-0.011
2300cc	7.54-8.34 @ 1.53	0.0015-0.0029	0.0015-0.0029		0.001-0.007

APPROXIMATE OIL PAN CAPACITIES

Engine	U.S. Measure	Imperial Measure
2000 cc	5 Qt. ①	4-1/8 ①
2300cc		

①Includes one quart with filter replacement

2,000/2,300cc engine specifications.

TORQUE SPECIFICATIONS

Component	Fastener Size	Torque (ft-lb)	Component	Fastener Size	Torque (ft-lb)
Auxiliary Shaft Gear Bolt	M10	28-40	Oil Pan Drain Plug	M14	15-25
Auxiliary Shaft Thrust Plate Bolt	M6	6-9	Oil Pan To Cylinder Block Bolts	M6	7-9
Belt Tensioner Bolt	Pivot M10	28-40		M8	11-13
	Adj. M8	14-21	Oil Filter Insert To Block	–	20-25
Camshaft Gear Bolt	M12	50-71	Oil Filter	–	①
Camshaft Thrust Plate Bolt	M6	6-9	Rocker Arm Cover Bolt	M6	4-7
Carb. To Carb. Spacer Stud	M8	7.5-15	Spark Plug To Cylinder Head	M14	10-15
Carb. To Spacer Nut	M8	10-14	Timing Belt Cover Bolt	M6	–
Carb. Spacer To Manifold Bolt	M8	14-21	Temperature Sending Unit To Cylinder Head	–	8-18
Connecting Rod Nut	M9	30-36 ⑤	Water Jacket Drain Plug	–	23-28
Crankshaft Damper Bolt	M14	80-114	Water Pump To Cylinder Block Bolt	M8	14-21
Cylinder Head Bolt	M12	80-90 ②	Exhaust Manifold To EGR Pipe – Connector	–	25-35
Decel Valve Nut	–	10-15	EGR Valve To Spacer Bolt	M8	14-21
Decel Valve To Intake Manifold – Adapter	–	22-28	EGR Tube To Exhaust Manifold (Connector)		8-12
Distributor Clamp Bolt	M10	20-28	EGR Tube Nut		8-12
Dist. Vacuum Tube To Int. Manifold – Adapter	–	5-8	Auxiliary Shaft Cover Bolt	M6	6-9
Exhaust Manifold To Cylinder Head Nut or Bolt	M10	16-23 ③	Cylinder Front Cover Bolt	M6	6-9
Flywheel To Crankshaft Bolt	M10	54-64	Water Outlet Connection Bolt	M8	14-21
Fuel Pump To Cylinder Block Bolt	M8	14-21	Inner Timing Belt Cover Stud	M8	14-21
Intake Manifold To Cylinder Head Nut or Bolt	M8	14-21 ④	Outer Timing Belt Cover Bolt	M6	6-9
Main Bearing Cap Bolt	M12	80-90 ②	Rocker Arm Cover Shield Bolt	M10	28-40
Oil Pressure Sending Unit To Cyl. Block	–	8-18	Thermactor Check Valve to Manifold		25-35
Oil Pump Pick-Up Tube To Oil Pump	M8	14-21	Fuel Filter To Carburetor		80-100 in-lb
Oil Pump Pick-Up Tube To Cylinder Block	M8	14-21			

① With oil or grease on the gasket surface hand-tighten until gasket contacts adapter face, then tighten 1/2 turn more.

② Step one in sequence 60 Ft-Lbs
Step two in sequence 80-90 Ft-Lbs

③ Step one in sequence 8 Ft-Lbs
Step two in sequence 16-23 Ft-Lbs

④ Step one in sequence 8 Ft-Lbs
Step two in sequence 16-23 Ft-Lbs

⑤ Step one 25-30 ft-lbs
Step two 30-36 ft-lbs

⑥ Step one: 8 vertical screws 4-7 ft-lbs
Step two: 2 angled screws 4-7 ft-lbs

IF NOT SPECIFIED ABOVE:

Component	Torque (ft-lb)	Component	Torque (ft-lb)
M6	6-9	M14	80-114
M8	14-21	1/4 – 18 Pipe	12-18
M10	28-40	3/8 – 18 Pipe	23-33
M12	50-71		

Note:
- All valves are in ft. lbs. unless otherwise noted.
- Oil threads with engine oil unless the threads require oil resistant or water resistant sealer.
- Standard torque limits above are applicable for all other functions not shown in the Special Torque chart.

DESCRIPTION	THREAD SIZE	FT-LBS
Auxiliary Shaft Gear Bolt	M10 X 1	32-36
Auxiliary Shaft Thrust Plate Screw	M6	5-8
Belt Tensioner Screw	M10	32-36
Camshaft Gear Bolt	M10 X 1	32-36
Camshaft Thrust Plate Screw	M6	5-8
Carburetor To Manifold Nut	M8	12-15
Connecting Rod Nut	M9 X 1	29-34
Crankshaft Pulley Bolt	M12 X 1.5	39-43
Cylinder Head Bolt	M12	①
Connector - Water Outlet	M8	12-15
Decel Valve Nut	1 - 12 UNF	27-30
Distributor Clamp Bolt	M8	12-15
Exhaust Manifold to Cyl. Hd. Nuts	M8	12-15
Flywheel to Crankshaft Bolt	M10 X 1	47-51
Front Cover - Upper Bolt	M6	6-9
Front Cover - Lower Bolt	M6	6-9
Fuel Pump to Cylinder Block Bolt	M8	12-15
Heat Shield Nut	M6	5-8
Intake Manifold to Cylinder Head Bolt	M8	12-15
Intake Manifold to Cylinder Head Nut	M8	12-15
Main Bearing Cap Bolt	M12	65-75
Oil Pump Cover to Body Bolt	M6	6-9
Oil Pump to Cylinder Block Screw	M8	12-15
Oil Pick Up Tube to Oil Pump Screw	M6	6-9
Oil-Pan Drain Plug	M14 X 1.5	15-20
Oil Pan to Block Bolts	M6	②

DESCRIPTION	THREAD SIZE	FT-LBS
Oil Filter to Block Insert	3/4-16 UNF	10-15
Oil Filter	3/4-16 UNF	1/2 Turn After Initial Seating
Rocker Arm Ball Stud Nut	M14 X 1.25	32-36
Rocker Arm Cover Screws	M6	③
Rocker Lubricating Pipe Screws	M6	4-6
Spark Plug to Cylinder Head	18 AM	14-20
Timing Belt Cover Spacer	M6	7-9
Timing Belt Cover Bolt	M6	6-13
Water Pump to Cylinder Block Bolt	M8	12-15
Water Pump to Cylinder Block Bolt	M10	26-31
PLUGS & FITTINGS		
Crankcase Hose to Inlet Manifold Connector	1/4-18 NPTF	9-11
Cylinder Head Core Plugs		43-58
Decel Valve to Intake Manifold Adapter	3/8-18 NPTF	13-17
Distributor Vacuum Tube to Intake Manifold Adapter	1/8-27 NPTF	9-11
Servo Connector to Inlet Manifold Blanking Plug	1/4-18 NPTF	9-11
Temperature Sender Unit to Head	1/8-27 NPTF	9-11
Temperature Sender Unit to Head Blanking Plug	1/8-27 NPTF	9-11
Oil Pressure Sender Unit to Cylinder Block	1/8-27 NPTF	9-11
Water Jacket Drain Plug	3/8-18 NPTF	15-18

① Step 1 14-29 ft-lb.
Step 2 36-50 ft-lb.
Step 3 65-80 ft-lb.

② Step 1 in sequence 1-2 ft-lb.
Step 2 in sequence 4-6 ft-lb.

③ Step 1 Torque (6) Rear Bolts from rear to front 4-6 ft-lb.
Step 2 Torque (2) Front Vertical Bolts 1-2 ft-lb.
Step 3 Torque (2) Lateral Bolts 4-6 ft-lb.
Step 4 Torque (2) Front Vertical Bolts 4-6 ft-lb.

2,300cc torque specifications (top) and 2,000cc torque specifications (bottom).

GENERAL SPECIFICATIONS

Engine	Compression Ratio	Bore and Stroke	Oil Pressure-Hot @ 1500 R.P.M.	Firing Order	Belt Tension (Ft-Lbs) ①	Compression Pressure PSI (Sea Level) @ Cranking Speed
2600 cc	8.2:1	3.545 x 2.630	40-55	1-4-2-5-3-6	New 140, Used 110	Lowest 75% of Highest
① All belts, used belt is any in operation for 10 minutes.						

APPROXIMATE OIL PAN CAPACITIES ①

Engine	U. S. Measure	Imperial Measure
2600 cc	5-1/4 Qt. ①	4-3/8
① Includes 1 quart with filter replacement.		

Cylinder Block

Cylinder block casting mark		A	
Cylinder arrangement		V formation 60°	
Number of main bearings		4	
Diameter standard cylinder bore		Class	Diameter
		1	3.543
		2	3.544
		3	3.545
		4	3.546
Diameter oversize cylinder bore	0.020 service		3.564
	0.040 service		3.584
Diameter main bearing bore		Red	2.386
		Blue	2.387
Thrust bearing width			0.890-0.892
Vertical inside diameter of fitted main bearing inserts	Standard	Red	2.244
		Blue	2.245
	Undersize	0.010	2.235
		0.020	2.225
		0.030	2.215
		0.040	2.205
Bores in cylinder block for camshaft bearings	Front		1.773
	No. 2		1.758
	No. 3		1.743
	Rear		1.728

Crankshaft

Diameter main bearing journals	Standard	Red	2.244
		Blue	2.243
	Undersize	0.010	2.234
		0.020	2.224
		0.030	2.214
		0.040	2.204
Clearance main journal to bearing insert	Standard		0.0005-0.002
	Undersize		0.0005-0.002
Thrust bearing width	Bearing journal		1.039
	Bearing inserts		1.034
Crankshaft end play			0.004-0.008
Diameter connecting rod bearing journals	Standard	Red	2.126
		Blue	2.125
	Undersize	0.010	2.116
		0.020	2.106
		0.030	2.096
		0.040	2.086

Connecting Rods

Vertical inside diameter of fitted connecting rod bearing inserts	Standard	Red	2.127
		Blue	2.126
	Undersize	0.010	2.117
		0.020	2.107
		0.030	2.097
		0.040	2.087
Clearance connecting rod bearing journal to bearing inserts	Standard		0.0005-0.002
	Undersize		0.0005-0.0025

2,600cc V-6 engine specifications.

Pistons

Piston diameter, service	Standard		3.542
	Oversize	0.020 0.040	3.562 3.582
Piston clearance			0.001-0.003

Piston Rings

Piston ring gap (piston installed)	Upper compression ring		0.015-0.023
	Lower compression ring		0.015-0.023
	Segment		0.015-0.055

Camshaft

Number of bearings			4
Diameter camshaft bearings	Front		1.650
	No. 2		1.635
	No. 3		1.620
	Rear		1.605
Inside diameter of bushings	Front		1.652
	No. 2		1.637
	No. 3		1.622
	Rear		1.607
Camshaft end play			0.001-0.004
Thrust plate thickness	Standard	Red Blue	0.156 0.157
	Oversize	Red Blue	0.161 0.162
Cam lift			0.255
Cam heel-to-toe dimension.			1.338-1.346

Cylinder Head, Valves

Valve seat angle (in cylinder head)				45°
Valve stem diameter	Intake	Standard		0.316
		Oversize	0.008 0.016 0.024 0.032	0.324 0.332 0.340 0.348
	Exhaust	Standard		0.315
		Oversize	0.008 0.016 0.024 0.032	0.323 0.331 0.339 0.347
Valve stem bore diameter in cylinder head	Intake and exhaust	Standard		0.318
		Oversize	0.008 0.016	0.326 0.334
Valve lift, intake and exhaust				0.373
Valve clearance (cold)	Intake			0.014
	Exhaust			0.016
Intake valve	Opens			20° BTDC
	Closes			56° ABDC
Exhaust valve	Opens			62° BBDC
	Clooos			74° ATDC
Valve tappet diameter				0.874

Camshaft Bearings

Distance from the front face of the cylinder block to the rear side of the assembled bearing (±0.010)	Front	0.831
	No. 2	6.559
	No. 3	11.319
	Rear	17.091

Engine Support Torque Limits Ft-Lbs

Front Supports	2600 cc	Rear Supports	2600 cc
Support Bracket to Engine	12-24	Crossmember to Frame Bracket Through Bolt (Nut)	20-30
Support Bracket to Insulator	20-30	Insulator to Crossmember	20-30
Insulator to Frame	20-30	Insulator to Transmission Bracket	20-30
		Transmission Bracket Attaching Bolt (Manual) Automatic	(20-30) 40-60

2,600cc V-6 engine specifications.

GENERAL SPECIFICATIONS

Engine	Compression Ratio	Bore and Stroke	Compression Pressure PSI (Sea Level) @ Cranking Speed	Oil Pressure-Hot @ 1500 R P M	Firing Order	Belt Tension (Ft-Lbs)①
2800cc	N.A.	3.66 x 2.70	Lowest Reading within 75% of highest	40-55	1-4-2-5-3-6	New 140, Used 110

① All belts except camshaft and thermactor drive belt: used belt is any in operation 10 minutes. Thermactor drive belt tension—New-80 lb.—Used-60 lb.

CYLINDER HEAD

Engine	Combustion Chamber Volume	Valve Guide Bore Diameter (Standard Intake and Exhaust)	Valve Seat Width		Valve Seat Angle	Valve Seat Runout (Maximum)	Valve Arrangement (Front to Rear)	Gasket Surface Flatness ①
			Intake	Exhaust				
2800cc	42.8-44.3	0.3174- 0.3184	0.06-0.079		45°	0.0015	IEEIEI (LH) IEIEEI (RH)	0.003 in any 6 inches, 0.006 overall

①Head Gasket Surface Finish R.M.S. 60-150

VALVE SPRINGS

Engine	Valve Spring Pressure Lbs @ Specified Length Pressure	Valve Spring Free Length Approximate	Valve Spring Assembled Height Pad to Retainer	Valve Spring Out-of-Square (Maximum)
2800cc	60-68 @ 1.585 138-149 @ 1.222	1.91	1-37/64 - 1-39/64	5/64

Wear Limit .... 54 @ 1.585

VALVES

Engine	Valve Stem To Valve Guide Clearance ①		Follower to Cam Clearance		Valve Head Diameter		Valve Face Angle ②	Rocker Arm Follower Ratio
	Intake	Exhaust	Intake	Exhaust	Intake	Exhaust		
2800cc	0.0008- 0.0025	0.0018- 0.0035	0.014 Hot	0.016 Hot	1.562 1.577	1.261 1.276	44°	1.46:1

①Wear Limit 0.0055

②Valve face runout .... Maximum 0.0020

VALVES (Continued)

Engine	Valve Stem Diameter							
	Standard		0.008 Oversize		0.016 Oversize		0.032 Oversize	
	Intake	Exhaust	Intake	Exhaust	Intake	Exhaust	Intake	Exhaust
2800cc	0.3167- 0.3159	0.3156- 0.3149	0.3238 0.3245	0.3228 0.3235	0.3317 0.3324	0.3307 0.3314	0.3474 0.3481	0.3464 0.3471

CYLINDER BLOCK

Engine	Cylinder Bore Diameter ①	Main Bearing Bore Diameter	Head Gasket Surface Flatness ②
2800cc	3.6614 3.6630	2.3866- 2.3874	0.003 in 6" 0.006 overall

①Maximum out-of-round 0.001
Wear Limit 0.005
Cylinder bore surface finish RMS . 15-38
Maximum Taper 0.001
Wear Limit 0.010

②Head gasket surface finish RMS . 60-150

CAMSHAFT

Engine	Lobe Lift ①		Theoretical Valve Lift @ Zero Lash		Camshaft	Camshaft Journal To Bearing Clearance ③
	Intake	Exhaust	Intake	Exhaust	End Play ②	Clearance
2800cc	0.2555		0.3730		0.0008-0.004	0.0010-0.0026

① Maximum allowable-lobe lift loss – 0.005. ② Wear Limit – 0.009. ③ Wear Limit – 0.006.

CAMSHAFT (Continued)

Item	Bearing	2800cc
Camshaft Journal Diameter Standard①	(No. 1)	1.6997 1.6505
	(No. 2)	1.6347 1.6355
	(No. 3)	1.6197 1.6565
	(No. 4)	1.6205 1.6073
Camshaft Bearings Inside Diameter	(No. 1)-(No. 4)	1.7730-1.7742
Camshaft Bearing Location ②	(No. 1)	0.000-0.010

① Camshaft journal maximum runout 0.005. Camshaft journal maximum out-of-round 0.0003.
② Distance in inches that the front edge of the bearing is installed towards the rear from the front of the cylinder block or pedestal.

CAMSHAFT DRIVE MECHANISM

Engine	CAMSHAFT GEAR OR SPROCKET Assembled Face Runout TIR Max	CRANKSHAFT GEAR OR SPROCKET Assembled Face Runout TIR Max
2800cc	0.007	0.005

CRANKSHAFT AND FLYWHEEL

Engine	Main Bearing Journal Diameter①	Main Bearing Journal Runout-Maximum ②	Main Bearing Journal Thrust Face Runout	Main Bearing Journal Taper Max	Thrust Bearing Journal Length	Main Bearing Surface Finish RMS Maximum	
						Journal	Thrust Face
2800cc	2.2433 2.2441	0.002	0.0015	0.0003	1.039 1.041	12	20

① Connecting rod and main bearing journal out-of-round maximum 0.0006. ② Wear Limit – 0.005

CRANKSHAFT AND FLYWHEEL (Continued)

Engine	Connecting Rod Journal Diameter ①	Connecting Rod Bearing Journal Maximum Taper	Crankshaft Free End Play ②	Flywheel Clutch Face Runout	Flywheel Ring Gear Lateral Runout	
					Standard	Automatic
2800cc	2.0464- 2.0472	0.0003	0.003-0.011	0.005	0.025	

1 Connecting rod bearing journal out-of-round maximum 0.0006.
② Wear Limit .... 0.012.

CRANKSHAFT BEARINGS

Engine	Connecting Rod Bearings			Main Bearings		
	To Crankshaft Clearance		Wall Thickness Standard①	To Crankshaft Clearance		Wall Thickness Standard ①
	Desired	Allowable		Desired	Allowable	
2800cc	0.0006-0.0015	0.0005-0.0022	Red 0.0548-0.0552 Blue 0.0552-0.0556	0.0006-0.0016	0.0005-0.0019	Red 0.07071-0.07098 Blue 0.07110-0.07138

① 0.002 U.S. Thickness Add 0.001 to Standard Thickness.

CONNECTING ROD

Engine	Piston Pin Bore Or Bushing ID	Connecting Rod Bearing Bore Diameter①	Connecting Rod Length Center To Center	Connecting Rod Alignment Maximum Total Difference②		Connecting Rod Assembly (Assembled To Crankshaft) ③
				Twist	Bend	Side Clearance
2800cc	0.9450-0.9452	2.2370-2.2398	5.1386-5.1413	0.006	0.004	0.004-0.011

①Connecting rod bearing bore maximum out-of-round and taper 0.0004

②Pin bushing and crankshaft bearing bore must be parallel and in the same vertical plane within the specified total difference at ends of 8-inch long bar measured 4 inches on each side of rod.

③ Wear Limit – 0.014

PISTON

Engine	Diameter①		Piston To Cylinder Bore Clearance	Piston Pin Bore Diameter	Ring Groove Width	2000 cc
	Standard	0.020 Oversize				
2800cc	3.6599 3.6615	3.6800 3.6812	0.001- 0.002	0.9450 0.9452	Upper Compression Ring	0.0803 0.0811
					Lower Compression Ring	0.1197 0.1205
					Oil Ring	0.1579 0.1587

①Measured at the piston pin bore centerline at 90° to the pin bore.

PISTON PIN

Engine	Diameter		To Piston Clearance	To Connecting Rod Bushing Clearance
	Length	Standard		
2800cc	2.835-2.866	0.9446-0.9448	0.0003-0.0006	Interference Fit

PISTON RINGS

Engine	Ring Width		Side Clearance			Ring Gap Width		
	Compression Ring		Compression Ring①			Compression Ring		
	Top	Bottom	Top	Bottom	Oil Ring	Top	Bottom	Oil Ring
2800cc	0.0778-0.0783	0.1172-0.1177	0.0020-0.0033		Snug	0.0150-0.0229		0.015-0.055 ②

①Wear Limit . . . . 0.006 ②Steel Rail

OIL PUMP

Engine	Rotor Type Oil Pump Relief Valve Spring Tension Lbs @ Specified Length	Drive Shaft To Housing Bearing Clearance	Relief Valve Clearance	Rotor Assembly End Clearance	Outer Race To Housing (Radial Clearance)
2800cc	13.6-14.7 @ 1.39	0.0014-0.0029	0.0015-0.0030	0.0011-0.0041	0.006-0.012

APPROXIMATE OIL PAN CAPACITIES

Engine	U.S. Measure	Imperial Measure
2800cc	5 Qt.①	4-1/8①

① Includes ½ quart with filter replacement

2,800cc V-6 engine specifications.

TORQUE LIMITS

	Thread	Ft-Lbs
Main bearing caps	M 12	65-75
Connecting rod bearing caps	M 8 x 1	22-26
Crankshaft gear	M 10 x 1	32-36
Camshaft gear	M 10 x 1	32-36
Crankshaft and balance shaft pulley retaining bolts	M 10 x 1	32-36
Threaded plugs in engine block front	M 36 x 1.5	42-45
Flywheel	M 10 x 1	45-50
Front cover	M 8	9-12
Water pump	M 6	6-12
Oil pump	M 8	10-12
Rocker shaft supports	M 10	32-36
Oil pan	M 6	2-4; 5-8
Rocker arm covers	M 6	2-4; 5-8
Intake manifold	M 8 x 1.25	2-6; 15-18
Cylinder head	M 12	30-40; 40-50; 65-80
Temperature sender unit	1/8"-27 NPTF	8-12
Spark plugs	M 14 x 1.25	22-28

2,600cc V-6 engine torque specifications.

Torque Limits

COMPONENT	TORQUE (ft-lb)	COMPONENT	TORQUE (ft-lb)
Camshaft Gear Bolt	30-36	Intake Manifold to Cylinder Block Stud	10-12
Camshaft Thrust Plate Bolt	12-15	Main Bearing Cup Bolt	65-75
Carburetor to Spacer Stud	10-12	Timing Pointer to Front Cover	5-7
Carburetor Spacer to Manifold Stud	5-7	Oil Pump Pickup Tube to Oil Pump	6-9
Connecting Rod Nut	21-25	Oil Pump Pickup Tube Bracket to Cylinder Block	12-15
Crankshaft Damper Bolt	92-103	Oil Pan Drain Plug to Oil Pan	15-20
Crankcase Vent Valve	11-14	Oil Pan Bolt to Cylinder Block	5-7
Cylinder Head Bolt	(1)	Oil Filter Insert to Cylinder Block	10-15
Decel Valve Nut	10-13	Oil Filter to Cylinder Block	(2)
Decel Valve to Intake Manifold Adapter	30-33	Rocker Arm Ball Stud Nut	9-25
Distributor Clamp Bolt	12-15	Rocker Arm Cover Bolt	3-5
Exhaust Manifold to Cylinuer Head Nut or Bolt	14-18	Spark Plug to Cylinder Head	14-22
Flywheel to Crankshaft Bolt	47-51	Water Jacket Drain Plug	14-18
Fuel Pump to Cylinder Block Bolt	12-15	Water Pump to Cylinder Block Bolt	6-9
Heat Shield Nut	12-15	Exhaust Manifold to EGR Tube Connector	25-35
Intake Manifold to Cylinder Head Bolt or Nut	15-18	All Other EGR Tube Fittings	5-6

(1) Step one in Sequence = 40 ft-lbs
Step two in Sequence = 50 ft-lbs
Step three in Sequence = 65-80 ft-lbs

(2) With oil or grease on gasket surface, hand-tighten until gasket contacts adapter face, then tighten 1/2 turn more.

2,800cc V-6 engine torque specifications.

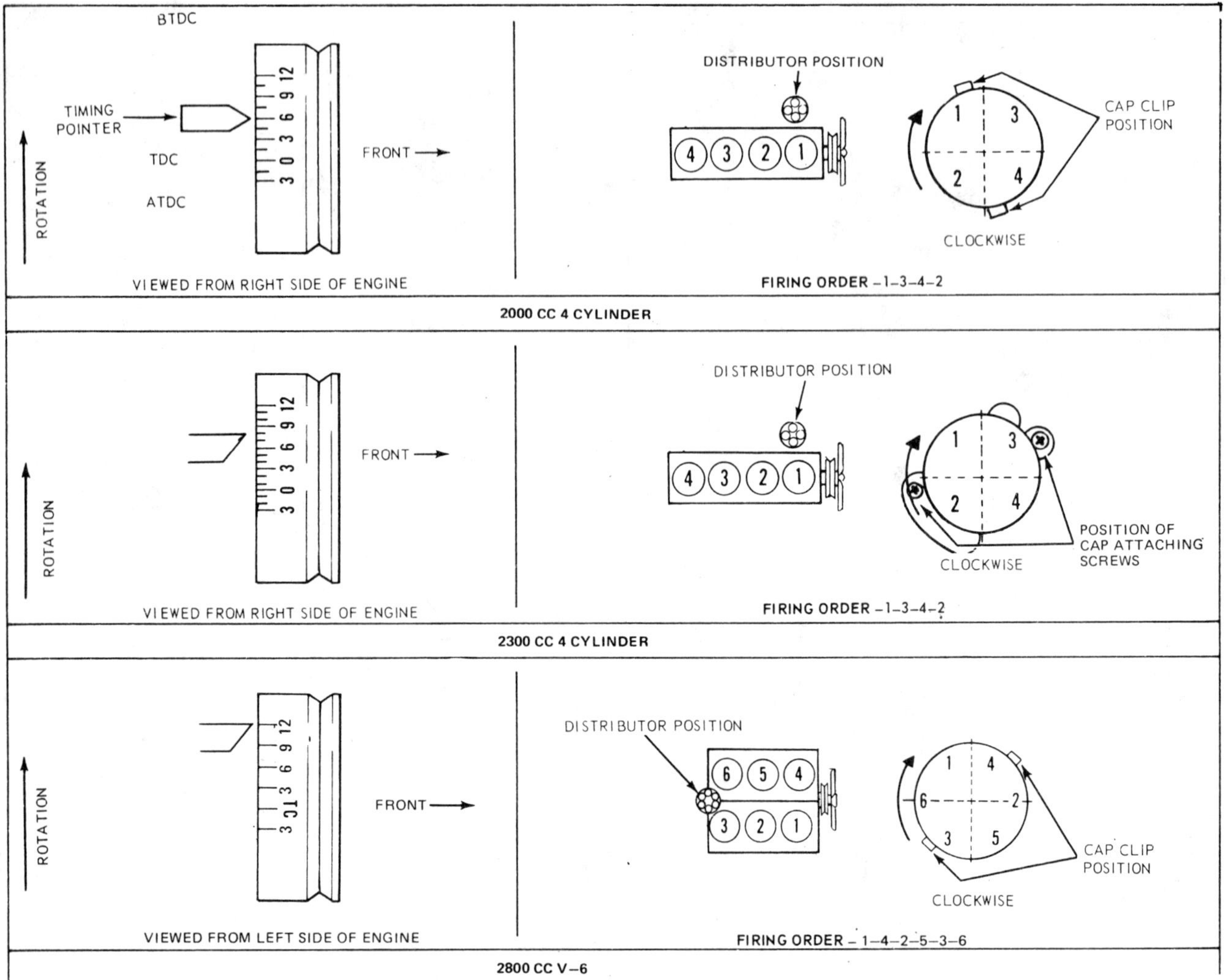

Ignition timing specifications.

ADJUSTMENT TORQUE SPECIFICATIONS (INTEGRAL CARRIER)

Description	Torque In. Lbs.	Torque Ft. Lbs.
Minimum torque required to tighten pinion flange nut to obtain correct pinion bearing preload		140 ①
Pinion Bearing Preload - (Collapsible spacer) ② Original Bearings New Bearings	6-12 17-32	
①If pinion bearing preload exceeds specification before this torque is obtained, install a new spacer. ②With Oil Seal.		

CLEARANCE, TOLERANCE AND ADJUSTMENTS (INTEGRAL CARRIER)

Description	Inches
Maximum Runout of Backface of Ring Gear	0.003
Differential Side Gear Thrust Washer Thickness	0.030-0.032
Differential Pinion Gear Thrust Washer Thickness	0.030-0.032
Differential Bearing Preload (Case spread across Differential) New Bearings Original Bearings	0.008-0.012 0.003-0.005

Description	Inches
Nominal Pinion Locating Shim	0.030
Available pinion Gear Shims in Steps of 0.001	0.008-0.024
Backlash between ring gear and pinion teeth	0.008-0.012
Maximum bqcklash variation between teeth	0.003
Maximum radial runout of U-joint flange in Assembly	0.010-T.I.R.

Specifications for the integral carrier rear axle.